Adult Development
and Aging

SECOND EDITION

Adult Development and Aging

JOHN C. CAVANAUGH

University of Delaware

Brooks/Cole Publishing Company

Pacific Grove, California

Brooks/Cole Publishing Company
A Division of Wadsworth, Inc.

Printed in the United States of America

10 9 8 7 6 5 4 3 2 1

Library of Congress Cataloging-in-Publication Data

Cavanaugh, John C.
    Adult development and aging / John C. Cavanaugh.
        p.   cm.
    Includes bibliographical references and indexes.
    ISBN 0-534-17250-4
    1. Adulthood — Psychological aspects.
    2. Aging — Psychological aspects.   3. Adulthood — Physiological aspects.   4. Aging — Physiological aspects.   5. Aging — Social aspects.   I. Title.
    BF724.5.C38   1992
    155.6 — dc20   92-2316

Psychology Editor: Kenneth King
Editorial Assistant: Gay Meixel
Production Editor: Vicki Friedberg
Text and Cover Designer: Ann Butler
Print Buyer: Barbara Britton
Art Editor: Nancy Spellman
Permissions Editor: Robert M. Kauser
Copy Editor: Jennifer Gordon
Photo Researcher: Stephen Forsling
Technical Illustrator: Susan Breitbard
Signing Representative: Art Minsberg
Compositor: Thompson Type, San Diego, CA
Printer: R. R. Donnelley & Sons, Crawfordsville, IN
Cover Art: David Hockney: *Mt. Fuji and Flowers*, 1972. Acrylic on canvas, 60 × 48 in. The Metropolitan Museum of Art, Purchase. Mrs. Arthur Hays Sulzberger Gift, 1972. (1972. 128) © David Hockney.

Acknowledgments are listed on page 534.

To Patrice,
the most wonderful wife
in the whole universe

BRIEF CONTENTS

CONTENTS

CONTENTS

xiii

CHAPTER 12

Where We Live   410

CHAPTER 13

Dying and Bereavement   444

CHAPTER 14

Looking Toward the 21st Century   480

PREFACE

THE NEED TO KNOW WHAT IT IS LIKE TO GROW old in modern society has never been greater. In most industrialized societies, the median age increases each year, meaning that the population as a whole is getting older. With the 21st century will come an unprecedented number of older adults, forcing us to rethink many of the assumptions we make about them. This rethinking will require the collective expertise of people in many fields — including academicians, gerontologists, social workers, medical professionals, financial experts, teachers, factory workers, technologists, and government workers. Every reader of this book, regardless of his or her area of expertise, will need to understand older adults in order to master the art of living.

Perhaps because of the need to know, the field of adult development and aging is changing at an ever-faster rate. Since the publication of the first edition of *Adult Development and Aging*, many new and exciting discoveries have been made. These developments led to this second edition, which provides an up-to-date look at these interesting and sometimes controversial findings. As was the case in the first edition, I have attempted to provide in-depth coverage of the major issues in the psychology of adult development and aging. To do so, while incorporating new material, meant some changes were in order.

THE SECOND EDITION

The second edition of *Adult Development and Aging* adds several new topics and provides expanded and updated coverage of many existing ones.

Major New Features

The most obvious changes in the second edition are the reorganization of some topics, the deletion of others, and the inclusion of a new chapter. The most important reorganizational feature is the application of the *biopsychosocial model* as a unifying framework for the book. The model is presented in Chapter 1 and is used throughout the text to organize and integrate the material. This model strongly emphasizes a multidisciplinary approach to the field, which is essential.

The opening chapters have been restructured to more coherently introduce the discipline. Chapter 1 now focuses on *developmental issues*, such as the definition of age and the nature-nurture and continuity-discontinuity controversies, as well as research methods. Chapter 2 in the second edition examines *diversity* in adult development and aging and includes demographics as well as ethnic and cross-cultural diversity.

New to the second edition is Chapter 5 on *information processing, human factors,* and *language processing*. These topics are very important issues in current research and offer additional information in the area of cognition and aging not included in the first edition. Chapter 5 provides extensive coverage of attention, which has recently been the focus of much theorizing. Also new are nearly all of the chapter introductions. These interest grabbers come from a variety of sources, including personal experience, anecdotes, media accounts, and folktales from around the world. These introductions are meant to demonstrate the variety of experiences adults have and the ways in which aging is incorporated into our cultures. Finally, several new pedagogical aids have been included, as will be described later.

New Topics and Expanded Coverage

In addition to the major differences, several new topics were added and topics in the first edition received additional coverage. Among the new topics are: *biological theories of aging* (Chapter 3), *brain-imaging techniques* (Chapter 3), *AIDS* (Chapter 3), *autobiographical memory* (Chapter 6), *reflective judgment* (Chapter 7), and *possible selves* (Chapter 8).

Every topic in the first edition has been updated, and some were expanded, including *the immune system* (Chapter 3), *working memory* (Chapter 6), *dementia* (Chapter 9), *life styles* (Chapter 10), *leisure* (Chapter 11), and *euthanasia* (Chapter 13).

WRITING STYLE

Although *Adult Development and Aging* covers complex issues and difficult topics, I use clear, concise, and understandable language. Many chapters were completely rewritten to achieve this goal, and many unnecessary terms from the first edition have been omitted. The text is aimed at upper-division undergraduate students. Although it will be helpful if students have taken an introductory psychology course, the text does not assume this background, and it should be comprehensible by students in many disciplines. Terms included in the end-of-book glossary and end-of-chapter key terms lists first appear in **boldface type**, and definitions are provided at that point in the text.

INSTRUCTIONAL AIDS

In addition to the chapter key terms lists, I have included several other features to help both students and instructors.

Boxes

Two types of boxes appear in the chapters. Boxes titled How Do We Know? draw attention to specific research studies that were discussed briefly in the main body of the text. These boxes supply additional information about the methodology and theory underlying the research to provide students with a more complete look at how empirical information is generated and some alternative interpretations of data.

The second type of box is titled Something to Think About. These boxes raise provocative and controversial issues, pose reflective questions, or draw attention to social problems. The point here is to get students to think about the implications of certain research findings or conclusions. These boxes may be used as a point of departure for class discussion.

Additional Reading

At the end of each chapter I have listed a few suggested readings for students interested in learning more about the topics. Readings have been chosen carefully to be current, readable, and important. Each suggestion contains a rating of the relative difficulty of the material based on undergraduates' evaluations.

Chapter Outlines, Chapter Summaries, and Review Questions

In order to assist students in organizing, learning, and studying the material, I have included three aids. *Chapter outlines* help orient students to the organization of the chapter and the major topics to be presented. *Chapter summaries* are organized by major sections and provide succinct statements of the main points. Numerous *review questions* are also presented in a topically organized format. These questions give students a means of testing themselves on the material.

INSTRUCTOR'S MANUAL AND STUDY GUIDE

The second edition of *Adult Development and Aging* is accompanied by an **instructor's manual**. Each chapter begins with a *lecture outline* that highlights the main points from the chapter. Additionally, information not in the text but that could be included in a lecture, some suggested activities, and a few excellent videos are noted. This information should assist the instructor in preparing lecture material from the text.

Each chapter also includes numerous *multiple-choice questions*. These items are four-choice items; none involve "all of the above" or similar alternatives. Correct answers are indicated. *Essay questions* are also provided. In all cases, the page in the text on which the material appears is listed. These items were compiled to facilitate the instructor's exam preparation.

New to this text is a **study guide** written by Bradley Caskey. Each chapter includes a preview section that contains focus questions and chapter outlines, a review section, multiple-choice questions, short-answer essay questions, and "After the Facts" discussion questions designed for critical thinking.

ACKNOWLEDGMENTS

Once again, it has taken many people to complete the second edition. The people at Wadsworth have been great. Ken King, senior editor, is truly a pleasure to work with, and he provided many valuable insights that helped improve the book. His continual belief in me and in this project is greatly appreciated; he is largely responsible for my being a textbook author.

I would also like to thank the reviewers of the manuscript, all of whom made excellent and thought-provoking suggestions: A. Regula Herzog, University of Michigan at Ann Arbor; Mildred Houanche, CUNY-City College; William Hoyer, Syracuse University; Shirley L. Lupfer, Memphis State University; Kevin MacDonald, California State University at Long Beach; and Jasmin T. McConatha, West Chester University.

This book would not have been possible without the support of my wife, Patrice. She is truly a gem. Not only did she tolerate my moodiness, long hours at the computer, and pile after pile of articles, journals, and books, but she was always there to give me encouragement whenever things were going badly. She is, without question, the most generous and giving person I've ever met.

Finally, a special thanks to Art Minsberg. Art was the marketing representative (and now a marketing director) who initially connected me with Wadsworth. He was the best and nicest rep I've known.

Adult Development and Aging

CHAPTER **1**

Introduction to Adult Development and Aging

ISSUES AND MODELS IN ADULT DEVELOPMENT AND AGING

The Nature-Nurture Controversy / The Continuity-Discontinuity Controversy / Moving from Issues to Models / The Mechanistic Model / The Organismic Model / The Contextual Model / Research Implications of Issues and Models / Practical Implications of Issues and Models / Moving to a Testable Approach

THE BIOPSYCHOSOCIAL MODEL

The Life-Span Perspective / The Interaction of Developmental Forces / Adopting the Model / Something to Think About: Using the Biopsychosocial Model

THE MEANING OF AGE

Age as an Index / Definitions of Age / Issues in Studying Age / Relationships Between Age and Developmental Influences

RESEARCH METHODS

Age, Cohort, and Time of Measurement / Developmental Research Designs / How Do We Know? Conflicts Between Cross-Sectional and Longitudinal Data / Representativeness and Adequate Measurement / Approaches to Doing Research / The Biopsychosocial Model and Research with Older Adults

Summary / Review Questions
Key Terms / Additional Reading

"To be 70 years young is sometimes far more cheerful and hopeful than to be 40 years old," wrote Oliver Wendell Holmes. In his day, about 100 years ago, being "70 years young" was unusual. Since then, industrialized countries have experienced an unprecedented explosion in the number of older adults. Because of technological advances, disease, famine, and childbirth no longer routinely claim lives before we can reach old age.

We are squarely in the midst of a monumental revolution: the fundamental restructuring of the population from one that is dominated by youth to one that now includes many older people as well. You have probably heard a great deal about this in the media: The median age in the United States passed 30 in the late 1980s, whole industries are now targeting middle-aged and older adult consumers, and services to older adults will increase in scope and cost for the foreseeable future.

There are three especially noteworthy reasons why it is important to learn as much as possible about what happens between the time one first becomes an adult and the time one dies:

1. *Older adults constitute a rapidly growing segment of the population.* At present, older adults represent the fastest growing age group in the United States. This means not only that the *number* of older adults will increase dramatically, but also that older adults will wield increasing political and economic power as we enter the 21st century. Their priorities and plans may differ from those of younger and middle-

aged adults, which will require creative use of the limited resources available.

2. *We want to understand older adults.* What is it like to grow old? Why are older people the way they are? What changes as people age? Why are there so many differences among people of the same age? These and many other questions about the nature of older adults point to a need to understand the adult developmental process and how this process unfolds for each individual.

3. *More older people means new jobs.* The increasing number of older adults will create employment opportunities. Many social service agencies, consumer product manufacturers, advertisers, and companies in the health care industry are increasingly targeting older adults for new areas of growth. New jobs will emerge as businesses begin to meet the needs of older adults. In the coming years, experts predict, this may well be the fastest growing segment of the economy.

This book deals with all of these issues by summarizing what scholars have learned about traversing adulthood and growing old. We have an advantage that the current population of older adults did not have: We are able to study what growing old will be like. Never before have we had the chance to prepare as well for old age.

This opportunity is provided by scientists in many disciplines who are all interested in a common goal: understanding the aging process. The field of study that examines the aging process is gerontology. More formally, **gerontology** is the study of aging from maturity (young adulthood) through old age, as well as the study of the elderly as a special group. Gerontology is a fairly new scientific discipline. For example, before the 1950s, researchers in the United States conducted only a handful of studies involving older adults (Freeman, 1979). One reason the study of older adults was so

long in coming, as Freeman points out, is that authors and scientists throughout history conceptualized the aging process as one of inevitable, irreversible decline. Consequently, nothing was to be gained by studying aging, since it was already thought to be beyond our power to improve or change the process.

We now know that this picture of aging was distorted and oversimplified. Aging involves both growth and decline. Still, many myths concerning old people survive: Older adults are often thought to be incompetent, decrepit, and asexual. These myths of aging lead to negative stereotypes of older people, which may result in **ageism**, a form of discrimination against older adults simply because of their age (Butler & Lewis, 1982). Ageism comes in many forms. It may be as blatant as believing that all old people are senile and are incapable of making decisions about their lives. Or it may be as subtle as dismissing an older person's physical complaints with the statement, "What do you expect for someone your age?"

This book will rebut these erroneous ideas. But it will not replace myths with idealized views of adulthood and old age. Rather, it will strive to paint an accurate picture of what it means to grow old today, recognizing that development across adulthood brings with it growth and opportunities as well as loss and decline.

To begin, we will consider the fundamental issues and models that form the foundation for studying adult development and aging. In particular, we will examine the nature-nurture and continuity-discontinuity controversies, as well as the mechanistic, organismic, and contextual models. Following that, we will adopt a framework to guide our interpretation of research and theory in adult development and aging—the biopsychosocial model. This model emphasizes the need to take a multidisciplinary view of adult development and aging. We will consider some basic definitions of age and will see that age can be viewed in many different ways. Finally, by examining various research methods, we will see how the information presented in this book was obtained.

ISSUES AND MODELS IN ADULT DEVELOPMENT AND AGING

Throughout history philosophers have wondered why and how people develop from birth to old age. Some of the greatest minds in Western civilization — such as Plato, Aristotle, René Descartes, John Locke, John Stuart Mill, and Charles Darwin — gave the question considerable attention. Their ideas reflect the same two core issues that underlie the modern study of human development (Lerner, 1986): the nature-nurture controversy and the continuity-discontinuity controversy.

Similarly, how people make sense of the grand plan of adult development and aging tends to fall into three views or models: mechanistic, organismic, and contextual. Each **model** is a metaphorical representation of reality that allows very complex phenomena, such as human development, to become more understandable (Pepper, 1942). Models are not testable, but they stimulate the creation of ideas, concepts, issues, and questions that *are* testable; in addition, models may suggest specific methods that can be used to address the issues.

Having a firm grasp on the issues and models of development is important, as it provides a context for understanding why researchers and theorists believe certain things about aging or why some topics have been researched a great deal and others have been hardly studied at all. For example, if you believe that a decline in intellectual ability is an innate and inevitable part of aging, you are unlikely to search for intervention techniques to raise performance. Similarly, if you believe that personality characteristics change across adulthood, you would be likely to search for life transitions.

The Nature-Nurture Controversy

The **nature-nurture controversy** can be summarized in two very different statements: "Your genes determine who you are, and that's that." "You are a product of your environment." At issue here is the extent to which inborn, hereditary characteristics (nature) and experiential, or environmental, influences (nurture) determine who we are.

Until relatively recently, theorists viewed adult development and aging from a nature position: Certain changes will occur inevitably, and one can do little to alter their course. This approach to aging can be seen in the works of such divergent writers as Shakespeare, who described old age in *As You Like It* as second childishness, and David Wechsler, who believed that intellectual development in adulthood meant an inevitable loss of skills. More recently, the pendulum has shifted to the nurture side. For example, in Chapter 7 we will consider evidence that the decline in performance on intelligence tests is not inevitable and is remediable.

Patterns of Nature-Nurture Interactions: Focus on Nature. How do nature and nurture interact? Anastasi (1958) points out that any specific hereditary factor can be reflected in any of several possible behaviors. Which behavior is observed depends on the environment present at any given time. For example, children born with Down syndrome have a specific genetic defect: an extra chromosome in the 21st pair. Although Down syndrome results in mental retardation, the degree of retardation depends in part on the child's environment. Children placed in an unstimulating environment are likely to be more severely retarded than children placed in a stimulating environment.

This same principle is being adopted in the study of some diseases associated with aging. For example, one theory of Alzheimer's disease holds that the illness has a genetic component (see Chapter 9). However, whether one actually gets Alzheimer's disease, and possibly even the course of the disease itself, is influenced by the environment. Specifically, the genetic predisposition hypothesis states that there has to be an environmental trigger for the disease to occur. Moreover, there is some evidence that providing a supportive environment for Alzheimer's patients improves their performance on cognitive tasks, at least for awhile.

One difficulty in focusing on nature in studying adult development and aging is that it is difficult to determine whether a particular behavior or disease has a genetic component. Having lived for many years already, adults pose tough problems for geneticists. Documenting a genetic component in a behavior that may have been part of their repertoire for many years is very difficult. For this reason, most research on genetics and aging focuses on disorders such as Alzheimer's disease and others like it (see Chapter 9) for which there is some evidence of a genetic component (such as an abnormal gene) that can be linked to certain behavioral patterns.

Anastasi (1958) also points out the range of effects of heredity on behavior. When the influences of heredity are strong and direct, effective intervention may not be possible. For example, there currently is no effective treatment for Huntington's disease, a genetic disorder that ultimately results in severe mental decline and death (see Chapter 9). In contrast, indirect effects of heredity, such as susceptibility to a disease like AIDS, may be changed. Increased education about how to protect oneself can reduce the risk.

Patterns of Nature-Nurture Interactions: Focus on Nurture. Just as the effects of heredity must be understood by considering the environment, so the effects of environment must be understood by con-

sidering heredity (Lerner, 1986). The issue is the breadth of the influence of the environment (Anastasi, 1958). In some cases environmental effects are narrow, having a minimal, temporary impact on only a few specific aspects of behavior. In other cases environmental factors affect a wide range of behaviors, and their influence lasts a long time.

As is the case with hereditary influences, environmental influences vary in how directly they influence behavior. For instance, the outcome of a specific type of environmental effect, such as social class, depends on the individual's inherited characteristics. Given equally supportive and cognitively rich environments, we would not expect a person in the late stages of Alzheimer's disease to profit from intervention as much as a normal middle-aged adult. Thus, even when we consider environmental influences, our genetic inheritance is important (Lerner, 1986). For example, assuming that all older adults will profit equally from cognitive training without taking into account their inborn characteristics is a mistake, as is assuming that a person cannot do a particular task simply because he or she is 70 years old.

Nature and Nurture. We have seen that nature and nurture interact to influence behavior. To understand behaviors, we must *simultaneously* consider the individual's inborn, hereditary characteristics and the individual's environment. Each of us is genetically unique and has unique interactions with a given environment. Both factors have to be considered together to yield an adequate account of why we behave the way we do. To explain an individual's behavior and discover where to focus intervention, we must look at the unique interaction for that individual between nature and nurture.

The Continuity-Discontinuity Controversy

The second major issue in developmental psychology is a derivative of the nature-nurture controversy. Given that people change over time, and given that rules govern these changes, how do these rules hold up across the life span? Can the same rules that describe you at one point be used to describe you at another point, or do we need to use different rules? If we can use the same rules to account for behavior at two different points, we have *continuity*. But if we need to use different rules at different times, we have *discontinuity* (Lerner, 1986).

The **continuity-discontinuity controversy** may appear rather straightforward; there is more to it, however, than establishing whether things are still the same or are different. The continuity-discontinuity debate is reflected in the competing views that adulthood is largely a matter of stability in behaviors and characteristics or that it is marked by significant and fundamental changes. The debate over the relative stability or change in behavior is especially heated in the areas of intellectual and personality development. We will consider these areas in Chapters 7 and 8.

The continuity-discontinuity issue lies at the heart of accounting for change within individuals. As we will see, two additional aspects of the controversy have major theoretical implications: description versus explanation and quantitative change versus qualitative change.

Description Versus Explanation. Think for a moment about the way you behaved when you were three years old. You can probably come up with a list of behaviors that have changed, as well as a list of behaviors that have stayed with you. The first things that may come to mind are specific behavioral differences, such as being less able to express yourself and being less able to open large doors. On the other hand, you may still cry sometimes when you are very happy or sad. Noting specific differences and similarities like these *describes* the changes that have occurred. To *explain* the differences, you would have to offer some reason, such as brain development (for language) and height (for opening doors).

Most of the research we will consider focuses on describing adults. Careful description is essential because we first need to know the areas in which adults change or stay the same before we can develop reasons why these patterns occur. Still, there have been a few attempts at explanation, most notably in cognitive development (Chapters 5, 6, and 7) and personality development (Chapter 8).

Quantitative Versus Qualitative Changes. Consider the following situation: A person is presented with a hypothetical dilemma concerning whether to stay with an alcoholic spouse. The nonalcoholic partner has given an ultimatum to the alcoholic — one more time coming home drunk, and the partner will leave. The alcoholic again comes home drunk. The dilemma: What should the nonalcoholic spouse do?

This problem typifies those often used to study intellectual development in adulthood and is solved differently depending on how old the respondent is (see Chapter 7). The explanation for the different solutions also varies, creating two different pictures of why people's responses change.

Age differences in solutions may reflect **quantitative change**, that is, a change in how much of something, such as knowledge, exists (Lerner, 1986). Perhaps people give different solutions because they have learned more about marriages over the years and so are drawing on more experience.

In contrast, perhaps the difference reflects **qualitative change**, meaning the fundamental way in which people think about the problem has changed. Qualitative change involves a difference in the essence of what exists. It is not a matter of more of the same, which characterizes quantitative change. Rather, in qualitative change we are dealing with a new quality or type of person (Lerner, 1986).

The notion of qualitative change has been adopted by many developmental psychologists. Writers such as Jean Piaget and Erik Erikson represent these qualitative changes as sequences of stages that individuals pass through on their way to maturity.

TABLE 1.1 Summary of issues and models in adult development and aging

The Nature-Nurture Controversy

The nature-nurture controversy involves the degree to which genetics and the environment influence human development. Most theorists agree that both must be considered simultaneously, and neither can be interpreted in isolation.

The Continuity-Discontinuity Controversy

The continuity-discontinuity controversy focuses on whether the same explanations (continuity) or different explanations (discontinuity) must be used over time to account for behavioral change. A continuity position typically emphasizes quantitative change, whereas a discontinuity position tends to emphasize qualitative or stagelike change.

The Mechanistic Model

The mechanistic model uses a machine metaphor, views environment as active and people as passive, views the whole as the sum of its parts, and emphasizes quantitative change.

The Organismic Model

The organismic model views people as complex biological organisms, views environment as passive and people as active shapers of their own development, views the whole as greater than the sum of its parts, and emphasizes qualitative change.

The Contextual Model

The contextual model views people in terms of the historical time period in which they live, views both environment and people as dynamically and mutually interactive, and views change as both quantitative and qualitative.

Moving from Issues to Models

The nature-nurture and continuity-discontinuity controversies provide an important basis for understanding the various viewpoints on adult development and aging (see Table 1.1). In fact, which side of each controversy theorists choose to emphasize becomes critical when they begin to build general models of development. As we will see, each model has its own combination of views on these controversies, which in turn creates very different ways of accounting for development.

The Mechanistic Model

The **mechanistic model** uses a metaphor of a machine to explain how best to understand humans. Machines are very complicated collections of interacting parts, which can be disassembled and studied separately. In short, the mechanistic model views the whole as the sum of the parts. Machines are also passive and reactive; they are incapable of doing anything on their own and rely on some environmental force to prompt them to action. We can clearly see that the mechanistic model's emphasis is on *nurture*. The mechanistic model views people as passive organisms that react to their environment; they do not initiate actions. Understanding human behavior comes from breaking down complex behaviors (such as memory) into less complex components (such as attention or sensory memory) and studying these components independently. For example, studying memory does not require taking emotions, goals, or motivation into account. The mechanistic model also emphasizes connections between environmental stimuli and observable behavior, rather than hypothetical concepts referring to internal processes. Finally, the mechanistic model focuses on *quantitative change*.

The Organismic Model

The **organismic model** views people as complex biological systems. However, the organismic model views the whole as more than the sum of its parts. That is, there is something that emerges from the interaction among the parts that is not predictable or understandable from focusing separately on the parts. For example, hydrogen is an extremely volatile substance that easily explodes, and oxygen provides a conducive atmosphere for fire. However, when two parts hydrogen and one part oxygen are combined appropriately, you get a substance that is used to put fires out—water. So it is with people; one cannot know what a person is like simply by knowing his or her constituent parts.

The organismic model also postulates that people are active participants in their own development. People control aspects of their lives, and in fact are responsible for initiating much of their intellectual and personal growth. Moreover, this development is headed to a particular goal or end state. Because the organismic model emphasizes *qualitative change*, it has provided the basis for stage theories of development, such as Piaget's theory of cognitive development (see Chapter 7) and Kohlberg's theory of moral reasoning (see Chapter 8).

The Contextual Model

The **contextual model** views human development in terms of the historical event, that is, the specific point in history in which it is occurring. How people in the late 20th century develop is different from the way people in the late 19th, or 10th, or 5th century B.C. developed. Each historical point

has a unique combination of social, psychological, cultural, and biological forces that shape the way we develop. For example, our ability to protect ourselves from diseases such as polio means that we can focus our attention on other health problems, such as AIDS. In turn, each generation influences the forces that will shape future generations; development of an AIDS vaccine would lessen the need to fear this disease for our great-grandchildren.

The contextual model also proposes that the whole is greater than the sum of its parts and views people as active shapers of development. However, it is not known where human development is headed; there is no set goal or endpoint to development. *Multidirectionality* is strongly emphasized, meaning that there is more than one path to successful aging. The contextual model accepts both quantitative and qualitative change, depending on the domain in question.

Research Implications of Issues and Models

How would different positions on the issues of development, as suggested by the three models, influence the way developmentalists study a problem? To answer this question, let us consider three researchers studying job satisfaction across adulthood.

The mechanist would be inclined to reduce behavior to a few principles of learning that hold true for all people, regardless of age, and would search for the environmental contingencies that govern behavior. Understanding job satisfaction may consist of mapping the contingency between productivity and salary, on the assumption that salary would be viewed as a reinforcer for good work.

In contrast, the organicist would concentrate on discontinuities across the life span. The job satisfaction issue would be approached by identifying the internal motivating factors for doing good work. The organicist might focus on a worker's desire to achieve or the thought processes that underlie self-concept at a given point in the life span.

Finally, the contextualist would describe the relationship of current behavior to behaviors earlier in life, to current cultural and social influences, and to future potentials. The contextualist would also be interested in describing the reciprocal interactions among all of these factors. Job satisfaction might be explored by trying to discern the congruity, or fit, between the personal needs of the individual and the opportunities provided by the environment.

Scientists working in different models ask fundamentally different questions about the nature of development. They collect different data and come to very different conclusions. Some criterion other than truth must be used to evaluate theories based on different models (Lerner, 1986). No one theory is intrinsically better than another. Consequently, Lerner suggests that theories be evaluated in terms of how well they describe and explain development, as well as their utility in developing ways to optimize human behavior.

Practical Implications of Issues and Models

The model one adopts has important research and practical implications. Models are used to develop and implement everything from educational systems to social programs. Let's consider the Smith family. The Smiths live in the inner city of a large metropolitan area. Their income is barely above the poverty level, but it is enough to make them ineligible for most subsidy programs. Their outlook on life is not highly optimistic. How will we help the Smiths?

A mechanist will believe that environmental factors need to be changed. Consequently, the mechanist will suggest housing programs, income maintenance, and other interventions in which the Smiths are subjected to some externally driven change. Such an approach will ignore factors such as whether the Smiths want the programs in question and whether they like what is happening. In short, if you change the environment, everything will fall into place.

In contrast, an organicist will be likely to do little or nothing. From this perspective the Smiths are responsible for their own development, and no outside intervention can change that. Attempts may be made to make the environment less of a hindrance, but the primary intervention will be to get them to become motivated to change. In other words, the family becomes responsible for its own behavior; the environment is innocent. This approach reflects a self-discovery, self-initiated, "pull yourself up by your own bootstraps" philosophy.

Finally, the contextualist will argue that in order to help the Smiths it is necessary to change the social context in which they live. Not only will change have to occur in the environment, but the Smiths will need to play a role as well. For example, housing reform will be ineffective unless the Smiths take advantage of the opportunity. The contextual perspective will play down the quick fix in favor of a more broad-based social policy.

We see these different perspectives every day. Politicians debate the relative merits of intervention programs from each point of view. In the United States we saw the failure of many mechanistic interventions instituted during the 1960s, and these programs underwent reform in the 1970s and 1980s. Perhaps in the future we will realize the vast complexity of the human condition and understand that complex problems require complex solutions.

Moving to a Testable Approach

Mechanistic, organismic, and contextual models each have merits. However, by themselves they do not provide a testable framework from which we can view adult development and aging. To facilitate our study we need just such a framework. Fortunately, a model exists that meets our needs: the biopsychosocial model. It is to this model we now turn.

THE BIOPSYCHOSOCIAL MODEL

The experience of being an adult and growing old can be approached from many perspectives: anthropological, sociological, biological, medical, political, psychological, and economic to name but a few. Each approach makes its unique contribution to research and theory. The task of the psychological perspective on adult development and aging is to explain how behavior becomes organized and, in some cases, how it becomes disorganized (Birren & Cunningham, 1985).

The Life-Span Perspective

The life-span perspective divides human development into two phases: an early phase (childhood and adolescence) and a later phase (consisting of young adulthood, middle age, and old age). The early phase is characterized by relatively rapid age-related increases in people's size and abilities. During the later phase, changes in size are slow, but abilities continue to develop as people continue adapting to the environment (Birren & Cunningham, 1985).

Viewed from the perspective of life-span development, adult development and aging are complex phenomena that cannot be understood within the scope of a single disciplinary approach (Baltes, Reese, & Lipsitt, 1980). Understanding how adults change requires input from a wide variety of perspectives (Riley, 1979).

Because aging is a lifelong process, human development never stops (Brim & Kagan, 1980).

Rather, there is a continuous process of development, socialization, and adaptation (Clausen, 1986). *Development* involves the processes that people need to attain their potential in any domain (physical size, intellectual abilities, social skills, and so on). For example, having the opportunity to go to college may foster curiosity, which in turn enables a person to learn more.

Riley (1979) also pointed out the mutual influences of social, environmental, and historical change. These influences relate to three concepts of time described by Neugarten and Datan (1973). *Life time* refers to the number of years a person has lived. In Chapter 4, we will examine some of the genetic (for instance, "long-life" genes) and environmental (such as, pollution and life style) factors that influence life time. *Social time* refers to the way that society determines the appropriate age for certain events to occur (such as, the right time to get married) and sets the kinds of age-related expectations on behavior (for example, how old people are supposed to behave). Finally, *historical time* refers to the succession of social, political, economic, and environmental events through which people live (the Depression, the Vietnam War, and Operation Desert Storm). Our lives are anchored in the major events of particular historical periods. As we will see later in this chapter when we consider the concept of cohort, these events affect people differently depending on their age and position in society when they occur.

These different notions of time come together for each of us in our social clock (Hagestad & Neugarten, 1985; Neugarten & Hagestad, 1976). A **social clock** is a personal timetable by which we mark our progress in terms of events in our lives. A social clock is based on our incorporation of biological markers of time (such as menopause) social aspects of time (such as graduating from college) and historical time (such as a particular presidential election).

The mutual influence between people and society is seen best in the concept of socialization.

Socialization refers to the ways in which people learn to function in society (see Chapter 2). Socialization demands that members of society conform their behavior, values, and feelings to society's expectations (Featherman, 1981). The roles we play as adults — such as parent, worker, grandparent, and retiree — reflect what we have incorporated from our observation of how society deals with people in these various positions. As people change their behaviors in particular roles, they in turn change society's expectations. For example, there have been significant changes in how men report they feel about taking care of children. Whereas a few generations ago social expectations dictated that men not change diapers, today many fathers report doing just that.

Finally, *adaptation* refers to modifying behavior in response to changing physical and social environments. We will see in Chapter 12 that changing the nursing home environment to allow residents to have a stronger sense of control may actually help them live longer. Adults of all ages respond to changes in their environment, and flexibility is a key aspect of healthy functioning.

The Interaction of Developmental Forces

Riley (1979) also stressed the lifelong interaction of the biological, psychological, and social forces of development; this interaction demands that we use a holistic multidisciplinary approach for studying adult development and aging. The implications of a holistic approach are profound. For example, if we want to understand what happens to a woman as she goes through menopause, we must consider what occurs biologically and how those events interact with the social myths surrounding menopause and the psychological characteristics of the woman at the time. Focusing on only one of these influences and ignoring the others results in a distorted view. We cannot understand a woman's ex-

perience during menopause if we only consider her hormonal changes.

Having to keep all of the factors in mind requires us to view behaviors as *emergent*. That is, how we act cannot be understood or predicted by breaking down complex behavior into simpler parts. There is something that happens when the pieces of human behavior are put together that goes beyond what one would expect from each piece alone. For example, you may have experienced the satisfaction of having the equation $E = mc^2$ finally make sense when you learned what the letters and the concepts truly meant. This "aha phenomenon" changes your understanding of how the world works. Even though you already knew something about energy (E), mass (m), and the speed of light (c), the new level of understanding you attained following your insight is not predictable based on the way you had previously organized the facts.

One useful way to organize the biological influences, psychological influences, and social influences on adult development and aging is the **biopsychosocial model**. The biopsychosocial model is depicted in Figure 1.1. The model has four major components: interpersonal factors, intrapersonal factors, biological and physical factors, and life-cycle factors (Fry, 1986; Lipowski, 1975). The arrows indicate that adult development and aging is the result of complex interactions among these four factors. These interactions suggest that understanding any one topic, such as physical illness, necessitates taking the other factors into account. Because we will be considering most components of the model more thoroughly in other chapters, we will only review them briefly here.

Interpersonal Factors. Interpersonal factors involve the kinds and quality of a person's relationships with other people, especially family members and friends, and with society at large. These influences fulfill many of our needs, such as for affiliation and love, as well as provide supportive networks for times of personal crisis. Important

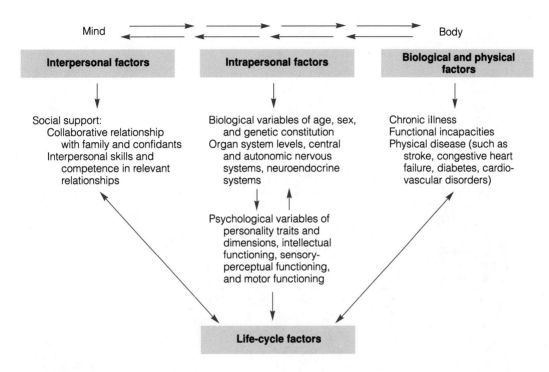

FIGURE 1.1   The biopsychosocial model

(Source: *Depression, Stress, and Adaptations in the Elderly: Psychological Assessment and Intervention* (p. 4) by P. S. Fry, 1986, Rockville, MD: Aspen. Reprinted with permission of Aspen Publishers, Inc. © 1986.)

developmental differences occur in the interpersonal realm, and will be explored in Chapters 9, 10, 11, and 12.

Intrapersonal Factors. Intrapersonal factors refer to two main types of influences. First, normal, health-related changes that are part of growing old place some constraints on what we are capable of doing. These changes will be described in Chapters 3 and 4. Second, psychological processes—personality, memory, intelligence, and so forth—provide the bases for interacting with the world and give us a sense of identity. The many patterns of age-related changes in these processes are described in Chapters 5, 6, 7, and 8.

Biological and Physical Factors. Biological and physical factors refer to illnesses, diseases, and forms of incapacity that disrupt our ability to function. These processes are not considered part of the

Life-cycle factors in the biopsychosocial model are important. For example, this woman's experience raising her child is different from the experience of a woman who becomes a mother at a much younger age.

normal aging process, although their occurrence may increase with age. These factors will be discussed in Chapters 3, 4, and 9.

Life-Cycle Factors. How one behaves at any specific point is strongly affected by one's past social, psychological, and physical experiences in conjunction with one's current functioning and beliefs about the future. Life-cycle factors provide a context for understanding how people perceive their current situation and its effects on them. Life-cycle factors imply that the same event may not have the same effects across the life span. Having a child may mean one thing at age 25 and something quite

different at age 45. Placing current life situations into a broader context is clearly important and has resulted in the life-span approach gaining popularity.

Adopting the Model

What the biopsychosocial model offers is a way to organize the myriad changes that occur over a lifetime. But it is not easy to adopt this holistic perspective once we begin to realize just how many different events occur in our lives. One metaphor that may help is to think of the life span as made

SOMETHING TO THINK ABOUT

Using the Biopsychosocial Model

It may seem that the biopsychosocial model's advantages are so obvious that researchers would have been using it for years. This is not the case. It is only in the past decade or so that psychological research has emphasized the need for multidisciplinary views about aging. Before this, most psychologists regarded aging as an inevitable decline, and they did not see the need for other views.

Adopting a biopsychosocial model, then, is a radical departure from the past. Working within this framework also means accepting that aging is an extraordinarily complex process. For one thing, it means that psychological aging is not an isolated phenomenon; it must be viewed in the context of biological and social aging as well.

For example, age differences in intelligence must be considered in the context of ongoing normative changes in the brain; these differences must also be regarded in terms of the important historical changes in education and technology that could affect the way people think. The fact that this book was written on a computer drastically simplifies the revision process, making it far easier to bring material up to date than it was even 30 years ago. Such changes profoundly affect the way people learn, which in turn affects what they learn, which can dramatically change underlying intellectual abilities.

To make the biopsychosocial model more personally relevant, take a minute to think about your own development. Think about the complex ways your life has been changed due to the interplay of biological, psychological, and social forces. See if you can identify why it makes more sense to think about all three of these forces being merged into a single explanation than trying to account for your behavior with any one of them. It's something to think about.

---

up of rhythms (Bohannon, 1980). Our bodies and our communities create biological, psychological, and sociocultural rhythms, all of which are embedded in the larger life-cycle rhythm. Each of these rhythms varies; some change daily, others only monthly or even more slowly. Every culture has its unique rhythm, and what we learn about one may not hold for another. Moreover, different cultures will have problems dealing with one another, since each moves to its own rhythm. Bohannon extends this point to different age groups, arguing that dysrhythmias can affect social relations between them so that they do not mesh well.

Only by studying adulthood and aging from a holistic perspective, both historically and cross-culturally, can we understand the rhythmic and dysrhythmic patterns within and across societies.

For this reason, we will use the biopsychosocial model throughout the book to remind us that adult development and aging is a complex interactive process. Take a minute to think about what the biopsychosocial model means as you read Something to Think About.

THE MEANING OF AGE

One of the most important aspects of studying adult development and aging is understanding the concept of aging itself. Aging is not a single process. Rather, it consists of at least three distinct processes:

primary, secondary, and tertiary aging (Birren & Cunningham, 1985). *Primary aging* refers to the normal, disease-free movement across adulthood. Changes in biological, social, or psychological processes in primary aging are an inevitable part of the developmental process; examples include menopause, decline in reaction time, and the loss of family and friends. Most of the information in this book falls under the primary aging heading. *Secondary aging* refers to developmental changes that are related to disease. The progressive loss of intellectual abilities in Alzheimer's disease and other diseases such as cancer are examples of secondary aging. Finally, *tertiary aging* refers to the rapid losses that occur shortly before death. As described more fully in Chapter 6, tertiary aging is sometimes associated with a phenomenon known as terminal drop, in which intellectual abilities show a marked decline in the last few years preceding death.

Increasingly, researchers are emphasizing that everyone does not grow old in the same way. While many people tend to show *usual patterns of aging* that reflect the typical changes with age, other people show *successful aging* in which few signs of change occur. For example, while most people tend to get chronic diseases as they get older, some people never do. What makes people who age successfully different? At this point, we do not really know for sure. It may be a unique combination of genetics, optimal environment, flexibility in dealing with life situations, a strong sense of personal control, and maybe even a bit of luck.

The main point to keep in mind throughout is that everyone's experience of growing old is somewhat different. Though you will have plenty of company if you should develop arthritis, how you learn to cope will be your unique contribution.

Age as an Index

When most of us think about age, we usually think of how long we have been around since our birth. This way of defining age is what is known as **chro-**

nological age. Chronological age provides a shorthand method to index time and to organize events and data by using a commonly understood standard: calendar time. Chronological age is not the only shorthand index used in adult development and aging. Gender, ethnicity, and socioeconomic status are others.

No index variable itself actually causes behavior. In the case of socioeconomic status, for example, it is presumably not the size of the person's bank account per se that causes charitable behavior. But this point is often forgotten when age is the index variable, perhaps because it is so familiar to us and so widely used. However, age (or time) does not directly cause things to happen, either. Iron left out in the rain will rust, but rust is not caused simply by time. Rather, rust is a *time-dependent process* involving oxidation in which time is a measure of the rate by which rust is created. Similarly, human behavior is affected by experiences that occur with the passage of time, not by time itself. What we study in adult development and aging is the result of time- or age-dependent processes, not the result of age itself.

What do we need to do in order to know whether some behavior is actually time dependent? Birren and Renner (1977) argue that we need to understand the underlying biological, social, and psychological processes that are all intertwined in an index such as chronological age. In short, what we need are better definitions of age that reflect the biopsychosocial model.

Definitions of Age

Age can be considered from each of the perspectives in the biopsychosocial model (Birren & Cunningham, 1985): biological, social, and psychological.

Biological Age. **Biological age** represents where a person is relative to his or her potential maximum life span. Biological age is assessed by measuring the functioning of the various vital, or life-limiting, organ systems, such as the cardiovascular system. These systems and the life-style factors that influence their functioning are discussed in Chapters 3 and 4. As we will see, with increasing age the vital organ systems typically lose their capacity for self-regulation and adaptation, resulting in an increased probability of dying. Through a healthy life style, it is possible to slow some of the age-related change processes and be functionally younger biologically than a lifelong couch potato. In contrast, someone who has the disease progeria, in which the body ages abnormally rapidly, is biologically much older than his or her peers. In short, biological age accounts for many health-related aspects of functioning in assigning an age to an individual.

Social Age. At some point in your life you have probably been told to act your age. There seem to be unwritten expectations of how individuals of a certain chronological age should act. Such unwritten expectations are what is meant by social age. More formally, **social age** refers to the specific set of roles individuals adopt in relation to other members of the society to which they belong. Social age is judged on the basis of many behaviors and habits, such as style of dress, language, and interpersonal style. Most important is the extent to which a person shows the age-graded behavior expected by society; this forms the basis by which a person is judged to be socially younger or older. If one is adopting new roles ahead of one's peers, that person is considered socially older. For example, Loretta Lynn, who married at 14, would be considered socially old in comparison with the typical age norm of 22 for first marriage. In contrast, if one adopts roles later than one's peers, then that person would be considered socially younger. Bette Midler, who had her first child when she was middle-aged, would be considered socially young; most women have their first child during their 20s.

Social age is especially important in understanding many of the family and work roles we adopt. When to get married, have children, make career moves, and so on are often influenced by what we think our social age is. Such decisions also play a role in determining our self-esteem and other aspects of personality. Many of the most damaging stereotypes about aging (such as that old people should not be having sex) are based on faulty assumptions about social age. We will consider these issues in more detail in Chapters 8, 10, 11, and 12.

Psychological Age. **Psychological age** refers to the abilities that people use to adapt to changing environmental demands. These abilities include memory, intelligence, feelings, motivation, and other skills that foster and maintain self-esteem and personal control. For example, 15-year-old Michelle who attends medical school would be considered psychologically older in the intellectual domain, because the large majority of her classmates are 22 or older. On the other hand, Mildred, a 60-year-old English major, would be thought of as psychologically young in the intellectual area, because the vast majority of her classmates are much younger.

Many myths about older adults stem from our misconceptions about the abilities that underlie definitions of psychological age. For example, many people believe that all types of memory and other intellectual capabilities decline precipitously in later life. As we will see especially in Chapters 5, 6, and 7, many of these beliefs are wrong, meaning that we need to revise the standards by which we judge psychological aging in these domains.

Issues in Studying Age

Despite potentially better alternatives, most researchers in adult development and aging continue to use chronological age as a primary variable of interest. You may wonder why, given the availability of more precise definitions of age.

Developmental research can be categorized on the basis of how it uses the variable of age (Birren & Cunningham, 1985). In the *developmentally*

Although chronologically older than most of her classmates, the woman on the right is psychologically younger than most of her same-age peers.

static approach the major goal of the researcher is to describe individuals in particular age groups. For instance, a researcher may be interested in how 21-year-olds and 30-year-olds behave on dates. In this case age is used mainly to define the boundaries of the investigation; the two groups would be studied at one point in time. In contrast, the *developmentally dynamic approach* seeks to understand the processes of change. The focus here is to understand how people develop, what characterizes change, and how change happens. In the developmentally dynamic approach, the researcher would be most interested in how 21-year-old daters evolve into 30-year-old daters. This would require following people for nine years, periodically testing them along the way.

The need for precision in defining the role of age is more important in the developmentally dy-namic approach. The ultimate interest of researchers in this approach is not the passage of time but rather the changes in behavior that emerge over time. These behavioral changes are only crudely indexed by chronological age (for example, not all 21-year-olds have the same amount of prior dating experience). Once this fact is recognized, however, there are two courses that could be followed.

First, chronological age could be replaced by one of the definitions described earlier that focus on some specific process, such as psychological change. This would put the focus on a more specific ability, which could then be tracked over time.

The second alternative is accepting chron-ological age as a *surrogate variable* (Birren & Cunningham, 1985) to represent the very complex, interrelated influences on people over time. Use of a surrogate variable such as age does not allow a researcher to state the cause of some behavior precisely, because the surrogate variable represents so many different things. If we say that memory for details shows an age-related decrease, we do not know whether the difference stems from biological processes, psychological processes, social processes, or some combination of processes. Even though chronological age is a crude index, however, it may provide useful information that can be used to guide future, more precise research that could narrow the number of explanations.

To date, most researchers have chosen to use chronological age as a surrogate variable. However, the strategy adopted over the past decade is to combine this use of chronological age with the concepts of primary, secondary, and tertiary aging. In particular, most of the research reported in this book focuses on primary (disease-free) aging. Participants in most studies are described as "healthy, community-dwelling adults." Although this tie between surrogate variables and primary aging is often not stated explicitly, it nevertheless offers an important way to document and understand the processes of aging that represent usual patterns of aging.

Relationships Between Age and Developmental Influences

Thus far, we have concentrated on how our interpretations of age data are clouded by a variety of influences. We come now to the issue of how the multiple determinants of adult development are related to age. Baltes (1979) identifies three sets of influences that interact to produce developmental change over the life span:

Normative age-graded influences are those biological and environmental factors that are highly correlated with chronological age. Some of these — such as puberty, menarche, and menopause — are biological. These normative biological events usually indicate major change. For example, meno-

pause is an indicator that a woman can no longer bear children. Other normative age-graded influences involve socialization and cultural customs, such as the time when first marriage occurs and the age when one retires. These influences typically correspond to major time-marker events, which are often ritualized. For example, many younger adults formally celebrate turning 21 as the official transition to adulthood, getting married is typically surrounded with much celebration, and retirement is often begun with a party as well. These events provide the most convenient way to judge where we are on our social clock.

Normative history-graded influences are events that most people in a culture experience at the same time. These events may be biological (such as epidemics), environmental (such as wars or economic depressions), or social (such as changing attitudes toward sexuality). Normative history-graded influences often endow a generation with its unique identity, such as the Depression generation or the Vietnam War generation. These influences can have a profound effect. For example, the emergence of AIDS during the 1980s fundamentally changed the attitudes toward dating and casual sexual relationships that had developed during the preceding decades.

Nonnormative influences may be important for a specific individual but are not experienced by most people. These may be favorable events, such as winning the lottery or an election, or unfavorable ones, such as an accident or layoff. The unpredictability of these events makes them unique. It is as if one's life is turned upside down overnight.

The relative importance of these three influences depends on the specific behaviors examined and the particular point in the life span when they occur (Hultsch & Plemons, 1979). For example, history-graded influences may produce generational differences and conflict. In turn, these interactions have important implications for understanding differences that are apparently age related.

Experiencing major historical events such as the Great Depression has a profound influence on subsequent development.

What makes the study of adult development and aging a bit different from other areas of psychology is the need to consider multiple influences on behavior. For gerontologists in particular, it is essential to consider the biopsychosocial factors. This makes research more difficult, if for no other reason than it requires considering more variables.

The usual approach to gathering data on adult development and aging has been to find ways to study the various factors that cause change over the life span in controlled settings (Maddox & Campbell, 1985; Nesselroade & Labouvie, 1985). However, some gerontologists advocate research on aging in the real world, and are using alternative methods that focus on the subjective experience of growing old. One alternative approach is naturalistic inquiry (Lincoln & Guba, 1985), which focuses on growing old in the real world rather than in the psychological laboratory. We will examine these approaches in this section. First, however, we must review the three major effects that explain differences between and within people over time.

In the next section we will specifically consider how these influences get incorporated into researchers' methods for learning about adults.

RESEARCH METHODS

As a part of psychology, the study of adult development and aging adheres to the principles of scientific inquiry that guide the parent discipline. Information concerning adult development and aging is gathered in the same ways as in other fields of psychology. Gerontologists also have the same problems as other psychologists: finding appropriate control groups, limiting generalizations to the groups included in the research, and finding adequate means of measurement (Kausler, 1982).

Age, Cohort, and Time of Measurement

Every study of adult development and aging is built on the combination of three fundamental effects: age, cohort, and time of measurement (Schaie, 1984).

Age effects reflect differences due to underlying processes, that is, biological, social, or psychological changes. Although usually represented in research by chronological age, age effects refer to inherent changes within the person and are not caused by the passage of time per se. As we established earlier in this chapter, a better approach would be to use a more specific definition of age (such as, biological, social, or psychological age).

Cohort effects are differences due to experiences and circumstances unique to the particular generation to which one belongs. In general, cohort effects correspond to normative history-graded influences. However, in studying cohort effects, it may not be easy to define what a cohort is. Cohorts can be specific, as in all people born in one particular year, or general, such as the baby boom cohort. As described earlier, each generation is exposed to different sets of historical and personal events (such as, World War II, home computers, educational opportunities). Later in this section we will consider evidence of just how profound cohort effects can be.

Time-of-measurement effects reflect differences stemming from social, environmental, historical, or other events at the time the data are obtained from the participants. For example, data concerning wage increases given in a particular year may be influenced by the economic conditions of that year. If the economy is in a serious recession, it is likely that pay increases would be small. In contrast, if the economy is booming, pay increases could be quite large. Clearly, whether you conduct your study during a recession or a boom will affect what you learn about pay changes. In short, when you decide to do your research could lead you to different conclusions about the phenomenon you are studying.

In conducting adult development and aging research, investigators have attempted to identify and separate the three effects. This has not been easy, because all three influences are interrelated. If one is interested in studying 40-year-olds, one must necessarily select the cohort that was born 40 years ago. In this case age and cohort are *confounded*, because one cannot know whether the behaviors observed are due to the fact that the participants are 40 years old or due to the specific life experiences they have had as a result of being born in a particular historical period. In general, confounding refers to any situation in which you cannot determine which of two (or more) variables is responsible for the behaviors you observe. Confounding of the three effects we are considering here represents the most serious problem in adult development and aging research.

Developmental Research Designs

What distinguishes developmental researchers from their colleagues in other areas of psychology is a fundamental interest in understanding how people change. Developmental researchers must look at the ways in which people differ across time. Doing so necessarily requires that they understand the distinction between age change and age difference. An *age change* occurs in an individual's behavior over time. A person's reaction time may not be as short at age 70 as it was at age 40. To discover an age change you must examine the same person at more than one point in time. An *age difference* is obtained when at least two different persons of different ages are compared. A person of 70 may have a longer reaction time than another person of age 40. Even though we may be able to document substantial age differences, we cannot assume that they imply an age change. We do not know whether the 70-year-old has changed since he or she was 40, and of course we do not know whether the 40-year-old will be any different at age 70. In some cases age differences reflect age changes, and in some cases they do not.

If what we really want to understand in developmental research is age change (what happens as people grow older), we should strive to design our research with this goal in mind. Moreover, different research questions require different research designs. We will consider the most common ways in which researchers gather data concerning age differences and age changes: cross-sectional, longitudinal, time-lag, and sequential.

Figure 1.2 helps to keep these different research designs straight, and shows how each of the designs relates to the others. The figure depicts a matrix containing each major effect (age, cohort, and time of measurement). Cohort is represented by the years down the left column. Time of measurement is represented by the years across the bottom. Age is represented by the numbers in the body of the table.

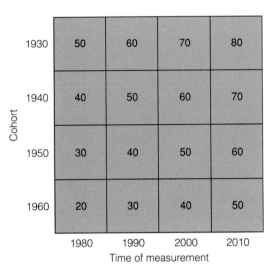

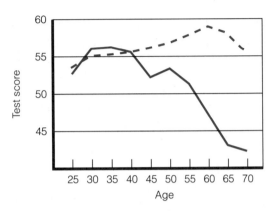

FIGURE 1.3 Cross-sectional (solid line) age differences and longitudinal (dashed line) age changes in intelligence for a verbal meaning test

(Source: "A Cross-Sequential Study of Age Changes in Cognitive Behavior" by K. W. Schaie and C. R. Strother, 1968, *Psychological Bulletin, 70*, 671–680. Copyright © 1968 by the American Psychological Association. Reprinted with permission.)

FIGURE 1.2 Matrix of time of measurement, cohort, and age (the cells in the body of the matrix), from which research designs can be constructed as described in the text

Cross-Sectional Designs. A **cross-sectional design** compares groups of people varying in age at one point in time. As such, it represents the developmentally static approach discussed earlier. Any single vertical column in Figure 1.2 represents a cross-sectional design. Cross-sectional designs allow researchers to examine age differences but not age change. The reason has to do with how any observed differences are explained.

Because all participants are measured at the same time, differences between the groups cannot be due to time-of-measurement effects. That leaves two possibilities: age change and cohort differences. Unfortunately, we cannot distinguish between them, which means that we do not know whether the differences we observe between groups stem from inherent developmental processes or from experiences peculiar to their cohort. To see this more clearly, take a careful look at Figure 1.2. Notice that the different age groups are automati-

cally formed when particular cohorts are selected, and vice versa. Thus, if the researcher wants to study people of a certain age at a particular time, he or she has no choice in choosing a cohort. This confounding of age and cohort is the major problem with cross-sectional studies.

Cross-sectional research tends to paint a bleak picture of aging. For example, early research on the development of intelligence across adulthood repeatedly showed large drops in performance with age (see Figure 1.3). The problem is that we have no way of knowing whether most people show the same developmental progressions; that is, we cannot address the issue of individual differences over time.

Despite the confounding of age and cohort and the limitation of only being able to identify age differences, cross-sectional designs dominate the research literature in gerontology. The reason is a pragmatic one: Because all of the measurements are obtained at one time, cross-sectional research can be conducted relatively quickly and inexpensively compared with other designs. As long as their limits are recognized, cross-sectional studies can provide a snapshot view of age differences that may provide insight into issues that may be followed up with other designs that are sensitive to age change.

Longitudinal Designs. A **longitudinal design** provides information about age changes; the strategy involves testing a single cohort over multiple times of measurement. Longitudinal designs represent the developmentally dynamic approach. A longitudinal design is represented by any horizontal row in Figure 1.2. A major advantage of longitudinal designs is that age changes are identified because we are studying the same people over time. But if age changes are found, can we say why they occurred?

Because only one cohort is studied, cohort effects are eliminated as an explanation of change. However, the other two potential explanations, age and time of measurement, are confounded. For example, suppose that we wanted to follow the 1930 cohort over time. If we wanted to test these individuals when they were 60 years old, we would have to do so in 1990. Consequently, any changes we identify could be due to changes in underlying processes or factors that are related to the time we choose to conduct our measurement. For instance, if we conducted a longitudinal study of salary growth, the amount of salary change in any comparison could stem from real change in skills and worth of the person to the company or from the economic conditions of the times. In a longitudinal study we cannot tell which of these factors is more important.

There are three additional potential problems with longitudinal studies. First, if the research measure requires some type of performance by the participants, we may have the problem of *practice effects*. Practice effects refer to the fact that performance may improve over time simply because people are being tested over and over again with the same measures. Repeatedly using the same measure on the same people may have significant effects on their behavior, may make the measure invalid, and may have a negative impact on the participants' perceptions of the research (Baltes, Reese, & Nesselroade, 1977).

Second, we may have a problem with *participant dropout*. Participant dropout refers to the fact that it is difficult to keep a group of research participants intact over the course of a longitudinal study. Participants may move, may lose interest, or may die. Suppose we want to examine the relationship between intelligence and health. Participant dropout can result in two different outcomes. We can end up with *positive selective survival* if the participants at the end of the study tend to be the ones who were initially higher on some variable; for example, the surviving participants are the ones who were the most healthy at the beginning of the study. In contrast, we could have *negative selective survival* if the participants at the conclusion of the study were initially lower on an important variable; for example, the surviving participants may have been those who initially weighed the least.

The extent to which the characteristics of the group change over time determines the degree of the problem. We may not know exactly what differences there are between those who return for every session and those who do not. What we do know is that the people who always return, in general, are more outgoing, are healthier, have higher self-esteem, and are more likely to be married than those who drop out (Schaie & Hertzog, 1985).

In any case, the result may be an overly optimistic picture of aging. Compare some typical results from longitudinal studies of intelligence, also shown in Figure 1.3, with those gathered in cross-sectional studies. Clearly, the developmental trends represented are quite different, a point we will examine again in Chapter 7.

The third problem with longitudinal designs is that our ability to apply the results to other groups is limited. The difficulty is that only one cohort is followed. Whether the pattern of results that is observed in one cohort can be generalized to another cohort is questionable. Thus, researchers using longitudinal designs run the risk of uncovering a developmental process that is unique to that cohort.

Because longitudinal designs necessarily take more time and are usually fairly expensive, they have not been used very frequently in the past. However, there seems to be a recognition that following individuals over time is badly needed in order to further our understanding of the aging process. Thus, longitudinal studies are becoming more common in the literature.

Time-Lag Designs. **Time-lag designs** involve measuring people of the same age at different times. Time-lag designs are represented in Figure 1.2 by any top-left to bottom-right diagonal. Because only a single age is studied, there are no age-related differences. Because each cohort is associated with a unique time of measurement, however, these two effects are confounded. Time-lag designs are used to describe characteristics of people at a particular age. But because they provide no information on either age differences or age change, time-lag designs are not frequently used.

Sequential Designs. Thus far, we have considered three developmental designs, each of which has problems involving the confounding of two effects. These effects are age and cohort in cross-sectional designs, age and time of measurement in longitudinal designs, and cohort and time of measurement in time-lag designs. These confoundings create difficulties in interpreting behavioral differences between and within individuals, as illustrated in How Do We Know? Some of these interpretive dilemmas can be alleviated by using more complex designs called sequential designs, which are shown in Figure 1.4 (Baltes et al., 1977; Schaie & Hertzog,

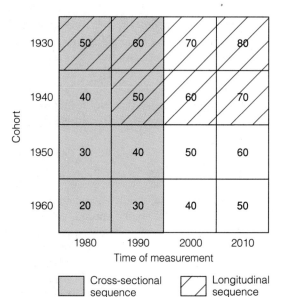

FIGURE 1.4 Matrix of time of measurement, cohort, and age, demonstrating sequential research designs. The first and second vertical columns illustrate cross-sectional sequences described in the text. The top two horizontal rows, likewise, illustrate longitudinal sequences mentioned in the text. (The three squares that are both shaded in red and striped are areas in the matrix where two sequences overlap.)

1985). Keep in mind, though, that sequential designs do not cure the confounding problems in the three basic designs.

Sequential designs build on the designs we have already considered. As shown in the figure, a *cross-sequential sequence* consists of two or more cross-sectional studies that are conducted at two or more times of measurement. These multiple cross-sectional designs each include the same age ranges; however, the participants are different in each wave of testing. For example, we might compare performances on intelligence tests for people between the ages of 20 and 50 in 1980 and then repeat the study in 1990 with a different group of people aged 30 to 60.

HOW DO WE KNOW?

Conflicts Between Cross-Sectional and Longitudinal Data

Cross-sectional and longitudinal research designs have several limitations. What may not be clear, however, are the major implications that each has on drawing conclusions about age differences. Recall that in cross-sectional research we examine different groups of people of different ages at one point in time, thereby confounding age and cohort. In longitudinal research we examine one group of people at many points, thereby confounding age and time of measurement.

As an illustration of how using these two designs can result in opposite conclusions about age differences, let's examine the case of intellectual development. For many years a debate raged in the literature over whether intelligence increased, decreased, or remained the same across adulthood. This debate was fueled in large part by conflicting findings based on cross-sectional research

and longitudinal research. Cross-sectional data documented clear age differences in intelligence with age. In contrast, longitudinal data showed no significant age differences. What conclusions could be drawn about each type of data? Which data are correct?

In the case of cross-sectional data, the age differences could reflect either true differences that occur with age or differences that are due to cohort, or generational, effects. For example, the fact that older people never learned computer skills in school whereas younger people did may make a difference in how well one performs on current tests of intelligence. The problem is that we cannot differentiate between these two equally plausible explanations.

In the case of longitudinal data, the lack of age effects could be a reflection of a true lack of change with age. However, it is also possible that only the brightest and healthiest people survived to be tested at the end of the study. This would mean that the characteristics of the sample at the end were significantly different from those of the sample at the beginning. In short, we ended up with

a very different group of people. Moreover, we also do not know whether the lack of difference is due to other aspects of the environment that serve to support intellectual performance. Perhaps there are new discoveries about maintaining intellectual performance that assist older people. We cannot sort out all of these different explanations.

As will be described in Chapter 7, neither type of data is entirely correct. It turns out that the confounding of age and cohort in the cross-sectional data was misinterpreted as showing *age* differences, when actually most of what are seen are differences due to *cohort*. The longitudinal data are problematic because of differential survival; that is, by the end of the research only the healthiest individuals remained. These survivors were not representative of the group that began the study.

This example illustrates the need for extreme caution in comparing the results of cross-sectional and longitudinal studies. We need to avoid making the same mistakes as researchers in the past. Fortunately, we have a viable solution: sequential designs.

Figure 1.4 also depicts the *longitudinal sequential* design. A longitudinal sequential design consists of two or more longitudinal designs that represent two or more cohorts. Each longitudinal design in the sequence would begin with the same age range and follow people for the same length of

time. For example, we may want to begin a longitudinal study of intellectual development with a group of 50-year-olds in 1980, using the 1930 cohort. We would then follow this cohort for a period of years. In 1990 we would begin a second longitudinal study on 50-year-olds, using the 1940 cohort, and follow them for the same length of time as we do the first cohort.

Schaie (1965, 1977) has argued that combining cross-sequential sequences and longitudinal sequences yields a "most efficient design." The combined design yields data that can be used to address most of the major questions that interest developmental researchers. As an example, let us consider Schaie's own research on intellectual development in adulthood. The research began with a simple cross-sectional study in 1956 in which participants aged 22 to 67 years from four cohorts were given tests of intellectual abilities. In 1963 as many of these participants as possible were retested, providing longitudinal data on age changes in each of the four cohorts. At the same time, new groups of participants between 20 and 70 years old were recruited and tested. These new participants formed a second cross-sectional study representing the same age groups that were tested in 1956. In 1970 both cross-sectional samples were retested, providing a second set of longitudinal data for the 1956 sample and the first for the 1963 sample. Finally, the 1963 sample was tested a third time in 1977, providing comparable 14-year spans for each of the two groups.

Although sequential designs are powerful and provide by far the richest source of information about developmental issues, few researchers use them because they are costly in terms of both money and time. Trying to follow many people over long periods of time, generating new samples, and conducting complex data analyses take considerable financial resources. Moreover, it took Schaie 21 years for all of the data to be gathered and an additional 5 years or so for the data to become widely published. Clearly, this type of commitment to one project is not possible for most researchers, especially those who are trying to establish themselves in the field. Additionally, in times of restricted research financing, the large sums needed for sequential designs may simply be unavailable.

Representativeness and Adequate Measurement

Research designs structure the approach we take in gathering our data. How we gather the data involves making assumptions about the behavior we plan on studying. In particular, we decide whether we are able to manipulate the situation to conduct an experiment, or whether we can only examine co-occurrences among behaviors to conduct correlational research. In addition, we might consider a technique called naturalistic inquiry that focuses on obtaining information about behavior in as natural a setting as possible.

There are two important research issues regardless of the approach chosen for data collection: representativeness and adequate measurement. **Representativeness** refers to the degree to which the participants in the research study reflect the characteristics of the group of people who make up the population of interest. For example, if one wants to know how grandparents and grandchildren interact, one would need to include grandparents of many different ages, ethnic backgrounds, socioeconomic statuses, and educational levels. Unless this diverse group is studied, one cannot be certain that the results of one's research will be true for groups of people who were not included. Because most of the research described in this book was conducted with white, middle-class, well-educated adults, we must be cautious in extending or generalizing the findings to ethnic minority groups or other underrepresented people.

Adequate measurement ensures that sound research tools are used to gather data. In particular, we must demonstrate that our measures are both reliable and valid. **Reliability** concerns whether a technique measures a variable consistently. For example, if we were to administer a self-esteem scale to a group of people on two occasions only a few days apart, we would need to find fairly consistent scores for both testing times to conclude that our measure is reliable. Reliability is an absolute must; data obtained from unreliable measures are worthless.

Whether a data gathering technique has **validity** refers to whether it measures what it is supposed to measure. For example, we must establish in fact that the self-esteem scale we are using indeed measures self-esteem. Validity may be established in several ways: comparing scores on this test of self-esteem to scores on other valid scales of self-esteem; evaluating how well this scale predicts scores on other related scales; seeing how well this scale corresponds to the true concept of self-esteem; or deciding how well this scale differentiates self-esteem from other personality traits and how well it agrees with similar notions such as self-concept. In general, the validity of a scale is harder to document than its reliability. And in the case of aging, few scales, even those used frequently, have been shown to be valid measures with older adults. Data obtained with such measures should be interpreted cautiously.

Approaches to Doing Research

The specific design you choose for your research will limit what you may conclude from your data, especially the inferences you may draw concerning age comparisons. Three basic approaches are used: experimentation, correlation, and naturalistic inquiry.

Experimental Design. Suppose we are interested in learning whether having people study a word list in various ways makes a difference in how many items people will remember. What we could do is to provide people of different ages with different types of instructions about how to study, and then see what happens when they are asked to remember the words. For example, we could tell one group each of younger and older adults to rehearse the

words in the list we will show them three times each, and not provide any special hints to a second group.

What we have done is an example of an **experiment**. The fundamental idea in an experiment is the manipulation of a key factor that the researcher believes is responsible for a particular behavior. In our case, the key variable being manipulated is the instructions for how to study. More generally, in an experiment the researcher is most interested in identifying differences between groups of people that are the direct result of the variable being introduced to various degrees across groups. The investigator exerts precise control over all important aspects of the study, including the variable of interest, the setting, and the participants. Because the key variable is systematically manipulated in an experiment, researchers can infer cause-and-effect relationships about that variable. In our example, we can conclude that type of instruction (how people study) causes better or worse performance on a memory test. Discovering such cause-and-effect relationships is important if we are to understand the underlying processes of adult development and aging.

An important distinction is made between *independent variables*, which are variables manipulated by the experimenter, and *dependent variables*, which are the behaviors or outcomes that are measured. In our example, the instructions that we give people would be the independent variable and the number of words people remember would be the dependent variable.

The results of experiments can come out in two ways. If everyone reacts the same way to the manipulation regardless of age, then we can conclude that the phenomenon under study may work in parallel ways across the age range examined. If younger and older adults improve their memory performance to equivalent degrees by rehearsing, then we could argue that rehearsal has the same benefit for both age groups. On the other hand, if one age group reacts very differently than the other to the manipulated variable, we obtain an age-by-condition interaction. Suppose the older adults benefited a great deal from rehearsing and the younger adults did not benefit at all. This age-by-condition interaction could mean that rehearsal instructions are only effective for older adults. In general, age-by-condition interactions are thought to imply that the underlying processes that produce the behavior being studied differ across age. By mapping out the conditions under which age-by-condition interactions are and are not present, we get a better picture of which psychological processes differ with age and which ones do not.

Finally, we must note that *age cannot be an independent variable because we cannot manipulate it.* Consequently, it is impossible for us to conduct true experiments to examine the effects of age on a particular person's behavior. At best, we can find *age-related effects* of an independent variable on dependent variables.

Correlational Design. In contrast to experiments, where the goal is to understand cause and effect, in **correlation** the goal is to uncover a relationship between two or more observed variables. For example, Cavanaugh and Murphy (1986) were interested in the relationship between anxiety and memory performance. They administered measures of anxiety and memory tests and calculated the correlations between the two. Their results showed that whether memory performance is related to anxiety depends on which measure of anxiety one chooses to use.

Correlational studies do not give definitive information concerning cause-and-effect relationships; for example, a correlation between intelligence and problem-solving ability does not mean that one causes the other regardless of how large the relationship is. However, correlational studies do provide important information about the strength of relationship between variables. Moreover, because developmental researchers are interested in

how variables are related to factors that are very difficult, if not impossible, to manipulate, correlational techniques are used a great deal. In fact, most developmental research is, at some level, correlational because age cannot be manipulated within an individual. What this means is that we can *describe* a great many developmental phenomena, but we cannot *explain* very many of them.

Naturalistic Inquiry. Since the late 1970s psychologists have become increasingly concerned that experimental and correlational approaches greatly oversimplify human behavior. In particular, both of these techniques rely on the assumption that the important factors that determine human behavior can be isolated and studied independently (Hesse, 1980). One approach that does not make this assumption is naturalistic inquiry (Lincoln & Guba, 1985).

Naturalistic inquiry assumes that human behavior is the result of complex, mutually dependent forces that cannot be studied in isolation. Human behavior must be studied in its natural environment and cannot be simulated in a laboratory. This approach relies on carefully conducted interactions between an inquirer (the researcher) and a participant. The information to be learned from the investigation may not be clear at the outset, but it will emerge as the study progresses. A common technique used in naturalistic inquiry is the in-depth interview, which provides a very rich set of data. Lincoln and Guba (1985) provide 14 principles that guide naturalistic inquiry, covering everything from selecting the appropriate participants, to conducting interviews, to extracting the key information, to reporting one's findings to others.

Naturalistic inquiry seems especially appropriate for research involving social interactions and such psychological issues as self-concept. Because these topics involve dynamic interchange, naturalistic inquiry provides a closer approximation of the real world than either the experimental or the correlational approach (Cavanaugh & Morton, 1989).

The Biopsychosocial Model and Research with Older Adults

Suppose you decide you want to learn something about age differences across adulthood with regard to people's judgments about their memory. Because little is known about this topic, you decide to adopt a cross-sectional approach (realizing the limitations that this decision brings). To make data collection maximally efficient, you develop a questionnaire that asks people about the adequacy of their memory in several different domains (names, faces, and so forth), how they think their memory has changed over the recent past, what kinds of tricks they use to remember, and how anxious they get when they have to remember. (Such a questionnaire really exists, as described in Chapter 6.)

Questionnaire in hand, you are now ready to collect data. Or so you may think. Actually, there are several issues to consider before dashing out and recruiting people to complete your survey, especially if you include older adults in your sample.

Recall that the biopsychosocial model draws attention to many factors that could influence research. Among these are participation rates of different groups, health, normative physiological and psychological changes, and life-cycle factors. Middle-class, fairly well-educated whites tend to be overrepresented in adult development and aging research; ethnic minorities tend to be underrepresented. Based on the biopsychosocial model, we would not necessarily expect research findings based on whites to generalize to other groups. Unfortunately, there are few data that address this issue.

Health has a powerful influence on psychological functioning. For example, we will see that chronic disease can influence intellectual functioning (Chapter 7), and that some diseases such as Alzheimer's, are marked by profound losses of psychological functioning (Chapter 9). As a result, researchers should include some minimal assessment of health in their investigations.

One frequently overlooked issue in conducting research with older adults concerns normative changes in vision and hearing (see Chapter 3). Older adults often have trouble reading small print that may be clearly seen by younger adults. Failure to correct for vision problems — by printing questionnaires in larger type — could result in missing or inaccurate data, or in older adults simply refusing to complete the survey. Likewise, hearing loss could lead to misinterpretation of interview questions or misunderstandings of verbal instructions.

Unlike psychology undergraduate students for whom research participation may be a course requirement, nonstudent adults who participate in research are typically volunteers. This may or may not cause problems in terms of the representativeness of your sample. It will, however, require you to make participation in your project sound attractive. Adults have many competing demands on their time, such as work, relationships, hobbies, and relaxation. Make the goals of the project clear, and argue that the findings will be important. Creative and properly applied research designs can yield important insights into adult development and aging.

SUMMARY

Issues and Models in Adult Development and Aging

1. The effects of any genetically linked trait depend on the environment in which the trait gets expressed; these effects vary from direct to indirect.

2. Environmental effects occur within a range set by genetically linked traits.

3. The focus on nature and nurture must be on how they interact.

4. Continuity and discontinuity lead to very different views on the course of adult development and aging.

5. Much of what we know about adult development and aging is description. We have few explanations for why or how these phenomena occur.

6. Quantitative versus qualitative changes in behavior lead to different views on the nature of change.

7. General models of adult development and aging are based on differing views on the nature-nurture and the continuity-discontinuity controversies.

8. The mechanistic model views people as machines; that is, as passive, reactive collections of interacting parts controlled by external stimuli, with a focus on quantitative change.

9. The organismic model views people as complex biological systems that are more than the sum of their parts. Emergence is a key idea, as are the notions that people are active shapers of their development, headed toward a goal, with an emphasis on qualitative change.

10. The contextual model focuses on the historical context in which people develop. It also views people as active, as more than the sum of their parts, and as having many possible goals. Change can be both quantitative and qualitative.

11. The various models lead to different methodologies for addressing research questions.

12. Social policy is influenced differently by each of the models.

The Biopsychosocial Model

13. The life-span perspective emphasizes that in order to understand adult development and aging, we must employ multiple perspectives in an interdisciplinary fashion.

14. Aging is a lifelong process that must be put into time perspective. How one regards one's development is determined in part by one's social clock, which is a result of socialization and adaptation.

15. The biopsychosocial model emphasizes four factors: interpersonal, intrapersonal, biological and physical, and life cycle.

16. Adopting the biopsychosocial model means being aware that aging is a complex process, with many determining factors.

The Meaning of Age

17. Three types of aging are distinguished: primary (disease-free), secondary (disease related), and tertiary (rapid loss with impending death).

18. Chronological age is a poor descriptor of time-dependent processes.

19. Better definitions of age include biological age, social age, and psychological age.

20. Developmental research can be categorized in terms of whether it is static (focuses on description) or dynamic (focuses on processes of change).

21. Chronological age can be used as a surrogate variable if better measures are unavailable.

22. Normative age-graded influences include all factors highly correlated with chronological age.

23. Normative history-graded influences are those experienced by an entire cohort, and are not necessarily related to chronological age.

24. Nonnormative influences are random events unrelated to age.

Research Methods

25. Age effects reflect underlying biological, social, or psychological processes.

26. Cohort effects reflect generational differences.

27. Time-of-measurement effects reflect influences due to the specific point in historical time when you are obtaining your information.

28. Developmental research designs represent various combinations of age, cohort, and time-of-measurement effects.

29. Cross-sectional designs examine multiple cohorts and age groups at a single point in time. They can only identify age differences.

30. Longitudinal designs examine one cohort over more than one point in time as members of the

cohort age. They can identify age change, but have several problems, including practice effects, drop-out, and selective survival.

31. Time-lag designs examine multiple cohorts of same-aged people and are rarely used.

32. Sequential designs involve more than one cross-sectional or longitudinal design.

33. Participants in a research study should reflect the composition of the population (representativeness). To the extent this is not the case, the results will have limited applicability.

34. Measures developed for younger adults may not be appropriate for older adults.

35. Experiments consist of manipulating one or more independent variables and measuring one or more dependent variables. Experiments provide information about cause and effect.

36. Correlational designs address relationships among variables; they do not provide information about cause and effect.

37. Naturalistic inquiry focuses on studying human development in its natural environment.

38. The biopsychosocial model emphasizes the need for examining multiple variables in research.

REVIEW QUESTIONS

Issues and Models in Adult Development and Aging

1. What are the two main controversies in developmental psychology? How do they relate to adult development and aging?

2. How do nature and nurture interact?

3. What is the continuity-discontinuity controversy? How does it relate to developmental theory?

4. What are the three models used to study human development? What are their characteristics?

5. What are the research and practical implications of the developmental issues and models?

The Biopsychosocial Model

6. What is the life-span perspective? What major points does it emphasize?

7. What is the biopsychosocial model? What implications are there for adopting this perspective?

The Meaning of Age

8. In what ways can age be defined? What are the pros and cons of each definition?

9. What developmental influences are associated with age? How do they differ?

Research Methods

10. What are age, cohort, and time-of-measurement effects? How and why are they important for developmental research?

11. What is a cross-sectional design? What are its advantages and disadvantages?

12. What is a longitudinal design? What are its advantages and disadvantages?

13. What differences are there between cross-sectional and longitudinal designs in terms of uncovering age differences and age changes?

14. What is a time-lag design?

15. What are sequential designs? What different types are there? What are their advantages and disadvantages?

16. What is meant by the notion of representativeness in a sample?

17. What is meant by the notion of adequate measurement? How does this relate to the reliability and validity of a measure?

18. What is an experiment? What information does it provide?

19. What is a correlational design? What information does it provide?

20. What is naturalistic inquiry?

21. How does the biopsychosocial model influence research design?

KEY TERMS

age effects One of the three fundamental effects examined in developmental research, along with cohort and time-of-measurement effects. Age effects test for the influence of time-dependent processes on development. (20)

ageism The untrue assumption that chronological age is the main determinant of human characteristics and that one age is better than another. (4)

biological age A definition of age that focuses on the functional age of biological and physiological processes rather than on calendar time. (16)

biopsychosocial model A framework for understanding human development that emphasizes the interactions among biological, psychological, and social influences. (12)

chronological age A definition of age that relies on the amount of calendar time that has passed since birth. (16)

cohort effects One of the three basic influences examined in developmental research, along with age and time-of-measurement effects. Cohort effects are differences due to experiences and circumstances unique to the historical time to which one belongs. (20)

contextual model A model that views people as dynamic, active, not reducible to parts, and not headed toward a specific end point. (9)

continuity-discontinuity controversy The debate over whether change in human development can be explained using the same rules (continuity) or different rules (discontinuity). (7)

correlation A relationship or association observed between two variables. (28)

cross-sectional design A study in which people of different ages from different cohorts are observed at one time of measurement to obtain information about age differences. (22)

experiment A study in which an independent variable is manipulated in order to observe its effects on a dependent variable so that a cause-and-effect relationship may be established. (27)

gerontology The study of aging from maturity to old age. (4)

longitudinal design A developmental research design that measures one cohort over more than one time of measurement in order to discover age changes. (23)

mechanistic model A model that uses a machine metaphor to view people as the sum of their parts, as passive receptors of environmental input, and that focuses on quantitative change. (8)

model A framework for understanding reality based on a metaphor. (5)

naturalistic inquiry A type of research based on studying people in their natural environments. (28)

nature-nurture controversey A debate concerning the relative influence of genetics and the environment. (5)

nonnormative influences Those influences on development due to chance or random events. (19)

normative age-graded influences Those influences on development that are closely related to a person's age. (19)

normative history-graded influences Those influences on development that are related to major social events. (19)

organismic model A view that people are complex organisms and active shapers of their environment, and that change is qualitative. (9)

psychological age A definition of age based on the functional level of psychological processes rather than on calendar time. (17)

qualitative change A view of change emphasizing differences in kind rather than in amount. (7)

quantitative change A view of change emphasizing differences in amount rather than in kind. (7)

reliability The ability of a measure to produce the same value on the same thing being measured over time. (26)

representativeness The degree to which a sample of research participants reflects the population from which they were drawn. (26)

sequential designs Types of developmental research designs involving combinations of cross-sectional and longitudinal designs. (24)

social age A definition of age emphasizing the functional level of social interaction skills rather than calendar time. (17)

social clock An internal set of developmental milestones used to mark one's progression through life. (11)

socialization The process by which people are taught the values and behaviors important in a particular culture. (12)

time-lag designs A developmental research design examining same-aged people from more than one cohort. (24)

time-of-measurement effects In developmental research, effects that are due to the point in historical time at which the data are collected. (21)

validity The degree to which an instrument measures what it is supposed to measure. (27)

ADDITIONAL READING

An excellent discussion of the concepts of time and age, as well as how we use them, can be found in

Hagestad, G. O., & Neugarten, B. L. (1985). Age and the life course. In R. H. Binstock & E. Shanas (Eds.), *Handbook of aging and the social sciences* (2nd ed., pp. 35–61). New York: Van Nostrand Reinhold. Medium difficulty.

A good introduction to the ideas underlying the life-span perspective is

Baltes, P. B. (1987). Theoretical propositions of life-span developmental psychology: On the dynamics between growth and decline. *Developmental Psychology, 23*, 611–626. Medium difficulty.

An excellent source for more information on the nature-nurture and continuity-discontinuity controversies, as well as the mechanistic, organismic, and contextual models, is

Lerner, R. M. (1986). *Concepts and theories of human development* (2nd ed.). New York: Random House. Easy to medium difficulty.

One of the best introductions to the issues involved in research designs is

Baltes, P. B., Reese, H. W., & Nesselroade, J. R. (1977). *Life-span developmental psychology: Introduction to research methods.* Pacific Grove, CA: Brooks/Cole. Easy to medium.

CHAPTER 2

Diversity

Laura Wheeler Waring, *Anna Washington Derry*, 1927. National Museum of American Art, Smithsonian Institution. Gift of the Harmon Foundation.

MRS. LOTTIE WATERS* IS AN AFRICAN-American 55-year-old great-grandmother born in a small town in southern Texas. She was delivered by her Aunt Elsie and Elsie's mother Lucy. Like her own mother, Lottie had her first child at 15; she did the best she could at raising her 5 children. When Lottie was unable to care for them, she gave them to Elsie to "keep" for a time, a common practice in her community. When Lottie's second daughter had her own child, named Kermit, Lottie joined the ranks of wise women, meaning women who were grandmothers. At the time, Lottie was 32 years old. As a wise woman, Lottie was expected to care for children, her own and others. All children, biological or not, were treated similarly; Lottie's biological children treated them all as siblings. Wherever she came across misbehaving children (whether or not they were her own), she was expected to speak to them and correct them. Wise women do not need permission from the biological parents to discipline children. It is their duty to teach any child if the opportunity presents itself. When Lottie was 52 and Kermit's first child was born, Lottie celebrated a double transition: She became the mother of a wise woman (Kermit's mother), and she herself had "twice reached the age of wisdom." Lottie was wise because she had "raised" two generations and was now working on a third. And she was wise because she could recite the family history that had been taught to her by previous wise women.

*This case is described in detail in J. W. Peterson (1990). Lottie Waters is not her real name.

Lottie Waters represents only one example of the rich diversity of adult development and aging. Her story drives home the point that what is expected or valued in one community (having children at a young chronological age) may not be valued in another (witness middle-class communities' fight against teenage pregnancy).

This chapter completes our introduction to adult development and aging by exploring it in broad social perspective, as we move from a personal level of analysis to a more encompassing level. First, we need to know who we are talking about: Who are the elderly, and how diverse a group are they? Then we will consider the notions of status and role, two of the central ideas in understanding diversity in adulthood from a biopsychosocial framework. Next, we will see how societies organize themselves based on age, creating age stratification systems that help to define the status and roles we have. Finally, we will consider the rich diversity in the experience of aging by focusing on two topics: ethnicity and culture. Ethnicity is an important consideration in the United States, which is populated by a wide variety of people with different backgrounds. We will conclude by seeing how cultures differ in their views of age and the aging process.

THE DEMOGRAPHICS OF AGING

As mentioned in Chapter 1, the numbers of the elderly population keep increasing. Each year another group of roughly 2 million adults joins the more than 30 million U.S. citizens who have reached what society calls old age. The best way to begin our study of this population is to start with some basic questions: How many older people are there? How rapidly is this number growing now compared to a few years ago? Are there more older men or older women? Are they married? What dif-

ferences are there among the various ethnic and minority groups in the United States? What population trends exist in the rest of the world?

Answering these and related questions involves describing the population demographics (size, growth, distribution) of older adults in the United States. Most of our demographic information comes from large-scale surveys such as the census, and much of the information can be easily categorized (for example, gender of the respondent). However, a desire to understand the demographics of older adults forces us to confront a difficult question: What is old age?

The most common definition of old age refers to crossing the arbitrary boundary of 65 years. There is nothing magical about that particular age, any more than there is about a legal drinking age of 21. Age 65 was selected as the official marker of old age in the United States in the Social Security Act of 1935. Age 65 has subsequently been adopted by virtually everyone around the world as the arbitrary marker of old age. As we will see later in this chapter, however, chronological age is a poor indicator of a person's physical, social, psychological, economic, or mental condition. Moreover, all people over age 65 are not the same. Some researchers argue that we should differentiate between the "young-old" (aged 65 to 74) and the "old-old" (aged 75 and over). Nevertheless, we will use the criterion of 65 in defining old age, keeping in mind the problems with using such an arbitrary index.

The population of older adults is constantly changing as new members enter the group and other members leave through death. With each new member comes a personal history reflecting a combination of many developmental influences. For example, the newest entrants into old age were born in the 1920s, meaning that they experienced the Depression and World War II and had more education, better medical care, and different occupational experiences than their predecessors. These experiential factors will be explored later in this chapter and will provide the basis for im-

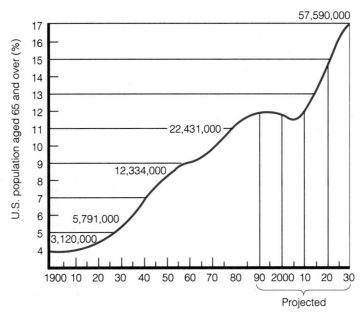

57,590,000

U.S. population aged 65 and over (%)

22,431,000

12,334,000

5,791,000

3,120,000

1900 10 20 30 40 50 60 70 80 90 2000 10 20 30

Projected

FIGURE 2.1 Population of Americans aged 65 and over, 1900–2030 (projected)

(Source: U.S. Bureau of the Census.)

portant discussions in other chapters. At this point it is important to recognize that the characteristics of older adults are changing rapidly. Approximately 60% of the current older population entered old age after 1975 (Uhlenberg, 1987). Clearly, this represents a substantial turnover in the older population.

How Many Older Adults Are There?

The number of older adults has grown steadily over the past century. Between 1900 and 1990 there was a 10-fold increase in the number of older adults (from 3 million to roughly 30 million). By 2010 nearly 10 million more are anticipated. Between 2010 and 2030 a major surge is expected as the members of the baby boom generation reach old age, increasing the number by a whopping 25 million in just 20 years. Following the baby boom surge, the rate of growth should slow and stabilize.

Older adults were only 4% of the total population in 1900 (see Figure 2.1). By 1990 this proportion had increased to over 12%, and it will increase to roughly 17% by 2030. Another way of looking at the proportion change is to look at how many older adults there are for every 100 children under age 18 in the population. In 1900 the population was truly young: there were only about 10 older adults for every 100 children. By 1990 the population had matured, with nearly 50 old people for every 100 children. By 2030, the U.S. Bureau of the Census projects, the number of older adults will actually exceed the number of children.

Not only is the population as a whole aging, but the older population itself has aged. Over the last 60 years, for example, the percentage of older adults who are over age 75 (the "old-old") has increased from 29% in 1930 to nearly 50% in 1990. This trend reflects the fact that technological advances in health care are enabling people to live longer than ever before.

What accounts for the differing rates of growth in the number of people in different age categories? The number of people entering old age in any one year depends on various combinations of three things: the number of people born 65 years earlier, the proportion of those born who survived to age 65, and the number of immigrants who joined this group over the years and are still living (Uhlenberg, 1987). For example, the proportion of men born during the early and mid-1920s who actually reach old age will be lower than slightly older or younger groups because of the numbers of men killed during World War II. Likewise, the surge in older adults during the first part of the 21st century will be due to the very large number of babies born between 1946 and 1960 (the baby boom).

Demographic projections are not always exact. Many unpredictable factors intrude that demographers cannot build into their models. For example, in industrialized countries, the scope of the influence of AIDS on the population as a whole remains to be seen, although it has had and will continue to have a significant impact on the gay male population. Its effects in the Third World (for example, Africa) are also likely to be devastating, especially in regions where more than half of the adult population is infected with the AIDS virus.

Clearly, these dramatic shifts in the composition of the population will have significant effects on daily life. From health care to city services and from wage scales to retirement benefits, the mechanisms of social support that all of us take for granted will undergo considerable stress as different groups vie for resources. Recognizing the prob-

Ethnic minority groups are the fastest growing segment of the older adult population.

lem and planning ahead for it may help us avoid intergenerational competition for resources.

Diversity of Older Adults

If all that we know about a person is that he or she is old, we know virtually nothing other than how many years the person has survived. Think about your own grandparents or other older adults that you know. There are undoubtedly many ways in which these people differ from one another. Perhaps some are very active tennis players while others act more like couch potatoes. Some are party animals while others would rather read a good book.

Older adults are not all alike, any more than younger adults or middle-aged adults are all alike. This diversity is what makes older adults such an interesting group to study. In this section we will consider some of the main ways in which older adults differ in ethnicity, gender, marital status,

TABLE 2.1   Gender ratio for all races aged 65 and over in 1980

Race	Age					
Men per 100 Women	*60–64*	*65–69*	*70–74*	*75–79*	*80–84*	*85+*
White	87	81	72	61	52	43
African American	80	73	69	63	60	50
Hispanic	86	76	77	76	73	61
Asian/Pacific Islander	84	93	109	89	67	60
Native American	87	77	82	74	66	59

(Source: American Association of Retired Persons. Reprinted with permission.)

employment and income, educational level, geographic distribution, and living arrangements. Many of these topics will be considered in more detail later in the book.

Ethnicity. One of the most important sources of diversity is ethnicity. It is important to realize that the status and resources of many elderly members of minority ethnic groups reflect social and economic discrimination that they experienced earlier in life. As a result many such elderly people are needy and malnourished and have poor access to medical care, little education, and substandard housing. This means that what may be true for white older adults may not be true for the aged who are from an ethnic minority group.

The elderly population in the United States has been growing faster among minorities than among whites (American Association of Retired Persons [AARP], 1988). In 1980 roughly 10% of the elderly population was nonwhite. This number is expected to increase to 15% by 2025 and to 20% by 2050. However, about 11% of whites are 65 or over, whereas this percentage is 8 for African Americans, 6 for Asian/Pacific Islanders, 5 for Hispanics, and 5 for Native Americans.

Examining the growth of the elderly population in the United States within ethnic minority groups reveals some interesting trends (AARP, 1988):

1. The elderly are the fastest growing segment of the African-American population. Between 1970 and 1980 elderly African Americans increased by 36% while the total African-American population was growing by only 16%.

2. Because Hispanics represent the fastest growing ethnic minority group, a substantial increase in the number of Hispanic elderly is anticipated.

3. The number of elderly from Asian or Pacific Island cultures has grown dramatically over the last 20 years, showing a fourfold increase.

4. Native-American elderly have increased faster than those of any other minority group. Between 1970 and 1980 alone the number of Native-American elderly increased by 65%, far higher than the rates for white or African-American elderly.

Gender Differences. Overall, elderly women outnumber elderly men (see Table 2.1), although the difference varies somewhat across racial and ethnic

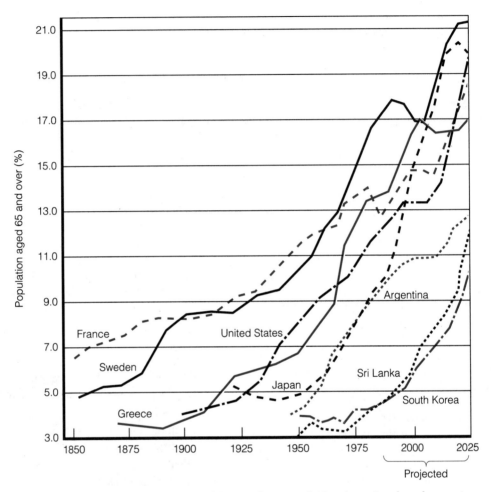

FIGURE 2.2 Trends in percentage of the population aged 65 and over in selected countries, 1850–2025 (projected)

(Source: "Aging and Worldwide Population Change" (pp. 173–198) by G. C. Meyers, 1985, in R. H. Binstock and E. Shanas (Eds.), *Handbook of Aging and the Social Sciences* (2nd ed.). New York: Van Nostrand Reinhold. Reprinted with permission of the Center of Demographic Studies, Duke University, and the author.)

groups. As indicated in the table, these differences become more pronounced at higher age levels. For example, in the age group over 85 there are only about 43 white men for every 100 white women, and there are 61 Hispanic men for every 100 Hispanic women.

Differences favoring women were not always the case, however. Until 1930 the gender ratio among the older population actually favored men. This situation was due in part to the predominance of male immigrants to the United States at the time. Additionally, many women died in young adulthood from complications of pregnancy and child-birth. Once mortality rates from childbearing declined, the gender ratio began to favor women (Uhlenberg, 1987). The current ratio is also partly explained by the fact that many more men than women died as a result of wars in this century. Finally, as will be explored later in this chapter and in Chapter 3, there are several health-related factors that tend to favor women.

International Perspectives

The changing demographics in the United States are not unique, as displayed in Figure 2.2. Note that other industrialized nations such as France, Japan, and Sweden show similar trends. All of these countries have relatively low birthrates and death rates and high standards of living. Although developed countries account for only one fourth of the world's population, they contain nearly one half of the world's older adults (Meyers, 1985).

In contrast to the developed countries, Third World countries, such as Sri Lanka, have relatively young populations. On the average only 4% of the people living in the Third World are over age 65. However, these countries will experience explosive growth in the elderly population over the next several decades (Meyers, 1985). Between 1980 and 2025, it is expected that the number of older adults living in less developed countries will quadruple; in developed countries the number will only double.

Such a large and rapid increase in the number of older adults will severely strain the limited resources of Third World countries. This division of increasingly scarce resources across age groups will become a major issue in the decades ahead. How these issues are handled will have tremendous significance as we head into the 21st century (see Chapter 14).

We will consider additional issues about aging in other societies and cultures later in this chapter.

At that point we will take another look at how well the different generations get along and how older people are treated in various places around the world.

STATUS AND ROLE

Are old people valued? This question is difficult to answer because it depends on which older adults you are inquiring about. As we will see, different ethnic groups and cultures have different ways of dealing with older adults. For example, African Americans' experience of aging differs from Hispanic Americans'. Moreover, African Americans have a different experience of aging in the United States than people who live in Africa. Why? In part, older adults in different ethnic groups and cultures have different status and occupy different roles.

Status and role are two basic elements that help define who we are and that influence our self-concept and well-being. For those reasons, they underlie much of the research and theory in social-psychological approaches to adult development and aging. Two major theories are used to study the impact of status and role; the structural perspective and the interactionist perspective. They differ in several ways, most importantly in their view of the flexibility and activity of the individual.

The Structural Perspective

Classical sociological theory concentrates on social structures, and it uses the concepts of status and role to define particular positions in society as well as the behavioral expectations associated with these positions. Rosow (1985) applies the *structural perspective* from classical sociological theory to adult development and aging. To him, **status** refers to a formal position in society that can be clearly and unambiguously specified and that may denote particular rights, privileges, prestige, and duties for the person. For example, traditional labels of "masculine," "elderly," and "minority" connote clusters of rights and privileges — such as senior citizen discounts or a seat on the subway — that may be independent of individual effort. People's statuses define the social contexts for evaluating others' behavior and serve to anchor people in the social structure. For example, a person having the status "elderly" who asks someone to give up his seat on the subway is evaluated differently from a person having the status "young adult" who makes the same request. Some U.S. mass transit systems even have signs in the vehicles making this distinction ("This seat reserved for elderly and handicapped passengers.").

Rosow (1985) defines **role** as the behaviors appropriate for any set of rights or duties. For example, people with a particular status are expected to behave in certain prescribed, or normative, ways. Those with the status of parent are expected to care for their children; parents who fail to look after their children violate the normal parental role. Rosow's approach emphasizes those roles that are essential to societal survival, such as parental roles and work roles. It should be noted, though, that people also engage in many personally meaningful roles that are not included in Rosow's system. For example, many people assume nonstatus roles as hobbyists, weekend athletes, church workers, and the like that are viewed as important but not vital to societal survival. The most important implication of Rosow's approach is that *old age in the United States represents status without a role*. In Rosow's view old age is a time of loss of social identity that cannot be prepared for.

Rosow's structural perspective is useful in describing the ways in which social structures influence the elderly through the predictable loss of certain social roles. Role loss is a major theme in psychosocial development; it is used to understand depression (Chapter 9), changes in relationships (Chapter 10), and changes in careers (Chapter 11). For example, it is believed that some of the adjustment problems experienced by some workers during retirement stem from the loss of meaningful work roles.

However, Rosow's argument has two problems. First, simply because people lose aspects of their social identity does not mean that their self-concept will suffer (Hagestad & Neugarten, 1985). The loss of the parental role when children leave home, for example, is hardly ever accompanied by serious psychological turmoil. Moreover, the opportunity to develop new informal roles through friendships could even bolster personal identity and counteract the effects of losses in societally essential social roles. Second, Rosow's view of the elderly as victims of society does not fit well with the considerable evidence that most older people successfully meet their environmental demands.

In sum, Rosow concentrates on the influence of society, which is clearly important, but tends to ignore the active role of the individual in negotiating the developmental changes in status and roles. This latter point is the focus of the interactionist perspective.

The Interactionist Perspective

According to the structural perspective, status and role are bestowed on individuals by society; individuals have little if any influence on them (Passuth & Bengtson, 1988). In contrast, the *interactionist perspective* emphasizes the individual's active interpretations of social structure as the main determinants of status and role (George, 1980; Passuth & Bengtson, 1988). Interactionists maintain that people subjectively define their own relationships to social structures and are able to mold and alter those relationships if necessary.

The interactionist perspective is important for three reasons. First, we often choose the particular status we occupy and the specific role we act out. If we do not like them, we may have the option to make changes. Second, not all roles have narrowly defined behavioral expectations but, rather, offer a range of optional behaviors. Parenting is an example of a role with a wide range of acceptable behaviors, because there is considerable flexibility in how one can rear children effectively. Third, people create many informal roles in areas of interest to them. For example, people who become mediators in a debate or dispute voluntarily assume the informal role of peacemaker; when a truce is declared, their role is over.

The most important idea proposed in the interactionist perspective of status and role is that *people are able to create and modify social structures*. The individual's interpretations and perceptions are necessary elements in any attempt to understand human behavior. The interactionist perspective has influenced a great deal of work in adult development and aging, most importantly in theorizing about the interplay of heredity and environment. Some cognitive-developmental theories emphasize the active interaction with and interpretation of the environment (Chapter 7), as well as perceptions of stress (Chapter 4). Additionally, the interactionist perspective has led to several theories of how people interact with their environment, the focus of Chapter 12.

Adopting the Best of Both Worlds

Certainly, neither the structural perspective nor the interactionist perspective is completely correct. Both have merit. Society does define some roles, such as "parent," "child," "teacher," or "student." However, society does not often specify the behaviors appropriate to that role in detail. For example, the role of "student" carries only general behavioral proscriptions; subtle differences in how you should behave in different classes are not mentioned. In these more ambiguous situations it is more useful to adopt an interactionist perspective

and consider how the person perceives his or her situation. Such a combined view helps us address the issue of how status is used to define a person's place in society.

Status and Treatment

In trying to understand ethnic and cultural differences in aging, it is important to make a distinction between the status older people have and how they are treated (Keith, 1990). Sometimes, the two go hand in hand; older adults are treated very well in societies that highly value their elderly. In other cases, however, there is a big difference between the two.

Some groups both value their elderly and engage in *gericide*, which is the practice of killing elderly people; this is a custom in roughly 20% of the world's societies (Glascock & Feinman, 1981). Although by Western standards this situation appears paradoxical, to the societies involved the practice is considered normal and necessary. Cultural meanings of gericide vary; death is not universally viewed as a bad thing, but sometimes as a regretted necessity or as a transition to another stage of existence (Keith, 1990).

Another important point about status and treatment is that many societies differentiate among the elderly. For example, Glascock and Feinman (1981) found than most of the societies they studied had two different categories of elderly: "intact" and "decrepit." For example, Nepalese men who have vision or hearing impairments lose status compared to nonimpaired men (Beall & Goldstein, 1986).

Status, Role, and Gender

Although in many societies men are often believed to have it better throughout much of the life span, most researchers agree that in most societies women age with less difficulty than men (Keith,

1990). However, there is much less agreement on why this is so.

Some researchers argue that because women in many societies live out their lives mainly in domestic settings, they face fewer difficult transitions in old age (Keith, 1990). For example, the household tasks that women perform in many societies may be more easily adapted with age than the tasks men perform. Additionally, the caregiving roles women perform may help establish stronger bonds with children and grandchildren, who in turn may care for them in old age. The power positions men occupy may not engender such caring feelings (Harrell, 1981).

Other researchers emphasize women's experience with discontinuities during their lives (Cool & McCabe, 1983). For example, in many patrilineal societies, when a woman marries, she must leave her parental home for a potentially harsh initiation into a household controlled by her husband's mother. Women in such societies also have learned to adjust to abrupt physiological changes such as pregnancy, lactation, and menstruation, so that when changes related to aging occur they are viewed with less shock than they would be by men (Keith, 1990).

Finally, women in many societies are simply better off in old age than they were when they were young. For example, the shift from an obedient bride to a powerful, dominant elderly head of the household represents a clear increase in power and status (Keith, 1990). In many nonindustrialized societies, women in late middle age are freer and more powerful because they no longer have behavioral restrictions put on them, they have authority over other relatives, and they become eligible for special status and privileges outside the family (Brown & Kerns, 1985).

In sum, the basis for women's improving status within many societies appears to be the separation of the domestic and public spheres (Keith, 1990). That is, young women in these societies are greatly restricted in what they are allowed to do, with most of their duties focused on domestic tasks. With increasing age, however, these strictures dissipate and women are allowed to assume roles of authority and power similar to those held by men. In some cases, such as some Pacific societies, there may even be a blending or "muting" of gender differences in roles during late life (Counts & Counts, 1985a).

People in every society of every age have certain status and are supposed to fulfill certain roles. As we have seen, sometimes status is bestowed by society, and sometimes it is a perception on the part of the person. The status of the elderly varies considerably with age and gender, and differs across societies. These variations provide a beginning insight into the great diversity of aging within and across societies. We will focus on this issue later in this chapter.

AGE STRATIFICATION

We have seen that status and role define a person's position in society. *Stratification systems* are universal processes of operationalizing status and role based on the distribution of valued things, such as prestige, esteem, wealth, privilege, and power (Streib, 1985). They are based on a variable or set of variables comprised of easily identifiable characteristics, such as age, race, gender, and social class. Once people have been stratified, society creates shared belief systems about these differences in order to reinforce the basis for the stratification systems (Dowd, 1980). Psychologists acknowledge the importance of these variables by including them in research as individual difference variables.

Of the many characteristics of people that form the basis for stratification systems, age is the most important in the study of adult development and aging (Riley, 1985; Streib, 1985). All cultures make distinctions based on age (Fry, 1988). Certain points in the life span, whether tied with ritual or not, mark the transition from one state (such as childhood) to another (adulthood). In the study of adult development and aging, consideration of how American and most other Western societies make such distinctions, and their importance in understanding behavior, led to the age stratification model (Riley, 1971, 1987; Riley, Johnson, & Foner, 1972).

The Age Stratification Model

The age stratification model grew out of an attempt by social gerontologists to discover normative patterns of aging that provide a broad appreciation of individual situations and the constraints put on people by social institutions (Passuth & Bengtson, 1988). As described below, the **age stratification model** is a way of describing and understanding how society makes distinctions in behavior, rights, privileges, and so forth. The model has become one of the most influential perspectives in the social-psychological study of aging (Passuth & Bengtson, 1988). The model is based on the fact that society holds different behavioral expectations through statuses and roles for people of different ages, thereby creating *age grades*, or age strata. Age grades place limits on the roles one has and the status one accrues. When you are told to act your age, for example, you are really being told to behave in accordance with a particular set of age-graded behavioral norms.

The set of social roles that one is allowed to perform depends on personal characteristics, societal structures, and the composition of one's birth cohort. As defined in Chapter 1, a birth cohort is a group of people born at the same time in history who age together. Each cohort is unique because it has its own characteristics, such as size and social class distribution, and each experiences its own set of historical influences that shape attitudes and behavior. For example, Elder (1974) showed that the

cohort of children who grew up during the Depression of the 1930s had different values as adults than other cohorts before or after. The members differed in expecting that their children's lives would be better than their own, among other things.

One goal of the age stratification model is to examine how successive birth cohorts move across time, a process termed *cohort flow* (Dowd, 1980). Cohort flow is important because as successive cohorts fill various statuses and roles, society changes as well. When a very large cohort such as the baby boom generation reached the labor market, for example, competition for jobs was far more intense than when the smaller Depression-era cohort entered. As this cohort ages, changes in advertising techniques (more middle-aged models), television programs, and other aspects of daily life will increase.

Age Stratification and Societal Significance

As noted earlier, the study of cohort flow is an important part of the age stratification model (Riley, 1985). Investigating how cohorts move from one age grade to another and how successive cohorts deal with the demands at a particular age stratum are the primary ways in which cohort flow is examined. One key discovery from studies of cohort flow is that age plays an important role in determining the degree of control that members of one cohort exert over others. This point, referred to as a cohort's **societal significance** (Uhlenberg, 1988), is best understood through the following example.

Suppose that all the members of a birth cohort (for example, those born within five years of one another) were suddenly removed from society. What would the consequences be? If the cohort were all people aged 25 to 29 or 45 to 49, major reorganizations would be required in families (to replace parents), in work settings (to fill numerous vacancies), in government (to occupy empty decision-making positions), in the news media (to report the changes), and so on. But what if the cohort were 75 to 79 years old? In contemporary American society, not much would change. Few of these individuals are parents of dependent children, are employed, hold government positions, and so forth. In short, few hold roles that are essential for keeping society functioning, as described in the structural perspective (Rosow, 1985).

Uhlenberg (1988) creates this scenario to drive home a point about age stratification and societal significance. A cohort is viewed as important, that is, as having societal significance, to the extent that the lives of its members are connected in significant ways within families and organizations and to the extent that it has access to power and money. Because the connections of people to families and organizations are the topics of Chapters 10 and 11, we will not dwell on them here. However, you should note that other types of connections to society are important, too: political affiliations, volunteer groups, and friendships.

People in different layers of society have different degrees of impact on others. Individuals higher in the stratification system have much more influence on those below them than vice versa. For example, 100 voters have little impact on a senator or member of Parliament, on the average, but 100 senators or members of Parliament have considerable impact on the average citizen. Such inequalities extend across many relationships, such as parents and children, executives and subordinates, haves and have-nots. Inequalities also exist across age groups. These inequalities do not mean that those in subordinate positions have no influence at all; 100 voters can begin a process of removing an elected official from office. The point is that power and rewards are more easily obtained by some groups than by others.

Inequality of influence is affected by three factors (Uhlenberg, 1988). First, position and influence are strengthened to the extent that individuals make decisions that affect others. In some hospitals or nursing homes middle-aged and younger adults exert considerable power over the elderly by deciding everything from when they go to bed or take a bath to what and when they will eat. Second, the ability to control how money is spent is directly associated with the power in a relationship. Husbands who control their wives' access to money wield considerable power, often limiting the wives' opportunities for employment or self-betterment. Third, differences in personal influence can be structured into relationships by giving them status differences. Job levels in corporations have different titles to reflect levels of influence.

To keep things relatively simple, we can analyze differences in degree of influence in activities or relationships by considering three groups: those with strong positions, those with weak positions, and those who are uninvolved with that particular activity or relationship (Uhlenberg, 1988). Table 2.2 presents an overall picture of various combinations of social activity and position of influence (strong, weak, uninvolved). Examples of the roles that would be included with each combination are listed in the body of the table. Cohorts whose members fall primarily in the "strong" column are those with the greatest societal significance.

Cohorts move from one column to another as they traverse adulthood. This implies that age norms may be present within different activity-position combinations. **Age norms** focus attention on behaviors that are expected for a cohort as it moves through adulthood toward old age. As we will see in the following discussion, social activities vary in terms of whether age norms for behaviors are present.

Social Institutions and Age Norms. In considering the combinations of activity and position in Table 2.2, you may have realized that society builds in different participation rates for people of different ages for some activities and not others. For example, American society has no strong age norms for political activity, being a volunteer, and being a friend. People of all ages are equally welcome. Some norms exist for media activities, but it is difficult to agree on them. Although there is evidence of a shift

TABLE 2.2 The structure of social activities based on combinations of social activity and position in activity

Domain of Social Activity	Position in Activity		
	Strong	*Weak*	*Uninvolved*
Household or family	Head or spouse	Dependent child	Single or group living
Economic arena			
Production of goods and services	Employer, boss, professional	Other workers	Retired or unemployed
Consumption of goods and services	Consumer with discretionary income to spend	Poor or dependent person	——
Politics	Legislator, executive, judge	Active citizen	Inactive citizen
Mass media	Writer, producer, director, actor	Consumer	Nonparticipant
Volunteer group	Board member, leader	Volunteer	Uninvolved
Friendship and caregiving	Active friend or caregiver	Dependent	Loner

in marketing strategies to include more older groups, the dominant market remains younger adults (Powell & Williamson, 1985). This situation is likely to change over the next decade, however, as the baby boom cohort continues to age. Signs of change are already apparent: More products are being designed and marketed for middle-aged adults, and the growing political clout of this generation was exemplified in the selection in 1988 of Senator Dan Quayle as a vice-presidential nominee. In short, there are no firm structural barriers in society to keep healthy older adults from being consumers of goods, services, and media products; active, voting citizens; friends; or members of clubs, churches, or other voluntary organizations (Uhlenberg, 1988).

In American society the strongest age norms lie in the domains of family and work. In the family domain two activities are guided by age norms: parenting children from birth through adolescence, and functioning as husband and wife. Both activities become much less likely with increasing age. Adults over 65 rarely have young children of their own, and becoming widowed is much more probable. Based on these two trends, Uhlenberg (1988) argues, the social institutions most necessary for societal functioning are structured to reduce the involvement of people as they grow older.

Age norms in the workplace are well known. The advent of mandatory retirement during the middle part of this century institutionalized the notion that older adults should not work. As we will see in Chapter 11, retirement involves a great deal more than just quitting work; for many it means a loss of identity and loss of influence.

Declining opportunities for healthy older adults to participate in family and occupational activities mean that the societal significance of cohorts diminishes in the later years of life. In part, this diminishing influence is related to cohort size, which also declines as members die. For example, with present mortality rates, the size of a cohort is reduced by half from age 75 to 85 (Uhlenberg, 1987). Furthermore, as members become incapacitated, they move from holding weak positions to becoming uninvolved; people with debilitating diseases are unable to attend church services, vote, or maintain even distant relationships with family members. This change also serves to reduce a cohort's societal significance.

Now that we have established that cohorts experience these changes in societal significance, we must turn to two important questions: How rapidly do the changes occur? What are the historical trends?

Developmental Trends in Societal Significance

We have seen that as cohorts age, they decline in influence, especially in the domains of family and work. Although it is impossible to know precisely how much of the decline is due to health factors or social factors, it is possible to estimate the effects of each. Figure 2.3 depicts the developmental progression in societal significance of the 1910–1914 birth cohort when the cohort members are from 55 to 99 years old (Uhlenberg, 1988). Three curves are shown, each representing a different pattern of societal significance. In each case the distance above the horizontal axis is the cohort's share of the total societal significance of the entire population.

The uppermost curve (B) is an approximation of the upper boundary for the societal significance for the 1910–1914 cohort in later life. The curve reflects the changing size of the cohort over time relative to the entire population, and it equates societal significance with sheer numbers of people. In 1970, for example, the cohort of 55- to 59-year-olds represented 7.9% of the population of the United States. This percentage, and hence the cohort's societal significance, declines steadily, so that by the time the members are between the ages of 95 and 99 (in the year 2010), they will represent

0.3% of the population. This curve represents primarily biological influences, since it is based entirely on mortality statistics. Thus, it represents what healthy, active older adults' societal significance would be in a society that was not age stratified.

The middle curve (C) represents the percentage of cohort members living in families. Being removed from a household that includes other family members means a loss of contact and social interaction. What this curve reflects is that older adults are less connected with others via family ties than are younger and middle-aged adults, thereby reducing societal significance below what would be expected based on biology alone.

The bottom curve (D) represents the further reduction in societal significance for a cohort based on retirement. More than any other change, separation from work removes older people from ties to others and reduces their influence. By the time the cohort is 65 to 69 years old, its societal significance is virtually negligible due to losses in family and work ties.

The importance of family and work ties in determining societal influence is also evident in Figure 2.3 in another way. Note that the middle and bottom curves actually begin higher than the top curve when the cohort is between the ages of 55 and 59. This implies that the family and work domains provide levels of societal significance well above that which would be expected by the size of the cohort alone. In a mere decade this influential position is nearly completely lost.

The key point in Figure 2.3 is the size of the discrepancy between the top curve, which is based only on numbers of people, and the bottom curve, which reflects the actual state of affairs. Contemporary American society eliminates a large number of people from influencing how that society operates by removing these people from positions of power within the system. As bad as this situation appears, however, it will get worse. Recall from Chapter 1 that the number of older adults in the

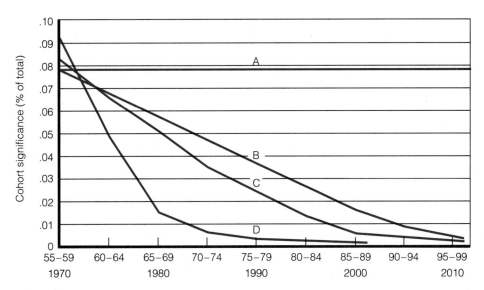

FIGURE 2.3 Alternative curves of a cohort's societal significance. **A**, no change in societal significance with age; **B**, societal significance proportional to cohort's relative size; **C**, societal significance proportional to cohort's relative familial involvement; **D**, societal significance proportional to cohort's relative familial and work involvement.

(Source: "Aging and the Social Significance of Cohorts" (p. 416) by P. Uhlenberg, 1988, in J. E. Birren and V. L. Bengtson (Eds.), *Emergent Theories of Aging*. New York: Springer.)

United States is increasing and will grow tremendously as the baby boom generation ages. By numbers alone, the top curve will be higher for the baby boomers, indicating that they could expect more societal significance. Unless current trends in retirement, parenting, and remarriage following the death of one's spouse are reversed, however, little change in the actual societal significance of old baby boomers will occur (Clark, Maddox, Schrimper, & Sumner, 1984; Uhlenberg & Chew, 1986).

Age Stratification and Socialization

As noted earlier, socialization is the process by which we internalize social values and expectations and ensure the smooth transition of cohorts. Socialization is by nature an active, reciprocal process that ties the individual to society and one generation to the next.

The Socialization Process. For many years the study of socialization was limited to investigating how children learn from their parents to be adults. The idea that adults are also socialized for many of their roles was not fully recognized until the 1960s (Brim, 1968). Socialization in adulthood mostly entails learning how to become a responsible member, participant, and contributor to society as well as acquiring a sense of teamwork, unity of purpose, and cooperation and consensus among age peers (Dannefer, 1988). Brim (1968) argues forcefully that adult socialization is equivalent to adult education, in that the goal is to bring about an integrated, consensual, and smoothly operating social order.

Much of the work on adult socialization focuses on the interaction between the socializer and the one being socialized (Dannefer, 1988). This research is based on the interactionist perspective discussed earlier, and it emphasizes that socialization is actually a two-way street. The socializer transmits a set of expectations that define the norms, roles, and values that the other person is supposed to accept. The one being socialized responds to these expectations, accepting some and modifying others, thereby providing feedback to the socializer.

The active, reciprocal process of socialization occurs in a variety of settings: parent-child interactions, formal teaching settings, marriage, employer-employee relationships, and so on. The common element of socialization settings is that they involve some type of relationship, whether it is formal or informal, explicit or implicit (Dowd, 1980).

This traditional view of socialization as a reciprocal process has been severely criticized (Dannefer, 1988; Passuth, 1984). The critics argue that this perspective implies that the goal of socialization is to stifle innovation and preserve what is perceived to be normative behavior in each succeeding cohort. Socialization strives for a certain sameness across cohorts, labeling variability in behavior as aberrant. For example, parents try to socialize their children to hold the same standards for behavior as they do. When their children act very differently, such as by wearing weird hairstyles, they attempt to eliminate these expressions of variation and individuality.

Dannefer (1988) argues that imposing uniformity is not a requirement of socialization. Rather, he contends, values and behavioral norms can be transmitted in a way that still allows room for variability. Look around at society, Dannefer says: There is considerable variability among people who hold the same values. People who take a general stance against abortion, for example, differ markedly in whether they are willing to sanction abortion in a few narrowly defined situations, such as rape or incest. Adult socialization involves transmitting not only a common set of values but also room to personalize them.

The general process of socialization can be broken down into more specific components. Two of the most important are anticipatory socialization and resocialization.

Anticipatory socialization is the process whereby people are prepared for changes in role or status (George, 1980). It involves learning about new norms and expectations that will accompany a role or status change. For example, most adults are socialized to assume the role of parenthood by their own parents, through parenting classes, and through books on the topic. Anticipatory socialization is often aided by giving the person the opportunity to practice the new role without actually assuming it. For instance, considerable knowledge about child care is gained by baby-sitting before having children of one's own.

Being able to anticipate role and status change is important. Unanticipated changes are usually more stressful and are more likely to result in poorer adjustment, at least in the short run (George, 1980). In Chapter 13 we will see that this is true concerning the death of a loved one. Moreover, preparing for role and status change is related to our sense of identity. Imagine how hard it would be if, for instance, we had no advance knowledge of what it was like to be a parent. If nothing else, the odds in favor of success would be low. Perhaps the frequently reported disillusionment in young adulthood after starting work (see Chapter 11) is actually the result of facing failure after one's anticipatory socialization has led to the expectation of success.

Research on anticipatory socialization shows that young people tend to anticipate many events during adulthood and base their behavior on past successes (Lowenthal, Thurnher, & Chiriboga, 1975; Sheehy, 1981). Anticipatory socialization for late-life events also occurs. For example, formal preretirement programs prepare workers by pointing out potential problems and raising important financial and psychological issues (Kamouri & Cavanaugh, 1986).

Resocialization involves a reorganization of one's expectations and occurs after a new role or status has been acquired. The degree of reorganization required depends on several factors, such as the amount of previous experience one has had and the amount of difference between one's previous and current role and status (George, 1980). In short, resocialization entails learning after the fact all the things that your mother never taught you.

When Does Adult Socialization Occur? Brim (1968) provides the most complete assessment of the situations in adulthood that involve socialization. Two of the most common are role and status transitions, as we discovered earlier. We know from Rosow's (1985) work that most of these transitions occur during young and middle adulthood, because old age has little status and few formal roles. Young adults receive considerable socialization for role and status changes, ranging from preparation for careers to marriage and parenthood. One of the changes for which older adults are socialized is the transition from being employed to being retired.

A second major time of socialization involves occupational changes. Moving from one job to another, being laid off, being promoted, and other job-related changes are often accompanied by preparatory training or resocialization.

Changes in the family cycle are also targets for socialization. We have already noted that socialization for the transition to parenthood is common. The family provides a major setting for the job of socializing one's children. Resocialization typically accompanies divorce, children's moving out, and widowhood. Although these preparation experiences are seldom formal, they are often quite extensive and occur through interactions with family and acquaintances.

Moving from one place to another often involves considerable anticipatory socialization (as one prepares) and resocialization (after one arrives). As will be noted in Chapter 12, anticipatory socialization is especially helpful when the elderly relocate.

How societies organize themselves on the basis of age reflects both natural biological differences and ideas developed within the culture. Although age grading is universal, how it gets played out varies considerably. As pointed out earlier with status and roles, it is precisely this diversity that makes the study of adult development and aging such a fascinating area. And it is to this diversity that we now turn.

ETHNICITY AND ADULT DEVELOPMENT

Before the mid-1960s research on adult development and aging was largely limited to the study of white males. Racial and cultural diversity was ignored (Jackson, 1985). The growing field of **ethnogerontology** seeks to draw attention to the influence that ethnicity has on the aging process. One of the problems in examining ethnic variations in aging is a general lack of research (Jackson, 1985). This lack of data is apparent throughout this book; much of our knowledge about ethnic variations in aging is confined to demographics. For example, we will see in Chapter 4 that we know some things about ethnic group differences in health and longevity. In contrast, we know very little about ethnic group differences in memory or cognitive development. Because examples of differences among

Ethnic identity is an important aspect of adult socialization from one generation to the next.

ethnic groups on many psychological dimensions are discussed throughout the book, we will focus here on the importance of ethnicity in aging.

Ethnic Groups

What does it mean to talk about an ethnic group or ethnicity? On the surface we probably have an intuitive feel for what ethnicity is when we use labels such as Polish American or Korean American. However, providing a scientific definition of ethnicity is difficult. Several attempts have been made, with varying degrees of success.

Schermerhorn (1970) defines an **ethnic group** as a collection of people within a larger society who have a common ancestry, memories of a shared historical past, and a cultural focus on one or more symbolic elements that they view as central to their identity as a people. These shared elements could involve kinship patterns, living patterns, religious affiliation, language, nationality, tribal identity, common physical features, or any of a host of other variables.

Although Schermerhorn's definition provides some precision, it also creates problems. For example, "Hispanic" would not qualify as an ethnic group because the Cubans, Puerto Ricans, Argentineans, Mexicans, and others do not share a common ancestry, nationality, or shared history. Moreover, ethnicity may not be easy to categorize. Children of a Hispanic father and a white mother would be difficult to classify in ethnic terms if the definition of ethnic group were based on biology.

Holzberg (1982) offers an alternative definition that defines *ethnicity* as social differentiation based on cultural criteria, such as a common language, customs, and voluntary associations, that foster ethnic identity and ethnic-specific social institutions and values. By this definition "Hispanic" would qualify as an ethnic group because of shared values, language, customs, and so forth. An additional advantage of Holzberg's definition is that it distinguishes between ethnic group and minority group; for example, being Irish would reflect an ethnic identity, but not a minority group.

Finally, it is essential to realize that ethnicity is a dynamic concept (Barresi, 1990). That is, ethnicity is not a label that someone is born with. Rather, it is a rich heritage that sets the stage for a continually evolving and emerging identity. Ethnic groups are developing right along with the people in them.

Ethnicity and Double Jeopardy

Most researchers agree that the experience of being old varies across ethnic groups. A controversial extension of this argument concerns whether being old and being a member of an ethnic minority group creates a situation termed **double jeopardy**. Talley and Kaplan (1956) originally used the term to refer to the situation of being simultaneously old and African American. At the time, elderly African Americans were perceived to be doubly jeopardized because they carried into old age "a whole lifetime of economic and social indignities" caused by racial prejudice and discrimination (National Urban League, 1964, p. 2). However, over the years the concept of double jeopardy has been expanded to include any individual, regardless of race, who has two or more traits that are socially undesirable, thereby subjecting him or her to prejudice and discrimination (Crandall, 1980).

Double jeopardy for elderly members of minority ethnic groups makes intuitive sense. For example, we have already seen that older adults normatively lose status. Coupled with the already lowered status of a minority ethnic group, becoming old would appear to put such individuals at a severe disadvantage. But as intuitively appealing as double jeopardy is, it turns out to be very difficult to document (Markides, Liang, & Jackson, 1990).

The problem appears to be twofold. First, researchers disagree on how to measure double jeopardy. M. Jackson and Wood (1976) operationalize it as existing whenever African Americans are more disadvantaged than whites in the same birth cohort. Jackson, Kolodny, and Wood (1982) define it as occurring when African Americans over age 65 are more disadvantaged than whites between 18 and 39 years old. Others (Cuellar & Weeks, 1980; Dowd & Bengtson, 1978) rely on subjective reports of members of minority ethnic groups concerning life satisfaction to define double jeopardy. Clearly, the lack of definitional consistency presents a problem: If researchers cannot agree on what double jeopardy is and how to measure it, then drawing conclusions from research is difficult.

Indeed, the second problem with the research literature on double jeopardy is inconsistent results. For one thing, cross-sectional research designs cannot address the notion that double jeopardy represents "a whole lifetime of economic and social indignities," as argued by the National Urban League (J. J. Jackson, 1985). Only longitudinal designs can address such questions, as pointed out in Chapter 1. Unfortunately, virtually all of the research on double jeopardy is cross-sectional. But even the cross-sectional studies yield conflicting results. Some report significant differences between elderly minority ethnic groups and elderly whites (M. Jackson et al., 1982; Register, 1981), while others find no differences (J. J. Jackson & Walls, 1978; Ward & Kilburn, 1983).

What are we to conclude? Perhaps the most reasonable position is to note that double jeopardy may not be a useful concept, because it focuses exclusively on social inequities without examining age changes in them and tends to ignore underlying variables other than ethnicity that may be the real causal factors (J. J. Jackson, 1985; Markides et al., 1990). For example, it is true that the average elderly white woman is better off financially than the average elderly African-American woman. As J. J. Jackson points out, however, marital stability and occupational and wage histories also differ between the two. Thus, we may be asking the wrong question if we ask whether differences in life satisfaction between the groups are due to racial differences that led to double jeopardy. Rather, we need to learn how marital, occupational, wage history, and other variables are related to disadvantages in old age that happen to correlate with ethnicity (J. J. Jackson, 1985; Schaie, Orchowsky, & Parham, 1982).

The role of ethnicity in adult development and aging is certainly important. What are needed, however, are (1) longitudinal investigations of the unique contributions of ethnicity to the experience of adulthood; (2) a stronger focus on variables other than race; and (3) work on how changes in society affect changes in the aging process of minority ethnic groups (Cool, 1987; J. J. Jackson, 1985; Markides et al., 1990).

Ethnicity and the Life Course

Recall that one of the key aspects of the biopsychosocial model is life-course influences, the notion that the meaning of events may change as people age. Although life-course influences are emphasized throughout this book, you may have noticed that we have avoided an important question: Where do the interpretive meanings of events come from in the first place?

The answer to this question is that we derive our interpretations of events from our culture, and, more fundamentally, from our particular ethnic group or subgroup (Barresi, 1990). The attitudes

and behaviors we learned when we were young shape our interpretations of events as adults, such as whether we are experiencing a life event "on time" or "off time" on our social clocks (see Chapter 1). For example, in some ethnic subgroups in the United States becoming a grandparent by age 30 is typical and considered on time. However, in other ethnic subgroups, having one's first child around age 30 is considered on time. The point is that whether behaviors are considered on or off time is heavily influenced by our particular ethnic heritage.

Of course, different perceptions of events could lead to differences of opinions or worse. One group may view another's perception as wrong and attempt to change it or to declare it unacceptable. On the other hand, perceptions may also change because of increased interaction among different groups. Teaching each other about our basic beliefs is important. Still, we need to keep in mind that people in ethnic groups different from our own may view the world in very different ways, and may have different experiences of being an adult as a consequence.

But intergroup conflict is not the only potential problem. As subsequent generations become increasingly exposed to alternative viewpoints, intergenerational conflict may result (Barresi, 1990). For example, ethnic elders may resent the younger generation's rejection of the traditional ways of doing things. To the elderly, traditions may represent more than a set of behavioral principles; these traditions may constitute a way of life that has helped them cope with a strange, sometimes hostile world and that ties them to their ancestral past (Barresi, 1990).

Ethnicity and Age

How various ethnic groups deal with age is fascinating. Some give increased status to older members of the group. Others make distinctions based on gender or other characteristics. Because of the complexity of this topic, the best we can do is to consider some snapshots by raising an important issue and discussing how a particular ethnic group deals with it. The first concerns the role that women play in the African-American community. This picture introduces a very important point: The very definition of the life course varies across ethnic groups. The second portrait concerns gender-based behavioral norms in the Hispanic community. Finally, we will look at how Korean Americans handle intergenerational relations.

As you consider each of these topics, keep in mind that many variations exist within each community. Just as there are many important individual differences among white communities, so are there differences within ethnic groups.

African-American Women. One of the most important roles that women in many ethnic groups play is to hold the various generations together (see Chapter 10). That is, the major kinship attachments tend to flow through mothers and grandmothers. As pointed out in Chapter 10, contact between generations tends to be fairly high and reasonably consistent across ethnic groups. However, factors such as average number of visits per month do not tell the whole story. There are very important and interesting differences among ethnic groups in what the visits mean and in how the notion of family itself is defined.

Elderly African-American women offer an interesting case in point. They tend to have much more flexible definitions of kinship than do white women, resulting in the absorption of grandchildren and "other relatives" into households headed by older women (Sokolovsky, 1990). In fact, older African-American women are roughly four times more likely than white women to live with dependent relatives under age 18. Tate (1983) finds that this makes a big difference in how younger people view the elderly: "It appears that absorbed nonindependent younger blacks are more likely to accept

their aged who become functionally impaired as a result of chronic conditions" (p. 99).

Many older African-American women do not measure age on a fixed continuum of time but rather in terms of important life events that help a person mature (J. W. Peterson, 1990). For example, the phrase "You grew today" is used to reflect this view. For this group, the ethnically important phases of the life cycle are: having a child, a sign of procreation; raising a child, a sign of maturity; and becoming a grandparent, a sign of having reached the age of wisdom. The terms *old age* and *aging* are not part of the language of this community, although they understand these concepts as used by white Americans. Note that ties to chronological age are absent. Children, however, are highly valued, and wise women are the ones who pass on the cultural and ethnic heritage. Thus it is knowledge, not possessions, that defines the importance of the role.

Status in this community is clearly attached to childbearing and not to chronological age. As a result, individuals who become mothers and grandmothers relatively young achieve the status; childless women, even those who are chronologically older, do not (J. W. Peterson, 1990). Most important is the experience that accrues with being a mother and grandmother. Life experience is what makes a woman wise.

Gender-Typed Age Norms Among Older Hispanics. As we discovered earlier in this chapter, the aged in the United States tend to have few well-defined roles. However, a case can be made that certain activities are reserved for older people by each social or ethnic group (Ward, 1984a). Bastida (1987) examined such a set in older Hispanic Americans.

A more detailed summary of the results of Bastida's study can be found in How Do We Know? In general, she found that Mexican, Puerto Rican, and Cuban elderly living in the United States were fairly similar to one another. Her most important

HOW DO WE KNOW?

Gender-Typed Age Norms Among Older Hispanics

Whether there are gender-related age-related norms for behavior has been a topic of research in social gerontology for several decades (Ward, 1984a). Expectations that people should act their age are fairly common, from childhood through adulthood. An important issue for gerontologists is whether these age norms actually constrain behavior, and, if so, how they are enforced. It would

also be important to know whether these constraints can be documented in different ethnic groups.

To find out, Bastida (1987) conducted an investigation of age norms and their enforcement among older Hispanic Americans. She used three methods to examine the norms: extensive fieldwork, during which structured interviews were conducted; detailed content analyses of the responses; and a three-member panel to check the interpretation of the transcripts of the interviews. Bastida studied 160 older adults representing Mexican, Puerto Rican, and Cuban groups who lived in predom-

inantly Hispanic communities, or barrios, and whose dominant language was Spanish. Information was collected about age identification; aging; heterosexual relationships, including courtship, marriage, and sexual behavior; demographic characteristics; and observations from the field team, which spent at least five hours a day at the senior centers where the participants were interviewed.

Extensive content analyses revealed that around 70% of the men and nearly 85% of the women used realistic qualifiers concerning their age when responding to questions.

---

discovery was that older Hispanics were quite realistic about their own aging: They knew that they were no longer able to do certain things. Sexual behaviors were not considered appropriate topics for conversation, and violators were sanctioned. Restrictions on behavior were generally more rigid for women than men; interestingly, women were usually the enforcers of the norms.

Intergenerational Relations Among Korean Americans. Korean Americans increased faster between 1970 and 1980 than any other ethnic group, with the exception of Mexicans and Filipinos (Kiefer et al., 1985). Koh and Bell (1987) were concerned about the adjustment of these immigrants, especially about potential disruptions in family relationships for the elderly. Elderly Koreans residing in the New York City area were asked about their

relationships with children and grandchildren, living arrangements, and need for services.

Koh and Bell report that nearly 70% of the participants wanted to live independently, a figure comparable to that for whites (see Chapter 12). Moreover, older Koreans reported frequent contact with their children, at least by phone; this is also characteristic of other ethnic groups (see Chapter 10). Older Koreans faced many problems common to immigrants: language barriers, poor housing, loneliness, low income, and transportation difficulties. Two thirds of the older Koreans could not read or speak English, which created serious problems in dealing with the majority culture. In contrast to life in Korea, where one's children represented the only source of assistance, older immigrants were more likely to go to social service agencies for help.

For example, one 76-year-old woman explained: "What do these wrinkles tell you? Well, I'm old and must be realistic about it." Despite the fact that half of the sample was between 55 and 66, none of the participants labeled themselves "middle-aged"; the younger portion of the sample preferred the term "of advanced age," whereas the oldest of the group preferred the expression *anciano*, or "very old." Participants openly admitted that age norms existed for grooming, courtship, marriage, and the ability to discuss sexuality. For example, there was a strong belief that one should dress

according to his or her age, avoid flirting and courting, and never discuss his or her sexual practices.

It turned out that women were much harsher than men when it came to enforcement of the norms. More than 80% of the women expressed disapproval of other women who violated the norms, whereas only a third of the men expressed the same sentiment. Punishment was usually meted out by women in the same age group; thus, there was a strong tendency for each age group to police its own members concerning conformity to age norms. Sex differences were also noted in how

men and women actively listened and in how they described their lovers.

Bastida's research is one of the best attempts at understanding how age norms operate naturalistically in a particular ethnic group. One important point that she noted was the general lack of differences among the three groups she studied, indicating that the age norms identified generalize across different Hispanic groups. Considerably more work remains to be done, not only with Hispanic Americans but with other minority ethnic groups as well.

In sum, Koh and Bell found that older Korean immigrants became similar to other ethnic groups in many respects in their living and relationship patterns. Their data suggest that these individuals accepted an intergenerational pattern more like that in the United States than that in their native Korea.

The Importance of Ethnic Identity in Later Life

The study by Koh and Bell on Korean immigrants raises an important issue: To what extent is it important or beneficial to maintain ethnic identity across adulthood?

Cool (1987) provides an analysis of this point. The pressure to maintain one's **ethnic identity**, or shared values and behaviors, is often pitted against

the pressure to assimilate into the larger society. Many researchers have explored the notion that ethnic identity, in fact, serves as a source of support for the elderly. For example, elderly Jewish residents of communities and nursing homes show a strong ethnic identity, whether or not Jewish traditions are supported (Hendel-Sebestyen, 1979; Holzberg, 1983; Meyerhoff, 1978). Royce (1982) argues that ethnic identity is important to the elderly because it provides a source of solidarity for people who might otherwise be cut off from society.

Luborsky and Rubinstein (1987, 1990) argue that ethnic identity is a life-course phenomenon that gains in importance with age. They interviewed elderly Irish, Italian, and Jewish widowers and found that many of them had rediscovered their ethnic identities in old age. They identified four intertwined life-course concerns that were related to the meaning of ethnicity. First, the meaning of ethnic identity in later life is based on issues of life-span development and family history. These issues include the differentiation and separation of the self from the family and the simultaneous integration in, participation in, and attachment to the family.

Second, ethnic identity derives meaning from the historical settings and circumstances in which key events are experienced. For example, the currently popular ethnic festivals engender a feeling of pride in one's heritage and a desire to identify with one's ethnic group. In contrast, times of national conflict tend to lower the desire to identify with ethnic groups connected to the countries on the other side. During World War II many people of Japanese origin were sent to internment camps, and those of German heritage often tried to hide their background. The effect of timing and historical events on ethnic identity illustrates the point made in Chapter 1 about the importance of history-graded influences on development.

Third, Luborsky and Rubinstein found that current ethnic identity in these elderly men was situationally evoked depending on the needs and goals of the individuals. For example, many older men found themselves in the position of family historian after the death of their wives, who had fulfilled these roles earlier. Consequently, they became aware again of their family heritage and traditions, which fostered the reawakening of ethnicity.

Finally, past ethnic identity and experiences continue to be reworked as we consider our current ethnic identity. In other words, how we defined ourselves in the past is continually rethought and updated throughout adulthood. During old age as we move toward integrity (see Chapter 8), we are especially prone to rethinking our earlier definitions of who we are. It turns out that our sense of self includes a healthy dose of ethnicity.

The importance of Luborsky and Rubinstein's research is that the aspects of ethnic identity that they uncovered may be common to many ethnic groups. Moreover, ethnic identity is inextricably intertwined with other personal characteristics in our sense of self, which is reworked across the life span. Thus, ethnic identity itself is truly a developmental concept and is not fixed within any person at any point.

Ethnicity and Acculturation

One of the challenges facing the United States is how to foster interaction among the various ethnic groups. Such interaction is always tricky, largely because the interacting groups may fear losing their ethnic identities in the process. One way this happens is through a process called **acculturation**, "the sociocultural adjustment occurring when two or more 'cultures' interact" (Roberts, 1987).

Societies in which one group is dominant are especially likely to pressure other groups to conform to their way of doing things. Language is a good example of how acculturation occurs. In the United States, a significant proportion of people speak a language other than English as their primary language; for most of these people, this language is Spanish. A heated debate is being waged over whether Spanish should be used in elementary schools to teach children who are native Spanish speakers. In contrast, Canada openly recognizes its French-speaking citizens and requires both English and French on all packages, official documents, and many scientific journals.

Whether or not it is official, acculturation is a stressful process. For example, we see in Chapter 4 that acculturation resulted in increased health problems for Mexican Americans. Acculturation of young adults in this ethnic group also affects the well-being of Mexican-American elders. Specifically, older Mexican Americans often report unhappiness over their adult children's failure to fulfill traditional parental care obligations (Markides &

Martin, 1983) despite clear evidence of strong intergenerational ties (Markides, Boldt, & Ray, 1986). Elderly first generation Japanese-Americans' (isseis') expectations about caregiving were tempered by the strong influence of American norms, which had been greatly adopted by their children (nisseis) (Masako & Liu, 1986).

A second area of research relating to acculturation focuses on feelings of alienation among recent immigrants. For example, Moon and Pearl (1991) found that recent Korean immigrants to the United States felt alienated. However, these feelings were related to age, length of time in the United States, and geographic location. Older Korean immigrants felt more alienated than their younger counterparts, and feelings of alienation decreased over time for both groups. Koreans who immigrated to locations with large Korean communities felt less alienated than immigrants moving to areas with small Korean communities. This latter finding emphasizes the importance of a supportive social network in helping people adjust to a new environment.

Although acculturation apparently has clear effects on the experience of aging, very few studies have examined the issue in detail. Moreover, we know even less about whether attempts at keeping ethnic traditions alive have any effect (positive or negative) on the stress associated with acculturation. As the population shifts in countries such as the United States toward the total number of individuals in minority ethnic groups outnumbering whites, we must begin to address these issues.

We have seen that ethnicity plays a very important role in understanding people's experience of adult development and aging. Our ethnic heritage gives us an interpretive framework that we can apply to the events happening to us. This interpretive framework continually evolves, however, as a result of exchange among different groups and generations. Although this dynamic change may produce conflict, it should be viewed as a rich source of emerging knowledge and behavior. Ethnic identity is clearly important to older adults, who use it to help define themselves as they near the end of their lives.

In sum, ethnicity is an important basis for understanding within-society variations in aging. We now turn our attention to cross-cultural variations.

AGING AROUND THE WORLD

Suppose your instructor gave you the following assignment: You are to choose three different cultures around the world on three different continents and make arrangements to study older adults in each. Your task is to make whatever observations are necessary to determine similarities and differences with your own culture.

Your first inclination may be to pick destinations based on where you would like to vacation — a reasonable strategy on the face of it. But you may run into a snag. In choosing your sites, it may occur to you that you need to know what a culture *is* before you can book your tickets.

In this chapter and elsewhere in this book we have used the word *culture* in many ways: as a focus of socialization, as a variable along which people differ, and as a way to organize behavior, to name a few. We have seen that whether a particular developmental theory holds up or whether a particular set of behaviors is observed across cultures is extremely important in evaluating its importance and generality. Even in our everyday speech we refer to people from different cultures, meaning that we do not expect them to be the same as us (although we may want them to become like us).

Culture, then, is an often-used concept, but it is not very well defined, nor is the term itself very old (Fry, 1988). The notion of culture dates only to the 19th century and the colonial expansion of Europe, when it was used as a way to convey obvious differences in the ways people did things in different parts of the world. However, culture rapidly became the most important concept in anthropological research (Fry, 1988). Originally, it meant tradition or the complex set of customs that people are socialized into, but more recently **culture** has been used to mean the ways in which people go about daily life (Fry, 1985; Ortner, 1974).

The study of aging in different cultures did not become a major area in anthropology until 1945 with the publication of Simmons's *Role of the Aged in Primitive Society*. Since the 1960s research in this area has grown considerably. Unfortunately, very little of this research has been conducted in a lifespan developmental framework. Instead, the goal has been to describe the lives of older and younger members of societies. In this section we will consider how the elderly fare in different cultures and how age itself is viewed.

Definitions of Age Across Cultures

Recall from Chapter 1 that the term *age* has many scientific meanings (chronological age, social age, psychological age, and so forth). It should come as no surprise that age also means different things across cultures. For example, the meaning of chronological age varies from nil to its formal incorporation into civil laws regulating behavior (Keith, 1990). In the United States, for instance, there are specific age requirements for obtaining a driver's license, becoming an elected official, and receiving retirement funds through Social Security. Usually, the need for explicit stipulation of age only occurs when citizenship principles go beyond direct kinship lines (Mayer & Muller, 1986). That is, only when social and civic laws involve more than regulating family behavior is there a need to specify age. Some authors (such as Mayer & Muller, 1986)

point out that the emergence of nations created the "periodized" life course. Indeed, some types of crime, such as juvenile delinquency, exist only because societies create categories of crimes that refer to people with certain age status; such crimes are often termed "status offenses" as a result.

In most traditional societies, chronological age per se makes little difference. Rather, what matters is *generation* (Keith, 1990). In many, chronological age was not even counted until Western colonialization began. Still, many societies only render chronological age because they have to and disregard it in assigning seniority to its members. This is especially apparent when a person younger in chronological age is given the privileges associated with generational seniority than a person who is older in terms of time since birth (Fortes, 1984). For example, if greater status comes with becoming a grandparent, then the status is bestowed at the birth of the grandchild regardless of the chronological age of the grandparent. Chronologically old people who never have grandchildren never acquire the status.

Ignoring chronological age in favor of some other standard works well for these societies. The problem is that researchers tend to be ethnocentric and try to use a chronological age standard anyway. While using this standard makes comparisons across cultures easier, it also masks important distinctions. One way around this problem would be for researchers to use both the custom of the society under study and a chronological standard for comparative purposes only.

Culture and the Life Course

If cultures vary in terms of how they view chronological age, then it only stands to reason that they should also differ in how they structure the life course (Keith, 1990). Differences here have important implications for using the biopsychosocial model across cultures. When different cultures have alternative views of the various parts of the life span, these views will alter the interpretation of personal events. According to the model, this will result in important differences in the experience of growing old. This means that whatever conclusions we draw from studying one culture may have little relevance to a culture that has a very different basis for defining the same events.

In some small societies, labels may be used to refer to different parts of the life span, such as "child," "young woman," "old man." However, these labels carry with them no status or specific roles. Other small societies have no labels; rather, when asked about a specific period during the life span they will list specific individuals as exemplars. Keith (1990) points out that societies in which the importance of specific periods of the life span is minimized tend to have several characteristics in common: small size, so that all members are known to each other; fluid social relations; and lack of personal property ownership. Societies without these characteristics, such as industrialized societies, tend to place far greater emphasis on periods in the life span.

Societies also differ in terms of the unit perceived as moving through the life course in the first place. Northern European ethnic groups, for example, think in terms of *individuals* moving through the life course. However, Meyer (1986) rightly notes that not only the individual as the unit of analysis but the life course itself are cultural creations that are not universal. For some cultures, life transitions are collective experiences shared, for instance, by entire families, not just one individual.

The notion of what it means to be a person also varies considerably across cultures. In middle-class communities in the United States, being a person means being independent (for example, heading a household) and having one's mental ability intact (Keith, Fry, & Ikels, 1990). But in some African cultures, full personhood is only attained if one has children and grandchildren (Sangree, 1989). And for followers of Confucianism, personhood is maintained after physical death as long as one's descendants tend the ancestral shrine.

With so many differences across cultures surrounding the life course, you may be wondering if there is any common cultural perspective. The answer is a qualified yes. The common ground across cultures in terms of views about the life course concerns reproductive status and responsibility (Keith, 1990). Cultures around the world make distinctions between people (usually women) who can and cannot have children, and assign different tasks to people of different age status. But even here there are subtle cross-cultural differences; for example, some cultures do not allow women to hold positions of authority until after they can no longer have children, while other cultures bar them from such positions altogether. By the same token, transitions that many Westerners view as abrupt and irreversible, such as death, are viewed quite differently by other cultures. Melanesian societies view death as a lengthy, reversible, and negotiable stage of life (Counts & Counts, 1985b).

Finally, how people view the life course is not necessarily uniform, even in the same location. Take the Guatemalan village of Atchatlan, for instance. Natives believe life is a well-worn path that everyone should follow as closely as possible. But Mestizos in the same village hold the view of wider Guatemalan society and perceive many possible paths through life (Fry & Keith, 1982).

Rituals and Life Transitions. Most cultures use rituals to mark changes over the life span. Typically, the most important rituals mark rites of passage. These rites are symbolic representations of the movement across the life span, and ritualize the passage from one stage to another. Rites of passage traditionally include three phases (Keith, 1990): separation, marginality, and reincorporation. These

Formal rituals such as bar mitzvahs and retirement parties are ways to mark transitions in age stratification systems. This initiation rite among the Xavante in Brazil reflects the universal nature of such rituals.

fully made these transitions themselves, they are seen as teachers or guides for the ritual passage. This is especially true in oral cultures, where, because there is no written language, older adults are the repositories of cultural wisdom and the keepers of the ritual itself.

Even in Western industrialized societies, the participation of older adults in rituals remains important. Although formal rites of passage may not occur on the broad societal level, rituals continue to be important at the religious, community, and family levels. For example, many religious groups have formal positions designated "elder," which are held by people perceived as having life experience and wisdom. Family rituals, such as Thanksgiving dinner, are often presided over by older members of the family, often in spite of declining health (Rosenthal & Marshall, 1988).

In general, rituals are important ways for older adults to maintain a feeling of being connected with other generations. Because rituals change very little over time, they also provide continuity across the life span; the rituals elderly adults assist in today are virtually the same as those they participated in as children and young adults. Family rituals are especially important in this regard in industrialized societies, as they offer one of the few formal opportunities for older adults to pass on important historical family practices and information to the younger generations.

phases may involve elaborate steps or may be collapsed to a few minutes. Initiates are typically dressed in different apparel to indicate their transition. (This is also true in many transitions as practiced in the United States; consider ritual garments used at baptisms, bar mitzvahs, and weddings, for example.)

Older adults play major roles in many cultural rites of passage. Because older people have success-

Patterns of Aging Across Cultures

We noted earlier that all societies consider age as one component of their organization (Halperin, 1987). How age-based organization is accomplished varies considerably from one culture to another. We will consider three types of societies as examples: egalitarian societies, ranked horticultural societies, and age-set systems.

Egalitarian Societies. **Egalitarian societies** are the oldest, smallest, and technologically simplest societies (Halperin, 1987). The members live by hunting and gathering in small, nomadic bands of extended families that come together or split apart according to seasonal variations in the availability of resources. Some examples of egalitarian societies in the world today are the Eskimo, the Kalahari !Kung, and the Tiwi of Australia.

Egalitarian societies rule themselves by consensus, and no individual has differential access to resources (Leacock, 1978). Class differences do not exist. Reciprocity and sharing the wealth form the basis for interaction; in times of need, everyone does without.

Age is an important characteristic of egalitarian societies. Among the !Kung, older men and women assume the role of managers who control water, the most important resource (Biesele & Howell, 1981). Apparently, the !Kung reserve this most important task for those who have the most experience. Additionally, elderly !Kung are the keepers of essential technical information about the seasonal fluctuations in food supplies. This knowledge about plants and animals makes the elderly a critical element in the survival of the !Kung in the Kalahari Desert. Because of their knowledge and their participation in decision making, older !Kung are cared for by their children and grandchildren (R. B. Lee, 1968). Because some degree of sophistication and expertise is needed for hunting and gathering, most of the physical labor is assigned to younger and middle-aged people; children and the elderly live a relatively leisurely life.

Another interesting use of age grading concerns diet. The !Kung have strict age-graded norms concerning what foods may be eaten. For example, only children and the elderly may eat ostrich eggs; the !Kung believe that ostrich eggs cause insanity in people of reproductive age (Biesele & Howell, 1981). A more scientific explanation is that the !Kung reserve the eggs — a relatively scarce but excellent source of protein — for those who may have difficulty chewing the hard-shelled alternative, the more plentiful mongongo nuts.

In other egalitarian societies, expectations of people at different ages also vary with gender. For example, the Mundurucu of the Brazilian Amazon Basin have differing expectations of women at various points along the life span (Y. Murphy & Murphy, 1974). During their childbearing years women are to remain passive, retiring, and demure, are not to seek male company, and are to occupy separate physical and social domains. After menopause, however, women can sit anywhere, can speak freely and with authority, and are typically deferred to by men.

In general, egalitarian societies use age to organize roles that need to be performed. Older adults, to the extent that the society can provide for them, continue to fulfill important roles of teaching and socializing.

Ranked Horticultural Societies. The relationship between age and other aspects of society becomes more complicated in **ranked horticultural societies**. These societies are relatively permanent residents of a particular area and are much larger than egalitarian societies. The most notable difference between the two is a clear ranking system in which "big men" and chiefs acquire a larger proportion of goods and power than other members of the society (Halperin, 1987). Big men are those who achieve power by creating a loyal following, whereas chiefs attain power by virtue of kinship connections. In most cases, such power is gained militarily; without this base, old men may be afforded status but little real power.

One example of a ranked horticultural society was that of the Coast Salish of the northwestern United States (Amoss, 1981). Among the Coastal Salish generational position defined the most important roles; political and economic power were in the hands of the old. In combination with high

SOMETHING TO THINK ABOUT

Modernization Theory and Respect for the Elderly

A major concern in studying aging in different cultures is to determine how older adults fare in different settings. One of the most influential theories that has guided this work is modernization theory. In brief, modernization theory provides a useful way of making comparisons between societies or within one society at different historical stages. It focuses on how a society is organized and dif-

ferentiated in an attempt to explain why the elderly are treated the way they are (Hendricks, 1982).

Modernization is a catch term closely associated with the Industrial Revolution of the 18th century, which began in Western Europe and continues to spread throughout the world today. The trend toward industrialization and subsequent urbanization, mass education, mass media, bureaucratization, wider dissemination of information, increased mobility, and rapid change brought about sweeping alterations in the traditional strata of society (Halperin, 1987; Silverman, 1987). As life got

more complex, modernization had an enormous impact on the life course. Periods of the life span that were unimportant in nonindustrialized societies, such as adolescence, became well recognized and formalized. Age grades became ways to label obsolete skills, as older people fell behind technological innovations.

Anthropologists and sociologists who examined the effects of these widespread changes on societies came to believe that modernization was largely responsible for the elderly's loss of prestige and power in industrialized societies (Cowgill & Holmes, 1972). Cowgill (1974)

---

kinship rank, age was the basis for redistribution of wealth. The elderly among the Coastal Salish were valued for their knowledge and experience concerning such things as hunting, house building, and canoe making, as well as being the information source for rituals. Older members were also important in holding extended families together.

Holding older members of ranked horticultural societies in esteem for their experience and knowledge indicates that increased societal complexity does not necessarily bring with it devaluation of the elderly (Foner, 1984). This point argues against **modernization theory**, which holds that devaluing of old age comes as a by-product of technological change and the growing obsolescence of older adults' skills. In ranked horticultural societies, age represents valued experience, not obsolescence. As

pointed out in Something to Think About, however, modernization theory controversially explains the tendency of more technologically advanced nations to devalue their elderly.

Age-Set Systems. One of the clearest examples of age grading occurs in some African cultures, in which age is a formalized principle of social organization that explicitly regulates the allocation of social roles (Foner & Kertzer, 1978, 1979; Kertzer & Madison, 1981). **Age-set systems** are groups of people who recognize common membership in a named grouping based on common age (Kertzer & Madison, 1981).

Formal age-set systems appear to share several commonalities (Fry, 1988). Because they are predominantly male, they tend to involve the distri-

points to four major culprits: advances in health technology, which kept more people alive longer and led to the development of retirement; advances in economic technology, leading to new jobs that made the skills of the elderly obsolete; urbanization, which led to young adults' migration away from the rural homes of the elderly; and mass education, which gave the young an advantage over the old. Several researchers have presented data supporting modernization theory from a variety of countries such as Bangladesh, Chile, and Turkey (Bengtson et al., 1975; Gilleard & Gurkan, 1987).

Although modernization theory is very popular, it has come under severe attack from some historians and anthropologists. Historians argue that there probably never was a time before the Industrial Revolution when older adults were uniformly treated with nothing but respect (Fischer, 1978; Quadagno, 1982; Stearns, 1977). Moreover, modernization theory tends to view all nonindustrialized societies alike in spite of their many differences. We have seen that these societies vary considerably in how they treat their elderly members, so to lump them all together is a serious oversimplification.

Anthropologists point out that modernization of a society does not affect all cohorts similarly (Foner, 1984); thus, as initially younger cohorts age, the effects of modernization are extremely difficult to determine.

Although modernization theory fails to account for variations among different societies and how they treat their aged, it has illustrated that when societies undergo major and fundamental change, one of the hardest hit groups is the old. Regardless of the adequacy of modernization theory in explaining how this happens, it still provides us with something to think about.

bution of power; for example, they determine who has the most political clout (Fortes, 1984). Physiological age tends to be ignored; rather, age assumes a social-structural or organizational meaning (Bernardi, 1985). Status and rights tend to be uniquely assigned to each age set, such as novice, warrior, or elder. In contrast to inequality across age groups, there tends to be considerable equality among members of an age group (Fry, 1988), although in some cases this egalitarianism is more apparent than real.

Although formalized age grading exists in many forms (Bernardi, 1985), and in many locations (for example, North and South America, East Asia, and Western Europe; see Keith, 1990), it has been studied most in East African cultures (Kertzer & Madison, 1981). Among the Latuka, for example, both men and women past a certain age belong to

an age set. The four age-set groupings in Latuka society are based solely on age; kinship and wealth are not considered. Within age sets there is no stratification for either gender. Labor is the responsibility of members of the two middle age sets; children and the elderly are exempt. In the Gada society each age set constitutes an egalitarian group collectively progressing through the social grades (Fry, 1988).

Similar systems operate elsewhere in Africa. For example, the Masai have explicit and comprehensive age-based organization of their society (Keith, 1990). On the surface, Masai in younger age grades enjoy egalitarian relationships, and individuals in older age grades maintain social control. But there is more to it than that. The egalitarianism of the young appears to be a reaction to their limited access to power and wealth, rather than a true egalitarian spirit. As individuals get older and gain access to power and wealth, egalitarianism disappears. Thus, the age grades carry with them very important meanings that are manifested in different behaviors.

There is some evidence that age-set systems existed in North and South America, but with some differences. For example, age sets were important only in young adulthood among the Akwe-Shavante of Brazil (Maybury-Lewis, 1984). On the Great Plains age sets and their accompanying rights were bought and sold to others as a means of passing through the age grades (Fry, 1988).

As noted earlier, very few age-set systems refer to women. Several reasons have been offered for this gender difference (Keith, 1990). Women in these societies tend to be tightly tied to familial roles, which may override age commonalities (Kertzer & Madison, 1981). That is, women may be less likely to participate in same-age group activities than men because child rearing can occur across a wide age range. It may be that women's associations with their peers may be more activity based than age based. Additionally, major life transitions for women in these societies have more to do with reproduction than age. Because of large individual differences in age at onset of menopause, for example, it may be easier to allow nature to define status changes. Viewed this way, formal age-set systems may be a way that men compensate for the lack of such obvious biological markers (Keith, 1990).

Finally, the status bestowed on older members of age-set societies does not necessarily mean that all old people wield great power. On the contrary, the acquisition of power solely on the basis of age is quite rare (Keith, 1990). In most age-set societies, old men have power because they control the key societal resources, such as cattle, and have acquired many wives. Power simply takes many years to acquire, making it highly unlikely that a younger man could achieve it.

Aging and Asian Cultures

Perhaps nowhere is the stereotype of revered older adults stronger in Americans' minds than in their view of how older people are treated in Asian cultures, especially in China and Japan. Americans envision a highly idealized image of honored elders who are greatly esteemed, veritably worshiped for their wisdom (Tobin, 1987)—an image that has been bolstered in the scientific literature (Palmore, 1975; Palmore & Maeda, 1985). The image is false in many respects; we will consider Japan as an example.

Tobin (1987) found Americans pictured the Japanese elderly to be highly respected, cared for, and happy with their lives. Although this view may have been accurate at one time, today the actual state of affairs is quite different (Plath, 1980; Tobin, 1987). Older people in Japan are faced with a gamut of pressing issues: declining health, housing shortages, and economic and familial problems. Younger Japanese wonder if their children will care for them when they grow old.

Western views on aging have begun to influence Asian societies and whittle away at time-honored cultural traditions (Martin, 1988). Japanese families are no longer as willing to care for their older members, due to increased migration, industrialization, and increased participation of women in the workplace. These changes in traditions are more apparent in urban areas than in rural areas. In response to these changes China and Japan have both passed legislation mandating that family members must care for frail elders (Goldstein & Goldstein, 1986; Kii, 1981).

Freed's (1990) research is typical of recent findings. She reported a growing reluctance among middle-aged Japanese families to care for their elderly parents until they are unable to care for themselves. The Japanese families in Freed's study expressed ambivalence and conflict, and recognized that caregivers usually experience considerable stress. The families felt that the only way around

Attitudes toward the elderly in Asian cultures may be changing as these countries become more urbanized and Westernized.

this was to adopt a martyr stance. The families in Freed's study were typical of other middle-class Japanese who are placing increasing demands on the government for supportive services so that their parents can maintain their independence. Such feelings conflict with the long-held Japanese tradition that elderly parents should be cared for by their oldest son's wife.

Idealized images of honorable elders are damaging because they are merely one-dimensional pictures. The truth is that the problems faced in Western countries concerning health care and support for older adults are also pressing issues for countries around the world, including those in Asia.

Consequences of Inequality

Using age to divide societies into various strata is universal, as we have seen. An important consideration of such stratification is how age grading affects the members of each stratum. This issue is relevant only for societies that also have power differentiation through big men, chiefs, elected officials, and the like, since in these societies people in certain age strata control those in other age strata. In this section we will consider four consequences of the combination of age and unequal distribution of power (Foner, 1984): the presence of old men at the top, the presence of old women at the top, the losses of the old, and generational conflict.

Old Men at the Top. As we have noted earlier, in many societies older men are the leaders. They have an advantage over younger men in controlling material resources and other property, accumulating wives, and exercising authority both at home and in the wider community (Foner, 1984). They are also primary keepers of knowledge about rituals and other practices. This combination of factors typically leads to their being held in considerable esteem by other members of society.

Control of property and material resources is an important benefit of old age. Older men may be the only ones allowed to conduct property transfers, hold farming rights, and allocate resources. Younger men depend on senior relatives for approval of marriages, which are often arranged among the elders.

Control of resources may include control of people as well. Such power allows those in charge to command the labor and support of others, and it is considered by some to be the most important source of older men's wealth and status (Moore, 1978). Having many children is a sign of power in many nonindustrial societies, as is the number of wives one has. Indeed, Moore (1978) argues that wives are the most treasured possessions of all. Having many children also enables the older men to show more hospitality, an important source of prestige, and to gain more wealth by marrying off many daughters.

Old Women at the Top. Later life is when women in many societies gain freedom, prestige, power, and respect (Foner, 1984). While they are young, women are at the mercy of both men and older women, and they are burdened with many restrictions on behavior and even diet.

Although the opportunities available to older women in nonindustrialized societies are not as great as they are for men, they are considerably better than they are for younger women. In many societies aging brings freedom to engage in previously prohibited behavior and to speak one's mind, some access to positions of political power, respect as a repository of wisdom and expertise, and ultimate authority over the household (Foner, 1984). For example, there is considerable documentation that among West African societies an older woman called the Queen Mother wielded considerable power, from selecting the new chief or king to running the affairs of the society when the king was away (Foner, 1984; Fortes, 1950; Wallace, 1971).

Most of the power held by older women involves the domestic arena (Foner, 1984; Fry, 1988). Older women have complete direction over younger adult women and children, with the senior wife in polygynous societies having the most authority. In many societies women gain prominence with age by becoming grandmothers. For example, LeVine (1978) notes that the most respected and powerful women in the Gusii culture were the oldest women with grandchildren, followed by other women with grandchildren, followed by women with married children. Married women with no children and unmarried adult women were at the bottom; they were at the mercy of everyone else. Similarly, in Chinese society older women who remained with the family could wield supreme authority over all other family members, even assuming control of the family's estate and affairs (Freedman, 1966).

With so much to gain, women in these societies eagerly anticipated growing old. Saddled with societal restrictions until after menopause, women greatly enjoyed their newfound freedom and respect. As Foner (1984) notes, the large discrepancy in power between men and women that is pointed out in sociological and psychological works diminishes significantly as women grow older.

Social Losses of the Old. The old are not always at the top in society. We know that well from observing our own culture, in which the elderly do not have a great deal of power. Putting older people at or near the bottom is not unique to Western culture, however.

In some societies physically and mentally competent older adults are stripped of their power and prestige in well-established ways. Ortner (1978) writes that among the Sherpa, property was dispersed before death, beginning with the first child's marriage. Sons were given a share of the land and a house; daughters were provided with cash, jewels, and utensils. Parents would do anything they could

to delay children's marriages, sometimes keeping them at home until they were in their 30s. However, eventually the youngest son married. According to custom, he inherited his parents' house. Parents became almost like servants, depending on the son for everything; they were left with virtually nothing. Property transfers before death also occurred in such diverse cultures as rural Ireland (Arensberg, 1968) and the Basque culture in Spain (Douglass, 1969).

Caring for physically or mentally incapacitated older adults was often difficult, especially in societies with few resources. In some cases frail older adults were cared for adequately, but in many they were not. Researchers have documented numerous societies that practiced abandonment or killing of incapacitated elderly (Glascock & Feinman, 1981; Maxwell, Silverman, & Maxwell, 1982; Simmons, 1945). In contrast, several reports have been made of societies like the !Kung who provide good care for their frail elderly (Goody, 1976; R. B. Lee, 1968; Simmons, 1945). Regardless of treatment, however, frail elderly people were usually stripped of any real or ceremonial authority they had.

Conflict Between Generations. One of the few universals in the study of aging in different cultures is the potential for **intergenerational conflict**. Young people the world over do not enjoy being subservient; they believe that older people are out of touch, and want greater power for themselves (Foner, 1984). Yet these feelings are almost never expressed openly. Why do the strains between young and old so often remain hidden beneath the appearance of stable relationships?

There are logical reasons for suppressing the bad feelings between generations (Foner, 1984; Fry, 1985): Open conflict could lead to homicide, which is outlawed; open conflict is disruptive to society; young people begin to grow old themselves and gain a share of the power; old and young simply accept inequality as a fact of life; intergenerational kinship ties defuse much of the hostility; and the age groups may simply avoid each other.

What we see in virtually every culture studied is a balance between the impatience in the young and the need for continuity in the old. The balance works by channeling each generation's assets appropriately: the energy of youth into productive activities, such as hunting, and the wisdom and experience of age into decision-making activities. This balance is often precarious, but it illustrates that the tensions between generations that we see in our own culture are not unique.

Normative generational tension is not the only source of conflict, however. Sometimes intergenerational conflict comes from unwanted social changes. For example, elderly Sherpa live in a Buddhist society that highly values old age; they own their own homes, are usually in excellent physical shape, and have children nearby to care for them if necessary. However, many of them feel dissatisfied and dependent because they cannot live with their younger sons as prescribed by their tradition; many of the sons have gone to take jobs elsewhere (Beall & Goldstein, 1982). For some other cultures, co-residence with children due to economic necessity may disrupt traditional authority structures favoring older family members, which may actually promote conflict (Keith et al., 1990).

Clearly, intergenerational conflict is a part of the life cycle insofar as younger adults want to take over from older adults. But to the extent that industrialization and other social changes create unintended conflict, we should carefully consider whether those changes are worth the price.

SUMMARY

The Demographics of Aging

1. Defining old age as 65 years is an arbitrary criterion.

2. The number of older adults has increased greatly since 1900 and will continue to increase through the first part of the 21st century.

3. Increases in the number of older adults in the United States is occurring faster among ethnic minorities than among whites.

4. There are more older women than men, mostly because women tend to live longer.

5. The most rapid increases in elderly are occurring in Third World countries.

Status and Role

6. Status and role are assigned by society and vary across age groups.

7. Individuals' interpretations of their status and role are more important than societal definitions of them.

8. Aspects of both the structural and interactionist perspectives are needed to understand the aging process.

9. Social status of older people varies across cultures. However, high status does not guarantee good treatment, nor does low status always imply poor treatment.

10. Women in most cultures have it better in old age than men, partly due to life experience and partly due to societal structures.

Age Stratification

11. Societies create age grades with different expectations for each level.

12. Societies assign differential degrees of importance and power to different age grades.

13. Each age grade has certain behavioral norms that people are supposed to follow. Age norms prescribe the types of activities people are expected to do (such as get married, seek employment, retire, and so forth).

14. In part, societal significance is determined by the number of people alive in the cohort and the amount of power the cohort wields. As cohort members age, their significance declines.

15. People are socialized into age norms of behavior by members of older cohorts. This process ensures continuity of essential values that define the culture.

16. Anticipatory socialization helps prepare people to assume new roles that accompany status changes.

17. Adult socialization occurs mainly for marriage, parenthood, and occupational changes, but not for old age.

Ethnicity and Adult Development

18. Ethnicity is a social differentiation based on such things as a common language and customs that foster similar identity and values.

19. The notion that older people in ethnic minority groups are at a double risk is not supported by research. Other variables, such as financial or marital status, are more important.

20. Much of our identity across the life span comes from our ethnic background.

21. There are considerable differences across ethnic groups in how they define old age and the status and roles they assign to older adults.

22. Older adults derive a considerable part of their well-being from their ethnic identity as it has evolved over the life course.

23. The process of acculturation is stressful for immigrants and can cause physical health problems as well as negatively affect well-being.

Aging Around the World

24. In many cultures, generation is more important than chronological age.

25. Different cultures vary in how they structure the life course. In some, there are specific labels for aspects of the life span (such as, "old woman").

26. Some societies do not focus on individual development, but more on cohort and interdependence.

27. All societies make distinctions based on reproductive status and responsibility.

28. Many cultures use rituals or rites of passage to mark life transitions in status and role.

29. Egalitarian societies rule by consensus and make no class distinctions. Age and gender are important characteristics, however.

30. Ranked horticultural societies make distinctions based on power and wealth, which are somewhat related to age.

31. Age-set systems make formal distinctions based on age, primarily among men.

32. The stereotype of the wise elder in Asian cultures is changing as societies adopt Western culture. Middle-aged children are increasingly reluctant to care for frail parents in the children's home.

33. In some societies, old men are in the most powerful positions due to an accumulation of wealth, power, and women.

34. In other societies, old women speak freely, gain power, and wield authority on an equal footing with men.

35. In many societies, however, older adults lose power and prestige.

36. Intergenerational conflict is a universal phenomenon.

REVIEW QUESTIONS

The Demographics of Aging

1. What is the definition of old age? How was this criterion chosen?

2. What trends have there been during the 20th century concerning the number of older adults in the population?

3. How do ethnic groups compare to one another in terms of the number of and growth in elderly members?

4. How do the numbers of older men and women compare? Why are there differences in numbers?

5. What trends exist in the elderly populations of various countries around the world?

Status and Role

6. What are the structural and interactionist perspectives? How do they differ in terms of people's acquisition of status and role?

7. How are status and the treatment of older adults related?

8. How are status, role, and gender related in various societies?

Age Stratification

9. How do societies stratify themselves on the basis of age?

10. What is the connection between age grades and societal significance?

11. How does societal significance vary across age grades?

12. How do people learn age norms of behavior? In particular, for what roles are most people prepared?

Ethnicity and Adult Development

13. What is ethnicity?

14. What is the current interpretation of the double jeopardy hypothesis?

15. How is ethnicity important in later life?

16. What are the effects of acculturation?

Aging Around the World

17. How do different cultures vary in terms of their use of chronological age to define status and roles?

18. What role do rites of passage play in many cultures?

19. What similarities and differences are there among egalitarian societies, ranked horticultural societies, and age-set systems?

20. How are older adults treated in Asian cultures? Why are traditional values changing?

21. What are the patterns of status and role in societies with old men at the top and old women at the top?

22. How universal is intergenerational conflict? Why?

KEY TERMS

acculturation Process by which immigrants to a country are brought into the dominant culture. (58)

age norms Behaviors that are tied to a specific age in a given society. (46)

age-set systems People who recognize common membership in a particular group on the basis of age. (64)

age stratification model A way in which societies divide their population on the basis of age so that status and roles may be given differentially. (45)

anticipatory socialization Deliberate preparation for future roles by those already occupying them. (50)

culture A term that describes the way in which people go about their daily lives. (60)

double jeopardy The notion that being both old and from an ethnic minority group places one in an especially vulnerable position. (53)

egalitarian societies Groups that live by hunting and gathering, and rule themselves by consensus. (63)

ethnic group A socially identifiable group based on common language, customs, and voluntary associations that foster an identity. (52)

ethnic identity The personal integration of the shared values of an ethnic group. (57)

ethnogerontology The study of ethnicity in an aging context. (51)

intergenerational conflict Disagreement or conflict between the parental and child generations, usually over the issue of power. (69)

modernization theory A belief that the devaluation of age is an inevitable product of technological change. (64)

ranked horticultural societies Relatively localized groups of people who have developed clear social ranking systems. (63)

role A set of behaviors given to a person that one is expected to perform. (42)

societal significance The degree to which a particular cohort has power or can influence events in a society. (45)

status A formal position in society that can be unambiguously described. (41)

ADDITIONAL READING

A more thorough discussion of the demographics of aging can be found in

Uhlenberg, P. (1987). A demographic perspective on aging. In P. Silverman (Ed.), *The elderly as modern pioneers* (pp. 145–160). Bloomington, IN: Indiana University Press. Easy to medium difficulty.

An excellent summary of stratification systems and age is

Riley, M. W. (1985). Age strata in social systems. In R. H. Binstock & E. Shanas (Eds.), *Handbook of aging and the social sciences* (2nd ed., pp. 369–411). New York: Van Nostrand Reinhold. Medium difficulty.

A survey of the major differences between men and women across adulthood can be found in

Rossi, A. S. (Ed.). (1985). *Gender and the life course.* New York: Aldine-Atherton. Easy to medium difficulty.

Ethnic and cultural differences in aging are surveyed in

Gelfand, D. E., & Barresi, C. M. (Eds.). (1987). *Ethnic dimensions of aging.* New York: Springer. Medium difficulty.

Sokolovsky, J. (Ed.). (1990). *The cultural context of aging.* New York: Bergin & Garvey. Easy to medium difficulty.

CHAPTER 3

Physiological Changes

THE BIOPSYCHOSOCIAL MODEL

Intrapersonal Factors and Attempts at Explaining Aging / Biological and Physical Factors in Disease / Implications of the Biopsychosocial Model

THE BRAIN

Neurons / Structural Changes in the Neuron / How Do We Know? Brain Aging Is Not All Decline: Evidence for Dendritic Growth / Changes in Communication Among Neurons / Studying Brain-Behavior Relations: Imaging Techniques / Psychological Consequences of Brain Aging

THE IMMUNE SYSTEM

Changes in Immune System Cells / Antibodies and Autoimmunity / AIDS and Aging / Psychological Consequences of Changes in the Immune System

THE CARDIOVASCULAR SYSTEM

Cardiovascular Structure and Function / Cardiovascular Disease / Psychological Consequences of Changes in the Cardiovascular System

THE RESPIRATORY SYSTEM

Structural and Functional Changes / Respiratory Diseases / Psychological Consequences of Changes in the Respiratory System

THE SENSES

Something to Think About: Sensory Changes and Experiencing the World / Vision / Hearing / Taste / Smell / Somesthesis and Balance

THE REPRODUCTIVE SYSTEM

Reproductive Changes in Women / Reproductive Changes in Men / Psychological Consequences of Changes in the Reproductive System

APPEARANCE AND MOVEMENT

Appearance / Movement

**Summary / Review Questions
Key Terms / Additional Reading**

YOU CAN PROBABLY RECALL AS A CHILD LOOKING through your family photo albums and thinking the clothes and hairstyles your parents and grandparents wore looked ridiculous. Maybe you pointed to a picture and asked "Who's that?" only to be told that the young-looking person was your grandmother. You may have looked at the picture and wondered why her once-dark hair was now all gray, or why her once-smooth skin was now wrinkled.

That photographic experience may well have been the first time you realized that people change as they grow old. Grandparents were not born looking grandparental. It may also have been the first time you encountered age-related stereotypes of beauty. Over the years, as you were deluged with commercials about how to cheat the aging process by using this cream or that hair dye, you may have wondered how physical aging happens. Are aches and pains just part of the process? Will you have to give up sex? Will your brain waste away? Will you walked stooped over?

If you are a typical aging adult, the answer to these (and many other similar questions) is a resounding no. As you will see, biological and physical aging does bring certain inevitable changes. However, most of them will not force you to stop doing the things you enjoy now. In fact, there is little reason not to stay active well into old age. (Some of the best students in a ski class I took were in their mid-60s.) The good news is that the normative changes that we will consider do not mean that every organ system in our bodies is over the hill by age 30. Or ever. On the contrary, there is considerable variability in how rapidly our bodies age. Mounting evidence points to the fact that in many areas the aging process can be slowed significantly, as long as we take proper care of our bodies. Moderation and understanding age-related limits is the key.

Our goal in this chapter is to identify normal patterns of aging in body systems and to consider some deviations from these norms due to diseases in these systems. We will focus first on how the biopsychosocial model provides a framework for understanding biological and physiological change. Next, we will consider some of the normal changes that occur in several systems in the body. The topics will be organized roughly from the ones that are least visible to those that are fairly obvious: the brain, the immune system, the cardiovascular system, the respiratory system, the senses, the reproductive system, and appearance and movement.

THE BIOPSYCHOSOCIAL MODEL

The biopsychosocial model introduced in Chapter 1 is a way to keep important influences on adult development and aging in mind. Take a minute to review it. In our consideration of age-related changes in body systems in this chapter and of health promotion in Chapter 4, we will be focusing primarily on two aspects of this model: normative health-related changes in intrapersonal factors, and biological and physical factors in disease. However, we must keep in mind that the other aspects of the model (interpersonal factors, other intrapersonal factors, and life-cycle factors) are necessary for a complete understanding of biological and physiological aging. For example, a person who becomes seriously ill for the very first time at age 70 may view the situation differently than someone else who has had several serious illnesses throughout life.

The biopsychosocial model places considerable emphasis on the psychological consequences of physiological change. Whitbourne (1985) was one of the first to highlight this connection. She argued convincingly that only when physiological change is viewed in its proper psychological context (and vice versa) can we truly appreciate the impact of normative changes. Whitbourne's approach fits exceedingly well in the biopsychosocial model adopted here, and provides an additional framework for this chapter. We will explicitly consider the psychological context for each of the physiological changes we examine.

The focus in this chapter is on age-related changes in major body systems. Thus, we will emphasize normative changes in those intrapersonal factors involving major organ systems. To the extent that these changes are thought to be genetically programmed, we will consider hereditary issues as well. To begin, we will consider some of the attempts at explaining how changes in health-related intrapersonal factors occur.

Intrapersonal Factors and Attempts at Explaining Aging

Why does everyone who lives long enough grow old physically and eventually die? This important question addresses the physical aspects of intrapersonal factors in the biopsychosocial model (psychological issues is the other; see Chapter 1). It is also a question that has spurred several biologists and physiologists to come up with answers based on basic biological and physiological processes. Each answer, expressed as a theory, does a reasonable job at accounting for some of the normative changes we experience. However, no one theory accounts for them all.

Wear-and-Tear Theory. One intuitively appealing set of ideas argues that the body simply wears out. The **wear-and-tear theory** suggests that the body is much like a machine that gradually deteriorates over time. Although there is some evidence that certain age-related problems are the result of life-

long use (such as osteoarthritis), the wear-and-tear theory does not explain general aging.

Cellular Theories. A second family of ideas points to cellular causes. Hayflick (1987) found that cells grown in laboratory culture dishes could only undergo about 50 divisions at most before dying, with the number of possible divisions dropping depending on the age of the donor organism. Some people thought this so-called **Hayflick limit** could explain why cells inevitably die, but recent evidence suggests that things are more complicated. For example, Harrison (1985) reports that cells from some older adults double as often as those from younger adults. Thus, the role of the Hayflick limit in human aging remains unclear.

Another cellular theory is based on a process called **cross-linking**. According to this view, certain proteins in human cells interact randomly and produce molecules that get linked in such a way as to make the body stiffer. As described later, this process occurs in arteries, muscles, and skin tissue. In these systems, cross-linking provides interesting accounts for age-related changes. Unfortunately, cross-linking does not work very well for many other organ systems.

A related notion argues that aging is due to unstable molecules called **free radicals**, which are highly reactive chemicals produced randomly in normal metabolism. It is thought that free radicals cause cellular damage, which in turn impairs the functioning of the organ. Free radicals may play a role in some age-related diseases (for example, emphysema, atherosclerosis, and cancer), but how this happens remains unknown (Harman, 1987).

There is some evidence that spontaneous changes occur in DNA, the hereditary building block of the cell. Some versions of this idea argue that the problem lies with the inability of DNA to replicate itself when cells divide, while others argue that the fault lies with DNA repair systems. Presumably, mistakes in DNA could trigger destructive processes that could seriously impair organ functioning. At present, though, how problems involving DNA relate to human aging remains a mystery (Tice, 1987).

Metabolic Processes. A third set of theories concerns metabolic processes. One of these involves how many calories one eats. Evidence from experiments with rodents suggests that reducing calories lowers the risk of premature death, and slows down a wide range of normative age-related changes (Masoro, 1988). Although experimental evidence with humans is lacking, there are some suggestive cross-cultural findings. For example, Okinawans, who eat only 60% of the normal Japanese diet, have 40 times as many centenarians (people who are at least 100 years old) per capita as there are in Japan. Moreover, the Okinawan incidence of cardiovascular disease, diabetes, and cancer is half that of their Japanese counterparts (Monczunski, 1991).

A second metabolic process theory of aging involves how readily one adapts to stress (Shock, 1977). Although stress per se does not cause aging, the body's ability to deal with changes in temperature and physical exertion declines with age. For example, elderly adults are more likely to die of exposure to cold and are more affected by hot weather than are younger adults. Later in this chapter, we will see that the cardiovascular and respiratory systems have lowered capacities to deal with physical exertion as we age.

Programmed Cell Death. A growing number of scientists believe that aging is a highly regulated process that is based on genetically programmed cell death (Lockshin & Zakeri, 1990; Vijg & Papaconstantinou, 1990). That is, even in cases where cell death appears random, researchers now believe that such losses are part of a master genetic program. **Programmed cell death** appears to be a function of physiological processes, the innate ability to self-destruct, and the ability of dying cells to

trigger key processes in other cells. At present, we do not know how this self-destruct program gets activated, nor do we understand how it happens once underway. However, understanding programmed cell death may be the key to understanding how genes and physiological processes interact to produce aging. Currently, considerable research is being devoted to the role of programmed cell death in determining longevity (see Chapter 4).

Biological and Physical Factors in Disease

Many people view aging as synonymous with disease. They think that aging inevitably brings aches and pains, and that there is nothing that can be done to improve the situation. Fortunately, this view is false. In fact, as far back as Aristotle, aging has been distinguished from disease. Aging is always a universal and inevitable process; disease is not. Kohn (1985) suggests that there are three major ways to define disease:

1. Some diseases are universal, progressive, and inevitable with age. Atherosclerosis, a chronic disease of the blood vessels that is discussed later, is one example of this kind of disease.

2. Some diseases are age related, but are neither universal nor inevitable. Many forms of cancer are related to age (see Chapter 4), but are not experienced by everyone.

3. Some diseases are not age related, but their impact is greater the older one is. For example, not all forms of pneumonia are age related, as explained later in this chapter. However, death rates from pneumonia increase dramatically with age.

Kohn (1985) distinguishes normal aging from disease by the following criteria. Normal aging consists only of changes that are universal, progressive, and irreversible. These changes cannot be the result of some other process, such as disease, but must contribute to the increased vulnerability of the person to disease. According to these criteria, only processes that fit the first category of disease, such as atherosclerosis, would represent normal aging.

Kohn's definitions and criteria are important. One of the myths of aging is that debilitating disease is simply to be expected. This myth often results in otherwise treatable conditions not being treated solely because the person with the problem is old. In part, this myth is perpetuated through the interaction of biological and physical factors with life-cycle factors; aches and pains in older adults are interpreted differently than the same complaints in younger adults. Adopting Kohn's approach avoids these unfortunate stereotypes.

Implications of the Biopsychosocial Model

Although we do not yet have one unified theory of biological and physiological aging, the picture is becoming clearer. We know that there clearly are genetic components, that some body systems simply wear out, and that the body's chemistry lab produces incorrect products at times. From the perspective of the biopsychosocial model, these facts point toward the need to integrate basic biological and physiological processes with social and psychological ones. Throughout this chapter and Chapter 4, notice how changes in body systems and diseases are influenced by these other factors.

The implication of this interactive process is that the diagnosis and treatment of health-related concerns must also include many perspectives. It is not enough to have one's physical functioning checked in order to establish whether one is healthy. Rather, one needs not only a typical bodily physical, but also a checkup concerning psychological and social functioning. Finally, the results of

all of these examinations must be placed in the context of the overall life span by considering appropriate life-cycle factors.

THE BRAIN

"Star Trek" fans may believe that space is the final frontier, but for many scientists it is the brain. Our knowledge of its secrets increases exponentially each year; so do our questions. Unlocking its functions is tough enough; understanding how these functions change over time is an additional challenge. Compared with changes in other organs, the brain's specific changes that occur with age are difficult to see. There are few corollaries to the wrinkles we get on our skin or the shortness of breath we experience when we exercise. Evidence of brain changes is indirect — for example, forgetting someone's name or difficulty in solving a complex math problem. Yet concern about brain aging is high during adulthood due to the mistaken idea that senility is inevitable and universal. In this section we will separate the myth from the reality of brain aging. Let us begin by taking a look at some key brain structures.

The age-related changes in the brain that we will consider occur mainly at the level of individual brain cells, called neurons. The changes often begin very subtly; they are often difficult to document because they are microscopic in nature and are hard to tie to specific behaviors. Still, our knowledge of normative changes in the brain is growing very rapidly due to major advances in technology. Much of what we have learned over the past decade has come from highly sophisticated computer-enhanced imaging techniques and from careful research in microbiology.

In this section we will primarily consider changes that are currently viewed as normative.

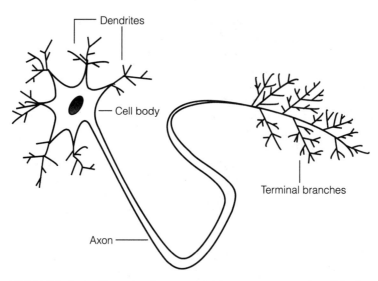

FIGURE 3.1 Example of a neuron. Major structures are the cell body, dendrites, axon, and terminal branches.

Abnormal brain aging, such as that which occurs in Alzheimer's disease, will be examined in more detail in Chapter 9.

Neurons

The cells that are the building blocks of the brain are the **neurons** (see Figure 3.1). As shown in the figure, neurons have several parts that play specialized roles in receiving, conducting, and transmitting information. At the left end of the neuron in the figure are the **dendrites**. They act like antennae; their responsibility is to pick up the chemical signals coming in from other nearby neurons much like TV antennae pick up signals from nearby stations. The signal is brought into the *cell body*, where it is converted into an electrochemical impulse and sent down the axon to the *terminal branches*. The terminal branches, shown at the right end of the drawing, act like transmitter stations. Chemicals called **neurotransmitters** are released at the terminal branches and carry the information signal to the next neuron's dendrites. The neurotransmitters are necessary for communication between neurons because neurons do not physically touch one another. The gap between the terminal branches of one neuron and the dendrites of another, across which neurotransmitters travel, is called the *synapse*.

We are born with roughly 1 trillion neurons of different sizes and shapes, which constitute all the neurons we will ever have. Neurons grow in size and complexity across the life span but, like heart-muscle cells, cannot regenerate (Bondareff, 1985). Once a neuron dies it is lost forever.

Structural Changes in the Neuron

Individual neurons undergo a wide variety of normative age-related changes. In most people, these changes produce little noticeable difference in behavior until very old age. However, when the changes are massive and occur more rapidly, disease is typically present. One problem in differentiating between normal and abnormal brain aging is that many of the same changes underlie both; as we will see in Chapter 9, for example, the defining characteristics of brain changes in Alzheimer's disease are also normative.

A second problem is that we have documented many neuronal changes, but we only understand the implications of a few. Tying specific brain changes to specific behaviors is very difficult. Much of this work relies on studies of people with brain injuries or disease, and is correlational. As we discussed in Chapter 1, this means that we cannot be certain that the brain changes found through imaging techniques, for example, actually caused the behaviors observed. Nevertheless, some consistent findings have been obtained, and we will consider them a bit later.

Cell Body and Axon. The most important change in the cell body and axon of neurons involves changes in the fibers contained there. Sometimes, for reasons we do not understand, neurons in some parts of the brain develop **neurofibrillary tangles**, in which fibers in the axon become twisted together to form paired helical, or spiral, filaments (Duara, London, & Rapoport, 1985). Large concentrations of neurofibrillary tangles are associated with behavioral abnormalities and are one defining characteristic of Alzheimer's disease, which is discussed in Chapter 9 (Bondareff, 1985). However, some degree of tangling occurs normally as we age. (This is an example of why it is sometimes difficult to tell the difference between normal and abnormal aging.)

Dendrites. When dendrites deteriorate, a person's ability to process information is impaired (Duara et al., 1985). Dendritic changes are complex. Scheibel (1982) maintains that dendrites of aging neurons are lost progressively, first from the outermost sections, but eventually from the entire dendritic structure. Ultimately the neuron is reduced to a stump with no dendrites, at which point it dies.

Buell and Coleman (1979) conducted a quantitative analysis in which they measured the length of the dendrites. Their results present a much different picture from Scheibel's. Buell and Coleman found that in normal aging, dendritic length of some neurons actually increases across adulthood. Only in abnormal aging, such as in Alzheimer's disease, do dendritic lengths decline. How Buell and Coleman came to this conclusion is examined in How Do We Know?

What should we conclude from this discussion? Do dendrites typically shrivel up and die or do they continue to grow and proliferate? It appears that both descriptions may be correct (Duara et al., 1985). Curcio et al. (1982) point out that in normal aging some neurons die while others, perhaps most, are prospering and continuing to grow. Thus, Scheibel's (1982) research provides a description of the degradation process, while Buell and Coleman's (1979) research describes the growth.

Plaques. Damaged and dying neurons sometimes collect around a core of protein and produce **neuritic plaques**. Neuritic plaques have been found in samples taken at autopsy from various parts of the brain (Kenney, 1982). Although the number of neuritic plaques increases with age, large numbers of them are not observed in normal brain aging until around age 90 (Adams, 1980). Until then high concentrations of neuritic plaques are considered characteristic of abnormal aging; for example, they are also indicative of Alzheimer's disease.

Because they are composed of degenerating neurons, neuritic plaques are believed to be a consequence, rather than a cause, of neural aging (Duara et al., 1985). As neuritic plaques become numerous, however, it is likely that they interfere with the normal functioning of healthy neurons (Bondareff, 1985).

Interpreting Neuronal Changes. Describing the effects of age-related processes on the brain is an

HOW DO WE KNOW?

Brain Aging Is Not All Decline: Evidence for Dendritic Growth

One of the dominant views of brain aging is the neuronal fallout model, which pictures brain aging as characterized by loss and decline. Over the last decade, however, researchers have discovered strong evidence for neuronal *growth* across adulthood. This line of work was pioneered by Buell and Coleman (1979), who were among the first to describe this growth process. How did they find their evidence?

Buell and Coleman obtained samples of brain tissue from 15 individuals during autopsy. These individuals represented three groups:

5 were neurologically normal middle-aged adults averaging 51.2 years; 5 were normal older adults, averaging 79.6 years; and 5 were older adults who had brain diseases, averaging 76 years. The samples of brain tissue were from the area of the brain near the hippocampus (a structure in the middle of the brain).

The key measurement was the length of the average dendritic segment, which was obtained by dividing total length of the dendrite by the number of segments it contained. The researchers found that the average length of a dendritic segment was significantly longer in the normal elderly brains than in the normal middle-aged brains, and both were significantly longer than those in the demented brains.

The findings clearly demonstrated continued growth of the dendrites in normal aging. Diseases such as Alzheimer's represent a failure of this process and actually involve a shrinking of the dendrites. Buell and Coleman were the first to definitively document growth in the brain during adulthood and aging. They speculate that there are two different populations of neurons in the normal older adult. One group consists of dying neurons, represented by the fallout model. The other group consists of surviving and growing neurons. Buell and Coleman argue that in normal aging the second group predominates until very late in life. How and when the shift from growth to decline occurs remains a mystery.

---

enormous task. Individual experience and programmed physiological changes interact to produce an intricate set of changes in an already enormously complex system. Moreover, once a neuron dies, all the connections it made are lost, possibly along with the behaviors based on those connections.

Buell and Coleman's (1979) landmark research is an example of the complexity of age-related changes. They documented the coexistence of both dying and growing neurons in the same individuals in different parts of the brain. Both decline and growth were present in the brains of all adults between the ages of 44 and 92 who were studied. Consequently, it appears that a complete model of the aging brain requires an understanding of both

why neurons die and why they continue to grow. It may be that the pattern of losses and gains represents an adaptive function. That is, we may be programmed to generate neuronal connections almost indiscriminately while we are young, thereby allowing as much learning to occur as possible. The normative losses accompanying aging would then represent judicious pruning of unused, redundant, unnecessary connections that can be removed without seriously compromising the person's ability to function.

The normative loss and growth pattern may also provide insight into abnormal brain aging. It could be that abnormal brain aging occurs when losses greatly outnumber gains before very old age. This is clearly the case in conditions such as Alzheimer's disease and related disorders, in which there is massive progressive loss of neurons in many areas of the brain.

Changes in Communication Among Neurons

Recall that because neurons do not physically touch one another, they communicate by releasing neurotransmitters into the synapse. Such communication is essential because behavior is governed by complex interconnections among many neurons. Understanding age-related changes in both the synapse and the neurotransmitters is also important for understanding changes in behavior (Bondareff, 1985).

Synapses. It is difficult to establish the pattern of age-related changes in synapses because two complex processes are occurring (Cotman & Holets, 1985). First, synapses are lost through neuronal degeneration and death. Second, new synapses are formed as a result of new learning and the continued growth of neurons. These two opposing processes result in no net change in the number of synapses, but they do produce changes in the configuration of synapses (Hoff, Scheff, Bernardo, & Cotman, 1982; Hoff, Scheff, & Cotman, 1982). In other words, the way in which neurons are organized and interconnected changes with age. Unfortunately, it is not clear how these organizational changes affect human behavior (Cotman & Holets, 1985).

Neurotransmitters. Changes in the level of neurotransmitters affect the efficiency of information transmission among neurons. Age-related changes occur along several neurotransmitter pathways, which are groups of neurons that use the same neurotransmitter (Rogers & Bloom, 1985).

One pathway in the brain that is responsible for controlling motor movements uses the neurotransmitter *dopamine*. As we age, the level of dopamine decreases (McGeer & McGeer, 1980). If this decline is extreme, we develop Parkinson's disease. As described in Chapter 9, Parkinson's disease is characterized by tremors and a shuffling walking style, as well as serious depression (Fry, 1986). Although there is no cure, the symptoms of Parkinson's disease can be alleviated by medications, such as L-dopa, which are converted into dopamine (Rogers & Bloom, 1985). The cause of the abnormal depletion of dopamine in Parkinson's disease is unknown (Dakof & Mendelsohn, 1986).

Age-related declines in the neurotransmitter *acetylcholine* are also well documented (Rogers & Bloom, 1985), and are linked with memory problems in old age (Drachman, Noffsinger, Sahakian, Kurdziel, & Fleming, 1980). Much current interest in acetylcholine is spurred by its link to both Alzheimer's disease and Huntington's disease (see Chapter 9). Some researchers speculate that there are causal connections between these diseases and abnormally low levels of choline acetyltransferase, an enzyme responsible for synthesizing acetylcholine (see Rogers & Bloom, 1985). Much of the search for drugs to alleviate the symptoms of Alzheimer's focuses on this and other enzymes related to acetylcholine.

Considerably less research has been conducted concerning age-related changes in levels of *serotonin*, a neurotransmitter that is involved in arousal and sleep (Rogers & Bloom, 1985). What little is known points to an age-related decline (Ponzio et al., 1982), which may underlie some of the age-related changes in sleep that are described in Chapter 4 (Frolkis & Bezrukov, 1979).

Studying Brain-Behavior Relations: Imaging Techniques

If we could peek inside your living, working brain, what would we find? The answer to this question turns out to be one of the most exciting avenues of research on brain development. Investigators can now use computer-enhanced images to assist in diagnosing disease and even to study the thinking brain. Researchers mainly use three imaging techniques to do this: computed tomography (CT) scans, magnetic resonance imaging (MRI), and positron emission tomography (PET). The first two (CT and MRI) are widely used not only in research but also in the diagnosis of brain diseases such as tumors and strokes. All three have provided fascinating insights into brain functioning.

Computed Tomography (CT). CT scans were the first of the high-tech imaging techniques, having been developed in the early 1970s by Hounsfield (1973). CT scans are created by passing highly focused X rays in various directions through a patient. The X rays are recorded by detectors, and computers are used to create a three-dimensional slice of the part of the body being studied. CT images produce shades of gray, which correspond to different types of tissue.

These days, CT scans of the brain are typically used only for medical diagnosis of tumors, strokes, and other conditions that produce brain lesions. For example, roughly 80% of strokes are detectable with CT scans within 24 hours after they occur (Wall, Brant-Zawadski, Jeffrey, & Barnes, 1981). CT scans also provide important information for recovery, as they can be used to monitor changes in the lesion. However, despite much excitement in the first few years after their development, CT scans were not highly useful in mapping cognitive functioning.

Magnetic Resonance Imaging (MRI). MRI comes closer to science fiction perhaps than any other imaging technique. Based on principles of molecular structure and magnetic fields, the basic idea in MRI is that one's molecules are reoriented and then restored to their normal configuration (Brown & Bornstein, in press). MRI devices are very large magnets and detectors that pick up radio frequencies that are shot through the body organ under study.

Like CT scans, MRI scans are excellent tools for diagnosing brain diseases. It is especially useful in assessing areas of damage due to hemorrhage and for evaluating damage to blood vessels and other soft tissues. MRI is typically better than CT in detecting small lesions and provides a more accurate assessment of the stage of the disease. However, MRI is much more expensive than CT, to the extent that MRI is used less often for routine screening purposes.

Positron Emission Tomography (PET). PET scans work on principles similar to the other two imaging techniques. In this case, a radioactive isotope is injected into the brain, and positrons (subatomic particles) are shot through from various directions. The positrons are detected and the information is processed by a computer. Two interesting aspects about PET scans make them especially useful for research. First, they measure glucose levels in the brain, thereby providing information about brain metabolism. Second, the computer-enhanced pictures are in color.

Measuring brain metabolism allows researchers to watch the brain at work. Individuals can be asked to think about something in particular, to solve a problem, or to learn a list of words while their brains are being monitored. This opportunity to observe a brain in action is currently not provided by CT or MRI (but scientists are trying with MRI). The fact that the pictures are in color enables researchers to know how active the brain is. For example, when the brain is hard at work, it uses more glucose; when it rests, it uses less. In PET scan pictures, high activity areas show up as red and low activity areas show up as blue.

PET scans have opened up many exciting avenues of research. For example, Caramazza and Hillis (1991) discovered what they think are separate areas in the brain for storing nouns and verbs. Other research, described in Chapters 5 and 6, has provided insights concerning basic information processing and memory. On the basis of these findings, some researchers are rethinking how the brain is organized. One recent idea is that the brain is organized into modules that control specific abilities, and that these modules are related to each other in complex ways (Hooper, 1991). Research studies using PET scans are being conducted at a frenzied pace, with new data and new insights appearing weekly. Within the next few years, it is possible that these data could revolutionize the assessment, treatment, and diagnosis of brain diseases, as well as help unlock the mystery of how the brain works.

Psychological Consequences of Brain Aging

Probably the worst stereotype about aging is that old people get senile. Older adults may even consider an insignificant memory lapse as evidence of impending senility, even though memory lapses normally occur throughout life (Cavanaugh, Grady, & Perlmutter, 1983).

In fact, the term *senility* has no valid medical or psychological meaning, and its continued use simply perpetuates the myth that drastic mental decline is a product of normal aging (Whitbourne, 1985). It is not. The diseases involving considerable loss of memory, emotional response, and bodily functions are dementias, which are described more fully in Chapter 9. But dementia is not a part of normal aging; only 15% of people over age 65 have dementia (Katzman, 1987). People who develop dementia may show severe and progressive impairments of memory, judgment, comprehension, and motor functions (Huff, Growdon, Corkin, & Rosen, 1987). It is fear of developing dementia that makes people interpret the slightest mental or physical mistake as symptomatic.

Nevertheless, several aspects of psychological functioning are affected by normal brain aging, which may, in turn, affect adults' adaptation to the environment (Whitbourne, 1985). For example, age-related declines in recent memory, described in Chapter 6, may be caused by neuronal losses.

These changes make it more difficult for older adults to complete daily routines that demand remembering information over time, and the elderly become less efficient at learning new facts and skills (Whitbourne, 1985). On the other hand, continued growth in some areas may be one reason why there is little evidence of age-related changes in experience-based problem solving, reasoning, and judgment, as described in Chapter 7 (Horn, 1982). This dual pattern of neuronal fallout and plasticity may be the underlying mechanism that explains why some intellectual functions decline with age and others do not. These different patterns of change are considered in detail in Chapter 7.

THE IMMUNE SYSTEM

One of the greatest milestones in medical history happened in this century: the conquering of many diseases. Illnesses that only a few generations ago were very serious problems, such as polio and diphtheria, are now rare in industrialized societies. Immunizations against these diseases were developed as a result of our increased knowledge of how the body's natural defense against disease works. This defense — the immune system — is a fascinating array of cells and processes: lymphocytes, antibodies, autoimmunity. Some of these exotic-sounding things (lymphocytes) help us fight infections by producing antibodies to invading viruses and germs. Other processes (autoimmunity) may provide the key to aging itself.

The study of the immune system has contributed greatly to the understanding of aging, primarily by describing the mechanisms that underlie changes in the susceptibility to disease. In particular, how immune system cells work and produce antibodies to invaders, how these cells are turned on and off, and what other body functions influence immune system functioning are a few of the discoveries that have been made in the last decade. Our knowledge has also been enhanced by studying immune system diseases such as acquired immune deficiency syndrome (AIDS) in terms of how the immune system is destroyed and how AIDS relates to other age-related disorders. In this section we will focus on the major changes seen with age that affect the body's ability to resist disease.

Changes in Immune System Cells

The human immune system is a highly advanced defense against invasion. The immune system itself consists of several parts, each with specific jobs to perform. One of the components, the **lymphocytes**, provides defense against malignant (cancerous) cells, viral infection, fungal infection, and some bacteria (Berkow, 1987). Typically, lymphocytes do not show age-related changes in number, at least not until one is over 90 years old (Lehtonen, Eskola, Vainio, & Lehtonen, 1990).

But major changes occur in how well lymphocytes work. For one thing, older adults' immune systems take longer to build up defenses against specific diseases, even after an immunization injection. This could partially explain why older adults are more susceptible to infection (Terpenning & Bradley, 1991) and need to be immunized earlier against specific diseases such as influenza. One line of research in this area is investigating the possibility of administering substances such as growth hormones to older adults to stimulate the functioning of the lymphocytes; results thus far seem to indicate that when this is done, some specific lymphocyte functioning returns to normal (Nagel & Adler, 1988; Weksler, 1990).

Considerable interest arose during the 1980s over one type of lymphocyte, the natural killer cell. Natural killer cells provide a broad surveillance system to prevent tumor growth, although how this happens remains a mystery (Herberman & Callewaert, 1985). Natural killer cells have also been linked to resistance to infectious diseases and to a possible role in multiple sclerosis, a disease that typically manifests itself during young adulthood and early middle age (Nagel & Adler, 1988). However, age-related changes in the function of natural killer cells are not completely understood.

Antibodies and Autoimmunity

When lymphocytes confront an invader, one of their responses is to produce an **antibody**, which protects the body from future invasions. Although longitudinal data on changes in the level of antibodies are lacking, cross-sectional research indicates that antibody levels for some specific invading organisms differ across age. For example, levels of the antitetanus toxoid antibody decrease with age, especially in women (Nagel & Adler, 1988).

In normal, healthy adults the immune system is able to recognize organisms that are native to the individual; that is, the immune system does not produce antibodies to organisms that occur naturally. One of the changes that occurs with age, however, is that this self-recognition ability begins to break down, and the immune system produces *autoantibodies* that attack the body itself (Weksler, 1990). This process, termed *autoimmunity*, is thought to be partially responsible for tissue breakdown and perhaps for aging itself (Nagel & Adler, 1988).

AIDS and Aging

Since first being detected in the United States in the early 1980s, AIDS has received an enormous amount of publicity and research. An increasing number of adults over age 40 are being diagnosed with AIDS, and estimates are that by 1992 100,000 people over age 40 will have been diagnosed with AIDS (Kendig & Adler, 1990). Of this group, roughly 10,000 will be over age 60. Most of these people will have gotten the disease through a contaminated blood product or through unsafe sexual activity.

As far as we know, there is no age difference in the symptoms of AIDS shown by older and younger adults. However, older adults' health tends to decline faster once symptoms begin. The reasons for this more rapid decline are not entirely clear, although it may be due in part to the age-related changes in the lymphocytes described above. Scientists know, for example, that the immune system attempts to fight the AIDS virus (Kendig & Adler, 1990); it may be that older adults' lowered ability to fight infection in general may contribute to the faster progress of the disease.

Of particular concern to developmentalists is the severe cognitive impairment in some AIDS patients. The impairment appears similar to the problems that evolve in diseases such as Alzheimer's. We will consider AIDS-related cognitive impairment in Chapter 9 along with Alzheimer's disease.

Psychological Consequences of Changes in the Immune System

At a practical level, changes in the immune system are manifested by increased frequency of illness. Psychologically, being ill more often could lead to lowered levels of self-esteem and the adoption of illness roles. Additionally, many people believe that there is little that can be done; poor health is simply a product of aging.

Clearly, such beliefs are unwarranted. Chapter 4 provides considerable detail on health promotion and disease prevention, actions that are successful with adults of all ages. Moreover, immunizations are available for many diseases and should be part of an older adult's health program (Nagel & Adler, 1988). Immunizations against tetanus and diphtheria should be given about every 10

years as a booster. Vaccination against pneumococcal pneumonia can be accomplished in one dose; boosters are not recommended. Yearly immunization against influenza is also a good preventive measure.

As more older adults are diagnosed with AIDS, support systems specifically tailored for this group will be needed. As pointed out clearly in the biopsychosocial model, AIDS conjures up different meanings for older adults than it does for younger people. Moreover, because there will be more older adults with AIDS, more education of older adults about the disease will be necessary.

THE CARDIOVASCULAR SYSTEM

Odds are that you have a relative who has (or perhaps has died from) cardiovascular disease. More people in industrialized countries die from cardiovascular disease than from any other cause. This is probably why more attention has been paid to cardiovascular fitness over the past decade or so than to any other health issue.

Cardiovascular disease provides an excellent application of the biopsychosocial model. On the biological front, we have established that cardiovascular disease has important genetic links. Psychologically, certain personality traits have been linked with increased risk of disease. Socially, cardiovascular disease has been clearly tied to life style. Let's explore in more detail how these various forces come together.

Cardiovascular Structure and Function

The heart is an amazing organ. In a life span of 75 years, for example, the heart beats roughly 3 billion times, pumping the equivalent of about 900 million gallons of blood (Rockstein & Sussman, 1979). The heart itself consists of four chambers: the right and left atria and the right and left ventricles. Between each chamber and at each entrance and exit are the heart valves. These valves ensure that the blood flows in only one direction as the heart contracts during a beat.

Blood pressure is the ratio of the systolic pressure (the pressure during the contraction phase of a heartbeat) to the diastolic pressure (the pressure during the relaxation phase). This pressure is created by the ventricles, which are literally pushing the blood through the circulatory system. The numbers associated with blood pressure, such as $120/80$, are based on measures of the force that keeps blood moving through the blood vessels. Definitions of normal blood pressure are somewhat arbitrary (Kannel, 1985) and can vary depending on who is doing the defining and the age of the person who is having his or her blood pressure checked.

Structural and Functional Changes. Two important age-related structural changes in the heart are the accumulation of fat deposits and the stiffening of the heart muscle due to tissue changes. By the late 40s and early 50s, the fat deposits in lining around the heart may form a continuous sheet. Meanwhile, healthy muscle tissue is being replaced by connective tissue, which causes a thickening and stiffening of the heart muscle and valves. This replacement is serious, because these changes reduce the amount of muscle tissue available to contract the heart. The net effect is that the remaining good muscle must work harder. To top it off, the amount of blood that the heart can pump declines from roughly 5 liters per minute at age 20 to about 3.5 liters per minute at age 70.

The most important changes in the circulatory system involve the stiffening ("hardening") in the walls of the arteries. These changes are caused by calcification of the arterial walls and by replacement of elastic fibers with less elastic ones.

The combination of changes in the heart and the circulatory system results in a significant decrease in a person's ability to cope with physical stress. This is one reason why older adults — in contrast with younger and middle-aged adults — are more likely to have heart attacks while performing moderately exerting tasks, such as shoveling snow.

Cardiovascular Disease

Incidence rates for some cardiovascular diseases in men and women between 35 and 84 years of age are listed in Table 3.1. Note that for all diseases there is a dramatic increase in rate with age. Note also that for most of the diseases listed, rates in men are higher than rates in women. Although the overall death rate in the United States from cardiovascular disease declined by more than one third from the early 1960s to the mid-1980s due to better prevention (Kannel & Thom, 1984), the death rate in some ethnic minority groups such as African-Americans remains nearly double that in whites (U.S. DHHS, 1988).

The clear gender difference in cardiovascular diseases has been the topic of much interest and debate (Nachtigall & Nachtigall, 1990). Premenopausal women appear somewhat protected from cardiovascular disease due to estrogen. Because estrogen production drops dramatically in postmenopausal women (see discussion later in this chapter), their risk rises. However, not all premenopausal women have low risk. Women who have hypertension, who smoke, who have high levels of LDL (so-called bad cholesterol, discussed in Chapter 4), who are overweight, and who have diabetes are always at greater risk. Although estrogen replacement therapy for postmenopausal women is a popular (and controversial) medical strategy for lowering their risk, exercise and other behavioral approaches (described in Chapter 4) are considered better options.

TABLE 3.1 Incidence of major cardiovascular diseases per 10,000 people, as a function of age: United States, 1988

Age	Coronary Disease		Cerebrovascular Accident		Angina		Myocardial Infarction	
	Men	*Women*	*Men*	*Women*	*Men*	*Women*	*Men*	*Women*
35–44	42	7	2	4	8	5	21	2
45–54	108	33	20	12	30	21	54	9
55–64	202	99	40	26	74	54	91	25
65–74	227	136	92	80	52	51	119	51
75–84	247	236	196	112	25	94	168	90

(Source: U.S. Department of Health and Human Services, 1988.)

Ischemic Heart Disease. The most common heart disease in older adults is **ischemic heart disease**, which occurs in approximately 12% of women and 20% of men over 65 years of age (Lakatta, 1985). In this disorder the muscle cells of the heart receive insufficient oxygen because of poor circulation or partial blockages in the coronary arteries. Ischemic heart disease is a major contributing factor to congestive heart failure, a condition in which cardiac output and the ability of the heart to contract severely decline. In congestive heart failure, the heart enlarges, pressure in the veins increases, and there is swelling throughout the body.

Cardiac Arrhythmias. Irregularities in the heartbeat, termed *cardiac arrhythmias*, are fairly common in older adults (Lakatta, 1985). These disturbances include extra and uneven beats as well as fibrillation, in which the heart makes very rapid, irregular contractions. Why these changes occur is not entirely understood, but they may be related to the level of various salts (such as sodium and potassium) and minerals (such as calcium) in the bloodstream. Cardiac arrhythmias can be very dangerous, because they may alter the normal functioning of the heart. For example, arrhythmias involving the ventricles can cause sudden death.

Angina. Recall that one of the changes in the heart with age is a gradual reduction in blood flow. When this reduction becomes severe, the supply of oxygen to the heart muscle becomes insufficient, resulting in chest pain. Such pain, called **angina**, may feel like chest pressure, a burning pain, or a squeezing that radiates from the chest to the back, neck, and arms (Berkow, 1987). In most cases the pain is induced by physical exertion and is relieved within 5 to 10 minutes by rest. Treatment of angina is similar in adults of all ages; depending on when the angina occurs, patients are given nitroglycerine, beta-blocking agents, or calcium-blocking agents.

Myocardial Infarction. Perhaps the most dramatic age-related coronary disease is *myocardial infarction*, or heart attack. Myocardial infarction is especially serious for older adults; mortality following a heart attack is much higher for them (U.S. DHHS, 1988). Heart attacks occur when the coronary blood flow drops below the level needed to nourish the heart muscle. If sustained, the interruption kills the heart muscle. The interruption in blood flow may result from a spasm, a progressive buildup of fatty plaques that clogs the coronary arteries, or some combination of factors. The initial symptoms of myocardial infarction are identical to those of angina but are typically more severe and prolonged. Additionally, there may be general symptoms such as nausea, vomiting, sweating, and severe weakness. In as many as 25% of patients, however, chest pain may be absent. These "silent" heart attacks are more common in older adults, especially those with diabetes (Berkow, 1987). Treatment of heart attack victims of all ages includes careful evaluation and a prescribed rehabilitation program consisting of life-style changes in diet and exercise.

Atherosclerosis. **Atherosclerosis** involves the age-related buildup of fat deposits on and the calcification of the arterial walls (Berkow, 1987). Much like sandbars in a river or mineral deposits inside pipes, the fat deposits interfere with blood flow through the arteries. These deposits begin very early in life and continue throughout the life span. Some amount of fat deposit inevitably occurs, and is considered a normal part of aging. However, excess deposits may deveop from poor nutrition, smoking, and other aspects of an unhealthy life style.

Fat deposits sometimes provide points where a blood clot or other mass becomes stuck, completely blocking the blood flow. Such blockages are responsible for heart attacks and angina, and are one cause of cerebrovascular accidents (discussed next). Atherosclerosis may become so severe that the coronary arteries must be replaced surgically. This procedure, known as a coronary bypass, involves transplanting a blood vessel from another part of the body, usually the leg, to serve as a new coronary artery. Other techniques used to treat atherosclerosis in the coronary arteries include inserting a tiny catheter or a balloonlike device into the arteries and clearing the blockage, scraping deposits off artery walls, and using lasers to clear the arteries

(Bierman, 1985). For reasons not yet understood, blocked coronary arteries do not always produce noticeable symptoms, so that periodic checkups are very important.

Cerebrovascular Disease. In some cases, severe atherosclerosis occurs in blood vessels that supply the brain. When this happens, brain cells may not receive proper nourishment, causing them to malfunction or die. This situation is termed **cerebrovascular disease**. When the blood flow to a portion of the brain is completely cut off, a *cerebrovascular accident (CVA)*, or stroke, results (Berkow, 1987). Causes of CVAs include clots that block blood flow in an artery, or the actual breaking of a blood vessel, which creates a *cerebral hemorrhage*. The severity of a CVA and likelihood of recovery depend on the specific area of the brain involved, the extent of disruption in blood flow, and the duration of the disruption. Consequently, a CVA may affect such a small area that it goes virtually unnoticed, or it may be so severe as to cause death.

The risk of a CVA increases with age; in fact, CVAs are the third leading cause of death among the elderly in the United States (U.S. DHHS, 1991). In addition to age, other risk factors include being male, being African American, and having high blood pressure, heart disease, or diabetes. The higher risk among African Americans appears to be due to a greater prevalence of hypertension in this population.

Recovery following a stroke must take into account not only the physical effects but also the psychological ones. For example, the sudden loss of the ability to move or speak can have profound effects on a person's self-esteem and sense of independence. Both health care professionals and family members must provide support for maximal recovery.

Hypertension. As we grow older, blood pressure tends to rise. Although parents of adolescents may claim otherwise, the main reason for this blood pressure rise is structural change in the cardiovascular system. When blood pressure increases become severe, the disease **hypertension** results. Roughly 35% of the population between the ages of 25 and 74 have some degree of hypertension. The rate is somewhat higher among African Americans, for reasons we do not fully understand.

Hypertension is a very serious matter. Older adults with hypertension have three times the risk of dying from cardiovascular disease. The long-term risk for young adults with hypertension may even be greater (Kannel, 1985). Because hypertension is a disease with no clear symptoms, most people with hypertension are not aware that they have a problem. Regular blood pressure monitoring is the only sure way to find out if one has hypertension.

As will be discussed in Chapter 4, some of the causes of hypertension are not purely physiological. For example, stress and some diets have been shown to cause hypertension in some people. Interestingly, differences in rates of hypertension in some ethnic groups support the causal roles of stress and diet. Espino and Maldonado (1990) report that the rate of hypertension was higher among Mexican Americans who were more acculturated into the American life style. In fact, degree of acculturation was a better predictor of hypertension than socioeconomic variables such as income. They speculate that with acculturation comes higher levels of stress and the adoption of a less healthy diet that puts such people at risk. Poverty alone does not explain the difference. In short, the American life style can be fatally hazardous to health.

Psychological Consequences of Changes in the Cardiovascular System

Clearly, the most important psychological consequences of cardiovascular system changes are reflected in the things people do to try to avoid cardiovascular disease. The past few decades have witnessed some remarkable changes in people's awareness of life-style factors as causes of heart attacks and heart disease. Many people have dramatically altered their diets (eating less red meat and saturated fat) and begun exercising. As we will see in Chapter 4, these changes, especially in exercise, significantly affect psychological functioning. We will also see how specific personality variables (such as hostility or anger) play key roles in cardiovascular disease. For many people, the specter of heart attacks is sufficient to get them to the health club or to the nearest park for a vigorous workout.

THE RESPIRATORY SYSTEM

Most of us only become aware of our breathing in the midst of physical exertion. But for many older adults, shortness of breath is a routine (and quite unpleasant) experience. How much of this age-related problem is due to a decline in the effectiveness of the respiratory system is hard to say. Air pollution, infections, smoking, and other factors all cause damage that could be mistaken for the effects of aging. Consequently, it is impossible to determine the strictly normative changes of aging (Kenney, 1982); the changes described in this section should be viewed as the combined effects of aging and living in a polluted and disease-bearing environment.

Structural and Functional Changes

With increasing age, the rib cage and the air passageways become stiffer, making it harder to breathe. The lungs change in appearance over time, going gradually from their youthful pinkish color to a dreary gray, due mainly to breathing in carbon particles (from exhaust and smoke). The rate at which we can exchange oxygen for carbon dioxide drops significantly due to the destruction of the membranes of the air sacs in the lungs.

Changes in the maximum amount of air we can take into the lungs in a single breath begin in the 20s, decreasing by 40% by age 85 (Shephard, 1982). We also have a more difficult time dealing with increased need for oxygen during physical stress, as we cannot increase our air intake when we are old as much as we can when we are young. This further aggravates the shortness of breath problems older adults have (Kenney, 1982). However, there is some good news; as pointed out in Chapter 4, these changes in capacity can be moderated by regular exercise, even in old age (Buskirk, 1985).

Respiratory Diseases

The most common and incapacitating respiratory disorder in older adults is **chronic obstructive lung disease (COLD)**. Since the 1960s deaths directly attributed to COLD have tripled, due in part to better diagnosis but most importantly to increased long-term exposure to pollution (Burdman, 1986). In these diseases, the passage of air in the bronchial tubes becomes blocked, and abnormalities develop in the lungs. Smoking, air pollution, infection, heredity, allergies, and pollutants are the major causes. COLD is a progressive disease in which the prognosis is usually very poor (Burdman, 1986).

Emphysema is the most serious type of COLD and is characterized by the destruction of the membranes around the air sacs in the lungs (Lebowitz, 1988). This irreversible destruction creates "holes" in the lung, drastically reducing the ability to exchange oxygen and carbon dioxide. To make matters worse, the bronchial tubes collapse prematurely when the person exhales, thereby preventing the lungs from emptying completely. Emphysema is a very debilitating disease. In its later stages, even the smallest physical exertion causes a struggle for

air. People with emphysema may have such poorly oxygenated blood that they become confused and disoriented. The sad part about emphysema is that it is largely self-induced by smoking. The disease is rare in nonsmokers, and such cases are probably caused by environmental pollutants, such as secondhand smoke or high levels of dust (Burdman, 1986).

Although upper-respiratory infections decrease in frequency with age, lower-respiratory infections such as pneumonia increase (Burdman, 1986). Consequently, older adults are more likely to die of pneumonia and related respiratory diseases. This age-related increase in frequency of pneumonia may be due in part to a lack of exercise (Burdman, 1986).

Psychological Consequences of Changes in the Respiratory System

The effects of age-related changes in the respiratory system that people notice most are shortness of breath and subsequent fatigue during physical exercise. It can be extremely frightening for a person to feel out of breath. The level of activity at which shortness of breath is experienced declines across adulthood. Increased concern over especially serious episodes of shortness of breath is understandable, and subsequent declines in physical activity may result (which in the long run only makes matters worse). In some cases people may become overly cautious and withdraw from any form of exercise. Such withdrawal can have a detrimental effect on other aspects of physiological functioning (for example, the cardiovascular system). Moreover, as we will see in Chapter 4, regular exercise has significant beneficial effects because it helps maintain higher levels of respiratory functioning.

Whitbourne (1985) hypothesized that reduced respiratory functioning has negative effects on sense of competence. Feeling that one is out of shape may follow experiences of shortness of

SOMETHING TO THINK ABOUT

Sensory Changes and Experiencing the World

There are several universal, inevitable changes with age in our sensory systems: Vision, hearing, taste, smell, and touch are all affected. But beyond the obvious effects sensory changes have on everyday behaviors, we should consider the impact these changes have on how older adults experience the world. Imagine for a moment what it would be like to look down the supermarket aisle and not be able to see clearly due to the glare from the nicely polished floor.

Consider what it would be like to be unable to read the very small print on your medicine bottle label. Think about being in a situation where you cannot make out all the words that are being spoken to you. Picture yourself having to eat simply to obtain nourishment, and not from enjoyment of a well-prepared meal. Imagine trying to navigate an icy sidewalk when you have trouble with your balance.

These and other behavioral outcomes of sensory changes take getting used to. Even though there are easy, often inexpensive devices that can correct or help compensate for sensory changes (such as eyeglasses and hearing aids), many people

choose not to use them even if they are affordable. Wearing glasses and hearing aids may be considered a sign of one's aging, and many may not want to admit that they are getting old.

But corrective devices are not available to compensate for all sensory changes. For example, we have yet to invent a device that compensates for changes in temperature regulation or smell. Changes in these and related abilities potentially diminish the enjoyment of life. Consequently, we must not underestimate the importance of sensory changes as factors in understanding age-related changes in behavior. It's something to think about.

---

breath, which may ultimately lower a person's sense of well-being. This lowered sense of self-esteem may further reduce activity. The bottom line is this: Keep exercising!

THE SENSES

Have you ever watched middle-aged people try to read something that is right in front of them? If they do not already wear glasses or contact lenses, they typically move the material farther away so that they can see it clearly. This change in vision is one

of the first noticeable signs of aging as we enter middle age. These changes in our sensory systems challenge our ability to interact with the world and to communicate with others, as pointed out in Something to Think About. Some changes, such as those that impair our ability to smell, could even prove life threatening. In this section, we will consider changes in vision, hearing, taste, smell, somesthesis, and balance.

Vision

We rely extensively on sight in virtually every aspect of our waking life, from checking the time to combing our hair in the mirror. Perhaps because of our strong dependence on this sensory system, its age-related changes have profound and pervasive effects. Loss of vision is second only to cancer as the most feared consequence of aging (Verrillo & Verrillo, 1985). Although people vary in their extent of visual impairment, it is likely that you will eventually experience some form of visual impairment that requires treatment or that interferes with everyday life (Kline & Schieber, 1985).

The major changes in visual functioning can be grouped into two classes: changes in the structures of the eye and changes in the retina (Kline & Schieber, 1985). Structural changes begin to affect visual functioning during middle adulthood (around age 40). The most important structural changes are decreases in the amount of light that passes through the eye (termed *transmissiveness*) and in the eye's ability to adjust and focus (termed *accommodation*). Two diseases may result from structural changes. First, opaque spots called *cataracts* may develop on the lens, which seriously limits the amount of light transmitted. Cataracts are often treated by surgical removal and use of corrective lenses. Second, the fluid in the eye may not drain properly, causing very high pressure. This condition, called *glaucoma*, can cause internal damage and loss of vision. Glaucoma is a fairly common disease in middle and late adulthood.

The retina lines approximately two thirds of the interior of the eye. The specialized receptor cells in vision, the rods and the cones, are contained in the retina. They are most densely packed toward the rear and especially at the focal point of vision, a region called the macula. At the center of the macula is the fovea, where incoming light is focused for maximum acuity, as when one is reading.

Retinal changes usually begin in a person's 50s. With increasing age the probability of degeneration of the macula increases (Kline & Schieber, 1985). *Macular degeneration* involves the progressive and irreversible destruction of receptors from any of a number of causes. This disease results in the loss of the ability to see details; for example, reading is extremely difficult, and television is often reduced to a blur.

A second retinal disease that is related to age is actually a by-product of diabetes. Diabetes is accompanied by accelerated aging of the arteries, with blindness being one of the more serious side effects. *Diabetic retinopathy*, as this condition is called, can involve fluid retention in the macula, detachment of the retina, hemorrhage, and aneurysms. Because it takes many years to develop, diabetic retinopathy is more common among people who developed diabetes relatively early in life. Sadly, diabetic retinopathy is the leading cause of blindness in the United States (Lewis, 1979).

The structural and retinal changes in the visual system produce important changes in visual abilities. We will consider several changes: absolute and difference thresholds, sensitivity to glare, accommodation, acuity, and adaptation.

Absolute and Difference Thresholds. Research consistently demonstrates that older adults require a greater intensity of light than young adults to detect that something is out there (Kline & Schieber, 1985). The most important practical consequence of this change is that as we grow older, we tend to require higher levels of illumination to perform daily tasks. You may have noticed how bright your grandparents' living room is compared to yours. Older adults do not see as well in the dark, which may account in part for their reluctance to go places at night. Older adults also have more difficulty discriminating different levels of illumination, such as telling the difference between a 60-watt and a 75-watt light bulb.

Sensitivity to Glare. One possible logical response to the need for more light would be to increase illumination levels. However, this solution may not work, because we also become increasingly sensitive to glare beginning around age 40 (Kline & Schieber, 1985). This change is especially important for older drivers, because reflected sunlight can pose a more serious problem for them. Consequently, the need for more illumination must be balanced with the need to avoid glare (Fozard & Popkin, 1978).

Accommodation. Accommodation is the process by which the lens adjusts so that we can see nearby and faraway objects clearly. Considerable research demonstrates an age-related decrease in the ability to focus on nearby objects, a condition termed **presbyopia** (Kline & Schieber, 1985). Presbyopia is what makes middle-aged people hold reading material at increasing distances, and, once their arms become too short, forces them to get either reading glasses or bifocals.

As we age, the time we need to switch our focus from near to far (or vice versa) increases (Corso, 1981). This poses a major problem in driving. Because drivers are constantly alternating their focus from the instrument panel to other autos and signs on the highway, older drivers may miss important information because of their slower refocusing time (Panek & Rearden, 1986).

Acuity. **Acuity** refers to the ability to see detail and to discriminate different visual patterns. The most common way of testing visual acuity is the Snellen test — the familiar eye chart — consisting of a standardized series of letters or symbols in different sizes that must be read at a distance of about six meters. Acuity shows a slight but steady decline between the ages of 20 and 60, with a more rapid decline thereafter (Richards, 1977). The consequences of decreases in visual acuity range from annoying, such as the print of this book looking fuzzy, to potentially serious, such as difficulty in reading medicine bottle labels.

Adaptation. Adaptation is the change in sensitivity of the eye as a function of changes in illumination. There are two types of adaptation: **dark adaptation**, the adjustment of the eye to dark environments, and **light adaptation**, the adjustment of the

Age-related decline in visual acuity results in difficulty reading small print.

eye to bright environments. Going from outside into a darkened movie theater involves dark adaptation; going back outside involves light adaptation. Research indicates that the time it takes for both types of adaptation increases with age (Kline & Schieber, 1985); the data for dark adaptation are depicted in Figure 3.2. In addition, the final level of dark adaptation is less in older adults (Wolf, 1960). This means that as we age, it takes us longer to adapt to changes in illumination, making us more susceptible to environmental hazards for the first few minutes following the change. For example, older drivers take longer to recover visually from the headlights of an oncoming car, making

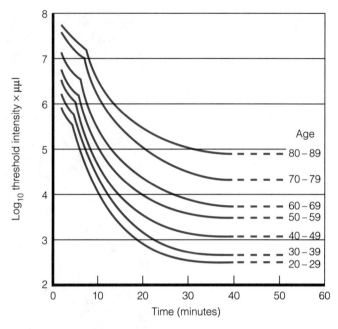

FIGURE 3.2 Dark adaptation as a function of age and time in the dark

(Source: "Dark Adaptation as a Function of Age: I. A Statistical Analysis" by McFarland et al., 1960, *Journal of Gerontology, 15,* 149–154. Copyright © 1960 The Gerontological Society of America. Reprinted with permission.)

them less able to pick up critical information from the highway in the meantime.

Psychological Effects of Visual Changes. Evidence of visual changes in everyday life has been documented through surveys of over 400 adults ranging in age from 18 to 100 (Kosnik, Winslow, Kline, Rasinski, & Sekular, 1988). The responses indicated a two- to sixfold decline in visual ability in everyday situations, depending on the skill required. Imagine the problems people experience performing tasks that most of us take for granted, such as reading a book, watching television, reading grocery labels, driving a car, and so on. Simply making things brighter is not the answer. For increased illumination to work, surrounding surfaces must not increase glare. Use of flat paint rather than

glossy enamel and avoiding highly polished floors are two steps that could be taken in designing environments. Details on dials, such as on stoves and radios, may be difficult to distinguish, as are some subtle facial features. As Whitbourne (1985) notes, these experiences may be especially difficult for people who always had good vision when young. Such people may simply avoid cooking or listening to their favorite music and become homebodies out of fear that they may not recognize a face.

People often do not recognize the extent of visual changes because these occur slowly over many years. Lack of awareness of these changes usually results in a failure to seek ways to compensate or correct for the problems. Most unfortunate are those individuals who believe that these decrements are simply a sign of aging and are untreat-

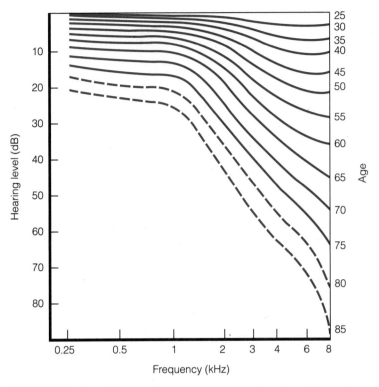

FIGURE 3.3 Ability to detect pure tones, as a function of age and frequency (data for men only)

(Source: U.S. Department of Health and Human Services.)

able. Many of the normal age-related changes in vision can be remediated. Periodic vision examinations can detect changes early, and correction of visual problems may help avert the internalization of these changes as potential threats to self-esteem.

Hearing

One of the most well-known changes in normal aging is the decline in hearing ability, which is quite dramatic across the life span (Olsho, Harkins, & Lenhardt, 1985). Age-related declines in hearing are progressive and may interfere with adaptation in later life. Significant hearing loss is widespread in older adults. If you have visited a housing complex for the elderly, you probably noticed that television sets and radios are turned up fairly loud in most of the apartments. Research indicates that nearly half of normal older adults have a relatively serious hearing impairment (Thomas et al., 1983). Men typically have greater loss than women, but this may be due to differential exposure to noisy environments (Olsho et al., 1985). Loss of hearing is gradual at first but accelerates during the 40s (Corso, 1984). This pattern can be seen quite clearly in Figure 3.3. Note in the figure that hearing loss with age is greatest for high-pitched tones, a condition called **presbycusis**.

Presbycusis. Presbycusis results from four types of changes in the inner ear (Olsho et al., 1985): (1) sensory, consisting of atrophy and degeneration of receptor cells; (2) neural, consisting of a loss of neurons in the auditory pathway in the brain; (3) metabolic, consisting of a diminished supply of nutrients to the cells in the receptor area; and (4) mechanical, consisting of atrophy and stiffening of the vibrating structures in the receptor area. Although the four types occur at different rates (12%, 31%, 35%, and 23%, respectively), rarely does an individual have only one of them (Schuknecht, 1974).

All of these types of presbycusis affect the ability to hear high-pitched tones. However, they differ in their effects on other aspects of hearing (Whitbourne, 1985). Sensory presbycusis has little effect on other hearing abilities. Neural presbycusis seriously affects the ability to understand speech. Metabolic presbycusis produces severe loss of sensitivity to all pitches. Finally, mechanical presbycusis produces loss across all pitches, but the loss is greatest for high pitches.

Hearing and Exposure to Noise. There is no doubt that lifelong exposure to noise has significant negative effects on hearing ability (Corso, 1981). Much of the research that established this relationship was conducted in industrial settings, but we now know that any source of sustained loud noise, whether from machinery or stereo headphones, produces damage.

An important question for developmentalists is whether older people are more susceptible to hearing damage from noise. The results of several experiments demonstrate convincingly that the answer is no. People of all ages can lose their hearing from living in noisy environments. More important, noise causes more damage than aging (Corso, 1981). Cross-cultural evidence suggests that hearing loss is less in cultures that have lower exposure to noise. Corso (1981) refers to the damaging effect of repeated, sustained noise on adults' hearing as "premature presbycusis." Because of these effects workers in many industries are required to wear protective earplugs in order to guard against prolonged exposure. However, the use of stereo headphones, especially at high volume, can cause the same serious damage and should be avoided. It is especially easy to cause hearing loss with headphones if you wear them while exercising; the increased blood flow to the ear during exercise makes hearing receptors more vulnerable to damage.

Psychological Effects of Hearing Loss. Because hearing plays an almost irreplaceable role in social communication, its progressive loss could have an equally important effect on individuals' adjustment. It is often argued that loss of hearing in later life causes numerous adverse emotional reactions, such as feelings of loss of independence, social isolation, irritation, paranoia, and depression. Substantial research indicates that older people with hearing loss are generally not socially maladjusted or emotionally disturbed as a result of hearing loss per se (Norris & Cunningham, 1981). However, there is often a strain on the quality of interpersonal relationships due to friends' and relatives' tendency to attribute emotional changes to hearing loss and their failure to communicate properly with a hearing-impaired person (Thomas et al., 1983).

Thus, hearing loss may not directly affect older adults' self-concept or emotions, but it may negatively affect how they feel about interpersonal communication. Knowledge of hearing loss problems and of ways to overcome them on the part of non-hearing-impaired individuals can play a large part in minimizing the effects of hearing loss.

Taste

Have you ever heard the expression "too old to cut the mustard"? It dates back to when people made mustard at home by grinding mustard seed and adding just the right amount of vinegar ("cutting the mustard") to balance the taste. If too much vinegar was added, the whole concoction tasted terrible, so the balance was critical. Many families found that elderly members tended to add too much vinegar, resulting in the saying.

Despite the everyday belief that taste ability changes with age, we know very little about what actually happens. Whatever age differences we observe are not due to a decline in the sheer number of taste buds, however. Unlike other neural cells, the number of taste cells does not change appreciably across the life span (Engen, 1982). Moreover, many adults over age 60 have no apparent loss of taste sensitivity. And even for those who do, the decreases are typically slight (Spitzer, 1988). Likewise, age-related differences in taste preference are not substantial, and may be due to a variety of factors including cultural experiences, the context in which the substances are consumed, or changes in the sensory areas in the brain. At present, however, it is impossible to distinguish among these possibilities. Finally, carefully conducted research shows no age differences in the ability to identify foods by taste alone (Murphy, 1985).

Psychological Effects of Changes in Taste. There is little question that older adults complain more about boring food (Schiffman & Covey, 1984; Whitbourne, 1985). The source of these complaints, however, cannot be predominantly physiological changes in taste. Age differences in taste are minimal; thus, the high incidence of food complaints among older adults is not based on changes in the ability to taste. The explanation appears to be that changes in the enjoyment of food are due to psychosocial issues (such as personal adjustment), to changes in smell (which we consider next), or to disease (Whitbourne, 1985). For instance, we are much more likely to eat a balanced diet and enjoy our food when we do not eat alone and when we get a whiff of the enticing aromas emanating from the kitchen.

Smell

"Stop and smell the roses." "OOOH! What's that perfume you're wearing?" "Yuk! What's that smell?" There is a great deal of truth in the saying "the nose knows." Smell is a major part of our everyday lives. How something smells can alert us that dinner is cooking, warn of a gas leak or a fire, let us know that we are clean, or be sexually arousing. A great many of our social interactions involve smell (or the lack of it). Billions of dollars are spent on making our bodies smell appealing to others. It is easy to see that any age-related change in sense of smell would have far-reaching consequences.

Researchers agree that the ability to detect odors remains fairly intact until the 60s, when it begins to decline fairly rapidly (Doty et al., 1984; Murphy, 1986; Schiffman & Pasternak, 1979). But people vary widely in the degree to which their abilities to detect odors are affected by age. Moreover, within the same individual, the degree of change depends on the odors being tested (Stevens & Cain, 1987).

These variations could have important practical implications. A large survey conducted by the National Geographic Society indicated that older adults were not as able to identify particular odors as younger people. One of the odors tested was the substance added to natural gas that enables people to detect leaks, a potentially fatal problem.

Changes in smell are greater than changes in taste (Stevens, Bartoshuk, & Cain, 1984; Stevens & Cain, 1985, 1986; Stevens, Plantinga, & Cain, 1982). Because much of the pleasure of eating comes from the odor of food, changes in smell are a major reason for the increase in food complaints with age.

Psychological Effects of Olfactory Changes. The major psychological consequences of changes in olfactory ability concern eating, safety, and overall pleasurable experiences. Odors play an important role in enjoying food and in protecting us from harm. Socially, decreases in our ability to detect unpleasant odors may lead to embarrassing situations in which we are unaware that we have body odors or may need to brush our teeth. Social interactions could suffer as a result of these problems. Smells also play a key role in remembering past life experiences. Who can forget the smell of cookies baking in grandma's oven when we were little? Loss of odor cues may mean that our sense of the past suffers as well.

Somesthesis and Balance

Knowing your body's position right now, feeling your lover's soft touch, experiencing the pain of a paper cut, and sensing a chill in the evening air are only a few benefits of somesthesis and balance. These abilities convey information about touch, pressure, pain, kinesthesis, outside temperature, and body orientation. Unlike the other sensory systems we have considered, the somesthetic system has multiple types of receptors and neural pathways, most of which convey specific information about bodily stimulation.

Touch Sensitivity. The distribution of touch receptors is not consistent throughout the body; the greatest concentrations are in the lips, tongue, and fingertips. Although touch thresholds increase with age in the smooth (nonhairy) skin on the hand (Axelrod & Cohen, 1961), touch sensitivity in the hair-covered parts of the body is maintained into later life (Kenshalo, 1977). Sensitivity to vibration decreases in the lower but not the upper part of the body beginning around age 50 (Kenshalo, 1977).

Temperature Sensitivity. The complex way in which our thermal regulation and sensing system works makes it difficult to research. The few studies on aging and temperature sensitivity suggest a meaningful increase in the threshold for warmth (Clark & Mehl, 1971). Although there is a slight increase in the cold threshold, this change appears minimal (Hensel, 1981; Kenshalo, 1979). These data appear to conflict with lowered tolerance of cold by older adults. However, the discrepancy may be due to different age effects between temperature sensitivity and temperature regulation (Whitbourne, 1985), but we do not know for certain.

Pain Sensitivity. Although there are many studies of age-related differences in sensitivity to pain, we still do not have a clear picture of what happens (Harkins & Kwentus, 1990). A major problem confronting researchers interested in pain threshold and pain tolerance (the highest level of pain that can be withstood) is that pain sensitivity varies across different locations on the body and with different types of stimulation. Moreover, experiencing pain is more than just a sensory experience; it involves cognitive, motivational, personality, and cultural factors as well.

Although older adults complain more about pain, the research evidence is conflicting. Data showing everything from decreased sensitivity to increased sensitivity can be found (Harkins & Kwentus, 1990). Corso (1987) notes that the problem is a lack of an appropriate definition of pain and a lack of understanding about how pain happens.

Kinesthesis. Do you know how your arms are positioned right now? If so, you have experienced your sense of body position, kinesthesis. Kinesthesis involves sensory feedback concerning two kinds of movements. *Passive movements* are instigated by something (or someone) else, as, for example, when your lover picks up your hand. *Active movement* is voluntary, as in walking.

Age-related changes in passive movements depend on the part of the body in question. For example, differences are not observed for passive movement of the big toe but are found for several joints, including the knees and the hips (Ochs,

Newberry, Lenhardt, & Harkins, 1985). However, age differences in active movements are not found. For example, judgments of muscle or tendon strain produced by picking up different weights do not differ with age (Ochs et al., 1985).

Balance. Information about balance is provided by the **vestibular system**, housed deep in the inner ear. The vestibular system is designed to respond to the forces of gravity as they act on the head and then to provide this information to the parts of the brain that initiate the appropriate movements so that we can maintain our balance.

Dizziness and vertigo are common experiences for older adults (Ochs et al., 1985). Dizziness is the vague feeling of being unsteady, floating, and light-headed. Vertigo is the sensation that you or your surroundings are spinning. These feelings are unpleasant by themselves, but they can also lead to serious injury from falls resulting from loss of balance.

The likelihood of falling increases with age. Falls may be life-threatening events, especially for those 75 and older (Ochs et al., 1985). Environmental hazards such as loose rugs and slippery floors are more likely to be a factor for healthy, community-dwelling older adults, whereas disease is more likely to play a role in institutionalized individuals. Increases in body sway, the natural movement of the body to maintain balance, occur with increasing age. Connections between the degree of body sway and likelihood of falling have been shown, with people who fall often having more body sway (Overstall, Johnson, & Exton-Smith, 1978).

Psychological Effects of Somesthesis and Balance. Sensations from the skin, internal organs, and joints serve critical functions. They keep us in contact with our environment, help us avoid falling, serve communication functions, and keep us safe. In terms of self-esteem, how well our body is functioning tells us something about how well we are doing. Losing bodily sensations could have major implications. Increased joint stiffness, loss of sexual sensitivity, and problems maintaining balance could result in increased cautiousness, loss of mobility, and decreased social interaction. How the individual views these changes is critical for the maintenance of self-esteem. Providing supportive environments that lead to successful compensatory behaviors can ameliorate the physical and social risks of lack of motor coordination.

THE REPRODUCTIVE SYSTEM

One of the most damaging stereotypes about older adults is that they have no desire for sexual contact. Nothing could be further from the truth. Many surveys show quite clearly that regardless of whether one is a grandparent or a newly married young adult, sexual desire still plays a major role in defining who we are. What is true is that human sexual behavior involves complex interactions among physiological and psychological factors. Age-related changes in these factors have important implications not only for sexual behavior but also for overall self-esteem and well-being.

Many of the major changes in our reproductive system begin during middle age. This has important psychological implications, as midlife is thought by many to be a key time for redefining ourselves (see Chapter 8). Such changes are most apparent in women, who undergo more dramatic physiological changes than men.

Reproductive Changes in Women

The major reproductive change in women during adulthood is the loss of the ability to bear children. This change begins in the 40s, as menstrual cycles become irregular, and by the age of 50 to 55 it is

Interest in sexuality and intimacy knows no age limits.

usually complete (Rykken, 1987). This transition during which a woman's reproductive capacity ends and ovulation stops is referred to as the *climacteric*. **Menopause** refers specifically to the cessation of menstruation. This end of monthly periods is accompanied by decreases in the levels of estrogen and progesterone, changes in the reproductive organs, and changes in sexual functioning (Solnick & Corby, 1983).

A variety of physical and psychological symptoms may accompany menopause due to decreases in hormonal levels (Solnick & Corby, 1983). These include hot flashes, chills, headaches, depression, dizziness, nervousness, and a variety of aches and pains. Although many women report no symptoms at all, most women experience at least some due to their fluctuating hormones. The psychological consequences of menopause, which are often tied to the so-called empty nest syndrome, will be explored more fully in Chapters 8 and 10.

There is some evidence of differences across ethnic groups in women's experiences before and after the climacteric (B. Jackson, Taylor, & Pyngolil, 1991). For example, studies of white women reveal a decrease in reported physical symptoms following climacteric. In contrast, African-American women reported more physical symptoms after climacteric than before. Although these differences could be due to the different age groups included in the various studies (B. Jackson et al., 1991), they also draw attention to the need to study the experiences of women from different ethnic and racial backgrounds.

Women's genital organs undergo progressive change after menopause (O'Donohue, 1987). The vaginal walls shrink and become thinner, the size of the vagina is reduced, the production of vaginal lubricant is reduced and delayed, and some shrinkage of the external genitalia occurs. These changes have important effects on sexual activity, such as an increased possibility of painful intercourse and a longer time needed to reach orgasm. However, maintaining an active sex life throughout adulthood lowers the degree to which problems are encountered.

Despite the physical changes, there is no physiological reason why most women cannot continue sexual activity and enjoy it well into old age. Whether this happens depends more on the availability of a suitable partner than on a woman's desire for sexual relations. This is especially true for older women. The Duke Longitudinal Studies of Normal Aging (Busse & Maddox, 1985) found that older married women were far more likely to have an active sex life than unmarried women. Those married women whose sex life had ceased attributed their lack of activity to their husbands, who agreed with the judgment. In short, the primary reason for the decline in women's sexual activity with age is the lack of a willing or appropriate partner, not a lack of physical ability or desire (Robinson, 1983).

Reproductive Changes in Men

Unlike women, men do not have a physiological (and cultural) event to mark reproductive changes. Men do not experience a complete loss of the ability to have children. However, men do experience a normative decline in the quantity of sperm (Rykken, 1987). Sperm production declines by approximately 30% between age 25 and 60 (Solnick & Corby, 1983). However, even at age 80 a man is still half as fertile as he was at age 25, and is quite capable of fathering a child.

With increasing age the prostate gland enlarges, becomes stiffer, and may obstruct the urinary tract. Prostate cancer becomes a real threat during middle age (Harman & Talbert, 1985); annual examinations are extremely important. The majority of men show no reduction in testosterone compa-

rable to the drop women experience in estrogen (Davidson et al., 1983). However, the men who do experience an abnormally rapid decline in testosterone production during their late 60s report symptoms similar to those experienced by some menopausal women, such as hot flashes, chills, rapid heart rate, and nervousness (Harman & Talbert, 1985).

Men experience some physiological changes in sexual performance. By old age men report less perceived demand to ejaculate, longer time to achieve erection and orgasm, and a much longer resolution phase during which erection is impossible (Rykken, 1987). Because men's conception of masculinity is often linked to the ability to achieve erection and subsequently reach orgasm, these normative changes may result in psychological stress (Rykken, 1987). Sexual satisfaction for men in later life is directly related to the degree to which they believe these myths of male sexuality. Erectile failure can damage confidence and self-esteem and support the mistaken idea that erection equals manhood. External factors such as career issues, alcohol consumption, poor health, and boredom can also lead to decreased activity.

As with women, as long as men enjoy sex and have a willing partner, sexual activity is a lifelong option. Mutual sharing derived from sexual activity can far outweigh any negative feelings that may accompany normal declines in performance (Weg, 1983).

Psychological Consequences of Changes in the Reproductive System

Engaging in sexual behavior is an important aspect of human relationships throughout adulthood. Healthy adults at any age are capable of having and enjoying sexual relationships. Moreover, the desire to do so normally does not diminish. Unfortunately, one of the myths in our society is that older adults cannot and should not be sexual. Many young adults find it difficult to think of their parents having a sexual relationship, and they find it even more difficult to think about their grandparents in this way.

Such stereotyping has important consequences. What comes to mind when you see an older couple being publicly affectionate? The reaction of many is that such behavior is cute. But observers tend not to refer to their own or their peers' relationships in this way. Many nursing homes and other institutions actively dissuade their residents from having sexual relationships, and may even refuse to allow married couples to share the same room. Adult children may verbalize their opinion that their widowed parent does not have the right to establish a new sexual relationship. The message we are sending is that sexual activity is fine for the young but not for the old. The major reason why older women do not engage in sexual relations is the lack of a socially sanctioned partner. It is not that they have lost interest; rather, they believe that they are simply not permitted to express their sexuality any longer.

APPEARANCE AND MOVEMENT

We see the outward signs of aging first in the mirror: gray hair, wrinkled skin, and the bulge around our middle. These changes occur gradually and at different rates. How we perceive that person staring back at us in the mirror says a great deal about how we feel about aging; positive feelings about the signs of aging are related to positive self-esteem (Berscheid, Walster, & Bohrnstedt, 1973).

How easily we move our changing bodies in negotiating the physical environment is also a major component of adaptation and well-being in adulthood (Lawton & Nahemow, 1973). If we cannot get around we are forced to depend on others, which lowers our self-esteem and sense of compe-

tence. Having a body that moves effectively also allows us to enjoy physical activities such as walking, swimming, and skiing.

Appearance

To get a complete picture of age-related changes in appearance, we will consider the skin, hair, voice, and body build separately.

Skin. For many people, realization that they are aging comes with their first awareness of creases, furrows, and sagging in their skin (Whitbourne, 1985). On that day, it makes no difference that these changes are universal and inevitable. Or that they are due to a combination of changes in the structure of the skin and its connective and supportive tissue and to the cumulative effects of damage from exposure to sunlight (A. M. Klingman, Grove, & Balin, 1985). What matters on that day is that they have seen their first wrinkle up close and personally.

Wrinkles result from a complex process. It takes four steps to make a wrinkle (A. M. Klingman et al., 1985). First, the outer layer of skin becomes thinner through cell loss, causing the skin to become more fragile. Second, the collagen fibers that make up the connective tissue lose much of their flexibility, making the skin less able to regain its shape after a pinch, for example. Third, elastin fibers in the middle layer of skin lose their ability to keep the skin stretched out, resulting in sagging. Finally, the underlying layer of fat, which helps provide padding to smooth out the contours, diminishes.

As much as people dislike wrinkles in American culture, it may come as a surprise to learn that much of the facial wrinkling experienced by adults is self-inflicted (A. M. Klingman et al., 1985). Facial wrinkles are not due solely (or perhaps even primarily) to age-related processes but also to chemical, physical, or other traumas. For example, many features of the old face, including wrinkles, are sunshine-induced: precancers, cancers, benign growths, blotches, saggy or stretchable skin, coarse skin, and yellow skin. Proper use of sunscreens and sunblocks slows the development of these problems (L. H. Klingman, Aiken, & Klingman, 1982). The message is clear: Young adults who are dedicated sun-worshippers will eventually pay a high price for their tans.

A lifetime of sun and of normative age-related processes makes older adults' skin thinner, gives it a leathery texture, makes it less effective at regulating heat or cold, and makes it more susceptible to cuts, bruises, and blisters (Fenske & Lober, 1990). The coloring of light-skinned people undergoes additional changes with age. The number of pigment-containing cells in the outer layer decreases, and those that remain have less pigment, resulting in somewhat lighter skin. In addition, age spots (areas of dark pigmentation that look like freckles) and moles (pigmented outgrowths) appear more often (A. M. Klingman et al., 1985). Some of the blood vessels in the skin may become dilated and create small, irregular red lines. Varicose veins may appear as knotty, bluish irregularities in blood vessels, especially on the legs (Bierman, 1985).

Hair. Gradual thinning and graying of the hair of both men and women occurs inevitably with age, although there are large individual differences in the rate of these changes (Kenney, 1982). Hair loss is caused by destruction of the germ centers that produce the hair follicles, whereas graying results from a cessation of pigment production. Men usually do not lose facial hair as they age; witness the number of balding men with thick bushy beards. In contrast, women often develop patches of hair on their face, especially on their chin. This hair growth is related to the hormonal changes of the climacteric (Kenney, 1982).

Voice. How one's voice sounds is one way we judge the age of a person. Younger adults' voices tend to be full and resonant, while older adults' voices tend to be thinner or weaker. Age-related changes in one's voice include lowering of pitch, increased breathlessness and trembling, slower and less precise pronunciation, and decreased volume. Some researchers (such as Benjamin, 1982) report that changes in the larynx (voice box), the respiratory system, and the muscles controlling speech cause these changes. However, other researchers contend that these changes result from poor health and are not part of normal aging (Ramig & Ringel, 1983). The question of whether changes in the voice are normative or mainly the product of disease remains unresolved.

Body Build. Two noticeable changes occur in body build during adulthood: a decrease in height and fluctuations in weight (Kenney, 1982). Height remains fairly stable until the 50s. Between the mid-50s and mid-70s men lose about half an inch, and women lose almost an inch (Adams, Davies, & Sweetname, 1970). Garn (1975) writes that this shortening is caused by compression of the spine from loss of bone strength, changes in the discs, and changes in posture. More details on changes in bone structure are provided below.

The experience of middle-age bulge is common. Typically, people gain weight between their 20s and their mid-50s, but lose weight throughout old age (Shephard, 1978). In old age the body loses muscle and bone, which weigh more than fat, in addition to some fat.

Psychological Consequences of Changes in Appearance. The appearance of wrinkles, gray hair, fat, and the like can have a major effect on an individual's self-concept (Sontag, 1972). Middle-aged adults may still think of themselves as young and may not appreciate others' references to them as old. Because our society places high value on looking young, middle-aged and older adults, especially women, may be regarded as less desirable on any number of dimensions, including intellectual capacity (Connor, Walsh, Lintzelman, & Alvarez, 1978). In contrast, middle-aged men with some gray hair are often considered distinguished, more experienced, and more knowledgeable than their younger counterparts.

Given social stereotypes, many women use any available means to compensate for these changes. Some age-related changes in facial appearance can be successfully disguised with cosmetics. Hair dyes can restore color. Surgical procedures such as face-lifts can tighten sagging and wrinkled skin. But even plastic surgery only delays the inevitable; at some point everyone takes on a distinctly old appearance (A. M. Klingman et al., 1985).

Not everyone tries to hide the fact that he or she is aging. Many older people accept changes in their appearance without losing self-esteem. For example, Barbara Bush made an important statement about accepting aging by not dyeing her hair. These individuals powerfully counterbalance the dominant youth-oriented view in American society.

Movement

Muscles. As we grow older, the amount of muscle tissue in our bodies declines (Whitbourne, 1985). This loss is hardly noticeable in terms of strength and endurance; even at age 70 the loss is no more than 20% (deVries, 1980). After that, however, the rate of change increases. By age 80 the loss in strength is up to 40%, and it appears to be more severe in the legs than in the arms and hands (Grimby & Saltin, 1983; Shephard, 1981). However, some people retain their strength well into old age. In one study, 15% of people over age 60 showed no loss of grip strength over a 9-year period (Kallman, Plato, & Tobin, 1990). Research evidence suggests that muscle endurance also diminishes with age, but at a slower rate (Spirduso & MacCrae, 1990). Men and women show no differences in the rate of muscle change (Spirduso & MacCrae, 1990).

Losses in strength and endurance in old age have much the same psychological effect as changes in appearance (Whitbourne, 1985). In particular,

these changes tell the person that he or she is not as capable of adapting effectively to the environment. Loss of muscle coordination (which may lead to walking more slowly, for example) may not be inevitable, but it can prove embarrassing and stressful. As will be discussed in Chapter 4, exercise can improve muscle strength. Interestingly, the rate of improvement does not seem to differ with age; older adults get stronger at the same rate as younger adults (Moritani & deVries, 1980).

Bones and Joints. Normal aging is accompanied by the loss of bone tissue from the skeleton (Exton-Smith, 1985). Bone loss begins in the late 30s, accelerates in the 50s (particularly in women), and slows by the 70s (Avioli, 1982). The gender difference in bone loss is important. Once the process begins, women lose bone mass approximately twice as fast as men (Garn, 1975). The difference is due to two factors: Women have less bone than men in young adulthood, meaning that they start out with less ability to withstand bone loss before it causes problems; and the depletion of estrogen after menopause speeds up bone loss (Heaney et al., 1982).

Figure 3.4 shows the changes that occur. Notice how the age-related process involves a loss of internal bone mass, which makes bones more hollow. Note that there is also a small age-related gain due to bone growth; however, this gain is limited to the outer surface of the bone. In addition to the changes shown in the figure, bones tend to become porous with age. All of these bone changes cause an age-related increase in the likelihood of fractures (Currey, 1984). Broken bones in older people present more serious problems than in younger adults. When the bone of an older person breaks, it is more likely to snap and cause a "clean" fracture that is difficult to heal. Bones of younger adults fracture in such a way that there are many cracks and splinters to aid in healing. This is analogous to the difference in breaking a young, green tree branch and an old, dry twig.

Women are especially susceptible to severe bone degeneration, a disease called **osteoporosis**.

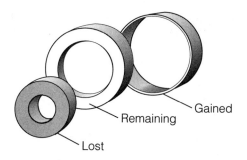

Gained
Remaining
Lost

FIGURE 3.4 Age changes in the surface of a tubular bone in women between ages 30 and 80. Note that bone loss occurs in the central portion of bone, making it weaker, and that the gain in bone occurs on the outer surface.

(Source: "Bone Loss and Aging" (p. 45) by S. M. Garn, 1975, in R. Goldman and M. Rockstein (Eds.), *The Physiology and Pathology of Aging*. New York: Academic Press.)

The loss of bone mass and increased porosity create bones that resemble laced honeycombs (Meier, 1988). Osteoporosis is the leading cause of broken bones in women (Exton-Smith, 1985). The disease appears more often in fair-skinned, white, thin, and small-framed women than in other groups; for example, rates are substantially lower in African-American women (Meier, 1988). Radiographic (such as X-ray) evidence suggests that at least 65% of all women over age 60 and virtually all women over age 90 are affected; in all, more than 20 million women in the United States have osteoporosis, with millions more at risk (Meier, 1988). Osteoporosis is also related to low bone mass at skeletal maturity, deficiencies of calcium and vitamin D, estrogen depletion, and lack of exercise (Meier, 1988). The gender, age, and race factors are probably related to differences on the other variables; for example, women tend to eat diets much lower in calcium than do men. Other risk factors include smoking, high-protein diets, and excessive alcohol, caffeine, and sodium intake (Exton-Smith, 1985).

The relationship of dietary calcium to osteoporosis is controversial (Meier, 1988). There is some

evidence that dietary supplements of calcium after menopause do not slow the rate of bone loss; benefits appear to accrue when the supplements are provided before menopause. The reasons why estrogen depletion affects bone loss are also not understood, mainly because the effects must be indirect, as there are no estrogen receptors in bone tissue (Meier, 1988). Although estrogen-replacement therapy may slow bone loss, this approach must be used cautiously because of potential side effects such as endometrial cancer. Additionally, estrogen therapy must be continued indefinitely, since bone loss speeds up as soon as the therapy is stopped. Finally, data showing that vitamin D metabolism plays a causative role in osteoporosis are clear; however, whether supplementary dietary vitamin D retards bone loss is less certain (Meier, 1988). Some research shows that vitamin D administered after menopause slows the loss of bone, while other research does not. As in the case of calcium supplements, however, the U.S. Food and Drug Administration endorses vitamin D supplements as a therapy for osteoporosis on the grounds that side effects are minimal and that there are some supportive data.

Age-related changes in the joints occur as a result of a degeneration of the protective cartilage (Exton-Smith, 1985). Beginning in the 20s cartilage shows signs of deterioration, such as thinning and becoming cracked and frayed. Over time the bones underneath the cartilage become damaged. If this process occurs to a great extent, the disease **osteoarthritis** results. Osteoarthritis is marked by gradual onset and progression of pain and disability, with minor signs of inflammation (Rogers & Levitin, 1987). The disease usually becomes noticeable in late middle age or old age, and it is especially common in people whose joints are subjected to routine overuse and abuse, such as athletes and manual laborers. Osteoarthritis is truly a wear-and-tear disease. Pain is typically worse when the joint is used, but redness, heat, and swelling are minimal or absent. Osteoarthritis usually affects the hands, spine, hips, and knees, sparing the wrists, elbows, shoulders, and ankles. Drugs are typically ineffective in treating osteoarthritis; effective approaches consist mainly of rest and nonstressful exercises that focus on range of motion.

A second and more common form of arthritis is **rheumatoid arthritis**, a more destructive disease of the joints (Rogers & Levitin, 1987). Rheumatoid arthritis also develops slowly, and typically affects different joints and different types of pain than osteoarthritis. Most often, a pattern of morning stiffness and aching develops in the fingers, wrists, and ankles on both sides of the body. Joints appear swollen. The typical therapy for rheumatoid arthritis consists of aspirin or other nonsteroidal anti-inflammatory drugs. Newer chemical therapies (such as methotrexate) and experimental drugs (such as cyclosporine) are showing promising results (Kremer, 1990). Rest and passive range-of-motion exercises are also helpful. Contrary to popular belief, rheumatoid arthritis is not contagious, hereditary, or self-induced by any known diet, habit, job, or exposure. Interestingly, the symptoms often come and go in repeating patterns.

Psychological Consequences of Changes in Movement. The changes in the joints, especially in arthritis, have profound psychological effects (Whitbourne, 1985). These changes can severely limit movement, thereby reducing independence and the ability to complete normal daily routines. Moreover, joint pain is very difficult to ignore or disguise, unlike changes in appearance. Consequently, the person who can use cosmetics to hide changes in appearance will not be able to use the same approach to deal with constant pain in the joints. However, as we will see in Chapter 4, participation in an exercise program appears to have some benefit. Older adults who suffer bone fractures face, in addition to the usual discomfort, several other consequences. For example, a hip fracture may force hospitalization or even a stay in a nursing home. For all fractures, the recovery period is considerably longer than that for a younger adult. Additionally, older people who witness friends or relatives

struggling during rehabilitation may reduce their own activities as a precautionary measure (Costa & McCrae, 1980a).

SUMMARY

The Biopsychosocial Model

1. Wear-and-tear theory suggests the body is much like a machine that gradually deteriorates over time.

2. Cellular theories suggest that there may be limits on how often cells may divide before dying and that certain proteins or molecules may react randomly.

3. Metabolic processes such as eating fewer calories or reducing stress may be related to living longer.

4. Some cells apparently are programmed to die at certain points.

5. Normal aging consists only of changes that are universal, progressive, and irreversible.

The Brain

6. Some neurons develop neurofibrillary tangles, fibers in the axon that are twisted. Large numbers of these are associated with Alzheimer's disease.

7. Some neurons lose dendrites with age, while others gain dendrites.

8. Damaged or dying neurons sometimes become surrounded by protein and form neuritic plaques. Large numbers of plaques are associated with Alzheimer's disease.

9. The ways in which neurons are interconnected change with age.

10. Several neurotransmitter levels decrease with age, including dopamine, acetylcholine, and serotonin.

11. Three types of brain imaging are used in research: computed tomography (CT), magnetic resonance imaging (MRI), and positron emission tomography (PET). Each provides important information about brain structures; PET also provides information on brain metabolism.

12. The term senility no longer has medical meaning, nor do all (or even most) older adults become senile.

13. Brain changes underlie many behavioral changes, including memory.

The Immune System

14. The number of lymphocytes does not change with age. However, they do not work as quickly or as well in older adults.

15. Some antibodies to specific diseases appear to decrease in number with age. In addition, people begin to develop autoimmunity, the development of antibodies that attack the body itself.

16. The number of older adults with AIDS is increasing.

17. Older adults health declines faster once AIDS symptoms begin.

The Cardiovascular System

18. Some fat deposits in and around the heart, as well as inside arteries, is a normal part of aging.

19. Overall, men have a higher rate of cardiovascular disease than women.

20. Several diseases increase in frequency with age: ischemic heart disease, cardiac arrhythmias, angina, heart attack, atherosclerosis, cerebrovascular disease, and hypertension.

The Respiratory System

21. The amount of air we can take into our lungs and how easily we can exchange oxygen and carbon dioxide decrease with age.

22. Chronic obstructive lung disease (COLD), such as emphysema, increases with age.

23. Shortness of breath due to age-related changes may result in a reduction of activity in the elderly.

The Senses

24. Several age-related changes occur in the structure of the eye, including opaque spots on the lens (cataracts), glaucoma, macular degeneration, and diabetic retinopathy.

25. Changes in visual functioning with age include: need for increased illumination, increased susceptibility to glare, difficulty seeing nearby objects (presbyopia), decreased acuity, and slower light and dark adaptation.

26. Age-related declines in the ability to hear high-pitched tones (presbycusis) are universal.

27. Exposure to noise speeds up and exacerbates hearing loss.

28. Psychologically, losses in hearing can reduce the ability to have satisfactory communication with others.

29. Age-related changes in taste are minimal.

30. The ability to detect odors declines rapidly after age 60 in most people. Changes in smell are primarily responsible for reported changes concerning food preference and enjoyment.

31. Changes in sensitivity to touch, temperature, and pain are complex and not understood.

32. Dizziness and vertigo increase with age, as do falls.

The Reproductive System

33. The transition from being able to have children to the cessation of ovulation is termed the climacteric; menopause refers to the end of menstruation. A variety of physical and psychological symptoms accompany menopause, including several in the genital organs.

34. No changes occur in the desire to have sex; however, the availability of a suitable partner for women is a major barrier.

35. In men, sperm production declines gradually with age. Changes in the prostate gland occur, and should be monitored by yearly examinations.

Appearance and Movement

36. Normative changes with age include: wrinkles, gray hair, thinner and weaker voice, decrease in height, and increase in weight in mid-life. Cultural stereotypes have an enormous influence on the personal acceptance of age changes in appearance.

37. The amount of muscle decreases with age, but strength and endurance only change slightly.

38. Loss of bone mass is normative; in severe cases, though, the disease osteoporosis may result. Osteoarthritis and rheumatoid arthritis may impair the ability to get around and function in the environment.

REVIEW QUESTIONS

The Biopsychosocial Model

1. What biological theories have been proposed to explain aging? How do they differ?

2. What are the differences between normal aging and disease?

The Brain

3. What structural changes occur in the neuron with age? How are these changes related to diseases such as Alzheimer's?

4. What happens to the interconnections among neurons with age?

5. What changes occur in neurotransmitters with age?

6. What types of brain imaging techniques are used and what structures and processes do they measure?

7. What are the relationships between changes in the brain and changes in behavior?

The Immune System

8. What changes occur in the immune system with age?

9. What happens in the development of antibodies as people grow older?

10. How is AIDS affecting older adults?

The Cardiovascular System

11. What changes occur in the cardiovascular system with age? What gender differences have been noted? Which cardiovascular diseases increase in frequency with age?

The Respiratory System

12. What changes occur in the respiratory system with age? How are respiratory diseases related to age?

The Senses

13. What age-related changes occur in vision?

14. What age-related changes occur in hearing?

15. What age-related changes occur in taste and smell?

16. What age-related changes occur in somesthesis, balance, and movement?

The Reproductive System

17. What age-related changes occur in women and men concerning their reproductive ability?

18. How does interest in sexual activity change with age? What constraints operate on men and women?

Appearance and Movement

19. What age-related changes occur in appearance?

20. What happens to muscle and bone tissue with age?

KEY TERMS

acuity Ability to see detail. (95)

angina A painful condition caused by temporary constriction of blood flow to the heart. (89)

antibody Type of immune system cell produced by lymphocytes that fights invading cells. (86)

atherosclerosis A process by which fat is deposited on the walls of the arteries. (90)

cerebrovascular disease A form of cardiovascular disease that involves the blood vessels in the brain. (90)

chronic obstructive lung disease (COLD) A family of age-related lung diseases that block the passage of air and cause abnormalities inside the lungs. (92)

cross-linking Random interaction among proteins that produces molecules that make the body stiffer. (77)

dark adaptation A process by which the eye adapts from a bright environment to a dark one. (95)

dendrites The part of the neuron that primarily receives incoming information from other nearby neurons. (80)

emphysema Severe lung disease that greatly reduces the ability to exchange carbon dioxide for oxygen. (92)

free radicals Deleterious and short-lived chemicals that cause changes in cells that are thought to result in aging. (77)

Hayflick limit The biological limit to the number of times a cell is able to reproduce, which is thought to be related to aging. (77)

hypertension A disease in which one's blood pressure is too high. (91)

ischemic heart disease The most common form of cardiovascular disease in older adults caused by decreased oxygen or poor circulation in the coronary arteries. (89)

light adaptation The process by which the eye adapts from a dark environment to a bright environment. (95)

lymphocytes Cells in the immune system responsible for fighting disease and other invading cells. (86)

menopause The cessation of menstruation in women. (102)

neuritic plaques A normative age change in the brain involving amyloid protein collecting on dying or dead neurons. Large numbers of plaques is a defining characteristic of Alzheimer's disease. (81)

neurofibrillary tangles A normative age-related change in the brain involving the production of new fibers in the neuron. Large numbers of tangles is a defining characteristic of Alzheimer's disease. (81)

neurons The basic cell in the brain. (80)

neurotransmitters Chemicals used for communicating between neurons. (80)

osteoarthritis A form of arthritis marked by gradual onset and progression of pain and swelling, primarily due to overuse. (107)

osteoporosis A degenerative bone disease more common in women in which bone tissue deteriorates severely. (106)

presbycusis The loss of the ability to hear high-pitched tones, a normative age-related change. (97)

presbyopia The normative age-related loss of the ability to focus on nearby objects, usually resulting in the need for glasses. (95)

programmed cell death The idea that some cells are genetically programmed to die at particular points in the life span. (78)

rheumatoid arthritis A destructive form of arthritis involving more swelling and more joints than osteoarthritis. (108)

vestibular system Sensory system in the inner ear that allows us to keep our balance. (101)

wear-and-tear theory A biological theory of aging stating that aging is due to the body simply wearing itself out. (77)

ADDITIONAL READING

There are several excellent sources of more detailed information on age-related biological and physiological changes. Basic overviews can be found in

Cart, C. S., Metress, E. K., & Metress, S. P. (1992). *Biological bases of human aging and disease.* Boston: Jones & Bartlett. Easy reading.

Spence, A. P. (1989). *Biology of human aging.* New York: Prentice-Hall. Easy reading.

Whitbourne, S. K. (1985). *The aging body.* New York: Springer. Medium to difficult.

An up-to-date professional-level overview can be found in

Schneider, E. L., & Rowe, J. W. (Eds.). (1990). *Handbook of the biology of aging* (3rd ed.). San Diego: Academic Press. Difficult reading.

CHAPTER 4

Health

IMAGINE FOR A MINUTE THAT YOU WERE BORN IN 1900, and what that would mean for your health. If you became ill, there would be no antibiotics to help you fight the infection — no immunizations against polio, measles, whooping cough, or a host of other diseases. No one knew the benefits of aerobic exercise, understood the dangers from smoking or from too much saturated fat, or how to treat cancer effectively. Coronary bypass surgery was not even a dream. Surviving childhood was a feat in itself; surviving to old age was highly unusual.

When it comes to health care, we are fortunate to live at the close of the 20th century. One of the most dramatic changes since 1900 has been the virtual elimination of acute disease as a primary cause of death in Western societies (Fries & Crapo, 1986). Early in the 20th century acute diseases such as tuberculosis, polio, measles, diphtheria, typhoid fever, and syphilis claimed tens of thousands of lives in the United States each year. Today, they kill relatively few. In fact, the risk of mortality in the United States from any of these acute diseases has been reduced by at least 99% since 1900. Contrary to popular belief, the rate of acute disease actually drops across adulthood; younger adults have the highest rate, older adults have the lowest.

More than any other factor, this reduction in the death rate from acute disease is responsible for the rapid increase in life expectancy in industrialized countries during the first half of the 20th century. Other factors — such as reduced risk of death during childbirth — played important roles, too. These changes have fundamentally altered our concepts of health and illness. Now when we think of illness and its relationship to age, we focus on chronic diseases such as cardiovascular disease (see Chapter 3). Chronic diseases have a slower onset than acute diseases, but last much longer. Developmental trends for chronic diseases are the opposite of those for acute diseases; younger adults have the lowest rates, older adults have the highest. Indeed, many older people have multiple chronic diseases that affect their health and well-being.

Changes in the conditions that cause death have also brought about changes in how we design health care. Since the 1960s, increasing emphasis has been put on preventive health care. Health promotion programs have become the focus of much research and funding, perhaps because they are primarily concerned with preventing chronic disease. Fries and Crapo (1986) comment that this change in the focus of prevention from acute to chronic disease has gone largely unnoticed, even though its implications for health care are enormous. Caring for someone afflicted with a serious chronic disease is typically much more expensive than treating an acute disorder. Indeed, much of the soaring cost of health care in industrialized countries is due to the cost of treating chronic disease.

A second fundamental change concerns the relationship between age and death. When acute diseases are important causes of death, as they were in the United States a century ago and as they still are in Third World countries, the relationship looks like the lower curve shown in Figure 4.1. Notice that the relationship is fairly linear, with the number of people living dropping regularly across age. But look what happens when acute diseases no longer kill large numbers of people, as in the United States today. As you can see in the top curve, the shape of the curve changes dramatically, taking on a more rectangular shape. This means that relatively few people die before old age; many more elderly people survive and many will have chronic diseases and be in poor health.

In this chapter we will consider several issues related to health and aging. The common theme linking them is that they all have some connection with life style, making them at least partly under our control. Although many of the findings and recommendations appear to be little more than common sense, we must remember that most people in Western society do not follow even the most basic guidelines for a healthy life style.

We will begin by considering how the elimination of many acute diseases, as well as the influence

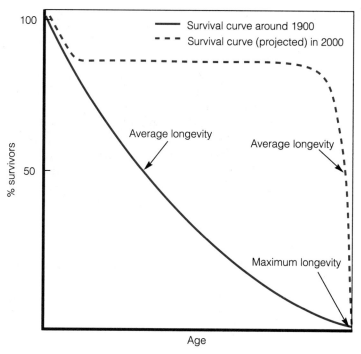

FIGURE 4.1 Survival curves

(Source: *Aging and Society*, edited by J. Bond and P. Coleman. Copyright 1990 by Sage Publications. Reprinted by permission of the publisher.)

of other factors, has increased the average number of years people live. Next, we will focus on one of the most pervasive influences on health — stress — and discover what some of these effects are. Following that, we will consider several specific aspects of life style: smoking, drinking, exercise, sleep, and nutrition. Each of these has important influences on the development of chronic disease. Because it is often an outcome of an unhealthy life style, cancer will be considered as an example of how these various influences may produce disease. Finally, we will conclude with a consideration of health promotion and disease prevention, with an eye toward helping ourselves develop healthier habits.

Throughout this discussion, you should keep the biopsychosocial model in mind. As pointed out in Chapter 3, the components being emphasized are intrapersonal factors and biological and physical factors. In this chapter, the interactive nature of these components will be especially important.

HOW LONG WILL WE LIVE?

One of the most important reasons why this book was written is that there are many more people living to old age than ever before. You have already seen far more older adults than your great-great-grandparents did even if they themselves lived to old age. The tremendous increase in the number of older adults has focused renewed interest in life expectancy. Knowing how long you are likely to live is not only important on a personal level for planning one's life, but also on a broader level for government agencies, service programs, the business world, and insurance companies. Why? The length of life has an enormous impact — from decisions about government health care programs (much higher costs to care for more chronically ill people) to retirement policy (a move to eliminate mandatory retirement) to how much one pays for life insurance (longer average lives mean cheaper rates). Longer lives have forced change in all of these areas, and will continue to do so well into the next century.

Life expectancy can be examined helpfully with the biopsychosocial model, as how long we live depends on complex interactions between our genetic heritage and our environment. You probably know people who have many relatives who live to very old age, and others whose relatives die rather young. It is true that tendencies toward long lives (or short ones, for that matter) tend to run in families. As we will see, our "long-life genes" play a major role in governing how long we are likely to live.

But the world in which we live can affect how long we live, too. Environmental factors such as disease or toxic chemicals modify one's genetic heritage and shorten one's lifetime, sometimes drastically. By the same token, other environmental factors such as quality medical care can sometimes fix genetic defects that would have caused early death, thereby significantly altering one's genetic heritage for the better.

Average and Maximum Longevity

The number of years one lives, as jointly determined by genetic and environmental factors, is called longevity. Researchers distinguish between two different types of longevity: average longevity and maximum longevity. **Average longevity** is commonly called average life expectancy. It refers to the age at which half of the individuals who are born in a particular year will have died. Average longevity is affected by both genetic and environmental factors, as we will see in the next section. For people in the United States average longevity has been increasing steadily over this century; recent estimates are presented in Figure 4.2. Note in the figure that the most rapid increase in average longevity occurred in the first half of this century. These increases in average longevity were due mostly to declines in infant mortality rates through the elimination of diseases such as smallpox and polio and through better health care. The decrease in the number of women who died during childbirth was especially important in raising average life expectancies for females. All of these advances in medical technology and improvements in health care mean that more people survive to old age, thereby increasing average longevity in the general population.

Maximum longevity refers to the oldest age to which any individual of a species lives. Although Methuselah is said to have lived to the ripe old age of 969 years, modern scientists are more conservative in their estimates of a human's maximum longevity. Most estimates place the limit at around 120 years (Fry, 1985), with the argument that the key body systems — such as the cardiovascular system — have limits on how long they can last. Whether this estimate of maximum longevity will change as new technologies produce better artificial organs remains to be seen. An important issue, of course, is whether extending the life span indefinitely would be a good idea.

Because maximum longevity of different animal species varies considerably, scientists have tried to understand these differences by considering important biological functions such as metabolic rate or relative brain size (Fry, 1985; Kirkwood, 1985). Unfortunately, none of these efforts has met with complete success (Walford, 1983). For example, why giant tortoises tend to live longer than we do remains a mystery.

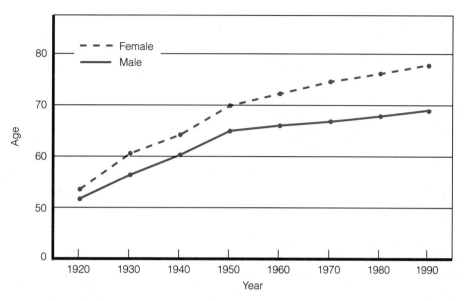

FIGURE 4.2 Life expectancy at birth, 1920–1990

(Source: U.S. Bureau of the Census.)

Genetic Factors in Longevity

A good way to increase one's chances of a long life is to come from a family with a history of long-lived individuals (Dublin, Lotka, & Spiegelman, 1946). For example, if your mother lives to at least age 80, roughly 4 years are added to your average longevity (Woodruff-Pak, 1988). Alexander Graham Bell was one of the first people to demonstrate systematically the benefits of coming from a long-lived family. Bell considered 8,797 of William Hyde's descendants and found that children of parents who had lived beyond 80 survived about 20 years longer than children whose parents had both died before they were 60. Evidence from research on twins also points toward the importance of genetics in determining longevity. Kallmann (1957) showed that even when identical twins lived in different environments, they died, on average, within three years

of each other, whereas fraternal twins died, on average, within six years of each other.

Having long- or short-lived relatives is not the only genetic effect on longevity. Some diseases also have a known genetic component. Two of the best known of these are cardiovascular disease (considered in Chapter 3) and Alzheimer's disease (discussed in Chapter 9). The effects of these diseases on average longevity is significant. For example, for each parent, grandparent, or sibling who dies of cardiovascular disease before age 50, one typically loses 4 years from one's average longevity.

One exciting line of research, the human genome project, is attempting to map all of our genes. This research and its spin-offs in microbiology and behavior genetics has already produced some astounding results in terms of genetic links to disease. In the past few years, genetic links have been identified for cystic fibrosis, Alzheimer's disease, and some forms of alcoholism. Some attempts are even being made at treating genetic diseases by implanting "corrected" genes into young children in the hopes that the good genes will reproduce and eventually wipe out the defective genes. Perhaps cures for genetic diseases that do not make their appearance until adulthood, such as Huntington's disease (see Chapter 9), may be developed in our lifetime.

Environmental Factors in Longevity

Although heredity is a major determinant of longevity, environmental factors also affect the life span (Schneider & Reed, 1985). Some environmental factors are more obvious: diseases, toxins, life style, and social class. The impact of some important diseases such as cardiovascular disease are discussed in this chapter. Environmental toxins, mainly encountered as air and water pollution, are an increasing problem. For example, mercury and other toxins in fish, cancer-causing chemicals in drinking water, and airborne pollutants are beginning to be recognized as major agents in shortening longevity. Life-style factors such as stress, exercise, smoking, drinking, and diet have received considerable attention since the 1980s. The impact of social class on longevity is due to the reduced access to goods and services, especially medical care, that characterizes many members of ethnic minority groups, the poor, and the elderly (AARP, 1991). Most of these people have either no or badly inadequate health insurance, and they cannot afford the cost of a healthier life style. For example, lead poisoning from old water pipes and from air pollution is a serious problem in large urban areas, but many people simply cannot afford to move. The sad part about most of these environmental factors is that we are responsible for them. Denying adequate health care to everyone, continuing to pollute our environment, living unhealthy life styles, and fail-

ing to address the causes of poverty have undeniable consequences: They shorten lives.

There are other less obvious but equally important environmental factors that affect how long we live. For example, marriage has a beneficial effect, as married people tend to live as much as five years longer than unmarried people (Woodruff-Pak, 1988). Apparently, having another person around to help take care of us, contribute to our financial stability, and help us regulate eating and sleeping habits can add years to our life. In fact, divorced men who live alone lose roughly nine years from their average longevity (Woodruff-Pak, 1988).

The full impact of environmental factors is seen best when they are considered in combination. For instance, the American Cancer Society has estimated that a nonsmoking married person living in a rural area can expect, on average, to live 22 years longer than an unmarried smoker who lives alone in a large city. The cumulative effects of environmental factors can clearly be substantial.

Ethnic Differences in Average Longevity

It has been known for a long time that people in different ethnic groups do not have the same average longevity at birth. For example, African Americans' average longevity at birth is roughly six and one-half years lower for men and about five years lower for women than it is for white Americans (National Center for Health Statistics, 1991). It is tempting to conclude that these differences reflect genetic factors alone. However, we have seen that environmental factors play a major role in determining longevity. Because the environmental variables differ substantially between the typical white person and the typical ethnic minority individual, it is wrong to focus on genetic factors as the explanation.

In fact, ethnic differences in average longevity are quite complex. Because they are at greater risk for disease and accidents (for instance, homicide), have much less access to good health care, and live less healthy life styles for economic reasons, a greater proportion of ethnic minority individuals die relatively young compared to their white counterparts. However, those from ethnic minority groups who manage to survive to old age actually tend to live longer, on average, than whites. For example, African Americans who are currently 85 years old can expect to live 1 year longer than 85-year-old white Americans (Woodruff-Pak, 1988).

The reason for the switch in average longevity advantage has to do mainly with the kinds of people from ethnic minority groups who survive to old age. Such people tend to be healthier, as they typically have made it to old age without the assistance of high quality medical care. Thus, until all people have equal access to health care and have equal opportunities to engage in healthy life styles, the degree to which genetic factors account for differences in average longevity will remain largely unknown.

Gender Differences in Average Longevity

Women tend to live longer than men. Indeed, throughout most of the life span, females' average longevity is substantially greater than that for males. (At birth, the difference in average longevity is roughly 7 years; at age 40 it is still 6 years.) However, by old age (age 85) women have only about a 1-year advantage (Woodruff-Pak, 1988).

How can we account for these data? Just as with ethnic differences, the relationship between gender and longevity is complex. Part of the reason is biological: Males are more susceptible to a variety of diseases and genetic defects than are females. As a result, more males die from these conditions in infancy and childhood. On the environmental side, males tend to be at greater risk for premature death due to war and work-related injuries and diseases

The fact that Bill is celebrating his 92nd birthday may reflect his genetic heritage. That he is surrounded by women reflects the substantial difference in average life expectancy between males and females.

(such as cancer from long-term exposure to dangerous chemicals). Men who successfully avoid these problems and survive to old age (especially beyond age 80) tend to live almost as long as their female counterparts.

As women assume more roles in the workplace that have traditionally been held by men, especially those that expose them to potentially life-shortening substances, the gender differences in average longevity could change. For example, cardiovascular disease increased in women during the middle part of the 20th century. And as we will see later in this chapter, smoking-related lung cancer in women was the only major cause of death to increase during the 1980s. The dynamic forces in the biopsychosocial model suggest that the gender differences may change even further as we enter the 21st century. For example, the current emphasis on health may help everyone live a little longer.

STRESS AND HEALTH

Stress is harmful to your health. One widespread (and erroneous) belief is that stress-related health problems occur mainly in people who hold certain types of jobs, such as air traffic controllers or high-level business executives. Lower-level employees are viewed as safe because they have little control over their working environment. Unfortunately, the relationships among job, stress, and health are not that simple. In fact, a carefully conducted study found that business executives had fewer stress-related health problems than waitresses, construction workers, secretaries, laboratory technicians, machine operators, farm workers, and painters (Smith, Colligan, Horning, & Hurrell, 1978). It appears that stress occurs most when people must be extremely vigilant, perform complex work, and meet time demands placed on them by others. Responsibility and decision making alone seem not to matter.

Just as the belief that executives are more prone to stress-related illnesses than laborers is more myth than fact, many other aspects of stress and its relationship to health are not understood very well. Indeed, the nature of the relationship of stress to age, gender, and ethnic or racial status remains underresearched and poorly understood. For example, in the 1980s more women than men in all age groups reported that stress had had a significant impact on their health in the previous year (U.S. DHHS, 1988). People between the ages of 30 and 44 reported the highest levels of stress, with those over age 65 reporting the lowest. The reasons underlying these differences are unknown.

The Meaning of Stress

Despite literally thousands of scientific studies on stress and its effects on health, scientists still cannot agree on a definition. To some, stress refers to something in the environment, as in "I am in a stressful relationship." Others see stress as a response to the environment, as in "I feel stress whenever I have to deal with a crisis." Finally, still others define stress as an interaction between environmental conditions and responses to them.

All three positions have been adopted by various theorists over the years. We will focus on two theories that have had the most impact on the investigation of stress: the general adaptation syndrome and the stress and coping paradigm.

Selye's General Adaptation Syndrome

The most influential person in the field of stress theory and research was Hans Selye (1956, 1979, 1982). Selye was almost single-handedly responsible for popularizing the notion that stress has physical effects. He was one of the first to conceptualize stress as a response to things in the environment. He used the term *stressor* to represent the environmental stimulus that caused the person to react and the term *stress* to represent the response to the stressor.

Selye described stress as a nonspecific response; that is, it is a precise response that can be triggered by any number of stressors (1956, 1979). Most of his work involved carefully describing this response, which became known as the general adaptation syndrome.

The **general adaptation syndrome** is the body's attempt to defend itself against stressors.

These freight car repairwomen work in a relatively dangerous and stressful occupation that could affect their health.

The syndrome consists of three stages. During the *alarm stage* the body's defenses against stressors are mobilized. The sympathetic nervous system, responsible for the fight-or-flight response, quickly goes into action. Epinephrine (adrenaline) is released; pulse, blood pressure, and respiration increase; more blood is diverted to the skeletal muscles; the sweat glands are activated; and the gastrointestinal tract is deactivated.

If the stressor continues, we enter the second phase, termed the *resistance stage*. During this stage we adapt to the stressor. The length of this stage depends on the potency of the stressor and how adaptable we are. Providing that adaptation is possible, the resistance stage can continue for a relatively long period. Outwardly, we look normal

during this stage. However, all is not well physiologically. Neurological and hormonal changes occur that Selye believed caused stress illnesses such as peptic ulcers, hypertension, hyperthyroidism, ulcerative colitis, and some forms of asthma. Additionally, Selye believed that continual adaptation to stressors weakened the immune system, making infections more likely. Later in this section we will examine research evidence for these stress-illness links.

But we cannot resist stress indefinitely. At some point the *exhaustion stage* is reached. The ability to resist is gone, and the body begins to break down. Depression is quite likely, and even death is a real possibility. Although rare, this situation can develop in people who are subjected to very long-term stressful situations, such as caring for someone who has Alzheimer's disease or other serious chronic illness.

Due to the changes in the immune, cardiovascular, and respiratory systems described in Chapter 3, older adults cannot withstand stress as long as their younger counterparts before their bodies begin to break down. This means two things. First, the resistance stage is shorter for older adults before exhaustion sets in. Second, older adults are more susceptible to stress-related illness.

The Stress and Coping Paradigm

A second very influential approach to stress is the **stress and coping paradigm**, developed by Richard Lazarus and his colleagues (Lazarus, 1984; Lazarus, DeLongis, Folkman, & Gruen, 1985; Lazarus & Folkman, 1984). Lazarus views stress not as an environmental stimulus or as a response but, rather, as the interaction of a thinking person and the event. How we interpret an event is what matters, not the event itself or what we do in response. Put more formally, stress is "a particular relationship between the person and the environment that is appraised by the person as taxing or exceeding his or her resources and endangering his or her well-being" (Lazarus & Folkman, 1984, p. 19). Note that this definition states that stress refers to a transactional process between a person and the environment, that the person's appraisal of the situation is key, and that unless the situation is considered to be threatening, challenging, or harmful, stress does not result.

Appraisal. Lazarus and Folkman (1984) describe three types of appraisals of stress. *Primary appraisal* serves to categorize events into three groups based on the significance they have for our well-being: irrelevant, benign-positive, and stressful. Irrelevant events have no bearing on us personally; hearing about a typhoon nowhere near land in the South Pacific while sitting in your living room in Boston is an example. Benign-positive appraisals mean that the event has good effects; a job promotion is a common example. Finally, stressful appraisals mean that you perceive an event, such as failing a course, as harmful, threatening, or challenging.

Secondary appraisal refers to our perceived ability to cope with harm, threat, or challenge. Secondary appraisal is the equivalent of asking three questions: "What can I do?" "How likely is it that I can use one of my options successfully?" "Will this option reduce my stress?" If you believe that there is something that you can do that will make a difference, stress is reduced and coping is successful.

Reappraisal involves being sensitive to changes in the situation. New information may become available that needs to be incorporated into your appraisal. For example, you may hear that the person you are dating is already married, a fact that, if true, would probably lead you to rethink your relationship. Reappraisal can either increase stress (if the person had lied to you before and is indeed married) or lower stress (if, perhaps, you discovered that the rumor was not true).

Coping. During secondary appraisal we may realize that we can do something to deal with the stress effectively. In other words, we could cope. Lazarus and Folkman view *coping* as a complex process. First, coping is an evolving process that is fine-tuned over time. Our first attempt might fail, but if we try again in a slightly different way we may be successful. Second, it is learned, not automatic. That is why we do not cope very well with stressful situations we are facing for the first time (such as the end of our first love relationship). Third, coping takes effort; it is something we work at. Finally, coping requires only that we manage the situation; we are not required to overcome or control it. Thus, we can cope with extreme weather even though we cannot control it.

How well we cope depends on several factors. Healthy, energetic people are better able to cope than frail, sick people. A positive attitude about yourself and your abilities is also important. Good problem-solving skills put you at an advantage in having several options with which to manage the stress. Social skills and social support are important in helping us solicit suggestions and assistance from others. Finally, financial resources are important; having the money to pay a mechanic to fix one's car allows nonmechanically inclined individuals to avoid the frustration of trying to do it themselves.

Aging and the Stress and Coping Paradigm. Two important areas of age differences in the stress and coping paradigm are the sources of stress and coping strategies.

Age differences have been described for the kinds of things that people report as everyday stresses (Folkman, Lazarus, Pimley, & Novacek, 1987). Younger adults experience more stress in the areas of finance, work, home maintenance, personal life, family, and friends than do older adults. These differences are probably due to the fact that the young adults are likely to be parents of small children and employed; parenting and work roles are less salient to retired older adults. The stresses reported frequently by older adults, coming mainly from the environment and social issues, may be more age related than role related. That is, environmental stress may be due to a decreased ability to get around rather than to a specific role.

Age differences in coping strategies are striking and consistent. For example, Blanchard-Fields and her colleagues have shown that younger adults tend to use defensive coping styles much of the time, whereas older adults choose coping strategies on the basis of whether they feel in control of the situation (Blanchard-Fields & Irion, 1988; Blanchard-Fields & Robinson, 1987; Irion & Blanchard-Fields, 1987). Even when people are faced with similar problems, age differences in coping style are apparent. For example, Felton and Revenson (1987) report that when trying to cope with their chronic illnesses, middle-aged adults were more likely to use interpersonal strategies such as information seeking than were older adults.

These age-related differences in coping strategies fit with developmental trends reported in personality reviewed in Chapter 8. In particular, there appears to be an age-related introversion that is reflected in increased passivity and more self-reflective behavior. It may be that these changes in personality are also reflected in the choice of a coping strategy.

Stress and Physical Illness

Considerable research has examined how stress causes physical illness. Zegans (1982) proposed numerous hypotheses about this connection. One of the most important of these involves the effects of stress on the immune system. Recall that Selye proposed that stress suppresses the activity of the immune system. Riley (1981) reports that increased levels of hormones called corticoids occur after prolonged stress and that they increase animals' vulnerability to viruses and possibly even cancer.

Research on humans has documented similar effects. Lower antibody levels and poorer functioning of some types of lymphocytes (see Chapter 3) have been demonstrated in students who were under stress during examination periods (Jemmott et al., 1983; Kiecolt-Glaser, Speicher, Holliday, & Glaser, 1984). Interestingly, personality differences influenced the degree to which the immune system was affected. People who were motivated by power rather than friendship (Jemmott et al., 1983), and people who were lonely (Kiecolt-Glaser et al., 1984) were affected most.

This line of research suggests that stress lowers the ability of the immune system to fight infection. This may be why we sometimes get ill shortly after a relatively prolonged period of stress (for example, during vacation after a very stressful time at work). Although the relationship between stress and the immune system may help explain one mechanism of the stress-illness connection, it is not the only one. Additional connections between stress and illness can be seen in examining specific diseases.

Headaches. Nearly everyone gets an occasional tension headache that is ascribed to stress. For most of us, headaches are relatively minor problems. However, for the 10% to 12% of people who must seek medical attention, headaches present major difficulties (Holyroyd, Appel, & Andrasik, 1983). Those who go to physicians do not do so because they have different kinds of headaches. Rather, they suffer from more serious or frequent headaches than the rest of us.

Holyroyd and colleagues (1983) describe two types of headache: tension headache and vascular headache. Migraine headache is a severe version of vascular headache caused by restriction followed by dilation of the cerebral arteries, causing intense, throbbing pain. Research dating to the 1960s has demonstrated that stress causes tension headaches to a much greater extent than vascular headaches.

Ulcers. Many years of research on both animals and people have confirmed the fact that stress causes ulcers. Ulcers seem most likely to occur when the stressful situation has strongly negative aspects that cannot be avoided, when it presents unexpected annoyances, and when it requires difficult decisions with little personal control (Smith et al., 1978). We will return to this issue in Chapter 8 when we consider personal control in more detail.

Cardiovascular Disease. Cardiovascular disease has several behavioral risk factors. One of the most provocative of these connections is between cardiovascular disease and self-imposed stress. Due to the work of M. Friedman and Rosenman (1974) we know that both personality and situational stress are related to cardiovascular disease. They identified two behavior patterns, which differ dramati-

cally in terms of the risk of cardiovascular disease. **Type A behavior pattern** is associated with high rates of cardiovascular disease. An opposite style, **Type B behavior pattern**, is not associated with cardiovascular disease.

Type A people are intensely competitive, angry, hostile, restless, aggressive, and impatient. They are also at least twice as likely as Type B people to develop cardiovascular disease, even when other risk factors such as smoking, diabetes, hypertension, and high serum cholesterol are taken into account. Furthermore, serious heart disease rarely occurs before age 70 except among Type A people. It does not seem to matter how much junk food Type B people eat, how many cigarettes they smoke, or how little exercise they get. They will probably not die prematurely from cardiovascular disease (Eisdorfer & Wilkie, 1977).

These findings led researchers and those involved in rehabilitating cardiac patients to advocate major changes in life style following heart attacks or other serious cardiovascular disease. The thinking was that if Type A behavior predisposed people to cardiovascular disease, then eliminating Type A traits would serve as a protective function. It appears, however, that the relationship between Type A behavior and cardiovascular disease is more complex.

Beginning in 1981, researchers began reporting a reversal in the relationship when the risk for secondary cardiovascular disease was examined. That is, researchers began studying individuals who had already had serious cardiovascular disease and investigated whether Type A or Type B people had a higher risk of developing additional heart diseases (such as having a second heart attack). The results were surprising and controversial. Contrary to the finding concerning risk of initial heart disease, Type A people actually recovered from their first heart attack better and had lower morbidity than Type B individuals (Case, Heller, Case, & Moss, 1985; Dimsdale, Gilbert, Hutter, Hackett, & Block, 1981; Shekelle, Gale, & Norusis, 1985). The strong-

HOW DO WE KNOW?

The Type A Controversy: Being Driven to Get Better

The controversy over whether Type A behavior is seriously detrimental to one's health has profound implications for treatment. It is a good idea, then, to take a closer look at one study that found an unexpected result.

Ragland and Brand (1988) examined the 22-year mortality of 257 men with heart disease. These men were part of the Western Collaborative Group Study, which uncovered the connection between Type A behavior pattern and coronary disease. Of these 257 men, 135 had symptomatic myocardial infarctions, 71 had silent myocardial infarctions, and 51 had angina; of those who had symptomatic myocardial infarctions, 26 died suddenly or within 24 hours of

the onset of symptoms. A follow-up through 1983 showed that 128 of the men had died, and their cause of death was coded from death certificates by 2 independent raters; 91 died of heart disease and 37 from unrelated causes. For the 91 men who died of heart disease, it was noted whether they died within 24 hours of symptom onset. The key analyses examined whether short-term and long-term outcomes were related differently to Type A and Type B patterns.

Results showed an almost identical mortality rate for Type A and Type B men who died within 24 hours of symptom onset. For long-term mortality, the fatality rate was 19.1 per 1,000 person-years for Type A and 31.7 per 1,000 person-years for Type B. Even when the data were examined in more detail, the Type A advantage never disappeared.

Although the results of the study point toward the conclusion that

Type A men who survive their initial bout with heart disease are more likely to survive in the long run, Ragland and Brand suggest several caveats. First, we do not know how Type A and Type B people actually respond to coronary disease. For example, one group may change their life style more completely than the other. Second, Type A men may be more likely to seek medical help for suspected heart disease. Finally, behavior patterns identified years before coronary disease is diagnosed may be meaningless; behavior patterns may have changed in the intervening years.

Still, the Ragland and Brand study points out that Type A and Type B behavior patterns have complex relationships with heart disease. The study also points out that we must be cautious in interpreting longitudinal data involving predictions over long periods.

---

est evidence for the reversal was reported by Ragland and Brand (1988), who examined 22-year follow-up data from the original Friedman and Rosenman study. Ragland and Brand (1988) also found lower morbidity following the first episode of serious cardiovascular disease in Type A people (see How Do We Know?).

Why do Type A people have a higher risk of first heart attack but a better chance of survival than Type B people? The answers are unclear. It may be that some of the characteristics of Type A

people that make them movers and shakers also motivate them overcome their disease. Indeed, researchers have noted that Type A people were much more likely to stick to diet and exercise regimens after heart attacks (Ragland & Brand, 1988) and have a more positive attitude about recovery (Ivancevich & Matteson, 1988). The laid-back approach of Type B people may actually work to their detriment during recovery.

Clearly, there is a need for caution in interpreting these findings. Type A and Type B patterns are just that — patterns. Only approximately 10% of the population is classified as a pure Type A or B. The rest of us fall somewhere in between. Additionally, the relationship between Type A behavior and cardiovascular functioning is obviously complex and varies between men and women of different ages (Harbin & Blumenthal, 1985). It is beginning to look as if it is the hostility and anger component of Type A behavior that is the risk factor, rather than the entire behavioral cluster (Ivancevich & Matteson, 1988). Moreover, virtually nothing is known about how the relationship between Type A and cardiovascular disease is affected by increasing age, if at all. These issues need to be more thoroughly researched before we can gain a firm understanding of the relationship between behavior and cardiovascular disease, and how this relationship varies with age.

Stress and Psychological Functioning

It is commonly believed that stress causes psychological problems. Despite years of research, though, there is little research support that even an accumulation of stressful life events causes depression, schizophrenia, or anxiety disorders. Dohrenwend (1979, p. 5) concluded that except for the death of a loved one or a very serious physical illness or injury, "it is difficult to find consistent evidence that other types of single life events can produce psychopathology in previously normal adults in societies free from war and other natural disasters." In order for stress to have a major influence on psychological functioning, Dohrenwend argues, three things must be present: (1) vulnerability from physical illness or injury, (2) undesirable life events, and (3) loss of social support. When all three factors occur simultaneously, psychopathology may result.

In contrast to the research on psychopathology, stress is related to other psychological processes. For example, Krause (1991) showed that certain kinds of stress, especially financial worries and fear of crime, promote social isolation in older adults. Moreover, chronic stressors of this sort foster a general distrust of other people, which in turn leads to additional isolation. This relationship is particularly strong in urban-dwelling older adults who are poor. Interestingly, Krause found that recent deaths were unrelated to distrust or to isolation. As we will see in Chapter 13, death often brings one's family and friends together.

Krause's research brings out an important point: Stressors fluctuate in importance across adulthood. For example, the pressures from work are typically more salient to younger and middle-aged adults than to older adults, but stressors due to chronic disease are often more important to older adults than to their younger counterparts. In other words, the life-cycle factors emphasized in the biopsychosocial model must be taken into account when considering what kinds of stress adults of different ages are experiencing.

Managing Stress

The treatment of stress has been approached in many different ways, based on the various definitions of stress. Thus, if stress is seen as coming from environmental stimuli, treatment involves modifying, escaping, or ignoring these stimuli. Unfortunately, this approach is often impossible; for example, it may be very difficult to quit a stressful job. Thus, most therapeutic efforts have focused on teaching people new ways to deal with the physical responses involved with stress or new ways to appraise the situation cognitively.

Managing the Response. Three methods have proven effective in dealing with the body's response to stress. Relaxation training is effective, particularly in controlling hypertension, insomnia, and tension headaches (Lavey & Taylor, 1985). Meditation or focusing attention so as not to dwell on negative thoughts is also effective. Shapiro (1985) concluded that meditation is as effective at reducing anxiety, phobias, and hypertension as relaxation training. Finally, biofeedback training also appears to be as effective as relaxation training at lowering muscle tension and skin temperature (Andrasik, Blanchard, & Edlund, 1985).

Changing the Appraisal. The best-researched cognitive approach to stress management is stress inoculation (Cameron & Meichenbaum, 1982; Meichenbaum, 1985; Meichenbaum & Cameron, 1983). The notion of stress inoculation is similar to vaccination against disease. The process first trains clients to identify the source of the problem (*conceptualization*); learn new and practice old coping skills (*skills-acquisition rehearsal*); and put these skills into practice (*application and follow-through*). Several problems have been successfully treated with stress inoculation (Hamberger & Lohr, 1984), including test anxiety, public speaking anxiety, and social anxiety (Jaremko, 1983).

Other Approaches. Some effective stress management techniques hardly require any work at all. One that millions of people have used for centuries (probably without knowing it) is pet ownership. Pets help lower their owners' stress and, at least for older adults, is associated with fewer visits to physicians (Siegel, 1990). Pet therapy is a rapidly growing approach used in nursing homes to help improve residents' morale and health (see Chapter 12). So the next time you take your dog for a walk or play with your cat, remember that you are doing it not just for them, but for your own health, too.

SMOKING

If everyone who smoked would stop today, that would do more to improve health than any other single step. In the United States alone roughly 320,000 deaths each year are related to smoking, and 10 million more people have smoking-related chronic diseases (U.S. DHHS, 1988). The American Cancer Society estimates that 75% of all cancers are due to either smoking or poor dietary habits.

These are sobering statistics. Although fewer older adults than younger or middle-aged adults smoke, the chronic diseases caused by smoking often are at their worst in old age. As we will see, this is because it usually takes years before the devastating effects become noticeable.

The rates of smoking vary not only with age but also with gender and ethnicity. Adult men tend to smoke more than adult women, although this difference is negligible in young adults. Among ethnic groups, Native Americans tend to smoke much less than whites, African Americans tend to smoke more, and Hispanics and Asian Americans smoke about the same as whites (U.S. DHHS, 1991). These differences in smoking rates result in different rates of smoking-related disease later in life; for example, lung cancer is relatively rare among elderly Native Americans.

The Hazards of Cigarette Smoking

The connection between cigarette smoking and cancer has been well documented since the 1960s. The United States Public Health Service notes that smokers have 10 times the incidence of lung cancer, 3 to 10 times the incidence of cancer of the mouth and tongue, 3 to 18 times the incidence of cancer of the larynx, and 7 to 10 times the incidence of bladder cancer as nonsmokers. Smoking plays a role in over half of all cancer deaths, and is directly responsible for 75% of all lung cancer; 9 out of every 10 people who develop lung cancer are dead within 5 years.

Cancer is not the only disease caused by smoking; as noted in Chapter 3, emphysema is primarily caused by smoking. The carbon monoxide and nicotine inhaled in cigarette smoke foster the development of atherosclerosis and angina (Wantz &

Gay, 1981). Men and women smokers have roughly twice the chance of dying of cardiovascular disease than nonsmokers (LaCroix et al., 1991). Women who smoke and take contraceptive pills for at least five years have an increased risk of heart attacks until menopause, even if they stop taking the pill (Layde, Ory, & Schlesselman, 1982). Smoking after the fourth month of pregnancy is linked with an increased risk of stillbirths, low birth weight, and perinatal death.

Clearly, smoking takes a frightening toll. But only among men has the prospect of lung cancer or other smoking-related disease significantly lowered smoking rates. The number of women smokers, especially among adolescents and young adults, is higher than ever. In fact, lung cancer has replaced breast cancer as the most common form of cancer among women. Among older women, lung cancer was the only major cause of death to show an increase during the 1980s, tripling in rate since the mid-1970s (U.S. DHHS, 1991).

The Hazards of Secondhand Smoke

The hazards of cigarette smoke do not stop with the smoker. Nonsmokers who breathe secondhand smoke are also at higher risk for smoking-related diseases, including chronic lung disease (U.S. DHHS, 1984), lung cancer (Pershagen, Hrubec, & Svensson, 1987; Sandler, Everson, & Wilcox, 1985), and heart disease (Garland, Barrett-Connor, Suarez, Criqui, & Wingard, 1985). Additionally, pregnant women who breathe secondhand smoke for as little as two hours a day at home or at work are more likely to give birth to infants who are of below average weight (Martin & Bracken, 1986). For these reasons many states and communities have passed stringent legislation severely restricting smoking in public areas, and smoking is not allowed at all on airplane flights within the United States.

Spouses of smokers appear to be especially vulnerable to the dangers of secondhand smoke. Nachtigall and Nachtigall (1990) report that wives of husbands who smoke are three times more likely to have heart attacks and other forms of cardiovascular disease. It is a sad legacy that smokers leave: Not only may they themselves die of a smoking-related disease but they may also kill their nonsmoking spouses.

Quitting Smoking

If you smoke and want to quit, how should you proceed? Many people successfully quit on their own, but others need formal programs. Whether a particular approach is effective depends on the individual; there is no one approach that works with everyone.

Most stop-smoking programs are multimodal, in that they combine a number of aspects from different therapeutic approaches. For example, Lando (1977) used several behavior modification techniques as well as booster sessions after therapy was over. Lando reported a 76% success rate, which is much higher than the typical 20% or 30% abstinence at 6- to 12-month follow-ups of other programs. It appears that the use of booster sessions is the key difference. Otherwise, the potential for relapse is quite high.

Because 70% to 80% of smokers who try to quit eventually relapse, Marlatt and Gordon (1980) investigated the relapse process itself. They concluded that for most people who have successfully quit smoking one cigarette is enough to create a full-blown relapse complete with feelings of utter failure. Marlatt and Gordon suggest that treatment programs take this into account and incorporate strategies to deal with these feelings caused by a slip.

Although some people may find formal programs helpful in their battle to stop smoking, as many as 95% of those who quit do so on their own, according to a survey by the United States Surgeon General's Office. Schachter (1982) speculates that people tend to go to clinics only after they have tried to quit on their own and failed. Thus, those who attend a clinic may not be a representative sample of smokers who try to quit; success rates at clinics of 20% to 30% may reflect success with the most difficult cases.

To date no one has convincingly demonstrated that one method of quitting smoking is more or less effective than another. It appears that what matter most are the person's commitment to quitting and being in an environment that fosters not smoking.

If you have successfully stopped smoking, you may wonder whether your health will ever return to normal. It takes considerable time, but eventually people who quit smoking return to a normal risk of disease. For example, within 10 to 15 years the risk of lung cancer has dropped to normal. Even in former smokers who did not quit until old age, the risk of death from cardiovascular disease returns to normal within a few years (LaCroix et al., 1991). The point is clear: If you don't smoke, don't start. If you do smoke, you're never too old to stop.

DRINKING ALCOHOL

The majority of Americans drink alcohol; roughly 10% abuse it (National Institute of Alcoholism and Alcohol Abuse [NIAAA], 1983). In fact, nearly half of all the alcohol consumed in the United States is drunk by only 10% of the drinkers. It is virtually impossible to escape being confronted with alcohol, either in person or through advertisements. For example, by the time you turned 18, you had already seen 100,000 television commercials for beer alone!

Clearly, alcohol presents a serious health problem when consumed in excess, especially over a long period. In this section we will examine some of the effects of alcohol and alcohol abuse and their relationship with age.

Alcoholism and Aging

Nearly 18 million Americans are heavy drinkers; roughly 11 million of them are alcoholics. Surveys conducted in the 1980s show that the incidence of problem drinking remains at a fairly constant rate of nearly 10% across adulthood (NIAAA, 1983; Post, 1987). Alcohol consumption tends to decrease with age, with drinking peaking between ages 30 and 44 and declining steadily thereafter (U.S. DHHS, 1988). Likewise, identification of individuals as alcoholics tends to peak by middle age. Two thirds of older alcoholics began drinking excessively earlier in life and persisted; only one third began abusing alcohol in old age (Scott & Mitchell, 1988).

Alcoholism is a form of **addiction**. That is, alcoholics demonstrate physical dependence on alcohol and withdrawal symptoms when they do not drink. Dependence occurs when a drug becomes so incorporated into the functioning of the body's cells that it becomes necessary for normal functioning. If the drug is discontinued, the body's withdrawal reaction is manifested in ways that are opposite to the effects of the drug. Since alcohol is a depressant, withdrawal symptoms include restlessness, irritability, and trembling. (Withdrawal from cocaine, in contrast, involves feeling tired and lethargic.) The disease of alcoholism results when the person becomes so dependent on the drug that it interferes with personal relationships, health, occupation, and social functioning.

Men are more likely than women to be diagnosed as alcoholics. However, the extent to which this reflects a true gender difference or a diagnostic bias is unclear. For example, many alcoholics are depressed, which has led some authors to speculate that women who are heavy drinkers are more likely to be labeled "depressed" rather than "alcoholic" (Kaplan, 1983). This diagnostic bias fits with the higher rate of women being labeled "depressed," discussed in Chapter 9.

For many years the problem of alcoholism and aging was ignored, perhaps because surveys indicated a drop in the average level of alcohol consumption beyond mid-life (NIAAA, 1983). However, a closer look at the data reveals that more recent cohorts drink more, possibly due to the current older generation's having been influenced by the Prohibition. This means that alcohol-related problems in older adults are likely to become more serious in future years as these heavier-drinking cohorts age (Wattis, 1983). In any case, professionals are taking a closer look at drinking and aging and are realizing that alcoholism is a serious problem for all age groups.

Negative Effects of Alcohol

Alcohol affects health directly and indirectly. The primary direct health problem for long-term heavy drinkers is liver damage (Eckhardt et al., 1981). Drinking more than five or six drinks per day causes fat to accumulate in the liver, which, over time, will restrict blood flow, kill liver cells, and cause a form of hepatitis. Continued heavy drinking results in cirrhosis, in which nonfunctional scar tissue accumulates. Cirrhosis is the leading cause of death in alcoholics.

A serious indirect result of long-term heavy drinking is **Wernicke-Korsakoff syndrome** (Eckhardt et al., 1981). Symptoms include severe loss of memory for recent events, severe disorientation, confusion, and visual problems. Wernicke-Korsakoff syndrome is actually caused by thiamine deficiency. Alcohol interferes with thiamine absorption (Thompson, 1978), and chronic alcoholics

typically do not obtain all of the nutrients that they need.

Heavy drinking has also been linked with heart disease, although the nature of the connection is unknown (Eckhardt et al., 1981). It appears that alcohol affects the constriction of the heart muscle, thereby lowering its efficiency.

Alcohol abuse has serious implications that specifically affect women. Heavy alcohol consumption reduces fertility (Greenwood, Love, & Pratt, 1983) and can cause menstrual periods to stop. Alcohol's negative effects on the pituitary and hypothalamus in the brain, and on thiamine absorption, appear to be the culprits. Drinking during pregnancy increases the risk of fetal alcohol syndrome. Babies born with fetal alcohol syndrome have facial abnormalities, growth deficiencies, central nervous system disorders, and mental retardation (Pratt, 1980, 1982).

Aging and the Negative Effects of Alcohol. The effect of alcohol on the brain and liver, and the level of blood alcohol following ingestion of a specific quantity of alcohol, appear to change with age (Scott & Mitchell, 1988). Older adults' cognitive functioning decreases more after a single drink than does that of younger adults (Jones & Jones, 1980). Early heavy drinking may result in premature aging of the brain (Ryan & Butters, 1980), but this evidence is highly controversial (Ryan, 1982; Scott & Mitchell, 1988).

Little research has been conducted on changes with age in the way in which the liver metabolizes alcohol. What is known suggests that the effects depend on the amount of alcohol consumed. Small amounts of alcohol in older adults slow the process by which other drugs may be cleared from the system; in contrast, high quantities of alcohol speed up this process (Scott & Mitchell, 1988). Another important difference between young and old drinkers concerns the level of alcohol in the blood. If the two groups are given equal doses of alcohol, older adults will have a higher blood-alcohol concentration (Scott & Mitchell, 1988). This age difference has important implications, since blood-alcohol levels provide an index of relative functional impairment; for example, an older adult does not have to drink as much alcohol as a younger adult to be declared legally intoxicated.

Benefits of Alcohol

Not all the effects of alcohol reported in the literature are negative. Results from several longitudinal studies have also demonstrated some positive health effects from light drinking (*no more than* the equivalent of two glasses of beer per day). Findings from the Kaiser-Permanente study (Klatsky, Friedman, & Siegelaub, 1981), the Alameda County study (Berkman, Breslow, & Wingard, 1983), the Framingham study (L. A. Friedman & Kimball, 1986; Gordon & Kannel, 1984), and the Albany study (Gordon & Doyle, 1987) documented lower mortality rates among light drinkers. Additionally, light drinkers may have a much lower risk of stroke than abstainers or heavy drinkers even after controlling for hypertension, cigarette smoking, and medication (Gill, Zezulka, Shipley, Gill, & Beevers, 1986).

Overall, the results reveal a U-shaped relationship between the amount of alcohol consumed and the mortality rate, with light drinkers having a lower death rate than either abstainers or heavy drinkers. The relationship seems to be stronger for men than it is for women, especially for men under 60.

Why does light drinking appear to have benefits? No one knows for sure. Apparently, the findings are unrelated to variables like group differences in personality such as impatience and aggressiveness (Kaufman, Rosenberg, Helmrich, & Shapiro, 1985); protection against the effects of fat deposits (Haskell et al., 1984), or poor research designs (Myers, 1983).

These benefits of drinking must be interpreted carefully. Light drinking *does not* mean getting drunk. Drinking to the point of intoxication, even on a very occasional basis, is potentially dangerous.

Quitting Drinking

Several approaches have been used to help problem drinkers achieve abstinence. The most widely known of these is Alcoholics Anonymous (AA). Founded in 1935 by two former alcoholics, AA follows a strict disease model of alcoholism. The program itself promotes personal and spiritual growth, with the goal being total abstinence. AA is based on the notion that problem drinkers are addicted to alcohol and have no power to resist it. Moreover, abstaining alcoholics are in the process of recovering for the rest of their lives.

Even though AA has a long history, very little research has been done to document its effectiveness (Peele, 1984), primarily because AA is an anonymous fellowship, making it difficult to follow people over time. The little research that has been done suggests that AA, while helping many different kinds of people, may be especially effective for people with lower educational levels or higher needs for authoritarianism, dependency, and sociability (Miller & Hester, 1980).

Psychotherapy is widely used in a variety of treatment settings, including Veterans Administration hospitals, care units in other hospitals, private treatment centers, and private counseling. These approaches include psychoanalysis (Blum, 1966), behavior modification (Wallace, 1985), psychodrama (Blume, 1985), assertiveness training (Materi, 1977), and group therapy (Zimberg, 1985). For any of these approaches to be effective, the primary goal should be sobriety (Zimberg, 1985). Moreover, long-term sobriety may require combining psychotherapy with other programs such as AA. No research has been done specifically examining success rates in these various programs as a function of age. In general, however, it appears that long-term sobriety of at least 3 years is achieved by no more than 30% of individuals seeking treatment (Armor, Polich, & Stambul, 1976; Wiens & Menustik, 1983). These data clearly indicate that the relapse potential for recovering alcoholics is very high.

EXERCISE

As far back as Hippocrates, physicians and researchers have known that exercise significantly retards the aging process. Recent evidence suggests that we can slow the process down by a decade or more (Thomas & Rutledge, 1986). Bortz (1982) and deVries (1983) report that the normative changes resulting from aging described in Chapter 3 resemble those seen in people of any age during a prolonged period of bed rest. For example, confining young, healthy men to bed for 3 weeks will decrease cardiac output by 25% and maximum breathing capacity and oxygen consumption by nearly one third (Bortz, 1982).

Types of Exercise

Exercise can be grouped into two categories (Thomas & Rutledge, 1986): aerobic and nonaerobic. **Aerobic exercise** places a moderate stress on the heart that is achieved by maintaining a pulse rate between 60% and 90% of the maximum. Maximum heart rate can be estimated by subtracting your age from 220. Thus, if you are 40 years old, the target range would be 108 to 162 beats per minute. The minimum time necessary to benefit from aerobic exercise depends on the intensity with which it is performed. For heart rates near the low end of the range, sessions should last roughly 60 minutes, whereas for high heart rates, 15 minutes may suffice. Examples of aerobic exercise include jogging at a moderate to fast pace, rapid walking, "jazzercise," swimming, and bicycling.

Nonaerobic exercise occurs when the heart rate does not exceed 60% of maximum for sustained periods. Nonaerobic exercise does not have the positive health benefits of aerobic exercise, as discussed next. Examples of nonaerobic exercise are stretching, some forms of weightlifting, and range-of-motion exercises.

Aerobic Exercise and Aging

What happens to you when you exercise (besides becoming tired and sweaty)? Physiologically, adults of all ages show improved cardiovascular functioning and maximum oxygen consumption, lower blood pressure, better muscle strength and endurance, increased joint flexibility, and better neuromuscular coordination (Smith & Serfass, 1981). Psychologically, people who exercise regularly claim to have lower levels of stress (Blumenthal et al., 1988), better moods (Simons, McGowan, Epstein, Kupfer, & Robertson, 1985), and better cognitive functioning. These effects are found even with low-impact aerobics (Hopkins, Murrah, Hoeger, & Rhodes, 1990). Interestingly, the general effects of exercise appear to be fairly consistent across age; older adults benefit from exercise and show patterns of improvement similar to those of younger and middle-aged adults. For example, the rate of heart disease is slowed in physically fit people even into the 80s (Posner et al., 1990).

The lack of significant age-related differences in the pattern of benefits from aerobic exercise is important. Recall from Chapter 3 that there are normative age changes in the cardiovascular, respiratory, skeletal, and muscular systems that reduce the efficiency with which they work. Available evidence supports the idea that aerobic exercise tends to slow these changes (see Smith & Serfass, 1981). In physiological terms, then, an elderly individual who exercises regularly could be in better condition than a younger adult who is sedentary.

The optimal way to accrue the benefits of exercise, of course, is to maintain physical fitness across the life span. In planning an exercise program, however, three points must be remembered. First, one should always check with a physician before beginning a program of aerobic exercise. Second, moderation is extremely important; more is not better. Paffenbarger, Hyde, Wing, and Hsieh (1986) made this point clear in their study of 16,936 middle-aged and elderly male Harvard graduates. They found that men who exercised moderately (walked 9 miles per week) had a 21% lower risk of mortality, while men who exercised strenuously (cycled for 6 to 8 hours per week) had a 50% lower mortality risk. However, men who engaged in extremely high levels of exercise (burning more than 3,500 calories per week) had a higher mortality rate than the other two groups. Third, the reasons why people exercise change across adulthood. Younger adults tend to exercise out of a concern for physical appearance, whereas older adults are more concerned with physical and psychological health (Trujillo, Walsh, & Brougham, 1991). This indicates that exercise programs may need to be marketed differently for adults of different ages.

Despite the many benefits of fitness and the increasing popularity of health spas, many adults simply do not exercise. For older adults, at least, the reason seems to be that they do not think they need to (U.S. DHHS, 1988). Women become less active earlier than men, and people with lower education become inactive sooner than college graduates (Ostrow, 1980). The consequences of inactivity, however, can lead to premature death. Blair and his colleagues (1989) documented that physically fit men and women live longer. They estimate that if everyone became fit, death rates could be reduced by 15% in women and 9% in men. There are role models for physical fitness, even for the elderly.

Older adults who engage in aerobic exercise are physiologically superior to many younger adults who are sedentary.

Wiswell (1980) notes that the late King Gustav of Sweden still played tennis regularly at 80 and that older Olympic champions functioned better than 25-year-olds who had sedentary jobs.

Finally, getting people to exercise aerobically is not always easy. Emery and Gatz (1990) reported problems in getting older adults to comply with exercise routines. They point out that exercise programs will need to take individual differences in interest and ability into account to be successful.

Indeed, social barriers and fears about the risks of exercising (for instance, falling down) keep many older women from participating in exercise programs (O'Brien & Vertinsky, 1991). Perhaps the best solution would be to educate older adults about the various types of exercise, and to make several programs available to allow older adults to choose the one that is best for them.

SLEEP AND AGING

How did you sleep last night? If you are elderly, chances are that you had some trouble. In fact, sleep complaints are quite common in older adults (Bootzin & Engle-Friedman, 1987). These complaints most often concern difficulty in falling asleep, frequent or prolonged awakenings during the night, early-morning awakenings, and just feeling like you didn't sleep very well. Effects of poor sleep are experienced the next day; moodiness, poorer performance on tasks involving sustained concentration, fatigue, and lack of motivation are some of the telltale signs. In this section we will consider the extent of sleep-related problems across adulthood and examine some of the reasons for them.

How Widespread Are Sleep Disturbances?

Results from national surveys and drug-use studies confirm that sleep disturbances increase with age. Mellinger, Balter, and Uhlenhuth (1985) reported that 45% of people between the ages of 65 and 79 had insomnia during the previous year. As we will see, many aspects of sleep decline with age. Interestingly, total sleep time over a 24-hour period does not change across adulthood (Webb & Swinburne,

1971), despite a significant drop with age in total sleep at night (Hauri, 1982). As you may have guessed, nap taking significantly increases with age (Zepelin, 1973).

Age-Related Changes in Sleep

The most consistent age-related difference in sleep is an increase in the frequency of awakenings as morning approaches (for example, Webb, 1982). Once awake, older adults have more difficulty getting back to sleep than younger adults. Webb and Campbell (1980) found that 50- to 60-year-olds took longer to fall back asleep after being awakened during the first 80 minutes of sleep than did 21- to 23-year-olds. Older adults also have more trouble falling asleep in the first place. Webb (1982) documented that it took women aged 50 to 60 twice as long to fall asleep initially as women aged 20 to 30.

Slight differences in REM (rapid eye movement) sleep have been noted between younger and older adults (Reynolds et al., 1985). Rather than increasing in duration over the course of the night as they do in younger adults, REM periods in older adults remain constant or decrease in length.

We have all experienced the negative effects of all-nighters on next-day mood and performance. We tend to lose our temper more quickly, tire more easily, and have more problems paying attention. These negative effects increase with age. For example, Webb and Levy (1982) found that middle-aged adults (40 to 49 years old) showed significantly poorer performance on auditory vigilance, addition, and mood scales after 2 nights of sleep deprivation.

Although the data clearly show differences in sleep with age, these differences do not always result in complaints of sleep disturbance (Bootzin & Engle-Friedman, 1987). Differences in REM sleep, for example, may go unnoticed, whereas increased awakenings during the night will be reported.

Sleep disturbances can result from both prescription and over-the-counter medications. Adverse reactions from drugs must be guarded against to help eliminate sleep disruptions.

Thus, we need to be sensitive to the different levels of awareness that adults have of underlying changes in sleep.

Causes of Sleep Disturbance

Sleep is affected by numerous factors (Bootzin & Engle-Friedman, 1987): physical disorders, medication, alcohol, caffeine and nicotine, stress, and sleep habits and naps.

Physical Disorders. The most common physical disorders that affect sleep are sleep-related respiratory problems (Bootzin & Engle-Friedman, 1987).

Among these are sleep apnea (a cessation of air flow for 10 seconds or longer occurring at least 5 times per night) and hypopnea (a 50% or greater reduction of air flow for 10 seconds or longer). Sleep apnea is the more common disorder, and it increases with age (Coleman et al., 1981).

Physical illnesses can also disrupt sleep because of discomfort or pain. Pain associated with arthritis is one of the most frequent causes of sleep disturbance in the elderly (Prinz & Raskind, 1978).

Medication. Both prescription and over-the-counter medications can disrupt sleep regardless of age (Karacen & Williams, 1983). For example, asthma medication may contain epinephrine, which may interfere with sleep if taken at night. Tricyclic antidepressants (discussed in Chapter 9) suppress REM sleep and can cause involuntary leg twitches. Several medications used to treat seizures, Parkinson's disease, and hypertension can increase nighttime awakenings.

Serious drug-induced sleep disturbances can be caused by sleeping pills and tranquilizers. Sleeping pills have two dangers. First, they lose their effectiveness within two weeks of continued use (Kales, Allen, Scharf, & Kales, 1970). Second, tolerance to them develops rapidly, so larger and larger doses are needed to produce an effect.

Sleeping pills and tranquilizers have several similar negative influences on sleep (Kales, Scharf, & Kales, 1978). They lower the amount of deep sleep and increase light sleep, decrease REM sleep on the night they are taken, and produce large REM rebound on subsequent nights. REM rebound is characterized by restless dreaming, nightmares, and fragmented sleep. Finally, they produce drug hangover effects and impaired motor and intellectual functioning as well as moodiness the next day. The carryover effects are probably due to the fact that many of these drugs remain in the bloodstream for days, resulting in the possibility that side effects could be observed for a relatively long period after the person has stopped taking the drug (Bootzin & Engle-Friedman, 1987).

Alcohol. The effects of alcohol on sleep are similar to those produced by sleeping pills and tranquilizers. In general, alcohol reduces REM sleep, and habitual heavy drinking produces fragmented sleep and several awakenings. Because alcohol is a depressant, it magnifies the effects of sleeping pills and tranquilizers, increasing the likelihood of fatal overdoses when they are combined.

Caffeine and Nicotine. You probably know that drinking a cup of regular coffee before bedtime is not usually a good idea if you want to go to sleep.

Smoking may have the same effect. The caffeine in the coffee and the nicotine in the cigarette produce insomnia or lighter and more fragmented sleep (Soldatos, Kales, Scharf, Bixler, & Kales, 1980). Reducing or eliminating excessive caffeine and nicotine can result in considerable improvement in sleep.

Stress. Stress is hazardous to your sleep. Even for people with no history of insomnia, worrying about exams, presentations, one's children, or one's spouse can cause sleep disturbances (Healey et al., 1981).

Sleep Habits and Naps. What do you do in your bedroom besides sleep? Do you read, talk on the telephone, watch television, snack, listen to music, or — worst of all — worry? All of these behaviors can be incompatible with falling asleep and are very common in insomniacs (Bootzin, 1977). The bed no longer is a cue for you to fall asleep; rather it becomes associated with arousal. The situation may become so bad that many insomniacs can seemingly sleep anywhere except in their own bed. In contrast, normal sleepers often have problems falling asleep anywhere other than their own bed (Bootzin & Engle-Friedman, 1987). The solution to the problem is relatively easy. At the first sign of insomnia get out of bed and go somewhere else. By maintaining the bed as a cue to go to sleep, many insomniacs quickly overcome their problem (Bootzin, 1977).

Another bad sleep habit is afternoon or evening naps (Webb, 1975). Such naps contain more deep sleep and less REM sleep. The night's sleep following one of these naps continues as if the nap were part of the night's sleep. That is, the entire night's sleep looks similar to the latter half of a normal night's sleep, containing more light and REM sleep and more awakenings (Webb, 1975). In contrast, morning naps have little effect on the subsequent night's sleep.

Taking naps whenever one feels tired has another, more serious effect. Adopting this strategy may cause disturbances in your *circadian rhythm*, or sleep-wake cycle. If such disturbances develop, an optimal sleeping time may never exist (Hauri, 1982), leading to chronic moodiness and fatigue. Disruptions of circadian rhythm are particularly common in hospital patients and the institutionalized elderly (Wessler, Rubin, & Sollberger, 1976). Additionally, excessive daytime sleepiness in the elderly may be indicative of an underlying disease and should be evaluated (Morewitz, 1988).

Treatment of Sleep Disorders

When most people have trouble sleeping, the first treatment they think of is medication. As we have seen, however, sleeping pills have little long-term effectiveness and several potentially serious side effects. Consequently, treatments other than medication have been the focus of considerable work (see Bootzin & Engle-Friedman, 1987; Borkovec, 1982). Two techniques that work well are stimulus-control instructions and progressive relaxation.

Stimulus-Control Instructions. The goals of stimulus-control instructions are to help the insomniac acquire consistent sleeping rhythms, to ensure that the bed is a cue for sleeping, and to dissociate the bed from other competing activities (Bootzin, Engle-Friedman, & Hazelwood, 1983). A typical set of instructions is shown in Table 4.1. Notice that these instructions get the person to only use the bed for sleeping (an exception is made for sex), and do not allow the person to lie in bed if he or she does not fall right to sleep. In short, stimulus-control instructions seek to instill good sleeping habits.

Instructions for controlling stimuli are the most effective treatment for insomniacs of various ages

TABLE 4.1 Typical stimulus-control instructions

1. Lie down intending to go to sleep only when you are sleepy.

2. Do not use your bed for anything except sleep; that is, do not read, watch television, worry, or eat in bed. Sexual activity is the only exception to this rule.

3. If you find yourself unable to fall asleep, get up and go into another room. Stay up as long as you wish, and then return to the bedroom to sleep. Although you should not watch the clock, get out of bed immediately if you still cannot fall asleep. The goal is to associate the bed with falling asleep *quickly*. If you are in bed more than 10 minutes without falling asleep and have not gotten up, you are not following instructions.

4. If you still cannot fall asleep, repeat Step 3. Do this as often as necessary throughout the night.

5. Set your alarm and get up at the same time every morning irrespective of how much sleep you got during the night. This will help your body acquire a constant sleep rhythm.

6. Do not nap during the day.

(Source: "Sleep Disturbances" (pp. 238–251) by R. R. Bootzin and M. Engle-Friedman, 1987, in L. L. Carstensen and B. A. Edelstein (Eds.), *Handbook of Clinical Gerontology*. New York: Pergamon Press. Reprinted with permission.)

(Bootzin, 1977; Borkovec, 1982; Lacks, Bertelson, Gans, & Kunkel, 1983; Puder, Lacks, Bertelson, & Storandt, 1983; Turner & Ascher, 1982). Simply restricting time in bed (a cornerstone of this approach) may do more to improve sleep habits in older adults than any other technique (Friedman, Bliwise, Yesavage, & Salom, 1991). Combining this approach with support and sleep-hygiene information appears to be even more effective (Bootzin et al., 1983).

Progressive Relaxation. Progressive relaxation includes several types of techniques, such as transcendental meditation, yoga, hypnosis, and biofeedback as well as traditional relaxation methods. The goal of all these approaches when used to treat sleep disturbances is to get people to relax at bedtime so that they will fall asleep faster. One widely used version of progressive relaxation involves the successive tightening and relaxing of the various muscle groups in the body. Since its development in the 1930s by Jacobson (1938), progressive relaxation has been the most widely prescribed and researched nonmedical therapy for sleep disturbances. There is now considerable evidence that it is effective in significantly shortening the time needed to get to sleep (Borkovec, 1982).

NUTRITION

How many times did your parents tell you to eat your vegetables? Or that you are what you eat? Most of us had many disagreements with our parents about food as we were growing up. As adults, we realize that diet is important to good health. Experts agree that nutritional status directly affects one's mental, emotional, and physical functioning (Guigoz & Munro, 1985; Steen, 1987). With increasing age this relationship becomes even more important, as health is determined in part by the cumulative effects of dietary habits over the years.

It is commonly believed that older adults as a group have poorer dietary habits than younger or middle-aged people and need to use vitamin and mineral supplements. This belief appears to be unfounded, at least until very old age (Lundgren, Steen, & Isaksson, 1987). This is not to say, of course, that older adults do not have nutritional problems. For example, the institutionalized el-

derly often suffer various nutritional deficiencies, such as thiamine, vitamin B12, and folic acid (Baker, Frank, Thind, Jaslow, & Louria, 1979). Economic factors often deny the aged poor adequate diets. Loss of one's partner, which causes one to eat alone, removes the important social component of sharing meals. Obtaining adequate nutrition is one of the most basic requirements for a health maintenance program; the poorer nutrition of many needy older people clearly contributes to their overall higher rate of chronic disease.

Establishing Dietary Requirements

Nutritional requirements, food and drink preferences, and eating habits change across the life span. You have probably noticed that adolescents and young adults seemingly require huge quantities of junk food, whereas middle-aged adults require more meats and vegetables. Seriously, though, there are important developmental differences in some dietary requirements.

Several age-related changes in the body affect nutrition. Body metabolism and the digestive process slow down. Age-related changes in vision may hinder older adults' ability to read food labels, recipes, stove settings, or menus. Changes in smell diminish the potential enjoyment of food. Poor teeth may interfere with the ability to chew, thereby limiting the foods a person can eat. Nearly half of all older adults take medications that can adversely affect appetite or how the body extracts nutrients from food. All of these factors need to be considered when planning meals and making recommendations for older adults.

We will consider several major requirements briefly. At this point it is important to note that eating a good diet in order to maintain good health is a lifelong duty. A diet that provides adequate vitamins, minerals, protein, and complex carbohydrates needs to be maintained throughout life.

Such a diet should be rich in fresh vegetables, fresh fruits, low-fat dairy products, legumes, and whole grains.

Proteins. Practically speaking, the protein needs of older adults are no different from those of younger adults (Steen, 1987). However, there is some evidence that protein metabolism in very old adults may be less efficient; if this is true, these individuals need more dietary protein (Munro & Young, 1978). People suffering from disease have greater protein needs at all ages (Isaksson, 1973).

Carbohydrates. Carbohydrates provide the energy that is necessary for maintaining metabolic, physical, and mental activity. Although energy needs decrease across adulthood, the recommended sources of carbohydrates remain the same, namely, whole grains, fruits, vegetables, and naturally occurring sugars. It should be noted that the refining processes for white flour and table sugar decrease the amount of B vitamins (only three of which are restored by enriched flour), vitamin E, and trace minerals.

Vitamins and Minerals. Old and young alike have the same needs for vitamins and minerals. Herbert (1988) reports that older adults do not need to adjust their vitamin intake and do not need vitamin supplements if they eat a well-balanced diet. Fads such as megavitamins should be avoided; the best advice is to get nutrition from food, not pills.

Diet and Health

Does what you eat affect how well you feel? Yes. Considerable evidence shows beyond doubt that dietary habits strongly influence physical health. Links have been established between serum cholesterol and cardiovascular disease and between various aspects of diet and cancer.

Diet and Cardiovascular Disease. The American Heart Association is quite clear in its recommendations concerning the amount of fat in our diet: Foods that are high in saturated fats—such as whole milk, butter, and processed foods containing coconut or palm oil—should be replaced with low-fat milk, margarine, and unsaturated fats from vegetable oils. Eggs and red meat should be limited and replaced by fish, white-meat poultry (without the skin), and legumes. Egg substitutes should be used whenever possible. Additionally, the association recommends limiting sodium intake; high levels of sodium have been linked to hypertension.

The main goal of these recommendations is to lower the level of serum cholesterol. You have probably heard that high cholesterol level is one risk factor for cardiovascular disease. While this is true, it is important to distinguish between two major types of cholesterol: **low density lipoproteins (LDL)** and **high density lipoproteins (HDL)**. Low density lipoproteins are thought to cause atherosclerosis (see Chapter 3). For this reason, LDL is sometimes referred to as bad cholesterol in the popular literature. High density lipoproteins are believed to actually help keep arteries clear and may even help break down LDL. Consequently, HDL is sometimes referred to as good cholesterol.

It is the ratio of LDL to HDL that is important in cholesterol screening. Relatively high levels of HDL are good; relatively high levels of LDL are bad. LDL levels have been linked to eating diets high in saturated fats; reducing these substances through diet modification is the easiest way to lower LDL levels. HDL levels can be raised through exercise, a diet high in fiber, and by modest amounts of alcohol intake (such as, one glass of beer per day). Finally, weight control is an important aspect in any overall diet plan.

Modifying one's diet to reduce LDL levels is effective in adults of all ages. For example, Löwik et al. (1991) found that older adults benefited just as much as younger adults from diet modification and weight reduction or control.

Diet and Cancer. The American Cancer Society has also issued extensive guidelines concerning diet. These recommendations include eating less fat and fewer salt-cured, smoked, and nitrite-cured foods; drinking less alcohol; and eating more fresh vegetables. The society points out that obesity greatly increases the risk of cancer. Excessive fat intake alone increases the chance of breast, colon, and prostate cancer. A high intake of commercially smoked meats (which contain nitrites and nitrates) is linked with stomach and esophageal cancer. Diets containing adequate levels of vitamin A may lower the risk of cancer of the larynx, esophagus, and lung. Similarly, high-fiber diets may reduce the risk of stomach and colon cancer.

Diet and Osteoporosis. As noted in Chapter 3, some researchers believe that diet can be used to prevent osteoporosis if it is begun in young adulthood. Because one of the causes of osteoporosis is a deficiency in calcium, diets should include foods that are high in calcium — for example, yogurt, broccoli, collards, turnip greens, salmon, sardines, oysters, and tofu. Interestingly, although protein is a daily requirement, too much protein can lead to loss of calcium through the urine.

In short, it is a good idea to become more aware of the things we eat and what effects they have. Eating should be both enjoyable and healthy.

CANCER

Cancer is the second leading cause of death in the United States, behind cardiovascular disease. Every year nearly 950,000 people are diagnosed as having cancer, and approximately 475,000 die. Over the life span, nearly one in every three Americans will develop cancer (U.S. DHHS, 1991). This ratio is likely to increase over the next few decades. Some researchers argue that as the rates of cardiovascular disease decline, cancer will become the leading cause of death in the United States (Manton, Wrigley, Cohen, & Woodbury, 1991). There is already mounting evidence that cancer is present in many individuals whose cause of death is officially listed as due to some other cause such as pneumonia (Manton et al., 1991).

One truly unfortunate aspect of these statistics is that many current deaths due to cancer are preventable. Some forms of cancer, such as lung and colo-rectal cancer, are caused in large part by unhealthy life styles. Others, including breast and prostate cancer, have high probabilities for cure if they are detected early. In this section we will consider some of the issues pertaining to cancer and age.

Cancer Risk and Age

The risk of getting cancer increases markedly with age (Young, Percy, & Asire, 1981). Figure 4.3 depicts the incidence rates for all forms of cancer as a function of age. As can be seen, the largest number of cases occurs in the age group 60–70. Notice that after age 40 the incidence rate increases sharply. For example, the incidence of cancer at age 50 is only about 400 cases per 100,000 people; by age 70, however, it has increased nearly 4-fold to over 1,500 cases. Overall, half of all cancer occurs in individuals over age 65.

Estimates of the annual age-specific incidence rates of the most frequent types of cancer in older adults show that rates are generally higher in men. Cancer of the lung, colon, rectum, pancreas, bladder, and stomach occur more often in men in all age groups. Overall, lung, colon, prostate (in men), and breast (in women) cancers are the most common.

It is not entirely known why the incidence of cancer is much higher in the elderly. Part of the

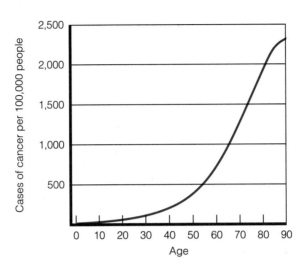

FIGURE 4.3 Age-related incidence of cancer

(Source: National Cancer Institute.)

reason is poor health habits over a long period of time, such as cigarette smoking and poor diets. In addition, the cumulative effects of exposure to pollutants and cancer-causing chemicals are partly to blame. As noted in Chapter 3, some researchers believe that normative age-related changes in the immune system, resulting in a decreased ability to inhibit the growth of tumors, may also be responsible.

However, research in microbiology is increasingly pointing to some genetic links (Ershler, 1991). For example, in colon cancer there appears to be a complicated series of five to seven specific genetic events that come into play. These changes, which occur over time, eventually produce a cancerous tumor. Age-related tissue changes have also been linked with the development of tumors, some of which become cancerous; some of these may be genetically linked as well. What remains to be seen is how these genetic events interact with environmental factors. Understanding this interaction process, predicted by the biopsychosocial model,

could explain why there are considerable individual differences across people in when and how cancer develops.

Screening and Prevention

The most effective way to address the problem of cancer is through increased use of screening techniques and changing life styles as a preventive measure. The American Cancer Society strongly recommends these steps for people of all ages, but older adults need to be especially aware of what to do. Table 4.2 contains guidelines for the early detection of some common forms of cancer.

One problem in cancer screening and prevention in the elderly is a reluctance on the part of some physicians to tackle the problem aggressively (List, 1987, 1988; Samet, Hunt, & Key, 1986). Whether this failure stems from the myth that older patients have substantially lower survival rates (actually, the survival rates are similar) or from some

TABLE 4.2   Suggested screening steps for cancer

Test	Sex	Age	Frequency
Health counseling and cancer checkup	M&F	>20 >40	Every 3 years Every year
Breast self-examination	F	>20	Once a month
Physical examination		20–40 >40	Every 3 years Once a year
Mammography		35–40 40–50 >50	Baseline Every 1–2 years Once a year
Pelvic examination	F	20–40 >40	Every 3 years Once a year
Pap test	F	At onset of sexual activity to age 65	Yearly for 2 exams, then every 3 years
Endometrial biopsy	F	At menopause in women at high risk	
Prostate check	M	>40	Once a year
Rectal examination	M&F	>40	Once a year
Stool guaiac test	M&F	>40	Once a year

(Source: Summarized from recommendations of the American Cancer Society, 1980.)

other set of reasons is unclear. For their part, many older adults are reluctant to request the necessary tests (List, 1988). In any event, regular cancer screening should be part of all older adults' program of health promotion and disease prevention.

HEALTH PROMOTION AND AGING

Throughout this chapter, we have seen that people have considerable potential for influencing the quality of their lives. Many of the key influences on longevity, and perhaps even the timing of some genetic influences, are under our control. The realization that how we conduct our lives matters is recognized most clearly in the field of health promotion. **Health promotion** reflects a shift from the traditional biomedical view of health toward the broader biopsychosocial view that includes individual life style, behavior, and the social and physical environment (Estes, Fox, & Mahoney, 1986). The World Health Organization recognizes that health promotion activities could have a profound effect on adults' health and could be accomplished for considerably less money than is currently spent on the practice of waiting for disease to occur and then instituting treatment (Kane, Evans, & Macfadyen, 1990). For example, of the 10 leading causes of death in the United States, at least 7 could be sub-

SOMETHING TO THINK ABOUT

Public Policy, Health Promotion, and Aging

Healthy life styles pay off. But many elderly people do not engage in behaviors that promote health and prevent disease for the simple reason that they cannot afford to. Many older adults rely on Medicare and Medicaid as their sole sources of health insurance. Both of these programs were begun in the mid-1960s when equal access to care was a major social concern. Both programs adhere tightly to the traditional biomedical model of disease; that is, illness and disease are covered, but health promotion is not. For example, treatment for pneumonia in the hospital or for a broken hip in a nursing home is usually covered. Going for a yearly physical examination that may prevent pneumonia is not.

This situation has led to cries for reform by researchers and practitioners alike. Among the recommendations for a new health care policy are these:

1. Health promotion policy must address not only physical needs but socioeconomic needs for adequate food, clothing, and housing as well. Changing life styles will have little effect if people have inadequate resources.

2. Health promotion should be targeted at all adults, so that all may have the potential for a happy and healthy old age.

3. Medical insurance reimbursement must begin to reward the promotion of health, not just the treatment of disease. Moreover, we must provide incentives to stay healthy.

4. Community health services must begin to work in cooperation rather than in competition

with one another. This cooperative network would include a broad spectrum of services, from walk-in clinics to hospitals to nursing homes.

5. Public policy and private policy must work together. Corporate health care plans must take advantage of community resources, and public policy must incorporate ideas from the business world.

6. We must emphasize the need for training professionals in promoting health.

All these goals are important, but to meet them we need to overcome a large hurdle: Instilling the value of health promotion requires that we change the current concept of waiting until one is ill to seek a physician. How can we change this attitude? It's something to think about.

---

stantially reduced if people changed just 5 habits: diet, smoking, lack of exercise, alcohol abuse, and living a stressful life style. However, as pointed out in Something to Think About, health promotion for the elderly will entail some fundamental shifts in our current thinking.

Despite the clear connections between life-style factors and health that gave rise to this movement, surprisingly little emphasis has been placed on health promotion in older adults. Minkler and Pasick (1986) note that the elderly are often ex-

cluded from health promotion programs for four reasons: (1) the focus of such programs is on extending life, and the elderly are not perceived as having a future; (2) the goal is usually preventing premature death, and the elderly are considered to be beyond that point; (3) the programs often promote looking youthful and preventing signs of aging; and (4) their focus is on avoidance of chronic disease, which is irrelevant for older adults since approximately 85% of them already have one chronic disease.

The view that health promotion comes too late for people over 65 is changing. It is now recognized that people of all ages benefit from changes in life style. We have noted several instances in this chapter; for example, recall that older adults benefit from stopping smoking as much as younger adults. The five habits listed above that have the greatest impact on health can be changed at any time in the life span, with positive outcomes accruing at all ages.

Taking control of aspects of our lives wherever possible does not only lead to better health. As we will see in Chapter 13, having a positive sense of control can in some cases literally keep us alive.

Psychologists and health care professionals will be challenged in the coming years with correcting misconceptions about health and age, and with emphasizing that the relationship between life style and health is true for people of all ages. The goal should be promoting healthy life styles for all adults.

SUMMARY

How Long Will We Live?

1. Average longevity increased dramatically in the first half of the 20th century, but maximum longevity remains at about 120 years.

2. Having long- or short-lived parents is a good predictor of your own longevity (not counting accidents, of course).

3. Living in a polluted environment can dramatically shorten longevity.

4. Different ethnic groups in the United States have different average longevity. However, these differences are primarily due to differences in nutrition, health care, stress, and financial status.

5. Women tend to live longer than men, partly because males are more susceptible to disease and environmental influences.

Stress and Health

6. According to Selye, the body's reaction to stress goes through three stages: alarm (mobilization of defenses), resistance (adapting to stressor), and exhaustion (breakdown of body).

7. According to Lazarus, stress results from a perception of an event as taxing or exceeding one's resources and as endangering one's well-being. Primary and secondary appraisal involve making a decision about whether an event is stressful. Coping entails trying to do something about the stressful event.

8. The kinds of events that are stressful and the types of coping strategies people use differ with age.

9. Stress lowers the immune system's ability to fight infection.

10. Stress is believed to have a causal role in some types of headaches, ulcers, and cardiovascular disease.

11. Type A behavior pattern is associated with higher risk of first heart attack but with lower risk of subsequent heart attacks than Type B behavior pattern.

12. Although stress is not directly related to psychopathology, it is related to certain behaviors such as social isolation.

13. Several approaches to stress management are effective, including relaxation, biofeedback, stress inoculation, and pet ownership.

Smoking

14. Smoking cigarettes causes several health problems: cancer, emphysema, cardiovascular disease, and low birth weight babies.

15. Breathing secondhand smoke can cause the same diseases as smoking.

16. Most people who want to quit smoking make several attempts before they are successful. No one formal program is superior; most people quit on their own.

Drinking Alcohol

17. Alcohol consumption peaks in middle age, but the incidence of problem drinking remains constant across adulthood. Gender bias is present in diagnosing alcoholism.

18. Most alcoholics die of cirrhosis, a liver disease.

19. Wernicke-Korsakoff syndrome is caused by a vitamin deficiency, and is often found in older, chronic alcoholics. The syndrome is a severe brain disorder affecting memory and awareness.

20. Older adults are more affected than younger adults by the same amount of alcohol.

21. Moderate drinking is associated with longer average longevity than abstinence or heavy drinking.

22. Several methods are available to help people stop drinking: Alcoholics Anonymous (AA), psychotherapy, and treatment centers.

Exercise

23. Aerobic exercise maintains a pulse rate between 60% and 90% of maximum; nonaerobic exercise does not.

24. Aerobic exercise has several benefits, even for older adults: improved physiological functioning and lower stress.

25. Moderate levels of exercise are more beneficial than high levels.

26. Low motivation to exercise is a major barrier to participation in older adults.

Sleep and Aging

27. Nearly half of older adults experience occasional insomnia. Waking up during the night is the most common age-related change. Slight changes in REM sleep also occur with age.

28. The negative effects of sleep loss increase with age.

29. Physical illness, sleep apnea, medications, alcohol, caffeine, nicotine, and stress can each cause problems with sleep.

30. The bed should be used only for sleeping and not for reading, watching TV, and the like.

31. Afternoon and evening naps can disrupt that night's sleep.

32. Stimulus-control instructions help insomniacs acquire consistent sleeping habits and help them associate the bed with sleeping only.

33. Progressive relaxation involves a systematic program of steps to get a person to relax and fall asleep.

Nutrition

34. Needs for vitamins, minerals, and protein do not change across adulthood. Older adults need less carbohydrates.

35. Eating high quantities of saturated fat is associated with atherosclerosis; eating lots of sodium is associated with hypertension.

36. Eating foods high in saturated fat, sodium, and nitrites may cause cancer of the breast, colon, and prostate. High fiber diets and foods containing vitamin A may lower the cancer risk.

37. Obtaining enough calcium and vitamin D possibly could help prevent osteoporosis.

Cancer

38. The risk of getting cancer increases markedly with age. The most common form of cancer is lung cancer.

39. Smoking and other life-style factors (such as diet) are major causes of cancer. There appear to be important genetic links in cancer.

40. There are several simple tests to detect cancer that should be taken regularly. Life-style changes are the best way to prevent cancer.

Health Promotion and Aging

41. Health promotion marks an important shift away from the approach of waiting until a disease appears before doing something about it.

42. Adults of all ages benefit from preventive medicine, but many programs ignore older adults.

REVIEW QUESTIONS

How Long Will We Live?

1. What is the difference between average longevity and maximum longevity?

2. What factors influence average longevity? What ethnic and gender differences have been found?

Stress and Health

3. Describe Selye's theory of stress.

4. Describe what stress is in the stress and coping paradigm. What is the appraisal process? What is meant by coping?

5. What are the major health consequences of stress?

6. What are Type A and Type B behavior patterns? What is the controversy associated with them?

7. What can be done to lower stress?

Smoking

8. What are the health risks from smoking? What happens from extended exposure to secondhand smoke?

9. How can people stop smoking?

Drinking Alcohol

10. How does alcohol consumption vary with age? What happens to the rate of alcoholism with age?

11. What are the negative effects of drinking? What benefits have been noted?

12. How can people stop drinking?

Exercise

13. What is the difference between aerobic and non-aerobic exercise?

14. What are the benefits of aerobic exercise? Why don't older people exercise as much as they should?

Sleep and Aging

15. How does sleep change with age?

16. What can cause sleep problems? How do these causes change with age?

17. What are some ways to improve the quality of your sleep?

Nutrition

18. How do nutritional needs change with age?

19. What problems can result from eating diets high in saturated fat or sodium?

20. How is diet related to osteoporosis?

Cancer

21. How does the risk of getting cancer vary with age?

22. What are some of the known causes of lung and colon cancer?

23. How can you prevent cancer?

Health Promotion and Aging

24. What is health promotion? How does it help?

KEY TERMS

addiction A disease in which one develops a physiological need for a particular substance, such as drugs and alcohol. (129)

aerobic exercise A form of exercise in which the pulse rate is high enough so that the cardiovascular system benefits. (132)

average longevity The length of time it takes for half of all individuals born in a certain year to die. (116)

general adaptation syndrome Selye's theory of stress consisting of the alarm, resistance, and exhaustion stages. (120)

health promotion A holistic approach to health that emphasizes disease prevention rather than waiting until the need for disease treatment. (142)

high density lipoproteins (HDL) So-called good cholesterol that helps prevent the buildup of fat deposits along arterial walls. (139)

low density lipoproteins (LDL) So-called bad cholesterol that is responsible for the buildup of fat deposits along arterial walls. (139)

maximum longevity The maximum length of time an organism can live, roughly 120 years for a human. (116)

nonaerobic exercise Exercise in which the heart rate does not exceed 60% of maximum. (132)

stress and coping paradigm An approach to stress emphasizing that it is people's perceptions of events rather than the events themselves that causes stress. (122)

Type A behavior pattern Behavior reflecting excessive competitiveness, time urgency, hostility, and aggressiveness. (124)

Type B behavior pattern Behavior reflecting relaxed, less-preoccupied life style in the absence of Type A behavior pattern. (124)

Wernicke-Korsakoff syndrome A result of long-term chronic vitamin deficiency causing severe memory loss. (130)

ADDITIONAL READING

The field of health psychology is expanding rapidly, and there are several good introductions to the research literature. Although it is not developmental in focus, the following is an excellent overview.

Feist, J., & Brannon, L. (1988). *Health psychology*. Belmont, CA: Wadsworth.

One of the best sources of easy-to-understand statistics on health, including discussions on aging and minority groups, is

Office of Disease Prevention and Health Promotion, U.S. Public Health Service. (1988). *Disease prevention/health promotion: The facts*. Palo Alto, CA: Bull Publishing Co.

An international perspective on health promotion and aging that also discusses health care policy is

Kane, R. L., Evans, J. G., & Macfadyen, D. (1990). *Improving the health of older people: A world view*. Oxford, England: Oxford University Press.

A good overview chapter of the specific relationships between health and behavior in the elderly is

Siegler, I. C., & Costa, P. T., Jr. (1985). Health behavior relationships. In J. E. Birren & K. W. Schaie (Eds.), *Handbook of the psychology of aging* (2nd ed., pp. 144–166). New York: Van Nostrand Reinhold.

An update on the research reviewed in this chapter was provided in

Elias, M. F., Elias, J. W., & Elias, P. K. (1990). Biological and health influences on behavior. In J. E. Birren & K.W. Schaie (Eds.), *Handbook of the psychology of aging* (3rd ed., pp. 79–102). San Diego: Academic Press.

A good resource on conducting exercise classes for older adults is

Lewis, C. B. (1990). *Health promotion and exercise for older adults: An instructor's guide*. Rockville, MD: Aspen.

CHAPTER 5

Information Processing

THE INFORMATION-PROCESSING MODEL

The Biopsychosocial Model and Information Processing / Sensory Memory

ATTENTION

Feature Integration Theory / Selectivity / Capacity / Vigilance / Attention Summary

PSYCHOMOTOR SPEED

Reaction Time Tasks / Age Differences in Components of Reaction Time / What Causes Age-Related Slowing? / Slowing Down How Much We Slow Down / How Do We Know? The Information-Loss Model / Psychomotor Speed Summary

HUMAN FACTORS AND AGING

Driving and Highway Safety / Home Safety / Accident Prevention / Something to Think About: Accidents and the Elderly

LANGUAGE PROCESSING

Language Comprehension and Sensory Systems / Language Comprehension and Information Processing / Implicit Memory

**Summary / Review Questions
Key Terms / Additional Reading**

IMAGINE THAT ONE DAY, JUST FOR THE FUN OF IT, you stroll into a Lamborghini dealership and are successful at getting the salesperson to let you take a Countach for a spin around the block. When you climb behind the wheel of the most expensive sports car you've ever seen in your life, your excitement almost gets the better of you. But as you start it up and ease into first gear, you are filled with utter terror. You suddenly realize that you must pay complete attention to what you're doing. After all, you wouldn't want to have an accident, would you? Now you are faced with the need to filter out everything — people's conversations, the radio, the sound of the wind whipping through your hair. How can you do it? More important, what abilities can you use to avoid an accident? If something happened on the road, how quickly could you respond? Would these abilities be any different in a younger adult than in an older adult? And, by the way, did you know that a Lamborghini Countach was a sports car before you read this? If so, how did you access this knowledge? If not, how did you incorporate this new knowledge?

These are the kinds of questions we will face in this chapter. This chapter begins a three-chapter sequence on cognition. In general, we will be examining how people process information from the world around them and make sense out of it. In this chapter, we will see how people pay attention to things, and what paying attention consists of. We will consider researchers' studies of how quickly people react to events, such as a car pulling into your lane on the highway. We will see how attention and other aspects of information processing are extremely important in understanding how accidents occur. Finally, we will consider some basic aspects of language processing. The remaining two chapters in the cognitive section will cover many aspects of memory (Chapter 6) and intelligence (Chapter 7).

THE INFORMATION-PROCESSING MODEL

How do we learn, remember, and think about things? Psychologists do not know for sure. About the best they can do is create models or analogues of how they believe our cognitive processes work. One of the most popular is the information-processing model, which is based on a computer analogue. Information enters the system and is transformed, coded, and stored in various ways. Information enters storage temporarily, as in a computer buffer, until it is sometimes stored more permanently, as in a computer disk. At a later time, information can be retrieved in response to some cue.

The **information-processing approach** is based on three assumptions (Neisser, 1976): (1) People are active participants in the process; (2) both quantitative (how much information is remembered) and qualitative (what kinds of information are remembered) aspects of performance can be examined; and (3) information is processed through a series of hypothetical stages, or stores. Researchers in adult development and aging usually distinguish a very brief sensory memory, a limited capacity primary (Poon, 1985) or working (Hultsch & Dixon, 1990) memory, a somewhat longer-term and larger-capacity secondary memory, and a relatively permanent and very large capacity tertiary memory. Researchers also focus on attention: the main way that information gets brought into the system for processing.

Using an information-processing model of memory raises three fundamental questions for adult development and aging: (1) Is there evidence of age differences in the various structural aspects (for instance, sensory memory, working memory, secondary memory, tertiary memory)? (2) What evidence is there for age differences in attention? (3) Are the differences observed in these structural aspects due to changes in how people bring information in, how they get information out, or both?

It will take us two chapters to answer these questions. In Chapter 5, we will focus on one structural aspect (sensory memory), on attention, and on two important related issues — processing speed and language processing. In Chapter 6 we will consider the remaining structural aspects, as well as address the reasons for age differences later in the system. Let's begin by considering how the biopsychosocial model applies to the information-processing model.

The Biopsychosocial Model and Information Processing

In Chapter 1, we saw that one of the key aspects of the biopsychosocial model was psychological variables, including sensory-perceptual functioning, motor functioning, and intellectual functioning. The information-processing model provides a fuller description of these variables, and specifies the ways in which they operate. The information-processing model emphasizes the complexity of human thinking and the need to be aware of a vast array of influences on performance. Likewise, the biopsychosocial model reminds us that we must place all of these influences into larger contexts; changes in the brain, for example, could dramatically alter the effects of any particular influence.

The most important aspects of the biopsychosocial model for information processing are the normative and disease-related biological, physiological, and life-style issues we considered in Chapters 3 and 4; the effects of psychopathology that we will examine in Chapter 9; and life-cycle factors — such as why adults of different ages interpret instances of forgetting differently (see Chapter 6). For example, underlying neural changes, cardiovascular disease, Alzheimer's disease, severe depression, and negative social stereotypes can all affect information-processing abilities as we age.

Sensory Memory

Each memory you ever have starts as a sensory stimulus. You can remember aspects of things you see or hear for only a fraction of a second. This ability is due to the earliest step in information processing, **sensory memory**, where new, incoming information is first registered. Sensory memory takes in large amounts of information very rapidly. However, unless you pay attention to this information very quickly, it will be lost. For example, try drawing a U.S. penny. (If you are not from the United States, try drawing a common coin in your own country.) Most people find this task difficult despite seeing the coins every day. Detailed information about pennies has passed through your sensory memory repeatedly, but because you failed to pay attention it was never processed to a longer-lasting store.

One way of studying sensory memory is to measure how fast incoming information gets into the system for subsequent processing. *Encoding speed* refers to how rapidly this storage occurs. Encoding speed has been studied extensively, with the evidence clearly displaying age-related decrements. For example, Cerella, Poon, and Fozard (1982) documented age-related slowing of encoding speed in processing letters. These results mean that *perceptual span*, the amount of visual information that one can handle at one time, declines with age.

A second way of studying sensory memory is to look for age differences in how quickly information can be passed from sensory memory to working memory. Some aspects of sensory memory appear not to differ with age; for example, there are no age differences in how efficiently information can be retrieved from sensory memory (for example, Poon & Fozard, 1980; A. D. Smith, 1975).

However, other aspects of sensory memory, such as susceptibility to backward masking, do show age differences. *Backward masking* involves presenting a target stimulus very briefly, followed by presenting another (masking) stimulus that diminishes the distinctiveness of the target. For example, you might be shown a letter (the target) very rapidly, followed quickly by a set of lines (the mask). Your job is to identify the target. By varying the interval between the target and the mask, researchers obtain an estimate of the degree to which the mask disrupts processing the target.

Numerous researchers have documented that susceptibility to backward masking increases slightly with age (Kline & Schieber, 1985). That is, the interval between the target and the mask needed for people to still be able to identify the target stimulus is slightly longer for older adults. This may not seem like much. As we will see, however, even slightly slower processing can produce important differences in performance.

Unfortunately, few researchers have studied sensory memory, so our knowledge is limited. Instead, most investigators focus on the way that information gets passed from sensory memory to working memory — attention.

ATTENTION

Several times during my educational career, teachers would catch me gazing out the window. "Pay attention!" they would say sternly, and then invariably call on me next. Of course, I would not know the answer. "I expect you to pay better attention to class!" would typically be their next remark.

You probably have had similar experiences. Someone asks you a question and you continue to stare off into space. You are driving along a long, boring stretch of interstate highway and suddenly realize you have gone 20 miles with no awareness at all of anything that you saw along the way. The examples are quite varied but the outcome is the same: Somehow we come to realize that lots of information was available to us that we never processed. In short, we simply did not pay attention.

These everyday experiences are so vivid to us that we would expect psychologists to have a clear handle on what attention is. William James's (1890) view that "we all know what attention is" reflects this belief. It turns out that vivid experiences can be misleading. Attention is actually quite difficult to pin down. About the best researchers can do is describe three interdependent aspects of attention (Posner & Boies, 1971): selectivity, capacity, and vigilance.

Selectivity in attention means that our ability to process information is limited. As we saw earlier, a great deal of information gets into sensory memory. However, this information only remains there for a very brief time. The next step, working memory, can only handle a small amount of information at a time (see Chapter 6). This creates a problem: how to go from a large capacity store to a very small capacity store. This situation is similar to the problem created when a large capacity freeway (say, eight lanes in one direction) must use a small capacity tunnel (two lanes in one direction). The potential traffic jam could be enormous, with many drivers simply opting to exit the freeway. The problem in the information-processing system is similar: a traffic jam of information trying to get from sensory memory to working memory. Much of it simply exits the system before it can be passed along.

Several theories have been postulated to explain where the bottleneck in information flow occurs (for a review, see Lachman, Lachman, & Butterfield, 1979). All agree that somehow information gets selected out for further processing, and

that this selection is part of attention. However, no one knows for sure how selectivity happens. Cognitive aging researchers primarily investigate selectivity by comparing visual search performance with nonsearch performance (Plude & Doussard-Roosevelt, 1990). Visual search tasks require you to find a specific target among several distractor stimuli. Nonsearch tasks make things easier; for example, visual cues could be given that provide prior information about where the target will be (Plude & Hoyer, 1985).

Capacity addresses the question of how much information can be processed at any given time. Most researchers view capacity as the pool of resources available to support information-processing activity. Underlying this idea is the key assumption that some processing occurs automatically while other processing requires effort. Automatic processing places minimal demands on attentional capacity. Some automatic processes appear to be "prewired" in the sense that they require no attentional capacity and do not benefit from practice; others are learned through experience and practice (Plude & Doussard-Roosevelt, 1990). In contrast, effortful processing requires some if not all of the available attentional capacity. Most of the tasks involving deliberate memory, such as learning the words on a list, require effortful processing. Cognitive aging researchers investigate both types of automatic processing and effortful processing, and then look at differences in performance across the two categories.

A second way of studying attentional capacity is to look at how well people perform multiple tasks simultaneously. For example, paying attention to a lecture in class while taking notes requires you to monitor two things (lecture content and what you are writing) at the same time. These divided attention and dual-task studies provide interesting information about differences and similarities across adulthood.

Vigilance or *sustained attention* refers to how well you are able to maintain vigilance in performing a task over a long period of time. In general, these tasks involve monitoring a display (such as a radar screen) for the appearance of targets (such as airplane blips). Fewer studies of age differences in sustained attention have been conducted than on either of the other two topics (selectivity and capacity).

Our examination of age differences in selectivity, capacity, and sustained attention will focus on visual information processing for several reasons (Plude & Doussard-Roosevelt, 1990): (1) The great majority of the research has examined visual processing; (2) the potential loss of vision is of great concern to older adults (see Chapter 3); and (3) age differences in visual processing are believed to generalize to other sensory modalities. Because of this emphasis we need to consider briefly how visual processing works.

Feature Integration Theory

Take a moment to look carefully at a picture in your room. Now that you've done that, close you eyes and describe to yourself what you saw. Your ability to do that required two basic processes. First, you had to extract key pieces of information from the picture. Second, you had to put these pieces together in order to figure out what was in the picture.

Feature integration theory (FIT); (Treisman & Gelade, 1980) is a formal way of expressing your experience. According to FIT, visual processing consists of two main steps: *feature extraction* and *feature integration*. Feature extraction involves paying attention to what you are seeing at each point and representing each dimension (color, shape, and so on) separately. Feature integration involves putting these separate dimensions together in order to make sense out of the visual stimulus. A key aspect of this process is that feature extraction and feature integration operate serially; that is, you can only process one part of the stimulus at a time.

FIT raises several interesting questions about aging and attention (Plude & Doussard-Roosevelt,

1990). Are there age differences in either or both aspects of processing? Do older people differ in the amount or kind of visual information they pick up? Are there differences in how quickly adults of various ages can perform feature extraction and feature integration? How do the age differences in vision discussed in Chapter 3 affect visual information processing? These are some of the questions we will address in the next three sections.

Selectivity

As we have seen, a small proportion of information in sensory memory gets selected for further processing. In this section we will consider evidence concerning age differences in selectivity by examining three lines of research: visual search, spatial cuing, and attention shifting. To preview a bit, age-related decrements are consistently found in visual search, but spatial cuing sometimes eliminates age differences (Plude & Doussard-Roosevelt, 1990). Age differences in the ability to shift attention appears to depend on the sensory modality being tested (McDowd & Birren, 1990).

Visual Search. Imagine yourself sitting at a computer terminal. You are told to push a key as fast as you can every time you see a red X, the target stimulus. So far, so good, you say. To make things difficult, sometimes you will see other letters or colors (green Xs, green Os, and red Os), the nontarget stimuli. The problem is that you have no idea where in the display the target will appear, so you must search for it among the nontargets.

This procedure is typical of visual search tasks, and was actually used by Plude and Doussard-Roosevelt (1989). Visual search tasks always involve responding to a specific stimulus, the *target*, and ignoring everything else, the *nontargets*. Such tasks measure attention selectivity because the main data involve *nontarget interference effects*; that is, the degree to which the nontargets interfere with your ability to respond only to targets. Usually, nontarget interference effects are a matter of *display size*; that is, how many nontargets are presented with the target. In the example above, it would be harder to find 1 red X amid 50 red Os than amid 5 red Os.

Performance on visual search tasks is measured either in terms of how quickly people respond (**reaction time**) or in terms of the number and kinds of errors they make. When performance data on visual search tasks are plotted as a function of display size, the slope of the linear function provides information about attention selectivity. A flat horizontal line, indicating zero slope, means perfect selectivity; nontargets never interfere with processing of the target. Positive slopes indicate some degree of nontarget interference, with higher positive slopes indicating more interference. Research consistently demonstrates that older adults show larger positive slopes than younger adults (Plude & Hoyer, 1985).

At this point we need to bring in feature integration theory. Recall that FIT has two components: feature extraction and feature integration. Problems with either component (or both) could produce increased nontarget interference, which we know is age related. Is there a way to tell which aspect of FIT is the source of the difficulty?

By using techniques like those in the example (red and green Xs and Os), Plude (1986; Plude & Doussard-Roosevelt, 1989) isolated the source as the feature integration component. Younger and older adults were equally able to extract information about the target (such as color) automatically. However, when it came time to put the pieces of information together (that is, specific letter and specific color), older adults were at a significant disadvantage. Thus, it appears that older adults are slower on visual search tasks not because they have problems picking up the separate pieces of information, but because they are slower at putting the various pieces of information together.

Spatial Cuing. Imagine sitting at the same computer terminal as before. This time, though, things are a bit easier. You are now told to watch for an asterisk somewhere on the screen; shortly after it appears, either the target or a nontarget stimulus will appear in exactly the same spot.

This procedure is known as **spatial cuing**. The idea behind it is to rule out certain other explanations for age differences in visual search tasks. For example, it may be that older adults decline in their ability to localize a target embedded among many nontargets. If this is true, telling them ahead of time where it will appear solves this problem.

When the spatial cue signals that a target will appear in that location, age differences in slopes disappear (Plude & Doussard-Roosevelt, 1990). As the actual locations of the targets move away from the locations of the cues, age differences reappear (Madden, 1990). In other words, when people know where to look, older and younger adults are equally able to identify targets. Hoyer (1987) extends this point by suggesting that some people accrue considerable experience and practice at looking for targets. These expert lookers are able to anticipate where a target is likely to appear, and may even be able to compensate for sensory changes. For example, highly experienced bird watchers find their feathered friends more quickly than novice bird watchers because they know what to look for up in the trees.

Thus, it appears that age-related differences in feature integration are due in turn to decrements in spatial localization ability. However, there are important qualifications. Age differences are eliminated only when the spatial cue provides unambiguous information about the target's subsequent position. When the cue is ambiguous (for instance, several asterisks appear and only one provides accurate information), age differences remain. This may suggest that other processes, such as generalized cognitive slowing (discussed later in this chapter), are also important for understanding age decrements in visual search. Additionally, experience and practice may play a role in eliminating age differences.

Attention Switching. Once again, you are back at your computer terminal. This time, however, you are asked to do two different things. Some of the time you are told to focus your attention on the center character in a five-character string, which will be the target. Let's call this the narrow attention condition. At other times, you are told to widen your attention to include all five characters. In this case, the target will be one of the peripheral characters. Let's call this the broad attention condition. Thus, the task requires you to switch your attention from one character to five characters. Hartley and McKenzie (1991) used this task to demonstrate that under some circumstances older and younger adults switch their visual attentional focus similarly.

Interestingly, Hartley and McKenzie's data do not agree with findings from research on adults' ability to switch attention on auditory tasks. For example, Braune and Wickens (1985) reported age differences in pilots' ability to switch their attention when information was presented verbally rather than visually. Several factors may account for these discrepancies, such as possible differences in the rates of change in vision and hearing or different types of changes in visual and auditory sensory memory. At this point, the reasons for differences in age-related decrements between visual and auditory attention switching remain unknown.

Selectivity and Irrelevant Information. Age decrements in selectivity appear to be greatest when tasks are complex and little information is available to assist performance. With advance information (such as spatial cuing), age differences are lessened. Why?

One popular hypothesis is that older adults have greater difficulty inhibiting processing of irrelevant information. That is, older adults do not focus their attention solely on target stimuli as much as younger adults do. This difference could explain why older people tend to be less accurate at

finding targets; they have to contend with processing information about nontargets as well.

There is considerable support for the inhibition idea. For example, McDowd, Filion, and Oseas-Kreger (1991) showed that when relevant and irrelevant information are both presented in the same modality (for example, visually), older adults distribute their attention more equally between the two types of information than do younger adults. However, when relevant information was presented in one modality (say, visually) and irrelevant information in another (auditorially), older and younger adults both showed similar patterns of attention allocation. Thus, it appears that older adults only have trouble selectively attending to relevant information when it and the irrelevant information are both presented in the same modality.

Capacity

Given that there is some evidence for age differences in *what* information is processed, are there also age differences in *how much* information is processed? That is the question faced by researchers studying attentional capacity. Investigating attentional capacity usually requires investigators to see how many things people can do at once by using divided attention tasks.

Divided Attention. Life is full of situations in which you need to do at least two things at once. Two common examples are listening to a lecture while writing in your notebook and driving a car while conversing with your passenger. Each of these situations requires you to monitor what is going on in at least two different domains. How well you are able to perform these multiple simultaneous tasks depends on how much attentional capacity you have available for each. To the extent that any one task requires a great deal of your capacity, your ability to do other things may be impaired.

In general, younger adults are better able to divide their attention between two tasks.

Research on **divided attention** is a good example of how conclusions about age differences can change. At one time, researchers were convinced that age-related decrements in divided attention were inevitable (Craik, 1977). But Somberg and Salthouse's research in 1982 changed all that. Researchers were amazed at their report of a lack of age differences on a divided attention task. Other researchers corroborated Somberg and Salthouse's findings (see Wickens, Braune, & Stokes, 1987).

Suddenly, researchers had to go back to the lab to try and account for these new data.

It now appears that everyone was right to some extent. Age differences are found on some divided attention tasks and not others. The explanation involves task complexity. When the divided attention tasks are relatively easy, age differences are typically absent. However, when the tasks become more complicated, age differences emerge (McDowd & Craik, 1988; Plude, Murphy, & Gabriel-Byrne, 1989; Salthouse, Rogan, & Prill, 1984). In other words, adults of all ages can perform multiple easy tasks simultaneously, but older adults do not do as well as younger adults when they must perform multiple difficult tasks at the same time.

Even though the task complexity interpretation greatly clarifies things, an important question remains: *Why* do older adults have more problems with performing more difficult tasks simultaneously? Many theorists and researchers believe that with increasing age comes a decline in the amount of available processing resources, which could account for poorer performance not only on attention tasks (Plude & Hoyer, 1985) but also on a host of others; see Salthouse (1988) for a review of these.

On the surface the notion of age-related decrements in processing resources offers a concise explanation of a wide range of age-related performance differences. But there is a nagging problem about the processing resource construct: It has never been clearly defined (Baddeley, 1981; Salthouse, 1985, 1988). In a carefully designed series of investigations, Salthouse and his colleagues set out to see what could be done (Salthouse, 1988; Salthouse, Kausler, & Saults, 1988). Their goal was to provide an empirical test of the processing resource explanation of age-related performance differences. Their results demonstrate that complete reliance on this idea is probably a mistake. Salthouse was able to show that although some kind of processing resource notion is a parsimonious explanation, the strong version of the resource decline idea that marks much current research has little empirical support. In other words, something besides a decline in processing resources is responsible for performance decrements with age.

Plude and Doussard-Roosevelt (1990) provide one possible answer. They argue that the problem stems back to age-related decrements in feature integration, at least when the multiple (and difficult) tasks are all visual. Complex tasks, they believe, require more features to be integrated, thereby differentially penalizing older adults.

In sum, it appears that divided attention ability per se does not differ with age. Rather, task complexity is the primary determinant of age-related decrements; older adults are at a disadvantage when they must perform two or more complex tasks simultaneously (Plude & Doussard-Roosevelt, 1990).

Vigilance

Did you ever think about the job that air traffic controllers have? They must sit in front of radar screens for hours keeping track of blips on the screen. Each blip represents an airplane, many of which have hundreds of people aboard. Air traffic controllers must sustain high levels of attention over long periods of time, as even the slightest error could have disastrous consequences.

Watching a radar screen is an excellent example of vigilance: the ability to sustain attention on a task for long periods of time. Researchers interested in studying age differences in vigilance use tasks very much like those performed by air traffic controllers. Investigators obtain two different measures of sustained attention: how many targets you correctly detect (*vigilance performance*) and the decrease in "hit" rate over time (*vigilance decrement*).

Compared to work on other aspects of attention, relatively little research has focused on vigi-

lance. What little there is suggests age-related decrements in vigilance performance but not in vigilance decrement (Parasuraman, 1987). This means that although older adults are not as accurate as younger adults in detecting targets, performance deteriorates at the same rate in both age groups. What causes this age difference in detection?

Parasuraman (1987) offers several suggestions. He points out that vigilance tasks are quite complex and require at least four different processes that could account for age differences: (1) alertness; (2) adaptation and expectancy; (3) sustained allocation of attentional capacity; and (4) development of automaticity. Parasuraman believes that only the first, alertness, is related to vigilance performance; the other three processes are related to vigilance decrement.

To preview, age differences are found only for alertness and the development of automaticity; no evidence of age-related decrements in adaptation or in capacity allocation have been reported.

Alertness. Age-related differences in alertness on vigilance tasks have been well established for many years. For example, Surwillo and Quilter (1964) demonstrated that older adults' poorer vigilance performance was correlated with lower physiological arousal. A longitudinal follow-up (Giambra & Quilter, 1988) verified this earlier finding. Thus, one good explanation of age differences in vigilance performance is age differences in arousal.

Adaptation and Expectancy. Suppose you were participating in a vigilance study involving monitoring a computer screen. The target is programmed to appear on the screen 10% of the time; the other 90% of the stimuli that appear will be nontargets. Prior to beginning, you are told one of two things: Either you are told the true probability of a target appearing (10%) or you are told an incorrect probability (50%). If a similar situation were presented to older and younger adults, would age differences emerge?

Parasuraman (1987) provides the answer — no. Although vigilance decrements were greater for the incorrect probability condition, older and younger adults were affected equally. Thus, both groups were able to adapt their performance to reflect how often they expected to see a target.

Capacity Allocation. As we saw earlier, the amount of attentional capacity a task requires can be manipulated by changing the complexity of the task. One way to do this is to degrade the perceptual quality of the target, such as making the blip dimmer on a radar screen or making a target letter harder to discriminate from other letters.

Parasuraman, Nestor, and Greenwood (1989) had younger and older adults perform a vigilance task under two conditions: normal and degraded. As might be expected, the degraded condition resulted in poorer vigilance performance and greater vigilance decrement than the normal condition. However, older and younger adults were affected similarly; no age differences as a function of condition were found.

Automaticity. Because vigilance tasks are highly repetitive, people's performance on them tends to improve for awhile and then plateau. If this plateau corresponds to a high rate of accuracy that is maintained over time, then the response is considered to have become automatic.

An interesting developmental question is whether there are age differences in the rates at which responses on vigilance tasks become automatic. Results from several studies suggest that there are. Several studies by Fisk (Fisk, McGee, & Giambra, 1988; Fisk & Rogers, 1987) and by Parasuraman (1987) show that only young adults' responses become automatic on vigilance tasks. Young adults' responses are typically accurate about 90% of the time after 10 sessions of training,

whereas older adults' responses are typically still only about 75% accurate after 20 or more training sessions.

Attention Summary

Research on age-related differences in attention point to two main conclusions. First, age differences are greatest when older adults are faced with having to perform complex tasks, especially more than one at a time. Second, these decrements appear to be localized in the feature integration process, where the various pieces of information picked up from a visual display are put together to figure out what the display is.

However, these conclusions do not answer an intriguing question: *Why* do these age-related decrements occur? At present, the leading possibility is a generalized cognitive slowing. It is to this possibility that we now turn.

PSYCHOMOTOR SPEED

You are driving home from a friend's house and all seems to be going well. Suddenly, a car pulls out of a driveway right into your path. You must hit the brakes as fast as you can or you will have an accident. How quickly can you move your foot from the accelerator to the brake?

This situation is a real-life example of psychomotor speed — making a quick motor movement in response to some sort of information that has been processed. In this case, the motor movement is switching your foot from one pedal to another, and the information is the visual stimulus of a car in your path.

Psychomotor speed is one of the most studied phenomena in adult development and aging research. Results from hundreds of studies point to a clear conclusion: People slow down as they get older. In fact, the slowing-with-age phenomenon is so well documented that many gerontologists accept it as the only universal behavioral change yet discovered. In this section we will examine some of the evidence for psychomotor slowing.

Reaction Time Tasks

Researchers use three types of reaction time tasks to study rapid responses to events: simple reaction time tasks, choice reaction time tasks, and complex reaction time tasks. We will consider each briefly.

Simple Reaction Time. Simple reaction time involves responding to one stimulus, such as pressing a button as fast as possible whenever a light comes on. Simple reaction time is usually broken down into two components: decision time and motor time. Decision time is the time it takes from the onset of the stimulus until the person begins to initiate a response. Motor time is the time needed to complete the response. Consistent age differences in overall simple reaction time and in each of its components have been reported (Borkan & Norris, 1980; Salthouse, 1985). Interestingly, the most noticeable difference between young and old is in the decision time component.

Choice Reaction Time. Tasks involving choice reaction time offer you more than one stimulus and require you to respond to each in a different way. For example, imagine being presented with two lights — one red and one blue. Your job is to press the left button every time the red light comes on and the right button when the blue light comes on. To perform well on such tasks you need to correctly identify the stimulus you see and decide which response goes with it (Fozard, 1981). Several researchers have found that older adults are slower on choice reaction tasks than younger adults (e.g., Salthouse & Somberg, 1982; Strayer, Wickens, & Braune, 1987).

Complex Reaction Time. The most difficult reaction time task involves complex reaction time, which requires you to make many decisions about when and how to respond. A good example of a complex reaction time task is driving a car: The number of stimuli is extremely large, and the range of possible responses is huge. Cerella, Poon, and Williams (1980) report that the magnitude of age differences in complex reaction time tasks increases as the task becomes more difficult. Thus, older adults become increasingly disadvantaged as situations demanding rapid response become more complex.

Age Differences in Components of Reaction Time

Although they may appear straightforward, reaction time tasks are actually quite complicated cognitively. In any reaction time task, you must: (1) perceive that an event has occurred, (2) decide what to do about it, and (3) carry out the decision (Welford, 1977). Successful performance in reaction time tasks involves many factors, including sensation, perception, attention, working memory, intelligence, decision making, and personality (Salthouse, 1985). Poor performance on reaction time tasks could be the result of a breakdown in any step in the process.

Because reaction time tasks involve complex mental activity, researchers must break reaction time down into components in order to discover which aspects show age differences (Goggin &

Stelmach, 1990). Typically, this means that investigators must manipulate variables that are related to reaction time. Two of these variables are especially important: response preparation and response complexity.

Response Preparation. Many driver education programs emphasize what is known as defensive driving. That is, instructors stress that you must be prepared for the unexpected at all times; you never know when an emergency situation could arise. This means that you need to be on your toes all the time. But suppose things were a little different. Suppose that there were only a handful of dangerous intersections along your route, and everything in between was completely safe. Getting close to one of these intersections would provide advance warning that you may need to make a quick response. Moreover, having this advance warning may even help you respond faster.

Providing such advance information is what happens in studies of **response preparation**. Researchers typically study the effects of response preparation in simple reaction time tasks by varying the amount or type of information provided about the impending presentation of a stimulus. For example, investigators might flash an asterisk right before presenting the target. Measuring reaction times when advance information is either present or absent allows researchers to address an important developmental question about reaction time: Do age differences in speed on reaction time tasks occur because older adults prepare poorly to make a response?

The answer appears to be yes. Several investigators report that older adults are especially vulnerable to ambiguous advance information or long delays between the advance information and the time at which the response must be made (Gottsdanker, 1982; Stelmach, Goggin, & Garcia-Colera, 1987). An example of the typical findings is shown in Figure 5.1 (Stelmach et al., 1987). Younger, middle-aged, and older adults were presented with differ-

ent kinds of preparatory information in advance of responding. This advance information varied in how much help it provided participants in knowing exactly what the response was to be, from very specific (level 0 uncertainty) to very nonspecific (level 3 uncertainty). You should notice two things in the graph. First, there is an orderly general slowing of responding, with a ranking of younger, middle-aged, and elderly adults from least slow to slowest. Second, older adults are especially hurt by ambiguity; notice that the difference between them and the middle-aged adults *increases* as the uncertainty level goes up.

One way that ambiguity can be introduced is by giving incorrect information about the response. For example, you could be led to believe that you will need to make a specific hand movement (for example, turn your hands palms up), only to find out at the time that you need to make a different hand movement (turn your hands palms down). Incorrect advance information forces you to reprogram your movements. When reprogramming is required, older adults are slowed down more than younger adults (Stelmach, Goggin, & Amrhein, 1988).

In sum, the research evidence shows that older adults are at a distinct disadvantage in reaction time tasks when they are not given specific advance information about the upcoming response. Such difficulties have many practical implications, the most important of which may be the effect on driving a car: Older people react more slowly to emergency situations.

Response Complexity. As we saw earlier, choice reaction time tasks and complex reaction time tasks involve decisions about which stimulus is present and which response needs to be made. These tasks make it possible to examine the effects of task complexity in several different ways. For example, the usual choice reaction time task involves using the same hand to push two different buttons. One way to complicate things is to require people to use both

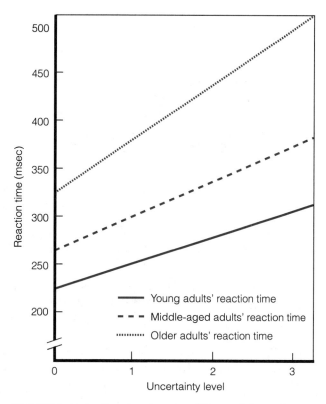

FIGURE 5.1 Reaction times in milliseconds for each age group plotted as a function of uncertainty. Notice that increased uncertainty slows older adults more than other groups.

(Source: "Movement Specification Time with Age" by G. E. Stelmach, N. L. Goggin, and A. Garcia-Colera, *Experimental Aging Research, 13*, 42. Copyright © 1987 by Beech Hill Enterprises, Inc. Reprinted with permission.)

hands simultaneously. Another way would be to not only require simultaneous use of both hands, but to have each hand move different distances in order to make the response.

Stelmach, Amrhein, and Goggin (1988) used these manipulations to study the effects of **response complexity** in younger and older adults. They found that older adults were more affected by increased complexity than younger adults. Older adults had difficulty coordinating movements of

both hands across different distances so that the movements would end simultaneously.

Light and Spirduso (1990) varied the complexity of response by having people make different movements with a microswitch. They also found that as response complexity increased, older adults proportionately slowed down more.

These findings fit well with the data from visual information-processing studies considered earlier. The results from both lines of research show that

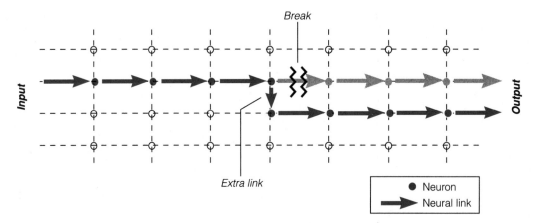

FIGURE 5.2 Schematic neural network. The network transmits signal from left to right. One link in the original, intact route is broken, forcing the signal to detour and adding one more link to the path for a total of nine.

(Source: "Aging and Information Processing Rate" (pp. 201–221) by J. Cerella, 1990, in J. E. Birren and K. W. Schaie (Eds.), *Handbook of the Psychology of Aging* (3rd ed.). San Diego: Academic Press. Reprinted by permission of Academic Press, Inc.)

adults experience increasing difficulty dealing with complexity in a variety of settings as they get older.

What Causes Age-Related Slowing?

The evidence documenting a normative decline with age in psychomotor speed is overwhelming. What causes people to slow down?

After many years of debate and several different ideas, researchers are zeroing in on an intriguing answer. Several theorists (e.g., Cerella, 1990; Myerson, Hale, Wagstaff, Poon, & Smith, 1990; Salthouse, 1985; Welford, 1988) argue that the reason people slow down has to do with age changes in neurons in the brain. Although there is disagreement about exactly what is happening, most researchers believe that physiological changes in the brain, rather than changes in higher-level cognitive processes, are responsible for age-related slowing. We will consider two variations on this theme: neural networks and information loss.

Neural Networks. One way to conceptualize thinking is to consider it as a computational process occurring on a neural network (McClelland, Rumelhart, & the PDP Research Group, 1986). In this approach, thinking involves making connections among many neurons. Efficient thinking means making the fewest number of necessary connections between the point at which information comes in and the point at which an answer (or thought) comes out. Each connection requires a certain amount of time, so how quickly you think depends on the number of connections you need to use.

For simplicity's sake, let's consider a simple reaction time task from this view of a neural network. The original neural pathway (in gray) of Figure 5.2 shows that, hypothetically, eight links are the minimum number needed to get the information from the input side to the output side. Using only eight links would therefore be the most efficient (that is, the fastest) way to process the information. Suppose, though, that one of the neurons dies. The revised route (in color) of Figure 5.2 shows what happens. Notice that an extra link is needed in order to bypass the break, bringing the minimum number up to nine links. Reaction time will be faster in the first case (using only eight links) than in the second (using nine).

Cerella (1990) builds a case that reaction times in older adults are slower because they must build many such bypasses. Based on sophisticated analyses of reaction time data, he constructed a set of mathematical equations that fit a neural network model and account for the research findings. His analyses show that reaction time data are extremely consistent with what would be expected in a brain undergoing systematic changes in how its neurons are interconnected.

Information Loss. Myerson and colleagues (1990) took a slightly different approach. They focused not so much on the links among neurons per se, but what happens during processing at each line. Their model is based on four assumptions:

1. Information processing occurs in discrete steps, and overall processing speed is the total of how long it takes to accomplish each step. This assumption is based on the same neural network model as Cerella used.

2. How long each step takes depends on how much information is available at the beginning of the step. For example, if the task you are doing requires you to identify particular letters, and if the quality of the printing is very poor, insufficient information may be available for you to make a rapid response. Additionally, as the task gets more complicated and you need more information, your processing speed slows down.

3. Information is lost during processing. This point is illustrated by thinking about photocopying a document. Each time the document is copied, there is a slight loss of quality. If the copy is then used to make a copy, more

quality is lost. Continuing this process several times nicely demonstrates Myerson's theory of how information gets lost during information processing.

4. The most important effect of aging is an age-related increase in the rate at which information is lost. To continue our example, age differences in information loss would be analogous to the quality of the copy deteriorating faster in an old photocopy machine.

Like Cerella's neural network model, Myerson's information-loss model accounts for a wide range of data. Myerson et al. are able to predict with a high degree of accuracy older adults' reaction times from young adults' performance, irrespective of task. As a result, they view age-related slowing as a global process that is not localized in specific age-sensitive components. How they arrived at this theory is discussed in How Do We Know?

Together, these models provide powerful explanations of age-related slowing. They also provide strong support for the biopsychosocial model by explicitly connecting a psychological process (making quick responses) with underlying physiological processes. As noted in Chapter 3, rapid advances are being made in understanding how the brain works. These advances clearly benefit our understanding of psychomotor speed and aging. However, the question remains: Is there a way to slow these age-related decrements in psychomotor speed?

Slowing Down How Much We Slow Down

Consider for a moment what it takes to be a successful race car driver: a fast car, lots of driving knowledge, and lightning fast reactions. On the face of it, auto racing sounds tailor-made for young adults. But few drivers in their 20s win major races like the Indianapolis 500. Many of the best drivers (like Rick Mears) reach the peak of their careers in

HOW DO WE KNOW?

The Information-Loss Model

How do researchers come up with new explanatory models? One way is to combine the results of many studies with one's own research, look for consistencies, and derive explanations. That is what Myerson, Hale, Wagstaff, Poon, and Smith (1990) did. As noted in the text, they tried to explain why people slow with age using four basic assumptions: (1) processing occurs in steps; (2) the duration of the step depends on the information available; (3) information is lost during processing; and (4) an age-related increase in the rate of information loss. Where did their final model come from?

First, Myerson et al. examined the results of over a dozen studies for trends in patterns of age differences. They then considered how well each of three possible explanations worked. The first alternative argues that even though older adults are slower, there are no real age differences in information-processing capabilities between older and younger adults. The second alternative was that the speed differences were due to age differences in some aspects of information processing but not others. The third alternative was that age differences in speed reflected age differences in all aspects of information processing.

Once the competing hypotheses were identified, the researchers set about systematically building a math-

ematical model to account for the data. Equations were derived for each alternative and used to try to predict the actual data. In only one case were the data adequately described, namely the third alternative. Specifically, only the equations based on Myerson and colleagues' four assumptions, combined into one equation, provided a good description of the data. In fact, this equation accounted for 99% of the variance in the speed of older and younger adults on different types of information-processing tasks.

This systematic approach to model building is representative of how good theories are developed. Theory building takes a great deal of painstaking effort, but the investment is well worth it.

---

their 30s. Or consider Paul Newman — the famous movie star and race car driver. He was racing successfully even in his late 50s. The data indicate that people in their 20s are faster than middle-aged adults, so how can older drivers still succeed?

It appears that at least two things make a difference: practice and experience. As we will see, both have been shown to make people respond faster. In addition, physical exercise also has a beneficial influence on reaction time.

Practice and Reaction Time. One way to see if age differences in psychomotor speed could be altered is by having people practice. Several studies over the years have examined this question (for example,

Berg, Hertzog, & Hunt, 1982; Leonard & Newman, 1965; Madden & Nebes, 1980; Plude & Hoyer, 1981; Salthouse & Somberg, 1982). The dominant finding is that practice results in considerable improvement among all age groups. However, age differences in overall level of performance are seldom eliminated completely with practice.

Experience and Reaction Time. One reason that middle-aged race car drivers are able to win has to do with experience. They have driven in many races and have accumulated a wealth of information about driving in these events. Veteran drivers know that younger drivers have quicker reflexes to get themselves out of an emergency situation. But be-

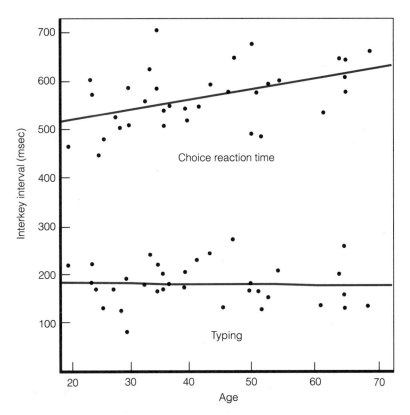

FIGURE 5.3 Comparison of speed in milliseconds of responding in choice reaction time task and typing as a function of age. Note how choice reaction time responses slow down with age while typing speed does not.

(Source: "Effects of Age and Skill in Typing" by T. A. Salthouse, 1984, *Journal of Experimental Psychology: General, 113*, 345–371. Copyright © 1984 by the American Psychological Association. Reprinted with permission of the author.)

cause of their experience, veterans are often able to avoid getting into trouble in the first place; they can anticipate what is likely to happen in front of them. This experience provides a way to compensate for slower psychomotor speed.

Researchers have studied real-world tasks to learn about the effects of experience on reaction time. Salthouse (1984) decided to examine performance in adults aged 19 to 72 on transcription typing. The typists in his study ranged in speed

from 17 to 104 words per minute, with ability and age being unrelated. Salthouse examined several components of reaction time, including choice reaction time, speed of repetitive tapping, and the rate at which people can substitute specific digits for letters (for example, 3 for *d*). Results are shown in Figure 5.3.

As you can see in the graph, there was age-related slowing on the choice reaction time task. Interestingly, however, there was no age effect for typing. Why? Both tasks involved pressing keys, so what was the difference? One measure revealed a difference favoring older adults: span of anticipation. This measure was derived from a manipulation of the number of simultaneously visible to-be-typed characters, and it was interpreted as an indication of how far ahead of the currently typed character the typist was focusing his or her attention. Because a greater span of anticipation minimizes the importance of the speed of psychomotor processes as a major factor in skilled typing, the larger span on the part of the older typists can be considered an extremely effective compensatory mechanism.

Thus, in some cases experience may allow older adults to compensate for psychomotor slowing. We will return to the notion of experience and how it benefits the aging process in Chapter 7.

Exercise and Reaction Time. As we noted in Chapter 4, one of the advantages claimed for aerobic exercise is improved cognitive performance. Most of this work is based on the effects of exercise on psychomotor speed. Several studies employing both simple and choice reaction time tasks document significant improvement in performance in older adults as a function of sustained exercise (Baylor & Spirduso, 1988; Rikli & Busch, 1986; Spirduso, 1980; Tomporowski & Ellis, 1986). That is, older adults who exercised regularly had significantly faster reaction times than sedentary older adults (Baylor & Spirduso, 1988).

These results do not mean that exercise affects all aspects of a reaction time task equally, however. Blumenthal and Madden (1988) demonstrated that the effects of exercise may be limited to the encoding and response components of a memory search task. In contrast, age appears to account for slower rates of memory search. Thus, the benefit of exercise for older adults' reaction time performance appears to stem from an enhancement of getting the information in and getting the response out. What happens in between may be relatively unchanged.

Psychomotor Speed Summary

Overall, research on psychomotor speed points to normative, age-related slowing. It appears that these differences are due to underlying changes in the brain. On tasks in which experience matters, older adults may be able to compensate for the loss of speed. When we combine the evidence of some age-related differences in attention, the picture that emerges is that the basic components of the information-processing system do not function as well in old age.

HUMAN FACTORS AND AGING

To this point, we have concentrated on age differences in basic aspects of the information-processing system. We have seen that in several areas older adults are at a disadvantage compared with younger (and often middle-aged) adults. However, most of the research we considered was based on esoteric tasks, such as finding the letter *X* in a visual display or pressing different keys for different color lights. If you are wondering what this work has to do with real life, you are not alone; many researchers wonder the same thing.

Making connections between laboratory research findings and everyday life is one aspect of human factors research. As a discipline, **human factors** tries to optimize the design of living and working environments (Charness & Bosman, 1990b). Human factors professionals deal with interesting problems in just about every conceivable area. For example, they may be asked to design an easy-to-use computer keyboard, the layout of a cockpit for a jumbo jet, or a safe environment for nursing home residents. Although most human factors work focuses on designing working environments, increased interest is being paid to everyday situations. For example, many of the safety features built into modern appliances (such as irons that automatically shut off) and automobiles (brake lights mounted in the rear window, for example) are the result of human factors research.

In order to make the most effective designs, planners must know as much as possible about their clients. This in turn requires integrating information about people's basic sensory and information-processing abilities. In the case of designs meant for older adults, planners need to understand the sensory changes described in Chapter 3 and those in basic information-processing abilities discussed in this chapter. Unfortunately, few human factors researchers have focused specifically on the needs of the elderly (Charness & Bosman, 1990b; D. B. D. Smith, 1990). Most of the previous work involves driving and other highway safety issues, as well as safety in the home.

Driving and Highway Safety

The vast majority of older adults live independently. Thus, access to workplaces, community services, leisure activities, and the like is an important consideration. Because roughly 80% of all trips made by older adults are in private automobiles (U. S. Department of Transportation, 1986), driving and highway safety are major issues for human factors research.

We have already noted that certain changes in vision, hearing, and information processing could cause problems for older drivers. For example, changes in light and dark adaptation and sensitivity to glare (see Chapter 3) and changes in psychomotor speed present challenges to elderly drivers. Older drivers themselves report several difficulties (Yee, 1985), from trouble reading highway signs and the instrument panel, to difficulty seeing the road, to problems reaching the seatbelt. Observational and other objective data suggest additional problems: trouble with backing up, changing

lanes, noting signs and warnings, turning properly, and yielding the right of way (McKnight, 1988; National Highway Traffic Safety Administration, 1988; Yanik, 1988).

Many of these problems could be solved by redesigning vehicles with older adults in mind. For example, instrument panel luminance levels could be higher and made more glare-free (Mourant & Langolf, 1976), and headlights could be redesigned (Mortimer, 1989). However, many other aspects of cars could be made more user-friendly for older adults (D. B. D. Smith, 1990): entry and egress, mechanical controls and locks, field of view, and safety features.

One example of an important driving problem that could be affected by vision and information-processing changes is identifying signs, especially at dusk. For example, Sivak, Olson, and Pastalan (1981) found that older drivers needed to be considerably closer to text signs at night in order to read them, despite the fact that they had been equated with the younger drivers for daytime vision. A follow-up study in which older and younger drivers were equated for both daytime and nighttime vision revealed no performance differences, emphasizing that visual defects, not age, cause the problem (Sivak & Olson, 1982).

Kline, Ghali, Kline, and Brown (1990) examined how well younger, middle-aged, and older drivers could read text and icon highway signs. Text signs have various messages printed on them, such as "men working" and "divided highway." Icon signs are picture versions of text signs following international conventions; for example a "men working" icon sign depicts a man using a shovel. Kline and colleagues showed that all age groups identified icon signs at greater distances than text signs. This effect was especially true at dusk. Most important, no age differences were found; older adults identified signs as well as younger adults. This finding is important, especially in view of the well-documented changes in vision and in visual information processing. Additionally, the distance at which older adults were able to identify the signs would provide enough time for them to prepare for any decisions, such as the need to exit or slow down.

Highway Accidents. Many people believe that older drivers are unsafe. However, testing that theory is difficult, primarily because older adults have very different driving habits than younger and middle-aged adults. Older adults drive fewer total miles, less at night, less in bad weather, less in rush hour traffic, and less on freeways and the open highway (D. B. D. Smith, 1990). The consensus among researchers is that if older adults do have any elevated accident risk, it is compensated for by changes in driving habits, at least until late life (e.g., National Highway Traffic Safety Administration, 1988; Williams & Carsten, 1989).

Psychologists approach the study of age and highway accidents by focusing on the role of skills known to be relevant to driving. Age, per se, does not lead to accidents; rather, it is decreased skills that can cause them (Panek, Barrett, Sterns, & Alexander, 1977). Barrett, Alexander, and Forbes (1977) identified three information-processing variables that are especially important in understanding automobile accidents: perceptual strategies, selective attention, and reaction time.

Several researchers have studied the relationship between measures of basic skills and on-the-road behavior. Rackoff and Mourant (1979) found that older drivers (aged 60–70) who scored more poorly than younger drivers (aged 21–29) on tests of visual search, embedded figures, and reaction time also took longer to extract important information while driving. Shinar, McDowell, Rackoff, and Rockwell (1978) reported that older drivers who were not as able to filter out irrelevant information were less effective in their visual search behavior on the road. Problems in selective attention are evident in accident victims' statements; "I never saw the other car" is a common example of a failure to detect important information. Moreover, older drivers have difficulty judging the speed of oncoming vehicles (Scialfa, Guzy, Leibowitz, Garvey, & Tyrrell, 1991).

An additional problem facing older drivers is that older adults tend to be taking more prescription and nonprescription medications than younger adults. Since many medications have side effects that could impair sensory, perceptual, and reaction time processes, all adults, but especially the elderly, need to be aware of these effects.

Given the number of potential problems facing older drivers, some researchers have emphasized a need for specialized training programs. A good example of this approach is the program created by Sterns and his colleagues (Sterns et al., 1978; Sterns, Barrett, Alexander, Valasek, and McIlvried, 1985; Sterns & Sanders, 1980). They developed an assessment and training program based on the sensory, perceptual, and reaction time processes involved in driving. Intensive and extensive retraining on deficient skills (such as looking down the road) were found to hold up two years after training. Importantly, short-term training was not effective.

In sum, many sensory and information-processing changes affect driving. However, human factors research on the use of icons on signs and training programs based on information-processing interventions effectively help older drivers compensate for these changes.

Home Safety

By far, the most important home safety issue is falls. As noted in Chapter 3, changes in the vestibular system as well as combinations of changes in the muscular and skeletal systems place older adults at much greater risk of falling down. Additional risk factors include information-processing changes involving attention and focusing on relevant information such as cracks in the sidewalk. Much human factors research on falls has focused on the role of stair construction in falls (Pauls, 1985). This research has resulted in the incorporation of several safety standards into U.S. building codes concerning such things as handrails, ramps, and grab bars.

Unfortunately, little human factors research has been conducted on other home safety issues. Many important problems remain, such as legibility of dials and controls on stoves and ovens, and the design and ease of use of hot water faucets, door locks, and windows.

Accident Prevention

We are exposed to environmental risks every day; at any moment we could slip on a throw rug, trip on the stairs, or run a stop sign. Maintaining a safe environment, then, cannot be obtained through eliminating risk entirely. Rather, it must be based on a balanced approach to minimizing risk wherever possible, instituting better assessment and screening procedures, and educating people about hazards (Singleton, 1979).

The key to addressing the problem of safety is to remember that age alone does not cause accidents. Rather, it is the decline in sensory and information-processing skills that is responsible for age-related increases in some types of accidents. However, there are large differences across (and even within) individuals in the rate and extent of such changes. Consequently, accident prevention strategies must be sensitive to individual differences rather than simply focusing on age. As pointed out in Something to Think About, incorporating this knowledge is desirable, but it may be difficult to accomplish this goal.

LANGUAGE PROCESSING

One of the most important information-processing abilities in everyday life is understanding and using language. Understanding what is said to you in a conversation, being able to read the note your

Age-related changes in sensory, motor, and physiological systems increase the likelihood that this woman may have an accident getting on or off the train.

friend just slipped to you, and having the ability to respond allows you to interact with others and maintain social ties.

For these reasons, language processing is an important area of research in information processing. Like human factors, it is based on interactions between sensory systems and basic information-processing abilities. Language processing researchers distinguish between language comprehension and language production. *Language comprehension* involves handling words coming into the

SOMETHING TO THINK ABOUT

Accidents and the Elderly

Accidents seldom "just happen," and many can be prevented. Accidental injuries become both more frequent and more serious in later life. Thus, attention to safety is especially important for older people.

Several factors make people in this age group prone to accidents. Poor eyesight and hearing can decrease awareness of hazards. Arthritis, neurological diseases, and impaired coordination and balance can make older people unsteady. Various diseases, medications, alcohol, and preoccupation with personal problems can result in drowsiness or distraction. Often mishaps are expressions of mental depression or of poor physical conditioning.

When accidents occur, older people are especially vulnerable to severe injury and tend to heal slowly. Particularly in women, bones often become thin and brittle with age, causing seemingly minor falls to result in broken hips.

Many accidents can be prevented by maintaining mental and physical health and conditioning and by cultivating good safety habits.

Falls are the most common cause of fatal injury in the aged. Proper lighting can help prevent them. Here's what we can do:

- Illuminate all stairways and provide light switches at both the bottom and the top.

- Provide night-lights or bedside remote-control light switches.

- Be sure *both* sides of stairways have sturdy handrails.

- Tack down carpeting on stairs, and use nonskid treads.

- Remove throw rugs that tend to slide.

- Arrange furniture and other objects so they are not obstacles.

- Use grab bars on bathroom walls and nonskid mats or strips in the bathtub.

- Keep outdoor steps and walkways in good repair.

Personal health practices are also important in preventing falls. Because older people tend to become faint or dizzy after standing too quickly, experts recommend rising slowly from sitting or lying positions. Both illness and the side effects of drugs increase the risk of falls.

Burns are especially disabling in the aged, who recover from such injuries more slowly. Here are some ways to avoid being burned:

---

information-processing system and figuring out what they mean. Knowing the definition of words or that the person sitting across the table just asked you to pass the salt are two examples of language comprehension. In contrast, *language production* means being able to produce an appropriate word or phrase when you are trying to say, or write, or think about something. A common example of language production is coming up with a person's name when you encounter them in a store.

Researchers have studied many aspects of both language comprehension and language production.

Much of this work has been done in the context of memory or intelligence research. For example, having people learn and remember word lists or text passages is commonly examined in memory research, and testing people's vocabulary knowledge is typical in intelligence research. Both of these areas rely heavily on language production because people's scores are based on how often and how well they produce correct responses. We will be considering these research areas in Chapters 6 and 7. In this section, we will focus on the basic processes of language comprehension.

- Never smoke in bed or when drowsy.

- When cooking, don't wear loosely fitting flammable clothing. Bathrobes, nightgowns, and pajamas catch fire.

- Set water heater thermostats or faucets so that water does not scald the skin.

- Plan which emergency exits to use in case of fire. Many older people trap themselves behind multiple door locks that are hard to open during an emergency. Install one good lock that can be opened from the inside quickly, rather than many inexpensive locks.

Motor vehicle accidents are the most common cause of accidental death among the 65–74 age group and the second most common cause among older people in general. Your ability to drive may be impaired by such age-related changes as increased sensitivity to glare, poorer adaptation to dark, diminished coordination, and slower reaction time. You can compensate for these changes by driving fewer miles; driving less often and more slowly; and driving less at night, during rush hour, and in the winter.

If you ride on public transportation:

- Remain alert and brace yourself when a bus is slowing down or turning.

- Watch for slippery pavement and other hazards when entering or leaving a vehicle.

- Have the fare ready to prevent losing your balance while fumbling for change.

- Do not carry too many packages, and leave one hand free to grasp railings.

- Allow extra time to cross streets, especially in bad weather.

- At night wear light-colored or fluorescent clothing and carry a flashlight.

Old people constitute about 11% of the population and suffer 23% of all accidental deaths. The National Safety Council reports that each year about 24,000 people over age 65 die from accidental injuries and at least 800,000 others sustain injuries severe enough to disable them for at least 1 day. Thus, attention to safety, especially in later life, can prevent much untimely death and disability. It's something to think about.

(Source: National Institute on Aging.)

Language Comprehension and Sensory Systems

Language comprehension is based initially on visual or auditory input. We saw in Chapter 3 that there are many important changes in each of these sensory systems that could influence how well or how easily we understand language. In vision, there are changes in light transmissiveness and accommodation that could affect how clearly we see letters or words. In hearing, changes in pitch perception may alter how well we hear certain sounds.

Earlier in this chapter we examined several changes in visual information processing that could also impact language comprehension. Most important, the data suggested that older adults have difficulty integrating different visual features. This could present problems when older adults read. One area we have not yet considered is understanding speech. It is to this topic we now turn.

Understanding Speech. Have you ever tried to have a serious conversation at a noisy party? You may have had trouble understanding what the person you were with was saying. Or perhaps you have been in a quieter environment like an art museum and couldn't quite pick up what the tour director was relating about the Monet masterpiece behind her. Both of these situations can be annoying and embarrassing. Constantly saying, "I can't hear you; would you repeat what you said?" is no fun.

Obviously, being able to hear plays an important role in understanding speech. Given the normative decline in hearing due to presbycusis (see Chapter 3), you may wonder whether people's ability to understand speech declines as well. Fortunately, presbycusis normally does not affect the pitches used in most speech sounds until around age 80. As a result, speech understanding is usually not seriously impaired until late in life. However, a few sounds in English, such as *s*, *ch*, and *sh* involve pitches that are affected earlier. Consequently, middle-aged and young-old adults (ages 60–75) may have trouble understanding these sounds (Brant & Fozard, 1990).

How well people understand speech is tested in two ways. *Speech recognition* is measured by presenting the listener with a list of spondee words: Spondaic two-syllable words are pronounced with equal emphasis on both syllables (some English examples are *airplane*, *baseball*, *birthday*, and *headlight*). *Speech discrimination* is tested with monosyllabic words that include the various sounds in English.

Several studies have documented an age-related decrement in both speech recognition and speech discrimination abilities, especially after age 50 (Corso, 1981; Olsho et al., 1985). Typical results are shown in Figure 5.4. Notice that age differences become especially pronounced when the listening situation is made more difficult, such as when there are other voices in the background or when speech is interrupted. Older adults also have difficulty understanding speech that is embedded in noise (Gordon-Salant, 1987).

How well people understand speech is also affected by how fast it is presented and whether the words are presented alone or in the context of regular speech. Stine, Wingfield, and colleagues examined these issues in a series of studies (e.g., Stine & Wingfield, 1987; Stine, Wingfield, & Poon, 1986; Wingfield & Stine, 1986). They looked for age differences in speech understanding by using compressed speech, which allowed them to use presentation rates between 200 and 400 words per minute. In addition, they manipulated whether words were presented in sentences, with normal voice inflections, in meaningless but grammatically correct strings, or in random order. Results demonstrated the power of context. When words were presented normally in sentences, older adults performed at over 90% accuracy even at 400 or more words per minute. However, when words were presented in random strings or without normal vocal cues, older adults performed poorly even at slower rates (around 250 words per minute).

Stine and Wingfield's work clearly shows how context affects older adults' understanding of speech. On one hand, context allows older adults to understand what is said even at very fast presentation rates. This finding is similar to the results from Salthouse's work on typing that we considered earlier. On the other hand, Stine and Wingfield's research also demonstrates how much older adults depend on context; their understanding of speech drops dramatically when contextual cues are not present. These effects get us into the realm of the role of information processing in language, to which we now turn.

Language Comprehension and Information Processing

How do words get processed beyond basic sensory systems so that we understand what they mean? This question has intrigued researchers for many years, and continues to be one of the most active areas in cognitive psychology. Some argue that lan-

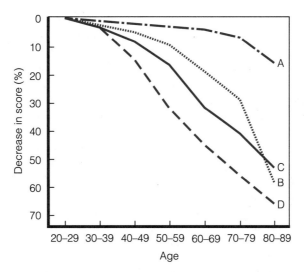

FIGURE 5.4 Decrease in percent intelligibility for speech as a function of age. Curves: **A** — unaltered speech; **B** — reverberated speech; **C** — overlapping speech with spondaic words; **D** — interrupted speech. For each curve, normal subjects 20–29 years served as zero reference.

(Source: "Hearing and Aging: Implications of Recent Research Findings" by M. Bergman, 1971, *Audiology*, *10*, 164–171. Reprinted with permission of S. Karger, AG.)

guage processing is the key to understanding a host of other processes, including understanding memory. If this is true, then age-related changes in language processing may underlie the age-related differences in memory we will discuss in Chapter 6. For example, Craik and Byrd (1982) claimed that age-related differences in language processing result in less richly encoded information that makes information less memorable. Their claim is based on the belief that older adults' information-processing abilities are compromised — due to less attentional capacity, drops in processing speed, and changes in working memory (see Chapter 6).

Numerous investigators have examined aspects of Craik and Byrd's claim (Light, 1990). We will consider this research under two general headings: richness and extensiveness of encoding and encoding deficits.

Richness and Extensiveness of Encoding. Suppose you and a friend hear the name Martin Luther King, Jr., as part of a lecture in history class. Suppose further that you are very familiar with him but your friend is not. You will have a distinct advantage over your friend in remembering him. Why?

When linguistic information comes in, you look for ways to connect it to other information you already know. (How this happens is described in detail in Chapter 6). The more connections you can make, the better off you will be later when you need to remember the name. Because your friend can only make a few connections, getting the name to stick in memory will be more difficult.

The number of different connections you create between incoming information and information already in your knowledge base is what is meant by rich and extensive encoding. If age differences in encoding occur, they could be manifested in two ways (Light, 1990). First, how knowledge is organized could change across adulthood, making it harder to keep connections intact. Second, it is possible that the processes by which connections get made change with age. However, neither appears to change substantially with age (Light, 1990).

Encoding Deficits. One school of thought is that extensive encoding underlies the ability to retrieve information. That is, information that is richly encoded is more easily retrieved. One way to test this is to ask people to judge whether a particular letter string is a word (called a lexical decision task). One variant of a lexical decision task involves showing people related words prior to the letter string (for example, show the word *nurse* and ask people to judge whether the letter string *d-o-c-t-o-r* is a word). Performing well on lexical decision tasks requires a fairly rich knowledge base. Adults of all ages are equally adept at lexical decision tasks. For example, Stern, Prather, Swinney, and Zurif (1991) showed that older and younger adults had equal automatic lexical access. However, as we will see in Chapter 6 older adults do worse on memory tests of the same words. This performance pattern of equivalent lexical access but poorer memory does not support the idea that poor encoding underlies memory problems.

A second issue concerning encoding deficits is the notion that older adults do not take advantage of contextual cues when they encode information. Specifically, Rabinowitz, Craik, and Ackerman (1982) believed that older adults do not tend to create distinctive context-specific encoding, but rather have a tendency to use the same approach each time. Although there is some support for Rabinowitz et al.'s position, several investigators disagree. We have already seen that older adults use sentence context to process rapid speech. Additionally, researchers have shown that older adults often do use context-specific information at encoding (for example, Howard, Heisey, & Shaw, 1986) and in naming words (Nebes, Boller, & Holland, 1986).

In sum, there is no support for the contention that basic linguistic processing is the basis for age-related differences in memory. Knowledge is organized similarly in younger and older adults, and tests of immediate comprehension as measured by word naming and lexical decision tasks show no age differences. What, then, accounts for memory problems? We will examine this issue in Chapter 6.

Implicit Memory

Although age differences in language processing do not appear to underlie age differences in memory, there is one area in which the two overlap. **Implicit memory** involves testing people's recollections of things, but without having people deliberately learn material. Typically, this is accomplished with a language task such as stem completion. In a stem completion task, you would be required to complete a word stem with the first word that comes to mind (for instance, con____). Previously, you may have been shown a list of words that contained a valid completion of the stem (such as con*tact*). If you have seen valid completions of the stems, you are more likely to use them later to complete the stems than you are to make up a different one (con*test*). The memory aspect of the task is that you remember the stem completion you were shown; the implicit part is remembering it without being told to do so.

Results from several studies demonstrate small differences in favor of young adults (Chiarello & Hoyer, 1988; Hultsch, Masson, & Small, 1991). Most important, it appears that implicit memory tests tap different cognitive processes than direct memory tests (such as deliberately learning and remembering a list of words). Hultsch and colleagues (1991) believe that implicit memory tests, such as stem completion, tap aspects early in information processing; direct memory tests, like those considered in Chapter 6, assess later steps.

SUMMARY

The Information-Processing Model

1. The information-processing model assumes an active participant, both quantitative and qualitative aspects of performance, and processing of information through a series of hypothetical stages.

2. Sensory memory is the first level of processing incoming information from the environment. Sensory memory has a very large capacity, but information only lasts there a very short time.

3. Age differences are found in two aspects of sensory memory: encoding speed and susceptibility to backward masking.

Attention

4. Three aspects of attention have been studied: selectivity, capacity, and vigilance. Selectivity involves choosing which information gets passed from sensory memory to working memory. Capacity refers to how much information can be processed at once. Some processes are automatic, placing little or no demand on attentional capacity; other processes require effort and put varying demands on capacity. Vigilance or sustained attention refers to how long you can maintain attention while doing a task.

5. Feature integration theory describes the process by which you encode important aspects of a stimulus (feature extraction) and then put those aspects together (feature integration).

6. Age-related decrements are found in visual search, primarily due to differences in feature integration.

7. Cuing spatial locations sharply reduces age differences when the cue provides unambiguous information.

8. No age differences are found on visual attention switching tasks, but are found on auditory tasks.

9. Older adults have more difficulty filtering out irrelevant information than younger adults.

10. Age differences in divided attention depend on the degree of task complexity.

11. Older adults are not as good as younger adults at detecting targets on vigilance tasks, but there are no age differences in the rate at which performance declines over time. Age differences are found on difficult vigilance tasks and in the degree to which performance becomes automatic.

Psychomotor Speed

12. Simple reaction time involves responding as quickly as possible to a stimulus. Choice reaction time involves making separate responses to separate stimuli as quickly as possible. Complex reaction time involves making complicated decisions about how to respond based on the stimulus observed.

13. Older adults do not prepare as well to make a response as younger adults.

14. As task complexity increases, age differences increase.

15. One explanation of age differences, based on neural networks, is that older people need more neuronal connections to make the response. A second possibility is that older adults lose more information at each step.

16. Although practice improves performance, age differences are not eliminated. However, experience allows older adults to compensate for loss of speed by anticipating what is likely to happen.

17. Regular exercise improves reaction time performance.

Human Factors and Aging

18. Human factors tries to optimize the design of living and working environments.

19. Older drivers have several problems, including reading highway signs, seeing at night, noting

warnings, and various operating skills. Changes in information-processing abilities could make older adults more susceptible to accidents.

20. Older adults are more likely to hurt themselves by falling at home than younger adults.

Language Processing

21. Language comprehension involves attaching meaning to incoming words. Language production involves coming up with an appropriate word or phrase.

22. Speech comprehension is usually not affected by presbycusis until age 80. However, a few sounds are affected earlier. Speech recognition and speech discrimination both decline with age.

23. Age differences are usually not found on lexical decision tasks.

24. Basic language processing deficits do not appear to be the cause of age differences in memory.

25. Older adults do slightly worse on stem completion tests than younger adults.

REVIEW QUESTIONS

The Information-Processing Model

1. What assumptions does the information-processing model make?

2. What is sensory memory? What age differences have been noted?

Attention

3. What aspects of attention have been studied? Define each of them.

4. What is feature integration theory? How does it help researchers understand age differences in attention?

5. What age differences have been reported in visual search? How can these age differences be reduced or eliminated?

6. What age differences have been noted on divided attention tasks? Why do these differences occur?

7. What age differences occur on vigilance tasks? What variables affect the magnitude of age differences?

Psychomotor Speed

8. What different types of reaction time tasks are used to study psychomotor speed? What age differences have been found on each?

9. How does task complexity affect age differences on reaction time tasks?

10. Describe the neural networks approach to accounting for age differences in reaction time.

11. How do practice and experience affect age differences in reaction time?

12. What effect does exercise have on reaction time?

Human Factors and Aging

13. What is human factors?

14. What problems do older drivers have, and what interventions can be applied to help them?

15. What accident risks do older adults face in their homes?

Language Processing

16. What is the difference between language comprehension and language production?

17. How do speech comprehension, speech recognition, and speech discrimination change with age?

18. What role do basic language processing deficits play in age differences in memory?

19. What age differences have been found on implicit memory tasks?

KEY TERMS

capacity A hypothetical construct referring to the amount of information that can be processed at a time. (152)

divided attention The ability to pay attention to more than one task at a time. (156)

feature integration theory (FIT) A theory of visual information processing consisting of two phases — feature extraction and feature integration. FIT explains a great deal of the age differences found in visual information processing. (153)

human factors The study of how people interact with machines and other objects in their environment. (166)

implicit memory A type of memory that occurs without one being aware that something has been remembered. (174)

information-processing approach The study of how people take in stimuli from their environment and transform them into memories; the approach is based on a computer metaphor. (150)

reaction time The speed with which one can make a response. (154)

response complexity The degree of difficulty associated with making a response in a reaction time task. (161)

response preparation The processes involved in getting ready to make a response in a reaction time task. (160)

selectivity The process by which information is chosen for further processing in attention. (152)

sensory memory The first step in the information-processing system responsible for receiving input from the environment. (151)

spatial cuing A technique in visual-processing research in which people are provided a hint concerning where the next target will occur. (154)

vigilance Maintaining attention to the same task over an extended period of time. (152)

ADDITIONAL READING

Additional information about aging and information processing can be found in

Cerella, J. (1990). Aging and information-processing rate. In J. E. Birren & K. W. Schaie (Eds.), *Handbook of the psychology of aging* (3rd. ed., pp. 201–221). San Diego: Academic Press. Moderate to difficult.

McDowd, J. M., & Birren, J. E. (1990). Aging and attentional processes. In J. E. Birren & K. W. Schaie (Eds.), *Handbook of the psychology of aging* (3rd. ed., pp. 222-233). San Diego: Academic Press. Moderate difficulty.

Many different aspects of language processing are discussed in

Light, L. L., & Burke, D. M. (Eds.) (1988). *Language, memory, and aging*. New York: Cambridge University Press.

CHAPTER 6

Memory

Andrew Wyeth, *Children's Doctor*, 1949. Brandywine River Museum, Chadds Ford, Pennsylvania.

There once lived a very old woman who one day decided that, because she had learned everything there was to learn, she might as well lie down and die. She called for her daughter to make her one last cup of tea. The daughter went over to the cold fireplace in the mother's cabin and scooped up a handful of ashes. "Why are you doing that?" asked the older woman. "My fireplace still has some hot coals," said the daughter. "I will go to my cabin, put a coal on top of these cold ashes, and carry it over to your fireplace without getting burned. Then I can start a fire to make some tea." On hearing this, the old woman got out of bed. "I've never heard of that before," she said. "I guess I won't have to die today."

T HIS FOLK TALE OF THE RURAL, SOUTHERN United States points out that learning something new every day is one of the things that keeps people motivated to live. Accumulating life experiences, such as learning how to carry a hot coal without getting burned, is a process that lasts as long as we live. These experiences also provide the basis for building a personal identity. It is the remembering of these experiences that tells us who we are and where we came from.

Memory is such a pervasive aspect of our daily lives that we take it for granted. From remembering where you keep your toothbrush to tying your shoes to timing soft-boiled eggs — memory is always with you. Moreover, it gives you a sense of identity. Imagine how frightening it would be to wake up and have no memory whatsoever — no

recollection of your name, address, your parents, or anything else.

Perhaps that is why we put so much value on maintaining a good memory in old age. Society uses memory as the yardstick with which to judge whether a person's mind is intact. Older adults are stereotyped as people whose memory is on the decline, people for whom forgetting is not to be taken lightly. Many people think that forgetting to buy a loaf of bread when one is 25 is all right, but forgetting it when one is 65 is cause for concern ("Do I have Alzheimer's disease?"). We will see that this belief is wrong. But there is no question that we have more at stake here than just another cognitive process. We are dealing with something that intimately involves our sense of self (Cavanaugh, Morton, & Tilse, 1989).

Most of the research described in this chapter views memory as an end in itself. That is, the goal is simply how well people perform the task of learning and remembering some material. Doing well on the memory test is the name of the game. Indeed, there are many situations in life that present similar demands. We may need to have considerable information at our fingertips in order to do well at games like *Trivial Pursuit*.

But many other situations in everyday life call for the use of memory to serve some other function. That is, we use memory as a means to an end. For example, we use memory when we summarize the most recent episode of our favorite soap opera, tell other people about ourselves, or reminisce about our high school days. In these situations we *are* using memory, but the point is not just how much we remember. More often, the idea is to facilitate social exchange, to allow other people to get to know us, or to give ourselves a shared past with others.

These different uses of memory raise some intriguing questions about adult development and aging. Are there differences in the ways in which adults of different ages use memory? How would these differences affect performance on traditional memory tests? What should our criteria be for good versus poor memory? These questions are something to think about as we explore what has been discovered about aging and memory. We will attempt to answer them by looking at memory from different vantage points. First, we will continue applying the information-processing model introduced in Chapter 5, and see what happens to secondary and tertiary memory. Second, we will focus specifically on how we keep information stored in memory and how we get it back out. An important aspect here will be how adults use different types of strategies to help themselves remember. Third, we will look at memory for discourse, and see how people vary in the kinds of information they remember from such things as prose passages and television. Fourth, we will consider several ways in which adults remember things in everyday life, and differences between these settings and laboratory research. Fifth, we will examine how we use memory as a yardstick by which we judge our competence. In particular, we will consider the processes by which we evaluate our memory. Finally, we will see how memory problems are assessed and how some problems may be treated.

INFORMATION PROCESSING REVISITED

In Chapter 5, you were introduced to the most widely used model of cognitive processes — the information-processing model. Recall that the information-processing model is based on a computer metaphor, and that different aspects of the model have different jobs to perform. In Chapter 5, we focused on the first two major components, sensory memory and primary memory, and on the

process of attention. Our focus in this section will be on the final three main components: working memory, secondary memory, and tertiary memory.

Working Memory

Working memory is a small-capacity store that deals with the items that are currently being processed (Stine, 1990). The capacity limitation of working memory operates like a juggler who can only keep a small number of items in the air simultaneously. Because working memory deals with information being processed right at this moment, it is also viewed as a kind of mental scratchpad. This means that unless we take direct action, the page we are using will get used up quickly and tossed away. For this reason, we need to have some way to keep information in working memory. The most important way in which information is held in working memory is through **rehearsal**, which involves either repeating items over and over or making meaningful connections between the information in working memory and information you already know (Craik & Lockhart, 1972; Kausler, 1985).

Many researchers propose working memory as the basis for understanding language processing difficulties encountered in later life (e.g., Kemper, 1988; Stine, 1990). This idea is based on the extremely important role that working memory is believed to play in information processing. For example, working memory is where all the action is during processing: It is where information obtains meaning and is transformed for longer storage. As a result, age differences here would have profound implications for just about all aspects of memory. The idea is that if information becomes degraded or is only partially integrated into your knowledge base, it will be very difficult for you to remember it.

There is growing evidence that the capacity of working memory declines somewhat with age (Salthouse, 1991), although the extent of the decline is still in doubt. Additionally, rehearsal ability declines, resulting in poorer quality information being passed along the system (Kausler, 1985). Salthouse (1991) believes that working memory is the key to understanding age differences in memory. Because older adults appear to lose some of the ability to hold items in working memory, Salthouse argues that this may limit older adults' overall cognitive functioning. Moreover, Salthouse points out that much of the apparent differences in working memory may in turn be related to speed of processing. That is, older adults' reduced working memory capacity may be due to their overall slower rate of processing, which we reviewed in Chapter 5.

However, there is some evidence that age differences in working memory are not universal. For example, working memory appears to depend on the type of information being used, and may even vary across different tasks (Daneman, 1987). Such differences complicate matters. It may be that the extent of age differences in working memory depend more on one's degree of expertise in a particular area than on age per se. Could practice eliminate age differences in working memory?

Campbell and Charness (1990) decided to look into the matter. They had young, middle-aged, and older adults learn and practice an algorithm for squaring 2-digit numbers (for example, learning how to calculate 57^2 in your head). Needless to say, this task is hard for the uninitiated; you not only need many facts about multiplication at your fingertips, but you also need to remember the results of all the intermediate calculations in order to get the correct answer.

Practicing the algorithm greatly reduced calculation errors for all age groups. However, the older group made more working memory errors (such as, leaving out steps in the calculation process). Moreover, practice did not substantially reduce age differences in the efficiency of working memory. These results imply two things. First, practice greatly enhances fact retrieval, as seen in the large reduction of calculation errors. Second, practice has only a minimal effect on improving working memory efficiency. Thus, it appears that although practice may help people retrieve information faster, it may not help them use it more efficiently. Age-related decrements in working memory efficiency appear to be normative.

Still, because research on working memory is relatively new, a great deal more needs to be done. Salthouse's attempt to link age differences in working memory with age differences in processing speed will open up new and exciting avenues for research. Campbell and Charness's differentiation between fact retrieval and working memory efficiency will help clarify the role of practice and expertise. For the moment, however, whether working memory is the key to understanding age differences in memory remains to be seen.

Secondary Memory

Secondary memory refers to what many people regard as the bread and butter of memory: the ability to remember rather extensive amounts of information over relatively long periods. Everyday life is full of examples — remembering routines, performing on an exam, summarizing a book or movie, and remembering an appointment. Memory researchers have adapted these examples and created a wide variety of tasks requiring individuals to remember long lists of information. These everyday and research-based examples are indications that secondary memory represents a very large capacity store in which information can be kept for long periods.

Because secondary memory includes so many of the day-to-day activities we adults perform, it

Activities such as spinning involve retrieving elaborate memory representations for each aspect of the activity as well as accurately monitoring what one is doing.

has been the focus of more research than any other single topic in memory development (Poon, 1985). Typically, researchers study secondary memory by having people learn a list of items and then asking them to recall or recognize the items. In a **recall** test, people are asked to remember information without hints or cues. Everyday examples of recall include telling everything that you can remember about a movie or taking an essay exam. **Recognition**, on the other hand, involves selecting previously learned information from among several items. Everyday examples of recognition include multiple choice tests and picking out the names of your high school friends from a complete list of your classmates.

Memory researchers use several techniques to study the variables that influence secondary memory performance. For example, they may vary the way that the information to be learned is presented (such as, in organized groups, with cues, or randomly); the speed at which it is presented; the familiarity of the material; and the conditions for remembering the items (for instance, giving recall cues or making a recognition test easy or hard).

The results from hundreds of studies on secondary memory point to several conclusions. Overall, older adults perform worse than younger adults on tests of recall, but these differences are less apparent or may be eliminated on tests of recognition (Poon, 1985). Older adults also tend to be less efficient at spontaneously using strategies, such as putting items into categories to organize information during study. When older adults are instructed to use organizational strategies such as categorization, however, they not only can do so but also show significant improvement in performance. These findings suggest that older adults are not as successful in situations requiring them to devise an efficient way to acquire disorganized information, especially when they will be expected to recall it later. When cues are provided during initial learning or at recall, or when memory is tested through recognition, older adults benefit considerably.

Age differences between older and younger adults can be reduced in several ways. First, slowing down the pace at which information is presented helps, especially when older adults can pace the task themselves. This finding fits well with the notion that aging brings a slowing in information processing (Cerella, 1990; see also Chapter 5). Second, allowing older adults to practice or to perform a similar task before learning a new list improves performance. Knowing what one is expected to do usually makes it easier to perform well. Interestingly, better memory performance after practice parallels similar improvements following practice on tests of skills related to fluid intelligence (see Chapter 7). Third, using material that is more familiar to older adults also improves their performance. For example, older adults do not remember words such as *byte* or *Walkman* as well as words such as *flapper* or *lizzie*.

What, then, can we conclude about secondary memory? It appears that older adults are disadvantaged when left on their own to face relatively rapid-paced, disorganized information. However, secondary memory performance appears to be quite flexible and manipulable, with improvements coming from a variety of sources. In later sections we will consider some attempts to explain why age differences occur and several ways in which secondary memory problems can be corrected.

Tertiary Memory

Information that needs to be kept for a very long time is housed in **tertiary memory**. Such information includes facts learned earlier, the meaning of words, past life experiences, and the like. Very little research has been conducted on age differences in tertiary memory, for a variety of reasons. For one thing it is difficult to design an adequate test of very long-term memory so that we know how to interpret performance. For example, we often cannot know whether an incident that someone recalls from the past is what actually happened, because we cannot verify the facts. Additionally, if a person does not remember a fact from years past, it may be due either to an inability to retrieve the information or to a failure to have learned the information in the first place. Some ingenious researchers, though, have managed to circumvent these problems and have studied two aspects of tertiary memory: knowledge base and autobiographical memory.

Knowledge Base. One way that researchers test tertiary memory is with questionnaires asking about events of public knowledge assumed to be available to everyone. A typical question would be to ask for the name of the spacecraft that exploded after launching in January 1986. Researchers who have examined adults' performance on tests of knowledge about the Challenger disaster and other events find little difference in performance across age groups (e.g., Botwinick & Storandt, 1974; J. L. Lachman & Lachman, 1980; Perlmutter, Metzger, Miller, & Nezworski, 1980).

Camp (1989) has conducted some interesting research on people's ability to combine pieces of information in tertiary memory in order to answer inference questions. The questions he asks are unlikely to have been encountered before, making this technique useful in exploring the kinds of information housed in tertiary memory. An example of one of Camp's questions might be: What horror movie character would want to avoid the Lone Ranger? Camp finds that older adults respond with the werewolf (who can be killed only with silver bullets, the Lone Ranger's trademark) as well as, and often better than, young adults. Camp argues that these findings indicate no age differences in tertiary memory, and may be evidence for improvement.

The lack of age differences in the knowledge base aspects of tertiary memory is not really surprising. The information we keep in tertiary memory is very similar to the information that relates to crystallized intelligence, such as world knowledge and vocabulary. As pointed out in Chapter 7, crystallized intelligence undergoes little if any change with age. Thus, it may be that tertiary memory is also related to this set of abilities.

Autobiographical Memory. One very important type of tertiary memory involves remembering information and events from your own life. These recollections, or autobiographical memory, provide each of us with a personal history and help define who we are. As important as autobiographical memory is, though, very few studies have looked at how well people remember things over the course of their lives.

One kind of personal information we remember are the names of our high school classmates. Bahrick, Bahrick, and Wittlinger (1975) tested high school graduates aged 17 to 74 for recall of their classmates' names and recognition of their faces in yearbook pictures. Recognition of faces was consistently over 90% up to 15 years after graduation. Amazingly, adults in their 70s could still recognize 70% of their classmates' names 48 years after graduation! Clearly, tertiary memory remains fairly good. The study also demonstrates that in some areas it is possible to assess the accuracy of very long-term memory. Being able to verify what individuals remember with some record of the true event is extremely important in evaluating our ability to remember over long periods of time.

The issue of verification is crucial in testing people's recollections of personally experienced events. Only in cases where records have been kept for many years is this usually possible. Coleman, Casey, and Dwyer (1991) examined records that were available from the Harvard Longitudinal Studies of Child Health and Development on individuals from birth to age 50. Detailed information was collected over the years on such things as which childhood diseases the participants had, whether they smoked cigarettes, and what kinds and how much food they ate. At age 50, participants completed a lengthy questionnaire about these issues, and their responses were compared with similar reports made 10 and 20 years earlier, as well as with the official records. Coleman and colleagues found amazing accuracy for information such as whether a person had ever been a smoker or had a particular disease such as chicken pox. In fact, half of the memories elicited at age 50 were *more* accurate than the memories for the same information elicited 10 years earlier at age 40! However, information about amounts of food consumed or about individual episodes was not remembered very well. Apparently, these events tend to blend together and are not stored as separate incidents.

What distinguishes events that are memorable from those that are not? What makes a moment we will remember the rest of our lives? Many people think that highly traumatic events are ones that are indelibly etched in our memories. If so, then people who survived Nazi concentration camps should have vivid memories of their experiences. Wagenaar and Groeneweg (1990) examined the testimony of 78 survivors of Camp Erika, a Nazi concentration camp in the Netherlands during World War II. Dutch police initially interviewed the survivors about their experiences between 1943 and 1948. In 1984, during a war crimes trial

SOMETHING TO THINK ABOUT

The Memory of Concentration Camp Survivors

One of the most common beliefs about autobiographical memory is that we can remember vivid details about especially important events in our lives. Indeed, researchers have identified so-called flashbulb memories in which people report minute details about what they were doing when they heard about a particular event, such as the assassinations of John F. Kennedy and Martin Luther King, Jr., or when the war with Iraq began.

This belief is especially strong when it comes to remembering traumatic events. Personal, detailed accounts of these events are an essential part of the judicial process; the lack of well-remembered details may mean a failure to obtain a conviction.

Juries often find it hard to believe that crime victims fail to remember key details of the event.

Recently, though, a provocative study on concentration camp survivors questions the assumption of detailed memories. As noted in the text, Wagenaar and Groeneweg report that many survivors of Camp Erika (a Nazi concentration camp) in the Netherlands could not remember basic details of their experience. Cognitive psychologists would argue that being in a concentration camp should have provided a classic flashbulb memory that should have lasted many years. Indeed, survivors reported remembering their experiences in vivid detail in their interviews with the Dutch press in the mid-1940s. After 40 years, though, the memories were gone for many people. Why?

We know that information in tertiary memory changes over time. For example, as we have new experiences we integrate them into our memory base. Over time, it becomes increasingly difficult to remember just the initial event. Additionally, people tend to not want to remember highly traumatic events. Rather, we want to forget them in the sense of learning to live with them. For example, after the loss of a loved one, people try to focus on the good events they shared rather than on the negative ones (see Chapter 13). "Getting on with one's life" is a familiar approach to such issues.

Wagenaar and Groeneweg's findings make us think about our own personal past. Just because we do not remember events in detail does not mean we have faulty memories. But by the same token, remembering details does not mean the events happened exactly as we remember them. All our recollections are selective interpretations of the past. It's something to think about.

---

for an accused Nazi collaborator, these witnesses gave sworn depositions about their experiences at Camp Erika.

As described in Something to Think About, the camp survivors' recollections were a mix of accurate and inaccurate information. In many cases memory was quite good; even 40 years later about half of the survivors remembered the exact date of their arrival at the camp and their entire identification number. They were able to recall the general conditions of the camp, overall treatment, and the like. However, they also had forgotten many important details, including in some cases their own brutal treatment. Wagenaar and Groeneweg point out that these forgotten details mean that even extreme trauma is no guarantee that an event will be remembered. Perhaps forgetting the horrors of being brutalized is a type of self-protection.

SOURCES OF AGE DIFFERENCES: STORAGE AND RETRIEVAL PROCESSES

Where do age differences between younger and older adults, especially in secondary memory, come from? Are older adults poorer at getting information into memory? Or do they get the information in just as well but have more difficulty getting it back out? Or is the problem a combination of the two?

Memory researchers have found that a two-stage model does a good job in accounting for age differences (Howe, 1988). In the two-stage model, the processes of getting information in and keeping it there are not considered separately but as one process, called **storage**. The second process, getting information back out, is termed **retrieval**. In the two-stage model information passes through three states (Howe, 1988): (1) an unmemorized state, in which information has not yet been learned; (2) a partially memorized state, in which the information is sometimes remembered and sometimes forgotten; and (3) a memorized state, in which the information is always remembered.

Age Differences in Storage

Results from several lines of research point to a clear age-related decrement in storage processes (Craik, 1977; Kausler, 1982; Poon, 1985). Most of this work attempts to examine various aspects of the storage process. Additionally, considerable research points to a decline in the efficiency of storage. Thus, another major line of research focuses on using memory strategies to improve efficiency.

Specific Components of Storage. Recall that an important process in working memory is rehearsal, and that one aspect of rehearsal is the ability to make sense out of incoming information. You typically do this by making connections between incoming information and information you already know. For example, if you are presented with the word *emu*, and are told that this is a bird that doesn't fly, you may try to think of other flightless birds. With some thought, *ostrich* may come to mind. Linking emu and ostrich would be an example of this type of rehearsal.

In a series of systematic studies, Howe (1988) examined this rehearsal process. He showed that the age-related decrement in storage processes may be due to age differences in how easily people make connections between incoming information and information that was previously stored in memory. Older adults have more difficulty making these connections than younger adults. Interestingly, however, once these connections have been made, older and younger adults maintain them equivalently. For example, older adults would be slower than younger adults at making the emu–ostrich connection, but once it is made both groups would remember it just as well.

Howe's research shows that we must be careful not to conclude that the entire storage process deteriorates with age. Rather, some aspects are probably more age sensitive than others.

The Use of Strategies. When confronted with large amounts of information that we need to remember, we tend to use various techniques that make the task easier and increase the efficiency of storage. These techniques are collectively referred to as **strategies**.

One extremely effective strategy for learning new information is to organize it. For example, consider your efforts to learn the information in college courses. It is much easier to learn the necessary facts of chemistry, psychology, literature, and so forth if you keep separate notebooks for each class. Imagine the potential for confusion if you simply

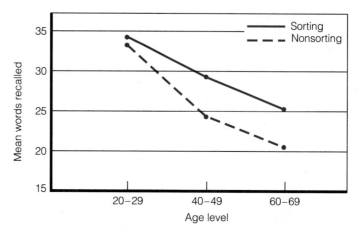

FIGURE 6.1 Mean number of words correctly recalled, as a function of age and sorting condition

(Source: "Adult Age Differences in Free Classification and Free Recall" by D. F. Hultsch, 1971, *Developmental Psychology*, *4*, 338–342. Copyright 1971 by the American Psychological Association. Reprinted with permission of the author.)

mixed all of the class notes together. Keeping them separate is an example of an organizational strategy.

There is substantial evidence that older adults do not spontaneously organize incoming information as often or as well as younger adults (Craik, 1977; Craik & Rabinowitz, 1984; Kausler, 1982). For example, older adults are less likely to take advantage of similarities in meaning among words (such as between *river* and *lake*) presented randomly in a list as a way to organize the items (Denney, 1974). Because the number of items remembered from such a list is highly related to the use of organization, younger adults outperform older adults on such tasks. Interestingly, older adults can use organization if they are told to do so (Schmitt, Murphy, & Sanders, 1981) or are experienced with sorting words into categories (Hultsch, 1971). This is clearly shown in Figure 6.1. However, the results of these manipulations are often short lived; older adults tend not to continue using organization over the long run if not required to do so.

The frequency of spontaneous use of other strategies also appears to decrease with age. For example, older adults are less likely to use imagery (forming pictures of items in one's mind) and other mnemonic memory devices (such as using the first letters of items to form a word, like *NASA*) (Kausler, 1982). When explicitly instructed to do so, however, older adults can use these and many other types of strategies. Moreover, their performance improves significantly compared with that of older adults who are not instructed.

Age Differences in Retrieval

Once we get information stored, we will at some point need to find it again and remember it. Researchers have agreed for many years that older adults have more difficulty retrieving information than do younger adults (Burke & Light, 1981; Craik, 1977; Kausler, 1982; Poon, 1985). This conclusion is based on research in three areas: (1) comparisons of performance using different types of retrieval; (2) comparisons of recall and recognition performances; and (3) studies of cued recall.

Specific Components of Retrieval. Researchers distinguish two general retrieval processes. *Heuristic retrieval* is any recovery process that produces both successes and failures. For example, when asked to give directions to a specific place, you remember some general steps ("I went south for awhile"). These general steps may or may not help you find the place again. Heuristic retrieval is used when information has been only partly learned, as when you have just moved to a new city and are unsure of street names. In contrast, *algorithmic retrieval* is any recovery process that produces error-free performance. Remembering that the street you turn left on is three blocks south of the big red office building will provide a distinctive tag or cue to remember the key information. Algorithmic retrieval is used when information has been learned very well, such as when you have lived in the same place a fairly long time and really know your way around.

An important issue is whether age differences are equivalent for both kinds of retrieval. Apparently, they are not. Howe (1988) has documented that age differences are substantially greater for algorithmic retrieval than for heuristic retrieval. This indicates that younger adults may be better than older adults at retrieving a specific piece of information correctly, but both age groups are just as good at using general retrieval strategies that do not guarantee success. For example, older adults are typically less successful than younger adults at remembering all of the detailed steps needed to give precise directions to a specific location.

Recall Versus Recognition. As noted earlier, two types of retrieval tests are generally used in research. In free recall tests no cues are given; a person is simply asked to remember all of the items on a list, for example. Recall tests are thought to place

heavy demands on the retrieval process, because you must generate all the cues for finding the correct information yourself. In contrast, recognition involves picking the newly learned item from a list of both newly learned and distractor items. Because the testing environment provides cues, recognition tests are thought to place fewer demands on retrieval processes.

Studies consistently show substantial age differences on recall tests but small or nonexistent differences on recognition tests (Poon, 1985). These performance differences mean older adults have less effective retrieval processes when they must generate their own retrieval cues. However, when cues are provided, such as in recognition tests, older adults' performance improves.

Cued Recall. In addition to recognition tests, there are other means to reveal the ways in which retrieval cues help people remember. For example, it is possible to provide cues in a recall task. *Cued recall* involves providing some hint, or aid, within the general constraints of a recall test. Examples would be asking you to remember all of the fruits in a word list you studied or to recall the capital of Nepal after I told you that its name begins with the letter *K*. Compared to their performances on free recall tasks, older adults benefit more than younger adults when cues are provided, but age differences are not eliminated (A. D. Smith, 1977).

Retrieval and Working Memory. Based on the evidence reviewed so far, age-related decrements in retrieval are clear. But where in the information-processing system is the problem?

One good candidate is working memory. Recall that working memory is where the memory processing activity takes place. Hasher and Zacks (1988) postulate that the retrieval problems older adults experience are due to changes in working memory. Specifically, they show that older adults have more trouble keeping irrelevent information out of working memory than younger adults. This irrelevant information takes up valuable space in working memory, and prevents older adults from using it for relevant information. For example, Gerard, Zacks, Hasher, and Radvansky (1991) report that older adults have increasing difficulty performing a speeded recognition test as the number of facts to be recognized goes up.

This research points out important links among different aspects of the information-processing system. No single component is responsible for all of the observed age differences in performance. Rather, it is a combination of changes that underlies these differences.

Relative Contributions of Storage and Retrieval Differences

Younger adults find it easier than older adults to store incoming information and organize it efficiently in order to retrieve it later. But this difference still leaves two questions unresolved: Are changes in memory with age primarily the result of decrements in storage, in retrieval, or in both? If both processes are responsible, then do both decline at the same rate? Based on the available evidence, the answers are that: (1) Changes in memory with aging are a consequence of decrements in both storage and retrieval; (2) these decrements are more substantial for retrieval; and (3) these decrements occur in specific subcomponents of storage and retrieval and do not generalize to all aspects of them (Howe, 1988).

The research on storage and retrieval processes is important for three reasons. First, it emphasizes that age-related decrements in memory are complex; they are not due to changes in a single process. Second, intervention or training programs must consider both storage and retrieval. Training people to use storage strategies without also training them how to use retrieval strategies will not work. Third, theories of how memory changes with age must take individual differences into account, especially differential rates of change in component processes.

Theories of memory development must consider both those components of processes that change and those that do not.

The picture that emerges is very similar to the one we will encounter in our consideration of intelligence in Chapter 7. Specifically, the question "Does memory change with age?" cannot be answered unless you look separately at the different aspects of memory. As we consider memory in different contexts in the rest of this chapter, we will see additional evidence of why this is true.

MEMORY FOR DISCOURSE

Adults of all ages spend a great deal of time reading books, magazines, and newspapers, and watching television programs and movies. Collectively, such material is termed *discourse*. Interest in whether there are age differences in how well people remember discourse is very strong. Indeed, how well adults remember prose, or text passages, is one of the fastest growing areas in memory research. In part, this rapid growth reflects the realization that prose (like a newspaper story) is something people need to remember in everyday life; word lists typically are not.

To preview a bit, we will see that age differences in remembering discourse are minimized when tasks are made more naturalistic by providing unlimited study time, using long text passages, and requiring only a general summary rather than details. However, younger adults appear to have a clear advantage in learning short passages and in remembering the details. These differences may become more important as we continue to move toward a society in which computerization makes rapid acquisition of large amounts of discourse mandatory (Meyer, 1987).

In this section we will mainly focus on adults' ability to remember information they have read.

TABLE 6.1 Proportion of statements correct for comprehension, probe recall, and recognition, as a function of age, vocabulary, and level of information

Measure	Young		Old	
	High Verbal	*Low Verbal*	*High Verbal*	*Low Verbal*
Comprehension				
Central	.98	.77	.99	.70
Plot-relevant	.81	.57	.79	.44
Plot-irrelevant	.61	.39	.59	.23
Probe recall				
Central	.95	.71	.92	.59
Plot-relevant	.74	.51	.80	.34
Plot-irrelevant	.29	.20	.26	.08
Recognition				
Central	.90	.81	1.00	.71
Plot-relevant	.77	.56	.89	.37
Plot-irrelevant	.38	.23	.34	.11

(Source: "Comprehension and Retention of Television Programs by 20- and 60-year-olds" by J. C. Cavanaugh, 1983, *Journal of Gerontology, 38,* 190–196. Reprinted by permission. © 1983 The Gerontological Society of America.)

Our primary concern will be to understand the person, task, and text variables that affect learning and remembering prose.

Person Variables

Sometime in your educational career you probably had to read a rather lengthy novel for a literature class. Providing you opted for the book rather than the video or *Cliff Notes* version, you probably were surprised at how much different your recollections of the story were compared to your classmates'. Many of these differences were due to person variables — characteristics about individuals that affect how they learn and remember.

One of the most researched person variables concerns education and verbal ability (Meyer &

Rice, 1983). There is general agreement that average- and low-verbal older adults (adults with mainly a high school education) perform significantly worse than younger adults (see Dixon & vonEye, 1984). The picture is less clear with high-verbal, college-educated older adults. Some researchers obtain age differences (Cohen, 1979; Light & Anderson, 1975) while others do not (Mandel & Johnson, 1984; Meyer & Rice, 1981). In related research examining memory for television programs, Cavanaugh (1983, 1984) also found no differences in high-verbal groups but significant differences in low-verbal groups. A representative set of results showing this differential connection between age and verbal ability is shown in Table 6.1.

Why is there such consistency regarding poor-verbal, lower-educated groups and such disagree-

Research on memory for text indicates that older adults usually remember the gist of the passage as well as do younger adults.

is a very difficult, 100-word vocabulary test. For example, adults who score in the 75th percentile on the vocabulary subtest of the WAIS-R score only at the 25th percentile of the Quick Test. Consequently, adults who score high on the vocabulary subtest may not be truly high on verbal ability. Meyer (1987) argues that many of the studies that found age differences in so-called high-verbal groups did not use sufficiently sensitive tests of verbal ability. Studies that included truly high-verbal adults found no age differences.

A second reason for the different patterns of age differences involves the strategies that readers use. Rice and Meyer (1985) asked young and older adults of both average- and high-verbal ability about the strategies they used while reading. Older, low-verbal ability adults reported using the fewest reading behaviors that foster good comprehension. Meyer (1987) argues that these data support the view that the lack of age differences between younger and older high-verbal adults is due to the older group's continued use of effective reading strategies. Meyer, Young, and Bartlett (1986) tested this hypothesis by training older average-verbal ability adults to use more effective reading strategies. Following five 90-minute training sessions, they used effective strategies more often and their text recall was substantially better.

How adults decide to retell a story is also important. Adams, Labouvie-Vief, Hobart, and Dorosz (1990) presented fables and nonfables to younger and older adults and examined their story recall styles. They found that older adults used a more integrative or interpretive style for nonfable passages, whereas younger adults used a more literal or text-based style. Age differences were not found for the fable passages. These findings mean that younger adults may spontaneously shift their recall style depending on the type of passage, whereas older adults may use a more consistently integrative style regardless of passage type.

Another person variable that affects performance is amount of prior knowledge. Hartley

ment concerning high-verbal, higher-educated groups? B. J. F. Meyer (1987) provides an insightful discussion of this question. She points out that the pattern of results may be due to the use of tests of verbal ability that are differentially sensitive to high ability levels. That is, some tests, such as the vocabulary subtest of the Wechsler Adult Intelligence Scale-Revised (WAIS-R), are poorer at discriminating people with high ability than other tests, such as the Quick Test (Borgatta & Corsini, 1964), which

(1989) found that text recall varied in relation to how much people knew about the topic beforehand. One way to test this is to look for pieces of topic-relevant information that people remember in retelling the story but that were not actually in the passage. If prior knowledge is an important factor, then you should see a fair amount of this relevant, but not presented, information. Older adults appear especially likely to put pieces of prior knowledge into their recall of new information (Hultsch & Dixon, 1983). Interestingly, how prior knowledge affects text recall also appears to vary with age (S. W. Smith, Rebok, Smith, Hall, & Alvin, 1983). Smith and colleagues found that young adults added prior knowledge to make unorganized stories make more sense, whereas older adults added prior knowledge to make already well-organized stories more interesting.

Task Variables

Just as the way tasks are presented affects secondary memory performance, these same variables also affect prose memory. One of the most important task variables is speed of presentation. Studies show that older adults are differentially adversely affected by rapid presentation (Cohen, 1979; Stine, Wingfield, & Poon, 1986). Specifically, between 100 and 120 words per minute (wpm) appears to be the critical speed for exceeding older adults' processing capability. Meyer and Rice (1989) report that the average reading speed for older adults is 121 wpm, compared with 144 wpm for younger adults. They note, however, that nearly half of their older adults read more slowly than 120 wpm; few younger adults read as slowly. Thus, older adults may be at a disadvantage when presented with text at speeds geared to younger adults. Indeed, when the speed-of-presentation variable is removed and participants can pace themselves, age differences are eliminated (Harker, Hartley, & Walsh, 1982; Meyer & Rice, 1981; Meyer et al., 1986).

Text Variables

In your personal experience you have undoubtedly found that all text material is not created equal. Some books or passages are very easy to read, comprehend, and remember, and others are not. Texts differ considerably in how all of the information they contain is organized. One way to think about text organization is to compare it to the outline form that is taught in composition classes. Some information is basic and is given prominence in the outline; other information simply expands the main points and is embedded in the outline. In a well-organized text the main ideas are all interrelated, and the passage is like a tightly woven tapestry. Such texts are more memorable, especially if you follow the built-in organizational structure.

Researchers have spent considerable effort examining whether there are age differences in memory for different kinds of information in texts. There appear to be no age differences in adults' memory for the major organizational elements of texts, such as the basic sequence of events or causal connections between events (Meyer & Rice, 1989; Meyer, Rice, Knight, & Jessen, 1979). However, remembering this kind of information does seem to be related to verbal ability; low- and average-ability adults are less able to use these organizational elements and remember fewer of them than high-ability adults (Meyer, 1983).

Because texts are constructed with information at different hierarchical levels of importance, a key question is whether there are age differences in memory for these different levels. Answering this question amounts to looking for age differences between memory for main ideas and memory for details. The literature on this issue is large and complex (Hultsch & Dixon, 1984; B. J. F. Meyer, 1987). In general, the data indicate two important points. First, when text is clearly organized, with emphasis on structure and the main ideas, older adults are just as good as younger adults in telling the difference between the main ideas and the details.

Second, verbal ability makes a big difference. Average-verbal older adults apparently do not benefit from advance signaling of important ideas, do not use the organizational structure to facilitate learning or retrieval as efficiently, and make fewer inferences about what they read. As a result, average-verbal older adults show a performance deficit compared with their younger average-verbal counterparts. In contrast, high-verbal older adults are very sensitive to the emphasis given to different pieces of information and to the overall structure of the text. In fact, they may be oversensitive to emphasis, since they tend to allocate more of their processing capacity to emphasized details than to the main ideas. Once again, it appears that verbal ability is more important than age in understanding the patterns of performance.

Still, there may be more to it. Price (1991) reports that middle-aged women who were enrolled in a graduate level gerontology course had different study strategies and motivation than younger students. The middle-aged women were more interested in learning concepts and how everything fit together; they were much less interested in learning facts. These findings are important, as they indicate that text structure and verbal ability may not be the only reasons for age differences in memory for text. Personal motivation may also be an important issue.

Text Memory and Secondary Memory

The research we have considered in this section is actually another way to examine secondary memory, since it involves learning large amounts of information and remembering it over time (Poon, 1985). Thus, it is useful to draw parallels between the two literatures and compare the important influences on memory for word lists and memory for text.

The most striking aspect about this comparison is that both are affected by a similar set of variables.

Performance on word-list tasks and text-memory tasks are influenced by pacing, prior knowledge or familiarity, and verbal ability. Note that age is not one of these influential variables. Being old does not necessarily mean that you cannot remember, especially if the situation provides an optimal opportunity to do so.

Because of the parallels between influences on prose retention and memory for word lists, some researchers have tried to blend the two approaches. One tactic is to look at the processes underlying prose memory by using related secondary memory tasks. For example, Spilich (1985) obtained age differences for some steps leading up to the understanding of text. In particular, older and younger adults may have different definitions of words and use different classifications for words. For example, the word *rap* may mean "to knock" to an older adult, whereas it may more likely mean "a form of music" to a younger adult. This may suggest that the associations formed in secondary memory for verbal material may differ for young and old. At a practical level, we should not assume that people of all ages understand the same meaning for a word or sentence.

MEMORY IN EVERYDAY LIFE

As we noted at the beginning of this chapter, memory is so integral to our everyday life that we take it for granted. Only recently has there been substantial interest in examining age differences in memory in everyday life (West, 1986a). However, this research is extremely important for three reasons. First, it may shed some light on the generalizability of findings based on laboratory tasks such as word-list recall. Second, new or alternative variables that affect performance could be uncovered. Third, research on everyday memory may force us to reconceptualize memory itself. In this section we will focus on two aspects of everyday memory that have received the most attention: spatial memory and memory for activities.

Spatial Memory

Every time you remember where you left your keys, find your way by locating a prominent building, successfully return home from the grocery store, and remember where your car is parked after coming out a different door, you are using **spatial memory** (Kirasic & Allen, 1985). We will consider the developmental trends in each of these abilities.

Memory for Location. Researchers test people's memory for location in three ways (Kirasic & Allen, 1985). One way is based on the psychometric approach to intelligence described in Chapter 7, in which relevant primary mental abilities such as spatial ability are tested. Results from this approach indicate that performance peaks by mid-life and decreases steadily thereafter.

The most common way to test people's memory for location is to present them with an array of objects, remove the objects, and ask the participants to reconstruct the array. Older adults do not perform this task as well as younger adults, regardless of whether the objects are household items (Attig, 1983; Pezdek, 1983; Waddell & Rogoff, 1981) or building locations on a map (Light & Zelinski, 1983; Ohta & Kirasic, 1983; Thomas, 1985). Charness (1981) found that younger chess players could reconstruct chess boards more accurately than older players, even though the two groups were matched for chess-playing ability. In contrast to this consistent picture of age decrement, West and Walton (1985) found no decline when they conducted interviews of young and old participants about the exact location in their home of common personal items such as keys. West and Walton argue that familiarity and the fact that

household locations are unlikely to change are the most likely reasons for the lack of age differences.

The third way to test spatial memory consists of actually carrying out tasks in real physical space. For example, Kirasic (1981) had older and younger adults plan the most efficient route possible in picking up items on a designated shopping list, and then actually go get them. The manipulation was the shopper's familiarity with the supermarket; some shoppers were tested in their usual supermarket, and others were tested in a different one. Younger adults performed equivalently in the two settings, whereas older adults performed better in the familiar environment.

Recall of Landmarks. Most studies of landmark recall involve the ability to place landmarks correctly on a map or other representation of a large-scale space. Young adults are more likely to organize their recall of a familiar downtown area based on spatial cues, which gives them an advantage in recalling correct location (Evans, Brennan, Skorpanich, & Held, 1984). In contrast, older adults' recall is influenced by frequency of usage, symbolic significance, natural landscaping, ease of finding the landmark, and uniqueness of architectural style (Lipman, 1991). In addition, there is some evidence that older adults are less accurate at locating landmarks on a scale model (Ohta & Kirasic, 1983) and at learning locations when the information is presented sequentially, as is often done in a travelogue or tour (Walsh, Krauss, & Regnier, 1981).

These results suggest that older and younger adults use different strategies to learn and remember landmarks. Older adults may be more likely to use experiential or personal relevance as a way to remember location, whereas young adults may use physical space cues.

Route Learning. Only a handful of studies has considered how people remember the way from one place to another. Sinnott (1984a) asked participants to describe routes to and around the hospital where they were undergoing a battery of tests and to recognize specific pathways that occurred en route from one area of the hospital to another. She found no differences with age on any of these tasks. Ohta (1981) also found no age differences in adults' ability to find unknown routes to a specific room when the known route was blocked. However, he did report that older adults were less accurate in drawing sketch maps of routes inside buildings. Ohta's findings provide additional support for age differences in algorithmic retrieval but not for heuristic retrieval.

A slightly different version of route learning involves plotting the shortest and most efficient route to accomplish a particular task. For example, suppose you were in a hurry at the supermarket, but needed to purchase several items. You would probably want to plot the most efficient route up and down the aisles that would allow you to get the items the quickest.

Kirasic (1991) tested younger and older adults at how well they could plan efficient routes in both familiar and unfamiliar supermarkets. She found no age differences in this ability, although older adults were better in the familiar store than they were in the unfamiliar store. Indeed, the only clear age difference Kirasic found was that younger adults were more efficient in learning store layouts.

Configurational Learning. **Configurational learning** requires people to combine spatial and temporal information so that they can recognize a location when they view it from a different perspective. Think about what you do when you go to a mall. You park your car and remember where it is based on the entrance you use. Suppose when you finish shopping you decide to leave the mall through a different door. Your ability to remember where your car is requires configurational learning; you recognize the parking lot even though you are viewing it from a different position.

When configurational learning is tested with unfamiliar locations, young adults sometimes outperform older adults (Ohta, Walsh, & Krauss, 1981). In contrast, no age differences are found in distance and directional judgments or in efficient route planning when familiar locations are used, such as one's hometown or a familiar grocery store (Kirasic, 1980; Kirasic & Allen, 1985). The hometown advantage is depicted in Figure 6.2. Notice the lack of an age effect when the locations used were familiar to all participants.

Memory for Activities

How many times have you been asked, "What did you do today?" or "What have you been up to lately?" To answer these questions, you must use a second major type of everyday memory — memory for activities. Researchers test activity memory with a wide variety of tasks, including following instructions, recalling activities performed in a research laboratory, and remembering to perform actions.

One of the major issues in activity memory research is whether people must expend cognitive effort or whether remembering what we do happens automatically. Kausler (1985) attacked this problem by separating activity memory into two parts. First, he argued that *storing* activities and actions performed in a laboratory is probably automatic, requiring no cognitive effort or resources. His view is supported by evidence that rehearsing the names of activities that participants perform does not affect performance. Second, he argued that *remembering* the activities one has performed involves cognitive effort, since reliable age decrements are observed. Indeed, organization, which requires cognitive effort, facilitates recall of activities (Bäckman, 1985; Bäckman & Nilsson, 1984, 1985).

In essence, Kausler contends that the recall of activities performed in a laboratory is a direct analogue to everyday life. Many everyday memory situations involve the intentional, effortful retrieval of information learned by doing things (such as, we learn the layout of the campus by walking around).

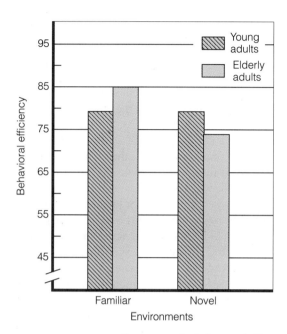

FIGURE 6.2 Differences in the behavioral efficiency of young and old adults while shopping in familiar and novel supermarkets

(Source: "Aging, Spatial Performance, and Spatial Competence" (pp. 191–223) by K. C. Kirasic and G. L. Allen, 1985, in N. Charness (Ed.), *Aging in Human Performance*. Chichester, England: Wiley. © 1985 John Wiley & Sons, Inc. Reprinted with permission of the publisher.)

In fact, activity memory may form the basis for acquiring much of our spatial memory.

A second major question in activity memory research is this: Does actually performing the actions help us remember them? It turns out that it does. Bäckman (1985) and Cohen and Faulkner (1989) both found that performed actions were remembered more accurately than activities that had only been watched.

There is an interesting twist to Cohen and Faulkner's (1989) study. They also report age differences in the accuracy with which people remember whether they in fact performed the action. Older adults are more likely than younger adults to say that they performed tasks that they in reality only

observed. Although more research on this issue is clearly needed, these findings have important implications. In situations where accuracy is crucial, such as in reporting one's recent activities to a physician or a police officer, older adults may be more likely to confuse what they saw with what they did.

A third focus of activity memory research involves examining whether the type of task performed has an effect on the likelihood that it will be remembered later. Kausler and Hakami (1983) found that older adults remembered doing problem-solving tests better than doing perceptual-motor, generic memory, and word list tests. The reason for such differences remains to be uncovered. West (1986a) suggests that better-remembered tasks may be more familiar and, thereby, more memorable.

The fourth area of activity memory research is one in which older adults are consistently superior: remembering to perform an action. This form of memory, termed **prospective memory** (Meacham, 1982), involves remembering to remember (Harris, 1984b). For example, when younger and older adults are asked to call a researcher at particular times, older adults are consistently better at remembering to do so (Moscovitch, 1982; Poon & Schaffer, 1982; West, 1984). Their secret is simple: They write down the number and message to be given. Younger adults rely on their own internal remembering strategies, which turn out to be less successful.

Everyday Memory Versus List-Learning Performance

How does performance on everyday memory tests stack up to performance on traditional laboratory word-list tests? Overall, age decrements in performance on everyday memory tasks are smaller than on list-learning tasks (West, 1986a). Why? Unfortunately we do not know for certain. One thing is clear, however. Older adults perform consistently better when they are confronted with information that is familiar, which in turn enhances the motivation to perform the task in the first place (Perlmuter & Monty, 1989).

Memory for Pictures. One of the areas in which performance on list-learning tasks and tasks closer to everyday life can be compared is memory for pictures. Researchers use a variety of things to study picture memory: faces, abstract drawings, line drawings, and complex scenes. Overall, studies show that older adults perform worse than younger adults in remembering many types of pictorial stimuli (A. D. Smith & Park, 1990). For example, older adults do not remember faces (Mason, 1986) or where objects are placed in a colored three-dimensional array or on a distinctive map (Park, Cherry, Smith, & Lafronza, 1990) as well as younger adults.

Still, we must not be too hasty in concluding that age differences found in the laboratory automatically generalize to the real world. Park and her colleagues examined many of the traditional issues in laboratory research, including context effects, retention intervals, and stimulus complexity (Park, Puglisi, & Smith, 1986; Park, Puglisi, & Sovacool, 1983, 1984; Park, Royal, Dudley, & Morrell, 1988). Whereas older adults were clearly worse at remembering words, their immediate memory for pictures was about as good as young adults'. Age differences were observed only when delayed tests were given, and then only at certain time delay intervals. This research shows that we need to be cautious even in generalizing the findings from laboratory list-learning tasks using words to list-learning tasks using pictures.

Many factors influence what people remember from pictures. One of the most important of these concerns what people expect to see, termed *schematic knowledge*. Suppose you were told that you would be shown a picture of a kitchen. Immediately, you would anticipate seeing a stove, refrigerator, sink, and other things that you commonly associate with a kitchen. Collectively, these items

form your kitchen schema. Now suppose that you were actually shown a picture of a kitchen for a brief time and asked to name the objects you saw. After recalling a few, you might realize that there were more objects there than you named. So, you might begin to guess what the others were, based on your kitchen schema.

Hess and Slaughter (1990) showed that older adults are more likely to use their schemas to fill in the blanks than younger adults. This appears especially likely when the scenes are not well organized, such as when a picture of a kitchen has the sink over the stove as opposed to beside it. These results fit with a wide body of literature suggesting that we tend to rely more on experience as we grow older in order to compensate for decrements in specific aspects of information processing (recall Salthouse's study of typing from Chapter 5) and memory. As we will see in Chapter 7, our knowledge base continues to improve into old age, giving us a good basis for using schemas.

Despite these innovative studies, the direct comparison between everyday memory and list learning is hampered by the lack of data establishing equivalent everyday tasks and list-learning tasks. We need a comprehensive analysis in which the memory demands of many everyday tasks and list-learning tasks are described. This analysis would provide a way to address the reasons for the presence or absence of age differences across different task domains.

SELF-EVALUATIONS OF MEMORY ABILITIES

How good is your memory? Are you absent-minded? Or are you like the proverbial elephant who never forgets anything? Like most people, you probably tend to be your own harshest critic when it comes to evaluating your memory performance. We analyze, scrutinize, nitpick, and castigate ourselves for the times we forget; we rarely praise ourselves for all the things we do remember, and we continue to be on guard for more memory slips. The self-evaluations we make about memory may affect our daily life in ways that traditionally were unrecognized.

The self-evaluations we make about memory are complex (Cavanaugh, 1989; Cavanaugh et al., 1989). They are based not only on memory and performance per se but also on how we view ourselves in general, our theories about how memory works, what we remember from past evaluations, and our attributions and judgments of our effectiveness.

Types of Memory Awareness

Interest in what people know about or are aware of concerning memory is an old topic in both philosophy and psychology (Cavanaugh & Perlmutter, 1982). Psychologists have dabbled with the topic for a century, studying everything from reports of children's awareness of problem-solving skills (Binet, 1903) to computer simulation of self-monitoring systems (Bobrow & Collins, 1975). In recent decades work on memory awareness has taken on a more developmental flavor. Researchers have focused primarily on two types of awareness. The first type involves consciousness of facts about memory, that is, knowledge about how memory works. This type of awareness is referred to as **metamemory**. For instance, you know that recall is typically harder than recognition, that memory strategies are often helpful, and that working memory is not limitless. Memory knowledge is most often assessed with questionnaires that ask about these various facts.

The second type of awareness, called **on-line awareness**, refers to the consciousness of what we are doing with our memory right now. We can

be aware of the process of remembering in many ways. At times we know how we are studying, how we are searching for some particular fact, or how we are keeping track of time for an appointment. At other times we ask ourselves questions while doing a memory task. For example, when faced with having to remember an important appointment later in the day, we may consciously ask ourselves whether the steps we have taken (writing a note) are sufficient.

The following sections provide closer looks at age differences in memory knowledge and on-line awareness. We will begin by considering the results obtained through questionnaires.

Age Differences in Metamemory

Researchers have explored age differences in metamemory mainly by using questionnaires (see Dixon, 1989, for a review). One of the best of these, the *Metamemory in Adulthood* instrument (Dixon & Hultsch, 1983), taps several different areas of knowledge about memory, including knowledge about strategies, tasks, change with age, and capacity.

The pattern of age differences in metamemory is interesting. Older adults seem to know less than younger adults about the internal workings of memory and its capacity, view memory as less stable, expect that memory will deteriorate with age, and perceive that they have less control over memory (Cavanaugh & Poon, 1989; Chaffin & Herrmann, 1983; Dixon & Hultsch, 1983; Zelinski, Gilewski, & Thompson, 1980).

The belief in inevitable decline with age appears to be especially reliable. Williams, Denney, and Schadler (1983) found that none of their participants over age 65 expected memory to improve over time. Their participants also said that decline was related to expectations, less use of memory, lower levels of memory demands, and inactivity. This belief is potentially damaging. For example, people who think memory inevitably declines may also believe that strategy training is useless (Person & Wellman, 1989), and may think that there is little point in exerting effort to try and remember something that does not come to mind immediately (Cavanaugh & Green, 1990). We will take a closer look at these negative views a bit later.

Interestingly, the belief in inevitable decline does not apply equally to all aspects of memory. Older adults view memory capacity as declining more rapidly than the use of memory strategies (Dixon & Hultsch, 1983). Similarly, adults report that different kinds of information present different likelihoods of being troublesome. For example, remembering names is universally problematic, but especially for older adults (Cavanaugh & Poon, 1989; Chaffin & Herrmann, 1983; Zarit, 1982). In contrast, remembering errands, appointments, and places appears to remain unchanged with age (Cavanaugh, Grady, & Perlmutter, 1983).

Although questionnaire studies of metamemory provide important information, they must be interpreted carefully (Cavanaugh & Perlmutter, 1982). Cavanaugh (1986–1987) discovered that how questions are worded makes a difference in how older adults respond. For example, when questions request a general overall rating of memory, older adults give more negative ratings than younger adults. But when the question pertains to a specific aspect of memory, such as memory for dates or errands, older adults' ratings are equivalent to those of younger adults.

Related work by Hertzog and his colleagues shows that how metamemory is organized may change across adulthood (Hertzog, Dixon, Schulenberg, & Hultsch, 1987; Hertzog, Hultsch, & Dixon, 1989). The facts people know about memory tend to form groups, or domains, of knowledge. As we age, the makeup of these domains may be a bit different. Because forgetting sometimes evokes strong emotional reactions in older adults, their memory knowledge may incorporate some of these feelings.

Age Differences in On-Line Awareness

On-line awareness involves knowing what you are doing mentally right now. The most popular way researchers usually study on-line awareness is by having people predict how well they will do on a memory task. One variation of this technique requires that people predict how well they will do *before* they get a chance to see the task. For example, you would be asked to predict how many words you think you could remember from a 20-item list without first being able to see the list. The second variation requires people to make performance predictions after they have seen the task. This time, you get to see the list first and then would be asked to predict how many words you will remember.

Predictions Without Experience. Estimating your performance without having a chance to see what you are up against is hard. You probably know from your own experience that guessing how well you will do on the first exam in a course is tough if you do not know anything about the exam style of the instructor. How well you think you will do depends on lots of test-related variables: item difficulty, fact versus concept questions, and the like.

When older adults are put in the position of having to estimate performance without seeing the task, they tend to overestimate how well they will do (for example, Bruce, Coyne, & Botwinick, 1982; Coyne, 1983; Mason, 1981; Murphy, Sanders, Gabriesheski, & Schmitt, 1981). For example, older adults typically predict that they will be able to remember more items than they actually can. Younger adults tend to be more accurate.

But older adults do not overestimate all the time. Camp, Markley, and Kramer (1983) asked older adults to predict recall of 15 words that were high in imagery, frequency, concreteness, and meaningfulness. When told to think about learning strategies, and then to make a prediction, older adults *under*estimated their performance. In this case, the need to think about strategies may have convinced older adults that the task was more difficult than it actually was. As a result, they gave lower estimates. Berry, West, and Scogin (1983) also found that older adults underestimated their performance when given everyday memory tasks.

Predictions After Experience. A much different picture of age differences emerges when participants have a chance to see the task before making a performance prediction. One way this is done is by asking people to rate their confidence that they will be able to remember each item on the list of words that will be learned. Results from several studies using this approach demonstrate that older adults are just as accurate in predicting their recall and recognition performances as younger adults (Lovelace, Marsh, & Oster, 1982; Perlmutter, 1978; Rabinowitz, Ackerman, Craik, & Hinchley, 1982). The usual finding is that, regardless of age, adults overestimate performance on recall tasks but underestimate performance on recognition tasks.

What can we conclude about age differences in on-line awareness? Older adults are at a disadvantage when asked to predict performance if they are given no information about the task. But when this information is forthcoming — either from direct experience, from instructions pertaining to important things to think about, or from a request for predictions on familiar everyday tasks — older adults do as well as younger adults.

CLINICAL ISSUES AND MEMORY TESTING

To this point we have been trying to understand the changes that occur in normal memory with aging. But what about situations where people have serious memory problems that interfere with their daily lives? How do we tell the difference between normal and abnormal memory changes? These are but two of the issues that clinicians face. They are often confronted with clients who complain of serious memory difficulties. Clinicians must somehow differentiate the individuals who have no real reason to be concerned from those with some sort of disease. What criteria should be used to make this distinction? What diagnostic tests would be appropriate to evaluate adults of various ages?

Unfortunately, there are no easy answers to these questions (Erickson, Poon, & Walsh-Sweeney, 1980; Poon, 1986). As we have seen, the exact nature of normative changes in memory with aging is not yet understood completely. This means that we have few standards by which to compare people who may have problems. Second, we also do not have a comprehensive battery of memory tests that taps a wide variety of memory functions. Clinicians are left with hit-or-miss approaches and often have little choice but to piece together their own assessment battery (Poon et al., 1986).

Fortunately, the situation is changing. Since the mid-1980s researchers and clinicians have begun to work closely to devise better assessments. This collaboration is producing results that will help address the key questions in memory assessment: Has something gone wrong with memory? Is the loss normal? What is the prognosis? What can be done to help the client compensate or recover?

In this section we will consider some of the efforts being made to bridge the gap between laboratory and clinic. We will begin with a brief look at the distinction between normal and abnormal memory changes. Because abnormal memory changes could be the result of some other psychological or physical condition, we will consider links between memory and mental health, and with nutrition and medications. After that, we will consider some of the ways in which memory can be assessed in the clinical setting.

Normal Versus Abnormal Memory Aging

As we have seen, there are many normative changes in memory as people grow old, such as in working memory and secondary memory. Still, many aspects of memory functioning do not change, such as the ability to remember the gist of a story. Increasingly forgetting names or what you need at the supermarket, though annoying, appears to be a part of aging. However, we also know that there are some people who experience far greater changes, such as forgetting where they live or their spouse's name. Where is the line that divides normative memory changes from abnormal ones?

From a functional perspective, one way to distinguish normal and abnormal changes is to ask whether the changes disrupt a person's ability to perform daily living tasks. The normative changes we have encountered in this chapter usually do not interfere with a person's ability to function in everyday life. When problems appear, however, it would be appropriate to find out what is the matter. For example, a person who repeatedly forgets to turn off the stove or forgets how to get home is clearly experiencing changes that affect personal safety and interfere with his or her daily life. It would be appropriate to bring such changes to the attention of a physician or psychologist.

Recent advances in neuroscience, especially the study of brain-behavior relationships, has led to an explosion in our knowledge of specific diseases or brain changes that can create abnormal memory performance. For example, researchers can test for specific problems in visual and verbal memory by examining glucose metabolism with PET scans (Berardi, Haxby, Grady, & Rapoport, 1991; see Chapter 3 for a discussion of PET scans). Other brain-imaging techniques such as CT scans and MRI (see Chapter 3) allow researchers to find tumors, strokes, or other types of damage or disease that could account for poorer than expected memory performance. Certain changes in brain-wave patterns are indicative of decrements in verbal memory (Rice, Buchsbaum, Hardy, & Burgwald, 1991). Finally, significantly poorer than normal performance on neuropsychological tests of memory are also useful in establishing for certain that the memory changes observed are indeed abnormal (Tuokko, Gallie, & Crockett, 1990).

Some diseases, especially the dementias described in Chapter 9, are marked by massive changes in memory. For example, Alzheimer's disease involves the progressive destruction of memory beginning with recent memory and eventually including the most personal—self-identity. Wernicke-Korsakoff syndrome (see Chapter 4) involves major loss of recent memory, and sometimes a total inability to form new memories after a certain point in time.

The most important point to keep in mind is that telling the difference between normal and abnormal memory aging is often very difficult. There is no magic number of times someone must forget something before getting concerned. Because serious memory problems can also be due to underlying mental or physical health problems, it is imperative that these be thoroughly checked out in conjunction with obtaining a complete memory assessment.

Memory and Mental Health

Several psychological disorders involve distorted thought processes, which sometimes result in serious memory problems. The two disorders that have been the main focus of research are depression and dementia (see Poon, 1986); but other disorders, such as amnesia following a head injury or brain disease, are also important. Depression is characterized by feelings of helplessness and hopelessness (American Psychiatric Association, 1987; see Chapter 9). Dementia, such as Alzheimer's disease, involves substantial declines in cognitive performance that may be irreversible and untreatable (American Psychiatric Association, 1987; see Chapter 9). Much of the research on clinical memory testing is on differentiating the changes in memory due to depression from those involved in Alzheimer's disease.

Serious depression impairs memory. For example, severely depressed people show a decreased ability to learn and recall new information (Cohen, Weingartner, Smallberg, Pickar, & Murphy, 1982); a tendency to leave out important information (McAllister, 1981); a decreased ability to organize (Breslow, Kocsis, & Belkin, 1981); less effective memory strategies (Weingartner, Cohen, & Bunney, 1982); an increased sensitivity to sad memories (Kelley, 1986); and decreased attention and reaction time (Breslow et al., 1981; Cohen et al., 1982).

Clinical models of depression emphasize its effects on cognition in everyday life (Beck, 1967, 1976; Garber & Seligman, 1980). In general, seriously depressed individuals develop negative expectations, decreased concentration, and attentional deficits that result in poorer memory. In contrast, mildly depressed individuals show little decrement. Unfortunately, few researchers have asked whether the effects of depression on memory vary with age. What data there are suggest that once normative age differences in secondary memory are eliminated statistically, few differences remain. Thus, at this point the memory impairments that accompany severe depression appear to be equivalent across adulthood. However, much more research needs to be done before we have a clear answer. Additionally, we need to know more about the possible effects of mild and moderate levels of depression.

Alzheimer's disease is characterized by severe and pervasive memory impairment that is progressive and irreversible. As described in Chapter 9, the memory decrements in Alzheimer's disease involve the entire memory system, from sensory to tertiary memory. The important point here is that the changes that occur early in Alzheimer's disease are very similar to those that occur in depression. However, since depression is treatable and Alzheimer's disease is not, it is important to differentiate the two. This differentiation is the underlying reason for the major effort to develop sensitive and comprehensive batteries of memory tests. In Chapter 9 we will see how Alzheimer's disease and depression are diagnosed.

Memory, Nutrition, and Medications

Researchers and clinicians often overlook nutrition as a cause of memory failures in later life (Perlmutter et al., 1987). Unfortunately, we know very little about how specific nutrient deficiencies relate to specific aspects of memory. The available evidence links thiamine deficiency to memory problems in humans (Cherkin, 1984), and it links niacin and vitamin B_{12} deficiencies to diseases in which memory failure is a major symptom (Rosenthal & Goodwin, 1985).

Likewise, many drugs have been associated with memory problems. The most widely known of these is alcohol, which if abused over a long period is associated with severe memory loss (see Chapter 4). Less well known are the effects of other prescription and over-the-counter medications. For example, sedatives and tranquilizers have been found to impair memory performance (Block, DeVoe, Stanley, Stanley, & Pomara, 1985). We will consider some specific drugs in Chapter 9.

These data indicate that it is important to consider older adults' diets and medications when assessing their memory performance. What may appear to be serious decrements in functioning may, in fact, be induced by poor nutrition or specific medications. Too often, researchers and clinicians fail to inquire about eating habits and the medications people take. Adequate assessment is essential in order to avoid diagnostic errors.

Questionnaire Assessments of Memory Problems

People frequently complain or express concerns about their memory. Perhaps you have complained that you do not remember names or dates very well or often lose your keys. Because being aware of problems with your memory is a kind of meta-memory, memory complaints are also typically assessed with questionnaires. There are about a dozen questionnaires that assess memory complaints (Gilewski & Zelinski, 1986). These questionnaires assess a variety of memory situations, such as remembering people's names or remembering the time of year it is.

Memory complaints correlate moderately with performance on word-list and prose tasks, and with standardized clinical memory tests (Zelinski, Gilewski, & Anthony-Bergstone, 1990). In addition, memory complaints show a stronger relationship with depressed mood (Zarit, Cole, & Guider, 1981). These findings indicate that although memory complaints should not be considered an accurate account of a person's current memory ability, they may provide important information about performance problems related to how the person is feeling emotionally.

Gilewski and Zelinski (1986) strongly advocate the use of memory questionnaires in clinical practice, as long as they are not used as a substitute for memory tests and as long as they are multidimensional. For example, comprehensive questionnaires should tap such things as frequency of forgetting, perceptions of changes in memory over time, seriousness of memory failures, use of strategies, daily memory demands, memory for past events, and what efforts are made when forgetting occurs. The *Memory Functioning Questionnaire* (Gilewski, Zelinski, & Schaie, 1990) is one example of a comprehensive questionnaire that provides reliable and valid assessments of memory complaints.

Behavior Rating Scales

Behavior rating scales are instruments designed to assess memory from the viewpoint of an observer, usually a mental health professional (McDonald, 1986). The most common behavior rating scales that tap memory are structured interviews. These interviews vary in length from very short to extensive, which means that they also vary in how sensitive they are at picking up abnormal memory performance.

Most structured interviews were developed with an eye toward diagnosing dementia (see also Chapter 9). The most common of these are the various mental status examinations (Blessed, Tomlinson, & Roth, 1968; Folstein, Folstein, & McHugh, 1975; Kahn, Goldfarb, Pollack, & Peck, 1960). These rating scales are short and easy to administer and serve as screening devices for severe memory impairment. Items on these scales focus on orientation to time and place and contain simple memory tests such as spelling *world* backward. Mattis (1976) developed a more extensive mental status exam that provides a more complete view of cognitive processes. Mattis's scale examines primary memory and secondary memory more thoroughly than the other mental status exams.

Mental status exams are used to screen people for serious problems. That is, mental status exams provide a very crude estimate of memory functioning, not nearly as accurate as you would get from an extensive battery of tests. However, mental status exams are very quick and easy to administer, and are good at differentiating people with serious problems from the normal group.

A very important source of diagnostic information is a person who is close to the client. Spouses or adult children can provide different perspectives than health care professionals. Caregivers have known the person being assessed for a much longer time, and may be in a better position to assess subtle changes in performance over time.

They also provide important information about the severity of the problem that can be compared to information provided by the person being assessed. For example, the diagnosis of Alzheimer's disease is often furthered by examining the discrepancy between the client's assessment of memory functioning and the caregiver's assessment of the client's memory functioning (Reisberg et al., 1986). In the middle stages of the disease the clients' reports of memory problems drop, but caregiver's reports continue to increase.

Neuropsychological Tests

Although questionnaires and rating scales are important in clinical diagnosis, they are not enough. Increasingly, clinicians are advocating the use of tasks developed in the laboratory as part of research on basic memory processes in the clinic (Ferris, Crook, Flicker, Reisberg, & Bartus, 1986).

Ferris and Crook (1983) propose nine criteria for a comprehensive cognitive battery, including that it samples a variety of cognitive functions, is sensitive to deficits, takes less than one hour to administer, has high reliability and validity, and is of appropriate difficulty for the population being studied. They recommend that all aspects of memory (primary, working, secondary, and tertiary) as well as attention and perceptual-motor speed be included in this battery. These suggestions have been supported and adopted by many of the leading clinicians involved in research on abnormal memory changes (Corkin, Growdon, Sullivan, Nissen, & Huff, 1986; Mohs, Kim, Johns, Dunn, & Davis, 1986).

The tests clinicians use to evaluate memory are one aspect of neuropsychological tests. These tests are designed to assess specific brain-behavior relationships in a wide variety of domains, from general intelligence to particular aspects of memory. While most comprehensive neuropsychological tests include several memory tests, some are designed to focus primarily on memory functioning. For example, the *Wechsler Memory Scale-Revised* is a fairly comprehensive test that examines many different aspects of verbal memory. It includes a variety of tasks, such as serial learning, paired associates, and short prose passages. Others, such as the *Memory for Designs* test, focus on visual memory. In these tests, people are typically shown a picture (such as an octagon) and asked to draw it from memory.

A neuropsychological assessment should always be coupled with complete health screening. A key aspect of the biopsychosocial model is the interaction between physiology and behavior; memory performance is no exception. We will return to this issue in Chapter 9. In any case, a systematic comprehensive approach is absolutely essential in order to sort out potentially treatable causes of memory problems from those that are untreatable. If real problems are suspected, make sure you search for a clinic specializing in comprehensive assessment. Having someone simply administer a short questionnaire or a mental status exam is not enough.

REMEDIATING MEMORY PROBLEMS

Suppose that someone you love has gone through a comprehensive diagnostic process like that advocated above, and a problem was discovered. Is there anything that can be done to help? In most cases, the answer is yes. Camp (1989) relates that even in Alzheimer's disease people can learn new things. As described in How Do We Know? he was able to teach people with Alzheimer's disease the names of the staff who worked with them. Additionally, researchers have developed several different types of

HOW DO WE KNOW?

What's My Name? Memory Training in Alzheimer's Disease

Memory intervention programs have been used with many different populations. However, one of the most interesting target groups consists of people with Alzheimer's disease. As noted in the text (and in Chapter 9), Alzheimer's disease is characterized by a severe and progressive deterioration in memory functioning. As a result, anything that could help people remember would be an important contribution.

In a series of studies, Camp (see Camp & McKitrick, 1991) showed that people with Alzheimer's disease can successfully be taught the names of staff people. His technique involves *spaced retrieval*, which consists of progressively increasing the amount of time between the recall of the target information (that is, a person's name). In the procedure, the trainer shows the client a photograph of a person and says that person's name. After an initial recall interval of 5 seconds, the trainer asks the client to remember the name. As long as the client remembers correctly, recall intervals are increased to 10, 20, 40, 60, 90, 120, 150, and so on. If the client forgets the target name, the correct answer is provided, and the next recall interval is decreased to the length of the last correct trial. During the interval, the trainer simply engages the client in conversation to prevent active rehearsal of the information.

Amazingly, even people who previously could not retain new information for more than 60 seconds can remember names taught via spaced retrieval for intervals up to 5 weeks. Although there are individual differences in how long people with Alzheimer's disease remember information learned this way, and how well they transfer new learning from photographs to the real people, these results are extremely encouraging. The intervention requires no drugs, can be done in any setting, and involves social activity. The training can even be inserted into everyday activities such as playing games or normal conversation, making it comfortable and uninterventionlike for the client. Although the technique needs to be refined, spaced retrieval seems to represent an easily applied intervention.

---

memory training programs, many of which are effective even with persons with severe memory impairments (Wilson & Moffat, 1984). In this section we will examine some of the attempts at remediating memory problems and some of the individual differences that affect how successful these programs are.

Training Memory Skills

The notion that memory can be improved through acquiring skills and practicing them is very old, dating back to prehistory (Yates, 1966). For example, the story of the *Iliad* was told for generations through the use of mnemonic strategies before it was finally written down. Books that teach readers how to improve their own memory have also been around for a very long time (Grey, 1756). Interestingly, these old how-to books teach techniques that are virtually identical with those advocated in recent books (Lorayne & Lucas, 1974; West, 1986b).

J. E. Harris (1984a) lists four major methods of improving memory: internal strategies (forming an image of the information to be remembered in one's mind, for example), repetitive practice (rehearsing the information over and over), physical treatments (such as drugs), and external aids (for example,

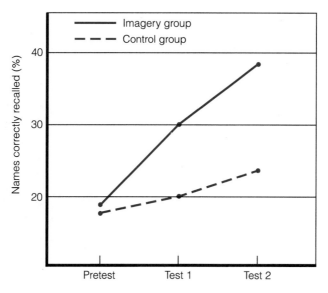

FIGURE 6.3   Proportion of names recalled at three points in the study. Pretest occurred in the first session before any training. Test 1 was after imagery training (in the imagery group) and after attitude training (in the control group). Test 2 was after both groups had received training in the face-name mnemonic.

(Source: "Imagery Pretraining and Memory Training in the Elderly" by J. A. Yesavage, 1983, *Gerontology*, *29*, 271–275. Copyright 1983 by S. Karger. Reprinted with permission.)

writing the information to be remembered on a notepad).

Training Internal Strategies. Most research on memory training concerns improving people's use of internal strategies that supply meaning and help organize incoming information (Bellezza, 1987). Examples of internal strategies include the method of loci (remembering items by mentally placing them in locations in a familiar environment), mental retracing (thinking about all the places you may have left your keys), turning letters into numbers, and forming acronyms out of initial letters (such as NASA from National Aeronautic and Space Administration).

Most memory improvement courses train people to become proficient at using one of these internal strategies. For example, Yesavage (1983) trained older adults to use images to help themselves remember people's names. As shown in Figure 6.3, this training was effective. Interestingly, certain personality traits may be associated with who benefits most from training. Gratzinger, Sheikh, Friedman, and Yesavage (1990) found that people who scored high on openness to experience (discussed in Chapter 8) performed better with imagery than other people. In particular, the fantasy subfactor of the openness dimension was related to greater improvement as a result of imagery training. It may be that people who find it easy to fantasize may be better at coming up with the imagery that helps them remember people's names.

Similar research has shown that training on most internal strategies improves memory significantly. For example, older adults have been successfully trained to use the method of loci as a way to help them remember items to be purchased at the grocery store (Anschutz, Camp, Markley, & Kramer, 1985). Unfortunately, these training programs have rarely been assessed over long intervals, so the degree of improvement after the course ends and how long this improvement lasts is largely unknown. One of the few exceptions was a three-year follow-up to the grocery shopping study (Anschutz, Camp, Markley, & Kramer, 1987). Although Anschutz and her colleagues found that loci were readily available, older adults had abandoned their use of the locus method as a memory aid. Clearly, more research needs to be conducted in order to understand why adults stop using internal memory strategies that are effective in improving recall.

Exercising Memory. A second approach to memory training is based on viewing memory as a mental muscle. This approach uses repetitive practice, which involves using specific memory exercises. Exercising memory on one type of task strengthens it, setting the stage for better memory in a variety of other tasks (Harris & Sunderland, 1981). For example, practicing how to organize a grocery list over and over will help you learn to organize other kinds of lists as well.

Exercising memory may have important benefits to a person during the rehabilitation process following an accident or stroke. For one thing, the person knows that something is being done about his or her memory problems. This may result in the belief that improvement is possible and that it is worth the effort. Second, evidence from both animal research (Wall, 1975) and human research (Black, Markowitz, & Cianci, 1975) indicates that early intervention with physical exercise promotes

A remedial program that emphasizes using external memory aids such as calendars is an effective intervention with cognitively impaired people.

recovery after damage to the motor cortex. Harris and Sunderland (1981) suggest that the same benefit may accrue if memory practice is begun at the first sign of loss.

Memory Drugs. Although considerable research has focused on the underlying neurological mechanisms in memory, little definitive information is available that can be easily translated into treatment approaches. For example, we still are not sure which neurotransmitters are primarily involved with memory. As a result, attempts to improve memory by administering drugs that act on certain

A cookbook can be an effective and helpful memory aid, no matter how often one has made black bean soup.

neurotransmitters have largely failed to produce long-term changes. This research is especially important for Alzheimer's disease and related disorders; we will return to it in Chapter 9.

External Memory Aids. External memory aids are objects such as diaries, address books, calendars, notepads, microcomputers, and other devices commonly used to support memory in everyday situations (Cavanaugh et al., 1983; Harris, 1980). Some external aids involve actually using some external device to store information (such as computers and date books), while others involve the use of external aids to cue action (for instance, setting a book out so you won't forget it).

Advocating the use of external aids in memory rehabilitation is becoming increasingly popular.

Zgola (1987) recommends external aids in working with Alzheimer's patients. For example, caregivers may label their kitchen cabinets to make it easier for the person with Alzheimer's disease to remember what is in them. Harris (1984a) suggests that for external cues to be most effective, they should: (1) be given close to the time that action is required, (2) be active rather than passive, (3) be specific to the particular action, (4) be portable, (5) fit a wide range of situations, (6) store many cues for long periods, (7) be easy to use, and (8) not require a pen or pencil.

Countering this trend toward greater use of external strategies, West (1986b) cautions that over-reliance on external aids can be a problem. She argues that memory is much like a muscle, which needs to be exercised in order to be kept in shape.

Consequently, we need to use internal strategies as much as possible, because they strengthen memory more than external strategies do. In practice, the best course is probably to use both.

Combining Strategies. Which memory strategy is best clearly depends on the situation. For example, remembering names probably demands an internal strategy whereas remembering appointments could most easily be helped by external strategies. For optimal improvement, the best approach is to tailor specific strategies to specific situations.

This is exactly what McEvoy and Moon (1988) did. They designed a comprehensive multiple strategy training program for improving older adults' memory in everyday situations. To remember names, older adults were taught an internal strategy emphasizing the need to associate new names with already-known information. In contrast, use of external aids and how to review them was used for remembering appointments such as occasional physician visits. McEvoy and Moon found that after training, participants had fewer complaints about their memory for names and faces, appointments, routine tasks, and spatial orientation.

McEvoy and Moon's study points out the importance of tailoring an intervention to fit the problem. What works best for one kind of information may not help us remember another. Moreover, their work also emphasizes the need for broad-based comprehensive intervention programs. Training people to only remember one kind of information is not helpful when their daily lives are filled with far more complicated demands.

Individual Difference Variables in Memory Training

As we have seen throughout this chapter, adults are a very heterogenous group when it comes to memory performance. For example, research reviewed earlier shows that verbal ability, prior knowledge,

and familiarity influence how well one performs on memory tasks. Treat, Poon, Fozard, and Popkin (1978) argued that individual difference variables should be considered when designing memory training programs, especially for older adults. Moreover, training may be more effective when changes in emotional status (Popkin, Gallagher, Thompson, & Moore, 1982) and feelings of self-efficacy (Berry, 1986; Cavanaugh et al., 1989) are major goals of the program. Yesavage, Sheikh, Tanke, and Hill (1988) found that the benefits of memory training depend on the specific needs of the client. Older adults who were highly verbal benefited most from a training program emphasizing ways to connect incoming information with information they already knew. In contrast, older adults who were highly anxious benefited most from training that included a relaxation component.

It is very unlikely that everyone will benefit equally from the same memory-training program. Some people may benefit most from training in the locus method, whereas others need training in the use of external aids. Only by tailoring programs to individual needs will long-term benefits be observed.

SUMMARY

Information Processing Revisited

1. Working memory is a small capacity store that deals with items currently being processed. Information is kept active through rehearsal. In general, working memory capacity and rehearsal decline with age.

2. In secondary memory, age-related decrements are typically found on recall tests but not on recognition tests. Older adults tend not to use memory strategies spontaneously as often or as well as younger adults.

3. In tertiary memory, age differences are typically not found in tests of the knowledge base. Some aspects of autobiographical memory remain intact for many years while others do not.

Sources of Age Differences: Storage and Retrieval Processes

4. Age-related decrements in storage may be due to decrements in rehearsal. Older adults do not spontaneously organize incoming information as well as younger adults.

5. Age differences are greater for algorithmic retrieval than for heuristic retrieval. Older adults benefit more than younger adults from retrieval cues, but age differences in performance are not eliminated. The locus of retrieval problems seems to be working memory.

6. Changes in memory with age are due to both storage and retrieval problems, but age-related decrements are greater for retrieval.

Memory for Discourse

7. Verbal ability is a major factor in determining age differences in discourse memory. Low-verbal older adults perform much worse than all younger adults; high-verbal older adults perform at least as well as high-verbal younger adults.

8. Age differences in performance are also influenced by the use of effective reading strategies, how a story is retold, and prior knowledge.

9. Higher presentation speeds may put older adults at a disadvantage.

10. With well-organized text, age differences are typically not found.

11. List learning and text memory are affected by similar variables.

Memory in Everyday Life

12. With familiar objects or locations, older adults often perform as well as younger adults. Older and younger adults use different strategies to learn locations. Older and younger adults appear equally able to learn a route and to perform configurational learning tasks.

13. Actually performing activities aids memory for older adults, but older adults are more likely to claim they performed actions they actually didn't.

14. Older adults are usually superior on prospective memory tasks.

15. Older adults are worse at remembering some types of pictures, but sometimes these differences are only found on delayed tests. Older adults are more likely to rely on their experience to help them remember scenes.

Self-Evaluations of Memory Abilities

16. Older adults typically believe that their memory will decline with age.

17. Older adults often overestimate how well they will do when making predictions without knowledge of the task. With task knowledge, age differences are usually absent.

Clinical Issues and Memory Testing

18. Whether memory changes affect daily functioning is one way to separate normal from abnormal aging. Brain imaging techniques allow localization of problems with more precision.

19. Dementia (such as Alzheimer's disease) and severe depression both involve memory impairment.

20. Certain vitamin deficiencies and medications can cause memory problems.

21. Scores on memory questionnaires correlate with depression.

22. Behavior rating scales are usually for diagnosing dementia, and include the various mental status exams.

23. Standardized memory tests help clinicians localize areas of memory problems and possible brain damage.

Remediating Memory Problems

24. Older adults can learn new internal memory strategies, but like all adults will usually abandon them over time.

25. Practicing remembering things helps to improve memory.

26. Use of memory enhancing drugs does not work over the long run.

27. External memory aids are very effective at improving memory.

REVIEW QUESTIONS

Information Processing Revisited

1. What is working memory? What age differences have been found? What role does working memory play in understanding age differences in memory?

2. What is secondary memory? How is it tested? What patterns of age differences have been found? What happens to the use of memory strategies with age?

3. What is tertiary memory? How does tertiary memory differ with age in terms of the knowledge base and autobiographical memory?

Sources of Age Differences: Storage and Retrieval Processes

4. What age differences have been found in storage processes?

5. What age differences have been found in retrieval processes?

6. How are these age differences related?

Memory for Discourse

7. What factors influence memory for discourse? What age differences have been uncovered related to these influences?

8. How do the patterns of age differences for discourse and list learning compare?

Memory in Everyday Life

9. What age differences are there in memory for location? What factors influence performance?

10. What difference does it make in accuracy in whether older and younger people actually performed the actions they need to remember?

11. What age differences are there in prospective memory?

12. How do younger and older adults compare at remembering pictures?

Self-Evaluations of Memory Abilities

13. What age differences are there in beliefs about memory?

14. What age differences have been found in making predictions about performance?

Clinical Issues and Memory Testing

15. What criteria are used to determine if there is a clinical problem with a person's memory?

16. What conditions involve significant memory problems?

17. How are clinical memory problems diagnosed?

Remediating Memory Problems

18. How much do older adults benefit from memory training programs?

19. What kinds of memory interventions work over time?

KEY TERMS

behavior rating scales Scales in which behavior is rated by an objective observer in order to make a diagnostic judgment. (204)

configurational learning Learning involving the combination of spatial and temporal information. (196)

metamemory Knowledge one has about how the memory system works and the kinds of things that influence it. (199)

on-line awareness Being aware of ongoing cognitive processes. (199)

prospective memory Remembering to do something in the future. (197)

recall A type of memory test in which no cues are provided. (183)

recognition A type of memory test requiring you to select the correct response from a list of alternatives. (183)

rehearsal The process by which information is kept alive in working memory. (181)

retrieval The process by which information that has been stored in memory is recovered and remembered. (187)

secondary memory An aspect of the information-processing system in which marked age-related differences in performance are observed. (182)

spatial memory The ability to remember where objects are located in the environment. (195)

storage The process by which information enters and is kept in memory. (187)

strategies The processes people use to help themselves remember. (187)

tertiary memory A large capacity aspect of the information-processing system. (184)

working memory A limited capacity aspect of information processing. (181)

ADDITIONAL READING

General overviews of memory research can be found in

Howe, M. L., & Brainerd, C. J. (Eds.). (1988). *Cognitive development in adulthood*. New York: Springer-Verlag. Moderate difficulty.

Poon, L. W., Rubin, D. C., & Wilson, B. (Eds.). (1989). *Everyday cognition in adult and late life*. New York: Cambridge University Press. Moderate to difficult.

An up-to-date discussion about memory in everyday life can be found in

West, R. L., & Sinnott, J. D. (Eds.). (1991). *Everyday memory and aging: Current research and methodology*. New York: Springer-Verlag. Moderate difficulty.

An excellent source of information about how memory is assessed in clinical settings is

Poon, L. W. (Ed.). (1986). *Handbook for the clinical memory assessment of older adults*. Washington, DC: American Psychological Association. Moderate to difficult.

CHAPTER 7

Intelligence

Jack Beal *Sydney and Frances Lewis* 1975 Washington and Lee University, Lexington, Virginia.

Once upon a time, there lived an old man with his beautiful daughter. She fell in love with a handsome lad, and the two married with the old man's blessing. The young couple led a happy life, except for one problem: The husband spent his time working on alchemy, dreaming of a way to turn base elements into gold. Soon enough, he ran through his patrimony, and the young wife struggled to buy food each day. She finally asked her husband to find a job, but he protested. "I am on the verge of a breakthrough!" he insisted. "When I succeed, we will be rich beyond our dreams."

Finally the young wife told her father about the problem. He was surprised to learn that his son-in-law was an alchemist, but he promised to help his daughter and asked to see him the next day. The young man went reluctantly, expecting a reprimand. To his surprise, his father-in-law confided in him, "I, too, was an alchemist when I was young!" The father-in-law inquired about the young man's work, and the two spent the afternoon talking. Finally the old man stirred with excitement. "You have done everything I did!" he exclaimed. "You are surely on the verge of a breakthrough. But you need one more ingredient to change base elements into gold, and I have only recently discovered this secret." The old man paused and sighed. "But I am too old to undertake the task. It requires much work."

"I can do it, dear father!" the young man volunteered. The old man brightened. "Yes, perhaps you can." Then he leaned over and whispered, "The ingredient you need is the silver powder that grows on banana leaves. This powder becomes magic when you plant the bananas yourself, and cast certain spells upon it."

"How much powder do we need?" the young man asked. "Two pounds," the old man replied.

The son-in-law thought out loud, "That requires hundreds of banana plants!"

"Yes," the old man sighed, "and that is why I cannot complete the work myself." "Do not fear!" the young man said, "I will!" And so the old man taught his son-in-law the incantations and loaned him the money for the project.

The next day, the young man bought some land, and cleared it. He dug the ground himself, just as the old man had instructed him, planted the bananas, and murmured the magic spells over them. Each day he examined his plants, keeping weeds and pests away, and when the plants bore fruit, he collected the silver powder from the leaves. There was scarcely any on each plant, and so the young man bought more land, and cultivated more bananas. After several years, the young man collected two pounds of the magic dust. He rushed to his father-in-law's house.

"I have the magic powder!" the young man exclaimed. "Wonderful!" the old man rejoiced. "Now I can show you how to turn base elements into gold! But first you must bring your wife here. We need her help." The young man was puzzled, but obeyed. When she appeared, the old man asked his daughter, "While your husband was col-

lecting the banana powder, what did you do with the fruits?"

"Why, I sold them," the daughter said, "and that is how we earned a living."

"Did you save the money?" the father asked.

"Yes," she replied.

"May I see it?" the old man asked. So his daughter hurried home and returned with several bags. The old man opened them, saw they were full of gold, and poured the coins on the floor. Then he took a handful of dirt, and put it next to the gold.

"See," he turned to his son-in-law, "you have changed base elements into gold!"

For a tense moment, the young man was silent. Then he laughed, seeing the wisdom in the old man's trick. And from that day on, the young man and his wife prospered greatly. He tended the plants while she went to the market, selling the bananas. And they both honored the old man as the wisest of alchemists.*

THIS OLD BURMESE FOLKTALE DRIVES HOME THE point that wisdom has long been associated with age. Surprisingly, psychologists have only recently become interested in wisdom, perhaps because they have been busy studying a related topic — intelligence. Another reason for not researching wisdom was the widespread belief that it would be a waste of time. At one time researchers and theorists were convinced that all intellectual abilities inevitably declined as people aged, due to biological deterioration. For instance, Wechsler (1958) wrote that "nearly all studies . . . have shown that most human abilities . . . decline progressively after reaching a peak somewhere between ages 18 and 25" (p. 135).

In the decades since Wechsler's pessimistic view, many things changed. Researchers discov-

*From A.B. Chinen (1989). In the ever after (pp. 31–33). Willmette, IL: Chiron. Reprinted with permission.

ered that intellectual development is an extremely complex process. It became evident that we cannot give simple yes or no answers to the question "Does intelligence decline with age?" And we continue to move farther away, rather than closer to, simple answers. Controversy is now quite common. For instance, Baltes and Schaie (1974) conclude that "general intellectual decline is largely a myth" (p. 35). Botwinick (1977) counters that "decline in intellectual ability is clearly a part of the aging picture" (p. 580).

Who is right? Does intelligence decline, or is that a myth? Does wisdom come with age? Answering these questions will be our goal in this chapter. Such widely divergent conclusions about age-related changes in intelligence reflect different sets of assumptions about the nature of intelligence, which are then translated into different theoretical and methodological approaches. We will examine three avenues of research on intelligence and age: the psychometric approach, the neofunctionalist approach, and the cognitive-process approaches. Along the way we will take a look at some attempts to modify intellectual abilities through training programs. But first, we need to consider the question of what intelligence is.

DEFINING INTELLIGENCE

What do we mean by intelligence? Is it being able to learn new things very quickly? Is it knowing a great deal of information? Is it the ability to adapt to new situations or to create new things or ideas? Or is it the ability to make the most of what we have and to enjoy life? Intelligence is all of these abilities and more. It is all of them in the sense that people who stand out on these dimensions are often considered smart, or intelligent. It is more than just these abilities because intelligence also involves the qualitative aspects of thinking style, or how one approaches and conceptualizes problems.

Intelligence in Everyday Life

Some intriguing work by Sternberg and his colleagues points out that intelligence involves more than just a particular fixed set of characteristics (Sternberg, Conway, Ketron, & Bernstein, 1981). They compiled a list of behaviors that laypeople at a train station, supermarket, or college library reported to be distinctly characteristic of either exceptionally intelligent, academically intelligent, everyday intelligent, or unintelligent people. This list of behaviors was then given to experts in the field of intelligence and to a new set of laypeople, who were asked to rate either how distinctively characteristic each behavior was of an ideally intelligent, academically intelligent, or everyday intelligent individual, or how important each behavior was in defining these types of intelligent individuals. Ratings were analyzed separately for the experts and the laypeople.

Sternberg and his colleagues found extremely high agreement between experts and laypeople on ratings of the importance of particular behaviors in defining intelligence. The two groups agreed that intelligence consisted of three major clusters of related abilities: problem-solving ability, verbal ability, and social competence. Problem-solving ability consists of behaviors such as reasoning logically, identifying connections among ideas, seeing all aspects of a problem, and making good decisions. Verbal ability includes such things as speaking articulately, reading with high comprehension, and having a good vocabulary. Social competence includes behaviors such as accepting others for what they are, admitting mistakes, displaying interest in the world at large, and being on time for appointments.

Sternberg also wanted to know how these conceptions of intelligence differed across the adult life span. To find out, individuals aged 25 to 75 were asked to list behaviors that they viewed as characteristic of exceptionally intelligent 30-, 50-, or 70-year-olds. Behaviors such as motivation, how much intellectual effort people exert, and reading were said to be important indicators of intelligence for people of all ages. But other behaviors were specific to particular points in the life span. For example, planning for the future and being open-minded were listed most often for a 30-year-old. The intelligent 50-year-old was described as being willing to learn, having a well-established career, and being authoritative. At age 70, intelligent people were thought to be socially active, up on current events, and accepting of change.

Intelligence and the Biopsychosocial Model

Sternberg and his colleagues' research provides an excellent example of the biopsychosocial model. Clearly, their respondents considered psychological and social functioning in their definitions. Moreover, respondents took the target person's life cycle into account; they listed somewhat different characteristics of intelligence depending on how old the target person was.

Throughout this chapter, you will see how studying intelligence forces researchers to consider all aspects of the biopsychosocial model. You will discover how physical health, cohort, life style, occupation, personality, and education all exert important influences on intellectual abilities. Perhaps in no other area is the evidence supporting the importance of using the biopsychosocial model as clear. Only when all of these influences are considered do we begin to get a picture of intellectual development across adulthood.

Research Approaches to Intelligence

Sternberg's work points out that many different skills are involved in intelligence, depending on one's point of view. Interestingly, the behaviors listed by Sternberg's participants fit nicely with the more formal attempts at defining intelligence that we will encounter in this chapter.

Some psychologists, such as Schaie and Horn, have concentrated on measuring intelligence as performance on standardized tests; this camp represents the **psychometric approach**. For example, the problem-solving and verbal abilities in Sternberg et al.'s study coincide with the notions of fluid and crystallized intelligence described in psychometric theories. Other researchers and theorists have reinterpreted the data obtained in the psychometric approach and have postulated the **neofunctionalist view**, which emphasizes individual differences and plasticity. Still others have been more concerned with the thought processes involved rather than with scores on tests; they take a **cognitive-process approach** to intelligence. This approach emphasizes developmental changes in the quality and styles of thinking. The age differences Sternberg found in which abilities their respondents thought were important correspond to the qualitative changes discussed by cognitive theorists.

In this chapter we will consider these theories and the research they stimulated. We will discover that each approach has its merits, and that whether age-related changes in intelligence are found depends on how intelligence is defined and measured.

THE PSYCHOMETRIC APPROACH

One way to define intelligence is to focus on individuals' scores on various tests of intellectual abilities and on how these scores are interrelated. This psychometric approach to intelligence has a long history; the ancient Chinese and Greeks used this method to select people for certain jobs, such as master horseman (Doyle, 1974; DuBois, 1968).

Because the psychometric approach focuses on the interrelationships among intellectual abilities, the major goal is to describe the ways in which these relationships are organized (Sternberg, 1985). This organization of interrelated intellectual abilities is termed the *structure* of intelligence. The most common way to describe the structure of intelligence is to picture it as a hierarchy (Cunningham, 1987).

Each higher level of this hierarchy represents an attempt to organize components of the level below in a smaller number of groups. The lowest level consists of individual test questions — the specific items that people answer on an intelligence test. These items can be organized into tests at the second level. The third level, primary mental abilities, reflects interrelationships among performances on intelligence tests. Interrelationships can also be uncovered among the primary mental abilities, which produce the secondary mental abilities at the fourth level. Third-order mental abilities in turn represent interrelationships among the secondary mental abilities. Finally, general intelligence at the top refers to the interrelationships among the third-order abilities.

Keep in mind that each time we move up the hierarchy we are moving away from people's actual performance. Each level above the first represents a theoretical description of how things fit together. Thus, there are no tests of primary abilities per se; primary abilities represent theoretical relationships among tests, which in turn represent theoretical relationships among actual performance.

So exactly how do researchers construct this theoretical hierarchy? The structure of intelligence is uncovered through sophisticated statistical detective work. First, researchers obtain people's performances on many types of problems. Next, the results are examined to determine whether performance on one type of problem — for example, filling in missing letters in a word — predicts performance on another type of problem — for example, unscrambling letters to form a word. If the performance on one test is highly related to the performance on another, the abilities measured by the two tests are said to be interrelated. In the psychometric approach large numbers of abilities that interrelate in this way are called a *factor*.

Most psychometric theorists believe that intelligence consists of several factors. Although estimates of the exact number of factors vary from a few to over 100, most researchers and theorists believe the number to be relatively small. We will examine two types of factors: primary mental abilities and secondary mental abilities.

Primary Mental Abilities

Early in this century researchers discovered the existence of several independent intellectual abilities, each indicated by different combinations of intelligence tests. The abilities identified in this way led Thurstone (1938) to propose that intelligence is composed of several independent abilities, which he labeled **primary mental abilities**. Thurstone initially examined seven primary mental abilities: number, word fluency, verbal meaning, associative memory, reasoning, spatial orientation, and perceptual speed. Over the years this list has been refined and expanded, resulting in a current list of 25 primary mental abilities that have been documented across many studies (Ekstrom, French, & Harman, 1979). These include such things as verbal comprehension, logical reasoning, and visual memory; descriptions of each ability are presented in Table 7.1. Because it is difficult to measure all 25 primary abilities in the same study, researchers following in Thurstone's tradition concentrate on measuring

TABLE 7.1   Primary mental abilities indicated by repeated research

Factor	Factor Label	Examples of Tests That Define the Factor
V	Verbal comprehension	Vocabulary, reading comprehension, understanding grammar and syntax
CV	Verbal closure	Scrambled words, hidden words, incomplete words
FW	Word fluency	Word endings, word beginnings, rhymes
FA	Associational fluency	Controlled associations, inventive opposites, figures of speech
FE	Expressional fluency	Making sentences, rewriting, simile interpretations
O	Object flexibility	Substantive uses, improving things, combining objects
SP	Sensitivity to problems	Improvements for common objects, listing problems, finding deficiencies
CA	Concept formation	Picture-group naming, word grouping, verbal relations
RL	Logical reasoning	Nonsense syllogisms, diagramming relationships, deciphering languages
I	Inductive reasoning	Letter sets, locating marks, classifications
RG	General reasoning	Word problems, ship destination, language rules
ES	Estimation	Width determination, spatial judgment, quantitative estimation
N	Number facility	Addition, division, mixed numerical operations
S	Spatial orientation	Card rotations, cube comparisons, boat positions
CS	Speed (gestalt) closure	Gestalt completion, incomplete pictures, concealed objects
CF	Flexibility of closure	Hidden figures, embedded figures, copying figures
VZ	Visualization	Form board, paper folding, surface development
P	Perceptual speed	Finding a's, number comparisons, identical pictures
FF	Figural flexibility	Toothpicks, planning patterns, storage
FL	Figural fluency	Decorations, alternate signs, make a figure
IT	Integration	Following directions, internalizing rules, manipulating numbers
MV	Visual memory	System-shape recognition, monogram recall, orientation memory
MS	Span memory	Digit span-visual, letter span-auditory, tone reproduction
MA	Associative memory	Picture-number pairs, first-last names, serial recall
MM	Meaningful memory	Recalling limericks, sentence completion, sentence recall

(Source: "Cognitive Factors: Their Identification and Replication" by Eckstrom et al., 1979, *Multivariate Behavior Research Monographs*, No. 79.2. Reprinted by permission.)

only a subset. Typically, this subset consists of five primary mental abilities: number, word fluency, verbal meaning, inductive reasoning, and space. How these five abilities fare with age will be considered next.

Age-Related Changes in Primary Abilities. The most comprehensive investigation of age-related changes in primary mental abilities is a study by Schaie that began in Seattle in 1956 (Schaie, 1983). Seven cohorts, representing people born between 1889 and 1938, were included; 162 people were tested in 1956, 1963, and 1970, and 250 others were initially tested in 1963 and retested in 1970 and 1977. Thus, it is possible to compare developmental trends on the 5 primary mental abilities listed earlier for 2 separate 14-year periods (1956–1970 and 1963–1977). This is exactly what Schaie and Hertzog (1983) did.

Schaie and Hertzog reported some complicated but interesting results. First, they found declines in performance on all 5 primary mental abilities after age 60 that were large enough to be of practical importance. That is, the amount of change in ability was likely to lead to decrements in everyday functioning. Second, there were also small drops in performance during the 50s; however, the impact that these changes had in a person's everyday life might be minimal. Schaie and Hertzog noted that the declines between ages 60 and 67 were greater than those observed between 53 and 60. This means that the pronounced decline in primary abilities after age 60 may have begun earlier. Finally, estimates of the size of the age effects differed when the data were analyzed cross-sectionally and longitudinally. Schaie and Hertzog were able to show conclusively that cross-sectional data gave a much more pessimistic view of intellectual decline than did longitudinal data. Moreover, individual differences were often found to be quite large, making it difficult to draw general conclusions about specific individuals.

In sum, Schaie and Hertzog's data show reliable declines in primary mental abilities after age 60 that may affect people's everyday lives. However, the limits of their research must be kept in mind. They only studied a small subset of the primary abilities. This is especially important because other abilities may show different developmental patterns. Also, the amount of variance accounted for by age never exceeded 9%, meaning that most of the differences in performance over time were due to something else. For these reasons, a complex theory may be needed to account for age differences in primary abilities (Horn, 1982). We will explore some of the variables needed in such a theory when we consider moderators of intellectual change later in the chapter.

Secondary Mental Abilities

Because so many primary mental abilities have been identified, some researchers think it may be easier to understand intellectual development by looking at interrelationships among them. Careful consideration of the relationships among the primary mental abilities has resulted in the identification of **secondary mental abilities**, which are broad-ranging skills, each composed of several primary abilities (Horn, 1982). At present, at least six secondary abilities have been found. Each of these is described in Table 7.2. Most of the developmental research and discussion of these abilities has been focused on two: fluid intelligence and crystallized intelligence.

Fluid and Crystallized Intelligence. Fluid and crystallized intelligence include many of the basic abilities that we associate with intelligence, such as verbal comprehension, reasoning, integration, and concept formation (Horn, 1978, 1982). Interestingly, they are associated with age differently, are

TABLE 7.2   Descriptions of major second-order mental abilities

Crystallized Intelligence (Gc)

This form of intelligence is indicated by a very large number of performances indicating breadth of knowledge and experience, sophistication, comprehension of communications, judgment, understanding conventions, and reasonable thinking. The factor that provides evidence of Gc is defined by primary abilities such as verbal comprehension, concept formation, logical reasoning, and general reasoning. Tests used to measure the ability include vocabulary (What is a word near in meaning to *temerity*?), esoteric analogies (Socrates is to Aristotle as Sophocles is to _____?), remote associations (What word is associated with *bathtub, prizefighting,* and *wedding*?), and judgment (Determine why a foreman is not getting the best results from workers). As measured, the factor is a fallible representation of the extent to which an individual has incorporated, through the systematic influences of acculturation, the knowledge and sophistication that constitutes the intelligence of a culture.

Fluid Intelligence (Gf)

The broad set of abilities of this intelligence include those of seeing relationships among stimulus patterns, drawing inferences from relationships, and comprehending implications. The primary abilities that best represent the factor, as identified in completed research, include induction, figural flexibility, integration, and, cooperatively with Gc, logical reasoning and general reasoning. Tasks that measure the factor include letter series (What letter comes next in the following series d f i m r x e ?), matrices (Discern the relationships among elements of 3-by-3 matrices), and topology (From among a set of figures in which circles, squares, and triangles overlap in different ways, select a figure that will enable one to put a dot within a circle and square but outside a triangle). The factor is a fallible representation of such fundamental features of mature human intelligence as reasoning, abstracting, and problem solving. In Gf these features are not imparted through the systematic influences of acculturation but instead are obtained through learning that is unique to an individual or is in other ways not organized by the culture.

Visual Organization (Gv)

This dimension is indicated by primary mental abilities such as visualization, spatial orientation, speed of closure, and flexibility of closure, measured by tests such as gestalt closure (Identify a figure in which parts have been omitted), form board (Show how cut-out parts fit together to depict a particular figure), and

(Source: "The Aging of Human Abilities" (pp. 847–870) by J. L. Horn, 1982, in B. B. Wolman (Ed.), *Handbook of Developmental Psychology.* © 1982 Reprinted with permission of Prentice-Hall, Inc., Englewood Cliffs, NJ.)

influenced by different underlying variables, and are measured in different ways.

Fluid intelligence refers to your innate ability independent of acquired knowledge and experience; that is, fluid intelligence refers to your basic information-processing skills. Fluid intelligence is reflected on tests of incidental learning and inductive reasoning, for example. **Crystallized intelligence** reflects knowledge that you have acquired through experience and education; it represents intelligence as cultural knowledge. Crystallized intelligence is reflected on tests of intentional learning—vocabulary, information, and comprehension, to name a few.

It is important to realize that any standardized intelligence test taps abilities underlying both fluid and crystallized intelligence. No single test of either ability exists, because each represents a cluster of underlying primary abilities. As a general rule tests that minimize the role of acquired, cultural knowl-

embedded figures (Find a geometric figure within a set of intersecting lines). To distinguish this factor from Gf, it is important that relationships among visual patterns be clearly manifest so performances reflect primarily fluency in perception of these patterns, not reasoning in inferring the patterns.

Auditory Organization (Ga)

This factor has been identified on the basis of several studies in which primary mental abilities of temporal tracking, auditory cognition of relations, and speech perception under distraction-distortion were first defined among other primary abilities and then found to indicate a broad dimension at the second order. Tasks that measure Ga include repeated tones (Identify the first occurrence of a tone when it occurs several times), tonal series (Indicate which tone comes next in an orderly series of tones), and cafeteria noise (Identify a word amid a din of surrounding noise). As in the case of Gv, this ability is best indicated when the relationships among stimuli are not such that one needs to reason for understanding but instead are such that one can fluently perceive patterns among the stimuli.

Short-Term Acquisition and Retrieval

This ability comprises processes of becoming aware and processes of retaining information long enough to do something with it. Almost all tasks that involve short-term memory have variance in this factor. Span-memory, associative-memory, and meaningful-memory primary abilities define the factor, but measures of primary and secondary memory can also be used to indicate the dimension.

Long-Term Storage and Retrieval

Formerly this dimension was regarded as a broad factor among fluency tasks, such as those of the primary abilities labeled associational fluency, expressional fluency, and object flexibility. In recent work, however, these performances have been found to align with others indicating facility in storing information and retrieving information that was acquired in the distant past. It seems, therefore, that the dimension mainly represents processes for forming encoding associations for long-term storage and using these associations, or forming new ones, at the time of retrieval. These associations are not so much correct as they are possible and useful; to associate *tea kettle* with *mother* is not to arrive at a truth so much as it is to regard both concepts as sharing common attributes (e.g., warmth).

edge involve mainly fluid intelligence; those that maximize the role of such knowledge involve mainly crystallized intelligence.

Developmentally, fluid and crystallized intelligence follow two very different paths, as depicted in Figure 7.1. Notice that fluid intelligence declines significantly as we grow older. Although our understanding of why this drop occurs is not yet complete, it may be related to changes in the underlying neurophysiological processes and to lack of prac-

tice. In particular, decline in fluid intelligence is associated primarily with decrements in the ability to organize information, the ability to ignore irrelevant information, the ability to focus or to divide attention, and the ability to keep information in working memory (Horn, Donaldson, & Engstrom, 1981).

In contrast, crystallized intelligence does not normally decline with age; indeed, it may even increase as a result of continued experience and life-

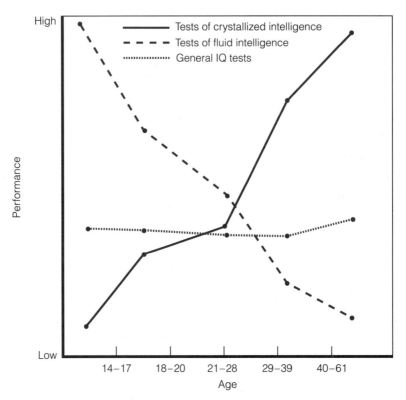

FIGURE 7.1 Performances on tests used to define fluid, crystallized, and general intelligence, as a function of age

(Source: "Organization of Data on Life-Span Development of Human Abilities" (p. 463) by J. L. Horn, 1970, in L. R. Goulet and P. B. Baltes (Eds.), *Life-Span Developmental Psychology: Research and Theory*. New York: Academic Press. Reprinted with permission.)

long learning. This makes sense because you are continually adding to your knowledge base by learning new words, acquiring new skills at home or work, and compiling information by reading, for example (Horn, 1982; Horn & Donaldson, 1980).

Considering intellectual development in terms of fluid and crystallized intelligence has proved useful for three reasons. First, it helps explain how older adults may be less able to perform tasks that are novel but may be as proficient as ever when it comes to situations that demand experience or practical knowledge. Second, the discovery that fluid and crystallized intelligence follow different developmental paths emphasizes that intellectual development is a complex process. Finally, research on fluid and crystallized intelligence has generated renewed interest in the interrelationships among intellectual abilities.

Although the concepts of fluid and crystallized intelligence are popular, they are not universally accepted. For example, they have been criticized as being nothing more than the product of statistical data analyses (Guilford, 1980). Additionally, there are alternative ways to interpret age differences that involve considering several personal and contextual variables (see Labouvie-Vief, 1977); this criticism is taken up in the next section.

Moderators of Intellectual Change

Based on the research we have considered thus far, two different developmental trends emerge: We see gains in experience-based processes, but losses in information-processing abilities. The continued growth in some areas is viewed as a product of lifelong learning. The losses are viewed as an inevitable result of the decline of physiological processes with age.

A growing number of researchers, though, disagree with the notion that intellectual aging necessarily involves an inevitable decline in fluid abilities (Labouvie-Vief, 1977, 1981; Schaie, 1979). These researchers do not deny that some adults show intellectual decline. Rather, they simply suggest that these decrements may not happen to everyone to the same extent. They argue that there are many reasons besides age why performance differences occur. In this section we will explore some of the social and physiological factors that have been proposed as modifiers of intellectual development. These include cohort differences, educational level, occupation, personality, health and life style, mindlessness, and relevancy and appropriateness of tasks.

Cohort Differences. Do the differences in intellectual performance obtained in some situations reflect true age-related change or mainly cohort, or generational, differences? This question gets right to the heart of the debate over interpreting developmental research on intelligence. On the one hand, dozens of cross-sectional studies document significant differences in intellectual performance with age. On the other hand, several longitudinal

investigations show either no decrement or even an increase in performance (Labouvie-Vief, 1985).

The way to resolve the discrepancy between the two approaches involves comparing data collected over long periods of time from several samples and analyzed simultaneously in both cross-sectional and longitudinal designs. When this has been done, the results indicate that part of the apparent decline with age in performance on intelligence tests is due to generational differences rather than age differences (Schaie, 1979; Schaie & Hertzog, 1983; Schaie & Labouvie-Vief, 1974; Schaie & Parham, 1977).

As an example of what is meant by generational differences, let us consider a portion of the data reported by Schaie (1983). In analyzing data from his longitudinal study, he found significant cohort effects favoring the more recently born adults for the primary mental abilities of verbal meaning, space, number, inductive reasoning, and word fluency. In other words, scores on these primary abilities were related to when people had been born. There was a relatively constant gain in scores on reasoning from the 1889 cohort to the 1952 cohort, for example, even after other factors, including age, had been ruled out. These data suggest that older cohorts may be at a significant disadvantage on tests tapping the component skills of fluid abilities. It is important to note, however, that although cohort effects reduce the size of the age effects, they do not explain all of the age-related differences (Horn, 1982; Schaie & Hertzog, 1983).

Documenting cohort effects is one example of considering the context in which people develop, an important aspect of the biopsychosocial model. But cohort is a rather general concept, since there are many things that could differ from one generation to the next. Let's take a look at some of these more specific variables.

Educational Level. Even though researchers have known for many years that scores on intelligence tests are related to educational level (Miles & Miles,

1932), only since the late 1960s have investigators seriously considered the meaning of this relationship for intellectual development in adulthood. Several studies have now documented that differences in educational level can account for some of the age differences that emerge (Blum & Jarvik, 1974; Gonda, 1980; Granick & Friedman, 1973; Green, 1969; Schaie & Strother, 1968).

Granick and Friedman (1973) took into account the fact that older adults had less formal education, on the average, than younger adults. Once this relationship between age and education had been controlled for, the age-related decline in intelligence was significantly reduced. Other researchers have compared people within a particular generation who differed in education. For example, Blum & Jarvik (1974) found better intellectual performance among older adult high school graduates than among older adults who had finished only elementary school.

The importance of education for intellectual development during adulthood may go beyond the absolute number of years spent in school (Gonda, 1980). For one thing, more highly educated individuals may adopt life styles that foster the maintenance of cognitive abilities. Highly educated older adults are also the exception in their generation; opportunities to go to college were not as prevalent 50 years ago as they are now.

Taken together, these factors indicate that one source of the cohort effect may be differences in the type and amount of education. The evidence points to the maintenance of intellectual abilities in well-educated adults at least into old age. As more well-educated cohorts grow old, they may help change the stereotype of universal and inevitable intellectual decline with age.

Occupation. Think for a minute about the kind of job you currently have or would like to get. What kinds of intellectual skills does it demand? What similarities or differences are there between your chosen job (for example, school counselor) and a different one (say, accountant)? An interesting line of research concerns how the differences in cognitive skills needed in different occupations makes a difference in intellectual development (Labouvie-Vief, 1981). To the extent that a job requires you to use certain cognitive abilities a great deal, you may be less likely to show declines in them as you age.

Indirect support for this hypothesis comes from research showing that when older people are familiar with the tasks used in intelligence tests, they perform much better (Labouvie-Vief & Gonda, 1976). To the extent that people become practiced at thinking in a certain way, they may be less likely to show declines in that kind of thinking as they grow older. More direct support comes from Avolio and Waldman's (1987) research on employees at a coal mine, which is highlighted in How Do We Know?

Personality. We know very little about how personality factors mediate intellectual functioning. Botwinick and Storandt (1974) found that as women grew older, their effort and deliberation increased, even though their performance on measures of brain function decreased. It was as if these women tried harder to compensate for decrements in ability.

Lachman (1983) studied the nature of change in personality and intellectual factors in later life from a different perspective. Based on data collected on two occasions about two years apart, she examined the causal relationship between perceptions of one's own cognitive abilities and performance on several measures of intelligence. Most important, she found that people changed in their perceptions of their abilities over time. Interestingly, the nature of this change was related to people's initial level of fluid intelligence and sense of personal control over their life. High initial levels of fluid abilities and a high sense of internal control led to positive changes in people's perceptions of their abilities; low initial levels led to decreases in perceptions of ability. Thus, Lachman's results sup-

HOW DO WE KNOW?

Job as a Moderator of the Age-Aptitude Relationship

There is a growing realization that people's everyday experience affects their performance on tests of intellectual abilities. This experience can range from formal education to work skills.

Avolio and Waldman (1987) examined performance on standard personnel aptitude tests and how it related to age, education, and job type. The tests, used widely in personnel departments, measured space visualization, numerical reasoning, verbal reasoning, symbolic reasoning, and mechanical reasoning. Participants were a random sample of 131 employees at a coal mine in the western United States; 82% of the employees were men. Of the partici-

pants, 69 were from the production department, representing unskilled workers, and 62 were from the machinery department, representing skilled workers.

The results showed very different patterns of correlations between performance on the aptitude tests and age as a function of job type. These differences remained even after corrections for level of education were made. Unskilled workers from the production department showed relatively high negative correlations between age and performance, ranging from .37 between age and numerical reasoning to .57 for age and verbal reasoning. In contrast, skilled workers in the machinery department showed little relationship between age and performance; the strongest relationship was .32 between age and symbolic reasoning.

These results mean that there were very few differences between

older and younger workers in the machinery department on aptitude tests, whereas such differences were common in production department workers. These findings support the idea that everyday experience affects the maintenance of intellectual abilities. In particular, certain job activities may provide workers with continued practice with various cognitive skills, thereby preventing marked decline. As we will see in our discussion of training primary abilities, this use-disuse hypothesis appears to explain much of the age differences in performance.

We must keep in mind, however, that Avolio and Waldman conducted a cross-sectional study, examined only a small number of aptitudes, and tested only coal mine workers. Future research needs to include other occupations and skills and to examine performance from a longitudinal perspective.

---

port the view that initial levels of cognitive ability affect changes in how abilities are perceived; no evidence for the reverse relationship was found.

Hayslip (1988) investigated relationships between personality and ability from an ego development perspective (see Chapter 8). He was interested in establishing connections between how people view themselves and their level of intellectual ability. He found that anxiety over the adequacy of one's ideational ability and feelings about bodily integrity were related to crystallized intelligence, whereas using cognitive resources to deal

with reality and organizational ability related to fluid intelligence. These relationships suggest that individual differences in the maintenance of higher levels of intellectual functioning in later life may be motivated by the desire to protect oneself from feelings of worthlessness and loss of control over one's abilities.

Health and Life Style. One of the most difficult problems in any study of aging is the separation of normal processes from abnormal ones. So far our discussion of intellectual development has ignored this distinction; we have been concerned only with normal changes. However, we know that not everyone is healthy, experiencing only normal cognitive aging. Moreover, disease is a hit-or-miss proposition, affecting some people primarily physically, as in arthritis, and others primarily cognitively, as in the early stages of dementia. Thus, we need to consider how specific aspects of health influence intellectual ability.

The most obvious relationship between health and intelligence concerns the functioning of the brain itself. We noted in Chapter 3 that several normative age-related changes in brain structure affect functioning. Disorders such as Alzheimer's disease and head injuries may damage the brain. In some cases these problems get worse as the individual ages. Obviously, the more extensive the damage, the more significant the impairment of intellectual ability.

The connection between disease and intelligence has been established fairly well in the case of cardiovascular disease (Schaie, 1990). Wilkie and Eisdorfer (1971) found significant intellectual decline over a 10-year period in people with hypertension but no decline in people with normal or slightly elevated blood pressure. The effects of hypertension may be manifested behaviorally as declines in fluid intelligence (Horn, 1982). Interestingly, Schaie (1990) reports that people in the Seattle Longitudinal Project who declined in inductive reasoning ability (one aspect of fluid intelligence) had significantly more illness diagnoses and visits to physicians for cardiovascular disease.

Mindlessness. Langer (1985) offers an interesting explanation of the apparent decline in intellectual abilities in adulthood. She argues that cognitive processing occurs at two levels: a mindful level, at which we are aware of what we are doing and are actively involved with the environment; and a mindless level, at which we are unaware of what we are doing and are only passively involved with the environment. Mindlessness occurs when we allow

the situation to dictate our behavior, rather than stepping back and critically evaluating what we should be doing. Many times we go along with requests, for example, because everything seems to be correct: The con artist looks and acts like a bank executive, so we do not question his request to withdraw our savings. What we fail to do is ask ourselves whether the request is reasonable; we just go along because appearances say that we should.

Langer contends that mindlessness increases as we get older unless something is done to stop this rise. Moreover, older adults may engage in mindlessness at inappropriate times and appear incompetent. Unchecked increases in mindlessness may be part of the reason that institutionalized older adults seem less alert cognitively; that is, the institution may not foster mindfulness. In a provocative study Langer and Rodin (1976) demonstrated this point. When they increased mindfulness in nursing home residents by encouraging them to make decisions and by giving them responsibilities for plants, the residents became happier, healthier, and more alert and did better on memory tests.

Although Langer's notion of mindlessness is still controversial, it fits well with the widely held belief and research evidence that people who remain cognitively active — mindful, in Langer's terms — are those who show the least decline (Blum & Jarvik, 1974).

Relevancy and Appropriateness of Tasks. All of the psychometric tests used today trace their origin to Binet's original attempt to measure academic performance. Some researchers argue that the academic settings and skills that led to the development of these tests may not be equally important or relevant to adults. Consequently, it is argued that we need new tests that are based on the problems adults typically face.

To build new tests requires understanding what skills adults use in everyday situations. Scheidt and Schaie (1978) tried doing just that. They interviewed older adults in parks, senior centers, and similar locations and asked them to name situations that involved using intelligence. In all, over 300 situations were described; looking for a place to live and figuring out how to pay a debt were two common examples. These responses provide a very different starting point for developing tasks for an intelligence test than trying to figure out how to measure classroom learning potential.

Willis, Schaie, and Lueers (1983) also looked at practical measures of intelligence, but from a different perspective. They examined the relationships between seven primary mental abilities, measured by traditional tests, and eight categories of everyday tasks, measured by the ETS Basic Skills Test. The categories of everyday tasks included understanding labels on medical or household articles, reading street maps, understanding charts or schedules, comprehending paragraphs, filling out forms, reading newspaper and phone directory ads, understanding technical documents, and comprehending news text. Three scores on the skills test were calculated; two scores reflected different levels of comprehension and information processing (literal and inference) and the third was the total score. Correlations between the scores for primary abilities and basic skills were very high for the older adults, indicating that the two tests were measuring similar things.

When Willis and colleagues examined their data to see which of the primary abilities best predicted each of the eight categories of everyday tasks, some interesting findings emerged. They had expected their measures of crystallized intelligence to be the best predictors, on the basis that these everyday skills reflect cultural knowledge and should not decline with age. Much to their surprise, the measures of fluid intelligence, especially figural relations, were the best predictors most of the time. Moreover, older adults did not always perform as well as the younger adults on the everyday skills test. In fact, the younger adults obtained near-perfect scores, whereas the older adults were significantly below ceiling, on average.

The Willis study is important for two reasons. First, it shows that traditional tests of primary mental abilities may predict performance on everyday tasks. For supporters of the psychometric approach, these data show that a total rejection of traditional tests on the ground that they are inadequate may be unwarranted. Second, the findings also show that tests consisting of what appear to be more relevant tasks may tap some of the same components of intelligence that the traditional tests are thought to measure. This suggests that we might develop new tests that consist of familiar tasks but that still tap the components of intelligence identified in psychometric research.

The issue of task relevancy is still far from being settled, however. As we will see later, many researchers and theorists argue quite strongly that only by abandoning a purely psychometric approach and moving to a focus on everyday uses of intelligence will we advance our understanding of intellectual aging. As with most controversies, there is something to be said for both sides.

Modifying Primary Abilities

As we have seen, older adults do not perform as well on tests of some primary abilities as younger adults, even after taking the moderators of performance into account (Schaie & Hertzog, 1983). In considering these results, investigators began asking whether there was a way to slow down or even reverse the declines. Are the age-related differences that remain after cohort and other effects are removed permanent? Or might it be possible to reduce or even eliminate these differences if older adults were given appropriate training? Can we modify adults' intelligence?

Attempts to answer these questions have appeared with increasing frequency since the mid-1970s. Several types of tasks have been examined, ranging from tests of skills underlying primary mental abilities (Willis, 1987) to the information-processing skills necessary to drive a car (Sterns & Sanders, 1980). Of these, perhaps the most interesting and important research area is the attempt to modify primary abilities that show early and substantial declines.

Primary abilities that are known to begin to decline relatively early in adulthood — such as inductive reasoning, spatial orientation, memory abilities, and figural abilities (Baltes & Willis, 1982) — have been examined most closely in intervention research. Labouvie-Vief and Gonda (1976) focused on inductive reasoning. They measured performance on the training task (the Letter Sets Test) and on a new transfer task that participants had not seen during training (Raven's Progressive Matrices). Training was given to three groups. Members of the first group were told to give themselves self-directional statements and feedback. The second group combined these with additional statements that were designed to help them cope with anxiety and to emphasize self-approval and success. Members of the third group received unspecific training; they simply practiced taking the Letter Sets Test with no instructions or feedback. Labouvie-Vief and Gonda found that inductive reasoning could be increased through training. They also found evidence for transfer of the training effects, since the performance of the trained groups was also better on the Raven's Progressive Matrices.

Project ADEPT. A much more comprehensive training study, involving a series of short longitudinal studies, was Pennsylvania State University's Adult Development and Enrichment Project (ADEPT) (Baltes & Willis, 1982). The training studies conducted as part of ADEPT included two levels of intervention in addition to a no-training control group. All groups were equivalent at the outset.

The first level of intervention involved minimal direct training and had test familiarity as its goal. Participants were given the same tests on several occasions to familiarize them with test taking, so that the researchers could learn about the effects of repeated testing alone.

The second type of training involved interventions tailored specifically for each of the primary abilities tested. Each training package was based on a thorough task analysis of the thinking processes involved in each ability. The resulting training programs varied a little in specific details, but in general they focused on teaching the relational rules associated with each test problem, over five sessions. Training on figural relations, for instance, involved practice with paper-and-pencil tests, oral feedback by the experimenter, group discussion, and review of the kinds of problems involving figural-relations ability.

Overall, the ability-specific training resulted in improvements in primary abilities. But the ability to maintain and to transfer the training effects varied. Evidence for long-term and broad transfer effects were strongest for figural relations. Training effects were found for inductive reasoning and attention/memory, but these effects did not transfer as well to new tasks.

These findings from the training studies become impressive when we consider their implications. The size of Baltes and Willis's improvements in fluid abilities were equivalent to the average 21-year longitudinal decline in these abilities reported by Schaie (1983). The implication of this comparison is that the decline in primary abilities can be slowed or even reversed by proper intervention strategies. The results are even more exciting given that the training packages in ADEPT were fairly short: an average of five 1-hour sessions. Although the reversal of age-related declines in all primary abilities and the duration of the effects of training remain to be seen, it is clear that we need to revise our view of pervasive, universal decline in primary abilities.

Other Attempts to Train Fluid Abilities. Schaie and Willis have extended the findings from Project ADEPT (Willis, 1990). This research involves the participants in Schaie's longitudinal study in Seattle. In one study (Schaie & Willis, 1986) participants were assigned to 1 of 2 groups based on their performance over a 14-year period (1970–1984). One group showed significant decline on either spatial ability or reasoning ability, and the other group remained stable on these measures. Schaie and Willis then provided a five-hour training session on spatial ability and a similar session on reasoning ability for those who had declined. Training was also provided to the individuals who had remained stable, in order to examine the effects of training as a function of amount of decline.

Schaie and Willis found that the cognitive training techniques could reverse declines that had been reliably documented over the 14-year period. However, the effects of cognitive training were largely ability specific. That is, gains were largest when the training matched the ability being tested; only modest gains in abilities were found that were not trained.

Most exciting, the improvements for both spatial and reasoning abilities allowed people who had declined to return to their earlier levels of functioning. In addition, the training procedures even enhanced the performance of many older people who had remained stable. This finding demonstrates that not only is training effective in raising the performance of decliners, but it can even improve functioning in nondecliners beyond their initial levels (Willis, 1990).

Rather than simply training older adults on particular fluid abilities, Hayslip (1986) tried something different. He randomly assigned 414 community-dwelling older adults to 1 of 4 groups: inductive reasoning training, anxiety reduction, no training at all, or posttest only. Several measures of inductive reasoning and other measures of intellectual abilities were given before training, one week after, and one month after training. Hayslip found that both training groups improved their performance, with the induction training group having the highest level one month after training. However, he found little evidence of generalized training effects to other abilities. He concluded that at least part of the gain in performance was due to reductions in people's level of anxiety in taking tests of intellectual ability.

Considered together, the results from Project ADEPT, the data from Schaie and Willis's research, and Hayslip's work allow us to conclude that declines in fluid abilities may be reversible. But how long do the improvements last?

Long-Term Effects of Training. Getting older adults to do better on skills underlying fluid intelligence is impressive. Having those benefits last over time would be even better, as it would provide a powerful argument in favor of providing intervention programs to more people.

So far, the data look very promising. Willis and Nesselroade (1990) report results from a seven-year follow-up to the original ADEPT study. Participants were initially trained in 1979, and received booster training sessions in 1981 and 1986. Significant training effects were found at each point, indicating that people continue to benefit from cognitive intervention as they move from young-old to old-old age. Even people in their late 70s and early 80s continued to perform at levels better that they had 7 years earlier prior to training. In fact, 64% of the training group's performance was above their pretraining baseline, compared to only 33% of the control group.

These findings provide strong evidence that in the normal course of development no one is too old to benefit from training. Moreover, the improvements brought by training last for many years.

THE NEOFUNCTIONALIST APPROACH

In reaction to the traditional psychometric approach, particularly the research on moderators of intellectual abilities and training of fluid abilities, Baltes and his colleagues developed a second view of adult intellectual development, the neofunctionalist approach (see Baltes, Dittmann-Kohli, & Dixon, 1984; Dittmann-Kohli & Baltes, 1990).

Basic Concepts

The neofunctionalist approach asserts that there may be some intellectual decline with age but that there is also stability and growth in mental functioning across adulthood. It emphasizes the role of intelligence in human adaptation and daily activity. Four concepts are central to the neofunctionalist interpretation of existing research on adult intelligence: plasticity, multidimensionality, multidirectionality, and interindividual variability.

Plasticity. The first concept, plasticity, refers to the range of intraindividual functioning and the conditions under which a person's abilities can be modified within a specific age range. The research on training cognitive abilities described earlier (Project ADEPT, for example) indicates that there is considerable plasticity in intellectual functioning.

Multidimensionality. The second concept, multidimensionality, represents the idea that intelligence consists of a multitude of abilities with distinct structural relationships that may change with age (Horn, 1982; Sternberg, 1980). This idea was described earlier in our discussion of primary and secondary mental abilities. In short, intelligence consists of many abilities that are organized into several separate dimensions, which in turn are related to one another in complex ways.

Multidirectionality. The third concept, multidirectionality, refers to the distinct patterns of change in abilities over the life span, with these patterns being different for different abilities. For example, developmental functions for fluid and crystallized intelligence differ, meaning that the directional change in intelligence depends on the skills in question.

Interindividual Variability. The last concept, interindividual variability, acknowledges that adults differ in the direction of their intellectual development (Schaie, 1979). Schaie's sequential research indicates that within a given cohort some people show longitudinal decline in specific abilities, some show stability of functioning, and others show increments in performance (Schaie, 1979; Schaie & Hertzog, 1983). Consequently, a curve representing typical or average changes with age may not really represent the various individuals in the group.

The Dual-Process Model

Using these four concepts of plasticity, multidimensionality, multidirectionality, and interindividual variability, Baltes and his colleagues proposed the neofunctionalist approach as a dual-process model. Two interrelated types of developmental processes are postulated. The first process, termed *cognition as basic processes*, concerns developmental changes in the basic forms of thinking associated with information processing and problem solving. Cognitive development in this first process is greatest during childhood and adolescence, as we acquire the requisite skills to handle complex cognitive tasks, such as those encountered in school. The second process, *pragmatic intelligence*, relates the basic cognitive skills in the first process to everyday cognitive performance and human adaptation. Pragmatic intellectual growth dominates adulthood. In the terminology of the psychometric approach, the neofunctionalists argue that adulthood is predominantly concerned with the growth of crystallized intelligence. But they expand the notion of crystallized intelligence that we considered earlier to include skills that are needed to function in adults' everyday lives.

The dual-process model is an important step toward relating adult intelligence to successful functioning in one's environment. In this approach we must always be concerned with whether a prospective task is equally relevant for assessing adults' intelligence across the life span. Baltes and colleagues (1984) called for research examining what types of tasks are characteristic of adults' intellectual lives. As Scheidt and Schaie (1978) reported, these tasks are typically different from those found on traditional psychometric tests. Baltes and his colleagues argue that until more research like that of Scheidt and Schaie is done, we will learn little about how intelligence is applied to everyday life.

Denney's Model of Unexercised and Optimally Exercised Abilities

Although Denney does not explicitly characterize herself as a neofunctionalist, she has developed a model that also emphasizes the use of intellectual abilities in everyday life. Denney (1982) postulates two types of developmental functions. One of these functions represents unexercised, or unpracticed, ability, and the other represents optimally trained, or optimally exercised, ability. **Unexercised ability** refers to the ability a normal healthy adult would exhibit without practice or training. Fluid intelligence is thought to be an example of untrained ability, since, by definition, it does not depend on experience and is unlikely to be formally trained (Horn, 1982). **Optimally exercised ability** refers to the ability a normal healthy adult would demonstrate under the best conditions of training, or practice. Crystallized intelligence is an example of optimally exercised ability, since the component skills (such as vocabulary ability) are used daily.

Denney argues that the overall developmental course of both abilities is the same: They tend to increase until late adolescence or early adulthood

and slowly decline thereafter. These developmental functions are shown in Figure 7.2. At all age levels there is a difference in favor of optimally exercised ability, although this difference is less in early childhood and old age. As the developmental trends move away from the hypothetical ideal, Denney argues, the gains seen in training programs will increase. As we noted earlier in our discussion of attempts to train fluid intelligence, it appears that this increase occurs.

Practical Problem Solving. Denney's model spurred considerable interest in how people solve practical problems. Based on the model, adults should perform better on practical problems than on abstract ones like those typically used on standardized intelligence tests. Tests of practical problem solving would use situations like the following:

> Let's say that a middle-aged woman is frying chicken in her home when, all of a sudden, a grease fire breaks out on top of the stove. Flames begin to shoot up. What should she do? (Denney, Pearce, & Palmer, 1982)

Findings from studies examining how well adults solve problems like this are mixed (Cornelius, 1990; Denney, 1990). While most researchers find better performance on practical problems, how this performance differs with age is unclear. Some investigators (such as Denney & Pearce, 1989) find that performance peaks during midlife and decreases after that, as predicted by Denney's model. Other researchers (for example, Cornelius & Caspi, 1987) find continued improvement at least until around age 70.

What is clear is that performance on practical problems increases from early adulthood to middle age. Differences among studies occur in the age at which maximal performance is attained and in the direction and degree of change beyond midlife. It may be that Denney's model reflects the general shape of development, but exactly where peak

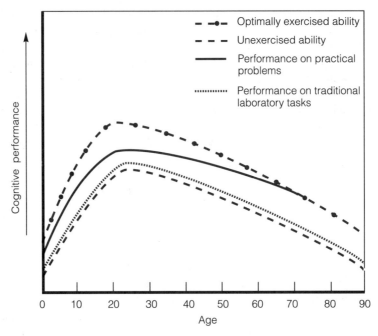

FIGURE 7.2 Developmental curves showing performance on practical problems and traditional laboratory tasks plotted against unexercised and optimally exercised abilities

(Source: "Aging and Cognitive Changes" (p. 820) by N. Denney, 1982, in B. B. Wolman (Ed.), *Handbook of Developmental Psychology.* Copyright © 1982. Adapted by permission of the author.

performance occurs depends on the task at hand. From a neofunctionalist's perspective, though, that would not be surprising. Individual variation is expected.

COGNITIVE-PROCESS APPROACHES

When I was a student, I always thought it was unfair when instructors simply marked the answers to complex problems right or wrong. I always wanted partial credit for knowing how to set up the problem and being able to figure out some of the steps. Although I didn't know it at the time, my argument paralleled one in the intelligence literature—the debate on whether we should pay attention mainly to whether an answer is right or wrong or to how the person reasons the problem through.

The psychometric approach we considered earlier is not concerned with the thinking processes that underlie intelligence; rather, psychometrics concentrates on interrelationships among answers to test questions. In contrast, cognitive-process approaches focus on the ways in which people think; whether a particular answer is right or wrong is not very important.

We will consider two theories that represent cognitive-process approaches. First, we will examine Piaget's theory and the recent discussions concerning possible extensions of it. Second, we will consider Schaie's theory, which represents a very different way of viewing intelligence. Both theories postulate that intellectual changes are mainly qualitative, even though they differ on many points. Let us see what each has to say.

Piaget's Theory

According to Piaget (1970), intellectual development is adaptation through activity. We create the very ways in which our knowledge is organized and, ultimately, how we think. Piaget believed that the development of intelligence stems from the emergence of increasingly complex cognitive structures. He organized his ideas into a theory of cognitive development that changed the way psychologists conceptualize intellectual development.

Basic Concepts. For Piaget, thought is governed by the principles of adaptation and organization. *Adaptation* refers to the process of adjusting thinking to the environment. Just as animals living in a forest feed differently than animals living in a desert, how we think changes from one developmental context to another.

Because all biological systems adapt, the principle of adaptation is fundamental to Piaget's theory. Adaptation occurs through *organization*, which is how the organism is put together. Each component part has its own specialized function, which is coordinated into the whole. In Piaget's theory the organization of thought is reflected in *cognitive structures* that change over the life span. Cognitive structures determine how we think. It is the change in cognitive structures, the change in the fundamental ways in which we think, that Piaget tried to describe.

What are the processes that underlie intellectual adaptation? Piaget defined two: assimilation and accommodation. **Assimilation** is the use of currently available knowledge to make sense out of incoming information. It is the application of cognitive structures to the world of experience that makes the world understandable. For example, a child who only knows the word *dog* may use it for every animal she encounters. So, when the child sees a cat and calls it a dog, she is using available knowledge, the word *dog*, to make sense out of the world — in this case the cat that is walking across the living room. The process of assimilation sometimes leads to considerable distortion of incoming information, since we may have to force-fit it into our knowledge base. This is apparent in our tendency to forget information about a person that violates a stereotype.

Accommodation involves changing one's thought to make it a better approximation of the world of experience. The child in our example who thought that cats were dogs eventually learns that cats are cats. When this happens, she has accommodated her knowledge to incorporate a new category of animal.

The processes of assimilation and accommodation serve to link the structure of thought to observable behavior. Piaget believed that most changes during development involved cognitive structures. His research led him to conclude that there were four structures (that is, four stages) in the development of mature thought: sensorimotor, preoperational, concrete operational, and formal operational. We will consider the major characteristics of each stage briefly. Because we are most interested in Piaget's description of adult thought, we will emphasize it.

Sensorimotor Period. In this first stage of cognitive development, intelligence is seen in infants' actions. Babies and infants gain knowledge by using their sensory and motor skills, beginning with basic reflexes (sucking and grasping) and eventually moving to purposeful, planned sequences of behavior (such as looking for a hidden toy). The most important thing that infants learn during the sensorimotor period is that objects continue to exist even when they are out of sight; this ability is called *object concept.*

Preoperational Period. Young children's thinking is best described as egocentric. This means that young children believe that all people and all inanimate objects experience the world just as they do. For example, young children believe that dolls feel pain. Although young children can sometimes reason through situations, their thinking is not based on logic. For example, a young child may believe that his father's shaving causes the tap water to be turned on because the two events always happen together.

Concrete Operational Period. Logical reasoning emerges in the concrete operational period. Children become capable of classifying objects into groups based on a logical principle, such as fruits or vegetables; mentally reversing a series of events; realizing that when changes occur in one perceptual dimension and they are compensated for in another, no net change occurs (termed *conservation*); and understanding the concept of transitivity (for instance, if A>B, and B>C, then A>C). However, children are still unable to deal with abstract concepts like love; for example, love to children is a set of concrete actions and not an abstract ill-defined concept.

Formal Operational Period. For Piaget, the acquisition of formal operational thought during adolescence marks the end of cognitive development. Because he argues that formal operational thinking characterizes adult thought, we will consider this level in some detail. Several theorists have commented on the characteristics of formal operational thought (Basseches, 1984; Kramer, 1983; Labouvie-Vief, 1980, 1981, 1984; Sinnott, 1984b). We will use these commentaries to focus on four aspects of formal operational thought: (1) It takes a hypothesis-testing approach (termed hypothetico-deductive)

to problem solving; (2) thinking is done in one framework at a time; (3) the goal is to arrive at one correct solution; and (4) it is unconstrained by reality.

Piaget describes the essence of formal operational thought as a way of conceiving abstract concepts and thinking about them in a very systematic, step-by-step way. Formal operational thought is governed by a generalized logical structure that provides solutions to problems that people have never seen and may never encounter. *Hypothetico-deductive* thought is similar to using the scientific method, in that it involves forming a hypothesis and testing it until it is either confirmed or rejected. Just as scientists are very systematic in testing experimental hypotheses, formal operational thinkers approach problem solving in a logical, methodical way.

Consider the situation when your car breaks down. When you take it for repairs, the mechanic forms hypotheses about what may be wrong, based on your description of the trouble. The mechanic then begins to test each hypothesis systematically. For example, the compression of each cylinder may be checked, one cylinder at a time. It is this ability to hold other factors constant while testing a particular component that is one of the hallmarks of formal operational thought. By isolating potential causes of the problem, the mechanic arrives at a correct solution very efficiently.

When we use hypothetico-deductive thought, we do so in order to arrive at one unambiguous solution to the problem (e.g., Labouvie-Vief, 1980, 1981, 1984; Labouvie-Vief, Adams, Hakim-Larson, Hayden, & Devoe, 1985). Formal operational thought is aimed at resolving ambiguity; one and only one answer is the goal. When more than one solution occurs, there is a feeling of uneasiness, and people begin a search for clarification. This situation can be observed in high school classes when students press their teacher to identify the right theory (from among several equally good ones) or the right way to view a social issue (such as abortion). Moreover, when people arrive at an answer, they are quite certain about it, because it was arrived at through the use of logic. When answers are checked, the same logic and assumptions are typically used, which sometimes means that the same mistake is made several times in a row. For example, you may repeat a simple subtraction error time after time when trying to figure out why your checkbook did not balance.

Formal operational thinking knows no constraints (Labouvie-Vief, 1984; Piaget, 1970). It can be applied just as easily to real or to imaginary situations. It is not bound by the limits of reality (Labouvie-Vief, 1980). Whether it is possible to implement a solution is irrelevant; what matters is that one can think about it. This is how people arrive at solutions to disarmament, for example, such as getting rid of all nuclear warheads tomorrow. To the formal operational thinker, the fact that this solution is logistically impossible is no excuse. The lack of reality constraints is not all bad, however. Reasoning from a Why not? perspective may lead to the discovery of completely new ways to approach a problem or even to the invention of new solutions.

Developmental Trends in Piagetian Thought. Considerable research has been conducted examining the developmental course of Piagetian abilities (Reese & Rodeheaver, 1985). Overall, the results are quite mixed and difficult to interpret, largely because the majority of studies are cross-sectional, the procedures used have strayed considerably from those described by Piaget, and the scoring criteria for performance are not systematized (Reese & Rodeheaver, 1985). Nevertheless, some general conclusions can be drawn (Papalia & Bielby, 1974; Rabbitt, 1977; Reese & Rodeheaver, 1985). We will consider the findings from research on formal operations and on concrete operations.

One serious problem for Piaget's theory is that many adults apparently do not attain formal operations. Several studies report that only 60% to 75% of American adolescents can solve any formal op-

How people think about issues such as abortion is largely a function of their cognitive developmental level.

erational problems (Neimark, 1975), and some estimate that no more than 30% of adults ever complete the transition to the highest levels of formal operational thought (Kuhn, Langer, Kohlberg, & Haan, 1977; Tomlinson-Keasey, 1972). Piaget (1972) himself admitted that formal operations were probably not universal but, rather, tended to appear only in those areas in which individuals were highly trained or specialized.

Older adults do not perform as well as younger adults on formal operational tasks (Clayton & Overton, 1973). Clayton and Overton also found that performance on the formal operational tasks was correlated with measures of fluid intelligence, thereby linking formal operational abilities to normative decline.

Extreme pessimism at these results may be unwarranted, however. Kuhn and her colleagues showed that as many as 94% percent of the adolescents in her research demonstrated formal operational thought after being given appropriate background and practice (Kuhn & Angelev, 1976; Kuhn, Ho, & Adams, 1979). Chandler notes that the lack of evidence for formal operations in the elderly may be more indicative of their lack of interest in doing formal operational problems than a lack of ability; older adults "generally dislike bookish, abstract, or childish tasks of low meaningfulness" (1980, p. 82). Tomlinson-Keasey (1972) points out that attainment of the highest levels of formal operations may even depend on preference, as well as personal experience and the cognitive structures that are available. These results imply that the estimates of how many people attain formal operations may be misleading, that formal operational thought is used only in specialized situations, and that adults' thinking is not described very well by Piaget. We will develop this last alternative in more detail later.

Because cross-sectional studies of formal operations showed a general lack of these abilities in adults, researchers have also focused on the development of concrete operations. Two types of tasks have been used most frequently: classification tasks and conservation tasks. In general, the results from these investigations support Papalia and Bielby's (1974) conclusion that cognitive operations decline in the reverse order of their acquisition. That is, the highest, most complex abilities are the last to be acquired but the first to be lost. However, investigations of concrete operations are all cross-sectional and involve highly specialized tasks. Thus, conclusions about age differences must be made with extreme caution.

Some studies document significant age differences between older adults and middle-aged adults in performance on classification tasks, with older adults being worse (Denney & Cornelius, 1975; Storck, Looft, & Hooper, 1972).

A much larger number of investigators have examined conservation abilities. Conservation tasks involve judgments about whether the amount of a substance has been changed after a particular manipulation. For example, an investigator might show two clay balls of equal size, flatten one of them, and ask you whether the lumps are still the same. Papalia (1972) found that conservation of substance, weight, and volume increased during childhood and declined in old age in the reverse order that they were acquired in childhood. Although some other researchers confirmed her findings (Papalia, Salverson, & True, 1973; Storck et al., 1972), other researchers found little evidence for loss of conservation abilities (Chance, Overcast, & Dollinger, 1978; Eisner, 1973; Papalia-Finlay, Blackburn, Davis, Dellmann, & Roberts, 1980). Still other researchers have obtained very inconsistent results, with age differences not showing any particular pattern (Hornblum & Overton, 1976; Hughston & Protinsky, 1978; Protinsky & Hughston, 1978).

Clearly, whether conservation abilities change across adulthood remains an open question. Attempts to explain the results by gender differences, educational level, intelligence, and even institutionalization have not succeeded (Reese & Rodeheaver, 1985). It may be that traditional concrete operational tasks, like traditional formal operational tasks, may not be interesting or challenging to older adults (Chandler, 1980).

Going Beyond Piaget: Postformal Thought

Consider the following problem (Labouvie-Vief et al., 1985, p. 13):

John is known to be a heavy drinker, especially when he goes to parties. Mary, John's wife, warns him that if he gets drunk one more time, she will leave him and take the children. Tonight John is out late at an office party. John comes home drunk.

Does Mary leave John? How certain are you of your answer?

When this and similar problems are presented to people of different ages, interesting differences emerge. Formal operational adolescents' responses clearly showed the ambiguity of the situation but also clearly reflected the need to search for the right answer. The ambiguity was considered a problem rather than an acceptable state of affairs. This is evident in the following answer:

It's a good chance that she would leave him because she warns him that she will leave him and take the children, but warning isn't an absolute thing. . . . And, I'd be absolutely sure that, well let's see . . . I'm trying to go all the way. I'm trying to think of putting everything [together] so I can be absolutely certain of an answer. . . . It's hard to be absolutely certain. "If he gets drunk, then she'll leave and take the children." I want to say yes 'cause everything's in that favor, in that direction, but I don't know how I can conclude that she does leave John. (Labouvie-Vief et al., 1985, pp. 17–18)

When adults were given the same problem, they handled it differently, for the most part. Their responses showed a combination of logic, emotion, and tolerance for ambiguity, as can be seen in the following example:

There was no right or wrong answer. You could get logically to both answers [yes or no]. . . . It depends on the steps they take to their answer. If they base it on what they feel, what they know, and they have certain steps to get an answer, it can be logical. (Labouvie-Vief et al., 1985, p. 41)

Based on a strict interpretation of formal operational thought, the adults who made responses like the second example showed little evidence of formal operational thinking. Thus, it could be argued that Labouvie-Vief and colleagues' research supports the data described earlier that point to declines in formal operational thought across adulthood. But not everyone agrees that the research examining formal operational thinking across adulthood points to loss. Rather than concluding that differences in performance reflect declines in ability, the results are seen as indicative of another, qualitatively different, style of thinking. This latter interpretation implies that Piaget's theory may need modification. Specifically, it has been proposed that these performance differences on Piagetian tasks reflect cognitive development beyond formal operations.

Developmental Progressions in Adult Thought. By the 1970s, it was clear that Piaget's contention that formal operations was the end point of cognitive development had serious problems. One of the first to formally propose an alternative model was Riegel (1973, 1976), who argued that formal operations was quite limited in its applicability. By the mid-1980s many other authors agreed (Basseches, 1984; Cavanaugh, Kramer, Sinnott, Camp, & Markley, 1985; Commons, Richards, & Kuhn, 1982; Labouvie-Vief, 1980, 1981; Sinnott, 1984b).

Riegel and other writers point out that Piaget is concerned with describing logical, hypothetico-deductive thinking in his stage of formal operations but that this is not the only kind of thinking that adults do. In addition, they argue that Piaget's stage of formal operations is primarily limited to explaining how people arrive at one correct solution. How adults discover or generate new problems and how they sometimes appear to accept several possible solutions are not explained. Finally, the fact that adults often limit their thinking in response to social or other realistic constraints appears to be in conflict with the unconstrained generation of ideas characteristic of formal operations.

For these reasons it has been proposed that there is continued cognitive growth beyond formal operations (Commons, Richards, & Armon, 1984; Commons, Sinnott, Richards, & Armon, 1989). **Postformal thought**, as it is called, is characterized by a recognition that truth (the correct answer) varies from situation to situation, that solutions must be realistic in order to be reasonable, that ambiguity and contradiction are the rule rather than the exception, and that emotion and subjective factors usually play a role in thinking.

In one of the first investigations of cognitive growth beyond adolescence, Perry (1970) traced the development of thinking across the undergraduate years. He found that adolescents relied heavily on the expertise of authorities to determine what was right and wrong. At this point thinking is tightly bound by the rules of logic, and the only legitimate conclusions are those that are logically derived. For Perry, the continued development of thinking involves the development of increased cognitive flexibility. The first step in the process is a shift toward relativism. Relativism in thought refers to realizing that more than one explanation of a set of facts could be right, depending on one's point of view. Although relativism frees the individual from the constraints of a single framework, it also leads to skepticism. Because one can never be sure if one is right or wrong, the skeptic may not try to develop knowledge further, which may lead to feeling confused or adrift. Perry points out that the price of freeing oneself from the influence of authority is the loss of the certainty that came from relying on logic for all the answers.

In order to develop beyond skepticism, Perry showed, adults develop commitments to particular viewpoints. In Perry's later stages adults recognize that they are their own source of authority, that they must make a commitment to a position, and that others may hold different positions to which they will be equally committed. In other words mature

thinkers are able to understand many perspectives on an issue, choose one, and still allow others the right to hold differing viewpoints. Thinking in this mature way is different from thinking in formal operational terms.

Perry's landmark research opened the door to documenting systematic changes in thinking beyond formal operations. Kitchener and King (1989) refined descriptions of the development of reasoning in young adults. They mapped the development of reflective judgment, which involves how people reason through dilemmas involving current affairs, religion, science, and the like. On the basis of well-designed longitudinal studies, they identified a systematic progression of thinking, which is described in Table 7.3. As you can see in the table, young adults move from a firm belief in an absolute correspondence between personal perception and reality to the recognition that the search for truth is a continuing, ongoing process that is never-ending.

Other researchers began looking at people's thinking across adulthood. For example, Kramer (1989; Kramer et al., 1991) identified three distinct styles of thinking: absolutist, relativistic, and dialectical. Absolutist thinking involves firmly believing that there is only one correct solution to problems and that personal experience provides truth. Adolescents and young adults typically think this way. Relativistic thinking involves realizing that there are many sides to any issue, and that the right answer depends on the circumstances. Young and early middle-aged adults often think relativistically. One potential danger here is that relativistic thinking can lead to cynicism or an "I'll do my thing and you do yours" approach to life. Because relativistic thinkers reason things out on a case-by-case basis based on the situation, they are not likely to be strongly committed to any one position. The final step, dialectical thinking, clears up this problem. Dialectical thinkers see the merits in the different viewpoints, but are able to synthesize them into a workable solution. This synthesis often

TABLE 7.3   Description of the stages of reflective judgment

Stage 1

View of knowledge   Knowledge is assumed to exist absolutely and concretely. It can be obtained with absolute certainty through direct observation.

Concept of justification   Beliefs need no justification since there is assumed to be an absolute correspondence between what is believed and what is true. There are no alternatives.

Stage 2

View of knowledge   Knowledge is absolutely certain, or certain but not immediately available. Knowledge can be obtained via direct observation or via authorities.

Concept of justification   Beliefs are justified via authority, such as a teacher or parent, or are unexamined and unjustified. Most issues are assumed to have a right answer, so there is little or no conflict in making decisions about disputed issues.

Stage 3

View of knowledge   Knowledge is assumed to be absolutely certain or temporarily uncertain. In areas of temporary uncertainty, we can know only via intuition and bias until absolute knowledge is obtained.

Concept of justification   In areas in which answers exist, beliefs are justified via authorities. In areas in which answers do not exist, since there is no rational way to justify beliefs, they are justified a-rationally or intuitively.

Stage 4

View of knowledge   Knowledge is uncertain and idiosyncratic since situational variables (for example, incorrect reporting of data, data lost over time) dictate that we cannot know with certainty. Therefore, we can only know our own beliefs about the world.

Concept of justification   Beliefs are often justified by reference to evidence, but still are based on idiosyncratic reasons, such as choosing evidence that fits an established belief.

Stage 5

View of knowledge   Knowledge is contextual and subjective. Since what is known is known via perceptual filters, we cannot know directly. We may know only interpretations of the material world.

Concept of justification   Beliefs are justified within a particular context via the rules of inquiry for that context. Justifications are assumed to be context-specific or are balanced against each other, delaying conclusions.

Stage 6

View of knowledge   Knowledge is personally constructed via evaluations of evidence, opinions of others, and so forth across contexts. Thus we may know our own and other's personal constructions of issues.

Concept of justification   Beliefs are justified by comparing evidence and opinion on different sides of an issue or across contexts, and by constructing solutions that are evaluated by personal criteria, such as one's personal values or the pragmatic need for action.

Stage 7

View of knowledge   Knowledge is constructed via the process of reasonable inquiry into generalizable conjectures about the material world or solutions for the problem at hand, such as what is most probable based on the current evidence, or how far it is along the continuum of how things seem to be.

Concept of justification   Beliefs are justified probabilistically via evidence and argument, or as the most complete or compelling understanding of an issue.

(Source: Adapted from "Sequentiality and Consistency in the Development of Reflective Judgment: A Six-Year Longitudinal Study," 1989, *Journal of Applied Developmental Psychology 10*, 73–95.)

produces strong commitment and a definite plan of action.

Notice that there is considerable agreement between the first two styles in Kramer's model and the progression described in the reflective judgment model. Both talk about moving from an "I'm right because I've experienced it" position to an "I'm not so sure because you're experience is different from mine" position. Both also provide insight into how young adults are likely to approach life problems. For example, Kramer (1989; Kramer et al., 1991) shows how different thinking styles have major implications for how couples resolve conflict. She demonstrates that only those couples who think dialectically truly resolve conflict; other thinking styles tend to result in resentment, drifting apart, or even breaking up. We will examine these very interesting findings in more detail in Chapter 10.

Labouvie-Vief proposes that adult thinking is also characterized by the integration of emotion with logic (Labouvie-Vief, 1980, 1981; Labouvie-Vief et al., 1985). She sees the main goal of adult thought as effectiveness in handling everyday life, rather than as the generation of all possible solutions. To her, adults make choices not so much on logical grounds but on pragmatic, emotional, and social grounds. Mature thinkers realize that thinking is a social phenomenon that demands making compromises and tolerating ambiguity and contradiction.

Consider the evidence that despite the possibility of pregnancy or of contracting AIDS or other sexually transmitted diseases, adolescents still tend not to use contraceptives when they have sexual relations. Why? Labouvie-Vief would argue that sexuality is too emotionally charged for adolescents to deal with intellectually. But is this a reasonable interpretation?

It may be. In a very provocative study, Blanchard-Fields (1986) asked high school students, college students, and middle-aged adults to resolve three dilemmas. One dilemma had low emotional involvement: conflicting accounts of a war between two fictitious countries, North and South Livia, each written by a supporter of one country. The other two dilemmas had high emotional involvement: a visit to the grandparents in which the parents and their adolescent son disagreed about going (the son did not want to go), and a pregnancy dilemma in which a man and a woman had to resolve an unintentional pregnancy (the man was anti-abortion, the woman was pro-choice).

Results are shown in Figure 7.3. Two important findings emerged. First, there were clear developmental trends in reasoning level, with the middle-aged adults scoring highest. Second, the high school and college students were equivalent on the fictitious war dilemma, but the high school students scored significantly lower on the grandparents and the pregnancy dilemmas. These findings suggest that high school students tend to think at a lower developmental level when confronted with problems that are especially emotionally salient to them. Although more evidence is certainly needed, Blanchard-Fields's findings provide support for the idea that emotion and logic are brought together in adulthood.

Whether the findings from research examining relativistic or other forms of postformal thought document qualitative cognitive growth is a topic of debate. For example, Kramer (1983) argues that it is possible to interpret relativistic and related thinking within Piaget's original framework. Her main point is that formal operations include the kinds of thinking described in the postformal literature. For instance, constraining possible solutions to only those that are realistic is simply a subset of generating all possible solutions, a defining characteristic of formal operational thought. Consequently, adult thinking may be different from adolescent thinking, but arguing for additional stages is not necessary. Cavanaugh and Stafford (1989) point out that because the roles of experience and education are not understood and because

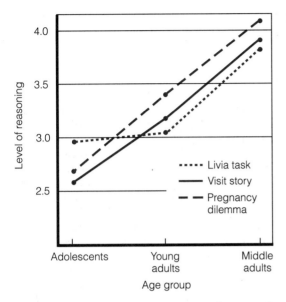

FIGURE 7.3 Level of reasoning as a function of age group and socioemotional task

(Source: "Reasoning on Social Dilemmas Varying in Emotional Saliency: An Adult Developmental Perspective" by F. Blanchard-Fields, 1986, *Psychology and Aging, 1*, 329. Copyright © 1986 by the American Psychological Association. Reprinted by permission of the publisher.)

the measures of postformal thought vary considerably from study to study, firm conclusions on the nature of adult cognitive development may be premature. Finally, Kramer and Woodruff (1986) showed that formal operations is not a prerequisite for relativistic thinking. On the contrary, it appears to be the other way around. However, it may be true that formal operations is a prerequisite for dialectical thinking (Cavanaugh et al., 1985).

The possibility of stages of cognitive development beyond formal operations is intriguing and has focused our attention on the existence of different styles of thinking across adulthood. It has certainly presented a counter to the stereotype of inevitable decline. However, the evidence supporting a separate stage of cognitive development beyond formal operations is limited and is open to different interpretations. More research is needed before we can decide one way or the other. As pointed out in Something to Think About, however, the resolution of this debate has important practical implications.

Schaie's Theory

Schaie (1977–1978) offers an alternative cognitive-process theory based on his research on adult intellectual development. He suggests that during childhood and adolescence the focus is on the acquisition of information and problem-solving skills. He contends that Piaget's theory is an example of a theory that explains this process. Schaie also thinks it is unlikely that we continue to develop more sophisticated ways to acquire new information beyond those described by Piaget. Therefore, if we are to understand what happens during adulthood, Schaie believes, we must shift our focus from how knowledge is acquired to how it is used.

As individuals move into young adulthood, they are no longer in a position to concentrate primarily on acquiring skills. As people begin careers and families, they concentrate more on achieving their goals. But to do so means that they must apply their knowledge to real-world problems, which involve social as well as abstract cognitive skills that are not measured well by most standardized intelligence tests. Schaie suggests that cognitive and social functioning begin to merge even more than in the past. Intellectual performance is likely to be best when tasks have, in his terms, "role-related achievement potential"; in other words, we do better on tasks when we are committed to them. Finally, a key theme in young adulthood is learning how to monitor oneself, keeping track of how things are going and how much progress is being made toward goals that may be years away.

SOMETHING TO THINK ABOUT

Practical Implications of Cognitive Stages

One of the most important questions we can ask about stage theories of cognitive development is whether the stages make a difference in human interaction. The answer to this question appears to be yes. When two persons who think at different levels try to interact, there may be a greater possibility for misunderstanding than when two people in-teract who operate at the same cognitive level.

Let's consider a situation in which a parent is dealing with an adolescent. Here we have the possibility of postformal thought coming into conflict with formal operational thought. Due to the nature of each mode of thinking, it is unlikely that the formal operational individual would concede to the wishes of the other if there was a sharp difference of opinion. It may be up to the post-formal individual to capitalize on his or her ability to see situations from multiple perspectives and frame the situation in a way compatible with the formal thinker. Moreover, the formal thinker would be less persuaded by an emotional argument than by a logical argument.

Think of situations in your own life when you have had sharp disagreements with another person. Was one reason for the disagreement a result of the way in which you both thought about the problem? How could you get around the limitations in thinking? How could you develop a strategy that would work with people of different levels of cognitive development? It's something to think about.

During middle age, Schaie believes, the emphasis shifts again. Once people have become competent and independent, they are in a position to assume responsibility for others. Covering the time from the late 30s to the early 60s, this stage involves learning to appreciate the effects that one's own problem solutions have on one's family and friends. Part of this realization comes from the need for many people to develop what Neugarten (1969) calls "executive abilities." An example of executive abilities would be skills necessary for understanding how an organization works. When you are responsible for developing a solution to a marketing problem, for example, both subordinates and superiors need to be kept informed of the progress, because they are affected by the decisions. Finally, it is often during middle age that people become involved in socially responsible organizations at work (such as unions) and the community (for example, the PTA).

Later in life the need to acquire new skills or to monitor the effects of decisions decreases. The future seems shorter, and retirement eliminates the need to deal with these effects. What happens now is a reintegration of intellectual abilities into a simpler form. The emphasis is on remaining intellectually involved in meaningful situations. In Schaie's words this stage "completes the transition from the 'What should I know?' through the 'How should I use what I know?' to the 'Why should I know?' phase of life" (1977–1978, p. 135). Intellectual endeavors in later life are influenced by motivational and attitudinal considerations more than at any other time.

In sum, Schaie's model is a competency-based approach to adult intellectual development. Standardized intelligence tests do not measure his stages very well. Consequently, little research has been done on his framework (Schaie, 1979). Still, Schaie's approach makes intuitive sense and stands as one of the few attempts to describe intellectual development from a life-span perspective. Once new assessment instruments are developed, it is likely that more work will be done on this framework.

EXPERTISE AND WISDOM

So far, one of the themes that emerges from our considerations of intellectual development is that older adults' performance is boosted when they are given familiar, everyday versions of problems. Why is that? Two possibilities are that age brings experience and wisdom. Both of these are believed to play a major role in providing adults with alternate ways to approach and solve real-life problems.

The focus in research on experience and wisdom is on what people know and how they use their knowledge to solve problems — in other words, how adults become more adaptive in their day-to-day world. Experience is typically studied in terms of expertise, or the degree to which you are an expert at something. Wisdom is more difficult to investigate, but researchers have come up with several novel ways to look at it.

Expertise

On many basic information-processing tasks, younger adults clearly outperform older adults. Yet, many people in their 60s and some in their 70s hold jobs that demand complex decision making,

abstract reasoning, and memory for a lot of information. How do they do it?

The most popular answer is that older adults compensate for poorer performance through their expertise. That is, through years of experience and practice, adults build up a wealth of knowledge about alternative ways to solve problems or make decisions that enables them to bypass steps needed by younger adults (Ericsson & Smith, 1991). In a way, this represents "the triumph of knowledge over reasoning" (Charness & Bosman, 1990a); experience and age can defeat skill and youth. In research terms, older people are sometimes able to compensate for declines in some basic intellectual abilities (for example, the information-processing skills underlying fluid abilities).

Figuring out exactly what expertise is turns out to be difficult. Charness and Bosman (1990a) point out that experts are identified at times because they use novel approaches to solve difficult problems, because they have extensive knowledge about a particular topic, or because they are highly practiced. For example, expert physicians diagnose diseases differently than novice physicians (Patel & Groen, 1986), chess masters quickly evaluate very complex board positions (Charness & Bosman, 1990a), and typists look ahead to help avoid mistakes (see Chapter 5).

Little research has been done on age differences in expertise. What we know is that expert performance tends to peak in middle age and to drop off slightly after that (Charness & Bosman, 1990a). However, the developmental decrements observed here are nowhere near as great as they are for underlying information-processing skills, secondary memory, or fluid intelligence. Thus, it appears that older adults may be compensating for underlying decline by relying more on their experience.

Notice that the different developmental trajectories for expertise and basic information-processing abilities apparently means that the two are not strongly related. How can this be? Rybash, Hoyer,

Young people have much to gain from taking advantage of the wisdom of the old.

and Roodin (1986) proposed a process called **encapsulation** as the answer. Their idea is that the *processes* of thinking (such as, attention, memory, logical reasoning) become connected to the *products* of thinking (such as knowledge about world history). This process of encapsulation allows expertise to compensate for decrements in underlying processing ability, perhaps by making thinking in the particular domain more efficient.

Becoming a more efficient thinker because one knows a great deal may help people come up with novel or creative solutions to problems. Let's consider briefly how creativity fares across adulthood.

Wisdom

We began this chapter with a tale about an old man's wisdom. Seemingly caught in a no-win situation with his son-in-law, the old alchemist comes up with an insightful and clever solution on how to turn base elements (dirt) into gold. Chinen (1989) points out that this tale highlights several aspects of wisdom: It involves *practical knowledge*, it is *given altruistically*, it involves *psychological insights*, and it is *based on life experience*.

Modern researchers and theorists agree with the writers of these wisdom tales. For example, Dittmann-Kohli and Baltes (1990) present a framework based on a view that wisdom is expert knowledge about the basic issues in life. They list five criteria of wisdom: (1) expertise in the practical aspects of daily living; (2) breadth of ability to define and solve problems; (3) understanding of how life problems differ across the life cycle; (4) understanding that the "right thing to do" depends on the values, goals, and priorities you have; and (5) recognition of the complexity, difficulty, and uncertainty in problems you face in life. Basically, a wise person is one who has "exceptional insight into human

Intellectual and creative abilities do not show across-the-board decline in adulthood. Like Henri Matisse, many individuals make great contributions in old age.

development and life matters, exceptionally good judgment, advice, and commentary about difficult life problems" (Smith & Baltes, 1990, p. 495).

Curiously, very little research has been conducted on wisdom. What little we know suggests that wisdom is not the same thing as creativity (Simonton, 1990); wisdom seems more related to the growth of expertise and insight while creativity is more associated with generating a new solution to a problem. Although wisdom has long been characterized as the province of the elderly, that may not be true. For example, Smith and Baltes (1990) had adults respond to hypothetical life-planning problems, such as whether to accept a promotion or whether to retire. The problems were presented as dilemmas facing fictitious people, and

participants had to reason out a solution. Contrary to the stereotype, Smith and Baltes found no association between age and wise answers. Instead, they found evidence of wisdom in adults of all ages. The key variable appears to be having extensive life experience with the type of problem given, not just life experience in general. Thus, given the right circumstances, a 35-year-old and a 75-year-old could give equally wise solutions to a life problem.

The picture of wisdom that is emerging appears to support the opening tale. Just as the old alchemist's response was based on his own specific experience with trying to make gold, so too our own wisdom comes from becoming experts at dealing with particular kinds of problems.

SUMMARY

Defining Intelligence

1. Experts and laypeople agree that intelligence consists of problem-solving ability, verbal ability, and social competence.

2. The psychometric approach focuses on performance on standardized tests. The neofunctionalist view emphasizes individual differences and plasticity. The cognitive-process approach emphasizes the quality and style of thought.

The Psychometric Approach

3. Primary mental abilities show normative declines with age that may affect performance in everyday life after around age 60.

4. Fluid intelligence refers to innate abilities that underlie the acquisition of knowledge and experience. Fluid intelligence normally declines with age.

5. Crystallized intelligence refers to acquired knowledge and experience. Crystallized intelligence does not normally decline with age.

6. Age-related declines in fluid abilities have been shown to be moderated by cohort, education, occupation, personality, health, life style, mindlessness, and task familiarity. Cohort effects and familiarity have been studied most. Although taking both into account reduces age differences, they are not eliminated.

7. Age differences in performance on familiar tasks are similar to those on standardized tests.

8. Several studies show that fluid intelligence abilities improve after direct training and after anxiety reduction. Improvements in performance match or exceed individuals' level of decline. Training effects appear to last for several years.

The Neofunctionalist Approach

9. Plasticity refers to the range within which one's abilities are modifiable. Multidimensionality refers to the many abilities that underlie intelligence. Multidirectionality refers to the many possible ways individuals may develop. Interindividual variability acknowledges that people differ from each other.

10. The first process in the dual-process model, cognition as basic processes, occurs mainly during childhood and adolescence. The second process, pragmatic intelligence, occurs mainly during adulthood.

11. In Denney's model, both unexercised and optimally exercised abilities increase through early adulthood and slowly decline thereafter.

12. Performance on practical problem solving increases through middle age.

Cognitive-Process Approaches

13. Key concepts in Piaget's theory include adaptation to the environment, organization of thought, and the structure of thought. The processes of thought are assimilation (using previously learned knowledge to make sense of incoming information) and accommodation (making the knowledge base conform to the environment).

14. According to Piaget, thought develops through four stages: sensorimotor, preoperations, concrete operations, and formal operations.

15. Older adults do not perform as well on tests of formal operations as younger adults, but results on tests of concrete operations are mixed.

16. There is growing evidence that the style of thinking changes across adulthood.

17. Postformal thought involves relativistic and dialectical thinking. Postformal thought is characterized by the integration of emotion and logic.

18. Schaie suggests that thinking in adulthood moves from a focus on acquiring information to executive abilities and teaching others to remain cognitively active.

Expertise and Wisdom

19. Older adults can often compensate for declines in some abilities by becoming experts, which allows them to anticipate what is going to be required on a task.

20. Knowledge encapsulation occurs with age, in which the processes of thinking become connected with the products of thinking.

21. Wisdom involves five criteria: expertise, broad abilities, understanding how life problems change, fitting the response with the problem, and realizing that life problems are often ambiguous.

22. Wisdom may be more strongly related to experience than to age.

REVIEW QUESTIONS

Defining Intelligence

1. How do laypeople and researchers define intelligence?

2. What are the three main ways that intelligence has been studied? Define each.

The Psychometric Approach

3. What are primary mental abilities? How do they change with age?

4. Define fluid and crystallized intelligence. How does each change with age?

5. What factors moderate age changes in fluid intelligence?

6. What benefits do older people get from intervention programs aimed at improving fluid abilities?

The Neofunctionalist Approach

7. What four concepts are key in the neofunctionalist approach? Define each.

8. What is the dual-process model? How does it trace intellectual development over the life span?

9. What are unexercised and optimally exercised abilities? How do their developmental paths differ from each other?

10. What are the developmental trends in solving practical problems?

Cognitive-Process Approaches

11. What are the key concepts in Piaget's theory?

12. What stages of cognitive development did Piaget identify? What age differences have been found in them?

13. What is postformal thought? What evidence is there that this stage is characteristic of adults?

14. Describe Schaie's theory of cognitive development.

Expertise and Wisdom

15. What is an expert? How is expertise related to age?

16. What is knowledge encapsulation?

17. What criteria are used to define wisdom? How is wisdom related to age?

KEY TERMS

accommodation A process in Piaget's theory in which knowledge is reorganized to better reflect the world. (235)

assimilation A process in Piaget's theory in which incoming information is interpreted in terms of knowledge already learned. (235)

cognitive-process approach A way of studying intellectual development that puts an emphasis on the ways in which people think rather than on the products of thinking. (218)

crystallized intelligence A type of secondary mental ability based on knowledge learned through education and experience. (222)

encapsulation A way in which the process of thinking becomes linked to the products of thinking so as to help compensate for age changes in cognition. (246)

fluid intelligence The basic intellectual abilities relating to information processing that are independent of life experience and education. (222)

neofunctionalist approach An approach to intelligence based on the view that people reflect many different patterns of aging. (218)

optimally exercised ability In Denney's theory, those intellectual abilities one would demonstrate under the best conditions of training or practice. (233)

postformal thought Reasoning beyond Piaget's level of formal operations involving the acceptance of multiple correct answers and a tolerance for ambiguity. (240)

primary mental abilities Intellectual abilities that represent basic information-processing skills. (219)

psychometric approach An approach to intelligence emphasizing the product of thinking rather than the process of thinking. (218)

secondary mental abilities Groups of primary mental abilities of which fluid and crystallized intelligence are two examples. (221)

unexercised ability In Denney's theory, the level of intellectual ability a normal adult would show without practice or training. (233)

ADDITIONAL READING

An excellent review of the psychometric approach and a discussion of developmental trends in psychometric intelligence can be found in

Horn, J. L. (1982). The aging of human abilities. In B. B. Wolman (Ed.), *Handbook of developmental psychology* (pp. 847–870). Englewood Cliffs, NJ: Prentice-Hall. Moderate to difficult.

Schaie, K. W. (1983). The Seattle Longitudinal Study: A twenty-one year exploration of psychometric intelligence in adulthood. In K. W. Schaie (Ed.), *Longitudinal studies of adult psychological development* (pp. 64–135). New York: Guilford. Moderately difficult.

A summary of the neofunctionalist perspective can be found in

Baltes, P. B., Dittmann-Kohli, F., & Dixon, R. A. (1984). New perspectives on the development of intelligence in adulthood: Toward a dual-process conception and a model of selective optimization with compensation. In P. B. Baltes & O. G. Brim, Jr. (Eds.), *Life-span development and behavior* (Vol. 6, pp. 33–76). New York: Academic Press. Moderately difficult.

Two excellent sources for descriptions of postformal thought are

Commons, M. L., Richards, F. A., & Armon, C. (Eds.). (1984). *Beyond formal operations: Vol. 1. Late adoles-*

cent and adult cognitive development. New York: Praeger. Easy to difficult.

Commons, M. L., Sinnott, J. D., Richards, F. A., & Armon, C. (Eds.). (1989). *Beyond formal operations: Vol. 2. Comparisons and applications of adolescent and adult developmental models*. New York: Praeger. Easy to difficult.

A good introduction to the topic of wisdom is

Dittmann-Kohli, F., & Baltes, P. B. (1990). Towards a neo-functionalist conception of adult intellectual development: Wisdom as a prototypical case of intellectual growth. In C. Alexander & E. Langer (Eds.), *Higher stages of human development* (pp. 54–78). New York: Oxford University Press.

CHAPTER 8

Personality and Moral Development

Alex Katz. *Supper*, 1974. Hood Museum of Art, Dartmouth College, Hanover, New Hampshire. Gift of Joachim Jean Aberbach.

*Already at the age of twenty-five you see the
professional mannerism settling down on the
young commercial traveller, on the young doctor,
on the young minister, on the young counsellor-at-
law. You see the little lines of cleavage running
through the character, the treks of thought, the
prejudices, the ways of the "shop" in a word, from
which the man can by-and-by no more escape
than his coat sleeve can suddenly fall into a new
set of folds. On the whole, it is best he should not
escape. It is well for the world that in most of us,
by the age of thirty, the character has set like
plaster, and will never soften again. (James,
1890, p. 121)*

ONE OF THE OLDEST DEBATES IN PSYCHOLOGY
concerns whether personality development
continues across the life span. From the earliest
days, prominent people argued both sides. William
James and Sigmund Freud, for example, believed
that personality was set by the time people reached
adulthood. Indeed, Freud thought that development was essentially complete in childhood. On
the other hand, Carl Jung asserted the viewpoint
that personality was continually shaped throughout
our lives. Aspects of personality come and go as
people's experiences and life issues change.

A century of research has done little to clarify the issue. We still have two main theoretical camps, one arguing for stability and the other for change. There is far less agreement on the developmental course of personality than for any other topic in adult development and aging. Theories and concepts abound. Data are contradictory, and results often depend on which specific measures researchers use. Perhaps the best way to achieve your own resolution of the controversy is through your own research project.

Most of us will eventually attend a high school reunion. It is amusing, so it is said, to see how our classmates have changed over the years. In addition to noticing gray or missing hair and a few wrinkles, pay attention to personality characteristics. For example, will Jackie be the same outgoing person she was as captain of the cheerleaders? Will Shawn still be as shy at 48 as he was at 18? In order to learn as much about your friends as possible, make careful observations of your classmates' personalities over the course of several reunions. Then, at the gathering marking 60 years since graduation, examine the trends you observed. Did your classmates' personalities change substantially? Or did they remain essentially the same as they were 60 years earlier?

How you think these questions will be answered provides clues to your personal biases concerning personality stability or change across adulthood. As we will see, biases about continuity and discontinuity are more obvious in personality research than in any other area of adult development.

Why should the area of personality be so controversial? The answer lies in the paradoxical beliefs we hold about personality itself. At one level we all believe that people have complex personalities that remain relatively constant over time. A stable personality makes it easier to deal with a person in different situations; when a person behaves in ways that violate our expectations, we act surprised. Imagine the chaos that would result if every week

or so everyone woke up with a brand new personality: The once easygoing husband is now a tyrant, trusted friends are now completely unpredictable, and our patterns of social interaction are in a shambles. Clearly, we must rely on consistency of personality in order to survive in day-to-day life.

Still, we like to believe that we can change undesirable aspects of our personalities. Imagine what it would be like if, for example, there were no way to overcome shyness, if anxiety were a lifelong, incurable curse, or if our idiosyncratic tendencies that cause others to tear their hair out could not be eliminated. Our assumption of the modifiability of personality is very strong indeed. The field of psychotherapy is a formal verification of that.

The biopsychosocial model provides a very helpful way to understand the arguments in personality theory and research. As pointed out throughout this book, the model emphasizes the complexity of influences on any specific issue; personality is no exception. Genetic factors and physical health exert important influences on personality and how it is expressed. Socialization influences which aspects of personality may be learned as we grow up and age. Life-course factors are especially important for theorists who emphasize that the issues people face change over time. Although there have been few attempts at integrating these influences in personality research, we need to keep them in mind in order to draw our own conclusions on the matter.

This chapter deals with stability and change in personality across adulthood. First, we will consider trait theories, which essentially assume stability in personality over time. In this section we will examine some impressive longitudinal research documenting long-term stability in many traits. Second, we will move to theories of ego development, which postulate normative change across the life span. In particular, we will consider Erikson's and Loevinger's theories, as well as popularized versions based on life transitions. Finally, we will consider a third alternative, cognitive theories, which argue that stability or change is largely under one's personal control. That is, people tend to remain the same unless they feel a need to change.

PERSONALITY TRAITS ACROSS ADULTHOOD

Consider the following anecdote:

> *Over the course of numerous encounters you notice that Michelle is always surrounded by a group of people. On closer observation you see why this is so. She walks up to people and initiates conversations, is at ease with strangers, is pleasant, and is often described as the "life of the party."*

What can we say about Michelle? One conclusion could be that she is an outgoing, or extraverted, person. How did we arrive at this judgment? We probably combined several aspects of her behavior into a concept that describes her rather concisely. What we have done is to use the notion of a personality **trait**. Extending this same reasoning to many areas of behavior is the basis for trait theories of personality. More formally, people's behavior is said to be understood in terms of attributes that reflect underlying traits. We use the basic tenets of trait theory when we describe ourselves and others with terms like calm, aggressive, independent, friendly, and so on.

Three assumptions are made about traits (McCrae & Costa, 1984). First, traits are based on comparisons of individuals, because there are no absolute quantitative standards for concepts such as friendliness. Second, the qualities or behaviors making up a particular trait must be distinctive enough to avoid confusion. Imagine the chaos that would result if friendliness and aggressive-

ness had many behaviors in common yet some that were vastly different. Finally, the traits attributed to a specific person are assumed to be stable characteristics. We normally assume that people who are friendly in several situations are going to be friendly the next time we see them. These three assumptions are all captured in the definition of a trait: A trait is any distinguishable, relatively enduring way in which one individual differs from others (Guilford, 1959, p. 6). Based on this definition, trait theories assume that little change in personality will occur across adulthood.

Most trait theories have several guiding principles in common. An important one for our present discussion concerns the structure of traits. Structure refers to the way in which traits are thought to be organized within the individual. This organization is usually inferred from the pattern of related and unrelated traits and is generally expressed in terms of dimensions. Personality structures can be examined over time to see whether they change with age.

Costa and McCrae's Model

Although many different trait theories of personality have been proposed over the years, few have been concerned with or have been based on adults of different ages. A major exception to this is the model proposed by Costa and McCrae (1988; McCrae & Costa, 1984, 1987; McCrae, Costa, & Busch, 1986). Their model is strongly grounded in cross-sectional, longitudinal, and sequential research. It consists of five independent dimensions of personality: neuroticism, extraversion, openness to experience, agreeableness-antagonism, and conscientiousness-undirectedness.

The first three dimensions of Costa and McCrae's model — neuroticism, extraversion, and openness to experience — have been the ones most heavily researched. Each of these dimensions is represented by six facets that reflect the main characteristics associated with it. The remaining two dimensions were added to the original three in the late 1980s in order to account for more data and to bring the theory closer to other trait theories. In the following sections we will consider each of the five dimensions briefly.

Neuroticism. The six facets of neuroticism are anxiety, hostility, self-consciousness, depression, impulsiveness, and vulnerability. Anxiety and hostility form underlying traits for two fundamental emotions: fear and anger. Although we all experience these emotions at times, the frequency and intensity with which they are felt vary from one person to another. People who are high in trait anxiety are nervous, high-strung, tense, worried, and pessimistic. Besides being prone to anger, hostile people are irritable and tend to be hard to get along with.

The traits of self-consciousness and depression relate to the emotions shame and sorrow. Being high in self-consciousness is associated with being sensitive to criticism and teasing and to feelings of inferiority. Trait depression refers to feelings of sadness, hopelessness, loneliness, guilt, and low self-worth.

The final two facets of neuroticism — impulsiveness and vulnerability — are most often manifested as behaviors rather than as emotions. Impulsiveness is the tendency to give in to temptation and desires due to a lack of willpower and self-control. Consequently, impulsive people often do things in excess, such as overeating and overspending, and they are more likely to smoke, gamble, and use drugs. Vulnerability refers to a lowered ability to deal effectively with stress. Vulnerable people tend to panic in a crisis or emergency and to be highly dependent on others for help.

McCrae and Costa (1984) note that, in general, people who are high in neuroticism tend to be high in each of the traits. High neuroticism typically results in violent and negative emotions that interfere with people's ability to handle problems or to get along with other people. We can see how this cluster of traits would operate: a person gets anxious and embarrassed in a social situation such as our class reunion, the frustration in dealing with others makes the person hostile, which may lead to excessive drinking at the party, which may result in subsequent depression for making a fool of oneself, and so on.

Extraversion. The six facets of extraversion can be grouped into three interpersonal traits (warmth, gregariousness, and assertiveness) and three temperamental traits (activity, excitement seeking, and positive emotions). Warmth, or attachment, refers to a friendly, compassionate, intimately involved style of interacting with other people. Warmth and gregariousness (a desire to be with other people) make up what is sometimes called sociability. Gregarious people thrive on crowds; the more social interaction, the better. Assertive people make natural leaders, take charge easily, make up their own minds, and readily express their thoughts and feelings.

Temperamentally, extraverts like to keep busy; they are the people who seem to have endless energy, talk fast, and want to be on the go. They prefer to be in stimulating, exciting environments and will often go searching for a challenging situation. This active, exciting life style is evident in the extravert's positive emotion; these people are walking examples of zest, delight, and fun.

An interesting aspect of extraversion is that this dimension relates well to occupational interests and values. People high in extraversion tend to be social workers, business administrators, and salespeople, or to have other people-oriented jobs. They value humanitarian goals and a person-oriented use of power. Individuals low in extraversion tend to prefer task-oriented jobs, such as architecture or accounting.

Openness to Experience. The six facets of openness to experience represent six different areas. In the area of fantasy, openness means having a vivid imagination and an active dream life. In aesthetics, openness is seen in the appreciation of art and beauty, a sensitivity to pure experience for its own sake. Openness to action refers to a willingness to try something new, whether it be a new kind of cuisine, a new movie, or a new travel destination. People who are open to ideas and values are curious and value knowledge for the sake of knowing. Open people also tend to be liberal in their values, often admitting that what may be right for one person may not be right for everyone. This outlook is a direct outgrowth of open individuals' willingness to think of different possibilities and their tendency to empathize with others in different circumstances. Open people also experience their own feelings strongly and see them as a major source of meaning in life.

Not surprisingly, openness to experience is also related to occupational choice. Open people are likely to be found in occupations that place a high value on thinking theoretically or philosophically and less emphasis on economic values. They are typically intelligent and tend to subject themselves to stressful situations. Occupations such as psychologist or minister, for example, appeal to open people.

Agreeableness-Antagonism. The easiest way to understand the agreeableness-antagonism dimension is to consider the traits that characterize antagonism. Antagonistic people tend to set themselves against others; they are skeptical, mistrustful, callous, unsympathetic, stubborn, and rude; and they have a defective sense of attachment. Antagonism may be manifested in ways other than overt hostility. For example, some antagonistic people are skillful manipulators or aggressive go-getters with little patience. In some respects these individuals have characteristics similar to the Type A behavior pattern (see Chapter 4).

Scoring high on agreeableness, the opposite of antagonism, may not always be adaptive either, however. These people may tend to be overly dependent and self-effacing, traits that often prove annoying to others.

Conscientiousness-Undirectedness. Scoring high on conscientiousness indicates that one is hardworking, ambitious, energetic, scrupulous, and persevering. Such people have the will to achieve (Dignam & Takemoto-Chock, 1981), that is, to work hard and make something of oneself. Undirectedness is viewed primarily as being lazy, careless, late, unenergetic, and aimless.

Research Evidence. Costa and McCrae have investigated whether the traits that make up their model remain stable across adulthood (e.g., Costa & McCrae, 1980b, 1988; Costa, McCrae, & Arenberg, 1980). Because their results are very consistent from study to study, we will consider the findings from the Costa, McCrae, and Arenberg study as representative. The data came from the Baltimore Longitudinal Study of Aging for the 114 men who took the Guilford-Zimmerman Temperament Survey (GZTS) on 3 occasions, with each of the 2 follow-up testings about 6 years apart.

What Costa and colleagues found was astonishing. Even over a 12-year period, the 10 traits measured by the GZTS remained highly stable; the correlations ranged from .68 to .85. In much of personality research we might expect to find this degree of stability over a week or two, but to see it over 12 years is noteworthy. Even when the researchers looked at individual scores, it was apparent that people had changed very little.

We would normally be skeptical of such consistency over a long period. But similar findings were obtained in other studies conducted over a 10-year span by Costa and McCrae (1977) in Boston, an 8-year span by Siegler, George, and Okun (1979) at Duke University, and a 30-year span by Leon,

HOW DO WE KNOW?

Personality Traits and Well-Being: Happy and Unhappy People

We all know what it feels like to be happy, and we also know what it feels like to be unhappy. But for researchers in personality, feelings are not enough. They want to identify the parts of our personalities that underlie being happy and being unhappy.

Costa and McCrae (1980b) examined the relationships between personality and happiness in three studies. Their participants were a subsample of 1,100 men who were members of the Normative Aging Study. The participants came from a variety of socioeconomic groups, and most were veterans. They were

asked to complete a series of four questionnaires over a three-month interval. These questionnaires measured personality traits and subjective well-being.

Results from the first investigation showed that similar relationships held between personality and well-being across a number of different scales. Moreover, different clusters of traits seemed to relate to happiness and unhappiness. Fear, anger, and poor impulse control were related to unhappiness, whereas sociability, tempo, and vigor related to happiness. Thus, it appears that happiness and unhappiness represent different aspects of personality; they are not two sides of the same coin.

In the second study Costa and McCrae tested this idea. Specifically, they examined whether neuroticism was differentially related to unhappiness and whether extraversion was

differentially related to happiness. Their suspicions were confirmed.

Having documented that different dimensions of personality influenced happiness and unhappiness, Costa and McCrae asked another question: Does this relationship hold over long periods of time, or is it limited to short-term mood changes? In the third study they compared scores on the personality tests administered 10 years earlier to current measures of happiness. They found that scores on the earlier personality tests accurately predicted current happiness or unhappiness.

This series of studies is representative of the careful research done by Costa and McCrae, which shows that personality is relatively stable over very long periods of time. It also should serve as a model of carefully thought-out, programmatic scientific inquiry.

Gillum, Gillum, and Gouze (1979) in Minnesota. Even more amazing was the finding that personality ratings by spouses of each other showed no systematic changes over a 6-year period (Costa & McCrae, 1988). Thus, it appears that individuals change very little in self-reported personality traits over periods of up to 30 years and over the age range of 20 to 90. As described in How Do We Know? these stable traits also relate to such things as being happy.

This is a truly exciting and important conclusion. Clearly, lots of things change in people's lives over 30 years. They marry, divorce, have children, change jobs, face stressful situations, move, and maybe even retire. Social networks and friendships come and go. Society changes, and economic ups and downs have important effects. Personal changes in appearance and health occur. People read volumes, see dozens of movies, and watch thousands of hours of television. But their underlying personality dispositions hardly change at all. Or do they?

Longitudinal Studies of Traits

Active to Passive Mastery. Neugarten and her colleagues (1964) provided some of the earliest findings based on interviews, projective tests, and questionnaires administered to a large, representative sample of adults between the ages of 40 and 80 over a 10-year span. They found that adaptational processes such as coping styles, life satisfaction, and strength of goal-oriented behavior remained stable. However, they also discovered a shift from *active mastery* to *passive mastery* among the men in their sample. Men at age 40 felt in control of their lives; they viewed risk-taking positively and believed that they had considerable energy to tackle problems head-on. By age 60, however, men viewed their environment as harmful and threatening and themselves as accommodating.

The shift from active to passive mastery has been observed in several cultures, including the Navajo and the Lowland and Highland Mayans of Mexico. With increasing age there is a tendency to accommodate the self to outside influences and a tendency for men and women to become more preoccupied with inner feelings, experiences, and cognitive processes. Gutmann (1978) argues that this increasing *interiority* reflects a normative shift in personality, and Neugarten (1973) points out that it is one of the best-documented changes in personality across adulthood. Although interiority reflects many of the characteristics of introversion, it also indicates that older adults tend to decrease their attachments to the external world.

The Berkeley Studies. Researchers in Berkeley, California, conducted one of the largest longitudinal studies on personality development. In this investigation the parents of participants being studied in

research on intellectual development were followed for roughly 30 years between ages 40 and 70 (Maas, 1985; Maas & Kuypers, 1974; Mussen, 1985). From the enormous amount of data gathered over the years, researchers were able to categorize men and women into subgroups based on their life styles (for instance, whether mothers were employed) and personality type. Based on the longitudinal follow-up data, gender differences were identified in terms of the best predictors of life satisfaction in old age. The data suggest that life style during young adulthood is the better predictor of life satisfaction in old age for women but that personality is the better predictor for men (Mussen, 1985).

Additional analyses of the Berkeley data provide other insights into personality development. Haan examined data from Q-sorts, a technique in which an individual arranges descriptors of personality into piles varying in the extent to which they reflect oneself (Haan, 1976, 1981, 1985; Haan, Millsap, & Hartka, 1986). Six dimensions of personality were derived from the Q-sort approach: self-confident–victimized (feeling comfortable with oneself and certain of acceptance by others); assertive–submissive (degree of direct and aggressive style of living); cognitively committed (degree of intellectual and achievement orientation); outgoing–aloof (degree of social enjoyment of others); dependable (degree of controlled productivity); and warm–hostile (degree of interpersonal giving and support) (Haan et al., 1986).

Haan and her colleagues found that orderly, positive progressions over time were observed for all of the personality components except assertive–submissive. When Haan tried to explain these developmental patterns, however, she ran into difficulty. Theories that predict stagelike progressions, such as those discussed later in this chapter, could not account for the results. Contrary to these theories, personality did not change in all areas simultaneously, nor was there evidence of change only during stage transitions. In other words, Haan's data suggest little support for the notion of general crisis followed by periods of stability. However, her data also did not indicate smooth, orderly changes across adulthood. The observation of several gender differences, the nonlinear trends over time, and the lack of equal improvement in all components indicates that personality development is a complicated process. Haan and her colleagues argue that changes in personality probably stem from life-cycle experiences that may force a person to change. We will consider a stronger version of this view later in the chapter when we examine cognitive theories of personality.

Some Specific Traits

As we have seen, researchers have identified numerous specific personality traits. Many of these are included in multidimensional personality tests such as the NEO. However, some are not. Two of the most researched traits in this latter category are life satisfaction and gender-role identity.

Life Satisfaction. Generally speaking, how is your life going right now? That is the issue researchers address when they investigate people's life satisfaction. Life satisfaction is not the same thing as mental health; one could conceivably be content with the way things are going but still have psychological problems. For example, some Alzheimer's disease victims are unaware of the extent of their memory loss, and will tell you that things are just fine. Life satisfaction has been studied more than almost any other aspect of personality. Hundreds of studies have examined adults' general feelings of well-being, morale, and happiness. In addition, many researchers have tried to discover the major ingredients in life satisfaction.

In one of the most ambitious studies of its kind, Cameron (1975) examined the life satisfaction of over 6,000 people ranging in age from 4 to 99. He concluded that life satisfaction — expressed as happiness, sadness, or neutral moods — was equivalent across all age groups. Satisfaction was determined primarily by social class, sex, and the person's immediate life situation, not by age. Likewise, Kozma and Stones (1983) found no relationship between age and life satisfaction in an 18-month longitudinal investigation. A review of 30 years of similar research led Larson (1978) to conclude that age had little bearing on overall life satisfaction. In general, three decades of research pointed to health as the single most important determining factor. Larson also noted that money, housing, social class, social interaction, marital status, and transportation had significant influence.

Specific personality factors also seem to have important effects on overall life satisfaction. McCrae and Costa (1983) found that both neuroticism and extraversion were related to happiness. Men who were high in neuroticism were more likely to feel dissatisfied and unhappy, and men high in extraversion were more likely to feel satisfied and happy. These relationships held regardless of the psychological maturity of the participants.

An interesting issue concerning life satisfaction is this: Does its nature change with age? In other words, does feeling happy at 75 mean the same thing as feeling happy at 25? People's feelings about life do not change in intensity with age, but the more qualitative aspects of feelings could be different. Life experiences during adulthood may have colored positive experiences during young adulthood with negative feelings, and negative experiences with positive feelings. The loss of a job in young adulthood may have been viewed very negatively at the time, for example, but the subsequent acquisition of a much better job in midlife changed this view to a far more positive one.

Older adults do not necessarily have more negative feelings and attitudes than younger adults. Increases in negative events such as poorer health, decreasing income, or death of one's spouse do not inevitably lead to increases in negative feelings. This lack of a relationship could be due in part to

The degree to which one is satisfied with aspects of life is not related to age.

changing expectations about life, which may offset the negative consequences of loss.

In sum, whether life satisfaction changes with age is a complex issue that depends much more on life experiences and their associated feelings than it does on age.

Gender-Role Identity Across Adulthood. What we consider to be appropriate personality traits for women and men reflect shared cultural beliefs of what is considered prototypically masculine and feminine styles (Williams & Best, 1990). In U.S. society, women are traditionally described as weaker, less active, and more concerned with affiliation, nurturance, and deference. Men are regarded as stronger, more active, and higher in autonomy, achievement, and aggression (Huyck, 1990). In addition, there are also gender-age stereotypes (Gutmann, 1987). Old men are seen as less stereotypically masculine or warrior-like and more as powerful elderly men striving for peace. Old women tend to be viewed as matriarchs overseeing extended families or as evil witches who use power malevolently. Some cultures view older adults as genderless, having lost the need for differentiated gender-role identity after they concluded their child-rearing duties (Gailey, 1987).

Because gender-role identity is most often viewed as a trait, the scales used to assess masculinity and femininity are grounded in trait theories of personality. Much of the research in this area was spurred by ego development theories (considered a bit later) that postulated a merging of masculine and feminine identities with age.

Evidence from several studies indicates that changes occur in the statements adults of different ages endorse about masculinity and femininity. In general, these findings show a tendency for older men and women to endorse similar self-descriptions. For example, data from the Berkeley studies document a move toward greater similarity between older men and women. Haan (1985; Haan et al., 1986) and Livson (1981) found that both men and women described themselves as more nurturant, intimate, and tender with age. Gutmann (1987), Sinnott (1986), and Turner (1982) reported similar findings. Overall, the data from these studies indicate that men and women appear most different in late adolescence and young adulthood and become increasingly similar in late-middle and old age (Huyck, 1990).

Longitudinal data on individual development is largely lacking. What evidence is available suggests that a majority (54%) of people remain in the same gender-role category over a 10-year period (Hyde, Krajnik, & Skuldt-Niederberger, 1991). However, this still means that a substantial number of people demonstrate change. As Hyde et al. (1991) note, however, we currently have no way of predicting who will change and who will not.

The move toward gender-role identity similarity may not always be apparent at the behavioral level. Although older men often indicate a greater willingness to develop close relationships, for example, few actually have the skills to do so (Turner, 1982). Troll and Bengtson (1982) argue that the change is more internal than external and tends to involve feelings about dependence and autonomy. Moreover, they point out that much of the change may be due to the failing health of elderly men. Because older wives tend to be healthier than their husbands, the balance of power may shift out of necessity to wives, and men may be forced to accept a more dependent role.

Whether the changes in self-assessments of gender-role identity reflect true changes in underlying personality traits is debatable. The lack of consistent behavioral evidence and the statistically small differences in some of the self-assessment data lead some authors to argue that no changes in personality occur (for example, Costa & McCrae, 1980b). In contrast, others see the convergence in self-assessments as evidence that older men and women transcend stereotypes to become essentially gender-free (Sinnott, 1986). Still others view any change in self-assessment, no matter how small, as at least personally relevant (Gutmann, 1987).

It will be interesting to see whether the trend toward similarity continues over the next few generations. Changes in how younger men and women view themselves as a result of women's new roles in society may shift the trend downward in age or may make it disappear altogether. As noted in Chapters 1 and 10, gender is one way that societies stratify themselves. Whether changes in self-report have any bearing on true behavioral change is something that only time will tell.

Conclusions About Personality Traits

What can we conclude from the research on the development of personality traits across adulthood? On the surface it appears that we have conflicting evidence. On the one hand, we have a definition of traits that requires stability. Costa and McCrae, among others, argue strongly for this position; they report that there is little evidence (and perhaps possibility) of change. On the other hand, Neugarten and the Berkeley group argue for change and stability. They say that at least some traits change, opening the door to personality development in adulthood. One partial resolution can be found if we consider how the research was done. Clearly, the overwhelming evidence supports the view that personality traits remain stable throughout adulthood when data are averaged across many different kinds of people. However, if we ask about specific aspects of personality in very specific kinds of people, we are more likely to find evidence of both change and stability.

A more important issue seems to be the role of life experiences. If a person experiences few events that induce him or her to change, then change is unlikely. In this view a person will be at 60 very much the same as he or she is at 30, all other factors being held constant. As we will see later in the section on cognitive theories, this idea has been incorporated formally into other theories of personality. On the basis of personality traits, then, we should have little difficulty knowing our high school classmates many years later.

EGO DEVELOPMENT ACROSS ADULTHOOD

Many theorists do not view personality in terms of traits. Rather, they prefer to view it is as the organization of needs, motives, dispositions, habits, and abilities that are used to reach certain higher-order goals. These goals are, in turn, set by biological instincts, cultural forces, or personal experience. The crucial aspect in these theories is the way in which individuals think about and combine these various influences. Viewing personality in this way has its roots in Freud's psychoanalytic theory. Over the years his work was extended and modified by many theorists, including his daughter Anna and several of his own students, such as Carl Jung. These theorists were concerned with **ego development** and the idea that we are constantly seeking ways in which to define our personal identity in everyday life. Ego development entails increasingly complex, more integrated, and more effective ways of dealing with reality and handling anxiety, and it is thought to be the basis for personality development across the life span.

Jung's Theory

Jung represents a turning point in the history of psychoanalytic thought. Initially allied with Freud, he soon severed the tie and developed his own ideas, which have elements of both Freudian theory and humanistic psychology. He was one of the very first theorists to believe in personality development in adulthood; this marked a major break with Freudian thought, which argued that personality development ended in adolescence.

Jung's theory emphasizes that each aspect of a person's personality must be in balance with all of the others. This means that each part of the personality will be expressed in some way, whether through normal means or through neurotic symptoms or in dreams. Jung asserts that the parts of the personality are organized in such a way as to produce two basic orientations of the ego. One of these orientations is concerned with the external world; Jung labels it "extraversion." The opposite orientation, toward the inner world of subjective experiences, is labeled "introversion." In order to be psychologically healthy, both of these orientations must be present, and they must be balanced. Individuals must be able to deal with the external world effectively and also be able to evaluate their inner feelings and values. It is when people overemphasize one orientation or the other that they are classified as extraverts or introverts.

According to Jung, there are two important age-related trends in personality development. The first relates to the introversion-extraversion distinction. Young adults are more extraverted than older adults, perhaps because of younger peoples' needs to find a mate, have a career, and so forth. With increasing age, however, the need for balance creates a need to focus inward and explore personal feelings about aging and mortality. Thus, Jung argued that with age comes an increase in introversion.

The second age-related trend in Jung's theory involves the feminine and masculine aspects of our personalities. Each of us has elements of both masculinity and femininity. In young adulthood, however, most of us express only one of them while usually working hard to suppress the other. In other words, young adults most often act in accordance with gender-role stereotypes appropriate to their culture. As they grow older, people begin to allow the suppressed parts of their personality out. This means that men begin to behave in ways that earlier in life they would have considered feminine, and women behave in ways that they formerly would have thought to be masculine. These changes achieve a better balance that allows men and women to deal more effectively with their individual needs rather than being driven by socially defined stereotypes. This balance, however, does not mean that there is a reversal of sex roles. On the contrary, it represents the expression of aspects of ourselves that have been there all along but that we have simply not allowed to be shown. We will return to this issue at the end of the chapter when we consider gender-role development.

Jung stretched traditional psychoanalytic theory to new limits by postulating continued development across adulthood. Other theorists took Jung's lead and argued not only that personality development occurred in adulthood but also that it did so in an orderly sequential fashion. We will consider the sequences developed by two theorists, Erik Erikson and Jane Loevinger.

Erikson's Stages of Psychosocial Development

The best-known life-span ego development theorist is Erikson (1982). According to him, personality is determined by the interaction between an inner maturational plan and external societal demands. He proposes that the life cycle is comprised of eight stages of development, summarized in Table 8.1.

The sequence of stages is thought to be biologically fixed.

Each stage in Erikson's theory is marked by a struggle between two opposing tendencies, both of which are experienced by the person. The names of the stages reflect the issues that form the struggles. The struggles are resolved through an interactive process involving both the inner psychological and the outer social influences. Successful resolutions establish the basic areas of psychosocial strength; unsuccessful resolutions impair ego development in a particular area and adversely affect the resolution of future struggles. Thus, each stage in Erikson's theory represents a kind of crisis.

The sequence of stages in Erikson's theory is based on the **epigenetic principle**, which means that each psychosocial strength has its own special time of ascendancy, or period of particular importance. The eight stages represent the order of this ascendancy. Because the stages extend across the whole life span, it takes a lifetime to acquire all of the psychosocial strengths. Moreover, Erikson realizes that present and future behavior must have its roots in the past, since later stages build on the foundation laid in previous ones.

Erikson argues that the basic aspect of a healthy personality is a sense of trust toward oneself and others. Thus, the first stage in his theory involves *trust versus mistrust*, representing the conflict that an infant faces in developing trust in a world it knows little about. With trust come feelings of security and comfort.

The second stage, *autonomy versus shame and doubt*, reflects children's budding understanding that they are in charge of their own actions. This understanding changes them from totally reactive beings to ones who can act on the world intentionally. Their autonomy is threatened, however, by their inclinations to avoid responsibility for their actions and to go back to the security of the first stage.

In the third stage the conflict is *initiative versus guilt*. Once children realize that they can act on the

TABLE 8.1 Summary of Erikson's theory of psychosocial development, with important relationships and psychosocial strengths acquired at each stage

Stage	Psychosocial Crisis	Significant Relations	Basic Strengths
1 Infancy	Basic trust versus basic mistrust	Maternal person	Hope
2 Early childhood	Autonomy versus shame and doubt	Parental persons	Will
3 Play age	Initiative versus guilt	Basic family	Purpose
4 School age	Industry versus inferiority	"Neighborhood," school	Competence
5 Adolescence	Identity versus identity confusion	Peer groups and outgroups; models of leadership	Fidelity
6 Young adulthood	Intimacy versus isolation	Partners in friendship, sex, competition, cooperation	Love
7 Adulthood	Generativity versus stagnation	Divided labor and shared household	Care
8 Old age	Integrity versus despair	"Mankind," "my kind"	Wisdom

(Source: *The Life Cycle Completed: A Review* by E. H. Erikson, 1982, New York: Norton. Reprinted with permission of W. W. Norton & Company, Inc. © 1982 by Rikan Enterprises Ltd.)

world and are somebody, they begin to discover who they are. They take advantage of wider experience to explore the environment on their own, to ask many questions about the world, and to imagine possibilities about themselves.

The fourth stage is marked by children's increasing interest in interacting with peers, their need for acceptance, and their need to develop competencies. Erikson views these needs as representing *industry versus inferiority*, which is manifested behaviorally in children's desire to accomplish tasks by working hard. Failure to succeed in developing self-perceived competencies results in feelings of inferiority.

During adolescence, Erikson believes, we deal with the issue of *identity versus identity confusion*.

The choice we make, that is, the identity we form, is not so much who we are but, rather, whom we can become. The struggle in adolescence is choosing from among a multitude of possible selves the one we will become. Identity confusion results when we are torn over the possibilities. The struggle involves trying to balance our need to choose a possible self and the desire to try out many possible selves.

During young adulthood the major developmental task, *intimacy versus isolation*, involves establishing a fully intimate relationship with another. Erikson (1968) argues that intimacy means the sharing of all aspects of oneself without fearing the loss of identity. If intimacy is not achieved, isolation results. One way to assist the development of

This actor is portraying King Lear, a Shakespearean character who experienced Erikson's struggle of integrity versus despair when he divided his kingdom among his children, who then fought among themselves and rejected him.

intimacy is to choose a mate who represents the ideal of all one's past experiences. The psychosocial strength that emerges from the intimacy-isolation struggle is love.

With the advent of middle age the focus shifts from intimacy to concern for the next generation, expressed as *generativity versus stagnation*. The struggle occurs between a sense of generativity (the feeling that people must maintain and perpetuate society) and a sense of stagnation (the feeling of self-absorption). Generativity is seen in such things as parenthood, teaching, or providing goods and services for the benefit of society. If the challenge of

generativity is accepted, the development of trust in the next generation is facilitated, and the psychosocial strength of care is obtained.

In old age individuals must resolve the struggle between *ego integrity and despair*. This last stage begins with a growing awareness of the nearness of the end of life, but it is actually completed by only a small number of people (Erikson, 1982). The task is to examine and evaluate one's life and accomplishments to verify that it has had meaning. This process often involves reminiscing with others and actively seeking reassurance that one has accomplished something in life. People who have progressed successfully through earlier stages of life face old age enthusiastically and feel that their life has been full. Those feeling a sense of meaninglessness do not anxiously anticipate old age, and they experience despair. The psychosocial strength achieved from a successful resolution of this struggle is wisdom. Integrity is not the only issue facing older adults; Erikson points out that they have many opportunities for generativity as well. Older people often play an active role as grandparents, for example, and many maintain part-time jobs.

Clarifications of Erikson's Theory. Erikson's theory has had a major impact on thinking about life-span development. However, some aspects of his theory are unclear, poorly defined, or unspecified. Traditionally, these problems have led critics to dismiss the theory as untestable and incomplete. The situation is changing, however. Other theorists have tried to address these problems by identifying common themes, specifying underlying mental processes, and reinterpreting and integrating the theory with other ideas. These ideas are leading researchers to reassess the utility of Erikson's theory as a guide for research on adult personality development.

Logan (1986) points out that Erikson's theory can be considered as a cycle that repeats: from basic trust to identity and from identity to integrity. In this approach the developmental progression is trust → achievement → wholeness. Throughout life we first establish that we can trust ourselves and other people. Initially, trust involves learning about ourselves and others, represented by the first two stages (trust versus mistrust and autonomy versus shame and doubt). The recapitulation of this idea in the second cycle is seen in our struggle to find a person with whom we can form a very close relationship yet not lose our own sense of self (intimacy versus isolation). Additionally, Logan shows how achievement — our need to accomplish and to be recognized for it — is a theme throughout Erikson's theory. During childhood this idea is reflected in the two stages initiative versus guilt and industry versus inferiority, whereas in adulthood it is represented by generativity versus stagnation. Finally, Logan points out that the issue of understanding ourselves as worthwhile and whole is first encountered during adolescence (identity versus identity confusion) and is reexperienced during old age (integrity versus despair). Logan's analysis emphasizes that psychosocial development, although complicated on the surface, may actually reflect only a small number of issues. Moreover, he points out that we do not come to a single resolution of these issues of trust, achievement, and wholeness. Rather, they are issues that we struggle with our entire lives.

One aspect of Erikson's theory that is not specified is the rules that govern the sequence in which issues are faced. That is, Erikson does not make clear why certain issues are dealt with early in development and others are delayed. Moreover, how transitions from one stage to the next happen is not fully explained. Van Geert (1987) proposes a set of rules that fills in these gaps. He argues that the sequence of stages is guided by three developmental trends. First, an inward orientation to the self gradually replaces an outward orientation to the world. This trend is similar to Jung's increase in introversion with age. Second, we move from using very general categories in understanding the world to using more specific ones. This trend is reflected in cognitive development, in that our earliest cate-

gories do not allow the separation of individual differences (for example, we use *dog* to mean all sorts of animals). Third, we move from operating with limited ideas of social and emotional experiences to more inclusive ideas. During childhood we may love only those people we believe are deserving, for example, whereas in adulthood we may love all people as representatives of humanity. By combining these three developmental trends, van Geert constructs rules for moving from one stage to another.

Although van Geert's approach has not been tested completely, his ideas fit with Erikson's theory and with other related data. For example, Neugarten (1977) points to an increase in interiority with age across adulthood, an idea very similar to van Geert's inward orientation. Cognitive developmental research (see Chapter 7) supports the development of more refined conceptual categories. Thus, van Geert's approach may be quite useful in understanding psychosocial development as well as in providing a way to identify the cyclic progression described by Logan.

Viney (1987) shows how other approaches to human development can add to Erikson's theory. As an example, she points to the sociophenomenological approach, which emphasizes that people change in how they interpret and reinterpret events. That is, the meaning of major life events changes from earlier to later in the life span. In a study that examined individuals between the ages of 6 and 86, she documented that the positive and negative descriptors that people used to characterize their lives changed considerably. Interestingly, these shifts in descriptors appear to parallel Erikson's stages. For example, adults over age 65 are more likely to talk about trying to get their lives in order or that they feel completely alone than are adults under age 65. Although Viney's research was not intended to be a direct test of Erikson's theory, her results indicate that we may be able to document his stages in research based on different approaches to development. Additionally, Viney's research may indicate that the themes identified by Erikson are applicable to many situations, including the way in which we view events.

Finally, some critics argue that Erikson's stage of generativity is much too broad to capture the essence of adulthood. For example, Kotre (1984) contends that adults experience many opportunities to express generativity that are not equivalent and do not lead to a general state. Rather, he sees generativity more as a set of impulses felt at different times in different settings, such as at work or in grandparenting. Only rarely, Kotre contends, is there a continuous state of generativity in adulthood. He asserts that the struggles identified by Erikson are not fought constantly; rather, they probably come and go.

Loevinger's Theory

Loevinger (1976) saw a need to extend the groundwork laid by Erikson both theoretically and empirically. For her, the ego is the chief organizer: the integrator of our morals, values, goals, and thought processes. Because this integration performed by the ego is so complex and is influenced by personal experiences, it is the primary source of individual differences at all ages beyond infancy. Ego development is the result of dynamic interaction between the person and the environment. Consequently, it consists of fundamental changes in the ways in which our thoughts, values, morals, and goals are organized. Transitions from one stage to another depend on both internal biological changes and external social changes to which the person must adapt.

Although Loevinger proposes eight stages of ego development, beginning in infancy, we will focus on the six that are observed in adults (see Table 8.2). An important aspect of her theory is that most people never go through all of them; indeed, the last level is achieved by only a handful of individuals. There is growing cross-sectional and

longitudinal evidence that these stages are age related (Cook-Greuter, 1989; Redmore & Loevinger, 1979). At each stage Loevinger identifies four areas that she considers important to the developmental progression: character development (reflecting a person's standards and goals); interpersonal style (representing the person's pattern of relations with others); conscious preoccupations (reflecting the most important things on the person's mind); and cognitive style (reflecting the characteristic way in which the person thinks). As we consider the ego levels important for adults, we will examine them in terms of these four areas.

A few adults operate at the *conformist* level. Character development at this stage is marked by absolute conformity to social rules. If these rules are broken, feelings of shame and guilt result. Interpersonally, conformists need to belong and show a superficial niceness. Of central importance is appearance and social acceptability. Conformists see the world only in terms of external tangibles, such as how one looks and if one behaves according to group standards. Thinking is dominated by stereotypes and cliches and is relatively simplistic.

Most adults in American society operate at the *conscientious-conformist* level. At this stage character development is marked by a differentiation of norms and goals; in other words, people learn to separate what they want for themselves from what social norms may dictate. People deal with others by recognizing that they have an impact on them and on the group as a whole. People at this level begin to be concerned with issues of personal adjustment and coping with problems; they need reasons for actions, and recognize that there are many opportunities in life from which they may choose. There is still concern with group standards, and the desire for personal adjustment is sometimes suppressed if it conflicts with the needs of the group.

The next level, the *conscientious* stage, is marked by a cognitive style in which individuals have a beginning understanding of the true complexity of the world. People at this stage focus on understand-

TABLE 8.2 Summary of Loevinger's stages of ego development in adulthood

Stage	Description
Conformist	Obedience to external social rules
Conscientious-conformist	Separation of norms and goals; realization that acts affect others
Conscientious	Beginning of self-evaluated standards
Individualistic	Recognition that the process of acting is more important than the outcome
Autonomous	Respect for each person's individuality; tolerance for ambiguity
Integrated	Resolution of inner conflicts

ing the role that the self plays; character development involves self-evaluated standards, self-critical thinking, self-determined ideals, and self-set goals. This level represents a shift away from letting other people or society set their goals and standards for them. Interpersonal relations are characterized by intensity, responsibility, and mutual sharing. People evaluate behavior using internalized standards developed over the years. They come to realize that they control their own future. Although more complex, conscientious people still think in terms of polarities, such as love versus lust or inner life versus outer appearance. But they recognize responsibility and obligation in addition to rights and privileges.

Loevinger postulates that the *individualistic* level builds on the previous (conscientious) level. A major acquisition at the individualistic level is a respect for individuality. Immature dependency is seen as an emotional problem, rather than as something to be expected. Concern for broad social problems and differentiating one's inner life from one's outer life become the main preoccupations. People begin to differentiate process (the way things are done) from outcome (the answer); for example, people realize that sometimes the solution to a problem is right but the way of getting there

involves hurting someone. The flavor of the individualistic person is an increased tolerance for oneself and others. Key conflicts are recognized as complex problems: dependence as constraining versus dependence as emotionally rewarding, and morality and responsibility versus achievement for oneself. The way of resolving these conflicts, however, usually involves projecting the cause onto the environment rather than acknowledging their internal sources.

At Loevinger's *autonomous* level comes a high tolerance for ambiguity with conflicting needs both within oneself and others. Autonomous individuals' interpersonal style is characterized by a respect for each person's independence but also by an understanding that people are interdependent. The preoccupations at this level are vividly conveyed feelings, self-fulfillment, and understanding of the self in a social context. Autonomous people have the courage to acknowledge and face conflict head-on rather than projecting it onto the environment. They see reality as complex and multifaceted and no longer view it in the polarities of the conscientious stage. Autonomous individuals recognize that there are multiple ways to view a problem, and are comfortable with the fact that other people's viewpoints may differ from their own. They recognize

Being committed to broad social concerns is the essence of Loevinger's individualistic phase of ego development.

the need for others' self-sufficiency and take a broad view of life.

The final level in Loevinger's theory is termed the *integrated* stage. Inner conflicts are not only faced but also reconciled and laid to rest. There is a renunciation of goals that are recognized to be unattainable. People at the integrated level cherish an individuality that comes from a consolidated sense of identity. They are very much like Maslow's (1968) self-actualized person; that is, they are at peace with themselves and have realized their maximum potential. They recognize that they could have chosen other paths in life but are content with

and make the most out of the one that they picked. Such people are always open to further growth-enhancing opportunities and make the most out of integrating new experiences into their lives.

Loevinger has spent decades developing the Sentence Completion Test, which provides a measure of ego development. The measure consists of sentence fragments (similar to "When I think of myself I _____") that respondents complete. Responses are then scored in terms of the ego developmental level they represent. Although it is a difficult instrument to learn how to use, the Sentence Completion Test has very good reliability. Trained coders have high rates of agreement in rating responses, often over 90% of the time.

Loevinger's theory is having an increasing impact on adult developmental research. One of its advantages is that because of the Sentence Completion Test it is more empirically based than Erikson's theory, so that researchers can document the stages more precisely. Loevinger's theory is the major framework for research examining relationships between cognitive development and ego development (King, Kitchener, Wood, & Davison, 1989). For example, Blanchard-Fields (1986) found ego level was the best predictor of young and middle-aged adults' reasoning on social dilemma tasks, such as what to do about an unwanted pregnancy. Likewise, Labouvie-Vief, Hakim-Larson, and Hobart (1987) reported that ego level was a strong predictor of the coping strategies used across the life span from childhood to old age. Both studies documented age-related increases in ego level that were associated with higher levels of problem-solving ability or with more mature coping styles.

Theories Based on Life Transitions

Jung's belief in a midlife crisis and Erikson's belief that personality development proceeds in stages laid the foundation for many later theorists' efforts. To get a flavor of what these theorists did, take a

SOMETHING TO THINK ABOUT

The Personal Side of Stage Theories

Studying stage theories generally makes us wonder how we stand. Evaluating our own ego development and other aspects of personality can be both fun and humbling. It can be fun in the sense that learning something about oneself is enjoyable and enlightening; it can be humbling in the sense that we may have overestimated how advanced we really are. There is another side to this personal evaluation, though, that is equally important.

Take a few moments and think back perhaps 5 or 10 years. What things were important to you? How well did you know yourself? What were your priorities? What did you see yourself becoming in the future? What were your relationships with other people based on? Now answer these questions from your perspective today.

If you are like most people, answering these questions will make you see the ways in which you have changed. Many times we are in the worst position to see this change, because we are embedded in it. We also find ourselves reinterpreting the past based on the experiences we have had in the meantime.

The focus of the stage theories we have considered is the change in the ways that we see ourselves. We do look at the world differently as we grow older. Our priorities do change. Take a few moments now and jot down how you have changed over the years since high school. Then write down how you see yourself now. Finally, write down how you would like to see your life go in the future. These ideas will give you something to think about now and again later when we consider Whitbourne's ideas about scenarios and life stories.

---

moment to think about your own life, as suggested in Something to Think About.

For many laypeople, the idea that adults go through an orderly sequence of stages that includes both crises and stability reflects their own experience. This is probably why books such as Gail Sheehy's *Passages* (1976) and *Pathfinders* (1981) are met with instant acceptance, or why Levinson's work (Levinson, Darrow, Kline, Levinson, & McKee, 1978) has been applied to everything from basic personality development to understanding how men's occupational careers change.

Compared to some theories of ego development such as Loevinger's, however, theories based on life transitions are built on shaky ground. For example, some are based on small, highly selective samples (such as men who attended Harvard) or surveys completed by readers of particular magazines. This is in contrast to Loevinger's large data base obtained with well-researched, psychometrically sound measures. Thus, the research methods used in studies of life transitions lead one to question the validity of their findings.

Second, it is impossible to tell whether the personal changes people report are due to true underlying changes in personality or to changing responses in the face of changing societal demands. That is, societies typically have certain tasks and roles that are assigned to people of different ages. It is possible that as our roles change with age we need to make adjustments in how we interact with the world, possibly resulting in changes in personality. To the extent this is true, transition-based theories are perhaps more appropriately viewed as theories of how people adapt to changing environmental demands rather than as theories of personality per se.

Finally, an important question about life transition theories is the extent to which they are real and actually occur to everyone. Life transition theories typically present stages as if they are universally experienced by everyone. Moreover, many have specific ages tied to specific stages (such as, age 30 or age 50 transitions). As we know from cognitive developmental research in Chapter 7, however, this is a very tenuous assumption. Individual variation is the rule, not the exception. What actually happens may be a combination of expectations and socialization. The experience of a midlife crisis, discussed next, is an excellent case in point.

In Search of the Midlife Crisis. One of the most important ideas in both Erikson's and Loevinger's theories based on life transitions is that middle-aged adults experience a personal crisis that results in major changes in how they view themselves. During a midlife crisis, people are supposed to take a good hard look at themselves and, hopefully, attain a much better understanding of who they are. Difficult issues such as one's own mortality and inevitable aging are supposed to be faced. Behavioral changes are supposed to occur; we even have stereotypic images of the middle-aged man running off with a much younger woman as a result of his midlife crisis.

Some research seems to document the crisis. Jaques (1965) reported that male artists went through a crisis precipitated by the recognition of their own mortality. Time since birth was replaced by time left to live in the minds of these middle-aged men. Levinson and his colleagues (1978) write that middle-aged men in his study reported intense internal struggles that were much like depression.

However, far more research fails to document the existence of a particularly difficult time in midlife. Baruch (1984) summarizes a series of retrospective interview studies of American women between the ages of 35 and 55. The results showed that women in their 20s were more likely to be uncertain and dissatisfied than were women at midlife. Middle-aged women only rarely mentioned normative developmental milestones such as marriage, childbirth, or menopause as major turning points in their lives. Rather, unexpected events such as divorce and job transfers were more likely to cause crises. Studies extending Levinson's theory to women have not found strong evidence of a traumatic midlife crisis either (Harris, Ellicott, & Holmes, 1986; Reinke, Holmes, & Harris, 1985; Roberts & Newton, 1987).

The midlife crisis was also missing in data obtained as part of the Berkeley studies of personality traits. Most middle-aged men said that their careers were satisfying (Clausen, 1981), and both men and women appeared more self-confident, insightful, introspective, open, and better equipped to handle stressful situations (Haan, 1985; Haan et al., 1986). Even direct attempts to find the midlife crisis failed. In two studies Costa and McCrae (1978) could identify only a handful of men who fit the profile, and even then the crisis came anytime between 30 and 60. A replication and extension of this work, conducted by Farrell and Rosenberg (1981), confirmed the initial results.

McCrae and Costa (1984) point out that the idea of a midlife crisis became widely accepted as fact due to the mass media. People take it for granted that they will go through a period of intense psychological turmoil in their 40s. The problem is that there is little hard scientific evidence of it. The data suggest that midlife is no more or no less traumatic for most people than any other period in life. Perhaps the most convincing support for this conclusion comes from Farrell and Rosenberg's (1981) research. These investigators initially set out to prove the existence of a midlife crisis, as they were firm believers in it. After extensive testing and interviewing, however, they emerged as nonbelievers.

Conclusions About Ego Development Theories

Ego development theories have had many influences on how people view adulthood. Most important, these theories helped establish the idea that personality development continues throughout life, and that this change occurs through personal struggle and transition. Much data, mostly based on Loevinger's theory, supports this view of change in adulthood, which may be linked to cognitive growth as well. Unfortunately, with the idea of change came a popular belief in age-graded crises such as the midlife crisis. Despite the lack of general empirical support for transitions that are tightly tied to chronological age, their intuitive appeal persists.

As more researchers implicitly adopt a biopsychosocial approach, ego development theories may become more attractive. As we have seen, they explicitly include biological, social, and experiential influences more so than most trait theories. However, the assumption that change across adulthood is a given puts ego development theories clearly at odds with much of the trait research. Moreover, ego development theory itself even holds open the prospect of stability; recall that very few individuals progress all the way through Erikson's or Loevinger's stages. What is needed is a resolution of this dilemma that admits the possibility of change but does not require it.

COGNITIVE THEORIES

Implicit in theories of ego development and in some of the research on traits is the notion that how we perceive the world is important. These perceptions emphasize the interaction between the person and the environment as the major force behind personality development. However, neither ego nor trait theories focus on how these perceptions are actually involved in personality development. Cognitive theories of personality development do. As we will see, in many respects cognitive theories offer a middle ground between trait and ego theories.

The basis of cognitive theories is your own conception of how your life should proceed. How you think things are is more important for personality development than how things really are. In other words, it is how you perceive yourself that matters, not what the scores on personality tests indicate. Personality development in adulthood is related to your awareness of changes in personal appearance, behavior, reactions of others, and an appreciation of the increasing closeness of death.

We will examine the work of two theorists whose research flows directly from a cognitive perspective. Hans Thomae developed a cognitive theory of personality based on his longitudinal research in Germany. Susan Krauss Whitbourne investigated people's own conceptions of the life course and how they differ from age norms and the expectations for society as a whole.

Thomae's Cognitive Theory of Personality

Thomae (1970, 1976, 1980) has offered a cognitive theory of personality that can also be viewed as a cognitive theory of aging. He lists three postulates that form the basis for explaining personality development, especially in terms of adjusting to one's own aging:

1. *Perception of change, rather than objective change, is related to behavioral change.* Only if we think we have changed over time will we act differently, regardless of whether other people think we have changed. This postulate, besides being fundamental to all cognitive theories of personality, also refers to people's belief in future change. Personality change is more or less likely

depending on whether the individual thinks that change is normative.

2. *People perceive and evaluate any change in their life situation in terms of their dominant concerns and expectations at that time.* They view the same problem differently depending on what stage of the life cycle they are in. For example, the main source of people's identity changes as they move from being a student to being a spouse, a worker, a parent, and so on. These different life stages motivate the person to perceive situations differently.

3. *Adjustment to aging is determined by the balance between people's cognitive and motivational structures.* If people perceive their life situation positively, believe that growth has occurred, and perceive change as complementing their interpretation of their current life stage, then adjustment to aging is possible.

Thomae's three postulates lead to the conclusion that personality change during adulthood cannot be reduced either to a happens–does not happen dichotomy or to a simple examination of scores on personality tests. Rather, personality change is in the personal eye of the beholder. Each of us has the potential to change, but whether it happens depends on our desire for change.

Thomae studied these processes of change in the Bonn Longitudinal Study of Aging in order to identify the most important components in the many pathways to successful aging (Thomae, 1976). The Bonn study differed in important ways from the other longitudinal studies we have encountered, mainly because it incorporated nearly all aspects of the biopsychosocial model. Data on personality were gathered from open-ended interviews and from unstructured, projective personality tests. In addition to these measures the Bonn study included measures of participants' social conditions, life history, future plans, intelligence, attitudes, and health. These additional variables gave Thomae a more complete picture of his participants than is typical in most longitudinal studies of personality.

From this large data base, Thomae identified 10 sets of interactions among biological, social, and perceptual-motivational processes that define the aging process in any specific person-environment context. More important, he found that adaptation in old age was not the result of one particular combination of the processes. Instead of one unique pattern of successful aging, Thomae found many. Despite the complexity of these interactions, however, Thomae noted that unless people's perceptions of themselves and of the situation require change, overall stability will be the most likely outcome.

Additional Supportive Research. At several points in this chapter, we noted that research conducted in other frameworks pointed to the importance of people's perceptions in understanding personality development. For example, recall that findings from the Berkeley studies provided strong support for the role of personal perceptions of the need for change in determining whether changes in traits occur (Haan et al., 1986). These findings are not unusual.

Chiriboga and his colleagues conducted an 11-year longitudinal study of the relationship between stressful life events and personality in people who were aged 16 to 65 at the beginning of the study (Chiriboga, 1984, 1985; Fiske & Chiriboga, 1985). They found that personality dimensions such as self-concept, life satisfaction, and interpersonal style were relatively stable over the 11 years. However, the degree of stability in these traits was directly related to the amount of stress experienced. Specifically, people who experienced the fewest stressful events were the least likely to change. These findings indicate that for personality traits to change, people must be confronted with a compelling reason such as stressful life events.

Research on stress itself supports Thomae's view. In Chapter 4 we saw that the most widely held theory of stress, the transactional framework, is based on the role of perceptions of the situation. That is, stress results from people's subjective appraisal of events. This approach provides the theoretical basis for much current work on caregiving as well (see Chapter 9).

Whitbourne's Life Story Approach

A second approach in the cognitive camp is based on Whitbourne's (1987) idea that people build their own conceptions of how their lives should proceed. The result of this process is the **life-span construct**, the person's unified sense of the past, present, and future.

There are many influences on the development of a life-span construct: identity, values, and social context are a few. Together, they shape the life-span construct and the ways in which it is manifested. The life-span construct has two structural components, which in turn are the ways in which it is manifested. The first of these components is the *scenario*, which consists of expectations about the future. The scenario translates aspects of our identity that are particularly important at a specific point into a plan for the future. The scenario is strongly influenced by age norms that define key transition points; for example, graduating from college is a transition that is normally associated with the early 20s. In short, a scenario is a game plan for how we want our lives to go.

Joan, a typical college sophomore, may have the following scenario: She expects that her course of study in nursing will be difficult but that she will finish on time. She hopes to meet a nice guy along the way whom she will marry shortly after graduation. She imagines that she will get a good job at a major medical center that will offer her good opportunities for advancement. She and her husband will probably have a child, but she expects to keep working. Because she feels that she will want to advance, she assumes that at some point she will

According to Whitbourne, this new Ph.D. graduate already has constructed a scenario of what he expects to happen in the next few years of his life.

obtain a master's degree. In the more distant future she hopes to be a department head and to be well-respected for her administrative skills.

Tagging certain expected events with a particular age or time by which we expect to complete them creates a social clock (see Chapter 1). Joan will use her scenario to evaluate her progress toward her goals. With each major transition she will check how she is doing against where her scenario says she should be. If it turns out that she has achieved her goals earlier than she expected, she will be proud of being ahead of the game. If things work out more slowly than she planned, she may chastise herself for being slow. If she begins to criticize herself a great deal, she may end up changing her scenario altogether; for example, if she does not

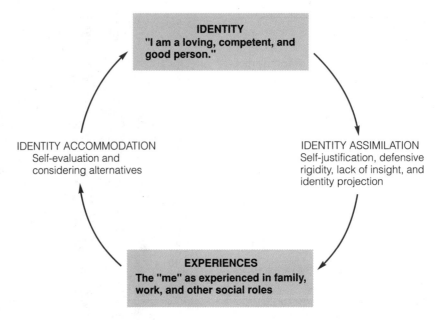

FIGURE 8.1 Whitbourne's model of adult identity processes

(Source: *The Me I Know: A Study of Adult Identity* by S. K. Whitbourne, © 1986, New York: Springer-Verlag. Reprinted with permission of the publisher.)

get a good job and makes no progress, she may change her scenario to one that says she should stay home with her child.

As Joan starts moving into the positions laid out in her scenario, she begins to create the second component of her life-span construct, her *life story*. The life story is a personal narrative history that organizes past events into a coherent sequence. The life story gives events personal meaning and a sense of continuity; it becomes our autobiography. Because the life story is what we tell others when they ask about our past, it eventually becomes somewhat overrehearsed and stylized. An interesting aspect of the life story, and autobiographical memory in general, is that distortions will occur with time and retelling (Neisser & Winograd, 1988). In the case of life stories, distortions allow the person to feel

that he or she was on time, rather than off time, in terms of past events in the scenario. In this way people feel better about their plans and goals and are less likely to feel a sense of failure.

Whitbourne (1986) conducted a fascinating cross-sectional study of 94 adults ranging in age from 24 to 61. They came from all walks of life and represented a wide range of occupations and life situations. Using data from very detailed interviews, Whitbourne was able to identify what she believes is the process of adult identity development based on an equilibrium between identity and experience. Her model is presented in Figure 8.1.

As can be seen, the processes of equilibrium are based on Piaget's concepts of assimilation and accommodation (see Chapter 7). Whitbourne has explicitly attempted to integrate concepts from cognitive development with identity development in order to understand how identity is formed and revised across adulthood. The assimilation process involves using already existing aspects of identity to handle present situations. Overreliance on assimilation makes the person resistant to change. Accommodation, on the other hand, reflects the willingness of the individual to let the situation determine what he or she will do. This often occurs when the person does not have a well-developed identity around a certain issue.

Not surprisingly, Whitbourne (1986) found that the vast majority of adults listed family as the most important aspect of their lives. It is clear that adults' identity as loving constitutes the major part of the answer to the question "Who am I?" Consequently, a major theme in adults' identity development is trying to refine their belief that "I am a loving person." Much of this development is in the area of acquiring and refining deep, emotional relationships.

A second major source of identity for Whitbourne's participants was work. In this case the key seemed to be keeping work interesting. As long as individuals had an interesting occupation that enabled them to become personally invested, their work identity was more central to their overall personal identity. This is a topic we will pursue in Chapter 11.

Although Whitbourne found evidence of life transitions, she found no evidence that these transitions occurred in stagelike fashion or were tied to specific ages. Rather, she found that people tended to experience transitions when they felt they needed to and to do so on their own time line.

Self-Concept and Possible Selves

Recall that in the cognitive view of personality it is the individual's subjective perception that matters, not objective reality. Self-perceptions and how they differ with age have been examined in a wide variety of studies and have been shown to be related to many behaviors. Changes in self-perceptions are often manifested in changed beliefs, concerns, and expectations. **Self-concept** is the organized, coherent, integrated pattern of self-perceptions (Thomae, 1980). It includes the notions of self-esteem and self-image.

Kegan (1982) attempted to integrate the development of self-concept and cognitive development. He postulated six stages of the development of self, corresponding to stages of cognitive development described in Chapter 7. Kegan's first three stages — which he calls incorporative, impulsive, and imperial — correspond to Piaget's sensorimotor, preoperational, and concrete operational stages (see Chapter 7). During this time, he believes, children move from knowing themselves on the basis of reflexes to knowing themselves through needs and interests. At the beginning of formal operational thought during early adolescence (see Chapter 7), he argues, a sense of interpersonal mutuality begins to develop; he terms this period *the interpersonal stage*. By late adolescence or young adulthood, individuals move to a mature sense of identity based on taking control of their own life and developing an ideology; Kegan calls this period *the institutional stage*. Finally, with the acquisition of postformal thought (see Chapter 7) comes an understanding that the self is a very complex system that takes into account other people; Kegan terms this period *the interindividual stage*. Kegan's (1982) work emphasizes the fact that personality development does not occur in a vacuum. Rather, we must not forget that the person is a complex integrated whole. Consequently, an understanding of the development of self-concept or any other aspect of personality is enhanced by an understanding of how it relates to other dimensions of development.

In one of the few longitudinal studies of self-concept, Mortimer, Finch, and Kumka (1982) followed a group of men for 14 years, beginning when the participants were college freshmen. They found that self-image consisted of four dimensions: well-being, interpersonal qualities, activity, and unconventionality. Well-being included self-perceptions concerning happiness, lack of tension, and confidence. Interpersonal qualities referred to self-perceptions concerning sociability, interest in others, openness, and warmth. The activity component consisted of self-perceptions of strength, competence, success, and activity. The unconventionality dimension indicated that men saw themselves as impulsive, unconventional, and dreamy. Clearly, what Mortimer and colleagues found concerning self-image is very closely related to Costa and McCrae's model of personality, described earlier in this chapter.

Over the 14-year period the men in the Mortimer et al. study showed little change as a group. The structure of self-concept remained stable. Some fluctuation at the level of self-image was noted, though. Both well-being and competence declined during college but rebounded after graduation. Self-perceptions of unconventionality declined after college. Sociability showed a steady decline across the entire study.

When the data were examined at the intraindividual level, it became clear that self-perceptions of confidence were related to life events. The course of a man's career, his satisfaction with career and marriage, his relationship with his parents, and his overall life satisfaction followed patterns that could be predicted by competence. For example, men whose competence scores remained above the group average experienced few problems related to their jobs and had higher marital and life satisfaction than men whose competence scores were below the group average.

Interestingly, a man's degree of confidence as a college senior influenced his later evaluation of life events, and it may have even set the stage for a self-fulfilling prophecy. Mortimer and colleagues suggest that these men may actively seek and create experiences that fit their personality structure. This hypothesis is supported by longitudinal research

on gifted women, whose high self-confidence in early adulthood becomes manifested as a high life satisfaction during their 60s (Sears & Barbee, 1978).

The results from the Mortimer, Finch, and Kumka (1982) study are strikingly similar to the data from the Berkeley studies described earlier in this chapter. Recall that data from these studies also support the idea that life events are important influences on personality development. In the present case, life events clearly influence one's self-concept. We will consider in the next section how adults explain why certain things or certain events happen to them.

Possible Selves. One important aspect of self-concept consists of ideas about different people we could become. In particular, we have aspects of self-concept representing what we could become, what we would like to become, and what we are afraid of becoming. Together, these aspects are called **possible selves** (Markus & Nurius, 1986). What you could or would like to become often reflects personal goals; you may see yourself as a leader, as rich and famous, or as in shape. What you are afraid of becoming may show up in your fear of being undervalued, or overweight, or lonely. Our possible selves are very powerful motivators; indeed, much of our behavior can be viewed as efforts to approach or avoid these various possible selves and to protect the current view of self (Markus & Nurius, 1986).

The topic of possible selves offers a way to integrate the trait and ego development research. On the one hand, possible selves tend to remain stable for at least some period of time, and are measurable with psychometrically sound scales (e.g., Ryff, 1991). On the other hand, possible selves may change in response to efforts at personal growth (Cross & Markus, 1991), which would be expected from ego development theory. In particular, possible selves facilitate adaptation to new roles across the life span. For example, a full-time mother who pictures herself as an executive once her child goes to school may begin to take evening courses to acquire new skills. Thus, possible selves offer a way to bridge the experience of the current self and your imagined future self.

Researchers have begun studying age differences in the construction of possible selves. Cross and Markus (1991) asked people aged 18 to 86 to describe their hoped-for and feared possible selves. Responses were grouped into categories (such as family, personal, material). Several interesting age differences emerged. In terms of hoped-for selves, 18- to 24-year-olds listed family concerns most often (for instance, marrying the right person). In contrast, 25- to 39-year-olds listed family concerns last; their main issues concerned personal things (like being a more loving and caring person). By age 40–59, family issues again became most common (such as, being a parent who can "let go" of my children). For 60- to 86-year-olds, personal issues were most prominent (for example, being able to be active and healthy for another decade at least).

All age groups listed physical issues as their most frequent feared self. For the two younger groups, being overweight, and for women, becoming wrinkled and unattractive when old were commonly mentioned. For the middle-aged and older adult groups, fear of having Alzheimer's disease or being unable to care for oneself were frequent responses.

Overall, adolescents and young adults were far more likely to have multiple possible selves, and to believe more strongly that they could actually become the hoped-for self and successfully avoid the feared self. By old age, though, both the number and strength of belief had diminished. Older adults were more likely to believe that both the hoped-for and feared selves were not under their personal control. These findings may reflect differences with age in personal motivation, beliefs in personal control, and the need to explore new options.

Ryff (1991) asked younger, middle-aged, and older adults to describe their present, past, future,

and ideal self. Rather than focusing on the categories of responses, Ryff focused on people's perceptions of change over time. In general, she found that younger and middle-aged adults saw themselves as improving with age, and expected to continue getting better in the future. In contrast, older adults viewed themselves as stable over time, but foresaw declining well-being in their future. Ryff points out that the older adults' results may reflect some degree of internalization of negative stereotypes about aging, especially as these respondents were all currently healthy and well educated. To the extent this is true, these data provide strong support for Thomae's belief that personal perception matters more than objective reality.

Taken together, the work on possible selves is opening exciting avenues for personality research. Possible selves offers a way to examine the importance of personal perception in determining motivation to achieve and change, as well as a way to study personality systematically with sound research methods. Because it provides an interesting bridge between different approaches to personality theory, it will likely be the focus of much research in the future.

Personal Control

Suppose you do not perform as well as you think you should have on an exam. Was it your own fault? Or was the exam too picky? How we answer such questions sheds light on how we tend to explain, or attribute, our behavior. The study of attributions is one of the major areas in social psychology and is the topic of numerous theories. Among the most important ways in which we analyze the cause of events is in terms of who or what is in control in a specific situation. **Personal control** is the degree to which you believe that your performance in a situation depends on something that you personally do. A high sense of personal control implies a belief that performance is up to you, whereas a low sense of personal control implies that your performance is under the influence of forces other than your own.

Personal control has become an extremely important idea in a wide variety of settings (Baltes & Baltes, 1986). For example, it is thought to play a role in memory performance (see Chapter 6), in intelligence (see Chapter 7), in depression (see Chapter 9), and in adjustment to and survival in institutions (see Chapter 12). Despite this range of research, however, we do not have a clear picture of developmental trends in people's sense of personal control.

Most of the research on personal control has been conducted using a locus of control framework. Locus of control refers to who or what one thinks is responsible for performance. Traditionally, researchers label people who take personal responsibility internal and people who believe that others (or chance) are responsible external. Evidence from both cross-sectional studies (e.g., Gatz & Siegler, 1981; Ryckman & Malikioski, 1975) and longitudinal studies (e.g., Lachman, 1985; Siegler & Gatz, 1985) is contradictory. Some find that older adults are more likely to be internal than younger adults, whereas others find older adults more likely to be external than younger adults.

Lachman (1986) argues that a major reason for the conflicting findings is the multidimensionality of personal control. Specifically, she shows that one's sense of control depends on which domain, such as intelligence or health, is being assessed. Moreover, she demonstrates that older adults often acknowledge the importance of outside influences on their behavior but still believe that what they do matters.

Indeed, Brandtstädter (1989) clearly showed that the developmental patterns of personal control vary considerably from one domain to another. For example, perceived control over one's development shows an overall age-related decrease. However, perceived marital support shows an age-related increase.

It appears that one's sense of personal control is a complex, multidimensional aspect of personality. Consequently, general normative age-related trends may not be found. Rather, changes in personal control may well depend on one's experiences in different domains and may differ widely from one domain to another.

Conclusions About Cognitive Theories

Although more research is needed, the cognitive theories have much to offer the study of adult personality development. Converging evidence from a variety of sources points to the conclusion that adults experience both change and stability and that the extent of each may be largely within their control. Adults may tend to remain the same unless they perceive a need to change. Future research is likely to integrate the theoretical framework of cognitive theories with the research methods used in studying ego development and traits, as is being done in the work on possible selves. This combination may provide an explanation for conflicting findings in those literatures and give us considerable insight into why some people seem to stay the same while others do not.

MORAL DEVELOPMENT

Suppose you are given the following problem:

In Europe a woman was near death from cancer. One drug might save her, a form of radium that a druggist in the same town had recently discovered. The druggist was charging $2,000, ten times what the drug cost him to make. The sick woman's husband, Heinz, went to everyone he knew to borrow the money, but he could only get together *about half of what the drug cost. He told the druggist his wife was dying and asked him to sell it to him cheaper or let him pay later. But the druggist said no. The husband got desperate and broke into the man's store to steal the drug for his wife. Should the husband have done that? Why? (Kohlberg, 1969, p. 379)*

Problems like this present a moral dilemma. One can think of many reasons why Heinz should or should not steal the drug. Researchers have recognized for a long time that how people answer, and the reasons that they give, reflect important aspects of their personality. Freud thought that morality was so important that he devoted an entire aspect of personality — the superego — to it.

Dealing with moral dilemmas raises several important points about morality. First, problems like the Heinz dilemma emphasize **moral reasoning**; the problem is a hypothetical one, and is aimed at getting people to think about the rules of ethical or moral conduct. The primary research emphasis in this approach is on people's rationale, or how well they think through the problem to justify their response.

But reasoning about hypothetical situations may not necessarily correspond with what a person would actually do if faced with the real situation. *Moral behavior* puts the focus on whether the person would in fact steal to get a drug to save someone else's life. In this case, researchers would be interested in learning about situations under which people either do or do not break the rules of society.

Finally, thinking about or facing moral dilemmas results in strong emotional feelings. *Moral emotions* that follow personal decisions are of interest, too. For example, feeling that you should put yourself at risk in order to save someone else, even at the risk of losing your life (altruism), or feeling that you should try to get away with something (such as cheating), are interesting topics.

In this section, we will consider Kohlberg's theory of the development of moral reasoning. As we will see, Kohlberg believes that moral reasoning develops in a stagelike sequence. However, we will also see that his theory has stimulated some very interesting debates, one of which rests on gender differences.

Kohlberg's Theory

Kohlberg (1984, 1987) believed very strongly that moral reasoning developed over the life span in a sequence of discrete stages. He grounded his theory in Piaget's theory of cognitive development (see Chapter 7); for example, Kohlberg assumed an invariant, universal sequence for everyone and that the stages represented qualitative changes in reasoning.

Kohlberg proposed that moral reasoning developed in three *levels* (preconventional, conventional, and postconventional) that consisted of two *stages* each. A person's level and stage of moral reasoning is measured by having him or her respond to several dilemmas like the Heinz problem. However, the evaluation is done in response to the Why? question, not to what the person should do. Kohlberg believed that it is the kind of reasoning people do that determines one's level and stage of moral reasoning, not what specific action they would take. In short, Kohlberg emphasized the *form* or *style* of moral reasoning (the rules people use) over the content of the response (the decision itself).

Table 8.3 presents a summary of the three levels and six stages in Kohlberg's theory, and Table 8.4 provides examples of responses to the Heinz dilemma at each stage. The two stages in the **preconventional level** reflect moral reasoning on the basis of personal gain. That is, one makes moral judgments by deciding what will maximize reward or minimize punishment, maintain one's power or status, and so forth. People who operate at this level have not internalized societal conventions; rather, their moral reasoning is based on "looking out for number one."

TABLE 8.3 An overview of the levels and stages that comprise Kohlberg's theory of moral development

Level and Stage	What Is Right	Reasons for Doing Right	Sociomoral Perspective
Level I — Preconventional Stage 1 — Heteronomous morality	To avoid breaking rules backed by punishment, obedience for its own sake, and avoiding physical damage to persons and property.	Avoidance of punishment, and the superior power of authorities.	*Egocentric point of view.* Doesn't consider the interests of others or recognize that they differ from the actor's; doesn't relate two points of view. Actions are considered physically rather than in terms of psychological interests of others. Confusion of authority's perspective with one's own.
Stage 2 — Individualism, instrumental purpose, and exchange	Following rules only when it is to someone's immediate interest; acting to meet one's own interests and needs and letting others do the same. Right is also what's fair, what's an equal exchange, a deal, an agreement.	To serve one's own needs or interests in a world where you have to recognize that other people have their interests, too.	*Concrete individualistic perspective.* Aware that everybody has his or her own interest to pursue and these conflict, so that right is relative (in the concrete individualistic sense).
Level II — Conventional Stage 3 — Mutual interpersonal expectations, relationships, and interpersonal conformity	Living up to what is expected by people close to you or what people generally expect of people in your role as son, brother, friend, and so on. "Being good" is important and means having good motives, showing concern about others. It also means keeping mutual relationships, such as trust, loyalty, respect, and gratitude.	The need to be a good person in your own eyes and those of others. Your caring for others. Belief in the Golden Rule. Desire to maintain rules and authority which support stereotypical good behavior.	*Perspective of the individual in relationships with other individuals.* Aware of shared feelings, agreements, and expectations that take primacy over individual interests. Relates points of view through the concrete Golden Rule, putting yourself in the other guy's shoes. Does not yet consider generalized system perspective.

Stage 4 — Social system and conscience	Fulfilling the actual duties to which you have agreed. Laws are to be upheld except in extreme cases where they conflict with other fixed social duties. Right is also contributing to society, the group, or institution.	To keep the institution going as a whole, to avoid the breakdown in the system "if everyone did it," or the imperative of conscience to meet one's defined obligations.	*Differentiates societal point of view from interpersonal agreement or motives.* Takes the point of view of the system that defines roles and rules. Considers individual relations in terms of place in the system.
Level III — Postconventional, or Principled Stage 5 — Social contract or utility and individual rights	Being aware that people hold a variety of values and opinions, that most values and rules are relative to your group. These relative rules should usually be upheld, however, in the interest of impartiality and because they are the social contract. Some nonrelative values and rights like *life* and *liberty*, however, must be upheld in any society regardless of majority opinion.	A sense of obligation to law because of one's social contract to make and abide by laws for the welfare of all and for the protection of all people's rights. A feeling of contractual commitment, freely entered upon, to family, friendship, trust, and work obligations. Concern that laws and duties be based on rational calculation of overall utility, "the greatest good for the greatest number."	*Prior-to-society perspective.* Perspective of a rational individual aware of values and rights prior to social attachments and contracts. Integrates perspectives by formal mechanisms of agreement, contract, objective impartiality, and due process. Considers moral and legal points of view; recognizes that they sometimes conflict and finds it difficult to integrate them.
Stage 6 — Universal ethical principles	Following self-chosen ethical principles. Particular laws or social agreements are usually valid because they rest on such principles. When laws violate these principles, one acts in accordance with the principle. Principles are universal principles of justice: the equality of human rights and respect for the dignity of human beings as individual persons.	The belief as a rational person in the validity of universal moral principles, and a sense of personal commitment to them.	*Perspective of a moral point of view from which social arrangements derive.* Perspective is that of any rational individual recognizing the nature of morality or the fact that persons are ends in themselves and must be treated as such.

(Source: "Moral Stages and Moralization" by L. Kohlberg, 1976, in T. Lickona (Ed.), *Moral Development and Behavior*. New York: Holt, Rinehart & Winston. Reprinted with permission.)

The **conventional level** (stages 3 and 4) reflects moral reasoning based on personal incorporation of societal and other individuals' (family, friends) expectations of you. A major theme here is following the rules; stage 3 is sometimes referred to as being a good girl or boy, and stage 4 as a law-and-order orientation.

Stages 5 and 6, the **postconventional level**, describe a view that reflects an understanding and application of the difference between basic human rights and obligations, on the one hand, and societal rules and regulations on the other. Human rights are those fundamental aspects of personhood that transcend time and culture; examples include life, liberty, the pursuit of happiness, and freedom. These rights apply equally to everyone. Rules and regulations, however, vary across time and culture. People who reason postconventionally use human rights as the basis for their moral judgments.

Influences on Moral Reasoning. Considerable research has documented several important influences on moral reasoning. Most important, it appears that overall cognitive developmental level is a major determinant of one's level and stage of moral reasoning. For example, Roodin, Rybash, and Hoyer (1984) suggested that postformal thought (see Chapter 7) may be necessary for attaining the postconventional level of moral reasoning.

Additionally, Kohlberg (1976) proposed that moral reasoning depends on the *sociomoral perspective* that one brings to the situation (see Table 8.3 for a discussion of the perspective accompanying each stage). Sociomoral perspectives are constructed through reciprocal person-environment interactions. Especially helpful environments are ones that (1) provide a wide range of opportunities for role-taking experiences so that people learn how other people or groups think and feel; and (2) put the person in real-life situations requiring moral decisions (such as a jury deliberating whether a person should be executed).

Development of Moral Reasoning

There is little doubt that moral reasoning develops. Colby, Kohlberg, Gibbs, and Lieberman (1983) presented findings from a 20-year longitudinal study that showed clear age trends. Over the 20-year period, reasoning at stages 1 and 2 dropped steadily. Reasoning at stage 3 increased until around age 18, when it dropped somewhat and leveled off. Finally, reasoning at stages 4 and 5 increased steadily, with stage 4 showing a much faster rate of increase. Note that stage 4 did not appear at all until early adolescence, and stage 5 was absent until the early 20s.

Kohlberg (1987) saw these results as reflecting a strong developmental trend. He argued that children and young adolescents reason at the preconventional level; most older adolescents and adults reason at the conventional level, and a few adults reason at the postconventional level. Apparently, only adults are able to reason morally based on universal principles of human rights.

Critiques of Kohlberg's Theory

Several cross-cultural studies have supported Kohlberg's claim of universality and invariance in his stages of development (Nisan & Kohlberg, 1982; Tietjen & Walker, 1985). Nevertheless, Kohlberg's theory has been criticized on two grounds.

Gilligan (1982) argues that Kohlberg's theory is more applicable to men's moral reasoning than to women's moral reasoning. For one thing, she points out that men tend to score higher (stage 4, on average) than women (stage 3, on average). Gilligan believes that this gender difference does not reflect a true difference in ability to reason. Rather, she argues that it reflects basic differences in what men and women bring into the moral decision-making situation. That is, Gilligan suggests that men and

TABLE 8.4 Responses at each stage to the Heinz dilemma

Stage 1

Pro

It's not really bad to steal the drug. It's not like he did not ask to pay for it first. The drug really isn't worth $2,000; at most it costs about $200. Also, letting your wife die would be the same as killing her — and God's commandments say that killing another person is wrong.

Con

Heinz shouldn't steal; he should buy the drug instead. Also, if he steals the drug he'd be committing a big crime and the police would put him in jail for a long time. Finally, God's commandments say that stealing is wrong.

Stage 2

Pro

Heinz should steal the drug because he'd be lonely and sad if his wife dies. He wants her to live more than anything else. Anyway, if he gets sent to jail (that would make him sad), but he'd still have his wife (and that would make him really happy).

Con

Heinz should not steal the drug if he doesn't like his wife a lot. Also, the druggist isn't really a bad person; he just wants to make a profit from all his hard work. That is what you are in business for, to make money.

Stage 3

Pro

If I were Heinz, I'd steal the drug for my wife. Heinz could not be so heartless as to let his wife die. The two partners in a marriage should naturally expect that they will come to each other's aid. Also, you can't put a price on life; and, any decent person should value life above anything else.

Con

Heinz shouldn't steal. If his wife dies, he cannot be blamed. After all, everybody knows that Heinz is not cruel and heartless, he tried to buy the drug legally. The druggist is the selfish one. He deserves to be stolen from.

Stage 4

Pro

When you get married, you take a vow to love and cherish your wife. Marriage is not only love, it's an obligation as well. Marriage is like a legal contract that must be obeyed. Also, by stealing the drug and going to court, Heinz will be able to show the members of his society how dumb the laws about stealing are. This might lead to positive changes in the judicial system.

Con

It's a natural thing for Heinz to want to save his wife, but it is still always wrong to steal. If everybody took the law into their own hands — like Heinz wants to do — his society would be in total chaos. In the long run, nobody in Heinz's society will benefit from this; not even Heinz and his wife!

(continued)

(Source: *Adult Development and Aging* (pp. 440–441) by J. W. Rybash, P. A. Roodin, and J. W. Santrock, 1991 (2nd ed.). Copyright © 1991 by Wm. C. Brown Publishers. Reprinted with permission.)

TABLE 8.4 Continued

Stage 5

Pro

The law is not set up to deal with the unique circumstances of the Heinz case. Taking the drug in this situation is not correct from a "legal" point of view. But, there may be a set of basic human rights (such as the right to life) that must be preserved regardless of what the law may happen to say. The law of the land should protect peoples' basic rights. It certainly isn't in this case. Therefore, Heinz should steal the drug.

Con

You cannot completely blame Heinz for stealing; but extreme circumstances do not really justify violating the law. This is because the law represents a commitment that Heinz and the other members of his society have made to one another.

Stage 6

Pro

Heinz has to act in terms of the principle of preserving and respecting life. It would be both irrational and immoral to preserve the druggist's property right to the drug at the expense of his wife's right to life. After all, people invented the concept of personal property; it is a culturally relative concept. Alternatively, the right of a person to claim their right to life should be absolute.

Con

Heinz is faced with the decision of whether to consider the other people who need the drug just as much as his wife. Heinz ought to act not according to his own feelings toward his wife but on his consideration of all of the lives involved.

women have different orientations to moral problems. Men tend to reason on the basis of abstract principles of justice, whereas women tend to reason based on their relationships with and responsibilities to others. These different orientations are due to different socialization patterns that begin in childhood. Consequently, Gilligan argues that Kohlberg's testing procedure and scoring are biased in favor of men, as they are grounded in a justice-based model. Research findings based on Gilligan's critique are equivocal; some investigators find the gender differences Gilligan predicts (Lyons, 1983) while others do not (Walker, deVries, & Trevethan,

1987). As a result, Gilligan's position remains controversial.

Rybash, Roodin, and Hoyer (1983) point out an age bias in Kohlberg's theory in favor of adolescents and young adults. They argue that the kinds of situations in Kohlberg's dilemmas are unlike those actually faced by adults in real life. As a result, older adults may be at an unfair disadvantage in responding to Kohlberg's problems. Indeed, Pratt, Golding, and Kerig (1987) provided strong supporting evidence for Rybash and colleagues' claim. The Pratt research found that older adults were more reflective when solving real-life problems than they were when solving Kohlberg's hypothetical dilemmas. Moreover, whereas younger and middle-aged adults were consistent in their stage of reasoning when given hypothetical and real-life problems, older adults were not.

Conclusions About Moral Development

It appears that moral reasoning develops in a stage-like manner well into adulthood. Moral reasoning seems to be linked to overall cognitive development. Kohlberg's stage theory has been criticized as gender and age biased, although some of the research on these issues is equivocal. Three lines of research are sorely needed: longitudinal studies, investigations of gender differences in the basis of reasoning, and studies of different types of problems in order to address possible age bias.

SUMMARY

Personality Traits Across Adulthood

1. A trait is a relatively stable characteristic.
2. Costa and McCrae's model has five components: neuroticism, extraversion, openness to experience, agreeableness-antagonism, and conscientiousness-undirectedness. Research consistently shows little change on these dimensions across adulthood.
3. There appears to be a shift from active to passive mastery during adulthood.
4. Evidence from the Berkeley studies shows that life style is a better predictor of life satisfaction for women, but personality is a better predictor for men. Additional evidence found no support for a life crisis model or for a continual change model of personality development. Gender differences were also apparent.
5. No age differences in life satisfaction are typically found, nor does the intensity of feelings change.

6. Evidence from several studies shows changes in the statements adults of different ages endorse about masculinity and femininity. The tendency is for older men and women to endorse similar statements.

Ego Development Across Adulthood

7. Jung emphasized dimensions of personality (masculinity-femininity; extraversion-introversion). Jung argues that people move toward integrating these dimensions as they age.
8. The sequence of Erikson's stages is: trust versus mistrust, autonomy versus shame and doubt, initiative versus guilt, industry versus inferiority, identity versus identity confusion, intimacy versus isolation, generativity versus stagnation, and ego integrity versus despair. Erikson's theory can be seen as a trust-achievement-wholeness cycle repeating twice.
9. Loevinger proposed eight stages of ego development, six of which can occur in adulthood: conformist, conscientious-conformist, conscientious, individualistic, autonomous, and integrated.
10. In general, life transition theories overestimate the commonality of age-linked transitions. Research evidence suggests that a crisis tied to midlife does not occur for most people.

Cognitive Theories

11. Thomae believes that personality changes to the extent that people think change is necessary. Evidence from research supports the view that the degree of stability depends on personal perception and life stress.
12. Whitbourne believes that people have a life-span construct: a unified sense of their past, present, and future. The components of the life-span construct are the scenario (expectations of the future) and the life story (a personal narrative history).
13. Self-concept is the organized, coherent, integrated pattern of self-perception. The events people experience help shape their self-concept.

14. Age differences in possible selves are more apparent in terms of hoped-for self than feared self. While younger and middle-aged adults view themselves as improving, older adults view themselves as declining.

15. Personal control is the degree to which you believe that performance depends on something you do. Age differences in the degree of personal control depend on the domain being studied.

Moral Development

16. Kohlberg's theory focuses on moral reasoning and emphasizes the rationale one gives in response to moral dilemmas rather than the content of the answer.

17. Kohlberg described three levels of moral reasoning: preconventional, conventional, and postconventional. Each level has two stages.

18. Overall cognitive development is related to level of moral reasoning.

19. Cross-cultural and other research supports the view that moral reasoning develops sequentially with age.

20. Gilligan criticizes Kohlberg's theory for gender bias. Research evidence is mixed, however.

21. An age bias may also be present in the types of situations included in the moral dilemmas used to measure moral reasoning.

REVIEW QUESTIONS

Personality Traits Across Adulthood

1. What is a trait?

2. Describe Costa and McCrae's five-dimensional model of personality. How do these dimensions change across adulthood?

3. What evidence is there for change in personality traits in adulthood?

4. What is the developmental trend across adulthood in life satisfaction?

5. How does gender-role identity develop across adulthood?

Ego Development Across Adulthood

6. Describe Jung's theory. What important developmental changes did he describe?

7. Describe Erikson's eight stages of psychosocial development. What cycles have been identified? How has his theory been adapted?

8. Describe Loevinger's theory of ego development, with particular emphasis on the stages seen in adults.

9. What evidence is there that a midlife crisis really exists?

Cognitive Theories

10. Describe Thomae's theory. What do personality stability and change depend on?

11. What is a life-span construct? Create your own scenario and life story.

12. What is self-concept? What shapes it?

13. What are possible selves? What developmental trends have been found in possible selves?

14. What is meant by personal control? How does it differ over age?

Moral Development

15. Describe Kohlberg's theory. What are the various levels and stages in his theory apparently related to?

16. What are some of the criticisms that have been raised against Kohlberg's theory? What evidence is there to support them?

KEY TERMS

conventional level In Kohlberg's theory, the third and fourth stages, which are based on the desire to maintain good interpersonal relations and to comply with society's rules. (284)

ego development An approach to adult personality development based mainly on Jung, Erikson, and Loevinger. This approach assumes a qualitative, stage-like progression. (263)

epigenetic principle In Erikson's theory, the notion that development is guided by an underlying plan in which certain issues have their own particular times of importance. (264)

life-span construct In Whitbourne's theory of personality, the way in which people build a view of who they are. (275)

moral reasoning In Kohlberg's theory, a type of thinking having to do with solving moral dilemmas. (281)

personal control The belief that what one does has an influence on the outcome of an event. (279)

possible selves Aspects of the self-concept involving viewing oneself in the future in both positive and negative ways. (278)

postconventional level In Kohlberg's theory, the highest level of moral reasoning, involving the use of universal principles of justice. (284)

preconventional level In Kohlberg's theory, the lowest level of moral reasoning involving construction of moral rules on the basis of avoiding punishment and the desire for personal pleasure. (281)

self-concept The total aspects of one's personality. (277)

trait A relatively stable, enduring aspect of personality. (255)

ADDITIONAL READING

General overviews of personality research and theories in adulthood can be found in

Wrightsman, L. S. (1988). *Personality development in adulthood.* Beverly Hills, CA: Sage Publications. Easy to moderate reading.

Bengtson, V. L., Reedy, M. N., & Gordon, C. E. (1985). Aging and self-conceptions: Personality processes and social contexts. In J. E. Birren & K. W. Schaie (Eds.), *Handbook of the psychology of aging* (2nd ed., pp. 544–593). New York: Van Nostrand Reinhold. Moderately difficult.

By his own admission, a good introduction to and summary of Erikson's theory is

Erikson, E. H. (1982). *The life cycle completed: Review.* New York: Norton. Easy to moderate.

An excellent example of the multidirectionality of personality development from the cognitive approach and a fine example of the interview method is

Whitbourne, S. K. (1986). *The me I know: A study of adult identity.* New York: Springer-Verlag. Easy to moderate difficulty.

A summary of Kohlberg's theory and Gilligan's objections to it can be found in

Gilligan, C. (1982). *In a different voice: Psychological theory and women's development.* Cambridge, MA: Harvard University Press. Relatively easy reading.

CHAPTER 9

Psychopathology and Treatment

Alberto Giacometti, *The Artist's Mother*, 1950. Oil on canvas, 35⅛″ × 24″. Collection, The Museum of Modern Art, New York. Acquired through the Lillie P. Bliss Bequest.

MARY LIVED BY HERSELF FOR 30 YEARS AFTER her husband died.* For all but the last five years or so of this period, she managed very well. Her children, who live in various parts of the country, visited her occasionally. Friends down the street looked in on her and cooked meals on occasion. Little by little, though, family members began noticing that Mary wasn't quite right; for example, her memory slipped, she sounded confused sometimes, and her moods changed without warning. Some family members attributed these changes to the fact that she was in her 80s. But when they discovered that she sometimes forgot about things in the refrigerator and then ate them even though they had molded and that she occasionally ate other strange things, they began to think differently. The family ultimately realized that she could no longer care for herself and that help had to be found. She moved to a type of group home but continued to deteriorate. She started having trouble remembering things from even a few minutes before. Names of family members became mixed up, at first, and later were forgotten. She began to wander. Finally, Mary had to leave the group home and be placed in a nursing home. The times when she was living in the present became fewer. Her physical abilities continued to deteriorate, until eventually she could not feed herself. Toward the end of her life she could not eat solid food and had to be force-fed. Mary died of Alzheimer's disease after more than 15 years of slow, agonizing decline.

Situations like this happen to families every day. Certainly, behavior like Mary's is not part of normal aging. But for families and even for professionals, it is not until something very strange happens that this realization occurs. When it does, it often results in tumultuous family upheaval. Depending on the particular problem, it may mean

*This case is true, but the names have been changed to protect confidentiality.

deciding whether to institutionalize a spouse or a parent — another very difficult process.

This chapter is about the people who do not make it through adulthood to old age in the normal way. This minority of adults develop disorders that cause them problems in their daily lives and that sometimes rob them of their dignity. The two ailments that present the most difficulty are depression and dementia, so those are the two that we will concentrate on. Other problems are troublesome as well. Some, such as physical difficulties and stress, were dealt with in Chapter 4. Others, such as paranoid disorders, occur rather infrequently.

As we consider different types of psychopathology, we will note how each is diagnosed, what is known about cause and treatment, and what families do when caring for a victim. In the final section we will consider some therapeutic techniques used in community outpatient clinics, nursing homes, and other institutions to try to provide the most supportive environment possible.

PSYCHOPATHOLOGY AND THE ADULT LIFE COURSE

Problems like the ones just described are considered to be sufficiently abnormal to most people to warrant the label "mental illness" or "mental disorder." What distinguishes the study of mental disorders, or *psychopathology*, in adulthood and aging is not so much the content of the behavior as its context, that is, whether it interferes with daily functioning. In order to understand psychopathology as it is manifested in adults of different ages, we must see how it fits into the biopsychosocial perspective outlined in Chapter 1.

Defining Mental Health and Psychopathology

The first issue confronting us in understanding psychopathology is how to distinguish it from mental health. It turns out that this is not easy. Most scholars avoid the issue entirely or try simply to say what mental health is not. What constitutes normal or abnormal behavior is hard to define precisely because expectations and standards for behavior change over time, over situations, and across age groups (Birren & Renner, 1980). Thus, what is considered mental health depends on the circumstances being examined.

Birren and Renner (1980) summarize several arguments concerning the nature of mental health and argue that mentally healthy people have the following characteristics: (1) a positive attitude toward self, (2) an accurate perception of reality, (3) a mastery of the environment, (4) autonomy, (5) personality balance, and (6) growth and self-actualization.

Alternatively, we could consider behaviors that are harmful to oneself or others, that lower one's well-being, and that are perceived as distressing, disrupting, abnormal, or maladaptive (Fry, 1986). Although this approach is used frequently with younger or middle-aged adults, it presents problems when applied to older adults. Some behaviors that would be considered abnormal under this definition may actually be adaptive under some circumstances for many older people (such as isolation, passivity, aggressiveness) (Birren & Renner, 1979). Consequently, an approach to defining abnormal behavior that emphasizes the consideration of behaviors in isolation and from the perspective of younger or middle-aged adults is inadequate for defining abnormal behaviors in the elderly (Gurland, 1973). For example, because of physical, financial, social, health, or other reasons, some older adults do not have the opportunity to master their environment. Depression or hostility may be an appropriate and justified response to such limitations. Moreover, such responses may actually help them deal with their situation more effectively and adaptively.

The important point in differentiating normal from abnormal behavior (or mental health from mental illness) is that behaviors must be interpreted in context. In other words, we must consider what else is happening and how the behavior fits the situation in addition to such factors as the age and other personal characteristics of the individual.

Taking a Biopsychosocial Approach to Psychopathology

Suppose two persons, one young and one old, came into your clinic, each complaining about a lack of sleep, changes in appetite, a lack of energy, and feeling down. What would you say to them?

If you evaluate them in identical ways, you might be headed for trouble. Just as we have seen in other chapters that older and younger adults may think differently or view themselves differently, the meaning of their symptoms and complaints may also differ, even though they appear to be the same. This point is not always incorporated into views of psychopathology. For example, some approaches assume that the same underlying cause is responsible for abnormal or maladaptive behavior regardless of age and that the symptoms of the mental disease are fairly constant across age. Although such models are often used in clinical diagnosis, they are inadequate for understanding psychopathology in old age. Viewing adults' behavior from a biopsychosocial perspective makes a big difference in how we approach psychopathology. Let's see why.

Interpersonal Factors. The interpersonal factors in the biopsychosocial model involve the nature of a person's relationships with other people, especially family members and friends. Important developmental differences occur in the interpersonal realm; for example, younger adults are more likely to be expanding their network of friends, whereas older adults are more likely to be experiencing losses. Thus, feelings of grief or sadness would be considered normal in older adults but might not be in younger adults (Parkes, 1972). Chapter 10 summarizes developmental changes in key relationships that may influence the interpretation of symptoms older adults have.

Intrapersonal Factors. Intrapersonal factors include variables such as age, gender, personality, and cognitive abilities. All of these variables influence the behaviors that people exhibit and affect our interpretation of them. For example, an older African-American woman who lives in a high-crime area may be highly suspicious of other people. To label her behavior paranoid may be inappropriate. In short, we must ask whether the behavior we see is appropriate for a person of this age, sex, personality type, ability level, and so forth.

Biological and Physical Factors. Various chronic diseases, limitations on functioning, and other ailments can provide an explanation of behavior. Because health problems increase with age (see Chapters 3 and 4), we must be increasingly sensitive to them when dealing with older adults. In addition, genetic factors often underlie important problems in old age. For example, many researchers believe Alzheimer's disease has a genetic component, and Huntington's disease is known to have a genetic cause. Physical problems may provide clues about underlying psychological difficulties; marked changes in appetite, for example, may be a symptom of depression. Moreover, some physical problems may even present themselves as psychological ones. For example, extreme irritability can be caused by thyroid problems, and memory loss

can result from certain vitamin deficiencies. In any case, physical health and genetic factors are extremely important dimensions to take into account in diagnosing psychopathology in adults, and should be among the first avenues explored.

Life-Cycle Factors. How one behaves at any point in adulthood is strongly affected by one's past experiences and the issues one is facing. These life-cycle factors must be taken into account in evaluating adults' behaviors. For example, a middle-aged woman who wants to go back to school may not have an adjustment disorder; she may simply want to develop a new aspect of herself. Likewise, an older man who provides vague answers to personal questions may not be resistant; instead, he may be reflecting his generation's reluctance to disclose one's inner self to a stranger. Most important, the meaning of particular symptoms may change with age. For example, problems with early morning awakenings may indicate depression in a young adult, but may be a result of normal aging in an older adult (see Chapter 4).

Issues in Clinical Assessment. Identification of mental disorders rests on accurate evaluation and assessment. Psychologists have a myriad of tests and measures at their disposal for assessing adults' functioning. Such assessment is a major problem if the person is elderly, because virtually all of the tests and measures were developed for use with young and middle-aged adults (Fry, 1986; Zarit, Eiler, & Hassinger, 1985). Very few tests have been standardized with the elderly, which means that we have little idea what a typical older adult would score, let alone one who is experiencing some problem.

An additional obstacle is that the primary diagnostic guide — the *Diagnostic and Statistical Manual (DSM III-R)* published by the American Psychiatric Association (1987) — does not provide different lists of symptoms for disorders based on the age of the individual. This problem stems from the use of the medical model as the basis for the DSM III-R. As we will see in the discussion of depression, for example, the symptom pattern differs for young and old adults in important ways.

Allowances need to be made when assessing older adults. For example, they tend to report their problems in more global terms than younger adults, and they may tire more easily during the assessment session (Fry, 1986). Consequently, adhering to rigid time schedules, limited standardized instructions, and specific wordings of questions may be inappropriate and result in incorrect decisions.

Integrating the Biopsychosocial Approach. A way to avoid many of the difficulties in the assessing of older adults is to integrate the biopsychosocial approach into the assessment process (Fry, 1986). Adopting this integrated model ensures that all relevant dimensions of functioning are assessed, a more holistic approach is adopted, mental health status is put into proper context, assessment sessions are shorter and more flexible, and the assessment addresses the person's ability to function in the natural environment. Additionally, an integrated approach attempts to document the client's problem, its antecedents and consequences, and the client's available resources and motivation; then it seeks to identify appropriate treatment options. The use of this integrated framework will allow the clinician to learn as much as possible about the person's problem, make a more accurate diagnosis, and recommend the most effective treatment.

As we consider specific types of psychopathology, we will emphasize the need to conduct comprehensive, multifaceted assessments based on the biopsychosocial approach. We will see that only when such assessments are made will the diagnosis and recommendations for treatment be appropriate.

DEPRESSION

Depression is one of the most common mental disorders and one of the most treatable (LaRue, Dessonville, & Jarvik, 1985). Estimates are that at any one point between 2% and 5% of all adults have a clinical depressive disorder; the odds across adulthood of ever having a depressive disorder are between 15% and 20% (Nolen-Hoeksema, 1988).

It is difficult to imagine anyone who has not felt down or blue at some point. Indeed, most older adults admit to having some depressive symptoms (Gallagher & Thompson, 1983). This does not mean, however, that most older adults are seriously depressed; researchers estimate that fewer than 1% of adults over age 60 are severely depressed (Blazer, Hughes, & George, 1987). In fact, the rate of severe depression among older adults (1%) is lower than that in younger age groups (roughly 4%) (Nolen-Hoeksema, 1988).

Women who are diagnosed as having a severe depressive disorder outnumber men in young adulthood and old age, but men outnumber women during the latter part of midlife (ages 55 to 64) (Leaf et al., 1988). This difference may reflect a gender bias on the part of clinicians, however, who may simply be more willing to diagnose depression in women (Feinson, 1987; Rodeheaver & Datan, 1988). For example, the much higher rate of diagnosed alcoholism in men during young adulthood and early middle age and a connection between alcoholism and depression suggest that depression in men is a common but undiagnosed problem (Turner, 1987). Other factors that reflect possible gender bias are also associated with the higher rates of clinical depression: being widowed (Vernon & Roberts, 1982); lower economic resources (Hirschenfield & Cross, 1982); and being in poorer health (Salzman & Shader, 1979). These data argue strongly that we need to be cautious in interpreting differential rates of depression in men and women.

TABLE 9.1 Comparison of criteria for major depression: Research Diagnostic Criteria (RDC) and DSM III-R

	RDC for Major Depressive Disorder (MDD)	DSM III-R Criteria for Major Depressive Episode (MDE)
Mood disturbance	One or more distinct periods with dysphoric mood or pervasive loss of interest or pleasure	Dysphoric mood or loss of interest or pleasure in all or almost all usual activities and pastimes
	In both systems, mood disturbance is characterized by descriptors such as depressed, sad, downhearted and blue, hopeless, down in the dumps, don't care anymore, or irritable. While this disturbance does not need to be dominant, it must be prominent and persistent. Momentary shifts from dysphoric mood to another serious emotional state such as anxiety or anger would preclude a diagnosis of major depression.	
Related symptoms	At least five of the following are required as part of the episode and four for probable MDD:	At least four of the following must be present regularly:
	1. poor appetite or weight loss, or increased appetite or weight gain 2. sleep difficulty (insomnia) or sleeping too much (hypersomnia) 3. psychomotor agitation or retardation (but not merely subjective feelings of restlessness or being slowed down) 4. loss of energy, fatigability, or tiredness 5. loss of interest or pleasure in usual activities, or decrease in sexual drive not limited to a period of delusion or hallucinating 6. feelings of worthlessness, self-reproach, or excessive or inappropriate guilt 7. complaints or evidence of diminished ability to think or concentrate (e.g., slowed thinking or indecisiveness) 8. recurrent thoughts of death or suicide, or any suicidal behavior	
Duration	Dysphoric features: 2 weeks for definite; 1–2 weeks for probable. Related symptoms: not specified but presumed at least 2 weeks.	Dysphoric features: not specified but presumed at least 2 weeks. Related symptoms: must be present nearly every day for at least 2 weeks.

(Source: *Clinical Geropsychology: New Directions in Assessment and Treatment* (pp. 14–15) by P. M. Lewinsohn and L. Teri (Eds.), 1983. Elmsford, NY: Pergamon Press. Copyright © 1983 by Pergamon Press, Inc. Reprinted with permission.)

Smallegan (1989) found higher rates of depressive symptoms in whites than in African Americans. In fact, upper-class African Americans reported the lowest level of symptoms of all the groups she studied. Because so few studies have included these individuals, however, Smallegan was unable to offer any explanation of this finding. Clearly, much more research is needed in examining ethnic group differences.

Diagnosis of Depression

The criteria for diagnosing depressive disorders are described in two classification systems: the DSM III-R (American Psychiatric Association, 1987) and the Research Diagnostic Criteria (RDC) (Spitzer, Endicott, & Robins, 1978). Although these two sets of criteria, summarized in Table 9.1, differ somewhat in their specificity, they are similar in viewing

	RDC for Major Depressive Disorder (MDD)	DSM III-R Criteria for Major Depressive Episode (MDE)
Exclusionary criteria	1. None of the following, which suggest schizophrenia, is present: delusions of being controlled, or of thought broadcasting, insertions, or withdrawal nonaffective hallucinations auditory hallucinations more than one month of *no* depressive symptoms but delusions or hallucinations preoccupation with a delusion or hallucination to relative exclusion of other symptoms or concerns definite marked, formal thought disorder 2. Does not meet criteria for schizophrenia, residual type.	1. Preoccupation with a mood-incongruent delusion or hallucination or bizarre behavior cannot be dominant in the clinical picture before or after the occurrence of an affective syndrome. 2. Mood disturbance cannot be superimposed on schizophrenia, schizophreniform disorder, or a paranoid disorder. 3. Organic mental disorder or uncomplicated bereavement is ruled out as a cause of mood disturbance.
Impairment of functioning	Sought or was referred for help during the dysphoric period, took medication, or had impairments in functioning with family, at home, at school, at work, or socially.	Not specified

depression as a multidimensional disturbance in biological, social, and psychological functioning (Gallagher & Thompson, 1983).

General Symptoms. The most prominent feature of clinical depression is **dysphoria**, that is, feeling down, or blue. Importantly, older adults may not label their down feelings as depression but, rather, as "pessimistic" or "helpless" (Fry, 1986). Older adults are also more likely to show signs of apathy, subdued self-deprecation, expressionlessness, and changes in arousal than are younger people (Caird & Judge, 1974; Epstein, 1976). It is common for older depressed individuals to withdraw, not speak to anyone, confine themselves to bed, and not take care of bodily functions. Younger adults may engage in some of these behaviors but to a much lesser extent.

The stereotype that most elderly are depressed is not supported. In fact, there is evidence that the rate of severe depression may decrease in old age.

The second major component of clinical depression is the accompanying physical symptoms. These include insomnia, changes in appetite, diffuse pain, troubled breathing, headaches, fatigue, and sensory loss (Lehmann, 1981). The presence of these physical symptoms in the elderly must be evaluated carefully. As noted in Chapter 4, some sleep disturbances may reflect normative changes that are unrelated to depression; however, regular early morning awakening is consistently related to depression, even in the elderly (Rodin, McAvay, & Timko, 1988). Alternatively, the physical symptoms may reflect an underlying physical disease that is manifested as depression. Indeed, many elderly people admitted to the hospital with depressive symptoms turn out to have previously undiagnosed medical problems that are uncovered only after thorough blood and metabolic tests (Sweer, Martin, Ladd, Miller, & Karpf, 1988). Because the incidence

of hypochondriasis (being overly concerned with one's health) increases with age, care must be taken to make sure that complaints about health are really related to depression (Gallagher & Thompson, 1983). Thoughts about suicide are particularly important, especially in the elderly, and should be considered a serious symptom (Osgood, 1985). Note that feelings one might expect to be evaluated, such as excessive worry or self-pity, are not included in the diagnostic criteria. This is because they are not unique to depression and do not help clinicians discriminate depression from other disorders (Spitzer et al., 1978).

The third characteristic is that the symptoms described must last at least two weeks. This criterion is used to rule out the transient symptoms that are common to all adults, especially after a negative experience such as receiving a rejection letter from a potential employer or getting a speeding ticket.

Fourth, other causes for the observed symptoms must be ruled out. For example, other health problems, neurological disorders, medications, metabolic conditions, alcoholism, or other forms of psychopathology can cause depressive symptoms. These must be considered in order to know how to treat the problem.

Finally, the clinician must determine how the person's symptoms are affecting his or her daily life. Is the ability to interact with other people impaired? Can he or she carry out domestic responsibilities? What about effects on work or school? Is the person taking any medication? Clinical depression involves significant impairment in daily living.

Women and Depressive Symptoms. As noted earlier, women tend to be diagnosed as being depressed more often than men. This has led some researchers to focus specifically on women's experience of depression in order to identify the kinds of symptoms they have. In a series of studies, Newmann, Engel, and Jensen (1990, 1991) looked at the patterns of symptoms women report and how these symptoms change over time. They found two different depressive syndromes and four different but related forms of psychological distress.

The two depressive syndromes differ on whether two key symptoms are present: dysphoria and feelings of guilt or self-blame. They are present in classic clinical depression, but appear to be absent in a version of depression called "the depletion syndrome of the elderly" (Fogel & Fretwell, 1985). Several other symptoms described above are common to the two different types (such as feeling worthless, losing interest in things, and various physical symptoms). Interestingly, four limited forms of psychological distress were found, each being independent of the others: sleep disturbances, loss of energy, loneliness, and self-deprecating attitude. These results clearly show that the symptoms of depression, as well as the syndrome itself, are far more complicated than most people imagine.

In their second study, Newmann and colleagues (1991) showed that the classic depressive syndrome declines in frequency with age whereas the depletion syndrome increases. These findings imply that the age-related declines in the frequency of severe depression discussed earlier probably reflect classic depression. Moreover, these results point to the need for very careful diagnosis of depression in women.

Assessment Scales. Assessing symptoms of depression is often done through the use of self-report scales, such as the Beck Depression Inventory (Beck, Ward, Mendelson, Mock, & Erbaugh, 1961), the Zung Self-Rating Depression Scale (Zung, 1965), the Center for Epidemiological Studies Depression Scale (Radloff, 1977), or standard interviews, such as the Hamilton Rating Scale for Depression (Hamilton, 1967). Because these scales were all developed on younger and middle-aged adults, they are most appropriate for these age groups. The most important difficulty in using these scales with older adults is that they all include several items assessing physical symptoms. Although the presence of such symptoms is usually

indicative of depression in younger adults, as we noted earlier such symptoms may not be related to depression at all in the elderly. For this reason Yesavage and his colleagues (1983) developed the Geriatric Depression Scale (GDS), which focuses exclusively on psychosocial aspects of depression. The GDS also has the advantage of having a simple yes-no response format, making it easier for older people to complete the scale.

An important point to keep in mind about these scales is that the diagnosis of depression should never be made on the basis of a test score alone. As we have seen, the symptoms observed in clinical depression could be indicative of other problems, and symptom patterns are very complex. Only by a thorough assessment of many aspects of physical and psychological functioning can a clinician make an accurate assessment.

Causes of Depression

Several theories about the causes of depression have been proposed. They can be grouped into two main categories: biological (or physiological) theories and psychosocial theories.

Biological and Physiological Theories. The most popular of the biological and physiological theories links depression to imbalances in or insufficient supplies of particular neurotransmitters (Maas, 1978; see Chapter 3). As we noted in Chapter 3, neurotransmitters are chemicals that provide the communication links between the neurons, or brain cells. Because most neurotransmitter levels decline with age, some researchers postulate that depression in the elderly is more likely to be a biochemical problem (Gerner & Jarvik, 1984). However, the link between neurotransmitter levels and depression is still unclear. The problem is that response to drug therapies has not yet been shown to be directly related to changes in neurotransmitter levels.

Other researchers argue that depression may be due to abnormal functioning of the hemispheres in the brain (Weingartner & Silberman, 1982). Neuropsychological tests, that is, tests that measure brain function, and electroencephalograms (EEGs) document abnormalities and impairments in the right hemisphere of persons diagnosed as having depression (Davidson, Schwartz, Saron, Bennett, & Goleman, 1979).

Depression is also linked to physical illness, especially in the elderly. Salzman and Shader (1979) and Verwoerdt (1980, 1981) note that there is considerable evidence that worsening physical health in the elderly often goes hand in hand with worsening symptoms of depression; expressions of guilt, crying, irritability, anxiety, and dependency are common. Among the physical diseases that often include obvious symptoms of depression are dementia, brain tumors, cerebrovascular disease, hypothyroidism, and cardiovascular disease (Fry, 1986). Given the connection between physical diseases and depressive symptoms, it is clearly important for the diagnostic process to include a complete physical examination.

Psychosocial Theories. By far, the most widely held belief is that depression is due to some psychologically traumatic event. Several themes emerge in this literature: loss, negative life events, internalization, and internal belief systems.

The most common theme of psychosocial theories of depression is *loss* (Butler & Lewis, 1982). Bereavement has been the type of loss receiving the most attention, but the loss of anything considered personally important could also be a trigger. Gaylord and Zung (1987) identified eight types of loss that may result in dysphoria or depression: loss of a loved one; loss of health or physical attractiveness; loss of job or caregiving roles; loss of personal possessions; loss of life style; failure of plans or ventures; loss of group membership or status; and loss of a pet. Moreover, these losses may be real and irrevocable, threatened and potential, or imaginary

and fantasized. In addition, the likelihood that these losses will occur varies with age. Middle-aged adults are more likely to experience the loss of physical attractiveness, for example, whereas older adults are more likely to experience the loss of a loved one.

The belief that *negative life events* cause depression is widely held. Indeed, major negative life events often trigger feelings of sadness and dysphoria. Additionally, some theorists view depression as resulting from a search for the self that uncovers negative or missing aspects of identity. These issues are especially important in understanding depression in midlife. It may be that events surrounding changes in employment and family result in a questioning of self, which in turn may result in dysphoria.

However, the research evidence suggests that events probably do not cause cases of severe depression (Fry, 1986; Gaylord & Zung, 1987). The lack of evidence for an event trigger for severe depression despite popular belief to the contrary probably reflects a difference of perspective. That is, feeling down is extremely common after experiencing a traumatic event; as noted in Chapter 13, it is a universal experience during the grieving process. When people experience these feelings, they may have a tendency to label themselves as "depressed." But as we have seen, feelings alone are not enough to indicate severe clinical depression. What happens following a significant loss is a much milder form of depression, which may in fact be a normal response to the situation (Blazer & Williams, 1980).

Internalization is a theme expressed in psychoanalytic theory. Freud viewed depression (or melancholia, in his terminology) as a profoundly painful dejection, cessation of interest in the outside world, loss of the capacity to love, and lowering of self-regarding feelings that resulted in severe self-reproaches (Mendelson, 1982). For Freud, this loss becomes internalized, and the displeasure felt toward someone else becomes focused on oneself.

Thus, in psychoanalytic terms, depression is hostility turned inward. The loss of self-esteem is also an important part of psychoanalytic theories of depression. In general, this loss comes from faulty aspects of how one presents oneself, the superego, the ideal self, and self-critical ego functions (Mendelson, 1982).

Internal belief systems underlie behavioral and cognitive theories of depression. This approach points to how people interpret uncontrollable events based on their internal belief system as causes (Nolen-Hoeksema, 1988). The idea behind these theories is that experiencing unpredictable and uncontrollable events instills a feeling of helplessness, which results in depression. Additionally, perceiving the cause of negative events as some inherent aspect of the self that is permanent and pervasive also plays an important role in causing feelings of helplessness and hopelessness. In short, according to this approach people who are depressed believe that they are personally responsible for their plight, that things are unlikely to get better, and that their whole life is a shambles.

One explanation for lower rates of depression in the elderly is based on the cognitive behavioral approach. Specifically, it is argued that older adults face fewer aversive and uncontrollable traumatic events than most stereotypes of aging suggest (Nolen-Hoeksema, 1988). It is also possible that there are cohort differences operating (Klerman, 1986); older generations have better strategies for dealing with their own depression, such as engaging in activities designed to get their minds off the problem. In some cases, changing older adults' negative attitudes about the acceptability of seeking help from mental health professionals for depression may be necessary (Nolen-Hoeksema, 1988).

Despite numerous studies attempting to find a psychological cause of depression, no definitive links have yet been established. What we know at this point is that certain experiences of loss and certain belief systems are often found in people with depression. However, we cannot conclude that

such things actually caused the person to become depressed. To establish those connections we will need carefully conducted longitudinal research. Finally, we need to remember from the biopsychosocial model that psychological events are not independent of biological ones. That is, experiencing loss could have implications for our neurotransmitter balance, which in turn could be a cause of depression.

Treatment of Depression

As we have seen, depression is a complex problem that can result from a wide variety of causes. We have also noted that depression can vary in severity — from fairly normal responses to traumatic events to very serious, life-threatening lack of concern for oneself. Thompson and Gallagher (1986) note that all forms of depression benefit from therapy. For the severe forms, it may be necessary to administer medications. In some cases of severe, long-term depression, electroconvulsive therapy may be required. For the less severe forms of depression, and usually in conjunction with medication for severe depression, there are various forms of psychotherapy.

Drug Therapy. Two families of drugs are used to combat severe depression. The most commonly used medications are the **heterocyclic antidepressants (HCAs)**. HCAs were formerly known as tricyclic antidepressants, but the recent marketing of monocyclic, bicyclic, and tetracyclic antidepressants led to the change in terminology (Berkow, 1987). Although HCAs are effective in at least 70% of cases, they are most effective with younger and middle-aged individuals (Berkow, 1987; Epstein, 1978). The main problem with HCAs in older age groups is that the elderly are more likely to have medical conditions or to be taking other medications that inhibit their use. For example, people who are taking antihypertensive medication or who have any of a number of metabolic problems should not take the tricyclic HCAs (Baldessarini, 1978). Moreover, the risk for side effects beyond the typical dry mouth reaction are much greater in the elderly (Epstein, 1978), although some of the newer HCAs have significantly lower risk. Because HCAs must be taken for approximately a week before the person feels relief, compliance with the therapy is sometimes difficult.

A second group of drugs that relieves depression is the **MAO inhibitors**, so named because they inhibit MAO, a substance that interferes with the transmission of signals between neurons. MAO inhibitors are generally less effective than the tricyclics and can produce deadly side effects (Walker & Brodie, 1980). Specifically, they interact with foods that contain tyramine or dopamine — mainly cheddar cheese but also others, such as wine and chicken liver — to create dangerously, and sometimes fatally, high blood pressure. MAO inhibitors are used with extreme caution in the United States, usually only after HCAs have proved ineffective. Research on other MAO inhibitors that have reduced risk is under way (Berkow, 1987).

If periods of depression alternate with periods of mania or extremely high levels of activity, a diagnosis of **bipolar disorder** is made (American Psychiatric Association, 1987). Bipolar disorder is characterized by unpredictable, often explosive mood swings as the person cycles between extreme depression and extreme activity. The drug therapy of choice for bipolar disorder is lithium (Berkow, 1987), which came into widespread use in the early 1970s. Lithium is extremely effective in controlling the mood swings, although we do not completely understand why it works. The use of lithium *must* be monitored very closely, because the difference between an effective dose and a toxic dose is extremely small (Mahoney, 1980). Because lithium is a salt, it raises the blood pressure, making it dangerous to use with individuals who have hypertension or kidney disease. The effective dosage level for lithium decreases with age; physicians unaware

of this change run the risk of inducing an overdose, especially in the elderly (Maletta, 1984). Compliance is also a problem, because no improvement is seen for between 4 and 10 days after the initial dose (Berkow, 1987) and because many individuals with bipolar disorder do not like having their moods controlled by medication (Jamison, Gerner, & Goodwin, 1979).

Electroconvulsive Therapy. Electroconvulsive therapy (ECT) is viewed by many people as an extreme and even cruel form of therapy. This perspective was probably justified in the past, when ECT was used as depicted in books and movies such as *One Flew Over the Cuckoo's Nest*. The popular perception is that ECT is used only for the most extreme mentally disturbed individuals; it was this view that forced Thomas Eagleton to withdraw his candidacy for the vice-presidency of the United States in 1972.

In fact, ECT is an extremely effective treatment for severe depression, especially in people whose depression has lasted a long time, are suicidal, have serious physical problems caused by their depression, and do not respond to medications (Salzman, 1975; Weiner, 1979). ECT is now tightly regulated, and it can be used only after review of each individual case (Walker & Brodie, 1980). ECT involves passing a current of 70 to 150 volts from one of the person's temples to the other for less than 1 second (Weiner, 1979). This results in a seizure similar to that experienced in severe forms of epilepsy. To prevent the person from injury, he or she is given a strong muscle relaxant. The effective voltage appears to increase with age, which means that treatments need to be spaced further apart and the person monitored more closely (Weiner, 1979).

ECT has some advantages (Salzman, 1975). Unlike antidepressant medications, it has immediate effects. Usually, only a few treatments are required, compared with long-term maintenance schedules for drugs. But ECT also has some side effects. Memory of the ECT treatment itself is lost.

Memory of other recent events is temporarily disrupted, but it usually returns within a week or two (Salzman, 1975).

The use of ECT with older adults was long thought to be very risky. However, research demonstrates that with careful monitoring the severely depressed elderly benefit considerably. Indeed, ECT may be safer for older adults with heart disease than HCA therapy (Salzman, 1975).

Psychotherapy. Psychotherapy is an approach to treatment based on the idea that talking to a therapist about one's problems can help. Often, psychotherapy can be very effective by itself in treating depression. In cases of severe depression, psychotherapy may be combined with drug or ECT therapy. Of more than a hundred different types of psychotherapy, two general approaches seem to work best with depressed people: behavior therapy and cognitive therapy.

The fundamental idea in **behavior therapy** is that depressed people receive too few rewards or reinforcements from their environment (Lewinsohn, 1975). Thus, the goal of behavior therapy is to get them to increase the good things that happen to them. Often, this can be accomplished by having people increase their activities; if they do more, the likelihood is that more good things will happen. Additionally, behavior therapy seeks to get people to decrease the number of negative thoughts they have, because depressed people tend to look at the world pessimistically. They get little pleasure out of activities that nondepressed people enjoy a great deal: seeing a funny movie, playing a friendly game of volleyball, having dinner with friends, or being with a lover.

To increase activity and decrease negative thoughts, behavior therapists usually assign homework — tasks that force clients to practice the principles they are learning during the therapy sessions (Gallagher & Thompson, 1983; Lewinsohn, 1975). This may involve going out more to meet people, joining new clubs, or just learning how to enjoy

life. Family members are instructed to ignore negative statements made by the depressed person and to reward positive self-statements with attention, praise, or even money.

An effective approach that incorporates Lewinsohn's (1975) behavioral approach but is presented in a less traditional therapeutic setting is the *Coping with Depression Course* (Lewinsohn, Steinmetz, Antonuccio, & Teri, 1984). The course adopts a psychoeducational approach, in that the principles of behavior therapy are embedded in an educational program. The advantage of a psychoeducational approach is that the stigma of receiving traditional psychotherapy is removed, since classes are held in a workshop setting. However, research indicates that the course is as effective as traditional behavior therapy for mildly and moderately depressed adults of all ages (Gallagher & Thompson, 1983).

Cognitive therapy for depression is based on the idea that depression results from maladaptive beliefs or cognitions about oneself. From this perspective, a depressed individual views the self as inadequate and unworthy, the world as insensitive and ungratifying, and the future as bleak and unpromising (Beck, Rush, Shaw, & Emery, 1979). In cognitive therapy the person is taught how to recognize these thoughts, which have become so automatic and ingrained that other perspectives are not seen. Once this awareness has been achieved, the person learns how to evaluate the self, world, and future more realistically. These goals may be accomplished through homework assignments similar to those used in behavior therapy. These often involve reattribution of the causes of events, examining the evidence before drawing conclusions, listing the pros and cons of maintaining an idea, and examining the consequences of that idea. Finally, individuals are taught to change the basic beliefs that are responsible for their negative thoughts. For example, people who believe that they have been failures all their lives or that they are unlovable are taught how to use their newfound knowledge to achieve more realistic appraisals of themselves (Gallagher & Thompson, 1983).

Cognitive therapy alone is also an effective treatment for mildly and moderately depressed adults of all ages. However, the process of change may take longer in older adults, who may also need more encouragement along the way. Despite the need for extra support, older adults are able to maintain the gains made during therapy as well as younger and middle-aged adults (Gallagher & Thompson, 1983).

The goal of **psychoanalytic therapy** is to alter the personality structure so that the individual can function more adaptively. Because the underlying cause of psychopathology is thought to lie in relationships earlier in life, much of psychoanalytic therapy deals with feelings about conflicts in past events and relationships. To achieve the goal of adaptive functioning, one of two approaches is used. In the first, *insight therapy*, the therapist helps the client gain insight into the maladaptive defenses and character defects causing the problem. Feelings about events and relationships earlier in life are discussed, and potential solutions are explored. In the second approach the goal is not insight but, rather, support of existing coping mechanisms to better face current problems. In *supportive therapy*, the strengthening of adaptive defenses and the replacement of maladaptive defenses is of primary concern. Both insight and supportive therapies are effective with adults of all ages.

Two versions of psychoanalytic therapy particularly useful with older adults are *life review therapy* and *reminiscence*. The goal of both therapies is to use the memories of previous events and relationships as ways to confront and resolve conflicts. Life review therapy and reminiscence can be done individually or in groups, and they can be unstructured or structured (by using particular topics as triggers). Although both approaches have become very popular and are claimed to be effective (Kaminsky, 1978; Lesser, Lazarus, Frankel, & Havasy,

1981), why they work and how remembering the past relates to specific cognitive and emotional processes are unknown (Merriam, 1980).

Suicide

Although one does not have to be depressed to commit suicide, depression is the most common reason (Osgood, 1985). Suicide represents a logical extension of depressed people's belief that they are unworthy, the future is bleak, and the world no longer has a place for them.

Every year, roughly 25,000 people in the United States commit suicide. Researchers believe that the true rate is much higher (Osgood, 1985), because most officials will rule that a death is accidental if at all possible to save the family from the stigma associated with suicide. Drug overdoses are often considered to be accidental, for example, as are most single-car accidents. The number of actual suicides could possibly be as high as 100,000 per year (Stenback, 1980).

Suicide and Age. The relationship between suicide rates and age changed considerably between the early 1960s and the 1980s (see Figure 9.1). Suicide rates for young adults (ages 20 to 35) showed a considerable increase, from between 8 and 12 per 100,000 people in 1962 to about 16 per 100,000 in 1980. However, suicide rates for middle-aged and elderly adults were much higher in 1962 (ranging from 20 to 29 per 100,000) than in 1980 (ranging from 15 to 19 per 100,000) (National Center for Health Statistics, 1988). Reasons for the changes are unclear, especially since some authors report contradictory data concerning the elderly (Osgood, 1985).

What is clear about the relationship between suicide and age is that older white males commit suicide at a much higher rate than any other group, perhaps as much as 3 times more than white males

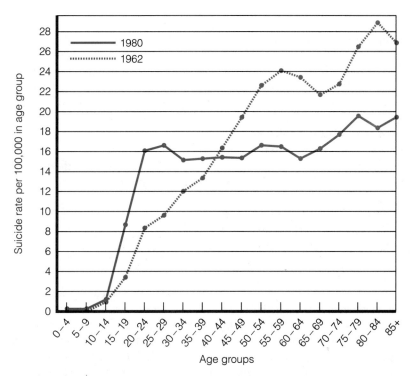

FIGURE 9.1 Cohort differences in suicide rates. Note that the rates of adolescent and young adult suicide were much higher in 1980, but the rates for other adult age groups were much lower.

(Source: National Center for Health Statistics.)

at age 20 (Sainsbury, 1986). Comparable statistics in other countries reveals an even wider gap: In Japan, the rate for those over 75 is 5 times higher than that for those aged 15 to 24, and in France the rate is 6 times higher (Palmore & Maeda, 1985).

In understanding these age differences, we must keep several important points in mind. Many more young people attempt suicide than actually succeed, with the ratio of unsuccessful attempts to successes about 7:1 (Stenback, 1980). Around midlife, however, the ratio switches, so that by old age successes outnumber unsuccessful attempts by

nearly 8:1 (Sendbeuhler & Goldstein, 1977). This switch has led many theorists to believe that suicide attempts by younger people are more often cries for help or acts of hostility directed at others, such as parents or lovers. In contrast, older adults seldom attempt suicide as a means of getting attention; rather, they are clearly interested in killing themselves and are far more deadly in their methods (Osgood, 1985).

The older adults who commit suicide are also much more likely to be physically ill than are younger suicide victims. About half of the elderly men and about one third of elderly women who commit suicide are seriously ill, many with cancer or a disease that affects the brain (Whitlock, 1986).

Suicide, Ethnicity, and Gender. Overall, white males have the highest rate of successful suicide. For white males, late adolescence and the first few years of adulthood show a relatively high rate, falling slightly through midlife and rising dramatically in late life. African-American and Hispanic males also show an early peak, but their rate stays substantially lower than white males in old age. Asian-American males show peak suicide rates in old age but at a lower level than whites. White women show a slight increase in suicide rate in midlife, followed by a decrease through old age. Finally, women in other ethnic groups have a low rate of suicide throughout adulthood.

The substantial difference in overall suicide rates between men and women may be misleading (Williams, 1977). More women than men *attempt* suicide, but more men than women *succeed* in killing themselves, primarily because men tend to use more lethal means (such as guns and jumping from high places), compared with women, who prefer less lethal methods (such as poison or sleeping pills).

No adequate explanation of women's suicide statistics has been offered. The notion that the peak in white women's rate during midlife reflects the empty nest syndrome is inadequate, because it fails to explain why women in other ethnic groups are able to experience the same event with no corresponding increase in suicide. Much more research needs to be done to understand these issues.

Depression Summary

Depression is a common form of psychopathology throughout adulthood. Symptom patterns are complex, especially among women, and are often due to underlying physical health problems. Adopting the biopsychosocial model helps put this complexity into perspective, as it emphasizes the interactions among physical, psychological, and life-course influences on feelings and behavior. Although behavioral forms of psychotherapy work quite well with adults of all ages, some serious forms of depression may require medication or other forms of treatment. One outcome of serious depression — suicide — is especially common in older men. Reasons for this age-related increase remain unknown.

ANXIETY DISORDERS

Imagine that you are about to give a speech before an audience of 500 people. In the last few minutes before your address, you begin to feel nervous, your heart starts to pound, and your palms get sweaty. These feelings, common even to veteran speakers, are similar to those experienced by individuals with anxiety disorders; a group of conditions that are based on fear or uneasiness. Anxiety disorders include anxiety states, in which feelings of severe anxiety occur with no specific trigger; phobic disorders, characterized by irrational fears of objects or circumstances; and obsessive-compulsive disorders, in which thoughts or actions are repeatedly performed for no apparent reason in order to lower anxiety. Anxiety disorders are diagnosed in as many as 10% of elderly women and 5% of elderly men, which is somewhat higher than in younger adults (Cohen, 1990).

Symptoms of Anxiety Disorders

Common to all of the anxiety disorders are physical changes that interfere with social functioning, personal relationships, or work. These physical changes include dry mouth, sweating, dizziness, upset stomach, diarrhea, insomnia, hyperventilation, chest pain, choking, frequent urination, headaches, and a sensation of a lump in the throat (Fry, 1986). These symptoms occur in adults of all ages, but they are particularly common in older adults due to loss of health, relocation stress, isolation, fear of losing control over their lives, or guilt resulting from feelings of hostility toward family and friends (Fry, 1986). Himmelfarb (1984) demonstrated the importance of these factors in understanding anxiety disorders in the elderly. After Himmelfarb statistically controlled the relationship between age and anxiety for such factors as health, quality of housing, and social support, the relationship was substantially reduced. Thus, we must be cautious in interpreting reports that the frequency of anxiety disorders increases with age. Such reports may be indicative of other, more important, factors.

Another important issue concerning anxiety disorders in older adults is that anxiety may be an appropriate response to the situation. For example, helplessness anxiety is generated by a potential or actual loss of control or mastery (Verwoerdt, 1981). Additionally, a series of severe negative life experiences may result in a person's reaching the breaking point and appearing highly anxious. Many older adults who show symptoms of anxiety disorder have underlying health problems that may be responsible for the symptoms. In all cases the anxious behavior should be investigated first as an appropriate response that may not require intervention. The important point is to evaluate the older adult's behavior in context.

Treatment of Anxiety Disorders

Both drug therapy and psychotherapy are used to treat anxiety disorders. **Benzodiazepines** are the most widely prescribed medications for anxiety (Fry, 1986). They include such drugs as Valium, Librium, Serax, and Ativan. Although benzodiazepines are effective with adults of all ages, they must be used very carefully with older adults. Effective dosage levels are lower in the elderly, and the potential for side effects is much greater. Most important, these drugs can cause decreased cognitive functioning, which may be mistaken for early dementia. In general, the benzodiazepines may cause drowsiness, loss of coordination, headaches, and lower energy levels. Moreover, because of the potential for addiction, the long-term use of these drugs should be avoided.

In most cases the treatment of choice for anxiety disorders is psychotherapy. A broad range of approaches is effective with adults of all ages. Of particular note are the relaxation techniques described in Chapter 4. These procedures help the anxious person learn to relax and to control the feelings of anxiety before they get out of hand. Other behavioral techniques such as systematic desensitization are especially effective with phobias. The advantage of these psychotherapeutic techniques is that they usually only involve a few sessions, have high rates of success, and offer clients procedures that they can take with them. Best of all, they have no long-term side effects, unlike their medical counterparts.

SCHIZOPHRENIA AND PARANOID DISORDERS

Some forms of psychopathology, referred to as psychoses, involve losing touch with reality and the disintegration of personality. Two behaviors that occur in some forms of these disorders are *delusions*, which are belief systems not based on reality, and *hallucinations*, distortions in perception. Two types of psychoses that occur in adulthood are schizophrenia and paranoid disorders.

Schizophrenia

Schizophrenia is characterized by the severe impairment of thought processes, including the content and style of thinking; distorted perceptions; loss of touch with reality; a distorted sense of self; and abnormal motor behavior (American Psychiatric Association, 1987). Individuals with schizophrenia show these abnormal behaviors in several ways: bizarre delusions (for example, that they are Jesus or that they are being spied on); loose associations (such as saying that they have a secret meeting with the president of the United States in the local bowling alley); hearing voices that tell them what to do; believing that they can read other people's minds; or believing that their body is changing into something else. Additionally, schizophrenic individuals tend to show very little or highly inappropriate emotionality (laughing hysterically at the news of a major tragedy, for instance). They are often confused about their own identity, have difficulty working toward a goal, and tend to withdraw from social contact.

Most researchers believe that schizophrenia occurs most often before age 45 (Post, 1987). When schizophrenic symptoms occur in late life, there is some question about whether they represent true schizophrenia, a paranoid disorder, or a form of dementia. These researchers assert that older adults tend to show different symptoms than younger or middle-aged adults; older adults' delusions focus more on sex and personal possessions, whereas younger adults' delusions are more likely to involve mystical or religious themes. Some researchers disagree, however, maintaining that there are few differences with age in the numbers of individuals who experience schizophrenic symptoms and no differences in the nature of the symptoms (Blazer, George, & Hughes, 1988). More research is needed to clarify the issue.

What is clear is that ultimately people with schizophrenia tend to show one of three outcomes. Some experience only one episode and are hospitalized for a brief period. Others show a gradual decrease in symptoms over time, perhaps as a result of living in institutions. Still others have symptoms that remain constant over their entire adult life span. In general, most older schizophrenic adults need some sort of structured care. The trend toward deinstitutionalization in the United States over the past few decades has resulted in many older schizophrenic adults ending up either in nursing homes, where the staff may have neither the training nor the time to respond effectively, or, unfortunately, as homeless street people.

Paranoid Disorders

The hallmark of paranoid disorders is a well-formed delusion. Most often, these delusions involve persecution ("People are out to get me"). The distinction between paranoid disorders and schizophrenia is fuzzy; indeed, one type of schizophrenia is termed paranoid type. In general, it is believed that hallucinations, loose associations, and absent or inappropriate emotions do not occur in paranoid disorders (American Psychiatric Association, 1987).

Beliefs in delusions can result in anger, resentment, or even violent acts. Because paranoid individuals are extremely suspicious and rarely seek help on their own, such people tend to come to the attention of authorities after having repeated run-ins with the police or neighbors, starting legal proceedings against others on mysterious grounds, or registering complaints about fictitious or distorted events.

Paranoid disorders are relatively rare among adults of all ages (about 1%) but tend to increase slightly with age (Post, 1987). Paranoid symptoms are commonly associated with dementia, as discussed later, as well as with the use of amphetamines. Fry (1986) notes that three conditions are associated with the onset of paranoid disorders at all ages but are especially important in late life: social isolation, marginal life circumstances and financial losses, and sensory losses — especially hearing loss. Some researchers argue that paranoid disorders in the elderly should not be viewed as illnesses at all but, rather, as minor maladjustments that should be considered only for their nuisance value. Due to these factors, the diagnosis of paranoid disorders needs to rule out other possible explanations for the behaviors.

Treatment of Schizophrenia and Paranoid Disorders

Traditionally, treatment of schizophrenia and paranoid disorders has emphasized medication. For schizophrenia, drug therapy consists of *antipsychotics*, medications that are believed to work on the dopamine system (see Chapter 4). Some of the more commonly used antipsychotics are Haldol, Thorazine, and Mellaril. These medications must be used with extreme caution in adults of all ages due to the risk of serious toxic side effects, especially the loss of motor control. Despite these risks antipsychotics are often used in nursing homes and other institutions as tranquilizing agents to control problem patients.

Drug treatment for paranoid disorders includes antipsychotics for the most severe cases and benzodiazepines for milder cases. Neither approach, however, is consistently effective.

In general, schizophrenic and paranoid individuals are difficult to treat in psychotherapy. The severe thought disturbances characteristic of schizophrenia make it difficult for therapists to work with clients. Because of their extreme suspiciousness, paranoid individuals may be reluctant to cooperate in psychotherapy. If these barriers can be overcome, however, there is some evidence that supportive therapy may be effective (Fry, 1986).

The goals of therapy for schizophrenic individuals tend to be adaptive rather than curative, that is, helping these people adapt to daily living rather than attempting to cure them. In contrast, the goal for paranoid individuals is more likely to be curative, that is, a significant reduction in delusionary thought, because the source of the delusions in many of these individuals is a lack of stimulation.

DEMENTIA

Probably no other condition associated with aging is more feared than **dementia**. In dementia people may literally lose their mind, being reduced from complex, thinking, feeling human beings to confused, vegetative victims unable even to recognize their spouse and children. Approximately 4.4 million older Americans, or roughly 15% of people over age 65, have some type of dementing disorder (Davies, 1988). Estimates are that the number may double in the next 50 years due to the increase in very old adults (Crook, 1987). Fewer than 1% of the people are afflicted at age 65, but the incidence rises sharply to 20% of those over 80.

Although there is a real basis for fearing dementia, it is important to realize that the vast majority of older adults are not demented. For many people, it is the fear of dementia that is the most serious problem; every time they misplace their keys they are apt to view it as a symptom of eventual dementia. It is hard to know how many older adults have unstated fears because they can no longer remember things in the same ways they did when they were younger. But as noted in Chapter 6, memory abilities show some normative changes with age. Consequently, it is important to realize that what many people believe are signs that they are becoming demented are actually quite normal.

The Family of Dementias

The term *dementia* does not refer to a specific disease but, rather, to a family of diseases that have similar symptoms. About a dozen forms of dementia have been identified. All are characterized by cognitive and behavioral deficits involving some form of permanent damage to the brain. Because dementia involves identifiable damage to the brain, it is also one of the diseases termed *organic mental disorders*. These criteria mean that dementia involves severe cognitive and behavioral decline and is not caused by a rapid onset of a toxic substance or by infection (American Psychiatric Association, 1987).

Dementias can be classified in several ways. For many years the age of the patient at diagnosis was used as the basis for classification. Dementias diagnosed in people younger than 60 to 65 years old were termed *presenile*, and those diagnosed in people older than 60 to 65 were termed *senile dementia*. Over the past two decades, however, this terminology has been declining in popularity and meaning, largely because new discoveries are revealing that age makes little difference in the types of underlying neurological changes (Crook, 1987). Thus, the trend is to refer to the various diseases by name rather than by the terms *presenile* and *senile*.

A second way to group dementias is more useful and important. Some dementias can be treated effectively, and a few can even be reversed. This distinction between reversible and irreversible dementias has profound implications for the patient.

Reversible dementia refers to a loosely defined set of disorders that are characterized by cognitive difficulties but that are treatable (Zarit & Zarit, 1983). **Delirium** is characterized by impaired awareness of self and surroundings, attention deficits, tendencies toward hallucinations and delusions, disorientation, changes in alertness, disturbed sleep patterns, and rapid changes in symptoms and their severity; memory may be affected (Lipowski, 1980). The common underlying factor is a disruption of cerebral metabolism; susceptibility to such metabolic disruptions increases with age. Indeed, the National Institute of Aging (1980) emphasizes that almost any internal disturbance can lead to cognitive symptoms in older adults.

Common causes of delirium include the toxic effects of medications (see Table 9.2) or drug interactions, infections, electrolyte imbalances, malnutrition, and potassium deficits. Symptoms may also appear following surgery, fractures, head injuries, changes in the environment, or the death of a close relative. Depression may manifest itself as cognitive impairment (Wells, 1979). The important point is that cognitive symptoms, especially in an older adult, do not necessarily indicate an untreatable, irreversible disease; careful diagnosis is critical. Unfortunately, such careful diagnoses are often unavailable because of the lack of physicians who specialize in geriatric medicine. As a result many older adults are misdiagnosed as having Alzheimer's disease when they actually have a treatable disorder such as delirium or depression. Additionally, physicians who are not geriatric specialists often dismiss serious cognitive or behavioral symptoms as part of normal aging, which they clearly are not.

In this section we will focus on dementias that are irreversible and degenerative. The most common and widely known of these is Alzheimer's disease, but others are important as well: multi-infarct dementia, Parkinson's disease, Pick's disease, Creutzfeld-Jakob disease, Huntington's disease, and normal-pressure hydrocephalus.

Alzheimer's Disease

Alzheimer's disease is the most common form of progressive, degenerative, and fatal dementia, accounting for perhaps as many as 70% of all cases of dementia (Davies, 1988). We have only recently

---

TABLE 9.2 Drugs that may cause cognitive deficits as side effects

---

Antidepressants used to treat depression

Benzodiazepines used to treat anxiety disorders

Bromocriptine used to treat Parkinson's disease

Carbamazepine used to treat seizure disorders

Cimetidine used to treat ulcers

Digoxin used to treat congestive heart failure and cardiac arrhythmias

Lithium used to treat bipolar disorder

Meclizine used to prevent dizziness or motion sickness

Neuroleptics used to treat psychotic disorders or severe behavior problems

Phenobarbitol used to treat seizure disorders

Phenytoin used to treat seizure disorders

Ranitidine used to treat ulcers

Scopolamine often used before surgery

---

realized how common Alzheimer's disease is, however. When Alois Alzheimer first described the sequence of changes in 1907, he was referring to a person 51 years old. For the next 60 years physicians believed that the disease was very rare and that it was a form of presenile dementia. It was not until Tomlinson, Blessed, and Roth (1970) showed that the same kinds of changes occurred in both early onset and late onset of the disease that physicians realized that age was not a factor. As a result virtually all that we know about Alzheimer's disease has been learned since 1970, with new discoveries coming almost daily.

The rapid growth in awareness that Alzheimer's disease is a major health problem resulted in the formation of the Alzheimer's Association in 1980. The association serves as a national advocacy group, sponsors workshops and research into the causes and treatment of the disease, and provides support groups for family caregivers. Nearly 200 chapters have been formed in communities throughout the United States, with roughly 1,000 family support groups (Lombardo, 1988). Another important function of the association is to provide information; its book *Understanding Alzheimer's Disease* (Aronson, 1988) provides a nontechnical summary of the disease and the complex family, ethical, and legal issues involved in it.

Neurological Changes in Alzheimer's Disease. The changes in the brain that characterize Alzheimer's disease are microscopic. This means that definitive diagnosis of the disease can be done only at autopsy; brain biopsies are an alternative, but the risks are so high that they are rarely performed (Crook, 1987). These progressive changes eventually cause so much destruction of the brain that the person dies. The microscopic changes that define Alzheimer's disease are neurofibrillary tangles, neuritic plaques, and granulovacuolar degeneration.

I thought my wife was just forgetting things.

Then she forgot my name.

ALZ EIMER'S

© 1988 Alzheimer's Disease and Related Disorders Association, Inc.

Someone to Stand By You.

The Alzheimer's Association is a nationwide group dedicated to providing information and support to family members of victims. For information on the association and the chapter nearest you, call the toll-free number: 1-800-272-3900.

Neurofibrillary tangles (see Chapter 3) are accumulations of pairs of filaments in the neuron that become wrapped around each other; when examined under a microscope, these paired filaments look like intertwined spirals. Neurofibrillary tangles occur in several areas of the brain, and the number of tangles is directly related to the severity of symptoms (Farmer, Peck, & Terry, 1976). *Neuritic plaques* (see Chapter 3) are spherical structures consisting of a core of **amyloid**, a protein, surrounded by degenerated fragments of dying or dead neurons. The plaques are also found in various

parts of the brain and are related to the severity of the disease (Blessed et al., 1968). Degeneration of neurons in some areas of the brain results in the formation of vacuoles, or spaces that become filled with fluid and granular material. Although *granulovacuolar degeneration* is a defining characteristic of Alzheimer's disease, its relationship to the severity of the disease is still unknown.

In addition to these three changes, atrophy of various parts of the brain has been found in Alzheimer's disease. However, brain atrophy is not a reliable indicator, since it is associated not only with Alzheimer's disease but also with many other diseases as well as normal aging (Crook, 1987).

Considerable research has uncovered specific deficits in neurotransmitters. Most notable is a marked decrease in the enzyme *choline acetyltransferase*, a marker for acetylcholine, a neurotransmitter involved in learning and memory (Davies & Maloney, 1976). The decline in acetylcholine appears to be caused mainly by the degeneration of the *nucleus basalis of Meynert* and surrounding structures in the base of the brain (Dekker, Connor, & Thal, 1991). These changes may be the cause of the drastic declines in cognitive functions associated with Alzheimer's disease. Other studies have revealed decreases in other neurotransmitters, including noradrenaline (Bondareff, Mountjoy, & Roth, 1982), serotonin (Gottfries, Roos, & Winblad, 1976), and dopamine (Gottfries, Gottfries, & Roos, 1969). Changes in these neurotransmitters may be related to other symptoms, such as agitation, sleep disturbances, and perceptual difficulties.

Although the changes occurring in the brains of Alzheimer's victims are substantial, we must use caution in assuming that they represent qualitative differences from normal aging. They may not. Gottfries (1985) notes that all of the changes seen in Alzheimer's disease, from cognitive changes to the changes in neurotransmitters, are also found in normal elderly people. To be sure, the changes in

Alzheimer's disease are much greater. But the important point is that Alzheimer's disease may be merely an exaggeration of normal aging and not something qualitatively different from it.

Symptoms and Diagnosis. The major symptoms of Alzheimer's disease are gradual changes in cognitive functioning: declines in memory, learning, attention, and judgment; disorientation in time and space; difficulties in word finding and communication; declines in personal hygiene and self-care skills; inappropriate social behavior; and changes in personality (Crystal, 1988; Davies, 1988). These symptoms tend to be vague in the beginning, and they mimic other psychological problems such as depression or stress reactions. For example, an executive may not be managing as well as she once did and may be missing deadlines more often. Slowly, the symptoms get worse. This executive, who once could easily handle millions of dollars, cannot now add two small numbers. A mother cannot set the table. A person who was previously outgoing is now quiet and withdrawn; a gentle person is now hostile and aggressive. Emotional problems become increasingly apparent, including depression, paranoia, and agitation. As the disease progresses, the patient becomes incontinent and more and more dependent on others for care, eventually becoming completely incapable of even such simple tasks as dressing and eating. In general, the symptoms associated with Alzheimer's disease are worse in the evening than in the morning, a phenomenon that is referred to as **sundowning** among caregivers.

The rate of deterioration in Alzheimer's disease is highly variable from one victim to the next, although progression is usually faster when onset occurs earlier in life (Bondareff, 1983). However, it is possible to identify a series of stages that the patient goes through (Reisberg, Ferris, de Leon, & Crook, 1982); these stages are summarized in Table 9.3. It is important to realize that many diseases cause the problems outlined in stages 1 and 2. In fact, fewer than 10% of those individuals at stage 2 will develop more serious cognitive impairment within several years of the clinical evaluation (Reisberg et al., 1985). Cognitive deficits such as those described in stage 3 typically indicate the presence of the serious decline characteristic of Alzheimer's disease (Reisberg et al., 1985).

Although a definitive diagnosis of Alzheimer's disease depends on an autopsy, the number and severity of behavioral changes allows clinicians to make increasingly accurate early diagnosis (Crook, 1987). In order for this earlier diagnosis to be relatively accurate, however, it must be comprehensive and broad. Table 9.4 provides the set of guidelines developed by a work group convened by the National Institute of Neurological and Communicative Diseases and Stroke (McKhann et al., 1984). Note that a great deal of the diagnostic effort goes into ruling out other possible causes for the observed cognitive deficits. This point emphasizes the fact that all possible treatable causes for the symptoms must be eliminated before a diagnosis of Alzheimer's disease may be made. Unfortunately, many clinicians do not conduct such thorough diagnoses.

As noted in Table 9.4, the clinical diagnosis of Alzheimer's disease consists of noting the history of the symptoms, documenting the cognitive impairments, conducting a general physical exam and neurological exam, performing laboratory tests to rule out other diseases, obtaining a psychiatric evaluation, performing neuropsychological tests, and assessing functional abilities (Crystal, 1988). The history or progress of the disease should be obtained from both the patient, if possible, and a family member. The questions asked must cover when the problems began, how they have changed, what the patient is capable of doing, and other medical problems.

TABLE 9.3 Stages of dementia as measured by the Global Deterioration Scale, with corresponding clinical phases and characteristics

GDS Stage	Clinical Phase	Clinical Characteristics
1. No cognitive decline	Normal	No subjective complaints of memory deficit. No memory deficit evident on clinical interview.
2. Very mild cognitive decline	Forgetfulness	Subjective complaints of memory deficit, most frequently in following areas: (a) forgetting where one has placed familiar objects and (b) forgetting names one formerly knew well. No objective evidence of memory deficit on clinical interview. No objective deficits in employment or social situations. Appropriate concern with respect to symptomatology.
3. Mild cognitive decline	Early confusional	Earliest clear-cut deficits. Manifestations in more than one of the following areas: (a) patient may have gotten lost when traveling to an unfamiliar location; (b) co-workers become aware of patient's relatively poor performance; (c) word- and name-finding deficits become evident to intimates; (d) patient may read a passage or a book and retain relatively little material; (e) patient may demonstrate decreased facility in remembering names upon introduction to new people; (f) patient may have lost or misplaced an object of value; (g) concentration deficit may be evident on clinical testing. Objective evidence of memory deficit obtained only with an intensive interview conducted by a trained geriatric psychiatrist. Decreased performance in demanding employment and social settings. Denial begins to become manifest in patient. Mild to moderate anxiety accompanies symptoms.
4. Moderate cognitive decline	Late confusional	Clear-cut deficit on careful interview. Deficit manifest in following areas: (a) decreased knowledge of current and recent events; (b) may exhibit some deficit in memory of one's personal history; (c) concentration deficit elicited on serial subtractions; (d) decreased ability to travel, handle finances, etc. Frequently no deficit in following areas: (a) orientation to time and person; (b) recognition of familiar persons and faces; (c) ability to travel to familiar locations.

(Source: "The Global Deterioration Scale for Assessment of Primary Degenerative Dementia" by B. Reisberg, S. H. Ferris, M. J. de Leon, and T. Crook, 1982. *American Journal of Psychiatry, 139*, 1136–1139. Copyright 1982 by The American Psychiatric Association. Reprinted with permission.)

GDS Stage	Clinical Phase	Clinical Characteristics
		Inability to perform complex tasks. Denial is dominant defense mechanism. Flattening of affect and withdrawal from challenging situations occur.
5. Moderately severe cognitive decline	Early dementia	Patient can no longer survive without some assistance. Patients are unable during interview to recall a major relevant aspect of current lives, e.g., their address or telephone number of many years, the names of close members of their family (such as grandchildren), the name of the high school or college from which they graduated.
		Frequently some disorientation to time (date, day of week, season, etc.) or to place. An educated person may have difficulty counting back from 40 by 4s or from 20 by 2s.
		Persons at this stage retain knowledge of many major facts regarding themselves and others. They invariably know their own names and generally know their spouse's and children's names. They require no assistance with toileting or eating but may have some difficulty choosing the proper clothing to wear and may occasionally clothe themselves improperly (e.g., put shoes on the wrong feet, etc.).
6. Severe cognitive decline	Middle dementia	May occasionally forget the name of the spouse on whom they are entirely dependent for survival. Will be largely unaware of all recent events and experiences in their lives. Retain some knowledge of their past lives, but this is very sketchy. Generally unaware of their surroundings, the year, the season, etc. May have difficulty counting from 10, both backward and, sometimes, forward. Will require some assistance with activities of daily living, e.g., may become incontinent, will require travel assistance but occasionally will display ability to travel to familiar locations. Diurnal rhythm frequently disturbed. Almost always recall their own name. Frequently continue to be able to distinguish familiar from unfamiliar persons in their environment.
		Personality and emotional changes occur. These are quite variable and include (a) delusional behavior (e.g., patients

(continued)

TABLE 9.3 Continued

GDS Stage	Clinical Phase	Clinical Characteristics
		may accuse their spouse of being an imposter; may talk to imaginary figures in the environment or to their own reflection in the mirror); (b) obsessive symptoms (e.g., person may continually repeat simple cleaning activities); (c) anxiety symptoms, agitation, and even previously nonexistent violent behavior may occur; (d) cognitive abulia (i.e., loss of willpower because an individual cannot carry a thought long enough to determine a purposeful course of action).
7. Very severe cognitive decline	Late dementia	All verbal abilities are lost. Frequently there is no speech at all — only grunting. Incontinent of urine; requires assistance toileting and feeding. Loses basic psychomotor skills (e.g., ability to walk). The brain appears to no longer be able to tell the body what to do. Generalized and cortical neurological signs and symptoms are frequently present.

The cognitive impairments are typically documented through a **mental status exam** (see Chapter 6), which is a brief series of questions tapping orientation ("What day is this? Where are you?"), memory, arithmetic ability (counting backward), ability to follow directions, motor skills (copying a design), and general information ("Who is the president now?"). The general physical exam and neurological exam help rule out other causes such as cardiovascular disease, nutritional problems, or strokes.

A series of laboratory tests must be conducted to rule out additional causes of the observed behaviors. Blood tests look for evidence of chronic infections and for abnormal levels of vitamin B_{12}, folic acid, and thyroid hormone. An EEG should be performed to rule out subtle seizures and to verify that the characteristic diffusely slow EEG pattern in Alzheimer's disease is present. Brain-imaging techniques such as MRI may be used (see Chapter 3). However, none of these imaging techniques provides conclusive evidence; at best they can rule out the presence of tumors, strokes, or other abnormalities (Crystal, 1988).

A psychiatric evaluation must be done to rule out any serious emotional problems that may be causing the observed deficits. A battery of neuropsychological tests should be administered to document the extent of the cognitive deficits and to provide additional information concerning the possibility of tumors or strokes. The functional abilities of the patient must be evaluated as well; these include instrumental daily activities, such as cooking and cleaning, and personal self-care skills, such as dressing and bathing.

Searching for a Cause. We do not know what causes Alzheimer's disease. One notion is that a

TABLE 9.4   Criteria for the diagnosis of probable Alzheimer's disease

1. Criteria for clinical diagnosis of *probable* Alzheimer's disease include

   • Dementia established by clinical examination and documented by Mini-Mental State Test (Folstein, Folstein, & McHugh, 1975), Blessed Dementia Scale (Blessed, Tomlinson, Roth, 1968), or some similar examination and confirmed by neuropsychological tests

   • Deficits in two or more areas of cognition

   • Progressive worsening of memory and other cognitive functions

   • No disturbance of consciousness

   • Onset between ages 40 and 90, most often after age 65

   • Absence of systemic disorders or other brain diseases that in and of themselves could account for progressive deficits in memory and cognition

2. Diagnosis of *probable* Alzheimer's disease is supported by

   • Progressive deterioration of specific cognitive functions, such as language (aphasia), motor skills (apraxia), and perception (agnosia)

   • Impaired activities of daily living and altered patterns of behavior

   • Family history of similar disorders, particularly if confirmed neuropathologically

   • Laboratory results of normal lumbar puncture as evaluated by standard techniques, normal pattern or nonspecific changes in EEG, such as increased slow-wave activity, and evidence of cerebral atrophy on CT with progression documented by serial observation

3. Other clinical features consistent with diagnosis of *probable* Alzheimer's disease, after exclusion of causes of dementia other than Alzheimer's disease, include

   • Plateaus in course of progression of illness

   • Associated symptoms of depression; insomnia; incontinence; delusions; illusions; hallucinations; catastrophic verbal, emotional, or physical outbursts; sexual disorders; and weight loss

   • Other neurological abnormalities in some patients, especially with more advanced disease and including motor signs, such as increased muscle tone, myoclonus, or gait disorder

   • Seizures in advance disease

   • CT normal for age

4. Features that make diagnosis of *probable* Alzheimer's disease uncertain or unlikely include

   • Sudden, apoplectic onset

   • Focal neurological findings such as hemiparesis, sensory loss, visual field deficits, and uncoordination early in the course of the illness

   • Seizures or gait disturbance at onset or very early in course of illness

5. Clinical diagnosis of *possible* Alzheimer's disease

   • May be made on basis of dementia syndrome, in absence of other neurological, psychiatric, or systemic disorders sufficient to cause dementia and in the presence of variations in onset, in presentation, or in clinical course

   • May be made in presence of second systemic or brain disorder sufficient to produce dementia, which is not considered to be cause of dementia

   • Should be used in research studies when single, gradually progressive severe cognitive deficit is identified in absence of other identifiable cause

6. Criteria for diagnosis of *definite* Alzheimer's disease are

   • Clinical criteria for probable Alzheimer's disease

   • Histopathological evidence obtained from biopsy or at autopsy

7. Classification of Alzheimer's disease for research purposes should specify features that may differentiate subtypes of the disorder, such as

   • Familial occurrence

   • Onset before age of 65

   • Presence of trisomy-21

   • Coexistence of other relevant conditions, such as Parkinson's disease

(Source: National Institute of Neurological and Communicative Diseases and Stroke.)

viral infection causes the changes in the brain (Davies, 1988). The viral idea is credible, because a virus appears to be involved in Creutzfeld-Jakob disease, another form of dementia. If a virus turns out to be responsible, though, it is probably slow acting. Unfortunately, scientists have not yet been able to detect a specific virus in the brains of people with Alzheimer's disease.

A second idea about a cause that has been widely reported is aluminum toxicity (Thal, 1988). The idea is that aluminum, which is deadly to brain cells, starts the chain of events leading to Alzheimer's disease. Although high concentrations of aluminum have been reported in some Alzheimer's disease victims, there is no evidence that links the use of aluminum in daily life, such as in cookware or deodorant, to Alzheimer's disease.

At present, the main focus of research is on a genetic link. The strong possibility that at least some forms of Alzheimer's disease are inherited is a major concern of families of disease victims. Breitner (1988) reviews the evidence to date and concludes that genetic factors may be a powerful determinant of Alzheimer's disease. Although there are several methodological difficulties in doing genetics research, it appears from some family trees and studies of relatives and twins that Alzheimer's disease shows an autosomal dominant inheritance pattern. An **autosomal dominant** pattern is one in which only one gene from one parent is necessary to produce the disease; this means that there is a 50% chance that the child of an affected parent will have the disorder. An autosomal dominant pattern for Alzheimer's disease makes sense, since we know that at least two other forms of dementia, Pick's disease and Huntington's disease, are autosomal dominant.

One exciting finding has linked a genetic mutation associated with amyloid protein to Alzheimer's disease. Goate and colleagues (1991) found that two families with early-onset Alzheimer's disease also had one altered amino acid in amyloid

protein, a molecule associated with the formation of neuritic plaques. If this finding holds up, it may be the clue that will unlock the mystery of Alzheimer's disease.

Some genetics research has also linked Alzheimer's disease with Down syndrome, a genetic form of mental retardation (Breitner, 1988). People with Down syndrome develop severe cognitive impairments and brain changes like those in Alzheimer's disease during middle adulthood and old age. Some researchers thought that the gene for Alzheimer's disease might be on the same chromosome responsible for Down syndrome, but the evidence is equivocal.

Even if a specific gene is identified, many questions about the cause of Alzheimer's disease will remain. Why does it take so long for the genetic defect to appear? What mechanism starts it? Why is there so much variation when it appears? Answers to these questions will help considerably in understanding how Alzheimer's disease develops.

Supposing that an autosomal dominant pattern were responsible, what would this mean for the relatives of Alzheimer's disease victims? Actually, it would depend on the relative's age. Even though the risk would always be greater, even at age 65 this increased risk would have little practical significance, because the overall incidence of Alzheimer's disease at this age is low. But by age 80 the risk to first-degree relatives would be roughly 25%, compared with 6% in the general population (Breitner, 1988). Although these numbers are not reassuring, they are considerably lower than the risk for many other autosomal dominant genetic diseases, such as Huntington's disease.

Tests can be developed to detect genes that transmit diseases via an autosomal dominant pattern. Such a test already exists for Huntington's disease. As discussed in Something to Think About, however, taking the test is not an easy decision, even when there is a high risk of passing the disease on to one's children.

SOMETHING TO THINK ABOUT

Genetic Tests for Dementia — Difficult Choices

When scientists discovered that they could determine whether or not someone was carrying the gene for Huntington's disease, they thought it would be a welcome relief to thousands of families. After all, Huntington's disease is a terrible scourge of adults in their 30s, 40s, or 50s that eventually institutionalizes and kills most of its victims. As noted in the text, those who have one parent with the disease run a 50-50 chance of having it themselves and, if they have children, of passing it on to them. So it seemed likely that the ability to determine in advance who would develop or escape the disease would be welcomed by affected families — allowing them to plan more practically about having children, choosing jobs, obtaining insurance, organizing finances, and pursuing social and leisure interests.

But the scientists were wrong. Only a small fraction of those at risk and close enough to obtain the test have done so. Why?

The answer is not with the test, which involves a genetic analysis of blood samples taken from the person being tested and from six or so family members. At present the test is administered at government expense on a trial basis at five medical centers: Columbia University, Johns Hopkins University, Massachusetts General Hospital, the University of Michigan, and the University of Minnesota.

Perhaps the answer lies in the fact that if the test, which is 99% accurate, comes back positive, there is a high probability that you will develop the disease yourself. In short, you learn that you face a long, terrible death.

Samuel L. Baily, former chairman of the National Huntington's Disease Association, chose not to have the test even though his mother died from Huntington's disease at age 58, 8 years after she was diagnosed. Baily, symptom-free at age 52, said that he would rather just take his chances with the disease, which had also killed his maternal grandfather. He prefers to live with the hope of not getting it than with the knowledge that he will.

Others choose a different course. Karen Sweeney, 28, who is married and has four children, told interviewers that she had to know (J. Brody, 1988). The stress of knowing that her mother and grandfather both died from the disease had taken its toll on her and on her marriage. After moving to Baltimore to be eligible for the Johns Hopkins testing program, Karen and her husband went through extensive counseling before the test. For Karen, the news was good: no Huntington's.

Certainly, Huntington's disease and all other forms of dementia are terrible, killer diseases. With research rapidly advancing on Alzheimer's disease, it is likely that a test for a genetic marker for it will be developed in the next decade. It is also likely that a test will be available before there is a cure. If you had relatives who had died from Alzheimer's disease or Huntington's disease, if you were planning to have a family, and if a test were available, what would you do? It's something to think about.

Intervention Strategies. Alzheimer's disease is incurable. However, much research has been done looking for ways to alleviate the cognitive deficits. Most of this work has focused on various drugs that could improve memory (Bartus, Dean, & Fisher, 1986; Crook, 1987; Thal, 1988). These drugs have included a wide variety of compounds aimed at improving cerebral blood flow or levels of various neurotransmitters. Although some drugs have been reported to aid cognitive functioning, these

Keeping persons with Alzheimer's disease involved in everyday activities is an important aspect of good caregiving.

successes have often been achieved with carefully selected patients on carefully selected tests (Crook, 1987). In terms of clinical application, none of the drugs has shown reliable improvements in a wide variety of patients (Thal, 1988).

In contrast to the poor picture for ameliorating cognitive performance, improving other behavioral problems is possible. Drugs that are used primarily in younger patients for the treatment of schizophrenia, such as thioridazine and haloperidol, are effective in lowering the severe psychiatric symptoms that develop during the course of Alzheimer's disease (Salzman, 1984). Similarly, antidepressants are effective in alleviating the depressive symptoms that typically accompany the early stages of the disease (Crook & Cohen, 1983), and sedatives may

be effective for sleep disturbances. However, these medications should be used with considerable caution, since dosage levels for older adults may be far lower than those for younger patients, and side effects may be much more serious (Salzman, 1984).

Several interventions that do not involve drugs are also available. Cognitive problems can be addressed by creating a supportive environment, such as labeling the contents of cupboards, and by using behavioral techniques to teach new strategies (see Chapter 6). Depression, irritability, wandering, and emotional problems can also be effectively dealt with through behavioral techniques. Most important in this regard is the introduction of a straightforward daily schedule in which meals, medications, and naps always come at the same time.

Environmental interventions — such as control of lighting, noise, and temperature in bedrooms — may also help alleviate sleep disturbances.

In the long run most Alzheimer's disease patients become completely dependent on others, leaving caregivers few intervention options. We will consider the burden on the family members in a later section.

Multi-Infarct Dementia

Until Tomlinson and colleagues' (1970) discovery that Alzheimer's disease was not rare, most physicians and researchers believed that most cases of dementia resulted from cerebral arteriosclerosis and its consequent restriction of oxygen to the brain. As described in Chapter 3, arteriosclerosis is a family of diseases that, if untreated, may result in heart attacks or strokes. For the present discussion it is the stroke, or *cerebral vascular accident (CVA)*, that concerns us. CVAs (see Chapter 3) result from a disruption of the blood flow, termed an *infarct*, which may be caused by a blockage or hemorrhage.

A large CVA may produce severe cognitive decline, but this loss is almost always limited to specific abilities. This pattern is different from the classic, global deterioration seen in dementia. However, it is believed that a series of small CVAs can produce this global pattern. This condition is termed **multi-infarct dementia** (Hachinski, Lassen, & Marshall, 1974). Multi-infarct dementia accounts for 10% to 15% of all cases of dementia (Crook, 1987).

The course of multi-infarct dementia is very different from that seen in Alzheimer's disease (Crook, 1987). Multi-infarct dementia has a sudden onset, and its progression is described as stepwise, or stuttering. This is in contrast to the insidious onset and gradual progression of Alzheimer's disease. The symptom pattern in multi-infarct dementia is highly variable, especially early in the disease. Again, this is in contrast to the similar cluster of cognitive problems shown by Alzheimer's disease patients.

Blass and Barclay (1985) report that the median survival of multi-infarct dementia patients is only two to three years, much shorter than that of Alzheimer's disease patients. They argue that the diagnosis of multi-infarct dementia should be reconsidered if the patient survives longer than two years without any evidence of additional CVAs.

The steps in diagnosing multi-infarct dementia are similar to Alzheimer's disease. Evidence of CVAs from diagnostic imaging (CT or MRI) and a history of cerebrovascular disease are usually the key factors (Davies, 1988). In a small percentage of cases, however, evidence of both Alzheimer's disease and multi-infarct dementia is found.

Unlike Alzheimer's disease, there are known risk factors for multi-infarct dementia that can be controlled. Among these are hypertension and others noted in Chapters 3 and 4. Attention to these factors earlier in life may well lower the risk of multi-infarct dementia considerably.

Parkinson's Disease

Parkinson's disease is known primarily for its characteristic cluster of motor problems: very slow walking, stiffness, difficulty getting in and out of chairs, and a slow tremor. These behavioral symptoms are caused by a deterioration of the neurons in the midbrain that produce the neurotransmitter dopamine (Lieberman, 1974). Administration of the drug L-dopa greatly alleviates these behavioral problems.

Recent research evidence established a link between Parkinson's-like symptoms and a soil-dwelling bacterium (*Discover*, Oct. 1990). The bacterium, *Nocardia*, is easily breathed in when you inhale dust. When laboratory mice were injected with the bacterium, they developed the motor symptoms associated with Parkinson's disease. Interestingly, when they were given L-dopa, the symptoms disappeared; when the drug wore off the symptoms returned. It is too early to tell whether a cause for Parkinson's disease has been discovered, but the link is intriguing.

The connection between Parkinson's disease and dementia was not generally recognized until the late 1970s. Researchers now estimate, however, that between 30% and 50% of people with Parkinson's disease will develop dementia (Boller, 1980). Interestingly, the changes occurring in the brain observed at autopsy, the symptoms, and the course of the dementia seen in Parkinson's disease are indistinguishable from those in Alzheimer's disease (Boller, Mizutani, & Roessmann, 1980).

Some researchers argue that the combination of Parkinson's disease and Alzheimer's disease is a disorder distinct from Parkinson's disease without dementia. Support for this belief comes from the fact that Parkinson's disease patients with dementia tolerate all anti-Parkinsonian drugs such as L-dopa very poorly compared with patients with Parkinson's disease without dementia (Lieberman et al., 1979). Why some people with Parkinson's disease develop dementia and others do not remains a mystery.

Pick's Disease

Pick's disease is a very rare form of dementia that is clinically very hard to discriminate from Alzheimer's disease. Nevertheless, it is quite distinct neuropathologically, that is, in terms of the structural changes in the brain. Some researchers and clinicians note that patients in the early stages of Pick's disease show little memory impairment but marked behavioral changes, such as social inappropriateness, loss of modesty, and uninhibited sexual behavior (Lishman, 1978). Neuropathological changes include striking atrophy of the frontal and temporal lobes, the absence of both senile plaques and neurofibrillary tangles, but the presence of so-called Pick's bodies in neurons (Davies,

1988). An interesting research question is why the cognitive changes in Pick's disease so closely resemble those in Alzheimer's disease even though the structural changes in the neurons are quite different. Perhaps a partial explanation is that the nucleus basalis of Meynert, a major source of acetylcholine, is destroyed in both diseases (Price et al., 1982). An additional interesting parallel is that Pick's disease appears to be determined by a single autosomal dominant gene (Sjogren, Sjogren, & Lindgren, 1952), the same genetic mechanism being investigated as a factor in Alzheimer's disease.

Creutzfeld-Jakob Disease

Creutzfeld-Jakob disease is another very rare form of dementia that is characterized by a relatively early onset, very rapid course (rarely more than two years), and severe changes in EEG patterns (Siedler & Malamud, 1963). These changes appear to be caused by severe neuronal degeneration, a very marked proliferation of *astrocytes* (star-shaped cells in the brain), and a spongy appearance of the gray matter in the brain. There are no senile plaques or neurofibrillary tangles (as in Alzheimer's disease), no massive atrophy (as seen in Pick's disease), and no vascular damage (as in multi-infarct dementia) (Lishman, 1978).

The most important aspect of Creutzfeld-Jakob disease is that it appears to be transmitted by a virus. It is known to be transmissible to chimpanzees (Gibbs et al., 1968) and to other animals from humans. There are also at least three confirmed cases of accidental transmission of Creutzfeld-Jakob disease from animals to humans (Crook, 1987). Moreover, the disease is clinically and neuropathologically related to kuru, a transmissible form of dementia found in the Fore linguistic tribe in New Guinea (Gajdusek, 1977). Gajdusek's research shows that the virus responsible is transmitted through the practice of cannibalism and has an incubation of many years. The research documenting that these forms of dementia are communicable earned these investigators a Nobel Prize and opened research to the possibility that Alzheimer's disease may also be caused by a virus.

Huntington's Disease

Huntington's disease is an autosomal dominant disorder that usually begins between the ages of 35 and 50. The disease generally manifests itself through involuntary flicking movements of the arms and legs; the inability to sustain a motor act such as sticking out one's tongue; prominent psychiatric disturbances such as hallucinations, paranoia, and depression; and clear personality changes, such as swings from apathy to manic behavior (Berkow, 1987). Cognitive impairments typically do not appear until late in the disease. The onset of these symptoms is very gradual. The course of Huntington's disease is progressive; patients ultimately lose the ability to care for themselves physically and mentally. Walking becomes impossible, swallowing is difficult, and cognitive loss becomes profound (Berkow, 1987). Changes in the brain thought to underlie the behavioral losses include degeneration of the caudate nucleus and the small-cell population, as well as substantial decreases in the neurotransmitters GABA and substance P. Although antipsychotic medications are sometimes used to control the psychiatric disturbances and agitated behaviors, they are only partially effective (Berkow, 1987). As noted earlier, a test is available to determine whether one has the marker for the Huntington's disease gene.

Normal-Pressure Hydrocephalus

Normal-pressure hydrocephalus is another rare form of dementia that is characterized by enlarged cerebral ventricles but normal cerebrospinal fluid pressure (Crook, 1987). The ventricles are the chambers in the brain that contain cerebrospinal fluid. This condition is caused most often by a head injury or hemorrhage deep in the brain (Hakim & Adams, 1965). The early symptoms are usually general cognitive deficits, hesitancy or shuffling during walking, and urinary incontinence (Berkow, 1987). The diagnosis can be confirmed through CT or MRI, which document the enlarged ventricles, but clinical observation of these three problems is usually sufficient (Mulrow, Feussner, Williams, & Vokaty, 1987). Treatment of the disease is usually through shunting: a procedure that helps drain the cerebrospinal fluid to lower the pressure. Many patients do not respond to this procedure, however, especially if the disease has been present a long time (Berkow, 1987).

Caring for Dementia Patients at Home

The changes that happen to a person who has a form of dementia are devastating, not only to the patient but also to the whole family. It is extremely difficult to watch a spouse, parent, or sibling go from being the independent, mature adult whom you knew to being a helpless shell who is oblivious to his or her surroundings.

Despite these formidable emotional issues, the vast majority of dementia patients are cared for by their family members at home. Until the mid-1970s little was known about their experience, and little information was available on effective home-care strategies. The appearance of Mace and Rabin's *The 36-Hour Day* in 1981 marked a major turning point; their book remains one of the best guides for families caring for a dementia patient. Throughout the 1980s and early 1990s, researchers have focused on two main lines of investigation concerning caregiving: identifying effective strategies of care and documenting the stress and burden felt by the family.

Because the majority of people with dementia have Alzheimer's disease, most of the research focuses on caregivers of these patients. The advice offered, however, applies to caregivers of all dementia patients.

Effective Caregiving Strategies. Aronson (1988) provides an excellent summary of the interventions and decisions that caregivers can make that will make the care of Alzheimer's patients as successful as possible. Key steps to be taken once a diagnosis is made include obtaining accurate information about the disease; involving the patient as much as possible in decisions; identifying the primary caregiver; reassessing the patient's living situation; setting realistic goals; making realistic financial plans; identifying a source of regular medical care; maximizing the patient's opportunity to function at his or her optimal level; making realistic demands of the patient; and using outside services as needed. The goal of these early steps is to build a broad support network of relatives, medical personnel, and service providers that may be needed later. The new responsibilities of family members require changes in daily routines; people adjust to these roles at different rates.

Many behaviors and situations that we take for granted need to be rethought when we find ourselves caring for an Alzheimer's disease patient. Dressing, bathing, and grooming become more difficult or even aversive to the patient. Use of Velcro fasteners, joining the patient during a bath or shower, and other such changes may be necessary. Nutritional needs have to be monitored, because patients may forget that they have just eaten or may forget to eat. Medications must be used with considerable caution. Changes in personality and sexual behavior need to be viewed as part of the disease. Sleeplessness can be addressed by establishing consistent bedtimes, giving warm milk or tryptophan, and limiting caffeine intake. Wandering is an especially troublesome problem because it is difficult to control; making sure that the patient has an identification bracelet describing the nature of the problem and making the house accident-

proof are two preventive steps. In severe cases of wandering it may be necessary to use restraints, but only under the direction of a health care professional. Incontinence, which usually occurs late in the disease, is a troubling and embarrassing issue for the patient; use of special undergarments or diapers or medications to treat the problem are two of the available options. It is important to realize that incontinence is not necessarily related to Alzheimer's disease. For example, stress incontinence, which is fairly common among older women, is unrelated to dementia.

One of the most difficult issues faced by caregivers concerns taking things away from the patient and restricting activity. Relatively early in the disease the patient will experience problems handling finances. It is not uncommon for patients to spend hundreds or even thousands of dollars on strange items, to leave the checkbook unbalanced and bills unpaid, and to lose money. Although the patient can be given some money to keep, it is necessary for someone else to handle the day-to-day accounts. Traveling alone is another problem. Families of dementia patients often wait until a major calamity occurs before recognizing their loved one's deteriorating condition. Instead, families should limit solo excursions to places within walking distance; all other trips should be made with at least one family member along. Driving is often a contentious issue, especially if the patient does not recognize his or her limitations. Once it is clear that the patient cannot drive, the family must take whatever steps are necessary. In some cases this entails simply taking the car keys, but in others it becomes necessary to disable the car. Suggesting that the patient could be chauffeured is another alternative.

Two rapidly growing options for caregivers are respite care and adult day care. **Respite care** is designed to allow family members to get away for a time. It can consist of in-home care provided by professionals or temporary placement in a residential facility. In-home care is typically used to allow caregivers to do errands or to have a few hours free, while temporary residential placement is reserved for a more extended respite, such as a weekend. Respite care is a tremendous help to caregivers. In one study there was marked improvement in family members' reports of problems after a two-week respite (Burdz, Eaton, & Bond, 1988). **Adult day care** provides placement and programming for frail elderly people during the day. This option is used most often by adult children who are employed. The demand for respite and adult day care far exceeds their availability, making them limited options. An additional problem is that many insurance programs will not pay for these services, making them too expensive for caregivers with limited finances. Even when services are available, however, many families do not use them until their informal support system begins to break down (Caserta, Lund, Wright, & Redburn, 1987).

In general, family members must change their entire daily routines in order to care for a dementia patient. Such complete alterations in habits, coupled with watching the deterioration in their loved one, create an extremely stressful situation.

Family Stress and Burden. Taking care of a person with dementia is an extremely stressful, time-consuming job. For many caregivers it becomes a full-time job, going from a situation that they control to one that controls them. In her book *Another Name for Madness* Marion Roach (1985) vividly describes what the process is like. She relates the range of feelings she experienced caring for her mother (who was in her early 50s when she was diagnosed with Alzheimer's disease): anger, frustration, worry, pity, guilt, and a host of others.

Researchers have documented what Roach and all other caregivers go through. The most commonly used term to describe the experience is burden (Teri, Truax, Logsdon, Uomoto, & Zarit, 1990). Burden relates to the experience of psychological stress and distress as the result of caring for

a frail elder. Most of the research on burden has been focused on caregivers of Alzheimer's disease patients, although some work has documented similar experiences in those caring for stroke patients and head-injured patients as well (Schulz, Tompkins, & Rau, 1988).

Caregivers experience considerable negative effects: chronic fatigue, anger, depression, loss of friends, loss of time to themselves, dissatisfaction with other family members, physical and mental strain, stress symptoms, less life satisfaction, and lower well-being (Kinney & Stephens, 1989; Zarit, Todd, & Zarit, 1986). Men tend to report higher levels of morale than women (Gilhooly, 1984; Zarit et al., 1986), perhaps because women become more emotionally involved in caregiving and care for more severely impaired patients. Married daughters caring for their parents often are forced to quit their jobs (Brody, Kleban, Johnsen, Hoffman, & Schoonover, 1987), whereas married sons often are not. Spouses who care for their partner report lower levels of physical health, mental health, and financial resources than spouses without such a burden (George & Gwyther, 1986; Gilhooly, 1984).

One important finding is that daughters are far more likely than sons to care for their parents (Brody, 1985). Moreover, daughters may have to deal not only with the problems of caregiving but also with resentments at having to assume a form of childrearing responsibilities in midlife. Compared with spouse caregivers, daughters have many more competing pressures such as career and family adding to their burden (Brody, 1985; Quayhagen & Quayhagen, 1988).

Considerable research documents that it is not a specific aspect of Alzheimer's disease or related disorders — such as wandering or incontinence — that causes these problems (Gilhooly, 1986; Zarit et al., 1986). Rather, it is the caregiver's perception of the situation that matters. For example, the perception that one's social support system is gone is a powerful predictor of the decision to

HOW DO WE KNOW?

Caregiver Burden: A Stress and Coping Approach

Caring for a dementia patient is a highly demanding and stressful job. Some researchers have begun to study the effects of caregiving by turning to the model of stress and coping proposed by Lazarus and Folkman (1984). Briefly, this model postulates that stress is the perception that one's resources are being taxed and that one is being threatened. To measure stress in this way, Lazarus and his colleagues developed the Hassles Scale, which measures whether stressful events have happened recently, and, if so, to what extent they were perceived as troublesome.

Kinney and Stephens (1989) adapted this idea to the caregiving situation. They believed that the amount of burden experienced by caregivers of Alzheimer's disease patients could be understood in Lazarus and Folkman's framework. Kinney and Stephens developed the 42-item Caregiving Hassles Scale. Each item on the scale is a commonly encountered situation, such as giving the patient a bath. Respondents indicate whether each event has occurred in the previous week and to what extent it represents a difficulty (on a four-point scale).

Caregivers of Alzheimer's disease patients reported many hassles. The most common ones involved assisting the patient with daily living (bathing, dressing) and dealing with cognitive limitations and behavior problems. The severity of perceived

problems correlated with poor caregiver-patient relations and higher levels of anxiety, hostility, and depression in caregivers. Hassles that were related to patients' behavior problems proved most troublesome; apparently, dealing with emotional outbursts and so forth presented serious problems for coping.

A key aspect of the Kinney and Stephens data is that the specific behaviors that were perceived as hassles varied a great deal across caregivers. This finding is in keeping with Lazarus and Folkman's notion that it is not *what* happens, but how you *perceive* what happens, that matters. Kinney and Stephens have provided a useful approach to the study of caregiving by applying a general model of stress and coping to a specific context.

---

institutionalize the patient, whereas the actual physical condition of the patient is not (George & Gwyther, 1986).

Some investigators of caregiver burden (Haley, Levine, Brown, Berry, & Hughes, 1987; Kinney & Stephens, 1989) have adopted a stress and coping approach based on Lazarus and Folkman's (1984) model, described in Chapter 4. In this approach it is the perception that one's resources are being taxed by the present situation that causes the burden, not the objective real situation. This approach, described in more detail in How Do We Know? fits

well with the data and should provide a useful framework for future research.

FAMILY INTERVENTION AND FAMILY THERAPY

Although many problems encountered during adulthood are best resolved at an individual level, other problems involve family factors and home relationships. These latter difficulties are best handled by working with the family as a whole. If adults are able to receive adequate help from family members and have a positive, collaborative relationship with them, their whole mental outlook, behavioral functioning, and adaptation to life is enhanced (Fry, 1986). Because family ties remain important throughout adulthood (see Chapter 10), family intervention is an important topic for adults of all ages. As we will see, because family therapy is effective for families confronting Alzheimer's disease, it is likely that this approach will continue to grow in popularity.

This section looks at the goals of family intervention and family therapy and discusses some important aspects of evaluating family dynamics. We will also consider some age-related issues pertaining to family dynamics that are important considerations in designing effective interventions.

What Is Family Therapy?

Family therapy views the family as an independent system of members who mutually influence one another (Haley, 1971). Consequently, changing the behavior of one family member means changing the whole family system. In addition, we must understand what particular roles are played by each member (parent, child, nurturer, martyr, and so forth) and how these roles are interrelated. Families also have certain rules that govern the communication among their members; these must be identified as well.

An assumption in family therapy is that functional families work toward the growth and development of their members, whereas dysfunctional families produce the distress or destruction of their members. These ends are achieved by implementing the roles and rules of the family.

The role of the family therapist is to identify the roles played by each member and the rules by which they play. Although there are several different ways in which these identifications are made and the therapy is carried out, all agree on the importance of improving the communication skills among family members as the first step.

Common Issues in Family Therapy with Older Adults

Issues addressed in family therapy reflect the variety of problems that occur in family relationships. When these problems involve older adults, however, they tend to focus on three themes (Fry, 1986): conflicts between spouses, conflicts between elderly parents and their adult children, and conflicts in communication and expectations.

Conflicts Between Spouses. One common problem confronting spouses of all ages is change in life circumstances. For middle-aged adults, these changes may include children's leaving home or a new job. For older spouses, these changes include retirement, loss of income, or physical incapacitation. In all of these cases such changes may reactivate earlier problems in the marriage. Despite feeling unhappy, many of these couples continue to live together out of fear of change or economic necessity. Conflict between the spouses may arise out of each party's resistance to change, inability to meet the other's needs, or feelings of being forced to adopt new and unwanted roles (such as a caregiver).

Conflicts Between Adult Children and Their Elderly Parents. When adult children become caregivers to their parents, conflict may result from the stress. Assuming additional responsibility for the management of an elderly parent often takes a high toll, as discussed earlier in this chapter. Elderly parents may try to assume control of the household, the spouses of the adult children may resent the extra duties put on their partners, or the adult children may resent their parents for disrupting the household. Additionally, older parents may be unfairly blamed for marital problems between adult children and their spouses. The results of such conflicts can be devastating to the family.

Problems of Communication and Roles. Many families cannot maintain open communication with all of their members, especially during times of conflict. Such open communication is clearly needed between adult children and their parents. What is often overlooked is that adult children need to be able to openly discuss matters with their parents but may not feel comfortable in doing so. For example, middle-aged adults may feel the urge to talk about their feelings with their parents, who have experienced middle-age firsthand, but the adult children may be reluctant to actually open up to their parents. Additionally, one generation may place excessive role demands on the other, such as the oldest generation expecting the middle generation to be perfect parents and high achievers in the workplace.

Techniques for Family Therapy

Herr and Weakland (1979) discuss several techniques for family intervention. Most important is *communication skills training,* in which family members learn how to listen to other family members and to express their own feelings more clearly. Early in the family therapy process it is important for the therapist to determine what the problems confronting the family really are and to uncover any hidden agendas a particular member has. Additionally, realistic goals for recovery must be set. It is also important for the therapist to ascertain how the family dealt with similar problems in the past and to determine which solution strategies worked and which ones failed. New alternatives are offered as needed. Also important is determining and explic-

itly stating the family rules for interaction and pointing out when these rules need to be changed. Finally, the family members must all agree on the nature and direction of change.

Several studies have documented that family therapy is effective in dealing with problems involving older adult family members (e.g., Cicirelli, 1986; Zarit & Anthony, 1986). Family therapy is often the approach of choice in addressing problems stemming from caregiving. For example, the increased ability to communicate feelings of guilt, anger, closeness, and love allows family members to deal with their feelings more adaptively.

WORKING WITH THE INSTITUTIONALIZED ELDERLY

Traditionally, one of the most underserved groups of older adults has been residents of nursing homes. However, these individuals can benefit significantly from a wide variety of intervention programs targeted for different levels of ability (Weiner, Brok, & Snadowsky, 1987). Indeed, nursing homes are one of the fastest growing areas of mental health intervention in developing strategies and programs. The ability of cognitively impaired individuals to benefit from such intervention has been sadly underestimated in the past; we now know that even people with moderately severe impairment can benefit. In this section we will consider some of the major techniques that are used with institutionalized elderly people to optimize their abilities.

A word of caution is needed before we begin our survey. These techniques have been widely adopted, but there is very little research evidence that they are effective. Although future research may demonstrate that these programs work, for the time being we must be careful not to assume that they will result in improvements in functioning.

Group activities such as coloring Easter eggs play an important role in fostering a sense of personal control and identity among the institutionalized elderly.

Sensory Training

Sensory training is aimed at bringing a person back in touch with the environment (Weiner et al., 1987). This technique is effective in getting highly regressed residents who have psychomotor, sensory, verbal, or cognitive deficits to reexperience their surroundings and remake social contacts. Sensory training begins with social introductions among group members, followed by body-awareness exercises and sensory stimulation. These activities stimulate social participation and sensory experience through the use of common objects. Having participants talk or think about their experiences also enhances cognitive activity.

Sensory training works best when groups are not too large, five to seven persons, and when they are conducted every morning, seven days a week.

The meeting place and time should always be the same, to eliminate confusion. Any materials that can be used to stimulate the senses — from cotton balls to sandpaper to different colored objects — are appropriate.

The major advantage of sensory training is that individuals who are usually excluded from other groups because of the sensory or cognitive impairments can benefit. And because no special equipment needs to be purchased, sensory training is inexpensive as well.

Reality Orientation

Reality orientation — based on repetition and re-learning — is a technique that was developed for the moderately confused resident (Stephens, 1975).

The key to reality orientation is that it is a 24-hour program that is integrated in the entire environment. The goal is to keep the resident in touch with what is going on in the world in every way possible.

Implementing a reality orientation program involves several things. Residents are addressed by a title such as Mr. or Mrs. unless they specify otherwise. Plenty of clocks and bulletin boards with calendars are placed in prominent locations. Name cards are used at meals. Activities are interesting and diversified and are announced on the public address system. Birthdays are recognized individually, and special meals are served on holidays. Visiting hours are liberal, and volunteers are encouraged to visit. Color-coded rooms and hallways are used. Independence is encouraged as much as possible. In short, everything that occurs in the institution is geared to keeping residents in touch with reality.

Research findings on the effects of reality orientation are mixed. It appears to be most beneficial for mildly disoriented individuals (Spayd & Smyer, 1988). Overall, reality orientation appears to improve individuals' knowledge of basic orienting facts (such as day, month, time) rather than providing them with a set of transferable skills for dealing with different environments (Hart & Fleming, 1985).

Attitude therapy is usually used in conjunction with reality orientation. Basically, attitude therapy aims at identifying each resident's primary interactive style, which is then dealt with by the staff in specified and consistent ways. For example, active friendliness is used with apathetic, withdrawn residents; passive friendliness, with frightened, suspicious residents; matter-of-factness, with manipulative residents; kind firmness, with depressed residents; and a no-demands approach, with angry, hostile residents. Attitude therapy is designed to reinforce adaptive behaviors and not to reinforce maladaptive behaviors.

Validation Therapy

In sharp contrast to reality orientation, validation therapy does not involve correcting a person's disorientation (Wetzler & Feil, 1979). For example, Anne believed that her son was a young infant, when in fact he was a middle-aged adult. Gentle attempts at reorienting her failed, partly because Anne could not remember the correct information over time. When Anne began to address a doll as her son, the staff was encouraged to talk to Anne about her son, such as how she cared for him and about his favorite foods or toys. The staff's acceptance of Anne's disorientation *validated* Anne's feelings. Such validation may keep residents from becoming agitated, as well as provide things for staff and residents to talk about. Note that the goal of validation therapy is not to correct disoriented statements, nor to confirm them. Rather, the goal is to validate the *emotions* incorporated in the disoriented belief in order to relieve distress (Spayd & Smyer, 1988).

Remotivation Therapy

Remotivation therapy is a structured program based on a set of standard topics intended to reawaken the interest of apathetic residents (Weiner et al., 1987). The program works by getting a group of 10 to 15 residents to discuss a topic such as clothing or food in a 5-step process: (1) creating a climate of acceptance by welcoming each member; (2) creating a bridge to reality by selecting a topic for discussion; (3) sharing the world of reality by asking the group members about the topic; (4) appreciating the world of reality by getting members to share their ideas or stimulating reminiscence; and (5) creating a climate of appreciation by noting the good contributions made by each member. Remotivation therapy should be conducted once or twice a week for between 30 minutes to an hour. The structured program lasts 12 weeks. Group leaders for remotivation therapy should have completed a 30-hour course in the technique at a training center, primarily because the program adheres to a rigid, precise format and requires preparation.

Additional Therapeutic Approaches

In addition to sensory training, reality therapy, validation theory, and remotivation therapy, a host of other interventions are used in institutions. Four of the more popular ones are activities and recreation therapy, milieu therapy, supportive group therapy, and pet therapy.

Activities and recreation therapy helps to optimize residents' functioning and improve their quality of life by getting them involved in physical and mental activities (Haun, 1965). A comprehensive program should include a wide variety of voluntary activities that can be performed individually, in small groups, and in large groups. The ability to choose activities is the key; whether it is playing solitaire or watching movies in a group, the benefits of participation are greater if it is the resident's choice (Weiner et al., 1987). Being able to make decisions fosters independence and self-esteem.

Milieu therapy takes a different approach. Rather than a staff member designing the program, the resident designs the environment so that it most closely reflects the kind of setting that he or she was used to before entering the nursing home (Weiner et al., 1987). This enables the resident to sustain social roles and puts responsibility for these roles on the resident rather than the staff. Residents in a milieu therapy program are placed together based on similarities in their primary needs, degree of independence, and degree of disability.

Many nursing homes and other residential facilities are beginning *supportive group therapy* for their residents. These groups serve many functions, but mainly they focus on promoting better human relationships, dealing with feelings of loneliness or inferiority, and encouraging coping (Hartford, 1980). These groups have been shown to increase residents' sense of personal control, life satisfaction, and trust (Moran & Gatz, 1987).

Pet therapy is one of the fastest growing techniques with institutionalized older adults (Brickel, 1984). Pets are used to enhance feelings of responsibility and control, trigger reminiscence, and promote social interaction. Short-term gains in positive feelings about oneself, well-being, and cognitive functioning have been reported, but few detailed studies of pet therapy have been conducted.

SUMMARY

Psychopathology and the Adult Life Course

1. Definitions of mental health need to reflect appropriate age-related criteria. Behaviors need to be interpreted in context.

2. Consideration of key interpersonal, intrapersonal, biological and physiological, and life-cycle factors is essential. Diagnostic criteria need to reflect age differences in symptomatology.

Depression

3. The rate of severe depression decreases with age.

4. Common features of depression include: dysphoria, apathy, self-deprecation, expressionlessness, changes in arousal, withdrawal, and several physical symptoms. Additionally, the problems

must last at least two weeks, not be caused by another disease, and negatively affect daily living.

5. Women are diagnosed with depression more frequently than men.

6. Many assessment scales are not sensitive to age differences in symptoms.

7. Possible biological causes of severe depression are neurotransmitter imbalance, abnormal brain functioning, or physical illness.

8. Loss is the main psychosocial cause of depression. Research evidence shows negative life events per se are unrelated to depression. Internal belief systems are also important.

9. Drugs, electroconvulsive therapy, and psychotherapy are all used to treat depression. Older adults benefit most from behavior and cognitive therapies.

10. Suicide rates in old age are relatively low except for white men. Ethnic differences are also apparent.

Anxiety Disorders

11. Symptoms include a variety of physical changes that interfere with normal functioning. Context is important in understanding symptoms.

12. Both drugs and psychotherapy are used to treat anxiety disorders.

Schizophrenia and Paranoid Disorders

13. Schizophrenia is a severe thought disorder with an onset usually before age 45.

14. Paranoid disorders are characterized by delusions, and are relatively rare in adults of all ages.

15. Treatment usually consists of using drugs; psychotherapy is not often effective alone.

Dementia

16. Reversible dementias such as delirium can be treated. Irreversible dementias such as Alzheimer's disease cannot.

17. Alzheimer's disease is a progressive, fatal disease that is diagnosed at autopsy through three neurological changes: neurofibrillary tangles, neuritic plaques, and granulovacuolar bodies.

18. Major symptoms of Alzheimer's disease include gradual and eventually pervasive memory loss, emotional changes, and eventual loss of motor functions.

19. Diagnosis of Alzheimer's disease consists of ruling out all other possible causes of the symptoms.

20. Current research suggests that Alzheimer's disease may be genetic, although other theories have been proposed.

21. Although no cure for Alzheimer's disease is available, interventions to relieve symptoms are advisable.

22. Multi-infarct dementia is caused by several small strokes. Changes in behavior depend on where in the brain the strokes occur.

23. Characteristic symptoms of Parkinson's disease include tremor and problems with walking. Treatment is done with drugs. A minority of people with Parkinson's disease will develop dementia.

24. Symptoms of Pick's disease show up early as behavioral, rather than memory problems. The disease appears to be genetic.

25. Creutzfeld-Jakob disease is caused by a virus. It has an early onset, very rapid course, and causes severe brain changes.

26. Huntington's disease is a genetic disorder that usually begins in middle age with motor and behavioral problems.

27. Normal-pressure hydrocephalus is a rare disorder caused by enlarged ventricles in the brain.

28. Caring for dementia patients at home can cause significant stress. Respite care and adult day care help caregivers deal with the stress and burden. Daughters and daughters-in-law do most of the caregiving.

Family Intervention and Family Therapy

29. Family therapy views the family as a dynamic system. All members participate in therapy.

30. Several issues are typically dealt with in family therapy: spousal conflict, parent-child conflict, and communication problems.

31. Communication skills training is the most important technique.

Working with the Institutionalized Elderly

32. Sensory training aims at getting a person back in touch with the environment.

33. Reality orientation is a technique based on repetition and relearning in an attempt to treat disoriented residents. The technique works best with mildly disoriented persons.

34. Validation therapy aims at dealing with the person's disorientation in an accepting, nonthreatening way.

35. Remotivation therapy seeks to get apathetic residents interested in activities.

36. Other techniques include activities and recreation therapy, milieu therapy, supportive group therapy, and pet therapy.

REVIEW QUESTIONS

Psychopathology and the Adult Life Course

1. How do definitions of mental health vary with age?

2. What are the implications of adopting a biopsychosocial model for interpreting mental health?

Depression

3. How does the rate of depression vary with age?

4. What symptoms are associated with depression? How do they vary with age and gender?

5. What biological causes of depression have been offered?

6. How is loss associated with depression?

7. What treatments of depression have been developed? How well do they work with older adults?

8. What is the connection between suicide and age?

Anxiety Disorders

9. What symptoms are associated with anxiety disorders?

10. How are anxiety disorders treated?

Schizophrenia and Paranoid Disorders

11. What are schizophrenia and paranoid disorders? How are they related to age?

12. What treatments are most effective for schizophrenia and paranoid disorders?

Dementia

13. What is the difference between reversible and irreversible dementia?

14. What is Alzheimer's disease? How is it diagnosed?

15. What causes Alzheimer's disease? What treatments are available?

16. What other types of dementia have been identified? What are their characteristics?

17. What happens when people care for dementia victims at home?

Family Intervention and Family Therapy

18. What is family therapy? How does it differ from individual psychotherapy?

19. What issues are typically dealt with in family therapy? How are they addressed?

Working with the Institutionalized Elderly

20. What are the main therapies used with institutionalized elderly?

21. What evidence is there that any of these techniques are effective?

KEY TERMS

adult day care A program in which older adults are housed during the day when they cannot care for themselves. Adult day care is often used with victims of Alzheimer's disease. (325)

Alzheimer's disease An irreversible form of dementia characterized by progressive declines in cognitive and bodily functions, eventually resulting in death. (310)

amyloid A type of protein involved in the formation of neuritic plaques in both normal aging and in Alzheimer's disease. (312)

autosomal dominant A type of genetic transmission in which only one gene from one parent is necessary for a person to acquire a trait or disease. (318)

behavior therapy A type of psychotherapy that focuses on and attempts to alter current behavior. Underlying causes of the problem may not be addressed. (303)

benzodiazepines A type of medication used to treat anxiety disorders. (307)

bipolar disorder A type of psychopathology characterized by both depression and mania. (302)

cognitive therapy A type of psychotherapy aimed at altering the way people think as a cure for some forms of psychopathology. (303)

delirium A treatable disease causing confusion and cognitive problems. (310)

dementia A family of diseases characterized by cognitive decline. Some forms of dementia are treatable and some are not. (309)

dysphoria Feeling down or blue, marked by extreme sadness; the major symptom of depression. (297)

family therapy A type of psychotherapy that views the family as a dynamic system, with a focus on working with all family members. (327)

heterocyclic antidepressants (HCAs) The most common form of drugs given to treat depression. (301)

internal belief systems An aspect of personality having to do with the issue of personal control, which is thought to be a key factor in psychosocial theories of depression. (301)

MAO inhibitors A type of drug used to treat depression that has potentially serious side effects. (302)

mental status exam A short screening device that tests mental competence, usually used as a brief indicator of dementia or other cognitive impairment. (316)

multi-infarct dementia A form of dementia caused by a series of small strokes. (321)

Parkinson's disease A form of dementia marked by tremor and difficulty in walking. (321)

psychoanalytic therapy Psychotherapy based on Freudian theory. (304)

respite care Providing relief to caregivers for some period of time. (324)

sundowning The phenomenon in which persons with Alzheimer's disease show an increase in symptoms later in the day. (313)

ADDITIONAL READING

An excellent source of general information about many types of psychopathology and therapies within a biopsychosocial perspective is

Fry, P. S. (1986). *Depression, stress, and adaptations in the elderly.* Rockville, MD: Aspen. Moderately difficult.

For an overview of assessment in a wide variety of situations with many different types of older adults see

Hunt, T., & Lindley, C. J. (Eds.). (1989). *Testing older adults.* Austin, TX: Pro-Ed. Moderately difficult.

An outstanding, very readable, and comprehensive resource on Alzheimer's disease, developed in conjunction with the Alzheimer's Association, is

Aronson, M. K. (Ed.). (1988). *Understanding Alzheimer's disease.* New York: Scribner's. Easy reading.

A readable overview of therapeutic interventions with people in nursing homes is

Weiner, M. B., Brok, A. J., & Snadowsky, A. M. (1987). *Working with the aged* (2nd ed.). Norwalk, CT: Appleton-Century-Crofts. Easy reading.

CHAPTER 10

Relationships

James Wyeth, *Breakfast at Sea*, 1984.

RELATIONSHIPS

Friendships / Love Relationships / How Do We Know? Choosing Mates Around the World

LIFE STYLES AND LOVE RELATIONSHIPS

Marriage / Singlehood / Cohabitation / Gay Male and Lesbian Couples / Divorce and Remarriage / Widowhood

PARENTHOOD

Deciding Whether to Have Children / The Parental Role / The Child-Rearing Years / When the Children Leave

FAMILY DYNAMICS AND MIDDLE AGE

Middle-Agers and Their Children / Middle-Agers and Their Aging Parents / Something to Think About: Hiring Surrogates to Care for Frail Elderly Parents

GRANDPARENTING

Styles of Grandparenting / The Meaning of Grandparenthood / Grandparents and Grand-children / Great-Grandparenthood

**Summary / Review Questions
Key Terms / Additional Reading**

IMAGINE YOURSELF MANY YEARS FROM NOW. YOUR children are all adults, with children and grand-children of their own. In honor of your birthday, they, along with your friends, have all gathered. As a present to you, they have assembled hundreds of photographs and dozens of videos from your life. As you begin looking at them, you realize for the first time how lucky you have been to have so many wonderful people in your life. You realize that it has been your relationships that has made your life fun and worthwhile.

Could you picture what it would be like going through life totally alone? Think of all the wonder-ful experiences you would miss — never knowing what friendship is all about, never being in love, never dreaming about children and becoming a grandparent someday, never being able to wish on a star that you and someone special could be to-gether. Our journey through life is not made alone. We are accompanied by many friends and relatives who love us and make us feel important. The same point was made years ago by the songwriter who said that people who need people are the luckiest people in the world. The bonds we form with friends and family get us through the good and bad times. The good is so much better and the bad is so much easier to take if we have someone to share them with.

How we express our mutual interdependence with other people differs according to the situa-tion — whether it be a family interaction, a love and sexual relationship, or a friendship. Relations that reflect love and attachment are especially impor-tant, since they are essential to survival and well-being throughout the life span. Although the nature of love in relationships is different at different ages, there is no doubt that men and women strive to attain it regardless of age (Reedy, Birren, & Schaie, 1981).

In this chapter we will explore some of the forms that our personal relationships take. First, we will consider friendships and love relationships and how they change across adulthood. Because love relationships usually involve a couple, we will explore how it is that two persons find each other and marry and how marriages develop. We will also consider singlehood, divorce, remarriage, and widowhood. Finally, we will take up some of the important roles associated with personal relationships, including parenting, family roles, and grandparenting.

RELATIONSHIPS

Friendships

What is a friend? Someone who is there when you need to share? Someone not afraid to tell you the truth? Someone to have fun with? The question is difficult to answer. But we all have an intuitive understanding that friendships are necessary, that they take work and time to develop, and that they play an important role in our daily lives.

Creating Friendships. A friendship, like any other intimate relationship, needs time to grow. It has been argued that friendships develop in three stages that reflect different levels of involvement. During the first phase there is only mutual awareness; people notice each other and make some judgment. This phase quickly passes to the second, termed *surface contact*, in which the two persons' behavior is governed by existing social norms and little self-disclosure occurs. In these first two stages

the people become what most of us call acquaintances. For a true friendship a third stage is necessary. As self-disclosure begins, the acquaintanceship moves into the mutuality stage, marking the transition to friendship. At this point the individuals probably start feeling a sense of commitment to each other and begin to develop private norms to guide their relationship. It is during this last stage that characteristics typically associated with close friendships — such as honesty, sincerity, and emotional support — emerge (Newman, 1982).

Developmental Aspects of Friendships. On the average, people tend to have more friends and acquaintances during young adulthood than at any subsequent period (Antonucci, 1985). Several reasons account for this age-related decrease. First, age-segregated and highly concentrated college campuses, which foster the development of friendships, give way to age-integrated work settings and neighborhoods, which make friendships somewhat more difficult to establish. Second, our typical geographic mobility during adulthood makes long-term close friendships difficult to maintain. Third, beyond the earliest years of adulthood, most people become too busy with their own families and careers to keep large friendship networks. Fourth, opposite-gender friendships typically diminish, probably because members of the opposite gender are perceived as threats to one's marriage (Huyck, 1982). Finally, the likelihood that members of one's friendship network will die increases with age.

Even though their numbers decline, friendships appear to become particularly important in later life. It may surprise you to learn that older adults' life satisfaction is largely unrelated to the quantity or quality of contact with the younger members of their own family but is substantially related to the quantity and quality of contacts with friends (Antonucci, 1985; Essex & Nam, 1987; Larson, 1978; Lee & Ellithorpe, 1982). The importance of maintaining contacts with friends cuts across ethnic lines as well. Ellison (1990) showed that happiness among African Americans is strongly related to the number of friends.

Why are friends so important to the elderly? Some researchers believe that one reason may be older adults' concern that they not become burdens to their families (Roberto & Scott, 1986). As a result they help their friends foster independence. This reciprocity is a crucial aspect of friendship in later life, since it allows the paying back of indebtedness over time. Also important, though, is that friends are fun for people of all ages. The relationships we have with family members are not always positive, but we choose our friends for their pleasure value (Larson, Mannell, & Zuzanek, 1986).

Gender Differences in Friendships. Men and women tend to have different friendship patterns and derive different things out of friendships. These differences originate in childhood and are most apparent during young adulthood (Fox, Gibbs, & Auerbach, 1985). Men tend to base friendships on shared activities or interests, whereas women tend to base them on intimate and emotional sharing. Men are more likely to go bowling or talk sports with their friends, whereas women may ask friends over for coffee to discuss personal matters (Huyck, 1982). The differences become even more apparent when the aspects of the self that are disclosed to friends are examined. In one study (Hacker, 1981) 25% of the women surveyed said that they revealed only their weaknesses to friends, whereas 20% of the men revealed only their strengths.

Huyck (1982) speculates that male confiding is inconsistent with the need to compete and provides a reason for men's reluctance to do so. Interestingly, the act of confiding, which is essential for true friendship, is a basis of the female standard of friendship. Arguably, this is the socially desirable model, one of the few times that women hold this position.

Sibling Friendships. The longest-term relationships we typically have in our lives are with our

Friendships remain important throughout adulthood.

siblings, because siblings usually outlive parents. For people over age 60, 83% report that they feel close to at least one brother or sister (Dunn, 1984). This closeness dates to childhood and adolescence and is based on shared family experiences.

Despite the length and importance of sibling relationships, very little research has examined their developmental course. Gold (1990) has identified different types of sibling interactions that reflect different patterns of emotional support, as well as closeness and frequency of contact. T. R. Lee, Mancini, and Maxwell (1990) showed that these different patterns result in different amounts and reasons for contact. That is, emotional closeness and geographical proximity result in the most frequent and positive contacts with siblings. Intimate, congenial, and loyal sibling relationships appear to be more characteristic of African-American siblings than white siblings (Gold, 1990). Gold speculates that such ethnic differences reflect different types of socialization toward siblings.

Ties between sisters are typically the strongest, most frequent, and most intimate (Cicirelli, 1980; Lee et al., 1990). Brother pairs tend to maintain less frequent contact (Connidis, 1988). Little is known about brother-sister relationships. Even though many older adults end up living with one of their siblings, we know virtually nothing about how or why this occurs.

Interestingly, what little we know about the roles siblings play comes from cross-cultural research. The degree to which siblings' roles are substitutable (for example, a father or his brother could serve as a male role model) or complementary (for example, it takes a man and a woman to form a father-mother couple) is important in many cultures. For example, in some Oceanic cultures, a gender-based division of labor results in complementary roles in the economic system (brothers are responsible for managing coconut palms while their sisters manage taro plots, for instance) (Feinberg, 1983). Some Irish-American men continue to farm land for their brother's widow, an example of substitutability (Salamon, 1982). Among the Ibaloi and Kankana-ey people in the Philippine highlands, there are even language terms to distinguish both gender and relative age (J. T. Peterson, 1990). These distinctions suggest a complex kinship structure that assigns specific tasks to specific genders at specific ages. Such practices occur in Western families (young girls may be given different tasks to perform than their older sisters), but we have no systematic data on them.

Clearly, there are major gaps in our understanding of sibling relationships. This is truly unfortun-ate, as our brothers and sisters play an important and meaningful role throughout our lives.

Love Relationships

Love is one of those things that everybody can feel but nobody can define adequately or completely. (Test yourself: How would you explain what you mean when you look at someone and say, "I love you"?) Despite the difficulty in defining it, love underlies our most important relationships in life. In this section we will consider the components of love and how it develops across adulthood.

The Components of Love. There is little consensus about the nature of love. What most researchers do is identify important concepts of love and then use them to create different categories of love. Sternberg (1986) conducted a series of detailed studies on people's conceptions of love and how love is manifested in different ways. Based on this research, Sternberg developed a theory of love based on three components: (1) *passion*, an intense physiological desire for someone; (2) *intimacy*, the feeling that one can share all one's thoughts and actions with another; and (3) *commitment*, the willingness to stay with a person through good and bad times. Based on different combinations of these three components, Sternberg identified seven forms of love:

1. *Liking*: intimacy but no commitment or passion
2. *Infatuation*: passion but no commitment or intimacy
3. *Empty love*: commitment but no passion or intimacy
4. *Romantic love*: intimacy and passion but no commitment
5. *Fatuous love*: commitment and passion but no intimacy
6. *Companionate love*: commitment and intimacy but no passion

7. *Consummate love*: commitment, intimacy, and passion

Ideally, a true love relationship such as marriage has all three components, although the balance shifts as time passes.

Love Across Adulthood. The different combinations of love that Sternberg identifies can be used to understand how relationships develop. Early in a relationship passion is usually high, but intimacy and commitment tend to be low. This results in infatuation: an intense, physically based relationship in which the two persons have little understanding of each other and a high risk of misunderstanding and jealousy. Interestingly, this pattern seems to characterize all kinds of couples — married, unmarried, heterosexual, and homosexual (Kurdek & Schmitt, 1986).

As the relationship continues, companionate love develops, a style characterized by greater intimacy and commitment but no passion. As Hatfield and Walster (1978) put it, "Passionate love is a fragile flower — it wilts in time. Companionate love is a sturdy evergreen; it thrives with contact." Sternberg (1986) compares infatuation to a drug addiction; in the beginning, even a small touch is enough to drive each partner into ecstasy. Gradually, though, one needs more and more stimulation to get the same feeling. Lovers eventually get used to the pleasures of passion with the same person, and passion fades. The wild passion of youth gives way to the deeper, committed love of adulthood.

Although the styles of love appear to differ with age, some important aspects of love relationships appear to maintain their same relative importance over time. Reedy, Birren, and Schaie (1981) examined 6 aspects of love relationships in 102 happily married couples: communication, sexual intimacy, respect, help and play behaviors, emotional security, and loyalty. As can be seen in Figure 10.1, the importance of some of love's aspects in satisfying relationships differs as a function of age. Overall, the findings support the idea that passion is relatively more important to younger couples, while tenderness and loyalty are relatively more important to older couples. Interestingly, sexual intimacy is equally important for young and middle-aged couples, and communication is more important to young couples than to any other group. Notice, however, that the relative rankings of the different components of love are the same for all age groups. Thus, although the particular weightings may vary, there are remarkable similarities across age in the nature of love relationships.

These results make intuitive sense. It is reasonable that young couples should focus more on communication, since they are still in the process of getting to know each other. Once this has occurred and people begin to anticipate their partner's reactions, they move to a love that is based more on security, commitment, and loyalty. Of course, all of this assumes that one has a partner to love in the first place. How we find one of these is the topic of the next section.

Selecting a Partner. How do we find someone to love? The process of mate selection has been researched a great deal over the years. Murstein (1982) synthesized this large literature and concluded that mate selection occurred in the United States in three stages: the stimulus stage, the values stage, and the roles stage. It should be noted that Murstein's conclusions tend to fall along traditional gender stereotypic lines, which means that they may only describe a subset of people.

In the first stage one or more interesting stimuli — such as physical attractiveness, intellect, or social status — make the two individuals notice each other. Physical attractiveness is an especially strong stimulus for many men. Women may look for attractive men, but they are also drawn to a person with status (preferring a leader to a follower), a good education, and a good job. But preferences do not necessarily become choices. Both men and women compare their perceptions of

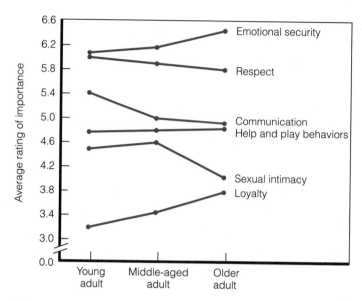

FIGURE 10.1 Developmental differences in components of love. Note that there are differences across age in the ratings of the different components but that the rank orders of the components are the same.

(Source: "Age and Sex Differences in Satisfying Love Relationships Across the Adult Life Span" by M. N. Reedy, J. E. Birren, and K. W. Schaie, 1981, *Human Development, 24,* 52–56. Copyright © 1981 by Karger. Reprinted with permission.)

themselves with their perceptions of someone they are attracted to; only when these two perceptions are about equal are they likely to approach the other person.

The hallmark of the second stage is a comparison of values. Couples discuss their attitudes toward work, marriage, religion, society, culture, and a host of other topics. The more similar their values, the more likely it is that their attraction to each other will deepen; it is true that "birds of a feather flock together." It is not true that "opposites attract," at least in terms of stable relationships.

Finally, as interactions become more frequent and intimate, each person develops roles within the relationship. Developing roles goes beyond the comparisons of values in the previous stage. It is a

way to see how each partner copes with the day-to-day aspects of the relationship, and it provides a forum to see whether the person accepts or shirks responsibility, is honest or deceitful, is moody or even-keeled, and so forth. In short, the roles stage provides a way to understand what makes the other person tick.

Overall, men tend to be quicker than women to think that they are compatible with their partner. Perhaps this is because men and women tend to have different ideas about love (Peplau & Gordon, 1985). Men tend to be more romantic; believing in love at first sight, feeling that there is only one true love destined for them, and regarding love as magical and impossible to understand. Women, on the other hand, tend to be cautious pragmatists who

HOW DO WE KNOW?

Choosing Mates Around the World

If you were a man living in India, how would the woman of your dreams differ from the ideal woman of a man living in Finland? Likewise, how do the desired men differ for women living in Nigeria and Great Britain? Buss and his colleagues decided to find out. They specifically examined the effects of culture and gender on mate preferences on a truly worldwide sample. Participants in the 37 samples (N = 9,474) represented 33 countries from 6 continents and 5 islands.

Participants were asked to complete measures concerning important factors in choosing a mate (such as, rating desired characteristics of potential mates) and preferences concerning potential mates (for example, ranking characteristics of potential mates from highest to lowest). Data were gathered by individuals in each country. In some cases, the survey items had to be modified to reflect the local culture. For example, many couples in Sweden, Finland, and Norway do not get married, opting instead simply to live together. In Nigeria, items had to reflect the possibility of many wives due to the practice of polygyny. Data collection in South Africa was described as "a rather frightening experience" due to the difficulty in collecting data from both white and Zulu samples. Finally, in some cases data were never received due to governmental interference or the lack of official approval to conduct the study. Such problems highlight the difficulty in doing cross-cultural research and the need to take local culture into account in designing research instruments.

As noted in the text, statistical analyses showed that each culture displayed a unique ordering of preferences concerning ideal characteristics. Despite the diversity, some common themes emerged. First, cultures tend to vary along a dimension referred to as *traditional-modern*. Countries such as China, India, Iran, and Nigeria represent the traditional end, while the Netherlands, Great Britain, Finland, and Sweden represent the modern end. In addition, the relative importance of education, intelligence, and refinement in choosing a mate is an important dimension along which countries vary.

Overall, Buss and his colleagues' results clearly demonstrate that mate selection is a complex process no matter where you live. The study also shows that socialization plays a key role in attractiveness; characteristics that are highly desirable in one culture may be highly undesirable in another.

---

believe that financial security is as important as passion in a relationship, that there are many people whom a person could learn to love, and that love does not conquer all differences.

How do these dimensions based on U.S. samples compare to cross-cultural evidence? In an extraordinary study, Buss and a large team of researchers (1990) identified the effects of culture and gender on mate preferences in 37 cultures worldwide. They had people rate and rank each of 18 characteristics (such as mutual attraction, chastity, dependable character, good health) on how important or desirable it would be in choosing a mate. These characteristics were based on ones used in U.S. research since the 1940s.

Buss found strong cultural effects, with each culture producing somewhat different preferences. A more detailed discussion of these is in How Do We Know? Chastity proved to be the characteristic showing the most variability across cultures; in some cultures it is highly desired, while in others it matters little. Interestingly, consistent gender differences emerged across cultures on the characteristics of earning potential (endorsed consistently more often by women) and physical attractiveness (endorsed consistently more often by men). Buss and his colleagues argue that the consistency of these gender differences across cultures supports evolution-based speculation about the importance of resources and reproductive value in mates. That is, in their respective search for mates, men around the world value physical attractiveness in women while women around the world look for men who will be good providers.

LIFE STYLES AND LOVE RELATIONSHIPS

Developing relationships is only part of the picture in understanding how adults live their lives with other people. Putting relationships in context is the goal of the following sections, as we explore the major life styles of adults. Because most people eventually get married, we will consider marriage first. Later, we will consider people who never get married, those who get divorced, people who are widowed, and those choosing homosexual relationships.

Marriage

Without question the vast majority of adults want their love relationships to result in marriage, although Americans are taking longer to achieve that. The median age at first marriage for adults in the United States has been rising for several decades. From 1960 to 1990 the median age for men rose about 3 years, from roughly 23 to 26, and the age for women rose nearly 4 years, from roughly 20 to 24 (U. S. Bureau of the Census, 1991). Although this increase in age at first marriage means that lifelong

singlehood is also increasing, more than 90% of American adults are still likely to get married for the foreseeable future.

As anyone who has tried it knows, marriage is hard work. Most of us also have an intuitive sense that certain factors — such as similarity of interests and values, age of the couple, and so forth — make a difference in the probability that a marriage will succeed. But we may not be aware of other important determinants. What is it, exactly, that keeps marriages going strong over time?

Factors Influencing the Success of Marriages. Although marriages, like other relationships, differ from one another, some general trends can be identified. One of the clearest is that marriages based on similarity of values and interests are the most likely to succeed (Diamond, 1986). Interestingly, the importance of **homogamy**, marriage based on similarity, extends across a wide variety of cultures and societies, as diverse as Americans in Michigan and Africans in Chad (Diamond, 1986).

A second important factor in enduring marriages is the relative maturity of the two partners at the time they are married. In general, the younger the partners are, the greater the odds that the marriage will not last, especially when the individuals are in their teens or early 20s (Kelly, 1982). In part, the age issue relates to Erikson's belief that intimacy cannot be achieved until after one's identity is established (see Chapter 8). Other reasons that marriages may or may not last include the degree of financial security (low security is related to high risk of failure) and pregnancy at the time of the marriage (being a pregnant bride is related to high risk of failure, especially in very young couples) (Kelly, 1982).

The Developmental Course of Marital Satisfaction. Considerable research has been conducted on marital satisfaction across adulthood. As shown in Figure 10.2, overall marital satisfaction is highest at

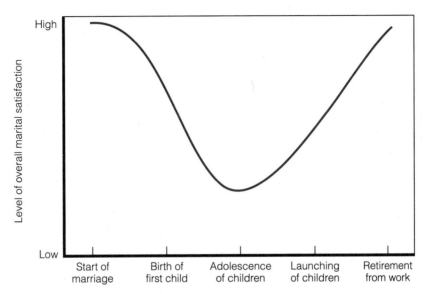

FIGURE 10.2 Composite graph of marital satisfaction across adulthood. As noted in the text, however, some couples do not show a significant decline in satisfaction.

the beginning of the marriage, falls until the children begin leaving home, and rises again in later life (Berry & Williams, 1987).

In its early days marriage is at its most intense. During this honeymoon phase, the couple spend considerable time together — talking, going out, establishing their marital roles, arguing, making up, and making love. In good marriages, in which husband and wife share many activities and are open to new experiences together, this honeymoon phase results in bliss and high satisfaction (Olson & McCubbin, 1983). When the marriage is troubled, the intensity of the honeymoon phase creates considerable unhappiness (Swenson, Eskew, & Kohlhepp, 1981).

During the honeymoon phase the couple must learn to adjust to the different perceptions and expectations each person has for the other. Many wives tend to be more concerned than their husbands with keeping close ties with their friends. Many women are also more likely to identify problems in the marriage and want to talk about them (Peplau & Gordon, 1985). The couple must also learn to handle confrontation. Indeed, learning effective conflict resolution strategies may be the most important thing a newly married couple can do for their marriage.

As the bliss of the honeymoon phase becomes a memory, marital satisfaction tends to decline, especially for many women. The decline in satisfaction holds for couples of diverse educational, religious, employment, age, and racial backgrounds (Glenn & McLanahan, 1981, 1982). The most common reason given for this drop is the birth of children. For most couples, having children means having substantially less time to devote to the marriage. As we will see in our discussion of parenthood, taking care of children is hard work, stealing energy that used to be spent on keeping the marriage alive and well (Glenn & Weaver, 1978). The fact that even childless couples experience a modest decline in marital satisfaction means that the drop is not totally due to having children. For example, Kurdek (1991a) found that declines in marital satisfaction over the first three years of marriage were related to lower education and failure to pool financial resources. However, whether being childless is a voluntary decision or due to infertility may make a big difference in marital satisfaction, with the latter group experiencing considerable stress (Matthews & Matthews, 1986).

By midlife, marital satisfaction hits rock bottom, and some differences between husbands and wives emerge (Turner, 1982). Husbands at all stages of the marriage tend to describe it in positive terms, whereas middle-aged wives tend to be more critical. For example, Lowenthal, Thurnher, and Chiriboga (1975) found that 80% of husbands, but only 40% of wives rated their marriages favorably in midlife. Wives' chief complaint was that their husbands were too dependent and clingy; interestingly, this difference in feelings is sometimes noted in newlyweds, but then it is husbands who describe their wives in such terms.

Marital satisfaction usually begins to rebound, at least temporarily, following the launching of adult children (Rhyne, 1981). The improvement is especially noteworthy in women, and it stems partly from the increased financial security after children leave, the relief from the day-to-day duties of parenting, and the additional time that wives have with their husbands.

For some middle-aged couples, however, marital satisfaction continues to be low. These couples tend to be ones who have grown apart but who continue to live together. In essence, they have become emotionally divorced (Fitzpatrick, 1984). For these couples, more time together is not a welcome change. Additionally, the physical appearance of one's partner is a contributor to marital satisfaction,

particularly for men (Margolin & White, 1987). Because age-related changes in women's appearance are viewed more negatively by society (see Chapter 3), some middle-aged men become increasingly disenchanted with their marriage.

Several studies report that marital satisfaction tends to be fairly high in older couples (Anderson, Russell, & Schumm, 1983; Lee, 1988; Maas & Kuypers, 1974). This level of satisfaction appears to be unrelated to the amount of past or present sexual interest or sexual activity (Bullock & Dunn, 1988) but is positively related to the degree of interaction with friends (Lee, 1988).

However, some researchers observe inconsistencies in satisfaction in long-term marriages (Ade-Ridder & Brubaker, 1983; Sporakowski & Axelson, 1984; Swensen & Trahaug, 1985). For example, Gilford (1984) reports that marital satisfaction among older couples increases shortly after retirement but decreases as health problems and age rise. Sporakowski and Axelson (1984) found that 80% of couples married at least 50 years recollected their marriages as being happy from their wedding day to the present. Surprisingly, however, only 28% of these couples named their spouse as being one of their closest friends.

The discrepant data concerning marital satisfaction in long-term marriages may be due to several factors. For one thing couples in this cohort were less likely to have divorced due to disagreement than those in more recent cohorts and may have developed detached, contented styles (Norton & Moorman, 1987). Older couples may also have different criteria for marital satisfaction than younger couples. Or they may not see the point in arguing anymore. Moreover, many older couples do not need to have their spouses be their best friends to be satisfied with their marriage. Also, Lee (1988) found lower marital satisfaction among older couples with working wives and retired husbands than among couples where both spouses were working or were retired. Unfortunately, our understanding of the dynamics of long-term marriages is extremely limited, so sorting out these possibilities must await further research.

Overall, marital satisfaction ebbs and flows over time. The pattern of a particular marriage over the years is determined by the nature of the dependence of each spouse on the other. When dependence is mutual and about equal, the marriage is strong and close. When the dependence of one partner is much higher than that of the other, however, the marriage is likely to be characterized by stress and conflict. Changes in individual lives over adulthood shift the balance of dependence from one partner to the other; for example, one partner may go back to school, become ill, or lose a job. Learning how to deal with these changes is the secret to long and happy marriages.

What Are Long-Term Marriages Like? Maybe you know couples who have celebrated their golden wedding anniversary. Perhaps you have even participated in such a celebration for your grandparents. You may have wondered how these couples managed to stay together for so long.

The answer to this question lies in considering types of marriages. Over the years several attempts have been made at describing types of marriages. For example, Cuber and Harroff (1965) asked middle-aged couples to describe what their marriages had been like. This approach yields different categories, but such descriptions are static; that is, they simply describe what couples are like at one point. Although point-in-time models are helpful, they do not capture the dynamics of marriage over the long haul. To do this requires longitudinal research.

Weishaus and Field (1988) conducted a longitudinal study of 17 couples married between 50 and 69 years that included measures of relationship quality over virtually the entire length of the couples' years together. The results of their research show that long-term marriages vary in their developmental trajectories. Moreover, couples show a real ability to roll with the punches and adapt to changing circumstances. For example, a spouse's serious illness may not be detrimental to the relationship and may even make the bond stronger. Likewise, couples' expectations about marriage change over time, gradually becoming more congruent.

Singlehood

During the early years of adulthood, most Americans are single. Current estimates are that 75% of men and 57% of women between the ages of 20 and 25 are unmarried. These percentages have been rising over the past few decades with the rise in median age of first marriage. Most single men and women enjoy this part of their lives, during which they have few responsibilities. For women, being single has the advantage of increasing the likelihood that they will go to college (Haggstrom, Kanouse, & Morrison, 1986).

Information about single people is very scarce. Beyond the contradictory popular images of singles as swingers on cruise ships and getaway weekends or as lonely people existing in quiet desperation, few scientific data are available. Perhaps the lack of research is due to the fact that relatively few adults never marry, so singlehood is treated as a transient state of little inherent interest. This situation may change as more people in recent cohorts remain single.

Deciding Not to Marry. Evidence drawn from several sources indicates that men and women typically decide whether to remain single between the ages of 25 and 30 (Phillis & Stein, 1983). One of the few consistent trends that emerges is a tendency for people with very little formal education (less than five years) and women with graduate training to remain single. Some speculate that highly intelligent women may choose career and personal freedom over marriage, or that these women stay single because they intimidate men with their superior earning power and career success (Doudna & McBride, 1981; Unger, 1979).

How the decision to remain single occurs has been the subject of much speculation. Different explanations have been offered for delayed marriage, including changes in sexual standards, the increased financial independence of women, various liberation movements, changing economic conditions, and changing conceptions of marriage (Safilios-Rothschild, 1977; Stein, 1978). However, some adults may simply postpone indefinitely the decision about whether to marry and slide into singlehood.

Because they spend a lifetime without a spouse, single adults develop long-standing alternative social patterns based on friendships. Women, especially, are highly involved with relatives — caring for an aged parent, living with a sibling, or actively helping nieces and nephews. Loneliness is typically not an issue; one study found that never-married women were comparable to married women (Essex & Nam, 1987), and other evidence argues that they are not socially isolated (Rubinstein, 1987).

The Single Role. Scientifically, we know very little about what it is like to be a single adult. There is some evidence to suggest that many never-married adults have more androgynous gender identities, have high achievement needs, are more autonomous, and want to maintain close relationships with others (Phillis & Stein, 1983). Singles may be acutely aware of their ambivalent feelings concerning their desires to have a successful career and their equally strong desires for intimacy. For many, this ambivalence is the reason they choose not to risk marriage.

Perhaps the two most difficult issues for single people are how to handle dating and others' expectations that they should marry. Both men and women experience role constrictions while dating: how sex should be handled, how to date without getting too serious too fast, and how to initiate a close friendship without coming on too strong. In addition, other people often assume that everyone gets married and sometimes force a single person to defend his or her status. This pressure to marry is especially strong for women as they near 30; frequent questions like "Any good prospects yet?" may cause women to feel conspicuous or left out as many of their friends marry.

Although attitudes are changing, it is still the case that people (especially women) who choose not to marry are often ostracized. Americans are extremely couple oriented, and as their friends marry, single people find their friendship networks shrinking accordingly. Moreover, such social behaviors as feeling sorry for never-married people compound our basic lack of understanding of them. Still, many never-married people report that they are quite happy: The satisfaction derived from careers and friendships is more than enough (Alwin, Converse, & Martin, 1985).

Cohabitation

Not being married does not mean having to live alone. Many unmarried adults live with other people who are not family members. Such living arrangements include sharing apartments and houses with other same-gender occupants. In the present context, however, we will define **cohabitation** as referring to two members of the opposite gender who live together but who are not married.

Over the last 25 years cohabitation has increased almost 60-fold. Proponents argue that it is a preparation for marriage; opponents may view it as living in sin. In this section we will consider who cohabits and why.

Who Cohabits? Although most attention is focused on college-age cohabitants, living together is certainly not confined to this age group. Research shows that cohabitants come from all socioeconomic backgrounds and represent all age groups. For instance, older couples sometimes choose cohabitation rather than marriage for financial reasons, and men who have less than a high school education or who are not attending college are more likely to cohabit (Glick & Norton, 1979). Other research shows that by the mid-1980s almost one third of all women between 20 and 29 had lived with an unrelated man (Tanfer, 1987).

Another group likely to cohabit is recent immigrants. For example, Muschkin and Myers (1989) report that cohabitation among second-generation Puerto Rican immigrants to the United States is higher than for first-generation individuals.

Attitudes Toward Cohabitation. In general, college students see cohabitation more as a relevant step toward marriage than as a permanent alternative to it. This is especially true of women, who are much more eager to marry their partners than are men (Blumstein & Schwartz, 1983). Cohabitation seems acceptable to students in a strong, affectionate, monogamous relationship that, they believe, will eventually lead to marriage. Partners emphasize the educational and socializing value of cohabitation; they describe it as a valuable learning experience that aids in personal growth and helps the couple evaluate their degree of commitment to each other (Macklin, 1978).

Gender differences in attitudes toward cohabitation have been noted. Men appear somewhat more open to cohabiting and do not feel the need for as strong an emotional commitment before living together. Women generally expect a deeper commitment and may feel exploited if it is absent (Macklin, 1988). Men are more likely to take it for granted that their partner will want to marry them, but, as noted earlier, women tend to be more eager to get married in order to achieve commitment (Blumstein & Schwartz, 1983).

Cohabitation Versus Marriage. For many, choosing whether to cohabit or to marry is a difficult and emotionally charged decision. Indeed, most cohabiting couples either marry or end the relationship in a relatively short period (Macklin, 1988). Cohabitants who do marry are very different from those who continue living together. Blumstein and Schwartz (1983) found that cohabitants who married held much more traditional views about the roles of men and women in society, were not avant-garde about their relationships, were more likely to pool their money and resources from the start, and saw each other in more flattering ways.

Considerable research has been aimed at uncovering differences between cohabiting and married couples. At first glance one might expect cohabiting couples to be more egalitarian than their married counterparts on the grounds that they must be more liberal and open-minded. However, this does not seem to be the case. Decision making, division of labor, communication, and satisfaction with the relationship do not appear to distinguish cohabiting and married couples (Yllo, 1978). Cohabiting couples are not more liberated in making financial decisions than married couples; when women have more power over the finances, cohabiting couples tend to fight as well (Blumstein & Schwartz, 1983). Finally, cohabitants do not engage in sex outside of their relationship any more often than do married couples (Phillis & Stein, 1983). Differences in the rate of nonmonogamous relationships are more related to cohort than to type of relationship, with younger couples more likely to engage in sex outside of their primary relationship (Blumstein & Schwartz, 1983).

In summary, research consistently shows many similarities between people who cohabit and people who marry. Many cohabiting couples tend to reflect the predominant social values and gender roles to the same degree as the couples who get married. Perhaps this is not surprising. After all, by their own admission many cohabiting couples view cohabitation as a prelude to, not a replacement for, marriage (Blumstein & Schwartz, 1983; DeMaris & Leslie, 1984).

Gay Male and Lesbian Couples

Less is known about the developmental course of gay male and lesbian relationships than about any other type. Perhaps this is because these relationships are not widely viewed as an acceptable alternative to traditional marriage. Besides the usual problems of instability and guilt that sometimes accompany other forms of cohabitation, gay male and lesbian couples experience several additional problems resulting from societal disapproval of such relationships. For example, the loss of one's mate cannot be openly mourned, since in many situations revealing one's gay or lesbian relationship may put one's job in jeopardy (Kimmel, 1978).

One of the major differences between cohabiting or married couples and gay male or lesbian couples is the frequency of sexual contact. On this dimension there is a difference between gay male and lesbian couples. On average, gay men, more than any other type of couple, begin sexual relations early in the relationship (Blumstein & Schwartz, 1983). However, after the relationship has lasted a few years, they have sex much less than the average married couple. Lesbian couples are more likely to have intense, intimate, monogamous relationships than are gay men, and they tend to have sex far less frequently than any other group (Blumstein & Schwartz, 1983). Lesbian couples are also more likely to stay together than are gay men.

Once the couple are together, several choices must be made, as is the case in any intimate relationship. For example, decisions need to be made about the style of the relationship — whether there will be clearly defined roles of nurturer and provider and whether the relationship will be sexually open (Blumstein & Schwartz, 1983). This latter issue is especially salient given the AIDS epidemic. Many gay men and lesbians have lost close friends to AIDS; relationship patterns have changed, especially in terms of sexual activity (Stall, Coates, & Hoff, 1988).

Gay male and lesbian relationships are similar to traditional marriages in many ways; financial problems and decisions, household chores, and power differentials are issues for all couples. Schneider (1986) reports that lesbian partners tend to divide household chores more equitably than cohabiting heterosexual couples. Moreover, gay male and lesbian parents do not differ substantially on most dimensions from heterosexual single parents (Harris & Turner, 1986).

Divorce and Remarriage

Through separation, divorce, and desertion, many adults make the transition from being married back to being single. (Later we will consider people who return to singlehood as the result of the death of their spouse.) These transitions are always stressful and difficult. The transition from being married to being single again involves important changes in both status and role expectations. For example, holidays may be difficult for individuals now unable to be with their children. In this section we will consider several issues in dealing with divorce and the decision to remarry.

Divorced Adults. Most adults enter marriage with the idea that the relationship will be permanent. Unfortunately, this permanence is becoming less attainable for more and more couples. Their early intimacy fails to grow. Rather than growing together, they grow apart.

Many factors may disrupt a relationship to the extent that a couple seeks divorce. We will consider attitudes toward divorce, changing expectations of marriage, gender differences, and demographic factors. We will also look at some of the problems facing divorced adults and the odds that they will enter into new relationships or marriages. But first it would be helpful to consider the facts: What are the odds of getting divorced?

Since reaching a post-World War II low during the 1950s, divorce rates for first marriages have been rising consistently at about 10% per year. (From 1960 to 1988 the actual increase was nearly 250%.) During the late 1980s the increase in the divorce rate slowed, although it is still too early to tell whether that trend will continue. Presently, at least one in every three households is affected by divorce. Based on current trends it is now estimated that couples who have recently married have no better than a 50-50 chance of remaining married for life (Fisher, 1987).

Statistics worldwide and from different periods indicate that marriages fail relatively quickly. Internationally, the peak time for divorce is 3 or 4 years after the wedding, or when the couple are in their late 20s. The United States reflects that trend, with half of all divorces occurring within the first seven years of marriage (Fisher, 1987).

Another way to approach the question of who is likely to get divorced is to examine personal demographic factors. One consistent factor related to divorce is ethnicity. African Americans are more likely than whites to divorce or separate (Glenn & Supancic, 1984). Hispanic groups show considerable variability; Mexican Americans and Cuban Americans have divorce rates similar to non-Hispanic whites, whereas the rate for Puerto Ricans is much higher (Bean & Tienda, 1987). Age is also important. The divorce rate for those who marry before age 20 is substantially higher than that for those who marry after age 20 (Glenn & Supancic, 1984). This difference is due in large part to the negative effects of premarital pregnancy on teenage couples. Higher frequency of attendance at religious services is related to lower divorce rates. Interestingly, in terms of religious preference, con-

servative Protestant denominations (for example, Nazarene, Pentecostal, Baptist) show relatively high divorce rates; rates for Protestants in general are higher than for either Catholics or Jews (Glenn & Supancic, 1984).

The factors that are good predictors of divorce are many of the same ones that argue against getting married in the first place (Udry, 1971). Differences on such dimensions as educational level, race, religion, or socioeconomic status produce marital discord more easily than do similarities.

One prominent reason given for the increase in divorce is that it is not perceived as negatively as it once was. Previous generations considered divorce the solution of last resort and held divorced adults in low regard, sometimes not allowing them to remarry. Even today, divorce is seen as a sign of failure — a pronouncement that the couple wish to end a relationship that they originally intended to last for a lifetime (Crosby, 1980). Still, divorced adults are not subjected to as many overt discriminations as they once were. So in some ways divorce has become a more acceptable, if not respectable, status.

Closely related to this change in attitude toward divorce is a shift in expectations for marriage. More people now expect marriage to be a positive experience and to be personally fulfilling. When a marriage fails to produce bliss, divorce is often pursued as the way to a new and better partner. In the past husbands and wives did not expect to understand each other, because the opposite gender was a natural mystery. Today, middle-class marriage partners have a more flexible view and expect each other to be a friend, lover, wage earner, and caregiver (Blumstein & Schwartz, 1983).

These changes are evident in the reasons that people give for divorcing. In 1948 recently divorced women cited cruelty, excessive drinking, and nonsupport as the most common reasons (Goode, 1956). By 1985 the reasons had shifted to communication problems, basic unhappiness, and incompatibility (Cleek & Pearson, 1985). Although women usually cite more reasons than men, as can be seen in

TABLE 10.1 Main reasons men and women give for divorcing

Reasons Women Give		Reasons Men Give	
1. Communication problems	70%	1. Communication problems	59%
2. Basic unhappiness	60%	2. Basic unhappiness	47%
3. Incompatibility	56%	3. Incompatibility	45%
4. Emotional abuse	56%	4. Sexual problems	30%
5. Financial problems	33%	5. Financial problems	29%
6. Sexual problems	32%	6. Emotional abuse	25%
7. Alcohol abuse by spouse	30%	7. Women's liberation	15%
8. Infidelity by spouse	25%	8. In-laws	12%
9. Physical abuse	22%	9. Infidelity by spouse	11%
10. In-laws	11%	10. Alcohol abuse by self	9%

(Source: Summarized from "Perceived Causes of Divorce: An Analysis of Interrelationships" by M. D. Cleek and T. A. Pearson, 1985. *Journal of Marriage and the Family, 47,* 179–191.)

Table 10.1 there is considerable agreement between the genders. The differences are interesting: Whereas 22% of women cite physical abuse as a significant cause of their divorce, only 3% of men do; and whereas 15% of men cite women's liberation as a cause, only 3% of women do.

These changes in reasons reflect a major shift toward no-fault divorce laws in the United States. In 1948, blame—such as infidelity or nonsupport—had to be established and was legally required for divorce. Today, blame is not a prerequisite, and reasons such as incompatibility are acceptable.

Although the changes in attitudes toward divorce have eased the social trauma associated with it, divorce still takes a high toll on the psyche of the couple. A nationwide survey in the United States revealed that divorce could impair individuals' well-being for at least five years after the event, producing a greater variety of long-lasting negative effects than even the death of a spouse (Nock, 1981). A longitudinal study of divorced people showed that they were more depressed than they had been when they were married (Menaghan & Lieberman, 1986). Divorced people living alone tend to be less happy than either married or cohabiting couples, with degree of unhappiness also related to the number of divorces one has had (Kurdek, 1991b).

Even though the psychological cost of divorce is high, divorced people do not wish they were still married. An intensive longitudinal study found that five years after the divorce only 20% of former partners thought that the divorce had been a mistake. Most approved of it, even if they had initially opposed it. However, most of the people said that they had underestimated the pain that the divorce would cause (Wallerstein & Kelly, 1980).

The nature of the effects of divorce changes over time. In the initial phase shortly after the breakup, the partners often become even angrier and more bitter toward each other than they were before the separation. These feelings are often fostered by lawyers, who may encourage partners to fight over property and custody of the children. Additionally, many partners underestimate their attachment to each other and may be overly sensitive to criticism from them. The increased hostility is often accompanied by periods of depression and disequilibrium, as patterns of eating, sleeping, drug and alcohol use, work, and residence change (Kelly, 1982).

Men have a more difficult time in the short run (Chiriboga, 1982). Most men report being shocked by the break, since it is usually the wife who files for divorce (Kelly, 1982). Husbands are more likely to be blamed for the problems, to accept the blame, to move out, and thereby to find their social life disrupted (Kitson & Sussman, 1982). Thus, although women are typically more distressed before the separation, men have more psychological and physical stress immediately after it (Bloom & Caldwell, 1981).

In the long run, however, women are much more seriously affected by divorce. The reasons are both social and economic. Women have fewer marriage prospects, find it more difficult to establish new relationships if they have custody of the children, and are at a major disadvantage financially. The financial problems of divorced women received considerable attention in the late 1980s as states passed laws to enforce child-support payments. Additionally, an ex-wife is not legally entitled to any of her former husband's Social Security benefits unless the divorce occurs after he has stopped working, nor does she share in pension or health benefits (Cain, 1982). These problems are especially important for middle-aged divorcees, who may have spent years as a homemaker and have few job skills.

Divorce in middle age or late life has some special characteristics. In general, the older the individuals are, the greater the trauma (Chiriboga, 1982), largely because of the long period of investment in each other's emotional and practical lives. Longtime friends often turn away or take sides, causing additional disruption to the social network.

Middle-aged and elderly women are at a significant disadvantage for remarriage — an especially traumatic situation for women who derived much of their identity from their roles as wife and mother. An additional problem for elderly divorced people is that even if the divorce occurred many years earlier, children and other relatives may still blame them for breaking the family apart (Hennon, 1983).

The difficulty in adjusting to divorce often depends on whether there are children. Childless couples tend to adjust more readily, probably because they can make a clean break and a fresh start.

For divorced people with children, the trouble typically begins during the custody battle. Despite much public discussion of joint custody, it is far more typical that one parent gains custody and assumes the role of two parents, while the other is reduced to an occasional visitor. More than 90% of the time the mother receives custody. The price she pays is very high. At the same time that her responsibilities as a parent are increasing, her financial resources are decreasing. On average, divorced mothers experience a 73% decline in their standard of living within the first year following divorce. In contrast, their ex-husbands typically enjoy a 42% rise (Weitzman, 1985). Child care is expensive, and most divorced fathers contribute less than before the separation. In fact, only about one third of all child-support payments are actually made.

Divorced fathers pay a psychological price (Furstenberg & Nord, 1985). Although many divorced fathers would like to remain active in their children's lives, few actually are. Two or more years after the divorce, only one child in five ever stays overnight with the father, and half of all children of divorce have not even seen their father in the previous year. The fact that about one quarter of divorced couples end up as bitter enemies (Ahrons & Wallisch, 1986) only makes matters worse for all concerned.

The problems between divorced people with children can be overcome (Ahrons & Rodgers, 1987; Wallerstein & Kelly, 1980). Some former

couples are able to get over their anger and cooperate with each other. This is especially true if the
couple had no children (Masheter, 1991). Adjustment is also helped if both or neither remarries.
Interestingly, it is easier for a new husband to accept
his wife's friendly relationship with her former husband than it is for a new wife to accept her husband's friendly relationship with his ex-wife.

Remarriage. Although divorce is a traumatic event,
it does not seem to deter people from eventually
beginning new relationships that typically lead
into another marriage. Nearly 80% of divorced
people remarry within the first 3 years (Glick &
Lin, 1986). However, rates vary somewhat across
ethnic groups. African Americans remarry a bit
more slowly than whites, and Hispanics remarry
more slowly than either of these other two groups
(Coleman & Ganong, 1990). Remarriage is much
more likely if the divorced people are young,
mainly because there are more partners available.
Partner availability favors men at all ages because
men tend to marry women younger than themselves. For this reason the probability that a
divorced woman will remarry declines with increasing age. Older divorced women with higher
educational levels are the least likely to remarry
(Glick & Lin, 1986), probably because of a shortage
of eligible unmarried older men and a lesser need
for the financial security provided by a man. However, several studies indicate higher well-being
among widows who remarried than among those
who remained single (Burks, Lund, Gregg, &
Bluhm, 1988; Gentry & Schulman, 1988).

Very little research has been conducted on second (or third or more) marriages. Remarried people
report that they experience their second marriage
differently. They claim to enjoy much better communication, to resolve disagreements with greater
goodwill, to arrive at decisions more equitably,
and to divide chores more fairly (Furstenberg,
1982). Indeed, most couples believe that they will
be more likely to succeed the second time around

(Furstenberg, 1982). For African Americans, this
appears to be true; divorce rates for remarriages are
lower than for first marriages (Teachman, 1986).
However, second marriages in general have a
slightly higher risk of dissolution than first marriages if one spouse has custody of children from a
previous marriage. Perhaps this optimism is the
only way that people can overcome the feelings of
vulnerability that usually accompany the breakup
of the first marriage.

Adapting to new relationships in remarriage
can be difficult. Hobart (1988) reports differences
between remarried men and women in this regard.
For remarried men, the preeminent relationship is
with his new wife; other relationships, especially
those with his children from his first marriage, take
a back seat. For remarried women, the relationship
with their new husband remains secondary to their
relationship with their children from the first marriage. Thus, the higher failure rate for second marriages involving stepchildren may stem from differences in the centrality of particular relationships
between husbands and wives.

Remarriage late in life tends to be happier than
remarriage in young adulthood (Campbell, 1981),
especially if the couple are widowed rather than
divorced. The biggest problem faced by older remarried individuals is resistance from adult children, who may think that the new spouse is an
intruder and who may be concerned about an
inheritance.

Because approximately 60% of all divorces involve children and because most divorced people
remarry, most second-marriage families face the
problems of integrating stepchildren. Unfortunately, we have almost no information about how
stepparents interact with their new families. For
example, we lack such basic information as the extent to which the factors that influence parent-child
relationships in first marriages are modified in subsequent marriages.

What little information we have suggests that
stepparents are more readily accepted by very

young or adult children and by families that were split by divorce rather than by death. Male children tend to accept a stepparent more readily, especially when the new parent is a man. However, children often feel that an opposite-gender stepparent "plays favorites" (Hetherington, Cox, & Cox, 1982). Adolescent stepchildren are especially difficult to deal with, and many second marriages fail because of this problem (White & Booth, 1985). To the extent that children still admire their absent biological parent, the stepparent may have feelings of inadequacy. Finally, stepparents and stepchildren alike often have unrealistic expectations for the relationship. Both parties need time to adjust to the new marriage (Hetherington et al., 1982).

There is essentially no socializing mechanism for becoming a stepparent. No consensus exists for how stepparents are supposed to behave, how stepparenting is to be similar or different from biological parenting, or how one's duties, obligations, and rights should be meshed with those of the absent biological parent. In many cases stepparents adopt their partner's children in order to surmount some of these problems. However, emotionally charged issues remain. It is clear that much more needs to be learned about the experience of stepparenting, and the status, rights, and obligations of stepparents need to be clarified.

Widowhood

Traditional marriage vows proclaim that the union will last "till death us do part." Experiencing the death of a spouse is certainly a traumatic event (see Chapter 13), and it is one that is experienced by couples of all ages. Widowhood is more common for women; over half of all women over age 65 are widows, but only 15% of the same-aged men are widowers. The reasons for this discrepancy are related to biological and social forces: Women have longer life expectancies and typically marry men older than themselves. Consequently, the average American married woman can expect to live 10 to 12 years as a widow.

The impact of widowhood goes far beyond the ending of a partnership. Because they have been touched by death, widowed people are often left alone by family and friends who do not know how to deal with a bereaved person. As a result, widows and widowers often lose not only a spouse but also those friends and family who feel uncomfortable including a single person rather than a couple in social functions. Additionally, widowed individuals may feel awkward as the third party or may even view themselves as a threat to married friends. Since going to a movie or a restaurant by oneself may be unpleasant or unsatisfying to widows or widowers, they just stay home. Unfortunately, others may assume that they simply wish or need to be alone.

Unlike some other cultures, U.S. society does not have well-defined social roles for widowed people. We even tend to show disapproval toward those who continue to grieve for too long. Since widowhood is most often associated with older women, the few social supports that are in place are largely organized for women.

Considerable research supports the notion that widowhood has different meanings for men and women. But the evidence is much less clear on the question of whether widowhood is harder for men or women. Let's consider what we know about these effects and meanings in order to appreciate the controversy.

In general, a woman's reaction to widowhood depends on the kind of relationship she had with her husband. To the extent that women derived their identities from their husbands and did things as a couple, serious disruptions will result (Lopata, 1975). But women whose lives are centered in individual interactions will experience far less loss of identity and typically make only small changes in their life style.

In a study of over 300 widows in Chicago, Lopata (1973, 1975) found 6 ways in which women dealt with the death of their spouse: (1) "Liberated" women had worked through their loss and moved on to lead complex, well-rounded lives; (2) "merry widows" had life styles filled with fun, dating, and entertainment; (3) working women were either still career oriented or had simply taken any available job; (4) "widow's widows" lived alone, valued their independence, and preferred the company of other widows; (5) traditional widows lived with their children and took an active role in their children's and grandchildren's lives; and (6) grieving women were willingly isolated and could not work through their husbands' deaths or were isolated because they lacked interpersonal or job skills, but they wished to become more involved.

Gentry and Schulman (1988) studied remarriage as a coping response in older widows. They interviewed 39 widows who had remarried, 192 who had considered remarriage, and 420 who had not considered it. They found that women who had remarried reported significantly fewer concerns than either of the other groups. Interestingly, the remarried widows were also the ones who recalled the most concerns immediately after the death of their spouse. Apparently, remarriage helped these widows deal with the loss of their husband by alleviating loneliness and emotional distress.

Many people feel that the loss of one's wife presents a more serious problem than the loss of one's husband. Perhaps this is because a wife is often a man's only close friend and confidant or because men are usually unprepared to live out their lives alone (Glick, Weiss, & Parkes, 1974). Men are often ill equipped to handle the routine and necessary tasks such as cooking, shopping, and keeping house, and they become emotionally isolated from family members. As more men become facile at housekeeping tasks, it remains to be seen whether these patterns will characterize future generations of widowers. Social isolation of widowers may become the most important factor in poor adjustment (Turner, 1982).

Men are generally older when they are widowed than are women. Thus, to some extent the greater overall difficulties reported by widowers may be due to this age difference. Indeed, if age is held constant, widows report higher anxiety than widowers (Atchley, 1975). Regardless of age, men have a clear advantage over women in the opportunity to form new heterosexual relationships; interestingly, though, older widowers are actually less likely to form new, close friendships than are widows. Perhaps this is simply a continuation of men's lifelong tendency to have few close friendships.

PARENTHOOD

Most Americans believe that it is normal, natural, and necessary to have children. We also tend to think that having children will be a joyful and fulfilling experience and that good parents are guided by their natural love for their children. These notions are applied especially to the mother, and belief in a maternal instinct is widespread. Unfortunately, it is unlikely that anyone possesses the innate ability to be a good parent. Perhaps this is the reason that adults often feel considerable anxiety over having children. "When are you going to start a family?" is a question commonly asked of young couples. But once the child is present, adults often feel inadequate. In the words of one new parent, "It's scary being totally responsible for another person." In this section we will explore some of the aspects of parenthood, including the decision process itself and the joys and pains of having children.

Deciding Whether to Have Children

At some point during an intimate relationship, couples discuss whether to have children. This decision is more complicated than most people think, because a couple must weigh the many benefits with the many drawbacks. On the plus side children provide a source of personal satisfaction and love, fulfill the need for generativity, provide a potential source of companionship, and serve as a source of vicarious experience (Frieze, Parsons, Johnson, Ruble, & Zellman, 1978). Children also present problems. In addition to the financial burden, children also change established interaction patterns. For instance, they disrupt a couple's sexual relationship and decrease by up to half the amount of time for shared activities. Moreover, having children is stressful. Rossi (1980) summarizes some of the most important sources of stress accompanying parenthood: cultural pressure to have children, possible involuntary or unplanned parenthood, irrevocability of having a child, lack of formal education for parenting, and lack of consensus about how to be a good parent.

Although most couples still opt to have children even when they recognize the stresses and strains, an increasing number of couples are remaining childless. These couples have several advantages over those who choose to have children. Child-free couples report having happier marriages, more freedom, and higher standards of living. But they must also face social criticism from the larger child-oriented society and may run the risk of feeling more lonely in old age (Van Hoose & Worth, 1982).

For many couples, having children of their own is not an option: One or both partners may be infertile. About one in six couples experiences fertility problems, and experts believe the problem is increasing. Both psychological factors (such as anxiety or stress) and physical factors (such as disease) may cause infertility. In women physical problems that can cause infertility include the failure to ovulate, fallopian tube blockage, endometriosis, abnormalities in the vaginal mucus, and untreated gonorrhea or chlamydia. In men they include faulty or insufficient sperm, varicoceles (a varicose enlargement of the veins of the spermatic cord), and blockage of the sperm ducts.

The Parental Role

The experience of being a parent is different for mothers than for fathers. Despite some recent changes, women are still responsible for meeting most of a child's day-to-day needs. Fathers are still expected to earn money and discipline the children. Being a mother and father, however, involves much more than these stereotypes.

In Western societies the status of being a full-time mother has varied over the last few decades. Traditionally, mothers have been thought to be crucial for the normal development of the child (Fields & Widmayer, 1982). Concerns about attachment, social and emotional growth, and intellectual development have largely reinforced this belief. As a result women often report feeling trapped and depressed when their first child is born. They are made to feel guilty about leaving their child to return to work, and many feel torn between working outside the home and mothering. (Indeed, whether day care affects children's development is still a hotly debated topic.) These feelings confront a majority of women in the United States; the government estimates that nearly two-thirds of all mothers with children under age six were employed in 1990.

Only in the last two decades or so has research focused on fatherhood (Pleck, 1983). Much of the existing research on fathers is devoted to examining the impact of their absence rather than to the positive benefits that they bring to relationships with their children (Biller, 1982). Compared with mothers, fathers do not interact with their babies as much, and these interactions tend to involve play rather than caretaking (Powers & Parke, 1982). Timing of fatherhood in the marriage appears to make a major difference in the amount of time that

The number of single parents is growing rapidly. Single mothers usually have a more difficult time financially than single fathers. Although being a parent — especially a single parent — can be difficult at times, there are many rewards.

fathers spend with their children. In general, men who become fathers in their 30s spend up to 3 times as much time in caring for preschool children as younger fathers (Daniels & Weingarten, 1982), feel less career pressure to divide their time, and have greater flexibility in their roles (Feldman, Nash, & Aschenbrenner, 1983).

Single Parents. One of the fastest growing groups of adults is single parents, most of whom are women. The increasing divorce rate, the large number of women who keep children born out of wedlock, and the desire of many single adults to have or adopt children are all contributing factors to this phenomenon. Being a single parent raises impor-

tant questions: What happens when only one adult is responsible for child care? How do single parents meet their own needs for emotional support and intimacy? Certainly, how one feels about being single also has important effects.

Some of the personal and social situations of single parents have been studied with these issues in mind. Many divorced single parents report feelings of frustration, failure, guilt, and ambivalence about the parent-child relationship (Van Hoose & Worth, 1982). Frustration usually results from a lack of companionship and from loneliness, often in response to the fact that most social activities are reserved for couples. Feelings of guilt may lead to attempts to make up for the child's lack of a father or mother, or they may result when the parent indulges himself or herself. Since they are sometimes seen as hindrances to developing new relationships, parents may experience feelings of ambivalence about their children. These feelings may also arise if children serve as a reminder of a former failure.

Single parents, regardless of gender, face considerable obstacles. Financially, they are usually much less well-off than their married counterparts. Integrating the roles of work and parenthood are difficult enough for two persons; for the single parent the hardships are compounded. Financially, single mothers are hardest hit. Emotionally, single fathers may have the worst of it; according to some research, their sleep, eating, play, work, and peer relations are badly affected, and they are more depressed than any other group of men (Pearlin & Johnson, 1977). Moreover, since most men are not socialized for child rearing, the lack of basic skills necessary to care for children may compound these problems.

One concern of particular importance to single parents is dating (Phillis & Stein, 1983). Indeed, the three most popular questions asked by single parents are "How do I become available again?" "How will my children react?" and "How do I cope with my own sexuality?" Clearly, initiating a new relationship is difficult for many single parents, especially those with older children. They may be hesitant to express this side of themselves in front of their children or may strongly dislike their children's questioning about or resentment of their dates. Moreover, access to social activities is more difficult for single parents; in response, organizations such as Parents Without Partners have been established to provide social outlets.

Overall, single parents seeking new relationships typically do so discreetly. Both mothers and fathers express concern about having dates stay overnight, although women feel more strongly about this (Greenberg, 1979). It would seem that single parents share the same needs as other adults;

it is fulfilling them that is the problem. Of course, many single parents learn how to deal with these issues and find fulfilling relationships.

The Child-Rearing Years

Raising children is a difficult job that is best described as a juggling act. Not only do you need to tend to the children's needs, but you need to maintain an intimate relationship with your spouse, help maintain a home, and probably maintain a career as well. Child rearing alone involves nurturing, socializing, and providing opportunities for intellectual and emotional growth. Throughout this process, parents need to develop their own style of parenting. Ideally, this should be a mutually interactive process between the parents and the children. All of these duties demand considerable attention, so it's no wonder why many parents get tired!

All of the issues discussed earlier concerning mothers and fathers and single parents come into play in child rearing. Initially, parents are often most concerned with doing things right, but this concern gradually subsides as parents gain experience. Indeed, most parents successfully figure out how to raise their children, helped in no small measure by the fact that children themselves are fairly resilient. Although parents tend to differ in style when children are very young, parents tend to become more similar in dealing with them as they become adolescents (Turner, 1982).

As we noted earlier, it is during the child-rearing years that marital satisfaction reaches its ebb. This finding is more understandable given the number of demands placed on parents.

When the Children Leave

One of the biggest events in a family occurs when one's children leave home to establish their own careers and families. For most parents, children's

Married couples are usually happier and more satisfied with their relationship after their children have left home.

empty nest can be important, as one mother complained: "My daughter was 21 when she married. It's not that I wanted her to stay with me, but I missed her terribly. I just felt so alone."

For many years this kind of reaction was thought to be universal in women. Children were assumed to be a central source of satisfaction for mothers. This belief has not been supported by contemporary research (Turner, 1982). For most parents, the departure of the youngest child is not a particularly distressing event. Many people even perceive it as a change for the better (Nock, 1982). Adolescents can be difficult to live with, so to be rid of conflict and challenges to parental authority can be a relief. As one parent said: "It's fantastic. I have more free time, less laundry, lower expenses, and my husband and I can do what we want when we want."

This mother described another important aspect of the postparental period. For the first time in many years, a couple are living by themselves. They must learn about each other again and adjust to a different life style without children. Most couples feel contentment over the successful completion of child rearing. They may now have the time to continue developing the intimacy in their relationship that brought them together years earlier. Research on marital satisfaction and personal happiness supports these notions (Turner, 1982). Marital satisfaction typically rises from the low point when one's children are teenagers to a high during the postparental period that is second only to the period of newlywedded bliss. It seems that it is the opportunity to recreate the interpersonal relationship that originally led the couple to marry that accounts for this upswing. Thus, for most couples, an empty nest is a happy nest.

But what if the nest does not become empty? When children refuse to leave home or repeatedly return after nominally moving out, parental distress is likely (Troll, 1975). This is especially true if the child is perceived to be delaying the transition to adulthood longer than the parents believe is rea-

departures are gradual; contact is still fairly frequent, and most ties are not cut. Eventually, the youngest child departs, creating a new situation for the middle-aged parents: the empty nest, or **postparental family**.

The departure of the youngest child can be a traumatic time. This is especially true for mothers who had defined their identity mainly in terms of their children. The psychological effects of the

sonable. Additionally, more adult children are returning home because they have difficulty finding employment and cannot afford housing, or experience financial problems following divorce. To the extent that these issues result in parent-child conflict, parents tend to be highly dissatisfied with the living arrangements and wish their child would leave (Aquilino & Supple, 1991). The outcome in this case is severely strained parent-child relationships. Empty nests are not only happy nests; they are also the nests that parents expect to have.

FAMILY DYNAMICS AND MIDDLE AGE

Family ties across generations provide the basis for socialization and for continuity in the family's identity. These ties are particularly salient for members of the middle-aged generation, precisely because they are the link between their aging parents and their young adult children. The pressure on this generation is considerable; in fact, middle-agers are often referred to as the **sandwich generation** to reflect their position between the old and the young.

In this section we will examine some of the dynamics between the middle-aged and their aging parents and between them and their young adult children. Along the way we will clear up some popular misconceptions about neglect of elderly parents and war between the generations.

Middle-Agers and Their Children

The relationship between parents and children improves considerably as the children become young adults. In fact, parents are likely to view their young adult children as friends (Troll & Bengtson, 1982). Middle-aged parents are still quite willing to help their adult children if needed, and they often provide financial assistance for college tuition, down payments on houses, and other major purchases. Young adults and their parents typically believe that they have strong, positive relationships, although the middle-aged parents tend to rate the relationship somewhat more positively than do their children. Still, most adult children and their middle-aged parents do not perceive a generation gap in their families (Troll & Bengtson, 1982).

Of course, this does not mean that conflicts are absent. About one third of middle-class fathers complain about their sons' lack of achievement and about their daughters' poor choice of husbands (Nydegger, 1986). And adult children do not necessarily approve of every aspect of their parents' lives either.

Despite these possible conflicts, being a parent of a young adult beginning college or a career is usually a source of pride. Moreover, the younger generation puts the middle generation, usually the mothers, in the role of **kinkeepers** — the people who gather the family together for celebrations and keep everyone in touch (Green & Boxer, 1986). Young adult children may be a source of encouragement; many middle-aged mothers go to college because their young adult children have urged them to, and many middle-aged fathers change life styles for the same reason. Young adults benefit from the experience and perspective of their parents, making it a truly mutual sharing.

However, middle-aged parents may get squeezed by the younger generation as well. The number of young adults living with their parents increased sharply during the 1980s, reaching 30% by mid-decade (Glick & Lin, 1986). Approximately one third of them were unemployed and could not support themselves. Of divorced adults in their 20s, 40% live with their parents, finding more emotional and financial support there than on their own (Glick & Lin, 1986). Thankfully from the middle generation's perspective, this situation is temporary; by the 30s only 17% of divorced adults live with their parents. As we noted earlier, middle-aged parents often take a dim view of adult children moving back home for long periods of time.

One of the most important ways in which middle-aged parents interact with their adult children comes when grandchildren arrive. Some of the best information on the relationship between parents and grandparents comes from studies of multigenerational families. For example, Cohler and Grunebaum (1981) studied the relationships among members of four multigeneration, working-class, Italian-American families. Most of their attention was directed toward the women, since they tended to be the key connectors between families (Troll, Miller, & Atchley, 1979).

Cohler and Grunebaum found that mothers and grandmothers maintained a close relationship due to socialization, role modeling, and the need for a source of information about parenting. The grandmothers in this study were not altogether pleased with the situation, however, and seemed annoyed that their daughters were demanding so much intimacy.

Similar close kinship bonds have been observed in several studies of African-American families (Hayes & Mindel, 1973; Stack, 1972; Stanford & Lockery, 1984). These kinship networks provide a wide variety of support, from financial aid for single parents to role models of parenting to a source of additional child care.

The middle generation often serves as a mediator between grandparents and grandchildren (Wood & Robertson, 1978). In fact, nearly two thirds of young adults between 18 and 26 said in one study that their parents had influenced their involvement with their grandparents (Robertson, 1976). How parents control the grandparent-grandchild relationship has been interpreted as making the middle generation the "lineage bridge across the generations" (Hill, Foote, Aldonus,

Carlson, & MacDonald, 1970, p. 62). We will consider additional aspects of grandparenting in a later section.

Middle-Agers and Their Aging Parents

In considering the relationship that middle-aged people have with their parents, two issues are most important. First, are they likely to ignore their elderly parents? Second, what do they do when confronted with a frail, elderly parent?

Frequency and Quality of Contact. One of the most widespread myths is that elderly parents are grossly neglected by their middle-aged children. At best, this myth has the middle-aged generation simply ignoring their parents; at worst, they put their parents into nursing homes and abandon them. The myth has been perpetuated by the beliefs that somewhere in the past, generations were much more devoted to each other than they are today and that today's children do not care for their parents the way they used to (Lee, 1985).

These beliefs are patently wrong. Although the proportion of older adults living with younger generations has declined over this century, the reason is financial independence of the elderly, not neglect (Lee, 1985). In 1900 programs such as Social Security or pension plans did not exist; older adults were forced to live with other family members just to make ends meet, not necessarily because they wanted to. What has increased is the number of older adults who live near one of their children; at least half of all older adults live within half an hour's drive of one of their children.

Frequency of contact between older parents and a middle-aged child remains high. Nearly 80% of elderly parents have seen their middle-aged child within the previous 2 weeks (L. Harris & Associates, 1981). This high visitation rate does not differ between rural and urban dwellers (Krout, 1988b) and continues even when older parents become ill. Adult children also seem to appreciate their parents more; middle age is a time for reevaluating one's relationships with parents (Farrell & Rosenberg, 1981; Helson & Moane, 1987).

Taking Care of Elderly Parents. Some middle-aged children, usually daughters, will have to care for at least one parent, most often a widowed mother in poor health. In fact, the gender difference in caring for an elderly parent is striking. Even after factoring out all demographic characteristics of the caregivers and care-recipients, daughters are over three times more likely to provide assistance with daily living tasks than are sons (Dwyer & Coward, 1991).

The decision to have a parent move in follows a relatively long period of time during which both generations live independently. This history of independence may create adjustment difficulties, since both parties must accommodate their life styles. Because most family caregiving of the elderly is done by spouses, situations in which adult children enter the picture usually involve a very old mother who, after caring for her now-deceased husband, is herself in poor health. For this reason taking care of elderly parents is most likely to confront adult children as they themselves are approaching old age.

Adult children who face caregiving are confronted with a dilemma. On the one hand, most feel a sense of responsibility to care for their parent and will do so if possible. But caring for aging parents is not without its price. Living together after years of separation is usually disliked by both parties; each would rather live alone. Conflicts typically arise due to differences in routines and life styles. Stress seems to result in such relationships in two primary ways (Robinson & Thurnher, 1979):

1. Adult children often have trouble coping with declines in their parents' functioning, especially mental deterioration. Misunderstandings of these changes may result in adult children's feeling ambivalent and antagonistic toward their parents.

2. Stress also results when the caregiving relationship is perceived as confining. If caring for aging parents seriously infringes on the adult child's life style or routine, the situation is likely to be perceived negatively.

How well do families cope? Considerable research clearly documents that middle-aged adults spend great amounts of time, energy, and money helping their elderly parents (Cicirelli, 1981; Shanas, 1980; Stoller, 1983; Stoller & Earl, 1983). One study reports that 87% of a sample of 700 elderly people received at least half of the help they needed from their children and other relatives (Morris & Sherwood, 1984). In fact, care provided by the family helps to prevent or at least delay institutionalization (Brody, 1981; Cantor, 1980).

Caring for a frail parent is not without cost. Besides the obvious monetary expense, caring for a parent exacts a high psychological cost. Even the most devoted child has feelings of depression, resentment, anger, and guilt at times (Halpern, 1987). Many middle-aged adults have just come through the financial expenses associated with child rearing and may need to plan for their own retirement. The additional burden of a frail parent puts considerable pressure on resources that were earmarked for other uses. These difficulties are especially acute for the children of victims of Alzheimer's disease and other chronic conditions (see Chapter 9).

Older adults in the United States may not be pleased with the prospect of living with their children. Independence and autonomy are important aspects of our lives, and their loss is not taken lightly. In fact, one study found that older adults were more likely than younger adults to express the desire to pay a professional for assistance than to ask a family member for help (Brody, Johnsen, Fulcomer, & Lang, 1983). Elderly parents are likely

SOMETHING TO THINK ABOUT

Hiring Surrogates to Care for Frail Elderly Parents

"It gets scary sometimes. You know, Mom would wander off or would forget where she was. We had to do something." The situation in the Smith household is a typical problem for a growing number of middle-aged people who are caring for their frail elderly parents. As noted in the text, the situation is bad enough when everyone is in the same household. But it presents even bigger problems when parents and children live in different cities.

The answer that many middle-aged adults have discovered is to hire surrogate children to care for their parents while they are at work. Surrogate care is one of the fastest growing segments of the health care industry, with over 600 companies in the United States by 1988, compared with fewer than 100 only 5 years earlier (Ricklefs, 1988). The increase reflects the rapid growth in the elderly population and the fact that most middle-aged caregivers must continue working to support themselves, their parents, and their own children. About half of the clients receiving surrogate care are elderly people whose children live far away — also indicative of the trend toward maintaining one's independence as long as possible.

Surrogate care costs as much as $30,000 a year for arranging and su-

pervising 24-hour home care and other related services, about the cost of a quality nursing home. But for many middle-aged adults who can afford it, the price is well worth it. Elderly people who may have been institutionalized are able to remain at home, and their children are able to provide for them.

Surrogate in-home services are not a panacea, however. They are largely unavailable outside of larger cities. Many health insurance plans do not pay for much of the service, which leaves out middle- and lower-income individuals. As the need for these services continues to grow into the next century, however, availability as well as subsidy programs will undoubtedly be hotly debated. It's something to think about.

to disapprove of receiving financial assistance from their middle-aged children; they may find it distasteful or demeaning to live with them and may accept help only if they feel they have no other choice (Hamon & Blieszner, 1990; Lee, 1985). Moreover, most elderly parents, even when they are ill, have a strong desire to make decisions about their needs.

Whether older parents are satisfied with the help that their children provide appears to be a complex issue (Thomas, 1988). Older adults in fairly good health, those who prefer to live near relatives, and those who endorse the idea that families should help are most satisfied with the help that their middle-aged children provide. On the

other hand, frail elderly parents, those who have little desire to live near their families, and those who prefer help from nonfamily sources are least satisfied.

Many people care for an aging parent, but it is often highly disruptive. Middle-aged adults often have few choices in how to provide care; many must quit their jobs because adequate alternatives are not available. One of the fastest growing issues pertaining to middle-aged adults is the availability of adult day care or other alternative programs. As explored in Something to Think About, more and more adult children are being forced to search for other means of care, primarily because the cost of caring for an aging parent is extraordinarily high.

GRANDPARENTING

Becoming a grandparent is an exciting time for most people and represents the acquisition of new roles (Robertson, 1977). Many grandmothers see their role as easier than mothering — affording pleasure and gratification without requiring them to assume major responsibility for the care and socialization of the child (Robertson, 1977). These days, becoming a grandparent usually happens while one is middle-aged rather than elderly, and it is frequently occurring as early as age 40 (Kivnick, 1982). Moreover, many younger grandparents have living parents themselves, making for truly multigenerational families.

Overall, surprisingly little research has been conducted on grandparents and their relationships with their grandchildren. We know that grandparents differ considerably in how they interact with grandchildren and in the meanings they derive from these interactions. We also know a little about how each group perceives the other and about the benefits of these relationships.

Styles of Grandparenting

Because grandparents, like all other groups, are diverse, how they interact with their grandchildren, termed their *grandparenting style*, differs (Neugarten & Weinstein, 1964). The most common style, characterizing about one third of grandparents, is called *formal*. These grandparents see their role in fairly traditional terms, occasionally indulging the grandchild, occasionally babysitting, expressing a strong interest in the grandchild, but maintaining a hands-off attitude toward child rearing — leaving that aspect to the parents. A second common style is used by the *fun seeker*, whose relationship is characterized by informal playfulness. The *distant* grandparent appears mainly on holidays, birthdays, or other formal occasions with ritual gifts for the grandchild but otherwise has little contact with him or her. A few grandmothers are *surrogate parents*, filling in for working mothers. Finally, a few grandfathers play the role of *dispenser of family wisdom*, assuming an authoritarian position and offering information and advice.

Little research has examined how grandparents develop different styles. It appears that grandparents under age 65 are more likely to be fun seeking, whereas those over 65 tend to be more formal. Whether this difference is due to the age of the grandparent, the age of the grandchild, or generational differences between younger and older grandparents is unclear. Some evidence points to a combination of factors. Grandparents tend to be more playful with younger grandchildren, but as both groups age, a more formal relationship emerges (Kahana & Kahana, 1970; Kalish, 1975).

Robertson (1977) offers an alternative description of grandparenting styles based on her study of 125 grandmothers. She identifies a social and a personal dimension of grandparenting. The social dimension emphasizes societal needs and expectations, whereas the personal dimension focuses on personal factors and individual needs. Four combinations of these dimensions are possible. The *appointed* type is high on both dimensions of grandmothering. These grandmothers are very involved with their grandchildren and are equally concerned with indulging them and with doing what is morally right for them. The *remote* type is detached and has low social and personal expectations about the grandmothering role. *Symbolic* grandmothers emphasize the normative and moral aspects of the grandmothering role, and they have few personal expectations. *Individualized* grandmothers emphasize the personal aspects of grandmothering and ignore the social or moral side of the relationship.

Additional support for Robertson's notion of social and personal dimensions comes from investigations of how grandparents influence their grandchildren's attitudes and life style. Many grandparents recommend religious, social, and vocational values through storytelling, giving friendly advice, or working together on special projects (Cherlin & Furstenberg, 1986). In return, grandchildren keep grandparents updated on current cultural trends.

The Meaning of Grandparenthood

Research has shown that people derive several positive meanings from grandparenthood. Kivnick (1982) administered a lengthy questionnaire to 286 grandparents. Based on the statistical procedure of factor analysis, Kivnick identified five meanings of grandparenting: centrality, or the degree to which grandparenting is a primary role in one's life; value as an elder, or being perceived as a wise, helpful person; immortality through clan, in that the grandparent leaves behind not one but two generations; reinvolvement with one's personal past, by recalling relationships with one's own grandparents; and indulgence, or getting satisfaction from having fun with and spoiling one's grandchildren.

When we compare the meanings derived by grandparents with the styles of grandparenting, there appear to be several similarities. For example, the notion that grandparents have a tendency to spoil or indulge their grandchildren appears as both a style and a meaning. Because of these apparent similarities, S. S. Miller and Cavanaugh (1990) decided to investigate whether there were any systematic relationships. They reported two major findings. First, most grandparents find several sources of meaning in being a grandparent. Second, there are few consistent relationships between the style of grandparenting and the various sources of meaning. J. L. Thomas, Bence, and Meyer (1988) also found that the symbolic meaning of grandparenthood was of little importance to the satisfaction derived from being a grandparent. Thomas (1986a, 1986b) reports that satisfaction with grandparenthood is higher in grandmothers and that the opportunity to nurture and support grandchildren is an important source of satisfaction.

What these results imply is that we may not be able to describe specific standardized styles or meanings of grandparenthood. This is not that surprising, because grandparents are so diverse. Moreover, to expect that there should be consistencies between how a 50-year-old grandfather interacts with a 2-year-old grandson and how an 80-year-old grandmother interacts with her 18-year-old grandson may be ridiculous. Grandparent-grandchild relationships may well be too idiosyncratic to be described in general terms (Bengtson & Robertson, 1985).

Grandparents and Grandchildren

The relationships between grandparents and grandchildren vary with the age of the child. Younger children (up to age 10 or so) tend to be closer to their grandparents than older children. Grandparents also tend to enjoy younger grandchildren more because they are so responsive (Kahana & Kahana, 1970). Still, many adolescents and young adults view their grandparents as a special resource and value their relationships with them. Most young adults think that adult grandchildren have a responsibility to help their grandparents when necessary and without pay (Robertson, 1976).

Relationships between grandparents and grandchildren may also vary with the gender of the child. Some authors have suggested that grandmothers and granddaughters have better relationships than do grandfathers and grandsons (Atchley, 1977; Hagestad, 1978). According to these writers, this may be due to the fact that the relationships are along the maternal kinkeeping line, supporting the speculation made in the previous section about middle-aged women and their role as kinkeepers.

When the grandparent-grandchild relationship is viewed from the child's perspective, another set of interesting findings emerges. When asked to provide written descriptions of their grandparents, children use a greater variety of descriptors for the grandparent with whom they have the more reciprocal relationship (Schultz, 1980). Children also attribute more perspective-taking ability and more feelings of attachment to their favorite grandparent.

A growing concern among grandparents is maintaining contact with grandchildren after a divorce of the parents (Johnson, 1988; Johnson & Barer, 1987). Indeed, in 1990 only half of the states in the United States had laws dealing with grandparental rights following divorce (Edelstein, 1990). In some cases contact is broken by the former in-laws. In other cases paternal grandmothers actually expand their family network by maintaining contact with their grandchildren from their sons' first marriage as well as subsequent ones (Johnson & Barer, 1987). Overall, however, maternal grandmothers whose daughters have custody have more contact with grandchildren following their daughters' divorces, and paternal grandmothers have less contact following their sons' divorces if their son does not have custody of the grandchildren (Cherlin & Furstenberg, 1986; Johnson, 1983).

Ethnic Differences. Grandparenting styles and interaction patterns differ somewhat among ethnic groups. In the United States, for example, African Americans, Asian Americans, Italian Americans, and Hispanic Americans are more likely to be involved in the lives of their grandchildren than are members of other groups. Differences within these ethnic groups are also apparent. Italian-American grandmothers tend to be much more satisfied and involved with grandparenting than Italian-American grandfathers, who tend to be more distant. Among Hispanic groups, Cuban Americans are least likely and Mexican Americans most likely to be involved with the daily lives of their descendants (Bengtson, 1985). African-American grandmothers under age 40 may feel pressured to provide care for a grandchild that they were not eager for, whereas those over age 60 tend to feel that they are fulfilling an important role. African-American men, though, perceive grandparenthood as a central role, and do so more strongly than white grandfathers (Kivett, 1991).

Kornhaber (1985) notes that styles of grand-parenting vary with ethnic background. This fact is highlighted by the case of an 18-month-old girl who had grandparents from two very different ethnic backgrounds: one pair Latin and one pair Nordic. Her Latin grandparents tickled, frolicked with, and doted over her. Her Nordic grandparents let her be but loved her no less. Her Latin mother thought the Nordic grandparents were "cold and hard," and her Nordic father thought his in-laws were "driving her crazy." The child, though, was perfectly content with both sets of grandparents.

Weibel-Orlando (1990) also reports variations between Native Americans and other groups. Among Native Americans, grandmothers tend to take a more active role than grandfathers. She also identified four main styles: distant, custodial, fictive, and cultural conservator. The first two parallel styles found in other ethnic groups, whereas the latter two are particularly Native American. Fictive grandparents are ones who fill in for missing or dead biological grandparents; cultural conservator grandparents actively solicit their children to allow the grandchildren to live with them in order to expose them to the Native-American way of life.

The Changing Role of Grandparents. Grandparenting is not what it used to be. Detachment rather than involvement increasingly characterizes grandparent-grandchild relations (Bengtson & Robertson, 1985; Kornhaber & Woodward, 1981; Rodeheaver & Thomas, 1986). There are many complex reasons for a more detached style. Increased geographic mobility often means that grandparents live far away from their grandchildren, making visits less frequent and the relationship less intimate. Grandparents today are more likely to live independent lives apart from their children and grandchildren. Grandmothers are more likely to be employed themselves, thereby having less time to devote to caring for their grandchildren. Because of the rising divorce rate, some grandparents rarely see grandchildren who are living with a former son- or daughter-in-law. Finally, grandparents are not seen as the dispensers of child-rearing advice that they

Interactions between grandparents and grandchildren vary among individuals and across age and cultures.

once were, so they tend to take a background role in order to maintain family harmony.

Most grandparents are comfortable with their reduced role and are quite happy to leave child rearing to the parents. In fact, those who feel responsible for advising their grandchildren tend to be less satisfied with the grandparenting role than those who feel that their role is mainly to enjoy their grandchildren (Thomas, 1986a).

Great-Grandparenthood

With increasing numbers of people (especially women) living to a very old age, the number of great-grandparents is rising rapidly. However, co-

hort trends in age at first marriage and age at parenthood also play a role. When these factors are combined, we find that most great-grandparents are women who married relatively young and had children and grandchildren who also married and had children relatively early.

Although little research has been conducted on this group, it is becoming clear that their sources of satisfaction and meaning differ somewhat from those of grandparents (Doka & Mertz, 1988; Wentkowski, 1985). Three aspects of great-grandparenthood appear to be most important (Doka & Mertz, 1988).

First, being a great-grandparent provides a sense of personal and family renewal. Their grandchildren have produced new life, renewing their own excitement for life and reaffirming the continuance of their lineage. Seeing their families stretch across four generations may also provide psychological support through feelings of symbolic immortality that help them face death. That is, they know that their families will live many years beyond their own lifetime. Second, great-grandchildren provide diversion in great-grandparents' lives. There are now new things to do, places to go, and new people to share them with. Third, becoming a great-grandparent is a milestone, a mark of longevity. The sense that one has lived long enough to see the fourth generation is perceived very positively.

For many reasons, such as geographic distance and health, most great-grandparents maintain a distant relationship with their great-grandchildren. Still, the vast majority (over 90%) are proud of their new status (Wentkowski, 1985). As we enter the 21st century and the number of elderly people increases, four-generation families may become the norm.

SUMMARY

Relationships

1. People tend to have more friendships during young adulthood than during any other period. Friendships in old age are especially important for maintaining life satisfaction.

2. Men tend to have fewer close friends and base them on shared activities. Women tend to have more, and base them on emotional sharing.

3. Sibling friendships tend to be strongest between sisters.

4. Passion, intimacy, and commitment are the key components of love. Although styles of love change with age, the priorities within relationships do not.

5. Selecting a mate works best when there are shared values, goals, and interests. There are cross-cultural differences in which specific aspects of these are most important.

Life Styles and Love Relationships

6. The most important factors in creating stable marriages are similarity, maturity, and conflict resolution skills.

7. For couples with children, marital satisfaction tends to decline until the children leave home, although individual differences are apparent, especially in long-term marriages.

8. Most adults decide by age 30 whether they plan on getting married. Never-married adults often develop a strong network of close friends.

9. Young adults usually cohabit as a step toward marriage, whereas older adults tend to cohabit for financial reasons. Cohabitation is only rarely seen as an alternative to marriage. Overall, more similarities than differences exist between cohabiting and married couples.

10. Gay male couples change more than any other type of couple in terms of frequency of sexual relations. Lesbian couples are more likely to stay together than gay male couples.

11. Currently, odds are 50-50 that a new marriage will end in divorce. Reasons for divorce show a lack of the qualities that make a strong marriage. Also, societal attitudes about divorce have eased and expectations about marriage have increased.

12. Recovery from divorce is different for men and women. Men tend to have a tougher time in the short run. Women clearly have a harder time in the long run, often for financial reasons. Difficulties between divorced partners usually involve visitation and child support.

13. Most divorced couples remarry. Second marriages are especially vulnerable to stress if stepchildren are involved. Remarriage in later life tends to be very happy.

14. Widowhood is more common among women because they tend to marry men older than they are, but widowed men are typically older. Reactions to widowhood depend on the quality of the marriage.

Parenthood

15. Although having children is stressful, most people do it anyway.

16. A substantial minority of couples have fertility problems.

17. Women still tend to perform most of the child-care tasks.

18. Single parents are increasing rapidly due to increased divorce, keeping children born out of wedlock, and a desire of many unmarried people to be parents.

19. Raising children demands considerable flexibility in juggling the competing time demands.

20. Most parents do not report severe negative emotions when their children leave. However, parents typically report distress if adult children move back.

Family Dynamics and Middle Age

21. Most parent-child relationships move toward friendship.

22. Middle-aged women often assume the role of kin-keeper to the family.

23. Middle-aged parents may get squeezed by competing demands of their children, who want to gain independence, and their elderly parents, who want to maintain independence.

24. Middle-aged adults do not abandon their parents. Contact is frequent and generally positive.

25. Caring for a frail parent is costly both financially and emotionally. Most elderly parents in the United States would prefer not to live with their children, however.

Grandparenting

26. Grandparents vary considerably in how they interact with their grandchildren, both in style and in frequency. Overall, grandparents tend to be more playful with children than the children's parents are.

27. People derive positive meaning from being a grandparent, and it is related to self-esteem.

28. Relationship characteristics vary with the age of the child. With younger children the emphasis is more on fun, but with young adults it is on common issues and a desire to learn about each other.

29. Maintaining contact with grandchildren following the parents' divorce is an important issue to many grandparents.

30. Ethnic differences in grandparent-grandchild relationships are apparent, especially in terms of child care.

31. Increased life expectancies make it more likely that children will have great-grandparents. Being a great-grandparent is an important source of personal and family renewal and provides diversion.

REVIEW QUESTIONS

Relationships

1. How does the number and importance of friendships vary across adulthood?

2. What gender differences are there in the number and type of friends?

3. What are the components of love? How do styles of love differ with age?

4. What characteristics make the best matches between adults? How do these characteristics differ across cultures?

Life Styles and Love Relationships

5. What are the most important factors in creating stable marriages?

6. What are the developmental trends in marital satisfaction? How do these trends relate to having children?

7. How do adults who never marry deal with the need to have relationships?

8. What are the reasons that people cohabit? How are cohabiting people and married people alike and different?

9. What are the relationship characteristics of gay male and lesbian couples?

10. What are the major reasons that people get divorced? How are these related to societal expectations about marriage and attitudes about divorce?

11. What characteristics about remarriage make it similar and different from first marriage? How does satisfaction in remarriage vary as a function of age?

12. What are the characteristics of widowed people? How do men and women differ in their experience of widowhood?

Parenthood

13. Why do couples decide to have children? What effects do children have on relationships?

14. How do couples divide child-care tasks during the child-rearing years?

15. What impact does children leaving home have on parents?

Family Dynamics and Middle Age

16. How do middle-aged parents relate to their children?

17. What roles do middle-aged mothers assume in the family?

18. What are the important issues facing middle-aged adults who care for their elderly parents?

19. How does independence relate to children, their middle-aged parents, and elderly parents?

Grandparenting

20. What styles and meanings of grandparenting do people demonstrate?

21. How do grandparents and grandchildren relate? How do these relationships change with the age of the grandchild?

22. What ethnic differences have been noted in grandparenting?

23. What are the important issues and meanings of being a great-grandparent?

KEY TERMS

cohabitation Two individuals living together who are not married. (348)

homogamy The notion that similar interests and values are important in forming strong, lasting interpersonal relationships. (344)

kinkeepers Members of the family, predominantly women, who maintain contacts with other family members across generational lines. (361)

postparental family A family in which the children have grown and left. (360)

sandwich generation A term referring to the middle-aged generation, which has both elderly parents and adult children. (361)

ADDITIONAL READING

One of the most complete and readable studies of all types of couple relationships (marriage, cohabitation, and gay male and lesbian relationships) is

Blumstein, P., & Schwartz, P. (1983). *American couples.* New York: Morrow. Easy reading.

A summary of family and marital relations in old age can be found in

Sussman, M. B. (1985). The family life of old people. In R. H. Binstock & E. Shanas (Eds.), *Handbook of aging and the social sciences* (2nd ed., pp. 415–449). New York: Van Nostrand Reinhold. Moderately difficult.

An excellent source of research on family issues is *Journal of Marriage and the Family*, which is a major outlet for investigations of aging and family. Reading level varies, but is typically moderately difficult.

A good description of family issues in midlife can be found in

Katchadourian, H. (1987). *Fifty: Midlife in perspective.* New York: W. H. Freeman. Easy reading.

CHAPTER 11

Work, Leisure, and Retirement

Jacob Lawrence, *Builders*, 1980. Courtesy SAFECO Insurance Companies, Seattle, Washington.

ONE OF THE MOST INTERESTING UNDERGRADuates I ever met was Earl. Earl was not a typical student. He was obviously older than the average undergraduate, but that's not why he stood out. What made Earl different was that he was preparing to embark on his third occupation. For 24 years he was in the Air Force, first as a pilot and later as a staff officer. His military experiences were often exciting but scary, especially when bullets ripped through his cockpit as he was flying missions over Vietnam. On returning to the United States, he taught some members of Congress and the Senate how to fly. He transferred to the staff of NATO, but dealing with politicians became so frustrating that he retired. At age 44 he began his second occupation, as an insurance salesman. Although he was promoted and did well, he became disenchanted and resigned after five years. At age 50 he went back to college to prepare for a third occupation, in physical therapy.

Earl has worked for all of his adult life. None of us should find that terribly exciting or unusual by itself. It is hard to imagine what adulthood would be like if we did not work. In fact, Sigmund Freud once wrote that love and work were the two defining aspects of adulthood. Work is such an important part of our lives that many people view themselves in terms of their occupation and judge others by theirs.

In this chapter we will seek answers to several questions: Why do people work? How do people choose occupations? How do occupations develop? What factors produce individual differences in occupational patterns? How do people spend time when they are not working? What happens to them after they retire? Along the way, we will see to what extent Earl and people like him are typical of workers in general.

As will become clear, research addressing these questions about work has focused primarily on middle-class white men; far less is known about women or about other ethnic groups. Although more research on women and on other ethnic groups is being conducted, we must be careful in applying existing research and theory to these other groups until data have been compiled.

We will be applying the biopsychosocial method to our consideration of work because it provides insight into several important issues. For example, the occupation you choose is partly influenced by the talents or skills you may have inherited from your parents, the kind of environment in which you grew up, and your overall physical and mental health. Likewise, the options you have are far greater than those available to your great-grandparents; in those days few people could go to college, and women and some ethnic groups were barred from certain occupations. Moreover, where you are in your life cycle makes a difference as well. Older adults may view working part-time at a fast food restaurant very differently than younger adults. Similarly, these same factors influence the decisions you make about how to spend your leisure time and about your retirement. For example, we will see that self-perceived ability to perform is important in leisure, and health is a leading predictor of early retirement. Thus, just as in the other domains we consider, work fits well in the biopsychosocial model.

THE MEANING OF WORK

In the 1960s the phrase "different strokes for different folks" was used to get across the point that people's motives and needs differ. Thus, work has different meanings for different people. Studs Terkel, the author of the fascinating book *Working* (1974), writes that work is "a search for daily meaning as well as daily bread, for recognition as well as cash, for astonishment rather than torpor; in short, for a sort of life rather than a Monday through Friday sort of dying. Perhaps immortality, too, is part of the quest" (p. xiii).

For some people, then, work is a source of prestige, social recognition, and a sense of worth. For others, the excitement of the activity or its creative growth potential makes work meaningful. But for most people, the main purpose of work is to earn a living. This is not to imply, of course, that money is the only reward in a job; things like friendships, the chance to exercise power, and feeling useful are also important. It is both the money that can be exchanged for life's necessities (and maybe a few luxuries, too) and the possibility for personal growth that provide the incentive for most of us to work.

Regardless of what they do for a living, people view their job as a key element in their sense of identity. This feeling can be readily observed when people introduce themselves socially: "Hi, I'm Kevin. I'm an accountant. What do you do?" One's job affects one's life in a whole host of ways, from living place to friends to clothes to how one talks. In short, the impact of work cuts across all aspects of life. Work, then, is a major social role of adult life. This role — one's occupation — provides an important anchor that complements our other anchor: love relationships.

Occupations and Careers

In understanding work roles, terminology is important. The term *occupation* is applied to all forms of work, but the term *career* is sometimes reserved for prestigious occupations. In this view a career is an elite institution in Western society (Stevens-Long, 1988). Ritzer (1977) argues that people who have careers stay in one occupational field and progress through a series of stages to achieve upward mobility, greater responsibility, mastery, and financial compensation. From this perspective, university professors and lawyers in a large firm have careers; assembly-line workers and secretaries do not.

Other authors disagree, viewing career as any organized path an individual takes across time and space — that is, any consistent, organized involvement in any role (Van Maanen & Schein, 1977). In this perspective physicians, carpenters, and homemakers have several careers simultaneously: as workers, spouses, citizens, and so forth.

In this chapter we will use the term *occupation* rather than career to refer to work roles. As we will see, occupations are highly developmental. Even young children are in the midst of the social preparation for work, as evidenced by pretend play and prodding questions from adults such as "What do you want to be when you grow up?" School curricula, especially in high school and college, are geared toward preparing people for particular occupations. We develop our interests in various occupations over time, and the changes that occur in occupations represent some of the most important events in the life cycle. Before we explore occupations as developmental phenomena, however, we need to consider how different occupations are associated with different levels of social status.

Social Status and Occupations

Workers in the United States are not all viewed as equally valuable. How people are treated is, in part, a function of the kind of work they do, which is given a particular status in society. Occupational status is correlated with intellectual ability and achievement, although not perfectly.

Five general levels of workers can be identified: marginal workers, blue-collar workers, pink-collar workers, white-collar workers, and executives and professionals. Where one falls in this hierarchy influences life style, well-being, and social recognition. We will consider the characteristics of each level briefly.

Marginal workers work occasionally, but never long enough with one employer to establish a continuous occupational history. In this sense they are similar to Super's (1980) unstable, or multiple trial, occupational patterns. (Super's theory is discussed later in this chapter.) Marginal workers' unstable working patterns are due to several factors, such as the lack of necessary language or other abilities, discrimination, a criminal record, or physical or mental disorders. The lack of steady employment has serious negative effects on most other aspects of their lives, such as increased marital distress.

Blue-collar occupations are those that do not require formal education past high school and may be based more on physical skills than intellectual skills. Blue-collar occupations vary tremendously, however, from unskilled labor to the highly complex trades of electricians and pipe fitters, for example. In general, there is little mobility in blue-collar occupations; moves typically reflect changes for better pay or job security or result from unemployment. One problem faced by blue-collar workers is being looked down on by supervisors and upper-middle-class professionals, and many express inferiority feelings (Terkel, 1974).

Pink-collar occupations are held primarily by women. These positions include office and clerical worker, bank teller, receptionist, and the like. Typically, these occupations do not pay high wages. Although men may hold some of these positions, such as bank teller, they do so only for short periods before they are promoted.

White-collar occupations are in offices rather than in factories or outdoors. Although the skills required are thought to be more intellectual than those needed for blue-collar occupations, white-collar workers are not always paid better. What they do get, however, is higher status. Many white-collar jobs require formal education beyond high school, although there is very little evidence that this education is always directly related to job performance. Unhappiness among white-collar workers comes mostly from their feeling that the extra time and expense for more education is not sufficiently rewarded, and from middle-level managers' feelings that they have little real effect on corporate decision making.

Executives and professionals have the highest status as well as the highest education. They are in the optimal position to control their own occupational development and to obtain the rewards that most other workers cannot. Comparisons among executives and professionals are usually not in terms of salaries but in how far and how quickly they progress.

OCCUPATIONAL CHOICE ACROSS ADULTHOOD

Our work life serves as a major source of our identity, provides us with an official position, and influences our life style and social interactions; therefore, choosing an occupation is a serious matter. Although most people think that occupational choice is something that is largely the province of young adults, much of what we will consider also holds true for middle-aged and older workers who are looking to change occupations either voluntarily or because they lost their jobs. As we will see later, more adults are changing occupations than ever before, and more are having to rethink the kinds of jobs they want to have. Moreover, as the downsizing trend in corporations continues, many adults may be forced to look for new employment in different fields.

From a developmental perspective, the decisions people make about occupations may change over time. As people face different life issues or achieve new insights about themselves, they may well decide that their best bet would be to change occupations. Additionally, occupational choices may reflect personal or social clocks (see Chapter 1); individuals of different ages may feel different degrees of pressure to make a certain occupational choice.

Regardless of age, three issues in deciding on an occupation are important: personality and interests, self-efficacy, and gender. Let's consider each in turn.

Personality and Interests

Although we tend to think of occupational choice as something done during adolescence or young adulthood, recent theories and research have increasingly adopted a life-course perspective (Adler & Aranya, 1984). The main theoretical frameworks for occupational choice have focused on aspects of one's personality (see Chapter 8).

Holland's Theory. Holland (1973, 1985) developed a theory based on the intuitively appealing idea that people choose occupations to optimize the fit between their individual traits — such as personality, intelligence, skills, and abilities — and their occupational interests. He categorizes occupations in two ways: by the interpersonal settings in which people must function and by their associated life style. He identifies six personality types that combine these factors; they are summarized in Table 11.1.

Support for Holland's personality types comes from other research examining the relationship between personality and occupational choice. Research comparing his types with Costa and McCrae's five dimensions of personality (see Chapter 8) suggests considerable overlap (Costa, McCrae, & Holland, 1984). For instance, his social and enterprising types fell into Costa and McCrae's extraversion dimension.

The congruence between traits and occupational selection in Holland's theory exists at the level of interest, not at the level of performance requirements per se. He predicts that people will choose the occupation that has the greatest similarity to their personality type. By doing this, they optimize their ability to express themselves, apply their skills, and take on new roles. Occupational satisfaction, for Holland, is maximized by having a good match between personality and occupation. Indeed, Spokane (1985) documented the relationship between such a congruence and occupational persistence, occupational choice, occupational stability, and work satisfaction.

Holland's theory does not mean that personality completely determines what occupation one chooses. The connection is that certain occupations are typically chosen by people who act or feel a certain way. Most of us would rather do something that we like to do than something we are forced to do. Thus, unless we have little choice due to financial or other constraints, we typically choose occupations on that basis. When mismatches occur, people usually adapt by changing jobs, changing interests, or adapting the job to provide a better match.

Although the relationships between personality and occupational choice are important, we must recognize that there are limits. Men and women are differentially represented in Holland's types (Costa et al., 1984). Regardless of age, women are more likely than men to be in the social, artistic, and conventional types. Additionally, Holland's theory ignores the context in which the decision is made. For example, he overlooks the fact that many people may not have much choice in the kind of job they can get because of external factors such as family, financial pressures, or ethnicity. There are also documented changes in congruence between personality type and occupation across adulthood (Adler & Aranya, 1984). In short, we must recognize that what occupation we choose is related not only to what we are like but also to the dynamic interplay between us and the social situation we are in.

Self-Efficacy

Occupational choice is strongly influenced by what we think of ourselves. Regardless of age, we evaluate our abilities in terms of our strengths and weaknesses. Since we are likely to shy away from doing things that we think we have little ability to do, we tend to choose occupations that match what we think we may be able to do. Bandura (1986) terms this self-evaluation process **self-efficacy**.

TABLE 11.1   Summary of Holland's personality types and their relationship to occupational choices

---

Investigative

The model type is task-oriented, intraceptive, asocial; prefers to think through rather than act out problems; needs to understand; enjoys ambiguous work tasks; has unconventional values and attitudes. Vocational preferences include aeronautical design engineer, anthropologist, astronomer, biologist, botanist, chemist, editor of a scientific journal, geologist, independent research scientist, meteorologist, physicist, scientific research worker, writer of scientific or technical articles, zoologist.

Social

The model type is sociable, responsible, feminine, humanistic, religious; needs attention; has verbal and interpersonal skills; avoids intellectual problem solving, physical activity, and highly ordered activities; prefers to solve problems through feelings and interpersonal manipulations of others. Vocational preferences include assistant city school superintendent, clinical psychologist, director of welfare agency, foreign missionary, high school teacher, juvenile delin-

quency expert, marriage counselor, personal counselor, physical education teacher, playground director, psychiatric case worker, social science teacher, speech therapist, vocational counselor.

Realistic

The model type is masculine; physically strong, unsociable, aggressive; has good motor coordination and skill; lacks verbal and interpersonal skills; prefers concrete to abstract problems; conceives of self as being aggressive and masculine and as having conventional political and economic values. Persons who choose or prefer the following occupations resemble this type: airplane mechanic, construction inspector, electrician, filling station attendant, fish and wildlife specialist, locomotive engineer, master plumber, photoengraver, power shovel operator, power station operator, radio operator, surveyor, tree surgeon, tool designer.

Artistic

The model type is asocial; avoids problems that are highly structured or require gross physical skills; re-

---

(Source: *Making Vocational Choices: A Theory of Vocational Personalities and Work Environments* (pp. 19–22) by John Holland, 1985. © 1985. Adapted by permission of Prentice-Hall, Inc., Englewood Cliffs, N.J.)

It is what we think we are good at that influences occupational choice, not what we are actually good at. In fact, the two are often completely unrelated (Panek & Sterns, 1985). Typically, the more efficacious that people judge themselves to be, the wider the range of occupational options they consider appropriate and the better they prepare themselves educationally for different occupational pursuits. People who have less confidence in themselves tend to limit their options, even when they have the true ability to engage in a wide range of occupations (Betz & Hackett, 1986; Lent & Hackett, 1987).

Self-efficacy theory also helps us understand differences between men and women and between whites and minorities in occupational choices (Bandura, 1990). Cultural practices that convey lower expectations for women, stereotypic gender roles, gender-typed behaviors, and structural barriers to advancement eventually lower one's self-efficacy. Consequently, women and minorities may limit their interests and range of occupational options by the belief that they lack the ability for occupations traditionally occupied by white men, even though they do not differ from white men in actual ability.

sembles the investigative type in being intraceptive and asocial; but differs from that type in that the person has a need for individualistic expression, has less ego strength, is more feminine, and suffers more frequently from emotional disturbances; prefers dealing with environmental problems through self-expression in artistic media. Vocational preferences include art dealer, author, cartoonist, commercial artist, composer, concert singer, dramatic coach, free-lance writer, musical arranger, musician, playwright, poet, stage director, symphony conductor.

Conventional

The model type prefers structured verbal and numerical activities and subordinate roles; is conforming (extraceptive); avoids ambiguous situations and problems involving interpersonal relationships and physical skills; is effective at well-structured tasks; identifies with power; values material possessions and status. Vocational preferences include bank examiner, bank teller, bookkeeper, budget reviewer, cost estimator, court stenographer, financial analyst, computer equipment operator, inventory controller, payroll clerk, quality control expert, statistician, tax expert, traffic manager.

Enterprising

The model type has verbal skills for selling, dominating, leading; conceives of self as a strong, masculine leader; avoids well-defined language or work situations requiring long periods of intellectual effort; is extraceptive; differs from the conventional type in that the person prefers ambiguous social tasks and has a greater concern with power, status, and leadership; is orally aggressive. Vocational preferences include business executive, buyer, hotel manager, industrial relations consultant, manufacturer's representative, master of ceremonies, political campaign manager, real-estate salesperson, restaurant worker, speculator, sports promoter, stock and bond salesperson, television producer, traveling salesperson.

Gender Differences

Men and women differ on many dimensions when it comes to choosing occupations. Men are groomed for future employment. Boys learn at an early age that men are known by the work they do, and they receive strong encouragement for thinking about what occupation they would like to have. Occupational achievement is stressed as a core element of masculinity. Important social skills are taught through team games, in which they learn how to play by the rules, to accept setbacks without taking defeat personally, to follow the guidance of the leader, and to move up the leadership hierarchy by demonstrating qualities that are valued by others.

Women have traditionally not been so well trained. The skills that they have been taught are quite different—how to be accommodative and supportive—and they have received little in the way of occupation-related skills (Shainess, 1984). However, the women's movement has stressed the importance of providing girls the necessary skills for occupations outside the home. Given that more than half of women are now employed and that this trend will probably continue, it is especially important that women be exposed to the same occupational socialization opportunities as men.

Attention to women's occupational choices is relatively recent (Betz & Fitzgerald, 1987), due mainly to the assumptions that women's primary roles were homemaker and mother and that occupations were important only to single women. Perhaps as a result of the influence of these stereotypes, occupational choices and developmental patterns differ between men and women. For example, one study found that male college seniors with a C+ average believed they were capable of earning a Ph.D. but that women with a B+ average thought they were incapable of doing so (Baird, 1973). Even a year after graduation women with an A average were no more likely to be attending graduate or professional schools than were men with a B average (Barnett & Baruch, 1978). These findings fit with self-efficacy influences on occupational selection discussed earlier, and they indicate the strength of the effects that early differences in socialization can have on subsequent occupational achievement.

One controversial topic in occupational selection concerns women's decisions to "specifically and intentionally avoid high-prestige occupations" (Barnett & Baruch, 1978, p. 133). Although this conclusion fits data cited earlier on women's likelihood to seek postgraduate training and the notion that women have a fear of success, we must be careful not to read too much into these findings. That is, women may be reluctant to enter high-status occupations because of genuine roadblocks, such as hiring and pay discrimination, rather than because they are afraid to try.

Although it is still too early to tell, as women continue to move into the work force, the ways in which they choose occupations are likely to become more similar to the processes that men use. Whereas research on occupational choice before the 1970s tended to focus on men, more recent research routinely includes women. Over the next

decade it is likely that we will see even fewer differences between men and women in the ways in which they decide to pursue occupations.

OCCUPATIONAL DEVELOPMENT

For most of us, getting a job is not enough; we would also like to move up the ladder. How quickly occupational advancement occurs (or does not) may lead to such labels as "fast-tracker" or "dead-ender" (Kanter, 1976). People who want to advance learn quickly how long to stay at one level and how to seize opportunities as they occur; others soon learn the frustration of remaining in the same job with no chance for promotion.

How we advance through our occupation seems to be related to several factors beyond those important in choosing an occupation. Among these are expectations, support from co-workers, priorities, and job satisfaction. All of these help us face what psychologists call early professional socialization, in other words, what we are expected to do in our occupation. Before we consider these aspects, however, we will look at a general scheme of occupational development.

Super's Theory

No one is more responsible for viewing occupations as developmental than Super. Over four decades, Super (1957, 1980) developed a theory of occupational development based on self-concept. He proposes that occupations progress through five distinct stages that result from changes in individuals' self-concept and adaptation to an occupational role: implementation, establishment, maintenance, deceleration, and retirement. People are located along a continuum of **vocational maturity** through their working years; the more congruent their occupational behaviors are with what is expected of them at different ages, the more vocationally mature they are.

The *implementation stage* occurs during late adolescence. During this time people take a series of temporary positions in which they learn first-hand about work roles. This socialization process includes learning about responsibility and productivity, co-worker friendships, and life styles of working adults. This series of positions helps individuals identify what types of occupations are attractive and fit their needs, self-concept, and expectations. Havighurst (1982) terms this period the *trial work period* and points out that it is typically very unstable.

The *establishment stage* begins with the selection of a specific occupation, which occurs during young adulthood, and continues through a period of years marked by stability, achievement, and advancement. During this time the typical worker may change jobs or positions within a company, but only rarely does he or she change occupations. For example, a person is likely to move from an entry-level to a supervisory position in the same company but is unlikely to go from working as an accountant to working as a plumber. During the establishment stage the worker's self-concept becomes more congruent with his or her occupation.

The third stage, termed the *maintenance stage*, is a period of transition that usually occurs during middle age (typically between ages 45 and 55). Workers begin to reduce the amount of time they spend in their work roles, mainly because they believe that they have either already accomplished their occupational goals or will never attain them. The drive to achieve diminishes, and simply maintaining one's occupation becomes dominant. This stage is reminiscent of Levinson and his colleagues' (1978) description of midlife development, described in Chapter 8.

As workers near 60, they begin the *deceleration stage*. Preparation for retirement begins in earnest for most people, interest in leisure activities increases, and the process of separating oneself from one's occupation begins. Whether this separation process is easy or difficult depends on how much of one's identity comes from one's occupation. To the extent that one identifies very strongly with one's occupation, the separation process is more difficult.

Finally, most workers enter the *retirement stage*, in which they stop working full time. Because the final sections of this chapter deal with the specific issues involved with retirement, we will not consider them here.

Super's framework is important because it emphasizes that occupations are not static once they are chosen. Rather, they evolve in response to changes in the person's self-concept. Consequently, occupations are a developmental process that reflects and explains important life changes.

Women and Occupational Development

For many years research on women's occupational development was based on the assumption that most women saw their primary roles as homemaker and mother (Betz & Fitzgerald, 1987). Consequently, descriptions of women's occupational development were predicated on this assumption, and continuous employment outside the home was viewed as nontraditional. This assumption is clearly wrong. Researchers' descriptions now reflect the fact that most women in the United States work outside the home.

Betz (1984) examined the occupational histories of 500 college women 10 years after graduation. Two thirds of these women were highly committed to their occupations, which for 70% were traditionally female ones. Most had worked continuously since graduation. Only 1% had been full-time homemakers during the entire 10-year period; 79% reported that they had successfully combined occupations with homemaking. Concerning occupational development, women in traditional female occupations were less likely to change occupations. If they did change, the move was more likely to be downward than were the changes made by women in nontraditional occupations.

Sex Discrimination. Even though the majority of women work outside the home, women in high-status jobs are unusual. It was not until 1981 that a woman was appointed to the U.S. Supreme Court; in 1991 Sandra Day O'Connor was still the only woman associate justice. Few women serve in the highest ranks of major corporations, and women are badly outnumbered in the faculties of most universities and colleges.

One intuitively appealing reason for the paucity of women in top-level jobs is work overload. Overload results when women with occupations outside the home are also expected to perform most of the day-to-day housekeeping chores and child care. Instead of one occupation, these women are expected to have two. Contrary to intuition, however, work overload is usually not a factor (we will come back to this topic later). Far more important is **sex discrimination**: denying a job to someone solely on the basis of gender.

Baron and Bielby (1985) pull no punches in discussing sex discrimination. "Our analyses portray [sex] discrimination as pervasive, almost omnipresent, sustained by diverse organizational structures and processes. Moreover, this segregation drastically restricts women's career opportunities, by blocking access to internal labor markets and their benefits" (Baron & Bielby, 1985, p. 245). Women are being kept out of high-status jobs by the men at the top.

Women sometimes refer to a **glass ceiling**, the level to which they may rise in a company but beyond which they may not go. This problem is most obvious in companies that classify jobs at various levels (as does the civil service). DiPrete and Soule (1988) found that the greatest disadvantage facing women occurred near the boundary between lower-tier and upper-tier job grades. Women tend to move to the top of the lower tier and remain there, whereas men are typically promoted to the upper tier, even when other factors, such as personal attributes and qualifications, are controlled. The U.S. government admitted in 1991 that the glass ceiling was not only real, but pervasive throughout the workplace.

Beyond discrimination in hiring and promotion, women are also the victims of pay discrimination. In many occupations men are paid substantially more than women in the same positions; indeed, on the average, women are paid only about three fourths or less of what men are paid. Why? Traditionally, the attitude was that men had families to support, whereas women were working just to have something to do. Obviously, this is untrue. Many working women are the primary, if not the sole, source of support for their family and should not be paid less. This issue of pay equity for men and women in the same position has been expanded to include the issue of **comparable worth**. The principle behind comparable worth is that women in traditionally female occupations (secretaries, nurses, teachers, and so forth) should not be paid less than men in traditionally male occupations (construction workers, factory workers, and so on), providing that the skills required in the job, the job level, and the perceived importance of the work are comparable. How these determinations are made has yet to be resolved. Comparable worth continues to be a controversial legal area, and it will undoubtedly be debated for several years to come.

Sex and pay discrimination against women are even more unjustified given the amount of effort that women devote to work. Some authors assert that family responsibilities keep women from devoting as much time to work as men. But Bielby and Bielby (1988) found no support for this assumption. In fact, they report that, on average, most women (65% to 70%) actually devote more time to work than do men with similar household responsibilities and occupations.

Although laws have been passed to prohibit discrimination in the workplace, real change is unlikely without fundamental changes in social attitudes. Until we inculcate the belief that men and women should be provided equal opportunities for all occupations and that everyone should be paid on the basis of the kind of work done rather than gender, these problems will remain.

Age Discrimination

Another structural barrier to occupational development is **age discrimination**, which involves denying a job or promotion to someone solely on the basis of age. The U.S. Age Discrimination in Employment Act of 1986 protects workers over age 40. This law stipulates that people must be hired based on their ability, not their age. Under this law employers are banned from refusing to hire and from discharging workers solely on the basis of age. Additionally, employers cannot segregate or classify workers or otherwise denote their status on the basis of age.

Age discrimination occurs in several ways (Snyder & Barrett, 1988). For example, employers can make certain types of physical or mental performance a job requirement and argue that older workers are incapable of it, or they can make cuts in the number of employees in an attempt to get rid of older workers by using mandatory retirement. Supervisors sometimes will use age as a factor in performance evaluations for raises or promotions, or in decisions about which employees are eligible for additional training.

Perceptions of age discrimination are widespread; nearly 700 federal court cases have been filed since 1970. Snyder and Barrett (1988) reviewed these cases and found that the employer had been favored about 65% of the time. Job performance information was crucial in all cases; however, this information was usually presented in terms of general differences between young and old. Surprisingly, many courts did not question inaccurate information or stereotypic views of aging presented by employers, despite the lack of scientific data documenting age differences in actual job performance.

On the basis of their review Snyder and Barrett argue that findings from gerontological research need to be given to federal courts to help clarify their decision making. Indeed, much of the research in this chapter supports the conclusion that older workers are capable of performing at high levels of competence.

Occupational Success

How do you know if you are successful in your occupation? A bumper sticker popular in the 1980s summarized one view: Whoever gets the most stuff wins. Indeed, for many people, occupational success is defined mainly in terms of how much money you earn. Jencks and his associates (1979) found that men's occupational success (defined in terms of salary) was related to four factors: (1) Family and ethnic background was the most important determinant. Sons of professional fathers earned the most, and whites outearned African Americans. (2) Number of years of formal education was the second most important factor, with more education related to higher income. (3) Intelligence was the third most important predictor of success; brighter people tend to earn more. (4) Personality traits were also significant predictors.

The Jencks et al. study showed that there was no single determinant of occupational success. Many factors, from family to luck, come together to influence how well we do in our occupation. It must also be remembered that not everyone defines occupational success in financial terms, so that the factors important in terms of pay may not be as important when success is defined in other ways (for instance, personal freedom, autonomy). Recall that people do not choose occupations solely on the basis of pay. Rather, they look for occupations that meet many varying personal needs as well.

Occupational Expectations

Individuals form opinions about what it will be like to work in a particular occupation based on what they learn in school and from their parents. People tend to set goals regarding what they want to become and when they hope to get there. This tendency is so common, in fact, that in their theory of adult male development Levinson and his colleagues (1978) maintain that forming a *dream*, as they put it, is one of the young adult's chief tasks.

A major task throughout one's occupation is to refine and update occupational expectations. Refining your dream typically involves trying to achieve your goal, monitoring your progress toward the goal, and changing or even abandoning your goal as necessary. For some, modifying goals comes as a result of failure (changing from a business major because one is flunking economics courses), racial or sexual discrimination, lack of opportunity, obsolescence of skills, economic reasons, or changing interests. In some cases one's initial choice may have been unrealistic; for example, nearly half of all young adults would like to become professionals (such as lawyers or physicians), but only one person in seven actually makes it (Cosby, 1974).

Whenever a person finds that he or she needs to modify occupational goals, stress usually results. And even though some goal modification is essential from time to time, it usually comes as a surprise that we could be wrong about what seemed to be a logical choice in the past. As Gina put it, "I really thought I wanted to be a flight attendant; the travel sounded really interesting. But it just wasn't what I expected."

Perhaps the rudest jolt for most of us comes during the transition from school to the real world, where things just never seem to happen the way the textbooks say that they are supposed to. This **reality shock** (Van Maanen & Schein, 1977) befalls everyone, from the young mother who discovers that newborns demand an incredible amount of time to the accountant who learns that the financial forecast that took days to prepare may simply end up in a file cabinet. The visionary aspects of the dream may not disappear altogether, but a hearty dose of reality goes a long way toward bringing a person down to earth and comes to play an increasingly important role in one's occupation and self-concept. For example, the woman who thought that she would receive the same rewards as her male counterparts for comparable work is likely to become increasingly angry and disillusioned when her successes result in smaller raises and fewer promotions.

A longitudinal study begun in 1956 by the American Telephone and Telegraph Company (AT&T) provides some of the best evidence available about one's dream and reality shock. In general, the research examined the variables related to personality and ability that could predict occupational success and satisfaction (Bray, Campbell, & Grant, 1974). The initial sample consisted of 422 white males in a pool of lower-level managers from which future upper-level managers would be chosen. Some participants were college graduates hired at the manager level, and the remainder were men without a college degree who had been promoted through the ranks.

The findings revealed considerable support for both Levinson's dream and a period of reality shock (Howard & Bray, 1980). Young managers began their occupations full of expectations but rapidly became more realistic. On average, by the time the college-educated men were 29 years old and the noncollege men were 34, the strong desire to seek additional promotions had decreased markedly. Two reasons for the decline were given. First, workers were concerned about disruption to the family due to the need to move following a promotion. Second, workers reported a lack of desire to devote more time to work, which would be required on entering upper-level management. Interestingly, these men were satisfied with their jobs. In fact, they found them challenging, and their intrinsic motivation levels did not drop despite their reluctance to advance.

Although the AT&T study provided important insights, its limitations must be recognized. The inclusion of only white males means that the developmental trends for other groups is largely unknown. Second, only white-collar workers with the potential of moving up the corporate ladder were studied. People in service, unskilled, and blue-collar jobs probably differ in important ways, since their potential for upward mobility is limited.

The Role of Mentors

Imagine how hard it would be to learn a new occupation with no support from other people around you. Being socialized into an occupation goes well beyond the relatively short formal training you receive. Much of the most critical information you need to know is usually not taught in training seminars. Instead, most people are shown the ropes by co-workers. In many cases, an older, more experienced person makes a specific effort to do this. Such a person is a **mentor** (Levinson et al., 1978). Although mentors by no means provide the only specific source of guidance in the workplace, they have been studied fairly closely.

A mentor is part teacher, part sponsor, part model, and part counselor. The mentor helps a young worker avoid trouble ("Beware of what you say around Bentley") and provides invaluable information about the many unwritten rules that govern day-to-day activities in the workplace (not working too fast on the assembly line, wearing the right clothes, and so on). As part of the relationship, a mentor makes sure that his or her protégé is noticed and receives credit for good work from supervisors. As a result, occupational success often depends on the quality of the mentor-protégé relationship. Consequently, mentors fulfill two main functions: improving the protégé's chances for advancement and promoting his or her psychological and social well-being (Kram, 1980, 1985; Kram & Isabella, 1985; Noe, 1987).

Playing the role of a mentor is also a developmental phase in one's occupation. Helping a younger employee learn the job fulfills aspects of Erikson's (1982) phase of generativity. In particular, the mentor is making sure that there is some continuity in the field by passing on his or her accumulated knowledge and experience. This function of the mentor is part of middle-agers' attempts at ensuring the continuity of society and accomplishing or producing something worthwhile (Erikson, 1982).

The mentor-protégé relationship develops over time. Based on her in-depth study, Kram (1985) proposes a four-stage sequence. The first stage, *initiation*, constitutes the 6- to 12-month period during which the protégé selects a mentor and they begin to develop their relationship. The second stage, *cultivation*, lasts from two to five years and is the most active phase of the mentoring relationship. This is the period when the mentor provides considerable occupational assistance and serves as a confidant. The third stage, *separation*, is the most difficult. It begins when the protégé receives a promotion, often to the level of the mentor. The protégé must emerge from the protection of the mentor in order to demonstrate his or her own competence. Both parties experience feelings of loneliness and separation. The final period is *redefinition*. In this period the protégé and mentor reestablish their relationship but with a new set of rules based more on friendship between peers.

Research on the selection of mentors by young adults reveals that potential mentors' interpersonal skills are the single most important factor (Olian,

The guidance provided by an older worker through the mentor-protégé relationship can be a key factor in successful career development.

Carroll, Giannantonio, & Feren, 1988). Additionally, protégés are attracted to mentors who are connected in the organization and who are older than themselves.

Some authors think that women have a greater need for a mentor than men (Busch, 1985). However, women seem to have a more difficult time finding an adequate mentor. One reason is that female role models who could serve a mentoring function are scarce, especially in upper-level management. Only 7% of the women in the work force are in administrative, executive, or managerial jobs, compared with 12% of men (U.S. Department of Labor, 1988). This is an unfortunate situation, especially in view of the fact that women who have female mentors are significantly more productive than women with male mentors (Goldstein, 1979). Although many young women report that they would feel comfortable with a male mentor (Olian et al., 1988), there are additional problems beyond

productivity. Several researchers note that cross-gender mentor-protégé relationships produce conflict and tension resulting from possible sexual overtones, even when there has been no overtly sexual behavior on anyone's part (Kram, 1985).

Occupational Priorities

What do you want from an occupation? Money? Fame? Glory? Your answers to this question are a function of your **occupational priorities**. Such things as fame, money, and helping others may motivate you to run for public office, work at a second job, or enter social work. If you know a worker's priorities, what he or she values most, then you are in a good position to understand what things about an occupation are probably satisfying or unsatisfying.

Much has been written about an apparent shift in priorities among young people today compared with a generation ago. For example, it is asserted that young people are no longer willing to be just another person in a corporate machine and that they value personal growth above monetary gain. As with most generalizations part of this notion is true and part is not. It does seem to be the case that today's college students are more concerned with occupations that have positive social effects. They also seem to desire occupations that are challenging and that offer the chance for personal growth. However, they still believe that hard work leads to fame and fortune and that material gains are an appropriate goal (Jones, 1980; Yankelovich, 1981).

Differences in occupational priorities were made clear in a second longitudinal study conducted by AT&T, begun in 1977, which was designed to parallel the original study started in 1956 (Howard & Bray, 1980). In the 1970s managers at AT&T were more diverse; almost half were women, and one third were minorities. No differences between the younger and older groups were found in intellectual ability (although the younger group was better educated), need for achievement, or personal work standards.

Key differences emerged in motivation for upward mobility, leadership, and desire for emotional support. The younger managers' expectations of rewards from work were much lower; they did not see most of their major rewards or life satisfactions coming from work. This view contrasted sharply with the older managers' high work motivation and early desire for promotion. The younger managers also had a lower desire to be responsible for subordinates and to direct others. Finally, they had a much stronger desire to provide emotional support to co-workers.

The findings at AT&T, depicted in Figure 11.1, are not unique. Other research has also documented the move away from materialism, power seeking, upward mobility, and competition toward an emphasis on individual freedom, personal growth, and cooperation (Jones, 1980; Yankelovich, 1981). Howard and Bray (1980) note that changes in workers' priorities may have significant implications for the effectiveness of our work socialization systems.

Expectation of a financially and personally rewarding occupation is praiseworthy. It may also be asking for trouble after reality shock hits, since very few jobs offer perfect combinations of material and personal rewards. As a result many people become disenchanted with their jobs. Terkel (1974) documented many of these reactions: "I'm a machine" (a spot-welder). "A monkey could do what I do" (a receptionist). "I'm an object" (a model). Disillusionment occurs in all types of occupations, from the assembly-line worker who feels like a robot to the high-level corporate executive who feels like a small piece of a giant machine. Such shattered expectations must have an effect on another important factor in occupational development: job satisfaction.

Job Satisfaction

What does it mean to be satisfied with one's job or occupation? In a general sense **job satisfaction** is the positive feeling that results from an appraisal of one's work (Locke, 1976). In research, specific aspects such as satisfaction with working conditions, pay, and co-workers are considered. In practice, American workers actually have a multidimensional conceptualization of job satisfaction.

Due to the complex nature of job satisfaction, most jobs end up being satisfying in some ways (such as achievement and power) and not in others (like pay and working conditions). Factors that make jobs satisfying at one time may become less important the longer one is in an occupation or as new concerns are raised in society. For example, concern over health and safety problems played a much more important role in job satisfaction in the late 1970s than they did a decade earlier (Quinn &

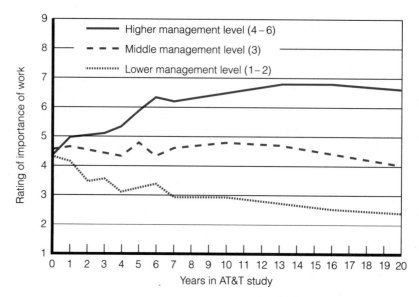

FIGURE 11.1 Changes in the relative importance of work at different levels of management in the AT&T study

(Source: *Career Motivation in Mid-Life Managers* by A. Howard and D. W. Bray, 1980, paper presented at the annual meeting of the American Psychological Association, Montreal. Reprinted with permission of the author.)

Staines, 1979). Additionally, occupational values change over time; military personnel and politicians have lost some of the prestige that they once had, while environmentally oriented jobs have increased in social worth. Given that the structural elements of a job (such as working conditions) affect satisfaction, an important question is whether the age of the worker is also related to his or her job satisfaction.

Almost all of the studies that have investigated the relationship between overall job satisfaction and age have found a low to moderate increase in satisfaction with increasing age (e.g., James & Jones, 1980; Schwab & Heneman, 1977). However, there are several important qualifications that need to be made in relation to this finding.

First, the results could be due to self-selection factors. That is, people who truly like their jobs may tend to stay in them, while people who do not may tend to leave. To the extent that this is the case, age differences in job satisfaction may simply reflect the fact that with sufficient time, many people eventually find a job in which they are reasonably happy.

Second, the relationship between worker age and job satisfaction is complex. Satisfaction does not increase in all areas with age. It appears that older workers are more satisfied with the intrinsic personal aspects of their jobs than they are with the extrinsic aspects, such as pay (Morrow & McElroy, 1987).

Third, increases in job satisfaction may not be due to age alone but, rather, to the degree to which there is a good fit between the worker and the job (Holland, 1985). From this perspective it is not surprising that increasing age should be related to increased job satisfaction: Older workers have had more time to find jobs that they like or may have resigned themselves to the fact that things are unlikely to improve, resulting in a better congruence between worker desires and job attributes (Barrett, 1978). A. T. White and Spector (1987) showed that the relationship between age and job satisfaction was due mainly to congruence and having an appropriate sense of control over one's job. Older workers also may have revised their expectations over the years to better reflect the actual state of affairs. Because expectations become more realistic and are therefore more likely to be fulfilled, job satisfaction increases over time (Hulin & Smith, 1965).

Fourth, work becomes less of a focus in men's lives as they age and achieve occupational success (Bray & Howard, 1983). This process of disengagement from work can begin as early as the 30s for men who are not advancing rapidly in their occupations, but it comes somewhat later for men who achieve some degree of success. Consequently, for many men it takes less to keep them satisfied due to lower work motivation.

Fifth, men may discover different sources of satisfaction. As men stay in an occupation longer, they begin to find satisfaction in different ways. For example, they derive pleasure from accomplishing tasks and from becoming independent in their work. Interestingly, lower-level managers become more nurturant as time goes on, but the men at the top of the hierarchy become progressively more remote and detached and less sympathetic and helpful (Howard, 1984).

Finally, there is a growing awareness that job satisfaction may be cyclical. That is, it may show periodic fluctuations that are not related to age per se but, rather, to changes that people intentionally make in their occupations (Shirom & Mazeh, 1988). The idea is that job satisfaction increases over time because people change jobs or responsibilities on a regular basis, thereby keeping their occupation interesting and challenging. This provocative idea of periodicity in job satisfaction is explored further in How Do We Know?

CHANGING OCCUPATIONS

In the past it was quite common for people to choose an occupation during young adulthood and stay in it throughout their working years. Today, many people take a job with the expectation that they will not be in it forever. Changing jobs is almost taken for granted; the average American will change jobs between 5 and 10 times during adulthood (Toffler, 1970). Some authors view occupational changes as positive; Havighurst (1982), for example, strongly advocates such flexibility. According to his view, building change into the occupational life cycle may help eliminate disillusionment with one's initial choice. Changing occupations may be one way to guarantee challenging and satisfying work, and it may be the best option for those in a position to exercise it (Shirom & Mazeh, 1988).

Factors Influencing Occupational Change

Several factors have been identified as important in determining who will remain in an occupation and who will change. Some of these factors — such as personality — lead to self-initiated occupation changes. Others, such as obsolescence and economic factors — cause forced occupational changes.

Personality. Personality is important in self-initiated occupational change. Recall that Holland (1985)

HOW DO WE KNOW?

Periodicity and Job Satisfaction

There is considerable evidence that job satisfaction tends to increase with age. Why this is true has been the subject of much debate. One hypothesis is that changes in job satisfaction are actually related to job seniority or job tenure. The idea is that satisfaction tends to be high in the beginning of a job, to stabilize or drop during the middle phase, and to rise again later. Each time a person changes jobs, the cycle repeats.

Shirom and Mazeh (1988) decided to study the cyclical nature of job satisfaction systematically. They collected questionnaire data from a representative sample of 900 Israeli junior high school teachers with up to 23 years of seniority. The questionnaire contained items concerning teachers' satisfaction with salary, working hours, social status, contacts with pupils, autonomy, opportunities for professional growth, and opportunities for carrying out educational goals. The focus of analysis was on year-to-year changes in satisfaction.

Using a statistical technique called spectral analysis, Shirom and Mazeh were able to show that teachers' job satisfaction followed systematic five-year cycles that were strongly related to seniority but unrelated to age. They noted that a major work-related change, a sabbatical leave, or a change in school characterized teachers' work approximately every five years. They concluded that each of these changes reinstated the cycle of high-lowered-high job satisfaction, which, when tracked over long periods, appears to show a linear increase in overall job satisfaction.

An important implication of Shirom and Mazeh's data is that change may be necessary for long-term job satisfaction. Although the teaching profession has change built into it (such as sabbatical leaves), many occupations do not (Latack, 1984). This option of changes in job structure and other areas should be explored for more occupations.

---

postulates that people with certain personality characteristics are suited to particular jobs. If a worker makes an initial selection and later comes to dislike an occupation, it may be because his or her personality does not match the job.

Several researchers have documented that personality factors and situational pressure combine to determine whether a person will remain in an occupation (for example, Clopton, 1973; Wiener & Vaitenas, 1977). For example, Wiener and Vaitenas found that lack of interest, incongruity with one's occupation, lack of consistent and diversified interests, fear of failure, or a history of emotional problems predicted occupational change. Age was not a predictor. Such findings support our earlier point that similar factors influence occupational choice throughout adulthood.

Obsolescence and Economic Factors. Sometimes people cannot choose whether they want to change occupations; they are forced to do so. For example, people may be forced to look for new occupations as a result of technological change (such as assembly-line workers being replaced by robots) or economic factors (economic recessions).

Technological change is occurring at an ever-increasing rate, such that the skills that one learns today may be obsolete in only a few years. When this occurs, individuals may find that they are forced into making occupational changes. As an example, many Americans with skills important in heavy manufacturing, such as making steel, were displaced in the late 1970s and 1980s as domestic plants closed. Thus, workers are being forced to retrain themselves as never before — either just to keep up with change or to learn about new employment opportunities. The latter reason is especially important; in 25 years at least one quarter of the readers of this book will hold jobs in fields or specializations that currently do not exist.

Layoffs are one primary impetus to change occupations. Layoffs occur most often during large economic recessions, such as the one during the early 1990s. Unlike most previous recessions in the United States, this time people in all types of occupations were affected, from blue-collar laborers to high-level corporate executives. In addition, some workers decide to seek new occupations because of personal economic factors, such as insufficient pay. For example, recently divorced women may need to find higher paying occupations, especially if child-support payments are not received.

Loss of One's Job

Changing economic conditions in the United States over the past few decades (such as increased competition from foreign companies), as well as changing demographics, have forced many people out of their jobs. Heavy manufacturing and support businesses (such as the steel, oil, and automotive industries) and farming were the hardest hit during the 1970s and 1980s. But no one is immune. Indeed, the corporate takeover frenzy of the 1980s and the recession of the early 1990s put many middle- and upper-level corporate executives out of work as well.

Losing one's job can have enormous personal impact (DeFrank & Ivancevich, 1986). Declines in physical health and self-esteem, depression, anxiety, and suicide are common (Lajer, 1982). Although the loss of one's job means the loss of income and status, these effects vary with age. Middle-aged men are more vulnerable to negative effects than older or younger men (DeFrank & Ivancevich, 1986). Moreover, the extent of the effects of losing one's job are related to the degree of

financial stress one is under and the timing of the loss (Estes & Wilensky, 1978). Childless couples and couples with young children suffer the most; couples whose children have left home or are independent fare better. Lajer (1982) reports that admission to a psychiatric unit following job loss is more likely for people who are over age 45 or who have been unemployed for a long period.

The effects of losing one's job emphasize the central role that occupations play in forming a sense of identity in adulthood. How one perceives the loss of a job plays a major role in determining what the long-term effects will be.

DUAL-WORKER COUPLES

At one time, most people in the United States pictured a two-parent home in which the father had an occupation and the mother stayed at home to raise the children. What 30 years will do! Today, only a clear minority of families fit this view. The vast majority consist of both parents working outside the home, largely because families need the dual income in order to pay the bills and maintain a moderate standard of living. As we will see, dual-worker couples experience both benefits and costs to this arrangement.

The experiences of most dual-worker couples are similar to those of Jan (a cashier at a local supermarket) and Tom (a worker at the nearby auto assembly plant). Jan and Tom are in their late 20s and have a 3-year-old daughter, Terri. Although they like the fact that their combined income lets them own a modest house, they also feel many strains.

"You know, at times I feel overwhelmed," Jan related. "It's not that Tom doesn't help around the house. But it's not as much as he could. Most days after work I have to pick up Terri from Mom's and then come home and prepare dinner. After a hard day, that's about the last thing I want to do. I guess I'm not very good at being a superwoman, or whatever they call it. I also still feel a little guilty leaving Terri with Mom; there are times when I think I ought to be home with her rather than out working."

"But look at what we've got now," Tom responded. "You used to complain about things a lot more. You should think about all the things we wouldn't have if you didn't work."

Jan and Tom's experiences point out the major gains and stresses reported by dual-worker couples. On the benefit side, their standard of living is higher, which allows them to have more material goods and provide better for their children. However, as Jan indicated, there are several stresses as well. For most dual-worker couples, the biggest problem is the division of housework duties.

Handling Multiple Roles

When both members of a couple are employed, who cleans the house, cooks the meals, and takes care of the children when they are ill? Despite much media attention and claims of increased sharing in the duties, women still assume the lion's share of housework regardless of employment status. Wives spend about twice as many hours per week as their husbands in family work and bear the greatest responsibility for household and child-care tasks (Benin & Agostinelli, 1988). Indeed, it is this unequal division of labor that creates the most arguments and causes the most unhappiness for dual-worker couples.

Husbands and wives view the division of labor in very different terms. Benin and Agostinelli (1988) found that husbands were most satisfied with an equitable division of labor based on the number of hours spent, especially if the amount of time needed to perform household tasks was relatively small. Wives, on the other hand, were most satisfied if the division favored them; their satisfac-

tion was unaffected by the total number of hours spent, but it was affected by the husband's willingness to perform women's traditional chores. Broman (1988) reports similar results with African-American dual-worker couples. In this study women were twice as likely as men to feel overworked by housework and to be dissatisfied with their family life.

Role conflict is another problem expressed by many dual-worker couples. Figuring out how to balance time at work and time with family confronts everyone. Many women were raised with motherhood as a major goal and feel torn between raising their children and continuing their occupation (Shainess, 1984). Guilt feelings may be exacerbated by others who feel that a woman who places her children in day care is not a good mother. Her partner may also have his own views that do not agree with hers, further compounding the problem.

However, it appears that most employed women and men manage to resolve the apparent tension between work and parenting. Women in one study were clear in their commitment to their careers, marriage, and children, and were successfully combining them without high levels of distress (Guelzow, Bird, & Koball, 1991). Contrary to popular belief, age of children was not a factor in stress level; only the number of children was important. Guilt was not an issue for these women. Men in the same study reported sharing more of the child-care tasks as a way of dealing with multiple role pressures. Additionally, low stress in men was associated with having a flexible work schedule that would allow them to care for sick children and other family matters. Together these findings are encouraging, as they indicate that more dual-worker couples are learning how to adaptively balance work and family.

It is often difficult for dual-worker couples to find time alone with each other, especially if both work long hours (Kingston & Nock, 1987). The amount of time together is not necessarily the most important issue; as long as the time is spent in

SOMETHING TO THINK ABOUT

Division of Labor and Role Conflict in Dual-Worker Couples

One of the largest issues facing American society in the 1990s is how dual-worker couples can balance their occupational and family roles. With the majority of couples now consisting of two wage earners, issues such as who does the household chores and how child care is arranged will become increasingly important.

Many people believe that work and family roles mutually influence each other. That is, when things go badly at work, family suffers, and when you have problems with your spouse, your work suffers. As noted in the text, such role conflicts and mutual interaction appear not to be the case. It is more of a one-way street. For the most part, problems at home have little effect on job performance, whereas trouble at work could spill over to your home life.

Negotiating agreeable arrangements of household and child-care tasks are critical. But truly equitable divisions of labor are the exception. Most American households with dual-worker couples still operate under a gender-segregated system: There are wives' chores and husbands' chores. There is no question that all of these tasks are important and must be performed to ensure domestic sanitation. There is also no question that these tasks take time. The important point for women is that it is not how much time is spent in performing household chores that matters but which tasks are performed. The research cited in the text indicates that what bothers wives the most is not that their husbands are lazy but that their husbands will not perform some "women's work." Men may mow the lawn, wash the car, and even cook, but they rarely run the vacuum, scrub the toilet, or change the baby's diaper.

It appears that husbands would be viewed much more positively by their wives if they performed more of the traditionally female tasks. Marital satisfaction would be likely to improve as a result. Moreover, the role modeling provided to children in these households would be a major step in breaking the transmission of age-old stereotypes. It's something to think about.

---

shared activities such as eating, playing, and conversing, couples tend to be happy.

Issues concerning balancing work and family are extremely important in couples' everyday lives. Learning how to deal with multiple roles is an important process in current industrial societies. We are creating patterns that will provide the anticipatory socialization for our children. Even now, most dual-worker couples feel that the benefits, especially the extra income, are worth the costs. Many dual-worker couples, however, have no choice but to try to deal with the situation as best they can: Both partners must work simply to pay the bills.

But what effects do family matters have on work performance and vice versa? Recent evidence suggests our work and family lives do not have equal influences on the other (Howard, in press). It appears that work stress has a far bigger impact on family life than family stress has on work performance. The relationship is extremely complex, but in essence the point is this: Work and family roles come together only when it comes to personal satisfaction. In all other respects, the two are quite separate. As discussed in Something to Think About, this means that couples need to take seriously the job of deciding how to divide up tasks.

Impact on Occupational Development

Besides the impact on their personal lives, dual-worker couples sometimes report negative effects on occupational development. The most obvious influence occurs when one partner decides to interrupt his or her occupation while the children are young and later reenters the labor force. Skills may have to be learned or relearned, and such returnees may find themselves competing with younger workers for the same positions.

What about people who do not interrupt their careers? Suppose you and your spouse have occupations in which you are both extremely happy. One day, your spouse comes home and tells you about an incredible opportunity for advancement. The problem is that the position is in another city 1,000 miles away. To remain together, you would have to quit your job and move. What would you do? It turns out that whether you are a husband or a wife makes an enormous difference; husbands' careers are clearly given higher priority. One survey showed that 77% of women and 68% of men said that a wife should quit her job if her husband were offered a good position in another city. In contrast, only 10% of the women and 18% of the men said that the husband should refuse the offer so that his wife could continue with her job (Roper Organization, 1980).

Some couples avoid making this decision. Rather than trying to decide whether the other partner should quit and move, an increasing number of people are living apart. Such living arrangements are common in some occupations — such as acting, politics, sports, and the military — and are becoming more popular among professional couples. (Other reasons for couples to live apart are less glamorous; spending time in prison is one example.) Although this arrangement may work for people who can afford to visit each other often, for many people the stress of long-distance relationships can be severe. Some couples eventually decide that the costs of separation are higher than

the benefits of maintaining both occupations, and they reunite. Others decide to make the separation permanent, and break up. Indeed, Rindfuss and Stephen (1990) found that married couples living apart are approximately twice as likely to get divorced compared to married couples living together. In this case, absence does not make the heart grow fonder.

LEISURE

Leisure is something that is important to each of us, and is something we intuitively understand. For researchers, though, leisure is hard to define. Many authors take the easy way out and define it as the opposite of work. In this case, leisure is any time not spent doing what you are employed to do. But this definition ignores time spent with your family and friends, as well as time spent sleeping. Leisure can also be viewed as a state of mind, like relaxation. In this case, only you know if you are being leisurely or not. This, too, is inadequate for research.

In the end, researchers often opt for the definition that leisure is time that one has to do things for pleasure. More formally, we can define leisure as "personally expressive discretionary activity, varying in intensity of involvement from relaxation and diversion . . . through personal development and creativity . . . up to sensual transcendence" (Gordon, Gaitz, & Scott, 1976). However, there are important differences in how men and women, as well as people in different ethnic groups, view leisure (Henderson, 1990). For example, one study of African-American women revealed that they viewed leisure as both freedom from the constraint of needing to work and as a form of self-expression (Allen & Chin-Sang, 1990).

Gerontologists have recognized the importance of leisure in maintaining positive well-being for many years (Cutler & Hendricks, 1990). Without question, leisure plays a major role in people's lives in terms of how they spend their time and the benefits derived from it. In this section we will examine how leisure fits in the life cycle, the types of leisure activities people do, and consider how leisure activities change over adulthood.

Leisure in the Life Cycle

In order to make sense of what adults of all ages do when they are not working, we must consider how leisure fits into various parts of the life cycle. This aspect of the biopsychosocial model explicitly emphasizes that leisure is influenced by many factors, and that its meaning depends heavily on the person involved. Which leisure activities you engage in are a result of things such as your personal preferences, what your friends like to do, and your health, physical ability, and past experiences. Only when leisure is viewed in this broader perspective can we understand age differences in adults' leisure activities.

One important constant across adulthood appears to be the importance of the quality of leisure activities rather than their quantity (Kelly, Steinkamp, & Kelly, 1987). That is, it is not how many leisure activities you engage in that matters; rather, it is how much you enjoy them. For example, people with severe physical limitations may derive more benefit from leisure activities than very healthy adults if benefit is based on the quality of social interaction (Kelly et al., 1987).

A second important factor is that one's sense of self changes with age (see Chapter 8), which is accompanied by changes in what people do to seek affirmation. Lawton (1985a) suggests that personal expectations may affect what older adults do for leisure activities. For example, older adults may not think that physical leisure activities (such as aerobics) are appropriate and may refuse to participate in them. Others may feel entirely differently. Still, if people of certain ages are made to feel uncom-

fortable in some activities, it is unlikely they will continue to participate.

Finally, we must look at the broad context in which leisure occurs. Individuals with spouses and families tend to engage in more communal or group activities than single adults. Moreover, leisure activities are also one way to meet new people. Many adults join clubs or health spas not only for the leisure and health benefits, but also because they present opportunities to make new friends.

Types of Leisure Activities

Virtually any activity that one engages in could be considered a leisure activity. To help organize the options, researchers have generally classified leisure activities into four categories: cultural — such as attending sporting events, concerts, church services, or meetings; physical — such as golf, hiking, aerobics, or gardening; social — such as visiting with friends or going to parties; and solitary — including reading, listening to music, or watching television (Bossé & Ekerdt, 1981; Glamser & Hayslip, 1985). Leisure activities can also be considered in terms of degree of personal involvement; examples of leisure activities organized along this dimension are listed in Table 11.2.

An alternative description of leisure involves the distinction between preoccupations and interests (Rapoport & Rapoport, 1975). Preoccupations are conscious mental absorptions: the fundamental needs that channel behavior into some outlets and not others. A preoccupation is much like daydreaming. Sometimes, preoccupations become more focused and are converted to interests. Interests are ideas and feelings about things one would like to do, is curious about, or is attracted to. Expression of interests occurs through various activities, such as jogging, watching television, painting, and so on.

Rapoport and Rapoport's distinction draws attention to a truism about leisure: Any specific

TABLE 11.2 Forms of leisure activity and how they vary in intensity of cognitive, emotional, or physical involvement

Very high intensity	Sexual activity
	Highly competitive games or sports
	Dancing
Moderately high intensity	Creative activities (art, literature, music)
	Nurturance or teaching (children's arts and crafts)
	Serious discussion and analysis
Medium intensity	Attending cultural events
	Participating in clubs
	Sightseeing or travel
Moderately low intensity	Socializing
	Reading for pleasure
	Light conversation
Low intensity	Solitude
	Quiet resting
	Taking a nap

activity has different meaning and value depending on the individual involved. For example, cooking a gourmet meal is an interest or leisure activity for many people; for professional chefs, however, it is work and thus is not leisure at all. Moreover, the same preoccupation (for instance, a sense of excitement) may be demonstrated in different activities, from watching a rare bird to climbing sheer rock cliffs.

Given the wide range of options, how do people pick the leisure activities they want to do? Apparently, each of us has a leisure repertoire: a personal library of intrinsically motivated activities that we do regularly (Mobily, Lemke, & Gisin, 1991). The activities that make up our repertoire are determined by two things: perceived competence (how good we think we are at the activity compared to other people our age) and psychological comfort (how well we meet our personal goals for performance). Other factors are important as well: income, interest, health, abilities, transportation,

education, and social characteristics. It is probable that how these factors influence leisure activities changes across adulthood, although exactly how this happens is currently unknown (Burrus-Bammel & Bammel, 1985).

Developmental Changes in Leisure

A national survey found age and cohort differences in leisure activities (L. Harris & Associates, 1975). As age increased, fewer of the activities that adults considered leisure involved strenuous physical exertion, while sedentary activities — such as reading and watching television — became more common.

Age differences have also been reported concerning the variety of leisure activities (Bray & Howard, 1983; Elder, 1974; Lowenthal et al., 1975). These studies indicate that young adults participate in a greater range of activities than middle-agers. Gordon et al. (1976) report that young adults prefer intense leisure activities, middle-agers focus more on less-intense home- and family-oriented activities, and the elderly further narrow the range and intensity of activities.

Longitudinal studies of changes in leisure activities show considerable stability over reasonably long periods (Cutler & Hendricks, 1990). In general, frequent participation in leisure activities during childhood continues into adulthood. Similar findings hold for the pre- and post-retirement years.

Correlates of Leisure Activities

Several variables are related to the kinds of leisure activities people choose. Adults may face barriers to leisure participation such as health problems and lack of transportation. These barriers are especially important for understanding participation of older adults and various ethnic groups. Indeed, health problems are the primary reason given when older adults explain their lack of participation in leisure activities (McGuire, Dottavio, & O'Leary, 1986).

Gender differences occur along several lines. For example, men are much more likely to participate in outdoor leisure activities such as hunting and fishing, whereas women are more likely to engage in cultural and home-based leisure activities (Lawton, Moss, & Fulcomer, 1986–87).

Type of residence also appears to matter. People who live in retirement housing participate more frequently in leisure activities than people living in typical neighborhoods (Moss & Lawton, 1982). Part of the reason for this finding is that retirement communities often provide structured activities for residents while many age-integrated neighborhoods and communities do not.

Consequences of Leisure Activities

What benefits do people derive from participating in leisure activities? Researchers agree that being involved in leisure activities is related to positive well-being (e.g., Kelly et al., 1987). The key aspect of this relationship is not the level of participation. Instead, how much satisfaction you derive from your leisure activities is more important in promoting well-being (Lawton et al., 1986–87). Indeed, an Israeli study showed that satisfaction with leisure activities is the crucial variable in the relationship between participation and well-being (Lomranz, Bergman, Eyal, & Shmotkin, 1988).

Leisure Summary

Leisure activities represent a major aspect of people's lives. Leisure is an important source of well-being across adulthood and offers ways of meeting new people. At the same time, we need to learn much more about how people spend their discretionary time. For example, we need to know how leisure activities vary across ethnic groups, how activity patterns may change with changing population demographics, and how economic factors influence which activities are realistically possible for people to pursue.

RETIREMENT

You probably take it for granted that someday, after working for many productive years, you will retire. But did you know that until 1935, when Social Security was inaugurated, retirement was rarely even considered by most Americans? Only since World War II have there been a substantial number of retired people in the United States. Today, the number is increasing rapidly, and the notion that people work a specified time and then retire is built into our expectations about work.

The enactment of Social Security and the advent of various pension and savings plans have been accompanied by profound changes in attitudes toward retirement. Most people now view it as a right — a rather curious view considering that work has long been considered virtually a moral obligation. It is this curious juxtaposition that makes retirement a very interesting topic.

As the number of retirees increases, several issues will be thrust to the forefront. Among them are early retirement, retirement planning, educational and work options for retirees, and health care for these individuals. We will explore many of these issues, as well as attitudes toward retirement and adjustment to it. But the first step in reaching these insights is to achieve a reasonably clear definition of it.

Defining Retirement

Like leisure, retirement is difficult to define. One way to look at retirement is to equate it with complete withdrawal from the work force. But this definition is inadequate; many retired people continue to work part time. Another possibility would be to define retirement as a self-described state. However, this definition will not work either because some African Americans define themselves as "disabled" rather than "retired" in order to qualify for social service programs (Gibson, 1987, 1991).

The most useful way to view retirement is as a complex process by which people withdraw from full-time participation in an occupation. The complexity of the retirement process must be acknowledged for us to understand what retirement means to people in different ethnic groups. For example, while middle-class whites often use a criterion of full-time employment to define themselves as retired or not, Mexican Americans use any of several different criteria depending on how the question is asked (Zsembik & Singer, 1990). We can approach our definition of retirement in three ways: as a process, as a paradox, and as a change.

Retirement as a Process. The process of retirement begins as soon as one thinks about what life after employment might be like. More thinking usually leads to some sort of planning, even if it is only to check with one's employer about available financial benefits such as Social Security or pension funds. (We will discuss the planning process in a later section.)

Retirement as a Paradox. Retirement involves the loss of two very important things that we derive from work: income and status. We might assume that losing these key aspects of one's life would be reflected in poor adjustment. The paradox of retirement is that despite these losses the majority of retirees say that they are satisfied; they like and enjoy being retired.

Retirement as a Change. Retirement involves change in almost every aspect of life. On the surface, such monumental change may appear overwhelming. But retirees have an advantage that is often overlooked. By the time they retire, they have already experienced several disruptive life transitions such as marriage, children leaving home, or moving; what they have learned from previous events provides the basis for adjusting to retirement. Clearly, retirement is complex. In the next few sections we will review some of the information available on retirement, including how to prepare for it and how to make the best of it.

Deciding to Retire

The decision to retire is an intensely personal one that involves carefully weighing several factors. Fortunately, the major predictors of the decision to retire — such as health, financial status, and attitudes toward retirement — have remained relatively constant for several decades. However, there are some important differences involving gender and ethnicity.

Health. One of the most important influences on retirement decisions is health, regardless of whether one is approaching mandatory retirement.

When these workers retired in 1949, a gold watch may have been all they had to look forward to. Today, options for most people are far greater.

Clark and Spengler (1980) report that poor health is one of the two main reasons that people retire early; financial security is the other (Ward, 1984a, 1984b). The importance of health cuts across ethnic group lines, especially in terms of early retirement. For example, health problems causing functional impairment is the main reason whites, African Americans, and Mexican Americans retire early (Stanford, Happersett, Morton, Molgaard, & Peddecord, 1991).

Financial Status. Feeling secure financially is another extremely important factor in deciding to retire. Many people have plans that involve money, such as traveling, and most would like to maintain their life style. Many corporations offer preretirement planning programs that provide advice about this topic.

Attitudes Toward Retirement. People with rewarding jobs typically do not look forward to retirement as much as do people with unrewarding jobs. For example, it has been known for years that blue-collar workers tend to desire retirement (as long as they have enough money) but that professionals and self-employed people may not. Being autonomous and having responsibility in a job is associated with more negative attitudes toward

People who own their own businesses, like this couple, are among the groups least likely to look forward to retirement.

retirement (Barfield & Morgan, 1978; Streib & Schneider, 1971).

Attitudes toward retirement for those in middle-level jobs, including clerical and service personnel, are best predicted by income. Workers with high incomes and those who have good pension plans are most favorable about retirement. This relationship is so strong and holds for such a wide range of middle-level jobs that some writers believe that it is the relationship between workers and money, not the one between people and work, that should be researched (Shanas, 1972).

Educational level is another important predictor of attitudes, but the connection is complex. For men, it appears that more education is accompanied by more negative feelings, but this could be due to the likelihood that such men are in more autonomous jobs (Sheppard, 1976). The evidence is contradictory for women. Sheppard (1976) reports that the most highly educated women are

positive about retiring and do so earlier. On the contrary, Streib and Schneider (1971) found that women with higher incomes, better education, and higher-status jobs tended to continue working longer. More research is needed in order to sort out the relationship between education and retirement attitudes, especially for women.

Age and cohort differences also influence attitudes. At one time it was believed that younger workers were more favorably disposed to retirement than older workers (Atchley, 1976). Contradictory evidence has been reported, however; Barfield and Morgan (1978) found that older cohorts were more favorably disposed to retire. These differences may reflect two changes in attitudes about retirement. First, workers may be becoming more receptive to the idea that employment does not last forever. It should be remembered that retirees who participated in earlier studies had largely begun working before retirement was commonplace. Second, many researchers have changed their assumption that retirement is "a major disruption of an adult's role and would tend to have deleterious consequences for the individual" (Streib & Schneider, 1971, p. 5). Rather, many investigators are viewing retirement simply as another normative life transition to which most people adjust positively.

Gender. Although most research on retirement decisions has focused on men, some work has examined women. George, Fillenbaum, and Palmore (1984) found that a married woman's decision to retire is predicted by her age and her husband's working, not by characteristics of her occupation. Campione (1987) found that a woman's decision to retire was related not only to her husband's wages but also to her own financial status independent of her husband. These discrepant findings may be due to changing demographics. That is, only in the past few years have women remained in the work force long enough to make the decision to retire based on their own wage history and financial security.

Ethnicity. Little research has been conducted on retirement decisions as a function of ethnicity. Important differences among ethnic groups about retirement are being uncovered, however, which emphasize the need for more research. As pointed out earlier, African Americans may not label themselves as "retired" for many reasons, ranging from socialization to the need to adopt the disability role in order to maximize their benefits (Gibson, 1987, 1991). Because many African Americans do not have the financial or other resources to retire and must continue to work into old age, researchers have often excluded them.

A few investigators have examined the characteristics of retired African Americans (Gibson, 1986, 1987; Irelan & Bell, 1972; J. S. Jackson & Gibson, 1985; Murray, 1979). These studies show that African Americans often do not decide to retire, since many may not have an occupation to

retire from. Instead, they appear to label themselves as either "retired" or "unretired" based on subjective disability, work history, and source of income. An important finding is that gender differences appear to be absent among African Americans; men and women base their self-labels on the same variables. Thus, findings based on white samples must not be generalized to African Americans, and separate theoretical models for African Americans may be needed (Gibson, 1987). The same is undoubtedly true for other ethnic groups as well.

Adjustment to Retirement

Everyone agrees on one point about retirement: It is a life transition that produces stress. Successful retirement requires responding to the challenges it presents and having a supportive network of relatives and friends. Before considering the research on whether people usually find retirement to their liking, we will look at three theoretical frameworks that help put the literature into perspective.

Work Styles. One way to conceptualize adjustment to retirement is by examining different combinations of work styles and life styles. Lowenthal (1972) suggests that past behavior and attitudes during their employment years influence people's adjustment to retirement. Thus, individuals who have always been strongly work oriented — viewing work as an end in itself — will be most likely to consider retirement traumatic. Lowenthal argues that unless highly work-oriented people find a substitute for work, retirement may be an unpleasant experience.

People who are less strongly oriented toward work as a means to social acceptance may view retirement as a crisis, but they will eventually adjust. Lowenthal suggests that these other-directed people may need to find a substitute for work, but usually this need is only temporary.

Three other groups complete Lowenthal's classification: the receptive-nurturant type, the autonomous type, and the self-protective type. Receptive-nurturant people are typically women who have lifelong commitments to emotional goals and intimacy. For them, the quality of the relationship with their partners is the key to adjustment in retirement. Provided the relationship is perceived as solid, retirement should present little difficulty for such people.

Many autonomous individuals are in occupations that allow them to decide when to retire. These people present a complex pattern of creativity, varied goals, and self-generativity. If retirement is voluntary, little disruption should be expected; however, mandatory retirement may lead to depression until reorientation is achieved.

Finally, the self-protective person often sees nothing special about retirement; it is simply another chapter in a life full of struggles. Dependency on or responsibility for others is not allowed. These individuals have always been detached or disengaged. As long as retirement does not require radical change, it does not produce a crisis.

Lowenthal's approach allows for a wide variety of possibilities. One common theme across the different types is that a redistribution of energy may be needed for successful adjustment to retirement; this change is reminiscent of the reevaluations that occurred earlier in development. Indeed, enduring aspects of personality and life style are useful in predicting adjustment to retirement (Maas & Kuypers, 1974; Neugarten, 1977).

Values. A second theoretical framework, suggested by Atchley (1976), is compatible with Lowenthal's. Atchley proposes that how the individual views the role of the job in his or her life determines the extent to which retirement is a crisis. If the job fulfills goals not achieved by other activities and if it is considered important throughout adulthood, retirement will demand a major reorganization of one's values. However, if one's goals have been attained or if one's job was never considered of primary importance, little reorganization will be necessary. Atchley agrees with Lowenthal in concluding that strongly job-oriented people seek substitutes for work or even second occupations after retiring; otherwise, these individuals are not able to sufficiently reorganize their lives.

Continuity. As we have seen, retirement involves important decisions. Atchley (1989) argues that any time middle-aged and older adults make adaptive choices, they attempt to build on the past. In other words, adults try to maintain continuity. Atchley believes this continuity occurs in two domains: internal and external. Internal continuity occurs when you want to preserve some aspect of yourself from the past, such as a specific personality trait or a skill, so that you see your past as sustaining and supporting your new self. External continuity involves maintaining social relationships, roles, and environments, such as living in the same neighborhood. To the extent that internal and external continuity are maintained, satisfaction with retirement is likely to be high.

Satisfaction. Once people retire, do they like it? The evidence suggests that they do. However, there is an interesting and important historical shift in the research findings. Numerous national cross-sectional surveys conducted from the 1950s to the late 1970s documented that as long as income and health were maintained adequately, satisfaction with retirement was high (e.g., Barfield & Morgan, 1978; Streib & Schneider, 1971).

By 1980, however, retirees' responses had begun to change; a significantly higher proportion of them, although generally satisfied with retirement, felt that they would prefer to work. These findings reflect retirees' increased concern over financial security. Indeed, two findings support this conclusion. First, the increase during the 1970s in the proportion of retirees preferring to work paralleled the increase in the inflation rate in the United States.

Second, retirees not collecting pensions were more likely to want to work than retirees on pensions.

In sum, there is little evidence to support the stereotypic view of retirement as leading inevitably to poor adjustment. On the contrary, research since the 1950s has shown consistently that most people are satisfied with retirement living. Although an increasing number of people express a desire to work, this response comes largely from financial pressures and not from a fundamental dislike for retirement. Positive adjustment outcomes do not imply, however, that reorganization and change are unnecessary. Such changes are vital to maintaining one's psychological well-being. Reorientation occurs in most aspects of one's life; we will examine three contexts in the next section: family, friends, and community.

Family, Friends, and Community

Retirement rarely affects only a single individual. No matter how personal the joys and sorrows of retirement may be, retirees' reactions are influenced by the social environment of their family, friends, and community. These social ties help us deal with the stresses of retirement, as they do in other life transitions. A long history of research verifies that social relationships help cushion the effect of life stress throughout adulthood. This support takes many forms: letting people know that they are loved; offering help if needed; providing advice; taking care of others' needs; just being there to listen. We should expect retirees who have close and strong social ties to have an advantage in dealing with change.

Family. Much attention has been focused on the role of intimate and family relationships in adjusting to retirement. Marriage has provided the framework for almost all of this work. Ideally, marital partners provide mutual support during the transition to retirement. Whether marriage actually

serves this function is unclear. The few studies specifically dealing with the connection between marital status and satisfaction with retirement provide conflicting results. Some evidence suggests that the never-married are as satisfied as married retirees, whereas divorced, separated, or widowed retirees are much less happy (Barfield & Morgan, 1978; Larson, 1978). It could be that never-married people prefer singlehood and become accustomed to it long before retirement. Additionally, the difficulties encountered by those whose marriages were disrupted indirectly emphasize the stabilizing effects of marriage. But it seems that whatever relationship exists holds mainly for men; marital status alone has little effect on older women's satisfaction (Fox, 1979). Furthermore, we know almost nothing about the link between the quality of retirees' marriages and satisfaction with retirement.

Possible benefits aside, there is little doubt that retirement has profound effects on intimate relationships. It often disrupts long-established patterns of family interaction, forcing both partners (and others living in the house) to adjust. Simply being together more strains the relationship. Daily routines need rearrangement, which may be stressful.

One common change that confronts most retired couples is the division of household chores. Although retired men tend to do more work around the home than they did before retirement, this situation does not always lead to desirable outcomes (Ingraham, 1974). For example, an employed husband may compliment his wife on her domestic skills; after retirement, however, he may suddenly want to teach her to do it correctly. Part of the problem may be that such men are not used to taking orders about how chores are supposed to be done. One former executive told interviewers that before he retired, when he said "Jump!" highly paid employees wanted to know how high. "Now, I go home, I walk in the door and my wife says, 'Milton, take out the garbage.' I never saw so much garbage" (Quigley, 1979, p. 9). Finally, part of the problem may be in the perception of one's turf; after retirement men feel that they are thrust into doing things that they, and their partners, may have traditionally thought of as "women's work" (Troll, 1971).

Retirees maintain and sometimes increase contact with their children, grandchildren, and other relatives. These contacts are viewed as an important component in retirees' lives. Still, independence between generations is associated with high satisfaction among retirees (Riley & Foner, 1968). This need for independence is underscored by the fact that visits with children sometimes have a depressing rather than a positive effect on older (65+) male retirees. Apparently, changing power relationships within the family are responsible; visiting children may serve to emphasize the father's loss of control over them.

Frequency of contact with other relatives does not appear to be related to life satisfaction among middle- and upper-middle-class retirees. That is, visiting relatives does not have negative effects, but it does not add to a retiree's overall satisfaction either (Lemon, Bengtson, & Peterson, 1972).

Friends. Intimate and family relationships are clearly important sources of support for retirees. However, they are not the only ones; friendship networks also provide support that often complements family networks. Friends sometimes provide types of support that, because of the strong emotional ties, families may be less able to offer: a compassionate, but objective listener; a companion for social and leisure activities; or a source of advice, transportation, and other assistance. The extent to which friends contribute to retirees' overall satisfaction is unclear, but seeing friends and having a confidant appear to be important (Lemon et al., 1972).

Older men have fewer close personal friends for support than older women (see Chapter 10). This difference may help explain the gender difference between marital status and satisfaction discussed earlier. Men, because of their fewer close relationships, may be forced to rely more on their wives for support.

Community. Since social ties are generally related to retirees' satisfaction, an important consideration is whether the social environment facilitates continuing old ties and forming new ones. The past few decades have witnessed the rapid growth of organizations devoted to providing these opportunities to retirees. National associations such as the American Association of Retired Persons provide the chance to learn about what other retirees are doing and about services such as insurance and discounts.

Numerous smaller groups exist at the community level; these include senior centers and clubs. Trade unions may also have programs for their retired members. Additionally, there are many opportunities for retirees to help others. One federal agency, ACTION, administers four programs that have hundreds of local chapters: Foster Grandparents, Senior Companions, the Retired Senior Volunteer Program, and the Service Corps of Retired Executives.

Retirement Planning

What do you need to do to plan for retirement? Is it just a matter of saving money? Or do people need to take psychological factors into account as well? Can prospective retirees anticipate and avoid some of the difficulties? For example, one common problem in adjusting to the retirement role is the abruptness of the transition from employment to unemployment. What processes might minimize the difficulties of this change?

One key element to successful retirement is preparation (Kamouri & Cavanaugh, 1986). Getting ready can take several forms: conscious or unconscious planning, informal or formal steps, and so on. One formal way to prepare for retirement is to participate in a **preretirement education pro-**

The Foster Grandparent Program, among others, provides a way for older adults to maintain meaningful personal roles.

gram. Such programs cover a wide variety of topics, from financial planning to adjustment; a typical content list is contained in Table 11.3. Campione (1988) found that men who do some preparing on their own, who are married and have families to plan for, who are healthy, and who have high occupational status are more likely to participate in formal preretirement programs. This profile reflects a strong bias in program participants; lower-income, minority individuals are not represented.

Every comprehensive planning program for retirement focuses on two key aspects: finances and attitudes. We will consider some of the ramifications of each.

Finances. Retirement, on average, involves a 50% reduction in income (Foner & Schwab, 1981). Obviously, if one is not prepared for this degree of income loss, financial pressures will be severe. Financial planning is necessary on several levels. First, most people are part of mandatory retirement plans such as Social Security. Although planning ends here for the majority of people, it is not enough. Many people also draw on pension plans provided by their employer. If possible, individuals should also save funds in anticipation of income loss, such as in individual retirement accounts. It must be recognized, though, that the majority of American workers cannot set aside sufficient funds to carry them through their retirement years in the life style they enjoyed before retirement.

Professionals who have the ability to plan for retirement tend to do it similarly, even across some ethnic groups. For example, African-American

TABLE 11.3 Topics in a typical preretirement education program

I. Deciding to retire: When is the right time?

II. Psychological aspects of aging
   A. Work roles and retirement
   B. Personal identity issues
   C. Retirement as a process, paradox, and change
   D. Effects on relationships with family and friends

III. Finances
   A. Social Security
   B. Pension
   C. Insurance
   D. Employment

IV. Legal aspects
   A. Wills
   B. Personal rights as senior citizens

V. Health
   A. Normal aging
   B. Medicare and Medicaid
   C. Issues in health insurance

VI. Where to live: the pros and cons of moving

VII. Leisure time activities
   A. Travel
   B. Hobbies
   C. Clubs and organizations
   D. Educational opportunities
   E. Volunteering

professionals tend to use financial planning strategies very similar to white professionals (Richardson & Kilty, 1989).

Attitudes. Aside from finances, one's attitudes about retirement probably have the most important effect on satisfaction (Foner & Schwab, 1981). Even if it only involves thinking about when to retire and looking forward to it, developing a positive attitude is central to more rapid adjustment to and enjoyment of retirement (Barfield & Morgan, 1978; Kimmel, Price, & Walker, 1978). It appears that more formal preparation, such as participation in preretirement programs, is associated with more positive attitudes (Friedman & Orbach, 1974), but this relationship may be due to the fact that people who already hold favorable attitudes are the most likely to plan.

The relationship between attitudes and participation in preretirement programs has been addressed by Kamouri and Cavanaugh (1986). They compared four groups of workers: retired workers who had participated in a preretirement program, retired workers who had not participated, employees in a preretirement program, and employees on the waiting list for a program. Kamouri and Cavanaugh found that workers who had the benefit of a program had a more realistic view of retirement than those who had not participated. The main benefit of participating in a preretirement program seemed to be realistic expectations that could be translated into a more positive attitude in the first few years of retirement. After about three years of retirement people who had not participated in the program were comparable in their attitudes to those who had, but they did note that their initial experiences had not been what they had expected.

SUMMARY

The Meaning of Work

1. Occupations are a reflection of socialization into the work role.

2. Five general levels of occupations can be distinguished: marginal, blue-collar, pink-collar, white-collar, and executives and professionals.

Occupational Choice Across Adulthood

3. Holland's theory is based on the idea that people choose occupations to optimize the fit between their individual traits and their occupational interests. Six personality types that represent different combinations of these have been identified.

4. Occupational choice is strongly influenced by what we think we would be good at, not necessarily what we actually are good at.

5. Men and women are socialized differently into occupational roles. Women may tend to downplay their ability while men may tend to overestimate theirs.

Occupational Development

6. Super proposed a developmental view of occupations based on self-concept and adaptation to an occupational role. Super describes five stages: implementation, establishment, maintenance, deceleration, and retirement.

7. Sex discrimination remains the chief barrier to women's occupational development. In many cases, this operates as a glass ceiling. Pay inequity is also a problem; women get paid a fraction of what men in similar jobs earn.

8. Denying employment to anyone over 40 because of age is age discrimination.

9. Important predictors of occupational success are family and ethnic background, level of formal education, intelligence, and personality.

10. Reality shock is the realization that one's expectations about an occupation are different than the reality one experiences.

11. A mentor is a co-worker who teaches a new employee the unwritten rules and fosters occupational development. Mentor-protégé relationships develop over time through stages like other relationships.

12. Occupational priorities include the reasons and motivation to work. Priorities change over time as a function of occupational and family development.

13. Older workers report higher job satisfaction than younger workers, but this may be partly due to self-selection; unhappy workers may quit. Other reasons include intrinsic satisfaction, good fit, lower importance of work, finding nonwork diversions, and life-cycle factors.

Changing Occupations

14. Important reasons why people change occupations include personality, obsolescence, and economic factors.

15. Losing one's job is a traumatic event that can affect every aspect of a person's life.

Dual-Worker Couples

16. Although many couples report feeling role conflict, most manage to solve the problem. However, time together often suffers.

17. Wives are far more likely to interrupt their occupational development for their husbands than husbands are for their wives.

Leisure

18. Quality of activity rather than quantity is a key to understanding why people engage in particular leisure activities. Other important factors include changing sense of self and family interests.

19. People develop a repertoire of preferred leisure activities.

20. The main reasons leisure activities change over adulthood are health or ability changes and self-perceptions.

21. Men are more likely to engage in outdoor and sports activities while women are more likely to engage in cultural or home-based activities.

22. Leisure activities produce positive well-being.

Retirement

23. Retirement can be viewed as a process, as a paradox, and as change. Overall, it is a way in which people withdraw from full-time employment.

24. The major predictors of retirement are health, financial status, attitudes toward retirement, gender, and ethnicity. Attitudes are influenced by income, education, age, and cohort.

25. Some ethnic groups have different definitions of or avoid using the term retirement.

26. People who are highly work oriented usually have a more difficult time with retirement than people who are less work oriented.

27. Retirement can also be understood in terms of a reorientation of values and a need for continuity.

28. Most people are satisfied with retirement.

29. Retirement affects all types of relationships. It may disrupt long-term friendships and produce stress. However, contacts are maintained with children and may even increase. Community participation options are increasing for retirees.

30. Preretirement education programs cover a variety of topics, including finances, attitudes, health, and expectations. Financial planning for retirement is essential.

31. Attitudes toward retirement are extremely important. Advance knowledge about what being retired is like helps dispel many misconceptions.

REVIEW QUESTIONS

The Meaning of Work

1. What different types of occupations have been distinguished? What are the characteristics of each?

Occupational Choice Across Adulthood

2. Briefly describe Holland's theory linking personality and occupational choice. What personality types did Holland identify? How are they related to occupational fit?

3. How is self-efficacy linked to occupational choice?

4. What gender differences have been identified that relate to occupational choice? How do men and women differ in terms of rating their own abilities and skills?

Occupational Development

5. Briefly describe Super's five-stage theory. How does self-concept fit into his model?

6. What are the major barriers to women's occupational development?

7. What is age discrimination and how does it operate?

8. What are the major predictors of occupational success?

9. What is a mentor? What role does a mentor play in occupational development?

10. How does the mentor-protégé relationship change over time?

11. What are occupational priorities and how do they change over time?

12. What is the developmental course of job satisfaction? What factors influence job satisfaction?

Changing Occupations

13. What are the major reasons that people change occupations?

14. What effects do people report after losing their jobs?

Dual-Worker Couples

15. How do dual-worker couples deal with role conflict?

16. What happens in dual-worker relationships when one partner is offered a promotion that involves a move? What other occupational development effects occur?

Leisure

17. What are the major reasons why people engage in leisure activities? What benefits occur?

18. What kinds of leisure activities do people perform?

19. How do leisure activities change over the life span?

20. What gender differences are there in leisure activities?

Retirement

21. In what ways can retirement be viewed?

22. What are the main predictors of the decision to retire? What predicts attitudes toward retirement?

23. How do people adjust to being retired?

24. What effects does retirement have on relationships with family, friends, and community?

25. What steps should people take to prepare for retirement?

KEY TERMS

age discrimination Denying employment or promotion to someone on the basis of age. Age discrimination is illegal in the United States. (383)

comparable worth The notion that people should be paid equally for similar work regardless of gender. (382)

glass ceiling An invisible barrier to the occupational development of women and minorities that allows them to advance to a certain level and no higher. (382)

job satisfaction How happy one is with one's job. (387)

mentor A person who teaches the informal rules of an organization. (385)

occupational priorities The reasons why one works, and how they are viewed by an individual. (386)

preretirement education program A program aimed at educating workers about the broad range of issues they will face in retirement, including health, adjustment, and finances. (404)

reality shock A term representing the realization that the real world does not work like a textbook. (384)

role conflict A clash between competing or incompatible sets of roles, most often seen in work versus family settings. (392)

self-efficacy The degree to which one thinks one is capable of performing or achieving something. (377)

sex discrimination Denying a person a position or a promotion solely on the basis of gender. (382)

vocational maturity In Super's theory, the degree to which one's occupational behaviors match what is expected of them at different ages. (381)

ADDITIONAL READING

An extensive review of research on older workers can be found in

Doering, M., Rhodes, S. R., & Schuster, M. (1983). *The aging worker: Research and recommendations*. Beverly Hills, CA: Sage Publications. Moderately difficult.

Excellent descriptions and case examples concerning couples and how they view work can be found in

Blumstein, P., & Schwartz, P. (1983). *American couples*. New York: Morrow. Easy reading.

An overview of retirement can be found in

Palmore, E. (Ed.). (1986). *Retirement: Causes and consequences*. New York: Springer. Moderate to difficult.

Two journals that are especially good sources of information about occupational development and occupational choice are *Journal of Vocational Behavior* and *Journal of Counseling Psychology*. Reading levels vary, but are typically moderately difficult.

CHAPTER 12

Where We Live

Grandma Moses, *Moving Day on the Farm*, 1951. Copyright © 1987, Grandma Moses Properties Co., New York. Anna Mary Robertson ("Grandma") Moses (1860–1961) became famous in old age for her paintings of American farm life.

L ET ME INTRODUCE YOU TO HENRY. HENRY, OR as his friends call him, Hank, has lived in the same neighborhood all of his 75 years. He grew up only a block or so from where he lives now, which is where he moved 53 years ago when he married Marilyn. Hank and Marilyn raised five children in their modest three-bedroom rowhouse; two still live across the city but the other three are scattered across the country. Hank has been living alone for the past several months, ever since Marilyn suffered a stroke and had to be placed in a nursing home. Hank's oldest daughter has been concerned about her father and has been pressing him to move in with her. Hank is reluctant — he likes knowing his neighbors, shopping in familiar stores, and being able to do what he wants. And he wonders how well he could adapt to living in a new neighborhood after all these years. He realizes that it might be easier for him to cope if he lived with his daughter, but it's a tough decision.

Hank's dilemma drives home an important point. People do not live in a vacuum; they live in environments. As perfectly obvious as this statement seems, it has only been in the last few decades that the living environments in which people operate have been studied systematically. And it is only more recently that researchers in adult development have given them much thought. The principle concern in the field of **environmental psychology** has been the interaction of people with the communities or institution's in which they live. The basic assumption is that "a person's behavioral and psychological state can be better understood with knowledge of the context in which the person behaves" (Lawton, 1980, p. 2). In other words, Hank's problem and the decision he needs to make can be understood better if we do not isolate his cognitive processes from the context and neighborhood in which his decision making takes place.

In this chapter we will see how differences in the interaction between personal characteristics and the living environment can have profound effects on our behavior and our feelings about ourselves. Several theoretical frameworks will be described that can help us understand how to interpret person-environment interactions in a developmental context. We will consider the communities and neighborhoods that influence us and that partially determine whether we will be happy. Similarly, there are several aspects of housing that play important roles in our lives. Because some people do not live in the community, we will take a close look at institutional environments, especially nursing homes. Finally, we will look at people on the move and examine the effects of community-based and institutional relocation. Even though we must sometimes consider the person separately from the environment, keep in mind throughout the chapter that in the end it is the interaction of the two that we want to understand.

Examining person-environment interactions highlights several important aspects of the biopsychosocial model. Where one lives is influenced by a host of variables: age, gender, ethnicity, physical health, mental health, finances, and availability of social support or a caregiver, to mention only a few. Many of these factors (such as gender) are ones we tend to overlook. Over the course of the chapter, we will specifically examine these influences in detail.

THEORIES OF PERSON-ENVIRONMENT INTERACTIONS

In order to appreciate the roles that different environments play in our lives, we need a framework for interpreting how people interact with them. Theories of person-environment interactions help us understand how individuals view their environments and how these views may change as people age. Because the field of environmental psychology has only recently been approached from a developmental perspective, few theories are well thought out (Scheidt & Windley, 1985). We will consider four that have received the most attention: competence and environmental press, congruence, stress and coping, and the loss-continuum concept.

All of these theories can be traced to a common beginning. Many years ago Kurt Lewin (1936) conceptualized **person-environment interactions** in the equation B = f(P,E). This relationship means that behavior (B) is a function of both the person (P) and the environment (E). Recent theorists have taken Lewin's equation and described the components in the equation in more detail. Specifically, their speculations concern what it is about people and about environments that combine to form behavior.

Most of these models emphasize the importance of people's perceptions of their environments. That is, while objective aspects of environments (for example, crime, housing quality) are important, personal choice plays a major role. For example, many people deliberately choose to live in New York or Atlanta, even though crime rates in those cities are higher than in Selma or Walla, and they have an opportunity to live in any of these locations. The importance of personal perception in environments is similar to the role of personal perception in cognitive theories of personality (see Chapter 8) and in concepts such as personal control. As we will see, these ideas, especially the notion of personal control, have been included in many approaches to understanding person-environment interactions.

Competence and Environmental Press

One way to express the person-environment interaction is by focusing on competence and environmental press (Lawton, 1982; Lawton & Nahemow, 1973). **Competence** is defined as the theoretical upper limit of an individual's capacity to function. Lawton and Nahemow (1973) believe that competence involves five domains: biological health, sensory-perceptual functioning, motor skills, cognitive skills, and ego strength. These domains are thought to underlie all other abilities, and they are lifelong. Unfortunately, the components of competence are not easy to measure. The problem is that there are very few measures of the components that do not involve the environment in any way. As noted in Chapter 3, for example, biological health is strongly related to the type of environment in which we live. Thus, in most research one must settle for a rough approximation of a person's true competence.

Environments can be classified on the basis of the varying demands that they place on the individual. To reflect this idea, Lawton borrowed the term **environmental press** from Henry Murray (1938). The demands that environments put on people (environmental press) can be any combination of three types: physical, interpersonal, or social. Physical demands include such things as having to walk three flights of stairs to one's apartment. Interpersonal demands include the various pressures we feel to get along with other people. Social demands include such things as the local laws or social customs that affect our lives.

Lawton and Nahemow's (1973) model is a combination of these ideas. They assert that behavior is a result of a person of a particular competence level acting in an environment of a specific press level. Furthermore, behavior is placed on a continuum from positive to negative and is thought to be manifested at two levels—as observable behavior and as affect, or feelings. Each of these elements is represented schematically in Figure 12.1.

Low to high competence is represented in the figure on the vertical axis, and the horizontal axis represents weak to strong press level. Points in the graph show various combinations of person-environment interactions. Most important, the shaded areas demonstrate that adaptive behavior and positive affect result from many different combinations of competence and press levels, not just one. As one moves farther away from these areas—due to a change in press level, for example—behavior becomes increasingly maladaptive, and affect becomes more negative. Notice that maladaptive behavior and negative affect also result from many combinations of competence and press levels. Finally, the area labeled **adaptation level** represents points where press is average for particular levels of competence. The adaptation level is where behavior and affect are normal, so we are usually unaware of them. Awareness increases as we move away from adaptation level.

As an example of Lawton and Nahemow's model, consider Rick. Rick works in a store in an area of Omaha, Nebraska, where the crime rate is moderately high, representing a moderate level of environmental press. Because he is very good at self-defense, he has high competence; thus, he manages to cope. Because the Omaha police chief wants to lower the crime rate in that area, he increases patrols, thereby lowering the press level. If Rick maintains his high competence, maladaptive behavior may result because he has more competence than is optimal for the new environment. But if instead of the police a street gang moved in, he would have to increase his competence and be more prepared in order to maintain his adaptation level. Other changes in the environment (such as arson

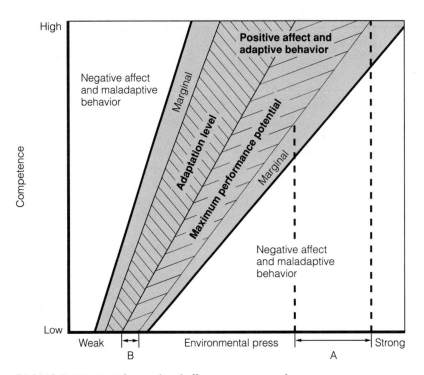

FIGURE 12.1 Behavioral and affective outcomes of person-environment interactions based on the competence–environmental press model. This figure indicates that an individual of high competence will show maximum performance over a larger range of environmental situations than will a less competent person. The range of optimal environments occurs at a higher level of environmental press (A) for the most competent person than it does for the least competent person (B).

(Source: "Ecology and the Aging Process" (p. 661) by M. P. Lawton and L. Nahemow, 1973, in C. Eisdorfer and M. P. Lawton, Eds., *The Psychology of Adult Development and Aging,* Washington, DC: American Psychological Association. Copyright © 1973 by the American Psychological Association. Reprinted with permission of the publisher and author.)

threats) or in his competence (such as a broken arm) would create other combinations.

Before leaving Lawton and Nahemow's model, we need to note an important implication that it has for aging. Notice that the less competent the individual is, the greater the impact of environmental factors. To the extent that individuals experience declines in health, sensory processes, motor skills, cognitive skills, or ego strength, they will be less able to cope with environmental demands. Thus, in order for older adults to maintain good adaptational levels, either changes to lower environmental press or interventions to raise competence would need to be undertaken.

The Congruence Model

Kahana's (1982) **congruence model** includes the ideas of competence and environmental press, but it applies them differently. In Kahana's view people vary in their needs, and environments differ in their ability to satisfy them. According to the congruence model, people with particular needs search for the environments that will meet them best. To the extent that a match exists, the individual feels content and satisfied; when a mismatch occurs, stress and discomfort result.

Congruence between the person and the environment is especially important when either individual or environmental options are limited. Limitations can occur for three reasons: (1) Environmental characteristics are restricted, such as when public transportation is unavailable for going shopping; (2) an individual's freedom is limited, such as when he or she must always eat at the same time every day; and (3) one believes that one has limited freedom, such as when one thinks that there is no way to get around despite a reliable bus system. Restricted environments are exemplified most clearly by institutions such as nursing homes and hospitals. Limits on individual freedom can result from age-related declines in competence. Self-perceptions of limited freedom reflect the belief that one's life is controlled by external forces, in the ways described in Chapter 9.

When applied specifically to the older adult, Kahana's congruence model shows that several points should be considered for optimizing the person-environment fit (Kahana & Kahana, 1983). Not only must the kind of situation be considered, such as whether the person is in a single-family, congregate, or institutional living arrangement, but personal factors must be weighed as well. Personal factors are very important because people vary in their needs. Some of us value autonomy and independence highly, for example, whereas others place less importance on them. We must be careful when designing programs and interventions for adults to take these individual differences into account. Otherwise, we may unintentionally increase the discrepancy between the person and the environment, resulting in increases in stress for the people we intended to help.

Kahana's model is especially useful when considering issues in institutional settings such as nursing homes and hospitals. Indeed, most of the research that has examined issues such as autonomy has been done in long-term care facilities (Collopy, 1988; Hofland, 1988). This makes sense when one realizes that it is in these settings that difficult decisions are most often made that involve trade-offs between personal freedom and institutional requirements (Collopy, 1988). We will return to Kahana's congruence model later when we focus on nursing homes.

Stress and Coping Theory

Schooler (1982) has applied Lazarus's cognitive theory of stress and coping (described in Chapter 4) to the understanding of the older person's interaction with the environment. The basic premise of Lazarus's theory is that people evaluate situations in order to assess their potential threat value. Situations may be evaluated as harmful, beneficial, or irrelevant. When situations are viewed as harmful or threatening, people also establish the range of coping responses that they have at their disposal for removing the harmful situation. This process results in making a coping response. Outcomes of coping may be positive or negative depending on many contextual factors.

Schooler (1982) argues that this perspective is especially helpful in understanding older adults because of their increased vulnerability to social and physical hazards. To test his ideas, Schooler evaluated retest data on a sample of 521 people drawn from a national sample of 4,000 institutionalized older adults. In particular, he examined the impact of three potential stressors (environmental change, residential mobility, and major life events) on health or morale. He also examined the buffering, or protective, effects of social support systems and ecological factors on the relationships among the stressors and outcomes. Consistent with the theory, Schooler showed that the presence of social support systems affected the likelihood that particular situations would be defined as threatening. For example, living alone is more likely to be viewed as stressful when one has little social support than when one has many friends who live nearby.

Schooler's work provides an important theoretical addition, because it deals with the relation between everyday environmental stressors and the adaptive responding of community-dwelling individuals. However, he admits that more research needs to be done, especially in the area of understanding how the threat-appraisal process varies with age across different environmental contexts.

The Loss-Continuum Concept

Pastalan (1982) views aging as a progressive series of losses that reduce one's social participation. This **loss continuum** includes children leaving, loss of social roles, loss of income, death of spouse or close friends and relatives, loss of sensory acuity, and loss of mobility due to poorer health. Because these losses reduce people's ability to partake fully in community resources, their own home and immediate neighborhood take on far greater importance. This increase in importance means that older adults are especially sensitive to even small environmental changes (Regnier, 1983; Rowles & Ohta, 1983).

The importance of the immediate neighborhood in the loss-continuum concept is illustrated by the fact that a one-block radius around homes in cities is critical. Beyond this radius the rate at which elderly people make trips for shopping or other purposes drops sharply (Silverman, 1987). Consequently, well-planned environmental changes, even those on a small scale, can have significant payoffs

for older adults. Pastalan (1982) himself views his approach as less a theory than a guide to practical change to facilitate the maintenance of competence and independence of older adults.

Common Theoretical Themes

It should be apparent that the four theories we have considered have much in common. Most important, all of them agree that the focus must be on the interaction between the person and the environment, not on one or the other. Another important theme is that no one environment will meet everyone's needs. Rather, a range of potential environments may be optimal.

As noted earlier, however, the study of person-environment interactions is very new and is not well systematized. There is little agreement on the set of environmental factors that must be accounted for or on which set of personal needs must be met for optimal satisfaction. It is also not clear whether there are developmental changes in person-environment interactions (Rowles & Ohta, 1983). Such transitions would be expected from the life-cycle dimension in the biopsychosocial model, but this approach has generally not been used in person-environment research (Silverman, 1987). However, one thing is clear: Elderly people require a broad range of living environments to satisfy their personal needs.

COMMUNITIES, NEIGHBORHOODS, AND HOUSING

The most general levels at which we can examine person-environment interactions are communities and neighborhoods. Communities are usually defined as geographic or political units like cities and towns. Neighborhoods are the parts of the larger community that groups of people identify with and often label; Flatbush in Brooklyn, Buckhead in Atlanta, and Watts in Los Angeles are some examples. In this section we will examine several aspects of communities and neighborhoods that have an impact on us and some personal factors that are important in considering the composition of the environment. We will also take a brief look at some crucial aspects of housing for the elderly.

Community Size

Among the most important dimensions of a community that affect the life satisfaction of the residents is community size, conveniently represented along the rural-urban continuum. Hundreds of studies have examined the effects of size on all kinds of personal characteristics, from overall life satisfaction to knowledge about the availability of services (e.g., Krout, 1988a, 1988b; Silverman, 1987). Some marked differences have emerged that are important for understanding person-environment interactions, especially among the elderly. In interpreting differences between rural and urban communities, keep in mind that size alone does not tell us why the differences emerge. Other factors such as economic or ethnic differences that were not or could not be measured may also be responsible.

Overall Satisfaction. In terms of overall life satisfaction the effects of community size are complex. No clear trends emerge for young adults, but both direct and indirect effects have been documented for older adults. Liang and Warfel (1983) used the results of surveys done nationally and in three states to study urban-rural differences in life satisfaction. They found that the large size of a community had a negative impact on the degree of actual and perceived integration into the community; in other words, people in large cities were less inte-

grated than people in smaller communities. However, feeling that one is a part of the community does not affect the life satisfaction of people living in large cities as much as it does that of people in small communities. In large cities health factors are more important. The importance of health as a predictor of satisfaction is highlighted by Lawton's (1980) finding that when health factors are controlled, no differences in satisfaction as a function of community size are observed.

Liang and Warfel's findings support results from several other studies and generations of folk wisdom concerning the informal social network (Lawton, 1985b). Rural communities often lack sufficient health care facilities, shopping centers, and so on. However, friends, neighbors, and family, collectively termed the **informal social network**, often make up for these shortcomings by providing some of the missing services, such as by visiting sick friends (Davis, 1980; Rowles, 1983). The more one feels like part of the community, the larger one's informal network and the higher one's life satisfaction (Rowles, 1983).

Still, many elderly people prefer to live in large cities because of greater opportunities for social interaction. In contrast to small towns, large cities have better public transportation, which greatly facilitates older adults' ability to maintain contact with their families, friends, and ethnic group (Rudzitis, 1984).

Complexity. A second way to examine urban-rural differences is to look at the complexity of the community (Taietz, 1975). Complexity refers to the degree of differentiation among the services available to a community. Taietz (1975; Taietz & Milton, 1979) and Krout (1988a) examined complexity in rural and urban communities in New York state in terms of older adults' knowledge of locally available social services, housing, retail trade, community planning, and medical specialties. Taietz found that higher complexity was associated with accurate information about facilities only in urban areas. As

A sense of community and friendliness tend to be higher among rural residents compared with their urban-dwelling counterparts.

complexity increased in smaller communities, accuracy of knowledge about available facilities decreased. Krout extended these findings by demonstrating that residents of smaller communities were less aware of services on average but that this relationship might vary with a particular personal need for a specific service. Krout's results are explored in more detail in How Do We Know?

Because accurate information is essential for appropriate use of community services, an accompanying decline in resource utilization would be expected in complex small communities. The end result is that individuals' life satisfaction may decline because they perceive needs that are not being adequately met. That is, even if services are available, as long as people think that they are not, their overall satisfaction may be adversely affected.

Ideal Communities. Finally, some studies have examined people's notions of what the ideal community ought to have. In a comprehensive investiga-

tion Blake and Lawton (1980) found that younger and older adults living in both rural and urban communities agreed that high-quality medical care, good schools, adequate numbers of good jobs, and a variety of stores should be available. However, several age and community differences emerged when comparisons were made of the absolute level of importance of these factors. Younger adults were most concerned about jobs and schools, and urbanites were more concerned about social facilities. Overall, older adults were more satisfied with the facilities available in their community than were younger adults.

Neighborhoods

Neighborhoods provide a setting for social interaction as well as a convenient location for obtaining goods and services. Most research on neighborhoods from a developmental perspective concerns

HOW DO WE KNOW?

Awareness of Services and Community Size

Lack of awareness of public services among the elderly has been cited as a major reason why many services are underutilized. However, few studies have examined the awareness levels of rural and urban elderly residents at the community level. One exception to this lack of research is a study conducted by Krout (1988a).

Krout surveyed a random sample of 600 elderly residents of a metropolitan county and a nonmetropolitan county in western New York. He was interested in how aware people were of various services as a function of three types of factors: predisposing, enabling, and need. Predisposing factors affect the likelihood that people become aware of services; they include such things as age, gender, race, marital status, education, home ownership, and contact with

children. Enabling factors facilitate or inhibit the use of services; household income and car ownership are two common ones. The need factor reflects various conditions, such as health problems, that affect the degree to which people seek out services.

Krout collected data in personal interviews. He asked respondents what they knew about eight types of services in their community: elderly visitors, home health, home help, home meals, hot luncheon sites, information-referral services, legal aid, and transportation. The greatest awareness was shown for transportation, home meals, and hot luncheon sites, all of which were familiar to at least 75% of the respondents. However, people living in the metropolitan county were more aware of services, in general, than were the nonmetropolitan residents.

When Krout subjected his data to further statistical analyses, he found that community size was the

best predictor of awareness. However, additional characteristics related to the personal factors were also important. For predisposing factors, young-old, nonwhite, better educated, married homeowners were more aware of services. For enabling factors, income was related to awareness. Finally, people with health problems or those who needed help with activities of daily living were more aware of services.

Krout's research shows that awareness of available services in one's community is more than a function of community size. It also appears that those who have specific reasons to know about services are also the ones who are aware of them. Krout's results must be interpreted with some caution, however, since he studied only elderly residents of two counties in New York. Whether the factors he found would generalize to other parts of the United States or to other Western countries remains to be seen.

---

people's perceptions of their neighborhood as a good place to live and the utilization of local services. One general finding from this work is that as people age, they become more dependent on their local environment (Regnier, 1983). With this in mind, we will focus on the factors of the neighborhood that are particularly important to the elderly.

People's perceptions of their neighborhoods not only affect how they behave there but also have an impact on their overall psychological well-being.

The important point here is that it is often the perception of the environment that matters, not necessarily the way things really are. The relationship between objective neighborhood characteristics (such as the actual number of stores) and well-being is modest at best (Lawton & Nahemow, 1979). This lack of relationship between objective indicators and subjective perception fits with the cognitive theories of personality (see Chapter 8) in which the emphasis is on what people believe to be true about themselves and not their scores on personality tests.

Crime. Crime is one important dimension related to individuals' perceptions of their neighborhoods. More than anything else, it is the fear of crime, rather than actually being a victim of crime, that affects overall well-being (Lawton & Yaffe, 1980). Moreover, a survey of middle-aged and elderly residents of Los Angeles showed that concern about being a victim of crime was more related to neighborhood crime rate than it was to age. However, this positive relationship between concern and crime rate was not constant for African Americans, Mexican Americans, and whites. That is, African Americans and Mexican Americans are less easily influenced by neighborhood crime rates than are whites (Janson & Ryder, 1983). In general, the data suggest that there is little evidence to support the view that most older adults live like prisoners in their homes out of fear (Lawton, 1985b). It appears that the perception of safety is the important consideration in satisfaction with one's neighborhood (Jirovec, Jirovec, & Bossé, 1985).

Structural Features. The age structure of neighborhoods as a factor in well-being has been examined in several studies. Lawton and Nahemow (1979) conducted an extensive examination of 31 characteristics of neighborhoods as factors in the well-being of 2,400 elderly tenants of planned housing projects. They found that living in a neighborhood with a high proportion of older adults was related to greater participation in activities, higher satisfaction with housing, and more interpersonal interactions with other tenants. Although these findings support the idea that there are benefits of living in a neighborhood with many similarly aged people, Lawton and Nahemow point out that the size of the benefits is small. Indeed, some older adults are more satisfied living where they have few age peers. It appears that the benefits of living near age peers

depend on the particular person; individual differences are large.

A study conducted by the Veterans Administration of 100 elderly men in Boston showed that perceived safety was by far the most important consideration in choosing a neighborhood (Jirovec et al., 1985). Interestingly, the other major characteristics listed — such as beauty, space, and antiquity — were aesthetic ones reflecting subjective, personal perceptions of the environment. Absent from this list were more traditional factors such as accessibility of resources or concentration of age peers.

When Lawton and Nahemow (1979) examined ethnic factors and neighborhood structure, they found parallel results. Specifically, friendship and activity patterns were highest for African-American elderly people when they lived in neighborhoods that had higher concentrations of African Americans. Overall, though, the results indicated that whites and African Americans were affected similarly by structural factors in the neighborhood.

Finally, people sometimes become attached to their neighborhoods. This may be especially true for older adults who have lived in the same place for decades and have become dependent on local services. This attachment may feed into one's general well-being by providing opportunities to reminisce about the past. Rowles (1980) suggests that reminiscing about the neighborhood may complement and accompany age-related increases in spatial constriction and dependence on the local area. As our society continues to be increasingly mobile, however, fewer of us will live in the same neighborhood all of our lives. Thus, it will be interesting to see whether our feelings of attachment to where we live change over the next few decades.

Ethnicity. Only a few researchers have considered race or ethnicity as important aspects of neighborhoods. Biegel and Farkas (1990) found that African-American elderly were less likely than white ethnic elderly to visit or borrow things from their neighbors. However, there were no differences in perceptions of how much help one's neighbors would provide if needed. Reasons for the differences in social visiting focus on neighborhood security; urban African Americans are more likely to live in neighborhoods with poor street lighting, higher crime rates, poor sidewalks, and inaccessible stairs.

One major resource available in the African-American community is the church. Indeed, the church in these communities is considered a frame of reference, a mediating institution, and a catalyst for economic, political, and social change (Eng, Hatch, & Callan, 1985). The church also serves as a primary means for social activity and interaction among its elderly members, and provides considerable support for older members and nonmembers alike who reside in the community (Taylor & Chatters, 1986).

Among white ethnic groups, attachment to neighborhood in older residents is uniformly high. For example, the clear majority of residents living in either single ethnic group or mixed ethnic group neighborhoods really liked their neighborhoods (Biegel & Farkas, 1990).

Housing

Over 20% of the households in the United States are headed by an adult over age 65, and the number of such households is growing more rapidly than the proportion of elderly in the general population (Silverman, 1987). Of these households headed by older adults, approximately 70% are owner occupied. Unfortunately, these homes are often old, in poor condition, and in less desirable neighborhoods than housing for younger and middle-aged adults. However, elderly homeowners have some advantages over renters; 86% of the homeowners have paid off their mortgage, whereas the renters

spend an average of 30% of their income on housing. Elderly renters also tend to live in poorer quality apartments than their younger counterparts.

Golant (1984) points out an important consideration about housing that is often overlooked. Most elderly homeowners and renters live in homes designed for younger cohorts that are inappropriate for the changing needs of older adults. For example, most housing is too large, built on multiple levels, and designed with few fixtures to compensate for changing perceptual and motor skills.

Despite the range of housing options, little developmental research has been conducted to examine the effects of these different arrangements on adults of various ages. Instead, gerontologists have primarily focused on age-segregated versus age-integrated housing. This research has been conducted in five settings: apartment complexes for the elderly, retirement communities, congregate housing, single-room-occupancy (SRO) hotels, and continuing care retirement communities.

Age-Segregated Versus Age-Integrated Housing. Most older adults live in age-integrated communities, where there are people of all ages. Increasingly, however, the elderly are opting for communities that are *age-segregated*, that is, exclusively for older adults. In the United States federally assisted age-segregated housing projects began in 1956. Although about 6% of older adults live in age-segregated housing, this number is still well below that in some European countries such as the Netherlands, Sweden, France, and West Germany (Silverman, 1987). Since the 1960s the impact of age-segregated housing on older adults has been the topic of considerable research.

Early studies by Rosow (1967) on middle- and working-class elderly people in Cleveland and by Messer (1968) on public housing residents in Chicago showed that high concentrations of older adults resulted in higher levels of social contacts and morale, especially for women. Later research

A positive aspect of living in age-segregated housing is the opportunity to socialize with one's peers.

supported these findings, but added some important cautions. For example, Lawton confirmed that age-segregated housing resulted in increased social participation, interaction with other tenants, and satisfaction with housing (Lawton, 1980; Lawton, Moss, & Moles, 1984). However, Lawton (1980) and Carp (1976) both point out that these findings may be a function of the kind of housing and the particular neighborhood studied. For example, the people whom Rosow studied lived in an old, established neighborhood with long-term friendship

patterns already in place. Whether the benefits of age-segregated housing extend to newer neighborhoods is a topic we will explore in the next few sections.

Apartment Complexes for the Elderly. Several researchers have conducted excellent studies of people living in apartment complexes for the elderly. Two research methods have been used: interviews and participant observation.

The classic interview study of apartment residents was done by Carp (1966, 1976) at Victoria Plaza in San Antonio. Carp not only collected baseline data but also conducted follow-up interviews for eight years following initial occupancy. In general, Carp found that the move to Victoria Plaza was associated with improved social and psychological well-being, lower mortality, a lower rate of institutionalization, improved health, and increased social participation as compared with remaining in one's original home. Although the people who moved to Victoria Plaza chose to do so and may not represent older people in general, they received many benefits.

Although the findings from other interview studies have not always been as impressive, they do tend to agree with Carp's overall conclusions that age-segregated apartments produce many benefits. For example, Lawton and Cohen (1974) and Messer (1967) both found improved well-being following a move to an age-segregated housing complex.

In contrast to interview studies, the investigator in **participant observation research** actually lives in the housing project. One of the best examples of such research was done by Hochschild (1973), who studied 46 low-income elderly residents, mostly widows, in San Francisco. An important characteristic of this project was the development of a *subculture:* a strong positive feeling distinctive to the occupants. That is, although they did not have a great awareness of what was happening in the community around them, they were well informed on the events that were relevant to their lives. They celebrated birthdays together; looked in on one another; shared information, shopping, and costs; and communicated with one another extensively. Hochschild viewed these new shared roles as replacements for roles lost in their former communities; these new roles protected the residents against loneliness.

In a much larger study Jacobs (1975) examined a high-rise apartment building for working-class elderly people on a college campus in Syracuse, New York. Unlike the complex studied by Hochschild, the one in Syracuse was large (over 400 residents) and ethnically diverse, with obvious tensions between the majority whites and the small number of African Americans. Additionally, the fact that some of the residents were frail was resented by others, who feared that the project would turn into a nursing home. Jacobs found that many residents were apathetic, passive, and isolated. Consequently, Jacobs concluded that a cohesive subculture would not result from simply putting people of the same age together. Rather, the emergence of a subculture depends on such factors as number, ethnicity, and health status.

In short, what we have learned from research on apartment complexes is that it takes much more than a collection of same-aged people to make a coherent, satisfying community. From a life-cycle perspective, past experiences, attitudes, and needs must be considered and taken into account. When these factors are considered and a subculture emerges, the positive impact of living in such settings is substantial (Longino, 1982).

Retirement Communities. Another rapidly growing form of age-segregated housing is retirement communities. In retirement communities not only is housing restricted to people of a given age, but the whole community is designed to cater to the needs of the elderly. For example, housing units are often one story, electric golf carts are a preferred mode of transportation, and activities are planned with the older adult in mind. From their beginning in the Sun Belt states, retirement communities are now appearing across the United States.

Despite the considerable publicity that retirement communities have received, surprisingly little research has been done on their effects on residents. What little there is points to two opposite conclusions. Survey studies show that retirement communities tend to have overwhelmingly white, relatively affluent, better educated, healthier, married older adults (e.g., Heintz, 1976). Life satisfaction among residents is high; few wish to move out, and social participation is high.

In sharp contrast, participant observation research paints a very different picture. Jacobs (1974, 1975) studied the geographically isolated community of Fun City southeast of Los Angeles. The typical resident there was lonely, unhappy, and in despair. Social participation was low; only around 500 of the nearly 6,000 residents were active in a club or organization. In terms of Lawton and Nahemow's environmental press model, an imbalance existed between high personal competence and low environmental demands, resulting in poor adaptation. Jacobs also reported strong racist attitudes toward African Americans, Hispanics, and Native Americans, which was thought to be responsible for the lack of minority residents.

It is unclear why the findings in the survey and participant observation studies were so discrepant. It may be that residents want to highlight only the good aspects on a survey and that the negative aspects must be uncovered by personal observations. Geographic location could also be a factor, as well as how good the match is between competence and environmental demands. Further research is clearly needed in order to resolve these issues.

Congregate Housing. Congregate housing represents an intermediate step between living independently and living in an institutional setting. Congregate housing includes what is sometimes called intermediate, communal, or community housing. The importance of congregate housing is that it provides a viable alternative to institutionalization for people who need supportive services in order to maintain their independence.

Great Britain has led the way in developing congregate housing. The complex usually has self-contained apartments that are linked to a central office for emergencies. A medical clinic with a full-time nursing staff is on the premises. Planned social activities are organized by a trained staff. Heumann and Boldy (1982) surveyed several British facilities and concluded that residents remained functionally independent longer and were more likely to avoid institutionalization than elderly residents of conventional housing.

Congregate housing in the United States has adopted the British model. Carlin and Mansberg (1984) showed that residents of a congregate facility in the northeastern United States were remarkably active in organizing and participating in activities. Their strong sense of cohesiveness was demonstrated by their sense of pride and mutual concern for the home and the residents. Ross (1977) also noted a strong sense of cohesiveness in her study of a congregate home for the working-class elderly in Paris.

The need for increased congregate facilities was identified as one of the most pressing housing needs in the United States a decade ago (U.S. Office of Technology Assessment, 1984). Estimates are that 3 million elderly people in the United States need some sort of assisted housing, with the number expected to increase dramatically over the next few decades. Because little is known about the optimal design of congregate facilities and the type of resident who will benefit most, however, social policy awaits more research on these issues. Such research would benefit from the theoretical perspectives outlined at the outset, with special attention on the relationship between competence and demands and the congruence between needs and services.

SRO Hotels. Rather than living in congregate facilities, some elderly want to maintain their indepen-

dence. The single-room-occupancy (SRO) hotel offers an alternative for people who desire a high degree of autonomy. SRO hotels are usually located in dangerous and dilapidated areas of inner cities (Lawton, 1980).

Erickson and Ekert (1977) classify SROs into three types: skid row hotels, the most deteriorated type with mainly male, low-income occupants; working-class hotels, relatively clean with house-keeping services and mostly male occupants; and middle-class hotels, more comfortable and expensive with equal numbers of male and female occupants and some activities. Several participant observation studies have shown that residents of skid row and working-class hotels are fiercely independent, have large social networks, have marginal relationships with family, show high mutual support, and are usually poor (Ekert, 1980; Sokolovsky & Cohen, 1983; Stephens, 1976; Teski, 1981). Survey research has documented similar findings; men living in SROs and on the street are in generally poorer health than their community-dwelling counterparts, and these health problems are related to stress, unfulfilled needs, relative youth, and contacts with agencies (Cohen, Teresi, & Holmes, 1988). Unfortunately, almost none of these data have been analyzed from a biopsychosocial perspective.

Most researchers agree that SROs play an important role in serving poor, independently minded elderly people. However, the number of SROs is rapidly diminishing, often because of urban renewal. For example, 89% of the SROs in New York City disappeared between 1970 and 1983 and were replaced with luxury housing (Sanjek, 1984). This substantial loss of SROs may be partially responsible for the increase in the homeless elderly, a connection that needs to be explored.

Continuing Care Retirement Communities. Continuing care retirement communities (CCRCs) offer a range of housing from independent housing through full nursing care (Sherwood, Ruchlin, & Sherwood, 1989). Financially, many CCRCs work

Between 25% and 30% of all homeless people are over age 60. Life on the street for the homeless elderly requires considerable survival skill and is extremely difficult, dangerous, and stressful.

differently than other housing options. Individuals pay a substantial lump sum when they move in and a monthly fee for as long as they remain there. Payments do not vary with the level of care. Because CCRCs are typically very expensive, residents tend to be wealthier, better educated, more involved, and are more likely to be unmarried and childless than the average older adult (Sherwood et al., 1989).

Little research has been conducted on CCRCs other than on the financial considerations (Parmelee & Lawton, 1990). Sherwood and colleagues (1989) showed that CCRC residents waited until late in life (usually their late 70s) before entering. They also showed that CCRC residents wanted the security of knowing that their future needs would be met.

Homeless Elderly. Although there are many housing options for older adults, the unfortunate truth is that some older people have nowhere to call home. No one knows for certain how many homeless people there are in the United States (estimates range from 250,000 to 2.5 million). Virtually every U.S. city of any size has an identifiable population of homeless people.

Between 25% and 30% of all homeless people are thought to be over age 60 (Cohen, Teresi, Holmes, & Roth, 1988). Moreover, homeless elderly represent every ethnic group and are heterogenous on many other dimensions as well (such as education, past occupation, gender). Reasons for homelessness vary (Martin, 1990). Some people lost their jobs and income and could not find affordable housing. Some are battered women. Some have serious mental health problems or drug or alcohol problems. Because most programs to aid homeless people are targeted at younger people and families, older homeless adults are often overlooked (Martin, 1990).

Living on the street requires many survival strategies. Just figuring out how to get something to eat or how to get a shower may require considerable skill. Maintenance strategies include denial, fantasy, and self-entertainment, and survival skills range from learning how to carefully pick through discarded food to sleeping sitting up to living totally in public view. Some cities have shelters, but these are often too small to meet the demand. Overall, life on the street is extremely difficult, dangerous, and stressful (Cohen et al., 1988).

At present, we know so little about the homeless elderly that it is even difficult to know what kinds of intervention programs might work. While providing adequate nutrition and a decent place to stay are clearly important, many other needs, such as physical and mental health, must also be met. Much more emphasis on the plight of homeless older adults is urgently needed.

Conclusions About Communities, Neighborhoods, and Housing

Although most of the research on communities, neighborhoods, and housing reviewed here focuses on how old people make out in various communities, it is important to realize that living arrangements in old age come from many decisions over the life span. Decisions about family size, kinship pattern, health care, occupational choices, and personal priorities all contribute to housing decisions in later life. Disruptions in these areas earlier in adulthood may have long-term carryover effects in old age.

The most important point to remember about communities, neighborhoods, and housing is that optimizing of the person-environment fit is the goal. Wiseman (1981) argues that the first step should be changing the person's level of competence or personal resources through such interventions as better health care and economic security. The second step would be to change the environment through relocation. The final strategy is to facilitate environmental interactions for the elderly, such as by instituting better transportation. What we need to know most of all is whether the success of these suggestions is related to normative developmental changes.

INSTITUTIONS

Although the majority of older adults live in the community, some do reside in institutions. At any moment approximately 5% of the population over 65 is living in an institution. This may seem to be a small number of people, especially in view of the dominant stereotype of disability and sickness in old age. Before we feel too relieved, however, we must also recognize that the probability that someone who lives past age 85 will spend at least some time in an institution is much higher than 1 in 20 — it is more like 1 in 4 (Johnson, 1987). Thus, the number of people who are potentially affected by institutions is rather large.

Institutions are very different environments from those we have considered so far. As we will see, the inhabitants of institutions differ on many dimensions from their community-dwelling counterparts. Likewise, the environment itself is markedly different from neighborhood and community contexts. But because many aspects on the institutional environment are controlled, it offers a unique opportunity to examine person-environment inter-actions in more detail.

In this section we will examine types of in-stitutions, the typical resident, and the psycho-social environment in institutions. Since virtually all of the adult developmental research in this field focuses on the elderly, we will concentrate on the older individual's experience of institu-tionalization.

Types of Institutions

The main types of institutions for elderly residents are nursing homes, personal-care and boarding homes, and psychiatric hospitals. Nursing homes house the largest number of elderly residents of institutions. They are governed by state and federal regulations that establish minimum standards for care. Two levels of care in nursing homes are de-fined in the federal regulations (Johnson & Grant, 1985). *Skilled nursing care* consists of 24-hour care requiring skilled medical and other health services, usually from nurses. *Intermediate care* is also 24-hour care necessitating nursing supervision, but at a less intense level. In actual practice the major differences between the two are the types and num-bers of health care workers on the staff. Perhaps for this reason, the distinction between skilled and in-termediate care is undergoing government review.

Personal-care homes and boarding homes may also be regulated by states; however, no federal guidelines for these types of institutions exist. These institutions are primarily very small, and they house people who need assistance with daily needs because of disabilities or chronic disorders such as arthritis but who otherwise are in fairly good health. The quality of care in these institu-tions varies widely.

In the past, psychiatric hospitals housed many more older adults than they do now. Elderly pa-tients who are admitted to psychiatric hospitals due to serious psychological disorders such as paranoia or severe depression stay there for a much shorter period than even 20 years ago. Since the mid-1960s elderly psychiatric patients have been increasingly dismissed and relocated in the community or in other institutions. Unfortunately, little research has been conducted to measure the adjustment of these individuals after relocation. Sometimes, older adults who suffer severe emotional or cognitive def-icits are often placed in nursing homes rather than psychiatric hospitals. However, some states have begun to stop this practice as well, arguing that nursing home placements are inappropriate for these individuals. Again, we have essentially no in-formation on how such people fare after being told they must leave or are denied entrance into a nurs-ing home.

Because they contain the majority of older adults who live in institutions, nursing homes have been the setting for almost all of the research on the effects of institutionalization. For this reason nurs-ing homes will be the focus of the remainder of this section. Caution should be exercised in generaliz-ing the results from nursing home research to other types of institutions. Differences in structure, staffs, and residents' characteristics make compar-isons of different types of institutions difficult. As a result we need more research on the experience of older residents of other types of institutions and on how these experiences compare with those of nurs-ing home residents. Additionally, as noted in Some-thing to Think About, funding for nursing homes will be an increasingly important issue in the com-ing decades.

Who Is Likely to Live in Nursing Homes?

Who is the typical resident of a nursing home? She is very old, white, financially disadvantaged, prob-ably widowed or divorced, and possibly without liv-ing children. These characteristics are not similar

SOMETHING TO THINK ABOUT

Financing Long-Term Care

The current system of financing long-term care in the United States is in very serious trouble. Nursing home costs in 1990 averaged about $25,000 per year and were far and away the leading catastrophic health care expense. Contrary to popular belief, Medicare pays only 2% of nursing home expenses, and the typical private insurance plan pays only an additional 1%. Most often, the typical nursing home patient must deplete his or her life savings to pay for care. Once patients become totally impoverished, they become dependent on Medicaid. This public subsidy for nursing home care cost over $20 billion in 1990 and is increasing rapidly. For example, government support of long-term care, which represented 0.45% of the gross national product in 1988, is expected to grow to 1.42% by 2050 (Wiener, 1988). How will we be able to finance the long-term health care system?

One option is through the private sector. This approach includes long-term care insurance, individual retirement accounts for long-term care, health maintenance organizations, and alternative housing arrangements such as congregate housing. Many of these options place the burden on individuals to come up with ways of financing their own care. The Brookings Institution estimates that by 2018 private long-term care insurance will be affordable by as many as 45% of older adults. However, these projections also indicate that at best, private insurance will lower Medicaid expenditures by only 2% to 5%. Such modest reductions in public support would also accompany individual retirement accounts, alternative housing, health maintenance organizations, and other options. Consequently, large subsidies from government will still be needed for long-term care regardless of what the private sector does.

Given that government subsidies for long-term care will be required for the foreseeable future, the question becomes how to finance them. Under the current Medicaid system older adults are not protected from becoming impoverished. Moreover, the way that the system is designed, the substantial majority of people needing care will ultimately qualify for the program once their savings are depleted. With the aging of the baby boom generation, Medicaid costs will skyrocket. If we want to continue the program in its current form, it is likely that additional revenues will be needed, perhaps in the form of taxes.

The questions facing us are whether we want to continue forcing older adults to become totally impoverished when they need long-term care, whether we want the government to continue subsidy programs, and whether we would be willing to pay higher taxes for this subsidy. How we answer these questions will have a profound impact on the status of long-term care over the next few decades. It's something to think about.

---

to the population at large, as discussed in Chapter 1. For example, men are underrepresented in nursing homes, as are minorities. At least some of the ethnic differences may be a matter of personal choice rather than institutional policy. For example, some older Mexican Americans remain in the community to be cared for by family and friends regardless of their degree of impairment (Eribes & Bradley-Rawls, 1978). However, Burr (1990) reports that the rates for institutionalizing older unmarried adults are converging for African Americans and whites, and the reasons for doing so are essentially the same (for example, poor health).

What are the problems of typical nursing home residents? For the most part, the average nursing home resident is impaired, both mentally and physically. Indeed, the main reason for institutionalization for almost 80% of nursing home residents is health. Still, placement in a nursing home is usually a last resort; over half of the residents come from other institutions such as general hospitals (Lawton, 1980).

Frail elderly people and their relatives alike do not see nursing homes as an option until other avenues have been explored. This may account for the numbers of truly impaired individuals who live in nursing homes; the kinds and amount of problems make life outside the nursing home very difficult on them and their families. In fact, if all other things are equal, the best predictor of who will be placed in a nursing home is the absence of a viable social support system (George, 1980).

The fact that older adults and their families do not see nursing homes as the placement of choice means that the decision was probably made reluctantly. In some cases individuals other than family members enter the decision process. One common situation involves older adults living in age-segregated housing projects, most of which have some type of policy concerning the level of functioning that residents must have to remain. In actual practice most housing projects have explicit policies in areas concerning safety and liability; for example, some have regulations that tenants who need constant monitoring or who are nonambulatory must move out. However, most of these regulations are deliberately vague concerning basic skills needed for daily living, such as the ability to maintain one's own apartment and about areas of personal behavior involving mental confusion, emotional instability, and drinking problems (Bernstein, 1982).

Bernstein surveyed the managers of 136 housing projects concerning their criteria for asking tenants to leave. She found substantial agreement across policies, which are summarized in Table 12.1. As can be seen, the most frequent reason for asking tenants to leave involved psychological functioning (mental ability, emotional stability, and so on). Tenants most often left voluntarily because they

needed constant supervision. Notice that these reasons (and most of the other criteria listed) are similar to the characteristics of the typical nursing home resident.

Characteristics of Nursing Homes

We can examine nursing homes on two dimensions: physical and psychosocial. Physical characteristics include factors such as size, staff-to-resident ratio, numbers and types of activities, and certification requirements. Unfortunately, very little research has been done comparing institutions on these dimensions. As a result we do not have a good idea of how much variance there is on these dimensions across nursing homes and when differences become important.

More is known about the effects of these dimensions on residents' psychosocial well-being. The combination of the physical, personal, staff-related, and service-related aspects of the nursing home makes up a milieu, a higher-order abstraction of the environmental context (Lawton, 1980).

Over the last decade several researchers have been conceptualizing the effects of the institutional milieu on residents. We are already familiar with Kahana's ideas; an expansion of the previous discussion will be presented here. A second investigator, Moos, has taken a somewhat different approach that emphasizes measurement; we will also consider his views in detail. Finally, we will consider some work by Langer from a social-psychological perspective.

The Congruence Approach. In describing her congruence theory, Kahana (1982) also discusses several dimensions along which person-environment congruence can be classified (see Table 12.2). She is especially interested in describing institutions so most of her research is aimed at documenting her dimensions in these settings.

TABLE 12.1 Most frequently mentioned reasons for asking tenants to leave housing projects or for their leaving voluntarily

	Projects Asked Tenants to Leave (%)	Projects' Tenants Left Voluntarily (%)
Tenant showed mental decline (senility, not mentally alert) or had problems such as emotional imbalance, aggressive behavior, paranoia, depression, etc.	61	27
Tenant was a potential health or safety hazard to self or others (accidents, fire, flooding, etc.).	32	10
Tenant needed daily supervision of activities, medication, and personal well-being.	30	67
Tenant had an alcohol abuse problem.	29	6
Tenant was bedridden and/or needed skilled nursing care facility (24-hour).	25	55
Tenant was a major disturbance or had a difficult personality.	22	0
Tenant had severe illness (stroke, heart, cancer, etc.).	18	39
Tenant had a general decline in health (frailty, deterioration, going downhill).	16	30
Tenant left to be with family members.	0	60
Tenant needed to have meals cooked or provided (if meals were on site, they were not frequent enough or tenant was unable to get to them).	0	20

(Source: "Who Leaves — Who Stays: Residency Policy in Housing for the Elderly" by J. Bernstein, 1982, *Gerontologist, 22,* 305–313. Copyright © 1982 by the Gerontological Society of America. Reprinted with permission.)

Kahana's approach emphasizes that personal well-being is not just the product of the characteristics of the institution and of the individual but also of the congruence between the individual's needs and the ability of the institution to meet them. People whose needs are congruent with the control provided by the institution should have the highest well-being. However, any number of factors could potentially be important in determining congruence, as is demonstrated by the large number of subdimensions in the congruence model.

Harel (1981) investigated which of these many factors in determining congruence was the most important in predicting well-being. Based on 125

Maintaining a social network is important, especially when living in a nursing home.

interviews in 14 nursing homes, Harel found that continuing ties with preferred members of the resident's social network was the most important variable. Meeting social needs, then, should constitute a major goal for institutions. Harel suggested that a resident services department be established in nursing homes as well as policies allowing greater opportunities for choice in socializing.

Attempting to establish congruence in the social domain may have direct benefits. Greene and Monahan (1982) demonstrated that the frequency of family visitation affected residents' level of impairment. Specifically, those residents who were visited often by their families had significantly higher levels of psychosocial functioning. This suggests that meeting social needs through visitation has a positive and direct effect on residents' well-being.

Moos's Approach. A second way to examine the person-environment interaction in institutions has been offered by Moos and his colleagues (Moos & Lemke, 1984, 1985). Moos believes that institutions can be evaluated in physical, organizational, supportive, and social climate terms. Each of these areas is thought to have an effect on the well-being of the residents.

Several scales have been developed to assess institutions on these dimensions. Moos's Multiphasic Environmental Assessment Procedure (MEAP), one of the most comprehensive, assesses four aspects of the facility: physical and architectural features; administrative and staff policies and programs; resident and staff characteristics; and social climate. Each area is measured by separate multidimensional scales. Together, information from the MEAP provides a complete picture that allows a judgment to be made about how well the facility meets residents' needs.

Moos's approach has the advantage that separate dimensions of the person-environment interaction can be measured and examined independently. For one thing, it establishes areas of strength and weakness so that appropriate programs can be devised. But perhaps more important, it may provide a basis for future efforts at developing rating systems for evaluating the overall quality of an institution. At present, questions like what really distinguishes good and bad nursing homes, for example, are unanswerable. Only further refinement of measures like those developed by Moos will give us a clue.

Social-Psychological Perspectives. Langer approaches the issue of person-environment interactions quite differently from either Kahana or Moos. She believes that the important factor in residents' well-being is the degree to which they perceive that they are in control of their lives (Langer, 1985).

To demonstrate her point, she conducted an ingenious experiment. One group of nursing home residents were told that staff members were there to care for them and to make decisions for them

TABLE 12.2 Environmental and individual dimensions of Kahana's congruence model with descriptions of important aspects of each

Segregate Dimension

Environment	Individual
a. Homogeneity of composition of environment. Segregation based on similarity of resident characteristics (sex, age, physical functioning and mental status).	a. Preference for homogeneity, i.e., for associating with like individuals. Being with people similar to oneself.
b. Change vs. sameness. Presence of daily and other routines, frequency of changes in staff and other environmental characteristics.	b. Preference for change vs. sameness in daily routines, activities.
c. Continuity or similarity with previous environment of resident.	c. Need for continuity with the past.

Congregate Dimension

Environment	Individual
a. Extent to which privacy is available in setting.	a. Need for privacy.
b. Collective vs. individual treatment. The extent to which residents are treated alike. Availability of choices in food, clothing, etc. Opportunity to express unique individual characteristics.	b. Need for individual expression and idiosyncracy. Choosing individualized treatment whether that is socially defined as "good" treatment or not.
c. The extent to which residents do things alone or with others.	c. Preference for doing things alone vs. with others.

Institutional Control

Environment	Individual
a. Control over behavior and resources. The extent to which staff exercises control over resources.	a. Preference for (individual) autonomy vs. being controlled.
b. Amount of deviance tolerated. Sanctions for deviance.	b. Need to conform.
c. Degree to which dependency is encouraged and dependency needs are met.	c. Dependence on others. Seeks support or nurturance vs. feeling self-sufficient.

(Source: "A Congruence Model of Person-Environment Interaction" by E. Kahana, 1982, in M. P. Lawton et al. (Eds.), *Aging and the Environment: Theoretical Approaches.* New York: Springer. Reprinted by permission of Dr. Eva Kahana.)

Structure

Environment	Individual
a. Ambiguity vs. specification of expectations. Role ambiguity or role clarity (e.g., rules learned from other residents).	a. Tolerance of ambiguity vs. need for structure.
b. Order vs. disorder.	b. Need for order and organization.

Stimulation–Engagement

Environment	Individual
a. Environmental input (stimulus properties of physical and social environment).	a. Tolerances and preference for environmental stimulation.
b. The extent to which resident is actually stimulated and encouraged to be active.	b. Preference for activities vs. disengagement.

Affect

Environment	Individual
a. Tolerance for or encouragement of affective expression. Provision of ritualized show of emotion (e.g., funerals).	a. Need for emotional expression. Display of feelings, whether positive or negative.
b. Amount of affective stimulation. Excitement vs. peacefulness in environment.	b. Intensity of affect, for example, need for vs. avoidance of conflict and excitement (shallow affect).

Impulse Control

Environment	Individual
a. Acceptance of impulsive life vs. sanctions against it. The extent to which the environment gratifies need immediately vs. postponed need gratification. Gratification-deprivation ratio.	a. Ability to delay need gratification. Preference for immediate vs. delayed reward. Degree of impulse need.
b. Tolerance of motor expression — restlessness, walking around in activities or at night.	b. Motor control; psychomotor inhibition.
c. Premium placed by environment on levelheadedness and deliberation.	c. Impulsive closure vs. deliberate closure.

about their daily lives. In contrast, a second group of residents were encouraged to make their own decisions concerning meals, recreational activities, and so forth. This second group showed marked improvements in well-being and activity level compared with the first group (Langer & Rodin, 1976). These improvements were still seen 18 months later; in fact, the second group also seemed to have lower mortality rates (Rodin & Langer, 1977).

Based on her findings, Langer became convinced that making residents feel competent and in control were key factors in promoting positive person-environment interactions in nursing homes. Langer (1985) points to several aspects of the nursing home environment that fail in this regard. First, the decision to institutionalize is often made by persons other than the individual involved. Staff members may communicate their belief that the resident is incapable of making any decision or may treat the resident like a child rather than like an adult who is moving to a new home.

Second, the label "nursing home resident" may have strong negative connotations. This is especially true if as a younger adult the person had negative preconceived ideas about why people go to nursing homes. A long history of social-psychological research shows that the individual may begin to internalize these stereotypic beliefs, even if they are unwarranted (Kelley, 1967). Other labels such as "patient" may have similar effects.

Third, the demonstration of tender loving care may serve mainly to reinforce the belief in one's incompetence. That is, in helping people perform basic tasks such as getting dressed we run the risk of increasing their level of incompetence and dependence on others. Again, providing assistance where none is needed may be a way in which the staff communicates its belief that the individual cannot fend for himself or herself at all.

The physical aspects of the environment may also reinforce the belief of no control. To the extent that the environment is unfamiliar or is difficult to negotiate, persons living in it may feel incompetent.

Mastering the environment increases feelings of control, but if this process is either not allowed or is made too easy, the outcome may be negative.

Finally, Langer (1985) argues that routine is also detrimental to well-being. If the environment is too predictable, there is little for people to think about; in Langer's terms we become mindless. In this state we are typically not aware of what we do; we behave as if we were on automatic pilot. If nursing home environments promote mindlessness, then individuals behave automatically and have difficulty remembering what happened even a short time before. When this occurs, the staff may view the person as incompetent. But since we all engage in mindless activity (for example, performing a series of complex but automatic functions while driving) about which we have no recollection (one often cannot recall anything about driving the last several miles), we cannot rationalize that this same mindlessness is indicative of incompetence in the elderly.

Other researchers have replicated Langer's basic findings in nursing homes (Schulz & Hanusa, 1979) and retirement communities (Slivinske & Fitch, 1987). Even though some researchers have failed to replicate Langer's research when nursing home residents are reexamined over longer periods (Schulz & Hanusa, 1978), the points raised concerning how nursing home residents should be treated are still very important. Whether the benefits of increased control last over the long run is still an open issue. Whether we should treat nursing home residents with respect is not.

RELOCATION

The United States is a highly mobile society. The time when people lived their entire lives in the same neighborhood has largely passed. Adults of all ages relocate, and many are already veterans by the time they reach 21. Regardless of one's age or previous experience, relocation is a challenge. Whether it is moving to a different floor in the dorm or across the country, moving disrupts our physical and social environments and tests our coping skills. Living in a house full of boxes and moving cartons is a hassle; leaving friends and family for a strange city hundreds of miles away is emotionally traumatic. But lots of things determine whether a move will be psychologically tolerable or a nightmare. Exactly what impact does moving have on psychological well-being? Does the type of relocation make a difference? What factors make adjustment after moving easier or more difficult?

In order to answer these questions, we will examine two types of relocation: community based and institutional. Community-based moves involve moving from one residence to another, regardless of whether the two are in the same neighborhood or a great distance apart. The key ingredient is that the person maintains an independent residence. In contrast, institutional relocations involve moving either from a community-based residence to an institution or from one institution to another. The major factor here is that the individual is not able to live independently in the community.

Community-Based Relocation

Community-based relocations are fairly common. Although younger adults are the most likely to move, middle-aged and older adults do relocate. Indeed, in 1990 approximately one third of adults over age 45 had moved within the previous 5 years. Community-based relocation is fairly common.

This pattern of mobility is not limited to the United States. Rogers, Watkins, and Woodward (1990) examined mobility patterns in the United States, Great Britain, Italy, and Japan. They found that the United States and Great Britain both show clear patterns of elderly migration to specific locations having high concentrations of older adults.

This pattern is less well defined in Italy and hardly occurs at all in Japan. It appears that family ties — strong in both these countries — along with few identifiable retirement regions combine to keep migration rates down.

Why People Move. Although many older adults head to the Sun Belt, many do not. In fact, recent trends indicate that the flight to warmer climates is slowing, and some elderly people choose to relocate to retirement communities in the North (J.W. Meyer, 1987). Regardless of where they go, why do they move in the first place?

In one of the few developmental studies on mobility, Speare and Meyer (1988) identified 4 reasons for moving mentioned by movers 55 and older that corresponded to changes in later life: amenity, kinship, retirement, and widowhood. *Amenity mobility* is based on a primary or secondary reason of climate change. *Kinship mobility* occurs because the person wants to be closer to relatives. *Retirement mobility* takes place in response to retirement, with climate and distance from relatives not a factor. *Widowhood mobility* occurs when a person desires to be closer to important members of the social support system other than the immediate family.

The characteristics of elderly movers differ somewhat based on the reason for moving. As summarized in Table 12.3, amenity and retirement movers are similar in that both groups are richer and better educated, own their own home, and are married. Kinship movers tend to be older than other types but in other respects are similar to other groups. Widowhood movers have significantly lower income, are older, but are also well educated and own homes. Additionally, amenity and retirement movers head to the South and West more often than other types, who relocate to all regions.

As older adults begin to have trouble performing tasks of daily living or when their health begins to fail, they are also likely to move (Longino, Jackson, Zimmerman, & Bradsher, 1991; Speare, Avery, & Lawton, 1991). For example, Longino et

TABLE 12.3 Percentages of movers and nonmovers aged 55 and older who fall into various descriptive categories

Independent Variables	Movers, by Reason					Nonmovers
	Amenity	Kinship	Retirement	Widowed	Other	
Age groups						
55 to 64	53.6	41.4	59.2	35.4	57.8	41.3
65 to 74	25.5	33.8	29.4	32.1	26.9	34.9
75 and over	21.0	24.8	11.5	32.5	15.3	23.8
Total	100.1*	100.0	100.1	100.0	100.0	100.0
Household types						
Single person	32.9	48.4	18.5	89.5	45.8	33.0
2 + persons	8.7	9.9	0.0	10.5	13.1	11.0
Married couple	58.4	41.7	81.5	0.0	41.1	56.0
Total	100.0	100.0	100.0	100.0	100.0	100.0
Previous tenure						
Homeowner	70.8	48.7	78.6	62.8	29.7	78.2
Renter	29.2	51.3	21.4	37.2	70.3	21.8
Total	100.0	100.0	100.0	100.0	100.0	100.0
Education (in years)						
0 to 7	8.7	13.2	6.9	17.4	20.2	14.5
8 to 11	27.1	39.6	25.2	25.2	28.3	30.9
12 to 15	50.3	34.8	55.7	33.7	39.5	41.8
16 +	13.9	12.3	12.2	23.7	12.0	12.9
Total	100.0	99.9	100.0	100.0	100.0	100.1
Income/poverty						
Below poverty	13.1	20.9	8.7	39.8	28.9	16.3
Below 2 × poverty	21.8	32.5	27.6	28.7	27.0	28.1
Above 2 × poverty	65.1	46.6	63.6	31.5	44.1	55.6
Total	100.0	100.0	99.9	100.0	100.0	100.0

(Source: "Types of Elderly Residential Mobility and Their Determinants" by A. Speare, Jr., and J. W. Meyer, 1988, *Journal of Gerontology, 43*, 574–581. Copyright © 1988 by the Gerontological Society of America. Reprinted with permission.)

*Totals may not equal 100 due to rounding off.

al. (1991) found that in adults over age 70, there was often a move between an amenity relocation and an institutional relocation that was precipitated by declines in one's ability to take care of daily tasks without assistance.

Factors Affecting Adjustment. Simply because relocation happens frequently does not diminish its psychological impact. One way to think about this aspect of relocation is to consider moving in terms of the psychological stress it introduces and the effects that stress has on a person's adjustment. When relocation is viewed this way, an important question comes to mind. Given that any relocation is potentially stressful, what variables influence an individual's perception of stress in community-based relocations?

Four variables appear to be important. Obviously, the degree to which familiar behavior patterns are disrupted is a consideration. Second, the sense of personal loss at leaving one's former residence also affects subsequent adjustment. To the extent that one was very attached to one's old home, adjustment to one's new home may be harder. A third variable is the distance involved in the move; the farther one moves, the greater the disruption of routines is likely to be. Finally, the reason for the move is very important. It is generally true that people who make voluntary moves perceive the relocation more positively than people who make involuntary moves.

Although the four variables of disruption, loss, distance, and reason are good predictors of stress in community-based moves, there are substantial individual differences in people's adjustment even for identical levels of loss, for example. How well one adjusts to relocation, then, is a function not only of disruption and so forth but also of several personal factors involving social status, social support, environmental variables, and perception of the move. These personal factors affect the perception of stress and facilitate or hinder the adjustment process. Since they are important factors in under-

standing how individuals cope with relocation, they will be considered more thoroughly in the following sections.

Social status factors such as occupation, education, and socioeconomic status provide an indication of where a person fits in the community and an index of life experience. Of the many social status variables that could influence adjustment to community-based relocation, only two have been studied systematically. Higher levels of education lead to better adjustment (Storandt, Wittels, & Botwinick, 1975), as does higher socioeconomic status, reflected in occupation and income (Rosow, 1967; Storandt et al., 1975). Because more highly educated people tend to have higher socioeconomic status, the two factors may operate together.

One thing is clear from this work. Our understanding of the influence of social status on adjustment to relocation is quite limited. Important factors such as marital status, race, and gender have not been examined very thoroughly as potential influences. Until such multivariate research is done, we will not know whether the influence of education and socioeconomic status holds independent of these other factors.

Social support systems provide both emotional and other types of assistance during relocation. We have already seen that maintaining friendships is an important factor in nursing home residents' well-being; the same is true for people who move. Research shows that good relationships with family and friends facilitate adjustment to relocation (George, 1980; Lawton, 1980).

Some research has examined changes in social support systems following relocation. Interestingly, it appears that people do not substitute relationships with one group for missing relationships with another. For instance, older adults whose children or other close relatives move away do not substitute friendships with age peers for the missing familial ties (Hochschild, 1973). The best possible situation is one in which old friendship and family bonds can be maintained and new ones developed.

Environmental variables such as the physical characteristics of the new residence and the nature of the new community affect adjustment. In particular, the issues of space, privacy, and convenience are important physical factors. Improvements on these dimensions will lead to better adjustment (Lawton, 1980). Additionally, people who move to communities having high proportions of same-age peers tend to adjust better (Rosow, 1967; Teaff, Lawton, Nahemow, & Carlson, 1978). This effect is probably due to the greater ease of forming new friendships when one is surrounded by people of similar age and background, thereby helping to build a new social support system.

People's *perception of the move*, such as what they believe to be their degree of control, has a direct bearing on how well they adjust, independent of the true situation. In general, if people think that they are being forced to move, adjustment problems are more likely to result (George, 1980).

If perception is viewed as a function of advance knowledge of the move, a contrasting picture emerges. Schooler (1982) found that when moves were expected, the outcomes were worse than when they were unexpected. He speculated that advance knowledge of an impending relocation might induce anxiety, which might be exacerbated by the trauma of the move itself. Interestingly, when expected relocations resulted in a better environment or when a confidant was available, the negative impact was reduced. However, Schooler did not take into account why people were moving or their attitudes about it, so the overall meaning of his results is somewhat unclear. Still, we should not dismiss his results; they point out that even when individuals know that they are going to move, some people may suffer from the anxiety induced by this knowledge.

Long-Term Effects. Most studies of adjustment to community-based relocation have followed the participants for only a short time after they move. Because short-term effects may differ from long-term effects, longitudinal investigations are required to address this possibility. All of the psychological consequences of moving that we have considered thus far are based on short-term assessments. In this section we will consider what we know about the long-term effects of moving in the community.

Two projects have examined adjustment of movers approximately a year after their voluntary relocation. Both involved older adults moving from independent community residences to housing projects designed specifically for the elderly, and both involved comparisons between movers and people who were on the waiting list for admission to the housing complex (termed *nonmovers* in this study).

In the first project participants were all eligible for low-income housing and had limited financial assets. They were tested on four areas relating to psychological adjustment: cognitive and psychomotor performance, health, activity level, and morale and well-being. Testing was done twice, five months before the move and nine months after. The results showed no differences between movers and nonmovers on any of the measures, so the investigators concluded that moving had no long-term adverse effects (Storandt & Wittels, 1975; Storandt et al., 1975; Wittels & Botwinick, 1974).

The second project involved individuals who wanted to move to Victoria Plaza in San Antonio. For those people who succeeded at getting into the project, the new residences offered considerably improved surroundings than had been available in the previous residence. Movers and nonmovers were tested three times: six months before the move and one and eight years after the move. Health, mortality rates, and well-being were measured. Results showed that on each test the movers were significantly better off than the nonmovers on every measure. Thus, when relocation involves significant improvements in one's physical surroundings, the benefits of moving or the costs of not moving are potentially very long-lasting (Carp, 1966, 1975, 1977).

Institutional Relocation

We saw in earlier discussion that although only about 5% of the people over age 65 reside in institutions at any one time, many more people spend at least part of their lives there. This means that many people face the transition from living in the community to living in an institution each year. As in community-based relocation, there is disruption in routines and in social relationships and a sense of loss from leaving the previous home.

From the previous discussion, and perhaps from personal experience, we might expect institutional relocation to be more difficult to deal with psychologically. After all, older and younger people view institutionalization with dread and see it as an admission that they are no longer competent enough to care for themselves. Admission to an institution also involves giving up a great deal of personal freedom and privacy. But do these factors necessarily imply that all institutional relocations result in negative outcomes?

Personal Factors Affecting Adjustment. To answer this question, we must consider many of the same personal factors affecting adjustment that are important in community-based moves: social status, social support, and involuntary versus voluntary relocation. Moreover, there are several other variables that must be considered in institutional relocation: physical and cognitive resources, personality factors, and preparation experiences.

Relocation to an institution is not random. As noted earlier, very old white women who are widowed or unmarried and who have minimal financial resources are the most likely to be institutionalized when they face serious health problems. Although these *social status* variables accurately predict who the typical relocator will be, they do not appear to predict level of adjustment in the institution.

Physical health and cognitive abilities facilitate institutional relocation (Tobin & Lieberman, 1976). Specifically, people in poor health and those who have experienced severe cognitive declines are more likely to have adjustment problems. Although inadequate physical and cognitive resources predict maladjustment, adequate resources do not guarantee successful relocation.

The importance of *social support* as a factor in adjustment to institutional relocation cannot be overemphasized. As indicated earlier, lack of a viable social support system is the best predictor of institutionalization (George, 1980). The maintenance of old support systems and the development of new ones after relocation to a nursing home eases adjustment (Greene & Monahan, 1982; Harel, 1981). Furthermore, close primary relationships are associated with better adjustment following relocation from one institution to another (Wells & Macdonald, 1981). These relationships provide residents with a source of continuity that enable them to deal better with an emotionally stressful event.

There appears to be a cluster of *personality traits* related to survival among nursing home residents: aggression, hostility, assertiveness, and narcissism (Tobin & Lieberman, 1976). Since people with these traits are not usually the easiest to get along with, it may seem surprising that such unpleasant characteristics are related to at least one aspect of adjustment. However, these traits may represent the only means by which a person can assert his or her individuality and dislike for the lack of personal freedom in the institution. In this sense these characteristics may represent a more adaptive response than passive acceptance, even though the latter behavior will win more friends among the staff.

Preparation for institutional relocation involves not only formal programs but also informal ones through friendship networks. A number of studies have shown that adjustment following relocation from one institution to another is better if residents are given a formal preparation program (e.g., Pino, Rosica, & Carter, 1978). Borup (1981) concluded that the major objective of these programs should be to help reduce the stress and anxiety associated with the relocation.

Whether relocation is *voluntary or involuntary* predicts adjustment in community relocation; involuntary moves are more stressful. Thus, we would expect that involuntary moves to institutions would also be more stressful. Unfortunately, almost no research has examined this issue. The problem is that most institutional relocations are involuntary so researchers have not considered this factor.

Type of Relocation and Adjustment. We have seen that many personal factors influence adjustment following institutional relocation. In order to understand the adjustment process itself, however, we must consider two types of institutional relocation: relocation from the community to an institution and relocation from one institution to another. We have alluded to these different types in our discussion of personal factors; we will now examine them in more detail. Since almost all of the relevant studies have concentrated on nursing homes as the setting, our survey will focus on this institution.

Three issues that are important in the adjustment process following relocations from the community to a nursing home have been investigated fairly intensely: person-environment fit, short-term versus long-term adjustment patterns, and factors immediately before institutionalization.

The appropriateness of the nursing home and of the services it provides is related to level of residents' morale one year after their relocation (Morris, 1975). People who are placed in inappropriate nursing homes have significantly lower morale than those who are appropriately placed. These findings once again show the importance of Kahana's (1982) notion of congruence, or person-environment fit.

In examining adjustment after a move from the community to a nursing home, a researcher must be careful to follow the residents for a sufficient length of time. This point was nicely demonstrated by Spasoff and his colleagues (1978). They found that life satisfaction was consistently high at one month and one year after relocation. However, 25% of the original sample had died and 15% had been moved to other nursing homes during the first year.

Clearly, the sample that was tested after one year was different from the one tested initially. Spasoff et al. (1978) demonstrated that investigators need to be sensitive to these changes in sample characteristics in order to avoid incorrect conclusions about long-term adjustment.

Tobin and Lieberman conducted a major longitudinal investigation of adjustment to moves from the community to nursing homes (Tobin & Lieberman, 1976). They were able to isolate the effects of relocation itself by examining three groups of people: a group that was waiting for admission to a nursing home, a group that had been in a nursing home for one to three years, and a sample that stayed in the community throughout the study. Five factors in adjustment (physical health, cognitive functioning, emotional states, emotional responsiveness, and self-perception) were measured at three times: before the institutionalization of the relocation group, two months after relocation, and one year after.

Most important, Tobin and Lieberman found that even before institutionalization the relocation group resembled the institutional group more than the community group. Moreover, the main influences on adjustment and identity after placement are those that lead to institutionalization in the first place. Following relocation, the first few months seem to be the most difficult, although some people experience relocation stress up to a year later. Thus, Tobin and Lieberman's results show that it is the elderly with the fewest personal resources to handle stress who are most likely to be involved in the stress of relocation from the community to a nursing home.

Few studies have examined the psychological adjustment process following relocation from one institution to another. Rather, investigators have looked at mortality rates as the measure of successful relocation. A highly controversial series of studies by Borup and his associates in the late 1970s and early 1980s spurred a heated debate over the connection between interinstitutional relocation and mortality (Borup, 1981, 1982, 1983;

Borup & Gallego, 1981; Borup, Gallego, & Heffernan, 1979, 1980).

Borup concluded from his own and others' research that relocation alone had no effect on residents' mortality. He argues that in some cases a moderate environmental change can even have a positive effect for reasons similar to Langer's concerning mindlessness. Finally, Borup attributes most of the apparent negative consequences of relocation to the length of time spent in the nursing home. That is, he feels that the same observations of decline would be made if residents remained in the same nursing home for the same period.

Borup's conclusions have been attacked by several authors (Bourestom & Pastalan, 1981; Horowitz & Schulz, 1983). Criticisms of Borup's research design and interpretations of his own and others' findings have been the main focus of these debates. These authors are also concerned that nursing homes will misapply Borup's results and abandon all attempts to make relocation less stressful. These critics force us to evaluate the evidence carefully, and they stimulate discussion on a very important topic.

The weight of the evidence points to the conclusion that interinstitutional relocation per se has little if any direct effect on mortality. Future researchers will be focusing on the question of psychological adjustment following such moves. It remains to be seen whether the findings from this research will prove as controversial as those from mortality research.

Relocation within the same institution occurs relatively frequently, such as when a new wing is built or a resident requests the move. As with interinstitutional relocation, past research has resulted in confusing data. In an attempt to clarify the issues, Pruchno and Resch (1988) examined one-year mortality rates in one group following room changes for reasons other than health and in a nonmover group matched for competence. Through advanced statistical analyses, Pruchno and Resch showed that the connection between mortality after relocation and initial competence was complex.

Mortality rates for movers who had high or low initial competence were lower than for the nonmover group. However, movers with moderate initial competence showed higher mortality levels. Pruchno and Resch argue that moving represented a positive and stimulating experience for residents with high or low competence, whereas those with moderate competence viewed the move as disruptive and confusing. The important point from this research is that mortality effects following a move may be related to the environmental cues that are most salient to the residents. That is, residents who notice the negative features of the move may be more at risk than those who focus on the positive aspects.

SUMMARY

Theories of Person-Environment Interactions

1. Environmental psychology focuses on the interactions between people and communities or institutions in which they live.

2. Person-environment interaction refers to the fact that behavior is a function of both the person and the environment.

3. Competence is the upper limit on one's capacity to function. Environmental press reflects the demands placed on a person. Lawton and Nahemow's model establishes points of balance between the two, called adaptation level.

4. Kahana's congruence model proposes that people search for environments that best meet their needs. The congruence model helps focus on individual differences and on understanding adaptation in nursing homes and other institutions.

5. Schooler claims that older adults' adaptation depends on their perception of environmental stress and their attempts to cope. Social systems and institutions may buffer the effects of stress.

6. The loss-continuum concept refers to adaptations based on the number and types of losses adults experience.

7. All theories agree that the focus must be on interactions between the person and the environment. No single environment will meet everyone's needs.

Communities, Neighborhoods, and Housing

8. Satisfaction with where one lives varies as a function of the quality of one's informal social network, degree of differentiation of services, and residents' expectations of what the community should be like.

9. Perception of their neighborhood affects people's overall well-being. Perceptions about crime and structural features also are influential.

10. Ethnic differences are widespread in terms of what a neighborhood is and the role it plays in people's lives.

11. Older adults live in a wide variety of housing: age segregated, age integrated, apartment complexes, retirement communities, congregate housing, SRO hotels, and continuing care retirement communities. Participant observation research has revealed subcultures that emerge in many types of housing.

12. A growing number of elderly are homeless.

Institutions

13. At any given point in time, only about 5% of older adults are in institutions.

14. Intermediate and skilled care nursing homes, personal care and boarding homes, and psychiatric hospitals are the main types of institutions in which older adults live.

15. The typical resident is female, white, very old, financially disadvantaged, widowed or divorced, and possibly without living children. Placement in nursing homes is seen as a last resort.

16. Kahana's congruence model emphasizes the importance of fit between the person and the nursing home. Members of residents' social network are especially important.

17. Moos's approach emphasizes evaluation of physical, organizational, supportive, and social climate aspects.

18. Langer emphasizes the importance of a sense of personal control in maintaining well-being and even staying alive.

Relocation

19. People move for many reasons, such as better climate, being closer to relatives, in response to retirement, or to be closer to friends.

20. Adjustment to relocation depends on the degree of disruption to familiar behavior patterns, sense of loss of residence, distance of the move, and whether the move is voluntary.

21. Individual difference variables affecting adjustment include social status, social support systems, environmental variables, and the perception of the move.

22. Important predictors of who will relocate include health, cognitive abilities, social support, and personality traits.

23. Preparation for relocation and voluntary relocation facilitate adjustment. Still, adjustment to different types of institutional relocation is a complex process that is not easily predicted.

REVIEW QUESTIONS

Theories of Person-Environment Interactions

1. What is environmental psychology?

2. What are person-environment interactions?

3. Describe Lawton and Nahemow's theory of environmental press. In their theory, what is adaptation level?

4. Describe Kahana's congruence model. In what settings is this model especially appropriate?

5. Describe the application of the stress and coping model to person-environment interactions. What kinds of things buffer stress?

6. Describe the loss-continuum concept.

7. What are the common themes expressed by the various theories of person-environment interactions?

Communities, Neighborhoods, and Housing

8. What factors affect satisfaction with where one lives?

9. What factors influence the perceptions of neighborhoods? What ethnic differences have been noted in neighborhood perceptions?

10. What kinds of housing do older adults live in?

Institutions

11. How many older adults live in institutions at any given point?

12. What types of institutions house older adults?

13. Who is most likely to live in a nursing home? Why?

14. How have the characteristics of nursing homes been studied? How do Kahana's approach, Moos's approach, and Langer's approach differ?

Relocation

15. Why do people move?

16. What factors influence adjustment to relocation?

17. What factors predict who is likely to relocate to an institution?

18. How do preparation and the degree to which the move is voluntary affect adjustment?

KEY TERMS

adaptation level In person-environment interactions, the point at which competence and environmental press are in balance. (413)

competence In person-environment interactions, the theoretical upper limit of a person's ability to function. (413)

congruence model In person-environment interactions, the notion that people need to find the environment in which they fit and that meets their needs the best. (415)

environmental press In person-environment interactions, the demands put on a person by the environment. (413)

environmental psychology The study of person-environment interactions. (411)

informal social network The people who provide support but who are not connected with any formal social service agency. (417)

loss continuum A theory of person-environment interactions based on the notion that social participation declines as personal losses increase. (416)

participant observation research An approach to research in which the experimenter lives among the people under study. (422)

person-environment interactions The interface between people and the world in which they live that forms the basis for development. (412)

ADDITIONAL READING

A good overview of person-environment interactions can be found in

Lawton, M. P., Windley, P. G., & Byerts, T. O. (1982). *Aging and the environment: Theoretical approaches.* New York: Springer. Moderately difficult.

Two chapters in a book edited by Philip Silverman summarize research on nursing homes and other living arrangements

Johnson, C. L. (1987). The institutional segregation of the aged. And Silverman, P. (1987). Community settings. Both are in P. Silverman (Ed.), *The elderly as modern pioneers.* Bloomington: Indiana University Press. Moderately difficult.

CHAPTER 13

Dying and Bereavement

Andrew Wyeth, *Beckie King*, 1946. Dallas Museum of Art, Gift of Everett L. DeGolyer.

THERE IS AN ANCIENT BUDDHIST STORY CALLED the Parable of the Mustard Seed. The parable tells of Kisa Gotami, a woman born in poverty who got married and, as was the custom, went to live with her husband's family. Because she was poor, his family treated her with contempt until she gave birth to a son, when she was treated with respect. Sadly, when the son was only a few years old, he died. Kisa was overcome with grief. She had liked the respect she had received since her son's birth so much that she wanted to try anything and everything to bring him back. She went from house to house, carrying her son, asking people for medicine for him. But everywhere she went people laughed at her, saying where did anyone ever find medicine for the dead. Kisa had no idea what they meant.

Now a certain wise man heard of this, and thought that Kisa must have been driven out of her mind with sorrow to set out on such a quest. He sent word to her that only the Teacher would know about medicine for her son. So, Kisa set out for a nearby monastery where the Teacher lived. When she arrived, she asked him for medicine for her son. Seeing that she was sincere, the Teacher told her to go into the city and, starting at the first house, knock on every door and in whatever house no one has ever died, fetch tiny grains of mustard seed for medicine.

Delighted at the prospect of finding medicine, she set off. Coming to the first house, she asked for the mustard seed. But when the seed was brought, Kisa realized she could not accept it because someone had died there. So she gave it back. On arriving at the second and the third and the fourth houses, Kisa encountered the same problem. Someone had died in each, and she could not accept the mustard seed. In fact, it would have been impossible to count the number of people who had died in the families she met.

Suddenly, she realized the truth. No family ever escapes the reality of death. She understood that this was what the Teacher wanted her to learn for herself. She now fully comprehended that all life is impermanent. Her grief for her son became easier to bear.

Kisa Gotami's lesson about grief is one that each of us must learn for ourselves. Death is not something we particularly like to think about, let alone face. Intellectually, we understand that all life is impermanent. Emotionally, we often try to shield ourselves from the truth, as Kisa did.

Indeed, Americans have a paradoxical relationship with death. On the one hand, we are fascinated by it. The popularity of news stories about murders or wars and the crowds of onlookers at accidents testify to that. Tourists often visit the places where famous people died or are buried. Many Americans stayed glued to their televisions watching the Gulf War in early 1991 as tens of thousands of people were killed. But when it comes to pondering our own death or that of people close to us, we have considerable problems — as La Rochefoucauld wrote over 300 years ago when he said that it is easier to look into the sun than to contemplate death. When death is personal, we become uneasy. We may not be as willing to watch CNN if it concerns our own death. It is hard indeed to look at the sun.

For most people in the United States, death is no longer a personal experience during childhood. We typically do not experience death up close as children; indeed, many Americans believe it is important to shield children from death. But just a few generations ago in America, and still in most of the world, death is part of people's everyday life experience. Children are present when family members die. Viewings and wakes are held in the home, and children are active participants in funeral services. In our technological times, perhaps we should consider what these changes in personal experience with death mean for life-span development.

In this chapter we will consider death from many perspectives. We will examine some of the issues surrounding how it is defined legally and medically. We will address several questions: Why do most of us avoid thinking about death? What it is like to die? How are dying people cared for? How do survivors grieve and cope with the loss of a loved one? Finally, we will consider two issues that transcend science: the possibility of an afterlife and the near-death experience.

DEFINITIONS AND ETHICAL ISSUES

From the dictionary's point of view, death is very simple: It is the transition between being alive and being dead. Similarly, dying is the process of making this transition. It all seems clear enough, doesn't it? But, as has been true with many other concepts in this book, death and dying are far more complicated and in fact are very hard to define.

The notions of death and dying are much like the notions of youth (or middle age or old age) and aging. We saw in Chapter 1 that it is extremely difficult to give precise definitions of these terms because age itself has many different meanings. Issues such as when middle age ends and old age begins have no easy answers. The same is true for death. What is death? When does death occur? The dictionary notwithstanding, it is very difficult in practice to give precise answers. As we will see, it depends on your perspective.

Sociocultural Definitions of Death

What comes to mind when you hear the word *death*? Black crepe paper or a cemetery? A driver killed in a traffic accident? Old people in nursing homes? A gathering of family and friends? A tran-

sition to an eternal reward? A car battery that doesn't work anymore? An unknowable mystery? Each of these possibilities represents one of the ways in which death can be considered in Western culture (Kalish, 1987). People in other cultures and traditions may view death differently. Because beliefs about death are not universal, it is important at the outset to realize that just because people around the world appear to use the same words or concepts that we do, they may not mean the same things.

For example, Westerners tend to divide people into groups based on chronological age, even though we recognize the limitations of this concept (see Chapter 1). Although we would like to divide people along more functional grounds, practicality dictates that chronological age will have to do. However, other cultures divide people differently. Among the Melanesians the term *mate* includes the very sick, the very old, and the dead; the term *toa* refers to all other living people. This distinction is the most important one, not the one between all the living and all the dead as in our culture (Counts & Counts, 1985b). Other South Pacific cultures believe that the life force may leave the body during sleep or illness, suggesting that sleep, illness, and death are considered together. In this way people "die" several times before experiencing "final death" (Counts & Counts, 1985b). For example, among the Kaliai, "the people . . . are prepared to diagnose as potentially fatal any fever or internal pain or illness that does not respond readily to treatment" (p. 150). Mourning rituals and definitions of states of bereavement also vary across cultures (Simmons, 1945). Some cultures have formalized periods of time during which certain prayers or rituals are performed. For example, Orthodox Jews recite the *Kaddish* after the death of a close relative, cover the mirrors in the house, and the men slash their ties as a symbol of loss. Family members may be prohibited from doing certain things (such as refraining from all social activities) for a specific period of time. Thus, in considering death, dying, and bereavement, we must keep in mind that the experiences of our culture may not generalize to others.

Meanings of Death. Kalish (1987) and Kastenbaum (1975) thought that death can be viewed in at least 10 ways: as an image, a statistic, an event, a state of being, an analogy, a mystery, a boundary, a thief of meaning, a basis for fear and anxiety, and a reward or punishment. These different ways of viewing death are a reflection of the diverse ways in which society deals with death. Kalish agrees with Kastenbaum's ideas: "Death means different things to the same person at different times; and it means different things to the same person at the same time" (Kalish, 1976, p. 483). Let's consider what these "different things" are.

In every culture there are *particular images or objects* that serve as reminders of death. For instance, a flag at half staff, sympathy cards, and tombstones all bring death to mind. People may try to avoid thinking about or viewing these reminders. Others may see these images and feel uneasy or may think about their own inevitable death.

Each year, numerous reports summarize death-related information: how many people died from certain diseases, traffic accidents, or murders, for example. These *mortality statistics* are vital to many organizations such as insurance companies (which use them to set premium rates for health and life insurance) and community planners (who use them to project needs for various services). But the statistics also tend to sanitize and depersonalize death by removing the personal context and presenting death as a set of numbers.

Whenever someone dies, it is an *event*. The legal community marks it with official certificates and procedures. Family and friends gather to mourn and comfort one another. Funerals or memorial services are held. Memorial funds may be established. All of these actions serve to mark a person's death and illustrate how death brings people together. The gathering is sometimes seen on a societal level;

the national mourning following the Challenger tragedy is an example.

What is it like to be dead? All answers to this question are examples of our belief in death as a *state of being*. Individual differences are the rule here, and particular beliefs are mainly a product of personal experiences and religious beliefs. Death may be thought of as a state of perpetual being, a state of nothingness, a time of waiting or of renewal, an experience that is much like this life, or an existence that involves a transformation of being. While we are alive, each of these views is equally valid; perhaps we will learn more when we make the transition ourselves.

In our language we have many sayings that use the notion of death as an *analogy* to convey the uselessness of people or objects: "That's a dead battery" or "You're a deadhead." In addition, some animals, such as opossums, use playing dead as a defense against predators. Finally, a person who is considered totally unimportant by family or acquaintances may be disowned and treated as if he or she were dead, and may even be referred to in conversations in the past tense.

Even though we know that death is inevitable, it is rarely a major topic for discussion or consideration. More important, because we have so little scientifically valid information about death, it remains an unanswered question, the ultimate *mystery* in our lives. Try as we might, death is one life event (like the moment that life begins) that is understood only when it is experienced. It is also one life event where it is impossible to do any advance work; one cannot even watch a daytime talk show to find out exactly what it is like to die and really be dead. Which, of course, is a major reason that we are typically afraid to die.

Regardless of how one views the state of death, it is seen as an end, or *boundary*, of one's earthly existence. When the end of a period of time is approaching, we tend to pay greater attention to it and to use the time remaining more effectively. For example, as students near the end of a term, they typically reprioritize the way in which they spend the remaining time (more studying and less partying in order to do well on their final exams and pass their courses). Consider how your use of time would change if you could assume 400 more years of life rather than 50 or 60. Would you continue doing what you are right now? Or would you do something different?

By the same token, as people's death becomes more imminent, how they use their remaining time becomes more important. For example, Kalish and Reynolds (1981) found that 29% of people over 60 thought about their death every day, compared with 15% under 40 and 11% between 40 and 60.

Interestingly, it also appears that people allot themselves a certain number of years to which they feel entitled. Although the exact number of years varies across the life span, most people feel that this amount of time is only fair; this view is termed the *just world view* by social psychologists (Kalish, 1987). If death becomes imminent many years before this perceived entitled length of life, the person is liable to feel cheated. If the number of expected years of life is exceeded, then death is seen to be playing by the rules; it is now all right to die.

Intellectually, we all know that we may die at any time, but in modern society the probability of death before old age is relatively low. This was not always true. In earlier centuries death occurred almost randomly across the life cycle, with many deaths among infants, young children, and women in childbirth. Aries (1974) believes that people in earlier times lived each day to the fullest because they knew firsthand that death really did occur to people of all ages.

Today, we are so convinced that we will live a long life that we let many days slip by. We delay fulfillment of dreams or ambitions until the later years, when illness or limited finances may restrict our ability to do what we had planned. In this sense death has *robbed us of the meaning of life*. We no longer take each day and use it for everything it is worth. As a result the conflicts of the later years (Erikson, 1982; see Chapter 8) involve questions of what life means, such as why we should bother learning new things since death is so close (Kalish, 1987).

Thinking about death may bring about feelings of *fear and anxiety*. Because so much research has examined this topic, we will consider it in detail later.

Many people believe that the length of life is a *reward or punishment* for how righteously or sinfully one lives. For example, the Hopi Indians believe that kindness, good thoughts, and peace of mind lead to a long life (Simmons, 1945). Similarly, a study of four ethnic communities in Los Angeles (African American, Hispanic, Japanese American, and white) found that over half of the respondents over 65 and about 30% of younger respondents agreed with the statement, "Most people who live to be 90 years old or older must have been morally good people" (Kalish & Reynolds, 1981). Finally, the Managalase, an Oceanic society, believe that simply remaining alive into old age is a sign of strength of soul, and their elderly are treated with more respect than in most societies (McKellin, 1985).

Legal and Medical Definitions

Sociocultural approaches help us understand the different ways in which people view death. But these views do not address a very fundamental question: How do we determine that someone has died? To answer this question, we must turn our attention to the medical and legal definitions of death.

Determining when death occurs has always been a judgment. Just as there is considerable debate over when life begins, so there is over when life ends. The solution typically has been for experts to propose a set of criteria, which are then adopted by society (Jeffko, 1979). For hundreds of years people accepted and applied the criteria known today as those defining **clinical death**, a

Among the Hopi, the length of life is believed to be tied to good deeds.

lack of heartbeat and respiration. Today, however, the most widely accepted criteria are those termed **brain death**:

1. No spontaneous movement in response to any stimuli

2. No spontaneous respirations for at least one hour

3. Total lack of responsiveness to even the most painful stimuli

4. No eye movements, blinking, or pupil responses

5. No postural activity, swallowing, yawning, or vocalizing

6. No motor reflexes

7. A flat electroencephalogram (EEG) for at least 10 minutes

8. No change in any of these criteria when they are tested again 24 hours later

In order for a person to be declared brain dead, all of these eight criteria must be met. Moreover, other conditions that might mimic death — such as deep coma, hypothermia, or drug overdose—must be ruled out.

It should be noted that the lack of brain activity in this definition is interpreted by most hospitals to require the complete absence of both brainstem and cortical activity. This point is important, as the famous case of Karen Ann Quinlan demonstrated. Quinlan's cortical functioning had stopped as the result of a deadly mixture of alcohol and barbiturates; however, because her brainstem was still functioning, she continued to survive on her own.

Based on this and similar cases, some professionals are beginning to argue that the criteria for death should include only cortical functioning. This approach, termed **cortical death**, would allow physicians to declare an individual who had no cortical functioning dead even when brainstem functioning continued. Under a definition of cortical death, Quinlan would have been declared legally dead years before she actually died. Proponents of a cortical death definition point out that those functions that we typically use to define humanness, such as thinking and personality, are located in the cortex. When these functions are destroyed, it is argued, the person no longer exists. Although the idea of cortical death as a definition has many adherents, it is not used as a legal definition anywhere in the United States.

Ethical Issues

An ambulance screeches to a halt. Emergency personnel quickly wheel a woman into the emergency room. She has no pulse and no respiration. Working rapidly, the trauma team reestablishes a heartbeat through electric shock. A respirator is connected. An EEG and other tests reveal extensive and irreversible brain damage, but her brainstem is not completely destroyed. What should be done?

This is an example of the kinds of problems faced in the field of *bioethics*, the study of the interface between human values and technological advances in health and life sciences. Specific issues range from whether to conduct research involving genetic engineering to whether someone should be kept alive by forced feeding or by a machine. In the arena of death and dying, the most important bioethical issue is euthanasia.

Derived from the Greek word meaning good death, **euthanasia** refers to the act or practice of ending a life for reasons of mercy. The moral dilemma posed by euthanasia becomes apparent when we try to decide the circumstances under which a person's life should be ended. In our society this dilemma occurs most often when individuals are being kept alive by machines or when someone is suffering from a terminal illness.

Euthanasia can be carried out in two very different ways. *Active euthanasia* involves the deliberate ending of someone's life. This can be done by the patient or someone else administering a drug overdose or using other means; by making it known that no extraordinary measures are to be applied to keep the person alive through, for example, a living will; or through ending a person's life without his or her permission by so-called mercy killing. For example, Dr. Jack Kevorkian, a physician in Michigan, created a "suicide machine" that in 1990 allowed Janet Adkins (who had Alzheimer's disease) and in 1991 Marjorie Wantz (who had a painful pelvic disease) to administer lethal doses of medication to themselves. In addition, Dr. Kevorkian provided expertise and equipment for multiple sclerosis victim Sherry Miller to end her life in 1991 by breathing carbon dioxide through a mask.

Cases of active euthanasia often provoke considerable public debate (Cutter, 1991), and physicians and family members who assist in suicides are sometimes prosecuted. Books such as *Final Exit* describing various types of lethal drug overdoses create controversy. In general, Western societies tend to view many forms of active euthanasia as objectionable if there is no clear evidence that the person in question wanted the action taken.

However, two ways exist to make such intentions known: living wills and durable power of attorney. The purpose of both is to make your wishes about the use of life support known in the event you are unconscious or otherwise incapable of expressing them. A durable power of attorney has an additional advantage: It names a specific person who has the legal authority to speak for you if necessary. Although there is considerable support for both (many states in the United States have laws concerning these documents), there are several problems as well. Foremost among these is that many people fail to inform their relatives about their living will, do not make their wishes known, or do not tell the person named in a durable power of attorney where the document is kept. Obviously, this puts relatives at a serious disadvantage if decisions concerning the use of life-support systems need to be made.

Some countries, such as the Netherlands, have taken a different route (Cutter, 1991). In 1984, the Dutch Supreme Court eliminated prosecution for physicians who assist in suicide if five criteria are met: (1) The patient's condition is intolerable with no hope for improvement; (2) no relief is available; (3) the patient is competent; (4) the patient makes the request repeatedly over time; and (5) two physicians agree with the patient's request. As more cases such as Karen Ann Quinlan, Janet Adkins, and Nancy Cruzan reach U.S. and other courts, societies will need to grapple with these very difficult ethical issues.

The second form of euthanasia, *passive euthanasia*, involves allowing a person to die by withholding an available treatment. For example, chemotherapy might be withheld from a cancer patient, a surgical procedure might not be performed, or food could be withdrawn. Again, these approaches are controversial. On the one hand, few would object to deciding not to treat a newly discovered cancer in a person in the late stages of Alzheimer's disease; treatment in such a case would only prolong and make even more agonizing an already certain death. On the other hand, many people would disagree with withholding nourishment

from a terminally ill person; indeed, such cases often end up in court. For example, in 1990 the U.S. Supreme Court took up the case of Nancy Cruzan, whose family wanted to end her forced feeding. The court ruled in *Cruzan v. Director, Missouri Department of Health* that unless clear and incontrovertible evidence is presented that an individual desires to have nourishment stopped (such as through a durable power of attorney or living will), a third party (such as a parent or spouse) may not decide to end it.

Most people find it difficult to decide how they feel about euthanasia. They opt for making case-by-case decisions that could vary with the circumstances. Physicians report that they would usually agree with passive euthanasia but only if authorized by the family. Active euthanasia is not generally supported, usually out of fear that it might be used against people who are not terminally ill or who are defenseless against such movements such as the cognitively impaired (Kieffer, 1979). The belief that one person should not kill another is deeply rooted in our society; for that reason euthanasia will be a much-debated topic for many years to come. Something to Think About explores some of the topics likely to be controversial.

The Price of Extraordinary Care

A growing debate in Western society concerns the financial, personal, and moral costs of keeping people alive on life-support machines. For example, many people argue that keeping older adults on life support makes little sense. They argue that such treatment is extremely expensive, that these individuals will soon die anyway, and if they do not they will be a burden on society. In these cases, it is argued, society would be better off simply allowing the person to die.

In contrast, many people — including many physicians — go to extraordinary lengths to keep very premature infants alive, despite high risks of

SOMETHING TO THINK ABOUT

Bioethics, Euthanasia, and Controversy

There is no universally accepted definition of death that is free from problems. In fact, each time the legal or medical definition of death is changed, a host of ethical issues must be confronted. Although most people in the United States now accept the brain death definition, when this criterion was being implemented it caused several problems. Perhaps the most troublesome issue was the introduction of life-support technology, both to prolong life and to keep organs available for transplant surgery. Under the prevailing definition of death at the time — clinical death — the act of turning off a

life-support system was considered murder, since death was defined solely as the lack of pulse and respiration. Since these bodily functions were present, even though artificially so, stopping them fell under the rubric of homicide in the criminal codes. Due to court decisions in cases like Karen Ann Quinlan's, the issue was resolved, and a different criterion of death was implemented.

Moving from a brain death criterion to a cortical death criterion would create new problems for bioethicists. Because this criterion requires only that activity cease in the cerebral cortex, the brainstem may still be intact and functional. In this case the patient might even have spontaneous pulse and respiration but would be considered dead. At this point some type of intervention would be needed to stop the brain-

stem functions. Would this be euthanasia? Under a cortical death criterion, no; the patient is already dead. But under a brain death criterion, such intervention would be active euthanasia and might even be viewed as murder. And under a clinical death criterion the patient would still be considered alive! Thus, the issues confronting physicians would be similar to those encountered during the shift from a clinical death criterion to a brain death criterion.

Whether American society will ever adopt a cortical death criterion remains to be seen. What is clear is that bioethicists must make the dilemmas clear, and we must make ourselves aware of the issues. What is at stake is literally a matter of life and death. It's something to think about.

---

permanent brain damage or physical disability. Some people point out that not only is the infant medical care often very expensive (an average of $2,000 per day for neonatal intensive care), but the potential cost to families and society if the person should need constant care could be enormous. Additionally, the emotional costs can be devastating to many families.

There are no easy solutions to these dilemmas. At present, there is no way to predict which premature infant will develop normally or which seriously ill older person will recover. But as the tensions among high-tech medicine, spiraling health

care costs, and people's ability to afford to pay continue to escalate, confronting these issues will become increasingly more common.

THINKING ABOUT DEATH: PERSONAL COMPONENTS

Being afraid to die is considered normal by most people. As one research participant put it, "You are *nuts* if you aren't afraid of death" (Kalish &

Reynolds, 1976). Still, most authors agree that death is a paradox (Schulz, 1978). That is, we are afraid of or anxious about death, but it is this same fear or anxiety that directly or indirectly causes much of our behavior. We will examine this paradox in the following sections. Specifically, we will focus on two questions: What is it about death that we fear or that makes us anxious? How do we show our fear or anxiety?

Death Anxiety

Death anxiety is difficult to pin down. Indeed, it is the ethereal nature of death, rather than something about it in particular, that usually makes us feel so uncomfortable. We cannot put our finger on something specific about death that is causing us to feel uneasy. Because of this, we must look for indirect behavioral evidence to document death anxiety. Techniques have varied considerably: projective personality tests, such as the Rorschach Inkblots; paper-and-pencil tests, such as Templer's Death Anxiety Scale; and measures of physiological arousal, such as galvanic skin response. Research findings suggest that death anxiety is a complex, multidimensional construct.

On the basis of several diverse studies using many different measures, it appears that death anxiety consists of several components. Each of these components is most easily described with terms that resemble examples of fear but cannot be tied to anything specific. Schulz (1978) concluded that the components of death anxiety included pain, body malfunction, humiliation, rejection, nonbeing, punishment, interruption of goals, and negative impact on survivors. To complicate matters further, it is possible to assess any of these components at any of three levels: public, private, and nonconscious. That is, what we admit feeling about death in public may differ considerably from what we feel when we are alone with our own thoughts.

In short, the measurement of death anxiety is complex, and researchers need to specify which aspect(s) they are assessing.

Considerable research has been conducted to learn what demographic and personality variables are related to death anxiety. Although the results are often ambiguous, some patterns have emerged.

Gender differences in death anxiety have been found inconsistently. Some researchers find that women score higher than men on questionnaire measures of death anxiety (e.g., Iammarino, 1975; Templer, Ruff, & Franks, 1971), but others do not (Dickstein, 1972; Nehrke, Bellucci, & Gabriel, 1977). When differences are observed, women tend to view death in more emotional terms, whereas men tend to view it in more cognitive terms (Degner, 1974; Krieger, Epsting, & Leitner, 1974; Wittkowski, 1981). Keith (1979) offers perhaps the best way of understanding the controversy. Keith's questionnaire combines items that measure death anxiety, perceptions of life after death, and general acceptance. Women apparently find the prospect of their own death more anxiety producing than men do, but they simultaneously have a greater acceptance of their own death. Acceptance and anxiety had always been thought to be antithetical, but they may not be (Kalish, 1985).

Several studies have demonstrated a complex relationship between death anxiety and religiosity, defined as being a churchgoing, denomination-affiliated person or as adhering to a traditional belief system (Feifel & Nagy, 1981; Templer, 1972). Although studies have documented the link between belief in an afterlife and degree of religiosity, the relationship between belief in an afterlife and death anxiety independent of religiosity needs further exploration (Kalish, 1985).

Few investigators have examined death anxiety in relation to ethnicity. Myers, Wass, and Murphey (1980) found that elderly African-American respondents in the American South expressed higher death anxiety than their white counterparts.

Bengtson, Cuellar, and Raga (1977) observed declines in death anxiety with age among three ethnic communities (African Americans, Mexican Americans, and whites) but did not find differences across the ethnic groups. Bengtson and colleagues (1977) also found that elderly African Americans were much more likely to expect a long life than either Mexican Americans or whites, confirming results obtained earlier by Reynolds and Kalish (1974).

Although the elderly think more about death than any other age group, they are less fearful and more accepting of it (Bengtson et al., 1977; Kalish & Reynolds, 1981; Keller, Sherry, & Piotrowski, 1984). Several reasons have been offered for this consistent finding (Kalish, 1987): Older adults have more chronic diseases, and they realistically know that these health problems are unlikely to improve over time; the probabilities are high that many members of their family and friendship network have died already; the most important tasks of life have been completed; and they have thought a great deal about their death. Kalish (1987) also suggests that a major reason for reduced death anxiety in later life is that the value and satisfaction of living are not as great.

Death anxiety may also be related to the occupation one has, the experiences one has had with the death of others, and how one views aging. Vickio and Cavanaugh (1985) found that among nursing home employees, those who had positive outlooks on older adults and on their own aging tended to have lower death anxiety. They also found that level of death anxiety was related to job; cooks and housekeepers tended to have higher anxiety than nurses and social service workers. The level of death anxiety was unrelated to the number of deaths among friends or relatives of the employee, but it was inversely related to the number of deaths among residents known by the employee.

Strange as it may seem, death anxiety may have a beneficial side. For one thing being afraid to die means that we often go to great lengths to make sure we stay alive. Because staying alive helps to ensure the continuation and socialization of the species, fear of death may serve as a motivation to have children and raise them properly.

Clearly, death anxiety is complex. We are uncertain on many of its aspects. Yet, we can see death anxiety and fear in action all the time in the many behaviors that we show.

How Do We Show Death Anxiety?

When we are afraid or anxious, our behavior changes in some way. One of the most common ways in which this occurs in relation to death is through avoidance (Kastenbaum, 1975). Avoiding situations that remind us of death occurs at both the unconscious and conscious levels. People who refuse to go to funerals because they find them depressing or who will not visit dying friends or relatives may be consciously avoiding death. Unconscious avoidance may take the form of being too busy to help out a dying person. Society provides several safeguards to help us avoid the reality of death, from isolating dying people in institutions to providing euphemisms for referring to death, such as saying that a person has "passed away."

A second way of showing fear or anxiety is the opposite of the first; rather than avoiding death, we challenge it (Kalish, 1984). In this case people deliberately and repeatedly put themselves in dangerous, life-threatening situations such as skydiving, auto racing, rock climbing, war, and so forth. These people have not been studied sufficiently to know whether they feel a need to assert their superiority over death. But interestingly enough, a study of pedestrian behavior at a busy intersection in Detroit revealed that people who took chances in crossing the street (for example, not looking before crossing, walking against the light, and jay-walking) were more likely to have thought about suicide and expected to live a significantly shorter time than more cautious pedestrians (Kastenbaum & Briscoe, 1975).

There are numerous other ways of exhibiting death anxiety. Some of the more common include changing life styles, dreams and fantasies, using humor, displacing fear or anxiety onto something else such as work, and becoming a professional who deals with death (Kalish, 1984). Such behaviors are indicative of large individual variations in how we handle our feelings about death. Still, each of us must come to grips with death and learn how to deal with it on our own terms.

Learning to Deal with Death Anxiety

Although some degree of death anxiety may be appropriate, we must guard against letting it become so powerful that it interferes with our normal daily routines. Several ways exist to help us in this endeavor. Perhaps the one most often used is to live life to the fullest. Kalish (1984, 1987) argues that people who do this enjoy what they have; although they may still fear death and feel cheated, they have few regrets. In a sense they "realize that [they] might die any moment, and yet live as though [they] were never going to die" (Lepp, 1968, p. 77).

Koestenbaum (1976) proposes several exercises and questions to increase one's death awareness. Some of these are to write your own obituary and plan your own death and funeral services. You can also ask yourself: "What circumstances would help make my death acceptable?" "Is death the sort of thing that could happen to me right now?"

These questions serve as a basis for an increasingly popular way to reduce anxiety: death education. Most death education programs combine factual information about death with issues aimed at reducing anxiety and fear in order to increase sensitivity to others' feelings. These programs vary widely in orientation, since they can include such topics as philosophy, ethics, psychology, drama, re-

ligion, medicine, art, and many others. Additionally, they can focus on death, the process of dying, grief and bereavement, or any combination of them. In general, death education programs appear to help primarily by increasing our awareness of the complex emotions that are felt and expressed by dying individuals and their families.

THINKING ABOUT DEATH: THEORIES OF DYING

What is it like to die? How do terminally ill people feel about dying? Are people more concerned about dying as they grow older? To answer these questions, a few scholars have developed theories of dying that are based on interviews and other methods. The point of these theories is to show that dying is a complex process and that our thoughts, concerns, and feelings change as we move closer to death. We will examine two ways of conceptualizing the dying process: a stage approach and a phase approach. We will also consider how the thoughts and feelings of dying people vary as a function of age.

The Stage Theory of Dying

Elisabeth Kübler-Ross became interested in the experience of dying as an instructor in psychiatry at the University of Chicago in the early 1960s. Over 200 interviews with terminally ill people convinced her that most people followed a sequence of emotional reactions. Using her experiences, she developed a sequence of five stages that described the process of an appropriate death: denial, anger, bargaining, depression, and acceptance (Kübler-Ross, 1969).

When people are told that they have a terminal illness, their first reaction is likely to be shock and disbelief. *Denial* is a normal part of getting ready to die. Some want to shop around for a more favorable diagnosis, and most feel that a mistake has been made. Others try to find reassurance in religion. Eventually, though, most people accept the diagnosis and begin to feel angry.

In the *anger* stage, people express hostility, resentment, and envy toward health care workers, family, and friends. Individuals ask, "Why me?" and express a great deal of frustration. The fact that they are going to die when so many others will live seems unfair. As these feelings begin to be dealt with and to diminish, the person may begin to bargain.

In the *bargaining* stage people look for a way out. Maybe a deal can be struck with someone, perhaps God, that would allow survival. For example, a woman might promise to be a better mother if only she could live. Eventually, the individual becomes aware that these deals will not work.

When one can no longer deny the illness, perhaps due to surgery or pain, feelings of *depression* are very common. People report feeling deep loss, sorrow, guilt, and shame over their illness and its consequences. Kübler-Ross believes that allowing people to discuss their feelings with others helps move them to an acceptance of death.

In the *acceptance* stage the person accepts the inevitability of death and often seems detached from the world and at complete peace. "It is as if the pain is gone, the struggle is over, and there comes a time for the 'final rest before the journey' as one patient phrased it" (Kübler-Ross, 1969, p. 100).

Although she believes that these five stages represent the typical course of emotional development in the dying, Kübler-Ross (1974) cautions that not everyone goes through all of them or progresses through them at the same rate or in the same order. In fact, we could actually harm dying individuals by considering these stages as fixed and universal. Individual differences are great, as Kübler-Ross points out. Emotional responses may vary in inten-

sity throughout the dying process. Thus, the goal in applying Kübler-Ross's theory to real-world settings would be to help people achieve an appropriate death. An appropriate death is one that meets the needs of the dying person, allowing him or her to work out each problem as it comes.

The Phase Theory of Dying

Instead of offering a series of stages, some writers view dying as a process with three phases: an acute phase, a chronic living-dying phase, and a terminal phase (Pattison, 1977a; Weisman, 1972). These phases are represented in Figure 13.1.

The acute phase begins when the individual becomes aware that his or her condition is terminal. This phase is marked by a high level of anxiety, denial, anger, and even bargaining. In time, the person adjusts to the idea of being terminally ill, and anxiety gradually declines. During this chronic living-dying phase, a person generally has many contradictory feelings that must be integrated. These include fear of loneliness, fear of the unknown, and anticipatory grief over the loss of friends, of body, of self-control, and of identity (Pattison, 1977b). These feelings of fear and grief exist simultaneously or alternate with feelings of hope, determination, and acceptance (Shneidman, 1973). Finally, the terminal phase begins when the individual begins withdrawing from the world. This last phase is the shortest, and it ends with death.

The notion of a **dying trajectory** was introduced to describe these three phases more clearly. A dying trajectory describes the length and the form of one's dying process. Four dying trajectories have been suggested, differing mainly in whether death is certain or uncertain (Glaser & Strauss, 1965, 1968; Strauss & Glaser, 1970):

1. Certain death is expected at a known time, such as when a woman is told that she has six months to live.

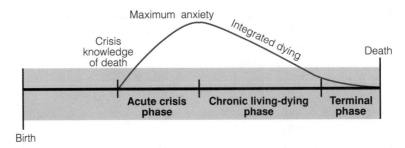

FIGURE 13.1 The phase theory of dying

2. Certain death is expected but at an unknown time, such as when the woman is told that she has between six months and five years to live.

3. It is uncertain whether the woman will die, but the answer will be clear in a known period of time; for example, exploratory surgery will resolve the issue.

4. It is uncertain whether the woman will die, and there is no known time when the question will be answered; for example, she has a heart problem that may or may not be fatal and could cause problems at some point in the future.

The last two trajectories are thought to produce the most anxiety due to their higher degrees of ambiguity and uncertainty. The acute phase is lengthened, and the overall trajectory is more difficult. It seems that knowing whether one is going to die plays an important role in the ability to deal with the problem and the degree of overall adjustment.

Although stages and phases of dying have not been researched very thoroughly, it seems that how people deal with their own death is a complicated process. Denial and acceptance can take many forms and may even occur simultaneously. People take a last vacation and update their will at the same time. It is becoming increasingly clear that it is not the task of health care workers or mental health workers to force someone to die in a particular way. There is no such thing as one right way to die. The

best we can do is to make sure that we stay in touch with the dying person's (and our own) feelings and are available for support. In this way we may avoid contributing to what could be considered a wrong way to die: being abandoned and left to die alone.

An Adult Developmental Perspective on Dying

Dying is not something that happens only to one age group. Most of us tend not to think about it, because we associate dying with old age. But babies die of sudden infant death syndrome, children die in accidents, and adolescents and young adults die from cancer. Death knows no age limits. Yet one person's death often seems more acceptable than another's (Kastenbaum, 1985). The death of a 95-year-old woman is considered natural; she had lived a long, full life. But the death of an infant is considered to be a tragedy. Whether or not such feelings are justified, they point to the fact that death is experienced differently depending on age: Treatment differs, and responses to others' losses differ. In this section we will briefly examine the personal side of how the age of a dying person (young adults and older adults) changes how death is viewed.

The old die mainly from chronic diseases, such as heart disease and cancer; young adults die mainly from accidents (Kalish, 1987). The diseases of older adults typically incapacitate before they kill, resulting in a dying trajectory of slow decline and eventual death. Because older adults and younger adults die in different ways, their dying processes differ (Kalish, 1985):

1. Financial costs for the elderly are higher due to the need for long-term care.

2. The elderly's need for health and human care is greater.

3. The elderly have more potential for leading a normal life during the early part of the dying process.

4. The elderly have a longer period to contemplate and plan for their death.

5. The elderly have more opportunity to see old friends or visit important places.

6. The elderly are more likely to die in institutions and are more likely to be confused or comatose immediately before their death.

7. More elderly women die without a spouse or sibling to participate in care, making them more dependent on adult children.

In short, the elderly take longer to die and are more likely to die in isolation than any other age group.

Many of the concerns of dying individuals seem to be specific to how old they are (Kalish, 1987). The most obvious difference comes in the extent to which people feel cheated. Younger adults are more likely to feel deprived of the opportunity to experience a full life than are middle-agers or older adults. Younger adults feel that they are losing what they might attain; older adults feel that they are losing what they have. Beyond these general differences, however, not much is known about how adults of various ages differ in how they face death. Most of the literature focuses on older adults. Clearly, we badly need more information about what it is like to be young or middle-aged and to be dying.

One important factor that affects dying older adults is that their deaths are viewed by the community as less tragic than the deaths of younger people (Kalish & Reynolds, 1976; Kastenbaum, 1985). Consequently, older adults receive less intense life-saving treatment and are perceived as less valuable and not as worthy of a large investment of time, money, or energy: "The terminally aged may be as helpless as a child, but they seldom arouse tenderness" (Weisman, 1972, p. 144). Many dying older adults reside in long-term care facilities where contacts with family and friends are fewer. Kalish (1987) writes that the elderly, especially the ill and those with diminished functional competence, offer less to their communities. Consequently, when their death occurs the emotional pain is not as great because the resulting losses are viewed as less significant and meaningful.

WHERE WILL WE DIE?

Where do most of us want to die? Surveys indicate that most older people would rather die at home but that this wish is not as important to middle-aged people (Kalish & Reynolds, 1976). Family members who had cared for relatives who died at home usually feel glad that it happened that way, even though about one third wonder whether home care was the right decision (Cartwright, Hockey, & Anderson, 1973).

Despite the expressed wishes of most people, the vast majority of us will not die at home among family and friends. Rather, approximately 75% of deaths occur in institutions such as hospitals and nursing homes (Lerner, 1970; Marshall, 1980). This increasing institutionalization of death has two major consequences (Schulz, 1978). First, health care professionals are playing a more important role in dying people's lives. This means that the medical staff is being forced to provide emotional support in situations largely antithetical to their main mission of healing and curing. This dilemma presents health care workers with problems that we will consider later.

A second important result of the institutionalization of death is that dying is being removed from our everyday experience. Not long ago, each of us would have known what it was like to interact with a dying person and to be present when someone died. Institutions isolate us from death, and some argue that the institutions are largely to blame for our increasing avoidance of death and dying people. Unfortunately, we cannot evaluate this opinion because we cannot randomly have some people die at home and have others die in hospitals in order to compare the effects of each in an experiment.

Dying in a Hospital Versus Dying at Home

As indicated earlier, the trend during the 20th century has been away from dying at home. What implications does this trend have? Certainly, some people still die at home either because their deaths occur unexpectedly or because they have chosen to remain at home. Yet even in these cases some people are still taken to a hospital where the official declaration is made (Marshall, 1980). In a technical sense, then, most people die at a hospital or other health care facility.

Perhaps the best explanation for this change relates to advances in health care itself. As health care became more effective, efficient, and technologically advanced, people needed to take advantage of hospital facilities in order to make certain that everything possible had been done. Even when a person's illness is terminal, there is a good chance that a lengthy hospital stay will result. Hospitals offer another major advantage compared to home: continuous care. Caring for a dying person is often time-consuming and draining and may require special medical expertise. Hospitals are typically better equipped to handle these demands.

All is not on the hospital's side, however. Autonomy and personal relationships usually suffer when

people are in a hospital (Kalish, 1984). People remaining at home have less difficulty on these dimensions; rigid visitation hours are the exception at home.

What, then, determines where we will die? Kalish (1984) offers six factors: physical condition, availability of care, finances, competence of institutions, age, and personal preference. Clearly, the particular health problem that a person has may dictate the context for dying. If it demands intensive or sophisticated medical treatment or if the degree of incapacitation is great, a medical facility is likely to be chosen.

Kalish notes that the availability of caregivers outside the health care institution plays a very important role. If an individual has several people who can care for him or her at home, an institution is a less likely choice. Overall, then, the best predictor of nursing home admission is the degree of social support available (George & Gwyther, 1986). However, caregivers must be more than just available; they must be willing to make the necessary sacrifices as well.

Finally, personal preference plays a role. Some people prefer to be at home in familiar surroundings with their family and friends when they die. Others, who fear that they will burden their loved ones or that emergency medical assistance will be unavailable, choose a hospital or nursing home. Kalish (1985) writes that dying at home is most appropriate when the person is reasonably alert and capable of interaction with others, when his or her health condition is beyond treatment, when dying at home would provide something meaningful to the person, and when death is imminent.

The Hospice Alternative

As we have seen, most people would like to die at home among family and friends. An important barrier to this choice is the availability of support systems when the individual has a terminal disease. In this case most people believe that they have no choice but to go to a hospital or nursing home. However, another alternative exists: a **hospice** (Koff, 1981). The emphasis in a hospice is on the quality of life. This approach grows out of an important distinction between the prolongation of life and the prolongation of death. In a hospice the concern is to make the person as peaceful and comfortable as possible, not to delay an inevitable death. Although medical care is available at a hospice, it is aimed primarily at controlling pain and restoring normal functioning. This orientation places hospices between hospitals and homes in terms of contexts for dying.

Modern hospices are modeled after St. Christopher's Hospice in England, founded in 1967 by Dr. Cicely Saunders. The services offered by a hospice are requested only after the person or physician believes that no treatment or cure is possible, making the hospice program markedly different from hospital or home care. The differences are evident in the principles that underlie hospice care: Clients and their families are viewed as a unit; clients should be kept free of pain; emotional and social impoverishment must be minimal; clients must be encouraged to maintain competencies; conflict resolution and fulfillment of realistic desires must be assisted; clients must be free to begin or end relationships; and staff members must seek to alleviate pain and fear (Saunders, 1977).

Two types of hospices exist: inpatient and outpatient. Inpatient hospices provide all care for clients; outpatient hospices provide services to clients who remain in their own homes. This latter variation is becoming increasingly popular, largely because more clients can be served at a lower cost.

Hospices do not follow a hospital model of care. The role of the staff in a hospice is not so much to do *for* the client as it is just to be *with* the client. A client's dignity is always maintained; often more attention is paid to appearance and personal grooming than to medical tests. Hospice staff members also provide a great deal of support to the

Hospices emphasize the importance of maintaining dignity and involving family members throughout the dying process.

client's family. At inpatient hospices visiting hours are unrestricted, and families are strongly encouraged to take part in the client's care (VandenBos, DeLeon, & Pallack, 1982).

Researchers have documented important differences between inpatient hospices and hospitals (Hinton, 1967; Parkes, 1975; VandenBos et al., 1982). Hospice clients were more mobile, less anxious, and less depressed; spouses visited hospice clients more often and participated more in their care; and hospice staff members were perceived as more accessible. In addition, E. K. Walsh and

Cavanaugh (1984) showed that most hospice clients who had been in hospitals before coming to a hospice strongly preferred the care at the hospice.

Although the hospice is a valuable alternative for many people, it may not be appropriate for everyone. Some disorders require treatment or equipment not available at inpatient hospices, and some people may find that a hospice does not meet their needs or fit with their personal beliefs. Walsh and Cavanaugh found that the perceived needs of hospice clients, their families, and the staff did not always coincide. In particular, the staff and family members emphasized pain management, whereas many of the clients wanted more attention paid to personal issues. The important point from this study is that the staff and family members may need to ask clients what they need more often, rather than making assumptions about what they need.

Although a hospice offers an important alternative to a hospital or other institution as a place to die, it is not always available. For example, older adults who are slowly dying but whose time of death is uncertain may not be eligible. Meeting the needs of these individuals will be a challenge for future health care providers.

CARING AND HELPING RELATIONSHIPS

The growing awareness that death is a developmental process and the fact that death no longer occurs as frequently at home have led to a substantial increase in the number of people who work with the dying. The contexts may vary (hospitals, hospices, nursing homes), but the skills that are required and the kinds of relationships that develop are similar. With this in mind, we will focus on the helping done by health care and mental health workers. As a prelude to this discussion, let us consider what it is like to work with the dying and the basic needs that must be met.

Working with Dying People

Most people think that it must be hard to work with individuals who are dying. They serve as reminders that we too will die someday. As indicated earlier, this is a scary proposition. The realization that we will die makes us question the value of things, since dying people are proof that we cannot control all aspects of our lives. Few of us really control when or how we die. Many dying people experience pain or are unpleasant to look at or be near, and all have a limited future. Most of us do not like to be reminded of these things. Finally, dying involves loss, and most of us do not seek out relationships with people when we know they are going to end painfully.

Despite these issues, many people work with the dying and have extremely positive experiences. Most of these individuals chose their occupation because of their interests. Yet they still experience stress and psychologically withdraw from their work. Although common, this withdrawal is not an inevitable part of working with people who are dying. As presented in the following sections, information about dying people and their needs may alleviate the need to pull away.

Needs of Dying People

There is consensus that dying people have three especially important needs: the need to control pain, the need to retain dignity and self-worth, and the need for love and affection (Schulz, 1978). The mission of the people who work with the dying is meeting these needs.

When a terminal disease is painful, an important need is pain management. Several approaches are available, such as surgery, drugs, hypnosis, and biofeedback. Particularly in the case of chemotherapy for cancer, the management of pain can sometimes become the major focus of intervention. In such cases it is especially important to consider additional issues such as compliance with the treatment.

The need for dignity and self-worth is extremely important. Recall that this was one of the needs stated most often by hospice clients in the Walsh and Cavanaugh (1984) study. Dignity can be enhanced by involving the dying person in all decisions that affect him or her, including control over the end of life. Loss of a sense of control can create serious psychological stress, which can have physical implications as well.

Showing love and affection to the dying can help reduce the fear of abandonment that many of us have. Love and affection can be communicated by touching or other physical contact, but it can also be shown by simply being present and listening, supporting, and reassuring the person that he or she is not alone.

How are these needs met? In addition to the family, health care and mental health workers share the responsibility. Let us consider how well they treat dying people.

Helping the Dying: Health Care Workers

How do health care workers deal with dying people? Do they confront the issues? What do they tell dying people about their condition? How do their clients feel about it? These are some of the questions that will concern us in this section. Although there is little research on these important topics, we can get some feel for the ways in which health care professionals handle death and dying.

Attitudes and Behaviors. Because the medical profession is oriented toward helping people and saving lives, death could be seen as a failure. Several researchers have shown that this was the perspective taken by many physicians and nurses in the past (Glaser & Strauss, 1965; Kastenbaum & Aisenberg, 1976; Pearlman, Stotsky, & Dominick, 1969). Most of this research documented that medical personnel in hospitals tended to avoid patients once it was known that they were dying. Indeed, one study found that nurses were slower to respond to the call lights of terminally ill patients than to those of other patients (Le Shan, in Kastenbaum & Aisenberg, 1976). Furthermore, when dying patients confront doctors or nurses with statements about death, such as "I think I'm going to die soon," the most common responses are fatalism ("We all die sometime"), denial ("You don't really mean that"), and changing the subject. These responses represent ways of not dealing with death.

How comfortable health care workers are in discussing death with dying people seems to be related to the amount of experience they have had with death, although the nature of the relationship is unclear. For example, some studies find that nurses' uneasiness increases with experience (Pearlman et al., 1969), while others find that experience makes it easier (Vickio & Cavanaugh, 1985). These discrepancies may stem from using interviews as opposed to questionnaires or from the general trend toward being open, honest, and supportive with people who want to talk about death. Indeed, there have been many calls in the medical literature for better communication with dying people (Kalish, 1985).

Changes in attitudes and behavior toward the dying may well reflect the spirit of the times (Kalish, 1987). During the 1980s there was a movement away from viewing science and technology as producing the ultimate in health care. Instead, the emphasis was increasingly on the relationship between health care workers and the dying person. At the same time the basic rights of the dying were being demanded, including the right to die with dignity. These changes at the societal level are probably the most important reasons for the shift in attitudes and behaviors over the past few decades.

Informing the Client. Should a patient be told that he or she is going to die? In the past this was only rarely done; most patients remained uninformed. The reasoning seemed to be that admitting the truth might accelerate the patient's decline, although it is also likely that it was done to protect the health care workers from facing death. This policy was typically followed regardless of the patient's wishes. For example, one comprehensive survey revealed that even though 75% to 90% of terminally ill patients indicated that they wanted to be told if they were dying, 70% to 90% of the physicians withheld that information (Feifel, 1965).

The majority practice today among medical personnel is to tell the patient the truth. Still, deciding whether to confront a person with the news that he or she is dying is a complex decision. For instance, sometimes it is not known for certain whether a person will live or die. Full disclosure often depends on the physical and mental health of the patient. However, most investigators believe that the physician or nurse can help the client achieve a good death by being honest, by letting clients take the initiative in requesting information, and by being available for support (Hinton, 1967).

Most terminally ill people understand that there is something seriously wrong with them even before they are officially informed. With this growing awareness comes the additional recognition that others know as well. If others are unwilling to talk about it, patients may engage in a *mutual pretense* with family, friends, and professionals. In mutual pretense everyone knows that death is coming soon, but everyone acts as if nothing serious is the matter. Mutual pretense is difficult to carry out over a long period, however, because it is likely that someone will break the rules and talk about the disease. Providing a supportive context in which the impending death can be discussed avoids the problem altogether.

When death occurs in a health care setting, it is often hidden from public view. In some cases extreme measures are taken, such as disguising bodies or hiding them in order to protect other patients. Such actions are interpreted by some as additional examples of health care workers' denial of death. Although the therapeutic value of protecting other patients has never been demonstrated, these practices continue in some places.

Helping the Dying: Mental Health Workers

Not all of the concerns of dying people involve their medical problems. Caring for the dying also entails meeting the psychological needs described by Kübler-Ross and others. We can separate the work done by mental health workers into two types: psychotherapy and paraprofessional counseling.

Psychotherapy. Dying people seek psychotherapy for many reasons. Sometimes, confronting our fears and anxieties is too difficult to handle on our own, and some professional help is needed. Concerns about work, conflicts with family, and financial matters may interfere with the ability to resolve the difficult psychological issues.

Conducting psychotherapy with the dying is often difficult. Use of the traditional hour-long session may be stressful if the client cannot sit that long or inconvenient if medical treatment needs to be continuous. Moreover, many psychotherapists have the same problems in dealing with death as medical personnel. When the therapist is forced to confront his or her own death anxiety and fear, it may hinder the psychotherapeutic process. And since many therapists use a medical model of pathology, dying people may not fit with their particular viewpoint. Most psychotherapists tend to focus on current problems and functioning rather than probing the distant past. Perhaps the best idea is to use the therapy to foster personal growth (Le Shan, 1969).

Paraprofessional Counseling. Working through anxieties and fears when one is dying does not always require a psychotherapist. In fact, most of the time it is accomplished by talking to relatives, friends, clergy, social workers, and medical personnel. The issues that are discussed are for the most part the same as those discussed with psychotherapists, and the feelings that are expressed are just as intense. Many people believe that having friends and family who are willing to listen and provide support is a key factor in resolving problems, although there is little research dealing with dying people.

SURVIVORS: THE GRIEVING PROCESS

Each of us suffers many losses over a lifetime. Whenever we lose someone close to us through death or other separation, we experience both grief and mourning. *Grief* refers to the sorrow, hurt, anger, guilt, confusion, and other feelings that arise after suffering a loss. *Mourning* concerns the ways in which we express our grief. These expressions are highly influenced by culture; for some mourning may involve wearing black, attending funerals, and observing an official period of grief, while for others it means drinking, wearing white, and marrying the deceased spouse's sibling. Thus, grief corresponds to the emotional reactions following loss, while mourning refers to the culturally approved behavioral manifestations of our feelings.

In this section we will examine how people deal with loss. Since the grieving process is affected by the circumstances surrounding the death, we must first differentiate between expected and unexpected loss. Next, because grief can be expressed in many ways, the differences between normal and abnormal reactions will be explored. Finally, how well we cope with the death of a loved one is related to the kind of relationship that existed. Thus, we will compare grieving following different kinds of loss.

Expected Versus Unexpected Death

For many years it has been believed that the intensity and course of grief depend on whether the death was expected or occurred suddenly and unexpectedly (Shand, 1920). Fulton (1970) labeled the two situations as "high-grief death" and "low-grief death." A high-grief death is one that is unexpected: for example, an accidental death. Low-grief deaths are expected: an example would be the death of a spouse following a long illness. According to Fulton, the main difference is not that people in one situation necessarily grieve more (or less) than those in another situation. Rather, when death is anticipated, people go through a period of anticipatory grief before the death that serves to buffer the impact of the loss when it comes.

Research on grief following expected versus unexpected deaths supports Fulton's basic point. The opportunity for anticipatory grieving has been shown to result in a lower likelihood of psychological problems one year after the death of a spouse (Ball, 1976–1977; Parkes, 1975), greater acceptance by parents following the death of a child (Binger et al., 1969), and more rapid recovery of effective functioning and subsequent happiness (Glick et al., 1974). However, anticipating the death of someone close does produce considerable stress in itself (Norris & Murrell, 1987).

However, that does not mean that people who experience the anticipated death of a loved one do not grieve. Indeed, Hill, Thompson, and Gallagher

The grief expressed by the Japanese following the death of Hirohito exemplifies the point that grief is experienced even though death may be anticipated.

(1988) found that the intensity of feelings per se do not differentiate widows whose husbands had been ill for at least one month prior to their deaths from widows whose husbands died unexpectedly.

The reasons why anticipated deaths result in quicker recovery are not yet fully understood. We know that the long-term effects of stressful events, in general, are less problematic if they are expected, so that the same principles probably hold for death. Perhaps it is the opportunity to rehearse what it would be like without the dying person and the chance to make appropriate arrangements that helps. In practicing, we may realize that we need support, may feel lonely and scared, and may take steps to get ourselves ready. Moreover, if we recognize that we are likely to have certain feelings, they may be easier to understand and deal with when they come.

Another difference between expected and unexpected deaths is that an anticipated death is often less mysterious. Most of the time we know why the person died. A sudden death from an accident is not as easy to comprehend, as there does not seem to be a good explanation for it. There is no disease to blame, and survivors may fear that it could just as easily happen to them. Knowing the real reason why someone dies makes adjustment easier.

Stages of Grief

How do people grieve? What do they experience? The process of grieving is a complicated and personal one. Just as there is no right way to die, there is no right way to grieve. Recognizing that there are plenty of individual differences, we will consider these patterns in this section.

Writers have found it convenient to describe the grieving process as consisting of several phases. Like the stages and phases of dying, the phases of grieving are not clearly demarcated, nor does one pass from one to another cleanly. The goal of this approach is simply to describe the major steps of recovery following a death. The phases reflect the fact that when someone close to us dies, we must reorganize our lives, establish new patterns of behavior, and redefine relationships with family and friends. Although there is an implied sequence to the phases, we must keep in mind that some people reexperience them over time and that progress through them is not always even or predictable.

The grieving process can be divided into three main phases: initial phase, intermediate phase, and recovery phase (Averill, 1968; Parkes, 1972; Pincus, 1976). Each phase has certain characteristics, and particular issues are more important at some points than others.

When the death occurs, and usually for a few weeks afterward, the survivor's reaction is shock, disbelief, and numbness. People often report feeling empty, cold, and confused, which serves to protect them from the pain of bereavement. The shock and disbelief typically continue for several days following the death and then give way to several weeks of sorrow and sadness, which are expressed mainly through crying.

Over time, one is expected to begin recovering from these feelings. As a result of this pressure survivors may suppress emotions. Unfortunately, suppression of feelings is often interpreted as a sign of recovery, which it certainly is not. Along with learning how to deal with sorrow, survivors must handle feelings of not being able to go on with life. Fortunately, most people eventually realize that these anxieties are not well founded and that they are actually hindering their own recovery.

Several weeks after the death, people begin to realize what life without the deceased person

means. Researchers point to three behavior patterns that characterize this second, or intermediate, phase. First, the bereaved person thinks about the death a great deal; feelings of guilt or responsibility are common. Second, survivors try to understand why the person died. They search for some reason for the death to try to put it in a meaningful context. Finally, people search for the deceased. They feel the person's presence and dream or even converse with him or her. Such behavior demonstrates a longing to be with the deceased, and it is often a reaction to feelings of loneliness and despair. Eventually, these feelings and behaviors diminish, and the bereaved person moves to the final phase.

Entry into the recovery phase of grief often results from a conscious decision that continued dwelling on the past is pointless and that one's life needs to move forward. Once this is recognized, recovery can begin. Behaviorally, the process takes many forms, with increased socializing one common example. It is not unusual to see marked improvement in the survivor's self-confidence. Emerging from a bereavement experience is an achievement. People are often more capable and stronger as a result of coping with such a tragic event. New skills may be developed, whether they be cooking, balancing a checkbook, or home repair.

In considering these phases of grief, we must avoid making several mistakes. First, grieving ultimately is an individual experience. The optimal process for one person may not be the best for someone else. Second, we must not underestimate the amount of time it takes to progress from the initial shock to recovery. To a casual observer, this may seem to occur over a few weeks. Actually, it takes much longer to resolve the complex emotional issues that we face during bereavement. Researchers and therapists alike agree that it takes at least a year for a person to be reasonably recovered, and two years is not uncommon. Interestingly, Weiss (1975) proposed a two-year period as the time needed for most people to recover from divorce. Finally, it should also be noted that *recovery* may be a misleading term. It is probably more accurate to say that we learn to live with our loss rather than that we recover. The impact of the loss of a loved one lasts a very long time, perhaps for the rest of one's life.

Normal Grief Reactions

The feelings experienced during grieving are intense, which not only makes it difficult to cope but also may cause one to wonder whether he or she is normal. A summary of college students' perceptions of normal responses is presented in Table 13.1. Many authors refer to the psychological side of coming to terms with bereavement as **grief work**. Vickio, Cavanaugh, and Attig (1990) found that college students were well aware of the need for grief work, correctly recognized the need for at least a year to do it, and were very sensitive to the range of emotions and behaviors demonstrated by the bereaved. In the following sections we will consider some of the most common reactions to bereavement.

Sorrow and Sadness. All the evidence we have suggests that intense feelings of sadness are the most common ones experienced during the grieving process (Kalish, 1985). Some studies have even found that these feelings of sadness can be so intense that they make the individual appear clinically depressed. For example, in the month following the death of their spouse, many widows display symptoms similar to those of depressed psychiatric clients. Many of these women lack a strong support system of family and friends (Kalish, 1981).

Denial and Disbelief. When death happens unexpectedly, a very common response is denial. Usually this response involves an intellectual recognition that the person has died but an inability or unwillingness to believe it. Sometimes denial is seen when a family starts to make plans that would

Grief provides a way to channel emotions, as in the Names Project, a memorial to people who died from AIDS.

normally have included the deceased person and then realizes the problem. At other times denial is shown when parents refuse to change the room of their deceased child or a widower continues to say "we." We must recognize that denial is sometimes adaptive and protective. Without denial during the first few days after the death, the pain might be overwhelming. Taken to extremes, however, denial can become very maladaptive.

Guilt. Guilt is probably the most complex reaction to death. Sometimes guilt arises because we have mixed feelings toward the person who died. We may be angry that he or she died yet relieved that we are not burdened with caregiving duties any longer. Perhaps the most common source of guilt is

TABLE 13.1 Perceptions of typical grief reactions following the death of a loved one

Type of Reaction	Occurs During Initial Period of Grieving (Percent Citing the Reaction)	Occurs During Intermediate or Long-Term Grieving (Percent Citing the Reaction)	Sign That Grieving Is Abnormal If Occurring Long After Loss (Percent Citing the Reaction)
Disbelief	32.5%	0.8%	2.7%
Denial	24.4	8.1	5.5
Shock	48.0	1.6	8.2
Sadness	80.5	80.5	0
Anger	52.8	39.0	10.0
Hatred	8.1	5.7	9.1
Guilt	12.2	10.6	0
Fear	8.9	1.6	0.9
Anxiety	4.9	4.9	0.9
Confusion	9.8	6.5	0
Helplessness	4.9	0.8	0
Emptiness	10.6	6.5	0
Loneliness	13.0	16.3	0
Acceptance	2.4	2.4	1.8
Relief	3.3	0.8	5.5
Happiness that person died	4.1	0.8	66.4
Lack of enthusiasm	0	3.3	0
Absence of emotions	1.6	1.6	4.5

(Source: *Perceptions of Grief Among University Students* by C. J. Vickio, J. C. Cavanaugh, and T. Attig, 1990, *Death Studies*, p. 236.)

what Kalish (1981) calls the "If only I had . . ." syndrome: "If only I had gotten home in time"; "If only I had made him go to the doctor earlier"; "If only I had expressed my feelings toward Mom while she was still alive." Guilt most often results from feeling that there was something one could have done to prevent the death, that one should have treated the person better while he or she was still alive, or that one is actually relieved that the person died. Such

feelings are commonplace in normal grief, but they must be monitored so that they do not become overwhelming.

Religious Beliefs. Many people find strength in their religious beliefs after experiencing the death of a loved one. For example, Pargament (1990; Pargament et al., 1990, 1991) has found that people often look to God as a way to deal with negative, traumatic life events. Death is one of the most common of these events that people cite as an example. Mainstream Christians in the United States, for instance, tend to view death as an event externally caused by God, as a loss, and as unchangeable. They look to their religion as a way to express their feelings of closeness to each other and as a way to understand what is happening to them (Pargament et al., 1991).

Parents whose children die may find comfort in their religious beliefs. For example, Cook and Wimberley (1983) report that parents who use religious coping tend to report three reasons for their beliefs: (1) reunion with the child in an afterlife; (2) the child's death as serving a noble purpose; (3) the death as punishment for parental wrongdoing. For these parents, religion serves as a compensatory mechanism that helps them work through their grief.

Anniversary Reactions. Resolving grief takes time, as we have seen. During that time, and for many years to come, certain dates that have personal significance may reintroduce feelings of grief. For example, holidays such as Thanksgiving that were spent with the deceased person may be difficult times. The actual anniversary of the death can be especially troublesome. The term **anniversary reaction** itself refers to changes in behavior related to feelings of sadness on this date. Personal experience and research show that recurring feelings of sadness or other examples of the anniversary reaction are very common in normal grief (Bornstein & Clayton, 1972).

Longitudinal Research Findings. Most research on how people react to the death of a loved one is cross-sectional. Norris and Murrell (1987) conducted a longitudinal study of older adults' grief work in which three interviews were conducted before the death, and one after. The results of their research are described in more detail in How Do We Know? Briefly, Norris and Murrell reported that

bereavement did not affect physical health; family stress increased as the death approached but diminished afterward; before the death, family stress was associated with worsening health; after the death, health worsened only if there had been no family stress before the death; and after the death, psychological stress always increased. The results of this study have important implications for interventions. That is, interventions aimed at reducing stress or promoting health may be more effective if done before the death. Additionally, because health problems increased only among those who felt no stress before the death, it may be that the stress felt before the death is a product of anticipating it. Lundin (1984) also found this to be the case in that health problems increased only for those experiencing sudden death.

Age Differences in Effects of Normal Grief on Health

Norris and Murrell's finding that bereavement per se has little direct effect on physical health caught some people by surprise. It had been assumed that losing a close loved one would have an obvious negative effect on the health of the survivor, especially if the survivor were elderly. After all, it is well known that older adults are more vulnerable to stress (see Chapters 3 and 4), and the loss of a loved one was assumed to be stressful.

Perkins and Harris (1990) decided to look at this issue carefully. In a cross-sectional study, they compared younger, middle-aged, and older adults who had experienced the loss of a spouse, sibling, or sibling-in-law in the previous five years. Surprisingly, they found that middle-aged adults were most likely to report negative physical health problems following bereavement, with younger and older adults reporting few health problems. Perkins and Harris argue that younger adults are able to deal with their losses because they are better equipped overall to handle stress. Because older adults have more experience with and anticipate such losses, they draw on their background in order to cope physically. In contrast, middle-aged adults have less experience and are also in the midst of dealing with their own mortality (see Chapter 8). As a result, the loss of a close family member is an emotionally unsettling reminder of their own fate.

Abnormal Grief Reactions

Not everyone is able to move through the phases of grief and begin rebuilding his or her life. Sometimes the feelings of hurt, loneliness, or guilt are so overwhelming that they become the focus of the survivor's life. Thus, what distinguishes normal from abnormal grief is not the kind of reaction but rather its intensity and duration (Schulz, 1985). For example, statements such as "I really feel that if I had gotten home from the store even five minutes earlier my husband would be alive" would be considered normal if made a month or so after the death. When made three years afterward, however, they would be considered abnormal. Likewise, intense feelings are normal early in the process, but if they never diminish they are classified as abnormal.

Elderly people who had difficulty coping with a death two years later were found to be different from good copers (Lund et al., 1985–1986). Poor copers expressed lower self-esteem before bereavement, were more confused, had a greater desire to die, cried more, and were less able to keep busy shortly after the death.

Overall, the most common manifestation of abnormal grief is excessive guilt and self-blame. In some people guilt results in a disruption of everyday routines and a diminished ability to function. People begin to make judgment errors, may reach a state of agitated depression, may experience problems sleeping or eating, and may have intense recurring thoughts about the deceased person. Many of these individuals either seek professional help

voluntarily or are referred by concerned family members or friends. Unfortunately, the long-term prognosis for people suffering abnormal grief responses is not good (Schulz, 1985).

Types of Loss and Grieving

Consider the following deaths from cancer: an adolescent, a middle-aged mother, and an elderly man. Our reaction to each of them is different even though all of them died from the same disease. The way we feel when someone dies is partially determined by how old that person was. Our society tends to view some deaths as more tragic or as easier to accept than others. Even though we really know that this approach has no research support, people nevertheless act as if it did. For example, people typically consider the death of a child as extremely traumatic, unless it occurred at birth. Or if one's parent dies when one is young, the loss is considered greater than if one is middle-aged and the parent is old. The point is that our society in a sense makes judgments about how much grief one should experience following different types of loss. We have noted that death is always a traumatic event for survivors. But unfortunately the survivors are not always allowed to express their grief over a period of time, or even to talk about their feelings. These judgments that society makes serve to impose arbitrary time limits on the grieving process, despite the fact that virtually all the evidence we have indicates that we should not do that. Let's consider three types of loss and see how these judgments occur.

Death of One's Parent. Most parents die after their children have grown. But whenever it occurs, parental death hurts. We lose not only a key relationship but also an important psychological buffer between us and death. We, the children, are now next in line. Indeed, when one's parent dies, it often leads the surviving children to redefine the

Family Stress and Adaptation Before and After Bereavement

What happens to a family that experiences the death of a loved one? Norris and Murrell (1987) sought to answer this question by tracking families before and after bereavement. As part of a very large normative longitudinal study, they conducted detailed interviews approximately every six months. The data concerning grief reactions constitute a subset of this larger study, in which 63 older adults in families experiencing the death of an immediate family member were compared with 387 older adults in families who had not been bereaved.

The measures obtained extensive information on physical health, including functional abilities and specific ailments; psychological distress; and family stress. The psychological distress measure tapped symptoms of depression. The family stress measure assessed such things as new serious illness of a family member, having a family member move in, additional family responsibilities, new family conflict, or new marital conflict.

The results were enlightening. Among bereaved families, overall

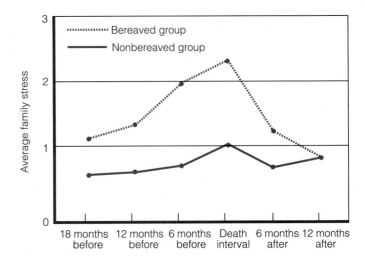

a

FIGURE 13.2 Family stress experienced by bereaved and nonbereaved groups. Part *a* shows stress over a 30-month period. Part *b* shows the relationship between health and stress before and after bereavement.

(Source: "Older Adult Family Stress and Adaptation Before and After Bereavement" by F. N. Norris and S. A. Murrell, 1987, *Journal of Gerontology, 42*, 609, 610. Copyright © 1987 by the Gerontological Society of America. Reprinted by permission of the publisher and author.)

family stress increased before the death and then decreased. The level of stress experienced by these families was highest in the period right around the death. Moreover, bereavement was the only significant predictor of family stress, meaning that it was the anticipation and experience of bereavement that caused

stress. Even more interesting were the findings concerning the relationship between health and stress. Bereaved individuals who reported stress before the death were in poorer health before the death than were bereaved persons who were not experiencing stress. However, bereaved individuals reporting prior

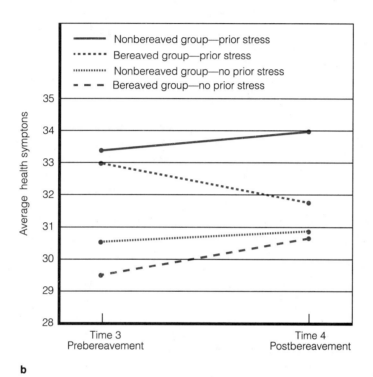

b

stress showed a significant *drop* in physical symptoms six months after the death; bereaved persons reporting no prior stress reported no change. The net result was that both groups ended up with about the same level of physical symptoms six months after bereavement. Both sets of results are depicted in Figure 13.2.

The Norris and Murrell study has two major implications. First, bereavement does not appear to cause poor health; the bereaved groups were not much different from the nonbereaved group in nonstressful families. Second, bereavement appears to result in a marked increase in psychological distress. In sum,

marked changes in psychological distress following bereavement are normal, but marked changes in physical health are not.

meaning of parenthood and the importance of time together (Malinak, Hoyt, & Patterson, 1979).

For most people, the death of a parent deprives them of many important things: a source of guidance and advice, a source of love, and a model for their own parenting style. It may also deny them the opportunity to improve aspects of their relationship with a parent. The loss of a parent is perceived as a very significant one; society allows us to grieve for a reasonable length of time.

Death of One's Child. The death of a child is generally perceived as a great tragedy since children are not supposed to die before their parents. It is as if the natural order of things has been violated. The loss is especially traumatic if it occurs suddenly, such as in sudden infant death syndrome or an automobile accident. But parents of terminally ill children still suffer a great deal, even with the benefit of anticipatory grieving. Mourning is always intense, and some parents never recover or attempt to reconcile the death of their child.

One of the most overlooked losses is the loss of a child through stillbirth, miscarriage, abortion, or neonatal death (Borg & Lasker, 1981). Attachment to one's child begins prenatally. His or her death hurts deeply, so to contend that the loss of a child before or at birth is not as tragic as the loss of an older child makes little sense. Yet parents who experience this type of loss are expected to recover very quickly and are often the recipients of unfeeling comments if these societal expectations are not met.

Finally, grandparents' feelings can easily be overlooked. They, too, feel the loss when their grandchild dies. Moreover, they grieve not only for the grandchild but also for their own child's loss (Hamilton, 1978). Grandparents must also be included in whatever rituals or support groups the family chooses.

Death of One's Spouse. More has been written about the death of a spouse than about any other type of loss. It clearly represents a deep personal loss, especially when the couple had a very long and close relationship. In a very real way when one's spouse dies, a part of oneself dies, too.

The death of a spouse is different from other losses. There is pressure from society to mourn for a period of time. Typically, this pressure is manifested if the survivor begins to show interest in finding another mate before an acceptable period of mourning has passed. Although Americans no longer define the length of such periods, many feel that about a year is appropriate. That such pressure and negative commentary usually do not accompany other losses is another indication of the seriousness with which most people take the death of a spouse.

Another important point concerning the loss of one's spouse involves the age of the survivor. Young adult spouses tend to show more intense grief reactions immediately following the death than do older spouses. However, the situation 18 months later is reversed. At that time older spouses report more grief than do younger spouses (Sanders, 1980–1981). Indeed, older bereaved spouses may grieve for at least 30 months (Thompson, Gallagher-Thompson, Futterman, Gilewski, & Peterson, 1991). The differences seem to be related to four factors: The death of a young spouse is more unexpected, there are fewer same-aged role models for young widows or widowers, the dimensions of grief vary with age, and the opportunities for remarriage are greater for younger survivors. Older widows anticipate fewer years of life and prefer to cherish the memory of their deceased spouse rather than to attempt a new marriage (Raphael, 1983).

Some longitudinal studies have examined the grief process in reaction to the death of a spouse. Dimond, Lund, and Caserta (1987) found that social support played a significant role in the outcome of the grieving process during the first two years after the death of a spouse. In particular, it is the quality of the support system, rather than the number of friends, that is particularly important.

Dealing with the death of one's spouse is often a very difficult process.

One interesting aspect of spousal bereavement concerns how the surviving spouse rates the marriage. Futterman, Gallagher, Thompson, Lovett, and Gilewski (1990) had bereaved older adults rate their relationships at 2, 12, and 30 months after the death of their spouses. Nonbereaved older adults were also studied as a comparison group. Bereaved widows and widowers rated their marriage more positively than nonbereaved older adults, indicating a positive bias in remembering a marriage lost through death. However, bereaved spouses' ratings were related to depression in an interesting way. The more depressed the bereaved spouse, the more positively the marriage was rated. In contrast, de-pressed nonbereaved spouses rated their marriage negatively. This result suggests that the loss of a positive relationship through death, as well as its consequences (for instance, loss of other social contacts), is viewed as a negative outcome.

IS THERE LIFE AFTER DEATH?

Most people believe that death does not mark the end of being. Although the exact nature of this belief in an afterlife varies widely across individuals and cultures, the themes are the same. We can examine these themes with two questions in mind. Is the belief in an afterlife just wishful thinking? Do we have any scientific indication that there may be reason to suspect another life or type of existence?

These were the questions that prompted Moody (1975, 1988) to interview children and adults who had had close calls with death, that is, **near-death experiences**. In many cases these people had been clinically dead, and in other cases they had come very close to dying. On the basis of these interviews Moody was able to identify several common reports for people of all ages, although individual experiences differed somewhat. The common aspects of the experiences include:

1. An awareness of a buzzing or drumming sound or possibly hearing oneself declared dead

2. Feeling oneself moving out of one's body and then quickly down a tunnel, funnel, or cave toward an intense light

3. Seeing or feeling the presence of dead relatives who are there to help one make the transition from this life

4. Sensing the light as a power or presence, sometimes interpreted or experienced as love, that makes one review one's own life rather than be judged

5. "Seeing" one's life pass in front of one's eyes as a kaleidoscopic view of one's own thoughts and deeds

6. Being instantly able to tap into knowledge of any sort

7. Being aware or being told that the time for one's death has not yet come and that one must return to finish the normal life span

Some of the people whom Moody interviewed resented having survived. For them, the near-death experience was extraordinarily pleasant, and they felt cheated. For most people, the close encounter with death gave them a new and more positive outlook on life. Many people changed their life styles, and some acquired a deep spiritual commitment. Most no longer feared death, because they felt that the knowledge of what it would be like had removed the mystery and doubt.

Moody makes no claims that these experiences prove that there is life after death. Nevertheless, he does believe that these data are significant, if for no other reason than that the experiences reported by his participants were remarkably similar. Subsequent verification of these reports have been offered (Moody, 1977; Siegel, 1980). As a result many people see the themes and consistency of the reports as evidence that there is life after death. Because belief in an afterlife is so common, this is not very surprising.

The believers in the evidence are not without their critics, however. Siegel (1980) uses evidence from biology, psychology, and anthropology to dismiss claims that the reports reflect experiences of an afterlife. Siegel tries to show how each of the common themes in these reports can be explained by known processes (such as hallucinations similar to those induced by drugs). He argues that because we know so little about the workings of the brain, it is more likely that the experiences reflect neurological processes than actual experiences of an afterlife.

Whose interpretation is correct? Unfortunately, the question is presently unanswerable and is likely to stay that way. But even if the claims of an afterlife are exaggerated, the belief in its potential existence is probably adaptive in this life. Many people are more likely to use death as a stimulus for personal growth if they think that something might follow it. Additionally, without the concept of an afterlife, death could result for some people in a devastating fear of total nonbeing. A belief in an afterlife may be nothing more than a way of denying the reality and the finality of death. But the adaptive value of this belief is truly great. If nothing else, it allows us to keep on living life to the fullest. And in the end, that is what it's all about.

SUMMARY

Definitions and Ethical Issues

1. Different cultures have different meanings for death. Some of the meanings in Western culture include images, statistics, events, state of being, analogy, mystery, and boundary. Death also makes people aware of whether they will achieve their goals and whether they will be rewarded or punished.

2. Three legal criteria of death have been proposed: clinical death, brain death, and cortical death.

3. Bioethics examines the interface between values and technological advances.

4. Two types of euthanasia are distinguished. Active euthanasia means deliberately ending someone's life. Passive euthanasia means ending someone's life by withholding treatment.

5. Keeping individuals alive with life support is not only financially costly, but can also take an emotional toll.

Thinking About Death: Personal Components

6. Most people exhibit some degree of anxiety about death. Individual difference variables include gender, religiosity, age, ethnicity, and occupation.

7. The main ways death anxiety is shown is by avoidance and by deliberately challenging it.

8. Several ways to deal with anxiety exist: living life to the fullest, personal reflection, and education.

Thinking About Death: Theories of Dying

9. Kübler-Ross's theory includes five stages: denial, anger, bargaining, depression, and acceptance.

10. People may be in more than one stage at a time and do not necessarily go through them in order.

11. An alternative view states that dying occurs in three phases: an acute phase, a chronic living-dying phase, and a terminal phase.

12. A dying trajectory describes a person's passage through the phases.

13. Older adults take longer to die and are more likely to die alone than any other group.

14. Age differences in the dying experience help put the meaning of dying into perspective.

Where Will We Die?

15. Most people want to die at home but actually die in a hospital.

16. The goal of hospice is to maintain the quality of life and to manage the pain of terminal patients.

17. Hospice clients are typically in better psychological status than hospital patients.

Caring and Helping Relationships

18. Many people have positive experiences working with dying people.

19. The most important things many dying people need are pain management, dignity, and self-worth.

20. Many physicians have difficulty dealing with terminal patients. Comfort in this regard depends on the amount of personal experience one has in dealing with death.

21. Most health care workers believe that terminal patients should be told that they are dying. However, some patients engage in mutual pretense and do not accept their condition. Likewise, death is often hidden in health care settings.

22. Psychotherapy and paraprofessional counseling often helps terminal patients deal with their condition.

Survivors: The Grieving Process

23. Grief is equally intense in both expected and unexpected death, but may begin before the actual death when the patient has a terminal illness.

24. Three main phases of grief have been identified: initial phase, intermediate phase, and recovery phase.

25. Dealing with grief usually takes at least one to two years.
26. Normal grief reactions include sorrow, sadness, denial, guilt, and religious beliefs.
27. Grief often returns around the anniversary of the death.
28. Middle-aged adults have the most difficult time dealing with grief.
29. Poor copers tend to have low self-esteem before losing a loved one.
30. Excessive guilt and self-blame are common signs of abnormal grief.
31. The death of a parent serves to remind people of their own mortality and deprives them of a very important person in their lives.
32. The death of a child is thought to be the most traumatic type of loss.
33. Loss of a spouse is a great loss of a lover and companion. Bereaved spouses tend to have a positive bias about their marriage.

Is There Life After Death?

34. Many people report near-death experiences having several similar components. Whether these experiences reflect life after death is open to debate.

REVIEW QUESTIONS

Definitions and Ethical Issues

1. What are the various sociocultural meanings for death?
2. What are the three legal criteria for death?
3. What are the criteria necessary for brain death?
4. What is bioethics and what kinds of issues does it deal with?
5. What are the two types of euthanasia? How do they differ?
6. What are the costs, both financial and psychological, of keeping someone on life support?

Thinking About Death: Personal Components

7. What is death anxiety? What factors influence death anxiety?
8. How do people demonstrate death anxiety?
9. How do people learn to deal with death anxiety?

Thinking About Death: Theories of Dying

10. Describe Kübler-Ross's stage theory of dying. How do people progress through the stages?
11. Describe the phase theory of dying. What is a dying trajectory?
12. How is age related to dying?

Where Will We Die?

13. Where do most people want to die? Where do they actually die?
14. What is hospice? How does hospice care differ from hospital care?

Caring and Helping Relationships

15. What is it like to work with dying people?
16. What needs do dying people have?
17. How do physicians and other health care workers deal with dying people?
18. How do mental health workers deal with dying people?

Survivors: The Grieving Process

19. What effects does an expected versus an unexpected death have on the grieving process?
20. What are the stages of grief? How long does grief usually last?
21. What are the differences between normal and abnormal grief reactions? What age differences are there in grief reactions?
22. How does the type of loss affect grief?

Is There Life After Death?

23. What is the near-death experience?

KEY TERMS

anniversary reaction Feelings of sadness and loneliness on holidays, birthdays, and on the anniversary of the loved one's death. (470)

brain death A definition of death that relies on the lack of an EEG as its primary criterion. (450)

clinical death A definition of death based on the lack of a pulse and respiration. (449)

cortical death A definition of death based on the lack of brain activity in the cortex. (451)

dying trajectory The pattern exhibited by a dying person in terms of the phase theory of dying. (457)

euthanasia Meaning "good death," the practice of allowing people who have a terminal illness to die. (451)

grief work The process by which people grieve. (468)

hospice An approach to assisting dying people that emphasizes pain management and death with dignity. (461)

near-death experiences Experiences related by people who have been near death or clinically dead involving feelings of floating, peace, and meeting deceased loved ones. (476)

ADDITIONAL READING

Several excellent books on death, dying, and bereavement are available. Summaries of the research can be found in

Kalish, R. A. (1981). *Death, grief, and caring relationships*. Monterey, CA: Brooks/Cole. Easy reading.

Kalish, R. A. (1987). Death and dying. In P. Silverman (Ed.), *The elderly as modern pioneers* (pp. 320–334). Bloomington: Indiana University Press. Relatively easy.

Kastenbaum, R. (1985). Death and dying: A life-span approach. In J. E. Birren & K. W. Schaie (Eds.), *Handbook of the psychology of aging* (2nd ed., pp. 619–643). New York: Van Nostrand Reinhold. Moderately difficult.

A discussion of death from an interdisciplinary view that includes historical and philosophical perspectives is

Stephenson, J. S. (1985). *Death, grief, and mourning: Individual and social realities*. New York: Free Press.

CHAPTER 14

Looking Toward The 21st Century

BY THE TIME YOU REACH OLD AGE, THE 21ST century will be well along. Technological advances will make commonplace what is only science fiction today. Our daily lives may be vastly different than they are right now. Life will undoubtedly be more complicated. You will probably have experienced firsthand many of the things discussed in this book: marriage, children, career changes, relocation, personal development, physical and cognitive changes, and so on.

For now, though, we must be content with gazing into a crystal ball. We know many things about adult development and aging to guide us, but there are many unknowns, too. Throughout this book we have made predictions about this future and guessed how older people may fare. Some of these predictions are positive; for example, it is likely that more people will live to advanced ages. Other forecasts are not so rosy; as more people live to a very old age, there will be more need for long-term care. These predictions represent our best guess about what life will be like in 40 years or so, based on what we know now and what is likely to happen if we continue the way we are going.

The purpose of this chapter is to pull together several crucial issues facing gerontologists as we approach the 21st century. This survey will not be exhaustive; rather, we will focus on two things: points that have been singled out for special concern, and areas where major advances may have a dramatic impact on our own development.

Three issues have been identified as trouble spots for the future. The first is the need for better research — a problem that underlies all others. Second, we will examine the growing crisis in health care and health policy. Third, we will consider the need for creating productive roles for the elderly.

Other issues concern areas of ongoing research that have the potential to revolutionize our own developmental course. Chief among these is research on biological and physiological aspects of aging. Also important are discoveries that are being made in the cognitive domain that challenge age-old stereotypes of aging.

THE NEED FOR RESEARCH

Throughout this book we have seen that adult development and aging are complex processes that we are far from understanding. Because the number of older people is rising and because we need more and better information, three issues need to be addressed in the near future if we are to optimize our own development into the next century. These are better research, health care, and productive roles.

The Need for Better Research

In Chapter 1 we considered various methods for conducting research on adult development and aging. Recall that of the major methods (cross-sectional, longitudinal, time lag, and sequential), longitudinal and sequential designs are the ones that tell us what we really want to know: whether a particular process or behavior changes over time. Cross-sectional research identifies only differences that are related to age; they may reflect true age change or merely cohort differences. But the vast majority of research we have considered in this book is cross-sectional. Longitudinal and sequen-

tial work is confined mainly to topics in cognitive and personality development. Where does this leave us?

The problem we are faced with is the possibility that much of what we know about adult development and aging may not reflect true age changes. Rather, it may largely reflect cohort differences that are, in turn, a reflection of the changes that have occurred in society over this century. Recall from Chapter 2 that the modernization of society has a strong influence that may differ across generations. This may mean that differences in intellectual skills or memory performance are due to changes in the skills needed by each succeeding generation to survive and adapt in daily life.

Cross-sectional research will never solve the problem, since age and cohort are always confounded. Longitudinal research addresses the issue of age change, but it is severely limited because the results may not generalize across cohorts. Sequential research appears to be our best and only way out. We must have reliable data on whether the differences we observe between age groups are something innate in humans or whether they are due more to historical experiential factors.

But improved research does not only mean using a different, more sophisticated design. It also means cutting across disciplines and incorporating findings from one field to interpret data from another. A good example is the need for truly interdisciplinary biopsychosocial research. The search for the genetic link in Alzheimer's disease, for instance, may also yield the key to why cognitive processes fail (see Chapter 9). Cognitive scientists and neurological scientists working together will make substantially more progress than either group working alone. Likewise, there may be a connection between changing levels of neurotransmitters and aspects of personality — mainly studied through psychopathology (see the discussion on depression in Chapter 9).

The point is that we need better research not

only to understand more about adult development and aging but also to know how better to commit resources for the future. As we will see, the most serious problem facing the United States concerning the elderly is health care; the lack of data collected over time from multiple cohorts seriously impairs our ability to plan for the future. Getting better information also means changing our research priorities from a system that rewards quantity (promoting more cross-sectional research) to one that rewards high quality (promoting more longitudinal and sequential research). Perhaps changing our priorities should be the place to start; otherwise, the future will arrive and we will still not have a data base.

CHANGING DEMOGRAPHICS

In Chapter 2 we noted several trends in the population of the United States during this century. These trends are not likely to change in the foreseeable future. Changes in the composition of the older adult population contribute to potentially critical issues that will emerge over the next few decades. One especially important area concerns the potential for intergenerational conflict.

Because the resources and roles in a society are never divided equally among different age groups, there is always a potential for conflict. One well-known intergenerational conflict is that between adolescents and their parents. Less well known is the potential for conflict between the middle-aged and the old (Uhlenberg, 1987). This type of conflict has not traditionally been a source of serious problems in U.S. society for several reasons: The elderly made up a small proportion of the population, family ties between adult children and their parents mediated conflict, and middle-agers were hesitant

to withdraw support from programs for the elderly. Despite these potent forces helping to prevent conflict, the situation is changing. To see this more clearly, let us project forward to the year 2030 when the baby boom generation will be old. Between now and 2030

1. The proportion of older adults will nearly double.

2. Older adults will be much more politically sophisticated and organized. They will be very well educated and will be familiar with dealing with the bureaucratic structure of a highly complex society.

3. Older adults will expect to keep their more affluent life style, Social Security, health care, and other benefits accrued through their adult life. They will believe that they are entitled to a comfortable retirement.

4. The ratio of workers to retirees will fall from its current level of roughly 3.5:1 to 2:1. Thus, to maintain the same level of benefits, the working members of society will have to pay much higher taxes than workers do now.

5. The increase in divorce that has occurred over the past two decades may result in a lowered sense of obligation on the part of middle-aged adults toward their absent parents. For example, will adult children feel obliged to care for an elderly father who left the family when they were very young?

6. The more rapid increase in minority elderly will force a reconsideration of issues such as discrimination and access to goods and services.

No one knows for certain what society will be like by 2030. However, the changes we have noted in demographic trends suggest the need for taking action now. The information contained in this book will provide a basis for this action.

HEALTH CARE

Especially in the United States, no problem will be more pressing in the coming years than the need for health care for older adults (J. A. Brody, 1988; Ferraro & Sterns, 1990; Wallack & Cohen, 1988). The number of elderly will increase dramatically over the next 30 to 40 years, most rapidly in the over-80 age group. By the year 2000 the over-80 group will constitute the largest single federal entitlement group, receiving well over $80 billion a year in benefits (Torrey, 1985). Health care costs for adults over age 65 will soar as the expenses for chronic and debilitating diseases mount. Long-term care is already in crisis; beds are in short supply, and the cost of the average nursing home is beyond the means of many (see Chapter 12). Information is also scarce, and statistical tools for analyzing it are often inadequate (National Research Council, 1988).

The growing concern over health care for the elderly prompted the National Research Council (NRC) to study the situation and to make several recommendations concerning future health care policy (NRC, 1988). These recommendations address several areas of special concern, as well as general issues.

The NRC identifies the financing of medical care for the elderly as the most important health policy issue facing the United States in the 1990s. The cost of care, who will pay for it, and how it will be financed are issues that *must* be addressed. The changes in Medicare and Medicaid during the 1980s and the growing realization that private insurance will need to become more heavily involved have had a significant impact on how health care is financed. We noted in Chapters 9 and 12 that many public and private insurance programs do not adequately cover the cost of quality long-term care. The trend toward increased reliance on individuals to either have their own health coverage or to pay for care themselves has profound implications for

people facing chronic debilitating conditions such as Alzheimer's disease. The NRC points to a lack of adequate data on the cost burden of such care, and it places high priority on obtaining this information.

How health care is delivered is a second issue facing American society. The diminishing number of physicians in rural areas and in some specialties, the closing of inner-city hospitals, and the lack of transportation to health care centers present significant problems to older adults, especially minority groups and the frail. The growth of for-profit care and business-oriented approaches to health care, not recognizing age differences in recovery time from illness, and increased competition also create barriers to quality health care for the elderly.

The NRC identifies the need for and cost of long-term care as major factors in the overall financing picture. Moreover, many of the issues cited earlier apply to long-term care facilities. Many nursing homes do not take Medicaid patients, for example, forcing some elderly poor to settle for lower-quality care or no care. We have no consistent program of data collection to determine how many people are likely to need long-term care in the future. Surveys also need to include facilities other than nursing homes, such as chronic disease hospitals, mental health facilities, rehabilitation centers, group homes, halfway houses, and residential facilities.

A smart investment strategy, according to the NRC, would be to spend health care dollars on health promotion and disease prevention. This approach would emphasize keeping oneself in good health to avoid the more expensive treatment programs. Generally speaking, paying for checkups and needed treatment early in the disease process is markedly less expensive than waiting until the disease has spread. Important intervention goals include promoting healthy activities and life style among older adults. Whether the federal government should finance prevention and promotion is an important policy decision.

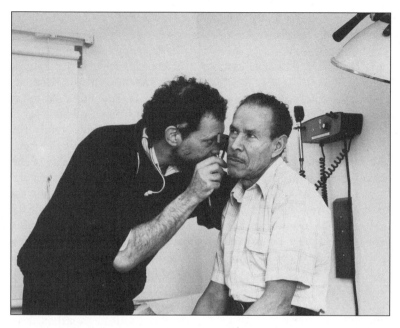

Screening for major health problems is an important component of health promotion.

Monitoring health care systems to ensure that people get the best care for their money and that care quality meets high standards are also important. Simply solving the financing problem is only half the battle. The health care industry must be held accountable for its actions.

Carrying out the NRC's recommendations will be expensive. By its own estimate, data collection alone may cost $15 billion to $20 billion or more. Such a high price tag makes one wonder whether the benefits would justify the expense. The answer is yes. We have too little information now to address the coming crisis in health care adequately (Hollander & Becker, 1988). To do the most good for the most people, policymakers need reliable data on which to base decisions about where to allocate federal dollars. Not collecting adequate information and not making appropriate policy decisions would be far more expensive, both in dollars

and in the quality of life of older people. Our goals should be to enable the elderly to stay healthy and functionally independent as long as possible, to provide access to quality health care of whatever type is appropriate, and to provide care in the least restrictive and most cost-effective environment (Somers, 1987). The issue facing us is whether we are willing to assume the cost burden. If not, we have unpleasant consequences to face.

PSYCHOLOGICAL CHANGES

The single most important contribution of psychology to the study of adult development and aging is its demonstration that much of the decline in psychological functioning is not an inevitable outcome of aging. We have seen again and again that while decrements in many areas are normative, the degree of change can be altered, sometimes significantly (for example, changes in fluid intelligence discussed in Chapter 7).

Although by now such information is hardly surprising to you, society has yet to fully appreciate its implications. American society retains a fairly negative view of age despite much data showing that such a view is wrong. In part, the problem stems from a general lack of appreciation for the diversity of aging; pick any two of your older relatives and you probably have two different models of what aging involves. Until recently, even scientists failed to acknowledge the enormous human variations in the ways in which people traverse adulthood.

Usual Versus Successful Cognitive Aging

With an appreciation of diversity and individual differences comes a realization that some people may even excel in old age. Rowe and Kahn (1987) understood this and distinguished between "usual" and "successful" aging. In usual aging, external factors heighten the effects of biological and physiological processes. In successful aging, external factors play either a neutral or a positive role. For example, consider the role of education in maintaining cognitive performance (see Chapter 7). Low levels of education are associated with significantly greater decrements; high levels of education are associated with maintenance of intellectual ability even into late life.

Other researchers have uncovered ways in which older adults clearly excel well beyond the range of younger adults. Smith and Baltes (1990) describe people who become experts in living, and in some cases greatly outperform younger adults at cognitive tasks. The point is that we simply do not know the absolute maximum that older adults can do. Perhaps it is time we found out.

Well-Being

People living in advanced technological societies potentially have access to several ways of extending their lives through material goods and high-quality health care. But in the drive to extend average longevity, an essential question has been ignored: Is it a good idea to blanketly extend life?

Researchers have yet to focus much attention on the issue of the quality of the extra years that technology buys. For example, are the years we add onto people's lives with improved medical care good, productive years? Or are they years in which one's health deteriorates and chronic diseases are numerous? Related to this issue is the notion that one could outlive one's *expected* longevity, that is, how long you *think* you will live. For example, if you think you will not live past 75, perhaps because no other relative in your family ever has, you may map out your life based on this assumption. But what do you do when you turn 76? This birthday wasn't planned, and you may feel confused as to what you should be doing with yourself.

These issues raise important questions that psychologists need to address for life in the 21st century. The degree to which old age brings well-being is vitally important; many times in this book we have seen the importance of maintaining well-being and feeling that you have some control over your life. Finding personal meaning in growing old will surely be an important topic for aging individuals and researchers alike.

SOCIAL CHANGES

What will older adults be doing in the 21st century? Some researchers see new roles as inevitable, if for no other reason than that there will be so many of them. Golant (1988) envisions that "the beginning decades of the 21st century will be

*Having older adults share their experiences and wisdom is one way of providing
productive roles for them in society.*

known as the Golden Era for Older People. While
our attention as this century closes is on the population we now refer to as Yuppies, in the 21st century the spotlight will be on the Yeepies; that is,
Youthful Energetic Elderly People Involved in
Everything" (p. 13). Whether or not Yeepies come
to pass remains to be seen. Nevertheless, there will
certainly be an emphasis on productive roles for
older adults.

Productive Roles for Older Adults

One of the key issues currently facing older adults
is the lack of formal social roles. Adults now relin-
quish many of the major roles of adulthood by the
time they reach old age. We have noted that older
cohorts experience major declines in societal significance as a result of these role losses. One of the

most important of these relinquished roles is work.
As more people enter retirement over the coming
decades, the issue of how to keep older adults connected with society will become more critical.

At present, older adults do the best they can to
create productive roles (Herzog, Kahn, Morgan,
Jackson, & Antonucci, 1989). Herzog and colleagues (1989) found that older adults participate
in many unpaid productive activities at levels comparable to their younger and middle-aged counterparts. These activities range from volunteering
in organizations, to providing informal help to
others, to home repair and housework. Few older
Americans currently get paid for what they do, although this is truer for older women than it is for
older men.

In an effort to develop guidelines for addressing the need to develop productive roles for older
adults, the Committee on an Aging Society (CAS)

of the Institute of Medicine and the National Research Council explored unpaid productive roles as one alternative (CAS, 1986). Unpaid productive roles are ones in which individuals make a significant contribution to society but are not given wages. The difference between paid and unpaid productive roles is sometimes arbitrary, and the work is often similar.

Voluntarism has a long, distinguished tradition in the United States. From Boy Scout troop leaders to friendly visitors in hospitals and nursing homes, millions of people donate their time freely each year. The CAS argues that we should look to older adults as a major source of volunteers in social and health services. It proposes that a systematic effort at providing unpaid productive roles for older adults would accomplish two things. First, it would increase the availability of some social and health services that could be provided by nonprofessionals. For example, existing programs such as Foster Grandparents could be enhanced, and new programs such as home visitation for the frail elderly could be started in many communities. Second, unpaid productive roles would give older people a formal way to maintain self-esteem and identity after retirement without having to be employed. Unpaid productive roles would enable them to retain societal significance by using their accumulated years of experience and expertise.

An important issue not directly addressed by the CAS is that volunteers often end up in clerical or social tasks, with little opportunity to have a direct say in the operation of the program. This is not an optimal situation, of course, since volunteers often come into the program with years of experience. This is especially true for older adults, who may view volunteer positions as low-status roles that do not take advantage of their experience.

The CAS gives most attention to the prospect of older volunteers (providing, of course, that the status and menial nature of volunteer work are addressed). It points out that declining federal and state support of social service programs through the 1980s has led to a serious shortage of people to provide these much needed services. The growing number of older people could be a resource in easing the impact of personnel cuts that have been made as a result of fewer dollars. Estimates are that between 35% and 40% of older adults already perform some sort of volunteer work, and projections are that this figure will increase (Kieffer, 1986). Thus, the potential pool is relatively large.

If a concerted effort is to be made to provide older adults with formalized roles through unpaid productive activities, several impediments to participation need to be addressed (CAS, 1986). Older people are often not actively recruited by organizations or are not encouraged to remain. Individuals are often expected to cover expenses such as transportation with little hope for tax deductions to help defray such costs. Unions are often reluctant to accept volunteers, viewing them as a way to displace paid employees. Some older adults themselves view voluntarism as a form of exploitation, feeling that volunteers are considered second-class citizens in organizations. The lack of adequate transportation for elderly people who do not drive means that people who might otherwise volunteer will not do so because they cannot get there.

How can we eliminate these barriers? First of all, we need to explicitly recognize that older adults have a wealth of experience and skill that should not be allowed to go to waste. Kieffer (1986) notes that this expertise of the elderly has been systematically and increasingly thrown away since the 1940s. We need to begin to draw on older adults as experts in much the same way as members of some nonindustrialized societies do. Second, we need to make positive appeals to older adults to become volunteers and share their knowledge. Third, there need to be incentives for volunteers, including increased recognition. Fourth, we need improved supervision, development, and management of volunteer programs. Providing services takes coordination of both government and business. Careful planning needs to be done, and programs have to be monitored to ensure that they provide optimal services. Finally, the impediments outlined earlier need to be removed. Most important, transportation to and from the volunteer site should be provided.

Well-planned and well-managed volunteer programs could become extremely cost effective, both in terms of the services they provide and the benefits to the volunteers. Social and health services that are currently unavailable could be provided at a fraction of the cost of identical programs using only a paid staff. Volunteers benefit by feeling more useful in society and regaining aspects of identity lost after retirement.

Volunteer programs are not a panacea, however. The CAS notes that volunteer programs should never be used as a way to cut corners or to eliminate needed professionals. Such programs should be viewed as a way to supplement existing services, not as a replacement for them. Used appropriately, however, voluntarism could be an effective way to reconnect older adults to society.

THE REALM OF DISCOVERY

Insights into the experience of adult development and aging are being achieved at an ever-quickening pace. Two areas that have had major impacts on the day-to-day experience of growing old are biological-physiological research and cognitive-developmental research.

Unlocking the Secrets of Aging

As we noted in Chapters 3 and 4, we have learned a great deal about the biology and physiology of aging. Our knowledge is increasing even more through research on diseases of aging, especially Alzheimer's disease. As noted in Chapter 9, Alzheimer's disease is thought by many to be qualitatively similar to normal aging. By combining research on both normal and abnormal aging, we may unlock the genetic basis of human aging in our own lifetime. Not even Ponce de León, the conquistador who searched for the fountain of youth, could have imagined that.

We already have the technology to greatly prolong life by curing diseases that only a few decades ago were major killers. High-tech surgical techniques make cataract operations routine. Open-heart surgery and cancer treatments that were only dreams in the 1960s are commonplace. Diagnostic techniques through computer-enhanced imaging allow physicians to detect problems even before they are manifested. Artificial joints make greater mobility a reality for many.

What might these changes mean to us? For one thing, they almost ensure that, barring accidents, virtually everyone will have the chance to live to a very old age. But more important is the prospect that in our lifetime we may have the ability to reverse the aging process itself. The implications of this possibility are mind-boggling. Bioethicists (see Chapter 13) would have to deal with the question of whose aging process could be reversed and under what circumstances it would be done. Would genetic engineering be routinely performed on victims of Alzheimer's disease or other genetic disorders? Could the average person have his or her aging process slowed? Who would decide? What impact would the significant slowing of aging have on society? How would we deal with the population increase?

These and other questions bring home the sobering fact that understanding the biological-physiological process of aging may create more problems than it solves. As pointed out many times in the text, we need to approach the problem from a *biopsychosocial* perspective and ask ourselves whether the outcome is in our best interest.

Interestingly, unlocking the secrets of aging would tend to exacerbate the health care problems facing the United States. Larger numbers of people living to unprecedented old age might completely overburden the system. This problem emphasizes the point that progress in one area may create additional dilemmas elsewhere. It also points out the need for careful planning and policymaking in the years ahead.

Understanding How We Think

Perhaps no other area of research in adult development and aging has forced more rethinking of stereotypes than work on intellectual and memory skills. From the earliest descriptions of older people to the present, the belief has been that with old age comes a marked diminution of cognitive ability. As we learned in Chapters 5, 6, and 7, however, researchers over the past two decades have discovered that this stereotype is only partially true.

In fact, aging does bring changes in cognitive abilities. Some people do decline, but others do not. Moreover, it is beginning to appear that even cognitive skills that we thought declined may actually be amenable to remediation. The discovery that one's predominant mode or style of thinking may change as one ages and that thought becomes reunited with emotion are revolutionizing the way in which psychologists view older adults. The effects are dramatic. We have gone from questioning whether we even needed to document the decline because we were so certain of it to being very cautious in discussing the developmental trends in relatively specific abilities, because we accept the fact that not all abilities change.

We are also witnessing a movement toward wondering how adults think in their everyday lives. This naturalistic shift, while not encompassing most cognitive-developmental research, nevertheless brings attention to the fact that adults develop compensatory strategies for dealing with cognitive aging. Differences that are obtained in the laboratory may be moot in the real world because we have learned how to deal with our limitations. In short, we may be realistic in our everyday cognitive activity without even knowing it.

What does the continued discovery of cognitive change across adulthood mean for the future? Perhaps above all, the discoveries since the early 1970s mean that a focus on lifelong learning will be even more pronounced in the 21st century. Colleges and universities may begin to actively recruit older adults into their academic programs. The image of older people being incapable of learning may be laid to rest, replaced by an image of older people teaching the young and learning from them.

SOME FINAL THOUGHTS

In this book you have seen a snapshot of what adult development and aging are like today. You have learned about their complexities, myths, and realities. But more than anything else, you have seen what we really know about the pioneers who have blazed the trail ahead of us.

In a short time it will be your turn to lead the journey. The decisions you make will have enormous impact on those who will be old: your parents, grandparents, and the people who taught you. The decisions will not be easy ones, but you have an advantage that the pioneers did not: You have the collected knowledge of gerontologists to help. With a continued concerted effort you will be able to address the problems and meet the challenges that lie ahead. Then, when you yourself are old, you will be able to look back on your life and say, "I lived long—and I prospered."

SUMMARY

The Need for Research

1. To answer the most important questions about adult development and aging, we need more lon-

gitudinal and sequential research that is multidisciplinary.

2. Better research will help us make better decisions about resource allocation in the future.

Changing Demographics

3. The rapid increase in the number of older adults between now and 2030 means that social policy must take the aging of the population into account.

4. Changing demographics will affect every aspect of life in the United States.

Health Care

5. The most pressing need in the United States is a comprehensive health care program that takes into account the high cost of caring for large numbers of people with chronic diseases, especially in long-term care.

6. A cost-effective approach would be to emphasize health promotion, especially in the elderly.

Psychological Changes

7. A distinction that is becoming more important is that between usual and successful aging. We need to learn more about how and why some people appear not to be affected very much by normative aging processes.

8. An important issue is the quality of life that people accrue through healthier life styles.

Social Changes

9. At a societal level, we need to develop productive roles for older adults. Current impediments to active participation need to be removed.

The Realm of Discovery

10. A major research emphasis over the next few decades will be on trying to unlock the genetic code for aging. However, ethical and practical issues need to be faced concerning a possible guarantee of a long life.

11. Lifelong learning will also be an important issue in the next decade.

REVIEW QUESTIONS

The Need for Research

1. What kinds of research are needed the most? Why?

Changing Demographics

2. What will the population in the United States look like in 2030?

3. What impact will these demographic characteristics have on social policy?

Health Care

4. Why is health care considered to be the most important issue facing the United States?

5. What kind of health care policy is needed? Why?

Psychological Changes

6. What is the difference between usual and successful aging?

7. What issues concerning older adults' well-being will be important in the years ahead?

Social Changes

8. What possible sources are there for productive roles for older adults?

9. What barriers currently exist to participation?

The Realm of Discovery

10. What effect would unlocking the secrets of aging have on society?

11. What are the important everyday life issues facing cognitive researchers?

REFERENCES

Adams, C., Labouvie-Vief, G., Hobart, C. J., & Dorosz, M. (1990). Adult age group differences in story recall style. *Journal of Gerontology: Psychological Sciences, 45*, P17–P27.

Adams, P., Davies, G. T., & Sweetname, P. (1970). Osteoporosis and the effect of aging on bone mass in women. *Quarterly Journal of Medicine, 39*, 601–615.

Adams, R. D. (1980). Morphological aspects of aging in the human nervous system. In J. E. Birren & R. B. Sloane (Eds.), *Handbook of mental health and aging* (pp. 149–160). Englewood Cliffs, NJ: Prentice-Hall.

Ade-Ridder, L., & Brubaker, T. H. (1983). The quality of long-term marriages. In T. H. Brubaker (Ed.), *Family relationships in later life* (pp. 21–30). Beverly Hills, CA: Sage Publications.

Adler, S., & Aranya, N. (1984). A comparison of the work needs, attitudes, and preferences of professional accountants at different career stages. *Journal of Vocational Behavior, 25*, 574–580.

Ahrons, C. R., & Rodgers, R. H. (1987). *Divorced Families: A multidisciplinary view.* New York: Norton.

Ahrons, C., & Wallisch, L. (1986). The relationship between former spouses. In D. Perlman & S. Duck (Eds.), *Intimate relationships: Development, dynamics, and deterioration* (pp. 269–296). Newbury Park, CA: Sage Publications.

Allen, K. R., & Chin-Sang, V. (1990). A lifetime of work: The context and meanings of leisure for aging black women. *The Gerontologist, 30*, 734–740.

Alwin, D. F., Converse, P. E., & Martin, S. S. (1985). Living arrangements and social integration. *Journal of Marriage and the Family, 47*, 319–334.

American Association of Retired Persons (AARP). (1988). *A portrait of older minorities.* Washington, DC: Author.

American Association of Retired Persons (AARP). (1991). *A profile of older Americans.* Washington DC: Author.

American Psychiatric Association. (1987). *Diagnostic and statistical manual (DSM III-R).* Washington, DC: Author.

Amoss, P. T. (1981). Coast Salish elders. In P. T. Amoss & S. Harrell (Eds.), *Other ways of growing old* (pp. 227–238). Palo Alto, CA: Stanford University Press.

Anastasi, A. (1958). Heredity, environment, and the question "how?" *Psychological Review, 65*, 197–208.

Anderson, S. A., Russell, C. S., & Schumm, W. R. (1983). Perceived marital quality and family life-cycle categories: A further analysis. *Journal of Marriage and the Family, 45*, 127–139.

Andrasik, F., Blanchard, E. B., & Edlund, S. R. (1985). Physiological responding during biofeedback. In S. R. Burchfield (Ed.), *Stress: Psychological and physiological interactions* (pp. 282–306). Washington, DC: Hemisphere.

Anschutz, L., Camp, C. J., Markley, R. P., & Kramer, J. J. (1985). Maintenance and generalization of mnemonics for grocery shopping by older adults. *Experimental Aging Research, 11*, 157–160.

Anschutz, L., Camp, C. J., Markley, R. P., & Kramer, J. J. (1987). Remembering mnemonics: A three-year follow-up on the effects of mnemonic training in elderly adults. *Experimental Aging Research, 13*, 141–143.

Antonucci, T. C. (1985). Personal characteristics, social support, and social behavior. In R. H. Binstock & E. Shanas (Eds.), *Handbook of aging and the social sciences* (2nd ed., pp. 94–128). New York: Van Nostrand Reinhold.

Aquilino, W. S., & Supple, K. R. (1991). Parent-child relations and parent's satisfaction with living arrangements when adult children live at home. *Journal of Marriage and the Family, 53*, 13–27.

Arensberg, C. (1968). *The Irish countryman: An anthropological study.* New York: Peter Smith.

Aries, P. (1974). *Western attitudes toward death: From the Middle Ages to the present* (P. N. Ranum, Trans.). Baltimore: Johns Hopkins University Press.

Armor, D. J., Polich, J. M., & Stambul, H. B. (1976). *Alcoholism and treatment.* Santa Monica, CA: Rand.

Aronson, M. K. (Ed.). (1988). *Understanding Alzheimer's disease.* New York: Scribner's.

Atchley, R. C. (1975). The life course, age grading, and age-linked demands for decision making. In N. Datan & L. H. Ginsberg (Eds.), *Life-span developmental psychology: Normative life crises* (pp. 261–278). New York: Academic Press.

Atchley, R. C. (1976). *The sociology of retirement.* Cambridge, MA: Schenkman.

Atchley, R. C. (1977). *The social forces in later life.* Belmont, CA: Wadsworth.

Atchley, R. C. (1989). A continuity theory of normal aging. *The Gerontologist, 29*, 183–190.

Attig, M. S. (1983, November). *The processing of spatial information by adults.* Paper presented at the meeting of the Gerontological Society of America, San Francisco.

Averill, J. R. (1968). Grief: Its nature and significance. *Psychological Bulletin, 70*, 721–748.

Avioli, L. V. (1982). Aging, bone, and osteoporosis. In S. G. Korenman (Ed.), *Endocrine aspects of aging* (pp. 199–230). New York: Elsevier Biomedical.

Avolio, B. J., & Waldman, D. A. (1987). Personnel aptitude-test scores as a function of age, education, and job type. *Experimental Aging Research, 13*, 109–113.

Axelrod, S., & Cohen, L. D. (1961). Senescence and embedded-figure performance in vision and touch. *Perceptual and Motor Skills, 12*, 283–288.

Bäckman, L. (1985). Further evidence for the lack of adult age differences on free recall of subject performed tasks: The importance of motor action. *Human Learning, 4*, 79–87.

Bäckman, L., & Nilsson, L.-G. (1984). Aging effects in free recall: An exception to the rule. *Human Learning, 3*, 53–69.

Bäckman, L., & Nilsson, L.-G. (1985). Prerequisites for the lack of age differences in memory performance. *Experimental Aging Research, 11*, 67–73.

Baddeley, A. (1981). The cognitive psychology of everyday life. *British Journal of Psychology, 72*, 257–269.

Bahrick, H. P., Bahrick, P. P., & Wittlinger, R. P. (1975). Fifty years of memory for names and faces: A cross-sectional approach. *Journal of Experimental Psychology, 104*, 54–75.

Baird, L. (1973). *The graduates.* Princeton, NJ: Educational Testing Service.

Baker, H., Frank, O., Thind, S., Jaslow, J. P., & Louria, D. B. (1979). Vitamin profiles in elderly persons living at home or in nursing homes versus profiles in healthy young subjects. *Journal of the American Geriatrics Society, 27*, 444–450.

Baldessarini, R. J. (1978). Chemotherapy. In A. M. Nicholi (Ed.), *The Harvard guide to modern psychiatry* (pp. 387–432). New York: Belknap.

Ball, J. F. (1976–1977). Widow's grief: The impact of age and mode of death. *Omega: Journal of Death and Dying, 7*, 307–333.

Baltes, M. M., & Baltes, P. B. (Eds.). (1986). *The psychology of control and aging.* Hillsdale, NJ: Erlbaum.

Baltes, P. B. (1979). Life-span developmental psychology: Some converging observations on history and theory. In P. B. Baltes & O. G. Brim, Jr. (Eds.), *Life-span development and behavior* (Vol. 2, pp. 255–279). New York: Academic Press.

Baltes, P. B., Dittmann-Kohli, F., & Dixon, R. A. (1984). New perspectives on the development of intelligence in adulthood: Toward a dual-process conception and a model of selective optimization with compensation. In P. B. Baltes & O. G. Brim, Jr. (Eds.), *Life-span development and behavior* (Vol. 6, pp. 33–76). New York: Academic Press.

Baltes, P. B., Reese, H. W., & Lipsitt, L. P. (1980). Life-span developmental psychology. *Annual Review of Psychology, 31*, 65–100.

Baltes, P. B., Reese, H. W., & Nesselroade, J. R. (1977). *Life-span developmental psychology: Introduction to research methods.* Pacific Grove, CA: Brooks/Cole.

Baltes, P. B., & Schaie, K. W. (1974). Aging and IQ: The myth of the twilight years. *Psychology Today, 7*, 35–40.

Baltes, P. B., & Willis, S. L. (1982). Enhancement (plasticity) of intellectual functioning: Penn State's Adult Development and Enrichment Project (ADEPT). In F. I. M. Craik & S. Trehub (Eds.), *Aging and cognitive processes* (pp. 353–389). New York: Plenum.

Bandura, A. (1986). *Social foundations of thought and action: A social cognitive theory.* Englewood Cliffs, NJ: Prentice-Hall.

Bandura, A. (1990). Reflections on non-ability determinants of competence. In J. Kolligan, Jr., & R. J. Sternberg (Eds.), *Competence considered: Perceptions of competence and incompetence across the lifespan.* New Haven, CT: Yale University Press.

Barfield, R. E., & Morgan, J. N. (1978). Trends in satisfaction with retirement. *The Gerontologist, 18*, 19–23.

Barnett, R. C., & Baruch, G. K. (1978). *The competent women: Perspectives on development.* New York: Halstead/Wiley.

Baron, J. N., & Bielby, W. T. (1985). Organizational barriers to gender equality: Sex segregation of jobs and opportunities. In A. S. Rossi (Ed.), *Gender and the life course* (pp. 233–251). New York: Aldine.

Barresi, C. M. (1990). Ethnogerontology: Social aging in national, racial, and cultural groups. In K. F. Ferraro (Ed.), *Gerontology: Perspectives and issues* (pp. 247–265). New York: Springer.

Barrett, G. V. (1978). Task design, individual attributes, work satisfaction, and productivity. In A. Negandhi & B. Wilpert (Eds.), *Current research in work organizations.* Kent, OH: Kent State University Press.

Barrett, G. V., Alexander, R. A., & Forbes, J. B. (1977). Analysis of performance measurement and training requirements for driving decision making in emergency situations. *JSAS Catalogue of Selected Documents in Psychology, 7*, 126 (Ms. No. 1623).

Bartus, R., Dean, R. L., & Fisher, S. K. (1986). Cholinergic treatment for age-related memory disturbances: Dead or barely coming of age. In T. Crook, R. Bartus, S. Ferris, & S. Gershon (Eds.), *Treatment development strategies for Alzheimer's disease* (pp. 421–450). New Caanan, CT: Mark Powley Associates.

Baruch, G. K. (1984). The psychological well-being of women in the middle years. In G. K. Baruch & J. Brooks-Gunn (Eds.), *Women in midlife* (pp. 161–180). New York: Plenum.

Basseches, M. (1984). *Dialectical thinking and adult development.* Norwood, NJ: Ablex.

Bastida, E. (1987). Sex-typed age norms among older Hispanics. *The Gerontologist, 27*, 59–65.

Baylor, A. M., & Spirduso, W. W. (1988). Systemic aerobic exercise and components of reaction time in older women. *Journal of Gerontology, 43*, P121–P126.

Beall, C., & Goldstein, M. C. (1982). Work, aging, and dependency in a Sherpa population in Nepal. *Social Science and Medicine, 16*, 141–147.

Beall, C., & Goldstein, M. C. (1986). Age differences in sensory and cognitive function in elderly Nepalese. *Journal of Gerontology, 41*, 387–389.

Bean, F., & Tienda, M. (1987). *The Hispanic population in the United States.* New York: Russell Sage Foundation.

Beck, A. T. (1967). *Depression: Clinical, experimental, and theoretical aspects.* New York: Harper & Row.

Beck, A. T. (1976). *Cognitive therapy and the emotional disorders.* New York: International Universities Press.

Beck, A. T., Rush, J., Shaw, B., & Emery, G. (1979). *Cognitive therapy of depression.* New York: Guilford.

Beck, A. T., Ward, C. H., Mendelson, M., Mock, J., & Erbaugh, J. (1961). An inventory for measuring depression. *Archives of General Psychiatry, 4,* 561–571.

Bellezza, F. S. (1987). Mnemonic devices and memory schemas. In M. A. McDaniel & M. Pressley (Eds.), *Imagery and related mnemonic processes: Theories, individual differences, and applications* (pp. 34–55). New York: Springer-Verlag.

Bengtson, V. L. (1985). Diversity and symbolism in grandparental roles. In V. L. Bengtson & J. F. Robertson (Eds.), *Grandparenthood* (pp. 11–25). Beverly Hills, CA: Sage Publications.

Bengtson, V. L., Cuellar, J. B., & Raga, P. K. (1977). Stratum contrasts and similarities in attitudes toward death. *Journal of Gerontology, 32,* 76–88.

Bengtson, V. L., Dowd, J. J., Smith, D. H., & Inkles, A. (1975). Modernization, modernity and perceptions of aging: A cross-cultural study. *Journal of Gerontology, 30,* 688–695.

Bengtson, V. L., & Robertson, J. F. (Eds.). (1985). *Grandparenthood.* Beverly Hills, CA: Sage Publications.

Benin, M. H., & Agostinelli, J. (1988). Husbands' and wives' satisfaction with the division of labor. *Journal of Marriage and the Family, 50,* 349–361.

Benjamin, B. J. (1982). Phonological performance in gerontological speech. *Journal of Psycholinguistic Research, 11,* 159–167.

Berardi, A., Haxby, J. V., Grady, C. L., & Rapoport, S. I. (1991). Asymmetries of brain glucose metabolism and memory in healthy elderly. *Developmental Neuropsychology, 7,* 87–97.

Berg, C., Hertzog, C., & Hunt, E. (1982). Age differences in the speed of mental rotation. *Developmental Psychology, 18,* 95–107.

Berkman, L. F., Breslow, L., & Wingard, D. L. (1983). Health practices and mortality risk. In L. F. Berkman & L. Breslow (Eds.), *Health and ways of living: The Alameda County study* (pp. 61–112). New York: Oxford University Press.

Berkow, R. (Ed.). (1987). *The Merck manual of diagnosis and therapy* (15th ed.). Rahway, NJ: Merck, Sharp, & Dohme Research Laboratories.

Bernardi, B. (1985). *Age class systems: Social institutions and politics based on age.* Cambridge: Cambridge University Press.

Bernstein, J. (1982). Who leaves — who stays: Residency policy in housing for the elderly. *The Gerontologist, 22,* 305–313.

Berry, J. M. (1986). *Memory complaints and performance in older women: A self-efficacy and causal attribution model.* Unpublished doctoral dissertation, Washington University, St. Louis.

Berry, J. M., West, R. L., & Scogin, F. (1983, November). *Predicting everyday and laboratory memory skill.* Paper presented at the meeting of the Gerontological Society of America, San Francisco.

Berry, R. E., & Williams, F. L. (1987). Assessing the relationship between quality of life and marital and income satisfaction: A path analytic approach. *Journal of Marriage and the Family, 49,* 107–116.

Berscheid, E., Walster, E., & Bohrnstedt, G. (1973). Body image. The happy American body: A survey report. *Psychology Today, 7*(6), 119–131.

Betz, E. L. (1984). A study of career patterns of women college graduates. *Journal of Vocational Behavior, 24,* 249–263.

Betz, N., & Fitzgerald, L. F. (1987). *The career psychology of women.* New York: Academic Press.

Betz, N. E., & Hackett, G. (1986). Applications of self-efficacy theory to understanding career choice behavior. *Journal of Social and Clinical Psychology, 4,* 279–289.

Biegel, D. E., & Farkas, K. J. (1990). The impact of neighborhoods and ethnicity on black and white vulnerable elderly. In Z. Harel, P. Ehrlich, & R. Hubbard (Eds.), *The vulnerable aged* (pp. 116–136). New York: Springer.

Bielby, D. D., & Bielby, W. T. (1988). She works hard for the money: Household responsibilities and the allocation of work effort. *American Journal of Sociology, 93,* 1031–1059.

Bierman, E. L. (1985). Arteriosclerosis and aging. In C. E. Finch & E. L. Schneider (Eds.), *Handbook of the biology of aging* (2nd ed., pp. 842–858). New York: Van Nostrand Reinhold.

Biesele, M., & Howell, N. (1981). The old people give you life: Aging among !Kung hunter-gatherers. In P. T. Amoss

& S. Harrell (Eds.), *Other ways of growing old* (pp. 77–98). Palo Alto, CA: Stanford University Press.

Biller, H. B. (1982). Fatherhood: Implications for child and adult development. In B. B. Wolman (Ed.), *Handbook of developmental psychology* (pp. 702–725). Englewood Cliffs, NJ: Prentice-Hall.

Binet, H. (1903). *L'etude experimentale de l'intelligence.* Paris: Schleicher.

Binger, C. M., Ablin, A. R., Feuerstein, R. C., Kushner, J. H., Zoger, S., & Mikkelson, C. (1969). Childhood leukemia — Emotional impact on patient and family. *New England Journal of Medicine, 280,* 414.

Birren, J. E., & Cunningham, W. (1985). Research on the psychology of aging: Principles, concepts, and theory. In J. E. Birren & K. W. Schaie (Eds.), *Handbook of the psychology of aging* (2nd ed., pp. 3–34). New York: Van Nostrand Reinhold.

Birren, J. E., & Renner, V. J. (1977). Research on the psychology of aging. In J. E. Birren & K. W. Schaie (Eds.), *Handbook of the psychology of aging* (pp. 3–38). New York: Van Nostrand Reinhold.

Birren, J. E., & Renner, V. J. (1979). A brief history of mental health and aging. In *Issues in mental health and aging: Vol. 1. Research* (pp. 1–26). Washington, DC: National Institute of Mental Health.

Birren, J. E., & Renner, V. J. (1980). Concepts and issues of mental health and aging. In J. E. Birren & R. B. Sloane (Eds.), *Handbook of mental health and aging* (pp. 3–33). Englewood Cliffs, NJ: Prentice-Hall.

Black, P., Markowitz, R. S., & Cianci, S. (1975). Recovery of motor function after lesions in motor cortex of monkey. In R. Porter & D. W. Fitzsimmons (Eds.), *Outcome of severe damage to the central nervous system* (pp. 65–70). Amsterdam: Elsevier.

Blair, S. N., Kohl, H. W., Paffenbarger, R. S., et al. (1989). Physical fitness and all-cause mortality: A prospective study of healthy men and women. *Journal of the American Medical Association, 262,* 2395–2401.

Blake, B. F., & Lawton, M. P. (1980). Perceived community functions and the rural elderly. *Educational Gerontology, 5,* 375–386.

Blanchard-Fields, F. (1986). Reasoning on social dilemmas varying in emotional saliency: An adult developmental study. *Psychology and Aging, 1,* 325–333.

Blanchard-Fields, F., & Irion, J. C. (1988). The relation between locus of control and coping in two contexts: Age as a moderator variable. *Psychology and Aging, 3,* 197–203.

Blanchard-Fields, F., & Robinson, S. L. (1987). Age differences in the relation between controllability and coping. *Journal of Gerontology, 42,* 497–501.

Blass, J. P., & Barclay, L. L. (1985). New developments in the diagnosis of dementia. *Drug Development Research, 5,* 39–58.

Blazer, D., George, L. K., & Hughes, D. C. (1988). Schizophrenic symptoms in an elderly community population. In J. A. Brody & G. L. Maddox (Eds.), *Epidemiology and aging: An international perspective* (pp. 134–149). New York: Springer.

Blazer, D., Hughes, D. C., & George, L. K. (1987). The epidemiology of depression in an elderly community population. *The Gerontologist, 27,* 281–287.

Blazer, D., & Williams, C. D. (1980). Epidemiology of dysphoria and depression in the elderly populations. *American Journal of Psychiatry, 137,* 439–444.

Blessed, G., Tomlinson, B. E., & Roth, M. (1968). The association between quantitative measures of dementia and of senile changes in the cerebral grey matter of elderly subjects. *British Journal of Psychiatry, 114,* 797–811.

Block, R., DeVoe, M., Stanley, B., Stanley, M., & Pomara, N. (1985). Memory performance in individuals with primary degenerative dementia: Its similarity to diazepam-induced impairments. *Experimental Aging Research, 11,* 151–155.

Bloom, B. L., & Caldwell, R. A. (1981). Sex differences in adjustment during the process of marital separation. *Journal of Marriage and the Family, 43,* 693–701.

Blum, E. M. (1966). Psychoanalytic views of alcoholism: A review. *Quarterly Journal of Studies of Alcohol, 27,* 259–299.

Blum, J. E., & Jarvik, L. F. (1974). Intellectual performance of octogenarians as a function of education and initial ability. *Human Development, 17,* 364–375.

Blume, S. B. (1985). Psychodrama and the treatment of alcoholism. In S. Zimberg, J. Wallace, & S. B. Blume (Eds.), *Practical approaches to alcoholism psychotherapy* (pp. 87–108). New York: Plenum.

Blumenthal, J. A., Emery, C. F., Cox, D. R., Walsh, M. A., Kuhn, C. M., Williams, R. B., & Williams, R. S. (1988). Exercise training in healthy Type A middle-aged men: Effects on behavioral and cardiovascular responses. *Psychosomatic Medicine, 50,* 418–433.

Blumenthal, J. A., & Madden, D. J. (1988). Effects of aerobic exercise training, age, and physical fitness on memory-search performance. *Psychology and Aging, 3,* 280–285.

Blumstein, P., & Schwartz, P. (1983). *American couples.* New York: Morrow.

Bobrow, D. G., & Collins, A. (1975). *Representation and understanding: Studies in cognitive science.* New York: Academic Press.

Bohannon, P. (1980). Time, rhythm, and pace. *Science 80, 1*(3), 18, 20.

Boller, F. (1980). Mental status of patients with Parkinson's disease. *Journal of Clinical Neuropsychology, 2,* 157–172.

Boller, F., Mizutani, T., & Roessman, V. (1980). Parkinson's disease, dementia, and Alzheimer's disease: Clinico-pathological correlations. *Annals of Neurology, 7,* 329–335.

Bondareff, W. (1983). Age and Alzheimer's disease. *Lancet, 1,* 1447.

Bondareff, W. (1985). The neural basis of aging. In J. E. Birren & K. W. Schaie (Eds.), *Handbook of the psychology of aging* (2nd ed., pp. 95–112). New York: Van Nostrand Reinhold.

Bondareff, W., Mountjoy, C. Q., & Roth, M. (1982). Loss of neurons or origin of the adrenergic projection to cerebral cortex (nucleus locus ceruleus) in senile dementia. *Neurology, 32,* 164–168.

Bootzin, R. R. (1977). Effects of self-control procedures for insomnia. In R. B. Stuart (Ed.), *Behavioral self-management: Strategies, techniques, and outcomes* (pp. 176–195). New York: Brunner/Mazel.

Bootzin, R. R., & Engle-Friedman, M. (1987). Sleep disturbances. In L. L.

Carstensen & B. A. Edelstein (Eds.), *Handbook of clinical gerontology* (pp. 238–251). New York: Pergamon Press.

Bootzin, R. R., Engle-Friedman, M., & Hazelwood, L. (1983). Insomnia. In P. M. Lewinsohn & L. Teri (Eds.), *Clinical geropsychology: New directions in assessment and treatment* (pp. 81–115). New York: Pergamon Press.

Borg, S., & Lasker, J. (1981). *When pregnancy fails.* Boston: Beacon.

Borgatta, E. F., & Corsini, R. J. (1964). *Manual for the Quick Word Test.* New York: Harcourt, Brace, & World.

Borkan, G. A., & Norris, A. H. (1980). Assessment of biological age using a profile of physiological parameters. *Journal of Gerontology, 35,* 177–184.

Borkovec, T. D. (1982). Insomnia. *Journal of Consulting and Clinical Psychology, 50,* 880–895.

Bornstein, P. E., & Clayton, P. J. (1972). The anniversary reaction. *Diseases of the Nervous System, 33,* 470–472.

Bortz, W. M. (1982). Disuse and aging. *Journal of the American Medical Association, 248,* 1203–1208.

Borup, J. H. (1981). Relocation: Attitudes, information network, and problems encountered. *The Gerontologist, 21,* 501–511.

Borup, J. H. (1982). The effects of varying degrees of interinstitutional environmental change on long-term care of patients. *The Gerontologist, 22,* 409–417.

Borup, J. H. (1983). Relocation and mortality research: Assessment, reply, and the need to refocus the issues. *The Gerontologist, 23,* 235–242.

Borup, J. H., & Gallego, D. T. (1981). Mortality as affected by interinstitutional relocation: Update and assessment. *The Gerontologist, 21,* 8–16.

Borup, J. H., Gallego, D. T., & Heffernan, P. G. (1979). Relocation and its effect on mortality. *The Gerontologist, 19,* 135–140.

Borup, J. H., Gallego, D. T., & Heffernan, P. G. (1980). Relocation: Its effect on health, functioning, and mortality. *The Gerontologist, 20,* 468–479.

Bossé, R., & Ekerdt, D. J. (1981). Change in self-perception of leisure activities with retirement. *The Gerontologist, 21,* 650–653.

Botwinick, J. (1977). Intellectual abilities. In J. E. Birren & K. W. Schaie (Eds.), *Handbook of the psychology of aging* (pp. 580–605). New York: Van Nostrand Reinhold.

Botwinick, J., & Storandt, M. (1974). *Memory, related functions and age.* Springfield, IL: Charles C Thomas.

Bourestom, N., & Pastalan, L. (1981). The effects of relocation on the elderly: A reply. *The Gerontologist, 21,* 4–7.

Brandtstädter, J. (1989). Personal self-regulation of development: Cross-sequential analyses of development-related control beliefs and emotions. *Developmental Psychology, 25,* 96–108.

Brant, L. J., & Fozard, J. L. (1990). Age changes in pure tone thresholds in a longitudinal study of normal aging. *Journal of the Acoustical Society of America, 88,* 813–820.

Braune, R., & Wickens, C. D. (1985). The functional age profile: An objective decision criterion for the assessment of pilot performance capacities and capabilities. *Human Factors, 27,* 681–693.

Bray, D. W., Campbell, R. J., & Grant, D. L. (1974). *Formative years in business.* New York: Wiley.

Bray, D. W., & Howard, A. (1983). The AT&T longitudinal studies of managers. In K. W. Schaie (Ed.), *Longitudinal studies on adult psychological development* (pp. 266–312). New York: Guilford.

Breitner, J. C. S. (1988). Alzheimer's disease: Possible evidence for genetic causes. In M. K. Aronson (Ed.), *Understanding Alzheimer's disease* (pp. 34–49). New York: Scribner's.

Breslow, R., Kocsis, J., & Belkin, B. (1981). Contribution of the depressive perspective to memory function in depression. *American Journal of Psychiatry, 138,* 227–230.

Brickel, C. M. (1984). The clinical use of pets with the aged. *Clinical Gerontologist, 2,* 72–74.

Brim, O. G., Jr. (1968). Adult socialization. In J. A. Clausen (Ed.), *Socialization and society.* Boston: Little, Brown.

Brim, O. G., Jr., & Kagan, J. (1980). Constancy and change: A view of the issues. In O. G. Brim, Jr., & J. Kagan (Eds.), *Constancy and change in human development* (pp. 1–25). Cambridge, MA: Harvard University Press.

Brody, E. M. (1981). Women in the middle and family help to older people. *The Gerontologist, 21,* 471–480.

Brody, E. M. (1985). Parent care as a normative family stress. *The Gerontologist, 25,* 19–29.

Brody, E. M., Johnsen, P. T., Fulcomer, M. C., & Lang, A. M. (1983). Women's changing roles and help to elderly parents: Attitudes of three generations of women. *Journal of Gerontology, 38,* 597–607.

Brody, E. M., Kleban, M. H., Johnsen, P. T., Hoffman, C., & Schoonover, C. B. (1987). Work status and parent care: A comparison of four groups of women. *The Gerontologist, 27,* 201–208.

Brody, J. (1988, August 29). New test for Huntington's creates difficult choices. *Atlanta Journal,* p. 2B.

Brody, J. A. (1988). Changing health needs of the ageing population. In D. Evered & J. Whelan (Eds.), *Symposium on research and the ageing population* (pp. 208–215). Chichester, England: Wiley.

Broman, C. L. (1988). Household work and family life satisfaction of blacks. *Journal of Marriage and the Family, 50,* 743–748.

Brown, G. C., & Bornstein, R. A. (in press). Anatomical imaging methods for neurobehavioral studies. In *Neurobehavioral aspects of cerebrovascular disease.* New York: Oxford University Press.

Brown, J. K., & Kerns, V. (Eds.). (1985). *In her prime: A new view of middle-aged women.* South Hadley, MA: Bergin & Garvey.

Bruce, P. R., Coyne, A. C., & Botwinick, J. (1982). Adult age differences in metamemory. *Journal of Gerontology, 37,* 354–357.

Buell, S. J., & Coleman, P. D. (1979). Dendritic growth in the aged human brain and failure of growth in senile dementia. *Science, 206,* 854–856.

Bullock, W. A., & Dunn, N. J. (1988, August). *Aging, sex, and marital satisfaction.* Paper presented at the meeting of the American Psychological Association, Atlanta.

Burdman, G. M. (1986). *Healthful aging.* Englewood Cliffs, NJ: Prentice-Hall.

Burdz, M. P., Eaton, W. D., & Bond, J. B. (1988). Effect of respite care on dementia and nondementia patients and their caregivers. *Psychology and Aging, 3,* 38–42.

Burke, D. M., & Light, L. L. (1981). Memory and aging: The role of retrieval processes. *Psychological Bulletin, 90,* 513–546.

Burks, V., Lund, D., Gregg, C., & Bluhm, H. (1988). Bereavement and remarriage for older adults. *Death Studies, 12,* 51–60.

Burr, J. A. (1990). Race/sex comparisons of elderly living arrangements. *Research on Aging, 12,* 507–530.

Burrus-Bammel, L. L., & Bammel, G. (1985). Leisure and recreation. In J. E. Birren & K. W. Schaie (Eds.), *Handbook of the psychology of aging* (2nd ed., pp. 848–889). New York: Van Nostrand Reinhold.

Busch, J. W. (1985). Mentoring in graduate schools of education: Mentors' perceptions. *American Educational Research Journal, 22,* 257–265.

Buskirk, E. R. (1985). Health maintenance and longevity: Exercise. In C. E. Finch & E. L. Schneider (Eds.), *Handbook of the biology of aging* (2nd ed., pp. 894–931). New York: Van Rostrand Reinhold.

Buss, D. M., et al. (1990). International preferences in selecting mates: A study of 37 cultures. *Journal of Cross-Cultural Psychology, 21,* 5–47.

Busse, E. W., & Maddox, G. L. (1985). *The Duke longitudinal studies of normal aging: 1955–1980.* New York: Springer.

Butler, R. N., & Lewis, M. I. (1982). *Aging and mental health* (3rd ed.). St. Louis: C. V. Mosby.

Cain, B. S. (1982, December 12). Plight of the grey divorcee. *New York Times Magazine,* pp. 89–90, 92, 95.

Caird, F. I., & Judge, T. C. (1974). *Assessment of the elderly patient.* London: Pittman Medical.

Cameron, P. (1975). Mood as an indicant of happiness: Age, sex, social class, and situational differences. *Journal of Gerontology, 30,* 216–224.

Cameron, R., & Meichenbaum, D. (1982). The nature of effective coping and the treatment of stress related problems: A cognitive-behavioral perspective. In L. Goldberger & S. Breznitz (Eds.), *Handbook of stress: Theoretical and clinical aspects* (pp. 695–710). New York: Free Press.

Camp, C. J. (1989). World knowledge systems. In L. W. Poon, D. C. Rubin, & B. Wilson (Eds.), *Everyday cognition in adulthood and late life* (pp. 457–482). New York: Cambridge University Press.

Camp, C. J., Markley, R. P., & Kramer, J. J. (1983). Spontaneous use of mnemonics by elderly individuals. *Educational Gerontology, 9,* 57–71.

Camp, C. J., & McKitrick, L. A. (1991). Memory interventions in Alzheimer's-type dementia populations: Methodological and theoretical issues. In R. L. West & J. D. Sinnott (Eds.), *Everyday memory and aging: Current research and methodology* (pp. 155–172). New York: Springer-Verlag.

Campbell, A. (1981). *The sense of well-being in America: Recent patterns and trends.* New York: McGraw-Hill.

Campbell, J. I. D., & Charness, N. (1990). Age-related declines in working-memory skills: Evidence from a complex calculation task. *Developmental Psychology, 26,* 879–888.

Campione, W. A. (1987). The married woman's retirement decision: A methodological comparison. *Journal of Gerontology, 42,* 381–386.

Campione, W. A. (1988). Predicting participation in retirement preparation programs. *Journal of Gerontology, 43,* S91–S95.

Cantor, M. H. (1980). The informal support system: Its relevance in the lives in the elderly. In E. Borgatta & N. McCluskey (Eds.), *Aging and society* (pp. 111–146). Beverly Hills, CA: Sage Publications.

Caramazza, A., & Hillis, A. E. (1991). Lexical organization of nouns and verbs in the brain. *Nature, 349,* 788–790.

Carlin, V. F., & Mansberg, R. (1984). *If I live to be 100 . . . Congregate housing for later life.* West Nyack, NY: Parker.

Carp, F. M. (1966). *A future for the aged.* Austin: University of Texas Press.

Carp, F. M. (1975). User evaluation of housing for the elderly. *The Gerontologist, 16,* 102–111.

Carp, F. M. (1976). Housing and living environments of older people. In R. H. Binstock & E. Shanas (Eds.), *Handbook of aging and the social sciences* (pp. 244–271). New York: Van Nostrand Reinhold.

Carp, F. M. (1977). Impact of improved living environment on health and life expectancy. *The Gerontologist, 17,* 242–249.

Cartwright, A., Hockey, L., & Anderson, J. L. (1973). *Life before death.* London: Routledge & Kegan Paul.

Case, R. B., Heller, S. S., Case, N. B., & Moss, A. J. (1985). Type A behavior and survival after acute myocardial infarction. *New England Journal of Medicine, 312,* 737–741.

Caserta, M. S., Lund, D. A., Wright, S. D., & Redburn, D. E. (1987). Caregivers to dementia patients: The utilization of community services. *The Gerontologist, 27,* 209–214.

Cavanaugh, J. C. (1983). Comprehension and retention of television programs by 20- and 60-year-olds. *Journal of Gerontology, 38,* 190–196.

Cavanaugh, J. C. (1984). Effects of presentation format on adults' retention of television programs. *Experimental Aging Research, 10,* 51–53.

Cavanaugh, J. C. (1986–1987). Age differences in adults' self-reports of memory ability: It depends on how and what you ask. *International Journal of Aging and Human Development, 24,* 241–277.

Cavanaugh, J. C. (1989). The importance of awareness in memory aging. In L. W. Poon, D. C. Rubin, & B. Wilson (Eds.), *Everyday cognition in adulthood and late life* (pp. 416–436). New York: Cambridge University Press.

Cavanaugh, J. C., Grady, J. G., & Perlmutter, M. (1983). Forgetting and use of memory aids in 20 to 70 year olds' everyday life. *International Journal of Aging and Human Development, 17,* 113–122.

Cavanaugh, J. C., & Green, E. E. (1990). I believe, therefore I can: Self-efficacy beliefs in memory aging. In E. A. Lovelace (Ed.), *Aging and cognition: Mental processes, self-awareness, and interventions* (pp. 189–230). Amsterdam: North-Holland.

Cavanaugh, J. C., Kramer, D. A., Sinnott, J. D., Camp, C. J., & Markley, R. J. (1985). On missing links and such: Interfaces between cognitive research and everyday problem solving. *Human Development, 28,* 146–168.

Cavanaugh, J. C., & Morton, K. R. (1989). Contextualism, naturalistic inquiry, and the need for new science: A rethinking of everyday memory aging and childhood sexual abuse. In D. A. Kramer & M. Bopp (Eds.), *Transformation in clinical and developmental psychology* (pp. 89–114). New York: Springer-Verlag.

Cavanaugh, J. C., Morton, K. R., & Tilse, C. R. (1989). A self-evaluation framework for understanding everyday memory aging. In J. D. Sinnott (Ed.), *Everyday problem solving: Theory and application* (pp. 266–284). New York: Praeger.

Cavanaugh, J. C., & Murphy, N. Z. (1986). Personality and metamemory correlates of memory performance in younger and older adults. *Educational Gerontology, 12,* 387–396.

Cavanaugh, J. C., & Perlmutter, M. (1982). Metamemory: A critical examination. *Child Development, 53,* 11–28.

Cavanaugh, J. C., & Poon, L. W. (1989). Metamemorial predictors of memory performance in young and old adults. *Psychology and Aging, 4,* 365–368.

Cavanaugh, J. C., & Stafford, H. (1989). Being aware of issues and biases: Directions for research on post-formal thought. In M. L. Commons, J. D. Sinnott, F. A. Richards, & C. Armon (Eds.), *Adult development: Vol. 1. Comparisons and applications of adolescent and adult developmental models* (pp. 272–292). New York: Praeger.

Cerella, J. (1990). Aging and information-processing rate. In J. E. Birren & K. W. Schaie (Eds.), *Handbook of the psychology of aging* (3rd ed., pp. 201–221). San Diego: Academic Press.

Cerella, J., Poon, L. W., & Fozard, J. L. (1982). Age and iconic read-out. *Journal of Gerontology, 37,* 197–202.

Cerella, J., Poon, L. W., & Williams, D. M. (1980). Age and the complexity hypothesis. In L. W. Poon (Ed.), *Aging in the 1980s* (pp. 332–340). Washington, DC: American Psychological Association.

Chaffin, R., & Herrmann, D. J. (1983). Self reports of memory abilities by old and young adults. *Human Learning, 2,* 17–28.

Chance, J., Overcast, T., & Dollinger, S. J. (1978). Aging and cognitive regression: Contrary findings. *Journal of Psychology, 98,* 177–183.

Chandler, M. J. (1980). Life-span intervention as a symptom of conversion hysteria. In R. R. Turner & H. W. Reese (Eds.), *Life-span developmental psychology: Intervention* (pp. 79–91). New York: Academic Press.

Charness, N. (1981). Aging and skilled problem solving. *Journal of Experimental Psychology, 110,* 21–38.

Charness, N., & Bosman, E. A. (1990a). Expertise and aging: Life in the lab. In T. M. Hess (Ed.), *Aging and cognition: Knowledge organization and utilization* (pp. 343–385). Amsterdam: North-Holland.

Charness, N., & Bosman, E. A. (1990b). Human factors and design for older adults. In J. E. Birren & K. W. Schaie (Eds.), *Handbook of the psychology of aging* (3rd ed., pp. 446–463). San Diego: Academic Press.

Cherkin, A. (1984). Effects of nutritional status on memory function. In H. J. Armbrecht, J. M. Prendergast, & R. M. Coe (Eds.), *Nutritional intervention in the aging process* (pp. 229–249). New York: Springer-Verlag.

Cherlin, A. J., & Furstenberg, F. F., Jr. (1986). *The new American grandparent: A place in the family, a life apart.* New York: Basic Books.

Chiarello, C., & Hoyer, W. J. (1988). Adult age differences in implicit and explicit memory: Time course and encoding effects. *Psychology and Aging, 3,* 358–366.

Chinen, A. B. (1989). *In the ever after.* Willmette, IL: Chiron.

Chiriboga, D. A. (1982). Adaptation to marital separation in later and earlier life. *Journal of Gerontology, 37,* 109–114.

Chiriboga, D. A. (1984). Social stressors as antecedents of change. *Journal of Gerontology, 39,* 468–477.

Chiriboga, D. A. (1985, November). *Stress and personal continuity.* Paper presented at the meeting of the Gerontological Society of America, New Orleans.

Cicirelli, V. G. (1980). Sibling relationships in adulthood: A life-span perspective. In L. W. Poon (Ed.), *Aging in the 1980s* (pp. 455–474). Washington, DC: American Psychological Association.

Cicirelli, V. G. (1981). *Helping elderly parents: The role of adult children.* Boston: Auburn House.

Cicirelli, V. G. (1986). Family relationships and care/management of the dementing elderly. In M. Gilhooly, S. Zarit, & J. E. Birren (Eds.), *The dementias: Policy and management* (pp. 89–103). Englewood Cliffs, NJ: Prentice-Hall.

Clark, R. L., Maddox, G. L., Schrimper, R. A., & Sumner, D. A. (1984). *Inflation and the economic well-being of the elderly.* Baltimore: Johns Hopkins University Press.

Clark, R. L., & Spengler, J. J. (1980). *The economics of individual and population aging.* New York: Cambridge University Press.

Clark, W. C., & Mehl, L. (1971). Thermal pain: A sensory decision theory analysis of the effect of age and sex on d', various response criteria, and 50 percent pain threshold. *Journal of Abnormal Psychology, 78,* 202–212.

Clausen, J. A. (1981). Men's occupational careers in the middle years. In D. H. Eichorn, N. Haan, J. Clausen, M. Honzik, & P. Mussen (Eds.), *Present and past in middle life* (pp. 321–351). New York: Academic Press.

Clausen, J. A. (1986). *The life course: A sociological perspective.* Englewood Cliffs, NJ: Prentice-Hall.

Clayton, V. P., & Overton, W. F. (1973, November). *The role of formal operational thought in the aging process.* Paper presented at the meeting of the Gerontological Society of America, Miami.

Cleek, M. B., & Pearson, T. A. (1985). Perceived causes of divorce: An analysis of interrelationships. *Journal of Marriage and the Family, 47,* 179–191.

Clopton, W. (1973). Personality and career change. *Industrial Gerontology, 17,* 9–17.

Cohen, C. I., Teresi, J. A., & Holmes, D. (1988). The physical well-being of old homeless men. *Journal of Gerontology, 43,* S121–S128.

Cohen, C., Teresi, J., Holmes, D., & Roth, E. (1988). Survival strategies of older homeless men. *The Gerontologist, 28,* 58–65.

Cohen, G. (1979). Language comprehension in old age. *Cognitive Psychology, 11,* 412–429.

Cohen, G., & Faulkner, D. (1989). The effects of aging on perceived and generated memories. In L. W. Poon, D. C. Rubin, & B. Wilson (Eds.), *Everyday cognition in adulthood and late life* (pp. 222–243). New York: Cambridge University Press.

Cohen, G. D. (1990). Psychopathology and mental health in the mature and elderly adult. In J. E. Birren & K. W. Schaie (Eds.), *Handbook of the psychology of aging* (3rd ed., pp. 359–371). San Diego: Academic Press.

Cohen, R. M., Weingartner, H., Smallberg, S. A., Pickar, D., & Murphy, D. L. (1982). Effort and cognition in depression. *Archives of General Psychiatry, 39,* 593–597.

Cohler, B. J., & Grunebaum, H. U. (1981). *Mothers, grandmothers, and daughters: Personality and child care in three-generation families.* New York: Wiley.

Colby, A., Kohlberg, L., Gibbs, J. C., & Lieberman, M. (1983). A longitudinal study of moral development. *Monographs of the Society for Research in Child Development, 48* (Whole #200).

Coleman, K. A., Casey, V. A., & Dwyer, J. T. (1991, June). *Stability of autobiographical memories over four decades.* Paper presented at the meeting of the American Psychological Society, Washington, DC.

Coleman, M., & Ganong, L. H. (1990). Remarriage and stepfamily research in the 1980s: Increased interest in an old family form. *Journal of Marriage and the Family, 52,* 925–940.

Coleman, R. M., Miles, L. E., Guilleminault, C. C., Zarcone, V. P., van den Hoed, J., & Dement, W. C. (1981). Sleep wake disorders in the elderly: A polysomnographic analysis. *Journal of the American Geriatrics Association, 29,* 289–296.

Collopy, B. J. (1988). Autonomy in long term care: Some crucial distinctions. *The Gerontologist, 28(Suppl.),* 10–17.

Committee on an Aging Society. (1986). *Productive roles in an older society.* Washington, DC: National Academy Press.

Commons, M. L., Richards, F. A., & Armon, C. (Eds.). (1984). *Beyond formal operations: Late adolescent and adult cognitive development.* New York: Praeger.

Commons, M. L., Richards, F. A., & Kuhn, D. (1982). Systematic and metasystematic reasoning: A case for levels of reasoning beyond Piaget's stage of formal operations. *Child Development, 53,* 1058–1069.

Commons, M. L., Sinnott, J. D., Richards, F. A., & Armon, C. (Eds.). (1989). *Adult development: Vol. 1. Comparisons and applications of adolescent and adult developmental models.* New York: Praeger.

Connidis, I. (1988, November). *Sibling ties and aging.* Paper presented at the Gerontological Society of America, San Francisco.

Connor, C. L., Walsh, R. P., Lintzelman, D. K., & Alvarez, M. G. (1978). Evaluation of job applicants: The effects of age versus success. *Journal of Gerontology, 33,* 246–252.

Cook, J. A., & Wimberley, D. W. (1983). If I should die before I wake: Religious commitment and adjustment to the death of a child. *Journal for the Scientific Study of Religion, 22,* 222–238.

Cook-Greuter, S. (1989). Maps for living: Ego development stages from symbiosis to conscious universal embeddedness. In M. L. Commons, J. D. Sinnott, F. A. Richards, & C. Armon (Eds.), *Adult development: Vol. 2. Models and methods in the study of adolescent and adult thought* (pp. 79–104). New York: Praeger.

Cool, L. E. (1987). The effects of social class and ethnicity on the aging process. In P. Silverman (Ed.), *The elderly as modern pioneers* (pp. 211–227). Bloomington: Indiana University Press.

Cool, L., & McCabe, J. (1983). The "scheming hag" and the "dear old thing": The anthropology of aging women. In J. Sokolovsky (Ed.), *Growing old in different cultures* (pp. 56–68). Belmont, CA: Wadsworth.

Corkin, S., Growdon, J. H., Sullivan, E. V., Nissen, M. J., & Huff, F. J. (1986). Assessing treatment effects: A neuropsychological battery. In L. W.

Poon (Ed.), *Handbook for clinical memory assessment of older adults* (pp. 156–167). Washington, DC: American Psychological Association.

Cornelius, S. W. (1990). Aging and everyday cognitive abilities. In T. M. Hess (Ed.), *Aging and cognition: Knowledge organization and utilization* (pp. 411–459). Amsterdam: North-Holland.

Cornelius, S. W., & Caspi, A. (1987). Everyday problem solving in adulthood and old age. *Psychology and Aging, 2,* 144–153.

Corso, J. F. (1981). *Aging sensory systems and perception.* New York: Praeger.

Corso, J. F. (1984). Auditory processes and age: Significant problems for research. *Experimental Aging Research, 10,* 171–174.

Corso, J. F. (1987). Sensory-perceptual processes and aging. In K. W. Schaie (Ed.), *Annual review of gerontology and geriatrics* (Vol. 7, pp. 29–55). New York: Springer.

Cosby, A. (1974). Occupational expectations and the hypothesis of increasing realism of choice. *Journal of Vocational Behavior, 5,* 53–65.

Costa, P. T., Jr., & McCrae, R. R. (1977). Cross-sectional differences in masculinity-femininity in adult men. *The Gerontologist, 17,* 50.

Costa, P. T., Jr., & McCrae, R. R. (1978). Objective personality assessment. In M. Storandt, I. C. Siegler, & M. F. Elias (Eds.), *The clinical psychology of aging* (pp. 119–143). New York: Plenum.

Costa, P. T., Jr., & McCrae, R. R. (1980a). Somatic complaints in males as a function of age and neuroticism: A longitudinal analysis. *Journal of Behavioral Medicine, 3,* 245–258.

Costa, P. T., Jr., & McCrae, R. R. (1980b). Still stable after all these years: Personality as a key to some issues in adulthood and old age. In P. B. Baltes & O. G. Brim, Jr. (Eds.), *Life-span development and behavior* (Vol. 3, pp. 65–102). New York: Academic Press.

Costa, P. T., Jr., & McCrae, R. R. (1988). Personality in adulthood: A six-year longitudinal study of self-reports and spouse ratings on the NEO Personality Inventory. *Journal of Personality and Social Psychology, 54,* 853–863.

Costa, P. T., Jr., McCrae, R. R., & Arenberg, D. (1980). Enduring dispositions in adult males. *Journal of Personality and Social Psychology, 38,* 793–800.

Costa, P. T., Jr., McCrae, R. R., & Holland, J. L. (1984). Personality and vocational interests in an adult sample. *Journal of Applied Psychology, 42,* 390–400.

Cotman, C. W., & Holets, V. R. (1985). Structural changes at synapses with age: Plasticity and regeneration. In C. E. Finch & E. L. Schneider (Eds.), *Handbook of the biology of aging* (2nd ed., pp. 617–644). New York: Van Nostrand Reinhold.

Counts, D., & Counts, D. (Eds.). (1985a). *Aging and its transformations: Moving toward death in Pacific societies.* Lanham, MD: University Press of America.

Counts, D. A., & Counts, D. R. (1985b). I'm not dead yet! Aging and death: Processes and experiences in Kalia. In D. A. Counts & D. R. Counts (Eds.), *Aging and its transformations* (pp. 131–156). Lanham, MD: University Press of America.

Cowgill, D. (1974). Aging and modernization: A revision of the theory. In J. Gubrium (Ed.), *Late life: Communities and environmental policy* (pp. 123–146). Springfield, IL: Charles C Thomas.

Cowgill, D., & Holmes, L. D. (1972). *Aging and modernization.* New York: Appleton-Century-Crofts.

Coyne, A. C. (1983, November). *Age, task variables, and memory knowledge.* Paper presented at the meeting of the Gerontological Society of America, San Francisco.

Craik, F. I. M. (1977). Age differences in human memory. In J. E. Birren & K. W. Schaie (Eds.), *Handbook of the psychology of aging* (pp. 384–420). New York: Van Nostrand Reinhold.

Craik, F. I. M., & Byrd, M. (1982). Aging and cognitive deficits: The role of attentional sources. In F. I. M. Craik & S. Trehub (Eds.), *Aging and cognitive processes* (pp. 191–211). New York: Plenum.

Craik, F. I. M., & Lockhart, R. S. (1972). Levels of processing: A framework for memory research. *Journal of Verbal Learning and Verbal Behavior, 11,* 671–684.

Craik, F. I. M., & Rabinowitz, J. C. (1984). Age differences in the acquisition and use of verbal information. In H. Bouma & D. G. Bouwhuis (Eds.), *Attention and performance* (Vol. 10, pp. 471–499). Hillsdale, NJ: Erlbaum.

Crandall, R. C. (1980). *Gerontology: A behavioral science approach.* Reading, MA: Addison-Wesley.

Crook, T. (1987). Dementia. In L. L. Carstensen & B. A. Edelstein (Eds.), *Handbook of clinical gerontology* (pp. 96–111). New York: Pergamon Press.

Crook, T., & Cohen, G. (1983). *Physician's guide to the diagnosis and treatment of depression in the elderly.* New Canaan, CT: Mark Powley Associates.

Crosby, J. F. (1980). Critique of divorce statistics and their interpretation. *Family Relations, 29,* 51–58.

Cross, S., & Markus, H. (1991). Possible selves across the life span. *Human Development, 34,* 230–255.

Crystal, H. A. (1988). The diagnosis of Alzheimer's disease and other dementing disorders. In M. K. Aronson (Ed.), *Understanding Alzheimer's disease* (pp. 15–33). New York: Scribner's.

Cuber, J. F., & Harroff, P. B. (1965). *Sex and the significant Americans.* Baltimore: Penguin.

Cuellar, J. B., & Weeks, J. R. (1980). *Minority elderly Americans: A prototype for area offices on aging (executive summary).* San Diego: Allied Home Health Association.

Cunningham, W. R. (1987). Intellectual abilities and age. In K. W. Schaie (Ed.), *Annual review of gerontology and geriatrics* (Vol. 7, pp. 117–134). New York: Springer.

Curcio, C. A., Buell, S. J., & Coleman, P. D. (1982). Morphology of the aging central nervous system: Not all downhill. In J. A. Mortimer, F. J. Pirozzola, & G. I. Maletta (Eds.), *Advances in neurogerontology: Vol. 3. The aging motor system* (pp. 7–35). New York: Praeger.

Currey, J. D. (1984). Effects of differences in mineralization on the mechanical properties of bone. *Philosophical Transactions of the Royal Society of London (Biology), 304(1121),* 509–518.

Cutler, S. J., & Hendricks, J. (1990). Leisure and time use across the life course. In R. H. Binstock & L. K.

George (Eds.), *Handbook of aging and the social sciences* (3rd ed., pp. 169–185). San Diego: Academic Press.

Cutter, M. A. G. (1991). Euthanasia: Reassessing the boundaries. *Journal of NIH Research, 3(5),* 59–61.

Dakof, G. A., & Mendelsohn, G. A. (1986). Parkinson's disease: The psychological aspects of a chronic illness. *Psychological Bulletin, 99,* 375–387.

Daneman, M. (1987). Reading and working memory. In J. R. Beech & A. M. Colley (Eds.), *Cognitive approaches to reading* (pp. 57–86). New York: Wiley.

Daniels, P., & Weingarten, K. (1982). *Sooner or later: The timing of parenthood · in adult lives.* New York: Norton.

Dannefer, D. (1988). What's in a name? An account of the neglect of variability in the study of aging. In J. E. Birren & V. L. Bengtson (Eds.), *Emergent theories of aging* (pp. 356–384). New York: Springer.

Davidson, J. M., Chen, J. J., Crapo, L., Gray, G. D., Greenleaf, W. J., & Catania, J. A. (1983). Hormonal changes and sexual function in aging men. *Journal of Clinical Endocrinology and Metabolism, 57,* 71–77.

Davidson, R. J., Schwartz, G. E., Saron, C., Bennett, J., & Goleman, D. J. (1979). Frontal vs. parietal EEG asymmetry during positive and negative affect. *Psychophysiology, 16,* 202–203.

Davies, P. (1988). Alzheimer's disease and related disorders: An overview. In M. K. Aronson (Ed.), *Understanding Alzheimer's disease* (pp. 3–14). New York: Scribner's.

Davies, P., & Maloney, A. J. F. (1976). Selective loss of central cholinergic neurons in Alzheimer's disease. *Lancet, 2,* 1403.

Davis, K. C. (1980). The position and status of Black and White aged in rural Baptist churches in Missouri. *Journal of Minority Aging, 5,* 242–248.

DeFrank, R., & Ivancevich, J. M. (1986). Job loss: An individual level review and model. *Journal of Vocational Behavior, 19,* 1–20.

Degner, L. (1974). The relationship between some beliefs held by physicians and their life-prolonging decisions.

Omega: Journal of Death and Dying, 5, 223.

Dekker, J. A. M., Connor, D. J., & Thal, L. J. (1991). The role of cholinergic projections form the nucleus basalis in memory. *Neuroscience and Biobehavioral Reviews, 15,* 299–317.

DeMaris, A., & Leslie, G. R. (1984). Cohabitation with the future spouse: Its influence upon marital satisfaction and communication. *Journal of Marriage and the Family, 46,* 77–84.

Denney, N. W. (1974). Classification abilities in the elderly. *Journal of Gerontology, 29,* 309–314.

Denney, N. W. (1982). Aging and cognitive changes. In B. B. Wolman (Ed.), *Handbook of developmental psychology* (pp. 807–827). Englewood Cliffs, NJ: Prentice-Hall.

Denney, N. W. (1990). Adult age differences in traditional and practical problem solving. In E. A. Lovelace (Ed.), *Aging and cognition: Mental processes, self-awareness, and interventions* (pp. 329–349). Amsterdam: North-Holland.

Denney, N. W., & Cornelius, S. W. (1975). Class inclusion and multiple classification in middle and old age. *Developmental Psychology, 11,* 521–522.

Denney, N. W., & Pearce, K. A. (1989). A developmental study of practical problem solving in adults. *Psychology and Aging, 4,* 438–442.

Denney, N. W., Pearce, K. A., & Palmer, A. M. (1982). A developmental study of adults' performance on traditional and practical problem-solving tasks. *Experimental Aging Research, 8,* 115–118.

deVries, H. A. (1980). *Physiology of exercise for physical education and athletics* (3rd ed.). Dubuque, IA: William C. Brown.

deVries, H. A. (1983). Physiology of exercise and aging. In D. W. Woodruff & J. E. Birren (Eds.), *Aging: Scientific perspectives and social issues* (pp. 285–304). Pacific Grove, CA: Brooks/Cole.

Diamond, J. (1986). I want a girl just like the girl . . . *Discover, 7(11),* 65–68.

Dickstein, L. S. (1972). Death concern: Measurement and correlates. *Psychological Reports, 30,* 563–571.

Dignam, J. M., & Takemoto-Chock, N. K. (1981). Factors in the natural language of personality: Re-analysis, comparison, and interpretation of six major studies. *Multivariate Behavioral Research, 16*, 149–170.

Dimond, M., Lund, D. A., & Caserta, M. S. (1987). The role of social support in the first two years of bereavement in an elderly sample. *The Gerontologist, 27*, 599–604.

Dimsdale, J. E., Gilbert, J., Hutter, A. M., Hackett, T. P., & Block, P. C. (1981). Predicting cardiac morbidity based on risk factors and coronary angiographic findings. *American Journal of Cardiology, 47*, 73–76.

DiPrete, T. A., & Soule, W. T. (1988). Gender and promotion in segmented job ladder systems. *American Sociological Review, 53*, 26–40.

Discover. (1990, October). Parkinson's bug. P.18.

Dittmann-Kohli, F., & Baltes, P. B. (1990). Toward a neofunctionalist conception of adult intellectual development: Wisdom as a prototypical case of intellectual growth. In C. Alexander & E. Langer (Eds.), *Beyond formal operations: Alternative endpoints to human development* (pp. 54–78). New York: Oxford University Press.

Dixon, R. A. (1989). Questionnaire research on metamemory and aging: Issues of structure and function. In L. W. Poon, D. C. Rubin, & B. A. Wilson (Eds.), *Everyday cognition in adulthood and late life* (pp. 394–415). New York: Cambridge University Press.

Dixon, R. A., & Hultsch, D. F. (1983). Structure and development of metamemory in adulthood. *Journal of Gerontology, 38*, 682–688.

Dixon, R. A., & vonEye, A. (1984). Depth processing and text recall in adulthood. *Journal of Reading Behavior, 26*, 109–117.

Dohrenwend, B. P. (1979). Stressful life events and psychopathology: Some issues of theory and method. In J. E. Barrett, B. M. Rose, & G. L. Klerman (Eds.), *Stress and mental disorder* (pp. 1–15). New York: Raven Press.

Doka, K. J., & Mertz, M. E. (1988). The meaning and significance of great-grandparenthood. *The Gerontologist, 28*, 192–197.

Doty, R. L. Shaman, P. Appelbaum, S. L., Giberson, R., Sikorski, L., & Rosenberg, L. (1984). Smell identification ability: Changes with age. *Science, 226*, 1441–1443.

Doudna, C., & McBride, F. (1981). Where are the men for the women at the top? In P. Stein (Ed.), *Single life: Unmarried adults in social context*. New York: St. Martin's.

Douglass, W. A. (1969). *Death in Murelaga: Funerary ritual in a Spanish Basque village*. Seattle: University of Washington Press.

Dowd, J. J. (1980). *Stratification among the aged*. Pacific Grove, CA: Brooks/Cole.

Dowd, J. J., & Bengtson, V. L. (1978). Aging in minority populations: An examination of the double jeopardy hypothesis. *Journal of Gerontology, 33*, 427–436.

Doyle, K. O., Jr. (1974). Theory and practice of ability testing in ancient Greece. *Journal of the History of the Behavioral Sciences, 10*, 202–212.

Drachman, D. A., Noffsinger, D., Sahakian, B. J., Kurdziel, S., & Fleming, P. (1980). Aging, memory, and the cholinergic system: A study of dichotic listening. *Neurobiology of Aging, 1*, 39–43.

Duara, R., London, E. D., & Rapoport, S. I. (1985). Changes in structure and energy metabolism of the aging brain. In C. E. Finch & E. L. Schneider (Eds.), *Handbook of the biology of aging* (2nd ed., pp. 595–616). New York: Van Nostrand Reinhold.

Dublin, L. I., Lotka, A. J., & Spiegelman, M. (1946). *The money value of a man*. New York: Ronald.

DuBois, P. H. (1968). A test dominated society: China 1115 B. C.–1905 A. D. In J. L. Barnette (Ed.), *Readings in psychological tests and measurements* (pp. 249–255). Homewood, IL: Dorsey Press.

Dunn, J. (1984). Sibling studies and the developmental impact of critical incidents. In P. B. Baltes & O. G. Brim, Jr. (Eds.), *Life-span development and behavior* (Vol. 6). New York: Academic Press.

Dwyer, J. W., & Coward, R. T. (1991). A multivariate comparison of the involvement of adult sons versus daughters in the care of impaired parents. *Journal of Gerontology: Social Sciences, 46*, S259–S269.

Dychtwald, K. (Ed.). (1986). *Wellness and health promotion for the elderly*. Rockville, MD: Aspen.

Eckhardt, M. J., Harford, T. C., Kaelber, C. T., Parker, E. S., Rosenthal, L. S., Ryback, R. S., Salmoiraghi, G. C., Vanderveen, E., & Warren, K. R. (1981). Health hazards associated with alcohol consumption. *Journal of the American Medical Association, 246*, 648–666.

Edelstein, S. (December 1990–January 1991). Do grandparents have rights? *Modern Maturity*, 40–42.

Eisdorfer, C., & Wilkie, F. (1977). Stress, disease, aging, and behavior. In J. E. Birren & K. W. Schaie (Eds.), *Handbook of the psychology of aging* (pp. 251–275). New York: Van Nostrand Reinhold.

Eisner, D. A. (1973). *The effect of chronic brain syndrome upon concrete and formal operations in elderly men*. Unpublished manuscript cited in Papalia & Bielby (1974).

Ekert, J. K. (1980). *The unseen elderly: A study of marginally subsistent hotel dwellers*. San Diego: Campanile.

Ekstrom, R. B., French, J. W., & Harman, H. H. (1979). Cognitive factors: Their identification and replication. *Multivariate Behavioral Research Monographs*, No. 79. 2.

Elder, G. H., Jr. (1974). *Children of the great depression*. Chicago: University of Chicago Press.

Ellison, C. G. (1990). Family ties, friendships, and subjective well-being among Black Americans. *Journal of Marriage and the Family, 52*, 298–310.

Emery, C. F., & Gatz, M. (1990). Psychological and cognitive effects of an exercise program for community-residing older adults. *The Gerontologist, 30*, 184–188.

Eng, E., Hatch, J., & Callan, A. (1985). Institutionalizing social support through the church and into the community. *Health Education Quarterly, 12*, 81–92.

Engen, T. (1982). *The perception of odors*. New York: Academic Press.

Epstein, L. J. (1976). Depression in the elderly. *Journal of Gerontology, 31*, 278–282.

Epstein, L. J. (1978). Anxiolytics, anti-depressants and neuroleptics in the treatment of geriatric patients. In M. A. Lipton, A. D. Mascio, & K. F. Killam (Eds.), *Psychopharmacology: A generation of progress* (pp. 1517–1523). New York: Raven Press.

Eribes, R. A., & Bradley-Rawls, M. (1978). Underutilization of nursing home facilities by Mexican American elderly in the Southwest. *The Gerontologist, 18*, 363–371.

Erickson, R., & Ekert, K. (1977). The elderly poor in downtown San Diego hotels. *The Gerontologist, 17*, 440–446.

Erickson, R. C., Poon, L. W., & Walsh-Sweeney, L. (1980). Clinical memory testing of the elderly. In L. W. Poon, J. L. Fozard, L. S. Cermak, D. Arenberg, & L. W. Thompson (Eds.), *New directions in memory aging* (pp. 379–402). Hillsdale, NJ: Erlbaum.

Ericsson, K. A., & Smith, J. (Eds.). (1991). *Toward a general theory of expertise: Prospects and limits*. New York: Cambridge University Press.

Erikson, E. H. (1968). *Identity: Youth and crisis*. New York: Norton.

Erikson, E. H. (1982). *The life cycle completed: Review*. New York: Norton.

Ershler, W. B. (1991). Cancer biology and aging. *Journal of NIH Research, 3(1)*, 50–52.

Espino, D. V., & Maldonado, D. (1990). Hypertension and acculturation in elderly Mexican Americans: Results from 1982–84 Hispanic HANES. *Journal of Gerontology: Medical Sciences, 45*, M209–M213.

Essex, M. J., & Nam, S. (1987). Marital status and loneliness among older women. *Journal of Marriage and the Family, 49*, 93–106.

Estes, C. L., Fox, S., & Mahoney, C. W. (1986). Health care and social policy: Health promotion and the elderly. In K. Dychtwald (Ed.), *Wellness and health promotion for the elderly* (pp. 55–70). Rockville, MD: Aspen.

Estes, R. J., & Wilensky, H. L. (1978). Life cycle squeeze and the morale curve. *Social Problems, 25*, 277–292.

Evans, G. W., Brennan, P. L., Skorpanich, M. A., & Held, D. (1984). Cognitive mapping and elderly adults: Verbal and location memory for urban landmarks. *Journal of Gerontology, 39*, 452–457.

Exton-Smith, A. N. (1985). Mineral metabolism. In C. E. Finch & E. L. Schneider (Eds.), *Handbook of the biology of aging* (2nd ed., pp. 511–539). New York: Van Nostrand Reinhold.

Farmer, P. M., Peck, A., & Terry, R. D. (1976). Correlations among neuritic plaques, neurofibrillary tangles, and the severity of senile dementia. *Journal of Neuropathology and Experimental Neurology, 35*, 367–376.

Farrell, M. P., & Rosenberg, S. D. (1981). *Men at midlife*. Boston: Auburn House.

Featherman, D. L. (1981). The life-span perspective in social science research. In American Association for the Advancement of Science (Ed.), *Policy outlook: Science, technology, and the issues of the eighties Vol. 2: Sources*. Washington, DC: U.S. Government Printing Office.

Feifel, H. (1965). The function of attitudes toward death. In Group for the Advancement of Psychiatry (Eds.), *Death and dying: Attitudes of patient and doctor* (pp. 632–641). New York: Mental Health Materials Center.

Feifel, H., & Nagy, V. T. (1981). Another look at fear of death. *Journal of Consulting and Clinical Psychology, 49*, 278–286.

Feinberg, R. (1983). The meaning of sibling on Anata. In M. Marshall (Ed.), *Siblingship in Oceania: Studies in the meaning of kin relations* (pp. 105–148). New York: University Press of America.

Feinson, M. C. (1987). Mental health and aging: Are there gender differences? *The Gerontologist, 27*, 703–711.

Feldman, S. S., Nash, S. C., & Aschenbrenner, B. G. (1983). Antecedents of fathering. *Child Development, 54*, 1628–1636.

Felton, B. J., & Revenson, T. A. (1987). Age differences in coping with chronic illness. *Psychology and Aging, 2*, 164–170.

Fenske, N. A., & Lober, C. W. (1990). Skin changes of aging: Pathological implications. *Geriatrics, 45(3)*, 27–35.

Ferraro, K. F., & Sterns, H. L. (1990). Epilogue: "2020 vision" and beyond. In K. F. Ferraro (Ed.), *Gerontology: Perspectives and issues* (pp. 357–360). New York: Springer.

Ferris, S. H., & Crook, T. (1983). Cognitive assessment in mild to moderately

severe dementia. In T. Crook, S. Ferris, & R. Bartus (Eds.), *Assessment in geriatric psychopharmacology*. New Canaan, CT: Mark Powley Associates.

Ferris, S. H., Crook, T., Flicker, C., Reisberg, B., & Bartus, R. T. (1986). Assessing cognitive impairment and evaluating treatment effects: Psychometric and performance tests. In L. W. Poon (Ed.), *Handbook for clinical memory assessment of older adults* (pp. 139–148). Washington, DC: American Psychological Association.

Fields, T. M., & Widmayer, S. M. (1982). Motherhood. In B. B. Wolman (Ed.), *Handbook of developmental psychology* (pp. 681–701). Englewood Cliffs, NJ: Prentice-Hall.

Fischer, D. H. (1978). *Growing old in America*. New York: Oxford University Press.

Fisher, H. E. (1987). The four-year itch. *Natural History, 96(10)*, 22–33.

Fisk, A. D., McGee, N. D., & Giambra, L. (1988). The influence of age on consistent and varied semantic-category search performance. *Psychology and Aging, 3*, 323–333.

Fisk, A. D., & Rogers, W. (1987, November). *Associative and priority learning in memory and visual search: A theoretical view of age-dependent practice effects*. Paper presented at the National Institute on Aging Conference on Aging and Attention, Washington, DC.

Fiske, M., & Chiriboga, D. A. (1985). The interweave of societal and personal change in adulthood. In J. Munnichs, P. Mussen, E. Olbrich, & P. G. Coleman (Eds.), *Life-span and change in gerontological perspective* (pp. 177–209). New York: Academic Press.

Fitzpatrick, M. A. (1984). A topological approach to marital interaction — Recent theory and research. *Advances in Experimental Sociology, 18*, 1–47.

Fogel, B. S., & Fretwell, M. (1985). Reclassification of depression in the medically ill elderly. *Journal of the American Geriatrics Society, 42*, 446–448.

Folkman, S., Lazarus, R. S., Pimley, S., & Novacek, J. (1987). Age differences in stress and coping processes. *Psychology and Aging, 2*, 171–184.

Folstein, M. F., Folstein, S. E., & McHugh, P. R. (1975). Mini-mental state: A practical method for grading the cognitive state of patients for the clinician. *Journal of Psychiatric Research, 12,* 189–198.

Foner, A., & Kertzer, D. I. (1978). Transitions over the life course: Lessons from age-set societies. *American Journal of Sociology, 83,* 1081–1104.

Foner, A., & Kertzer, D. I. (1979). Intrinsic and extrinsic sources of change in life course transitions. In M. W. Riley (Ed.), *Aging from birth to death: Interdisciplinary perspectives* (pp. 121–136). Boulder, CO: Westview.

Foner, A., & Schwab, K. (1981). *Aging and retirement.* Pacific Grove, CA: Brooks/ Cole.

Foner, N. (1984). *Ages in conflict: A cross-cultural perspective on inequality between old and young.* New York: Columbia University Press.

Fortes, M. (1950). Kinship and marriage among the Ashanti. In A. R. Radcliffe-Brown & D. Forde (Eds.), *African systems of kinship and marriage* (pp. 252–284). London: Oxford University Press.

Fortes, M. (1984). Age, generation and social structure. In D. Kertzer & J. Keith (Eds.), *Age and anthropological theory.* Ithaca, NY: Cornell University Press.

Fox, A. (1979, January). Earnings replacement rates of retired couples: Findings from the Retirement History Study. *Social Security Bulletin, 42,* 17–39.

Fox, M., Gibbs, M., & Auerbach, D. (1985). Age and gender dimensions of friendship. *Psychology of Women Quarterly, 9,* 489–502.

Fozard, J. L. (1981). Speed of mental performance and aging: Costs of age and benefits of wisdom. In F. J. Piorzzolo & G. J. Maletta (Eds.), *Behavioral assessment and psychopharmacology* (pp. 59–94). New York: Praeger.

Fozard, J. L., & Popkin, S. J. (1978). Optimizing adult development: Ends and means of an applied psychology of aging. *American Psychologist, 33,* 975–989.

Freed, A. O. (1990). How Japanese families cope with fragile elderly. *Journal of Gerontological Social Work, 15,* 39–56.

Freedman, M. (1966). *Chinese lineage and society: Fukien and Kwangtung.* London: Athlone.

Freeman, J. T. (1979). *Aging: Its history and literature.* New York: Human Sciences Press.

Friedman, E. A., & Orbach, H. L. (1974). Adjustment to retirement. In S. Arieti (Ed.), *American handbook of psychiatry: Vol. 1* (2nd ed., pp. 609–645). New York: Basic Books.

Friedman, L., Bliwise, D. L., Yesavage, J. A., & Salom, S. R. (1991). A preliminary study comparing sleep restriction and relaxation treatments for insomnia in older adults. *Journal of Gerontology: Psychological Sciences, 46,* P1–P8.

Friedman, L. A., & Kimball, A. W. (1986). Coronary heart disease mortality and alcohol consumption in Framingham. *American Journal of Epidemiology, 124,* 481–489.

Friedman, M., & Rosenman, R. H. (1974). *Type A behavior and your heart.* New York: Random House.

Fries, J. F., & Crapo, L. M. (1986). The elimination of premature disease. In K. Dychtwald (Ed.), *Wellness and health promotion for the elderly* (pp. 19–38). Rockville, MD: Aspen.

Frieze, I. H., Parsons, J. E., Johnson, P. B., Ruble, D. N., & Zellman, G. L. (1978). *Women and sex roles: A social psychological perspective.* New York: Norton.

Frolkis, V. V., & Bezrukov, V. V. (Eds.). (1979). *Aging of the central nervous system: Vol. 11. Interdisciplinary topics in human aging.* New York: Karger.

Fry, C. L. (1985). Culture, behavior, and aging in the comparative perspective. In J. E. Birren & K. W. Schaie (Eds.), *Handbook of the psychology of aging* (2nd ed., pp. 216–244). New York: Van Nostrand Reinhold.

Fry, C. L. (1988). Theories of age and culture. In J. E. Birren & V. L. Bengtson (Eds.), *Emergent theories of aging* (pp. 447–481). New York: Springer.

Fry, C. L., & Keith, J. (1982). The life course as a cultural unit. In M. W. Riley (Ed.), *Aging from birth to death: Sociotemporal perspectives.* Boulder, CO: Westview.

Fry, P. S. (1986). *Depression, stress, and adaptation in the elderly.* Rockville, MD: Aspen.

Fulton, R. (1970). Death, grief, and social recuperation. *Omega: Journal of Death and Dying, 1,* 23–28.

Furstenberg, F. F., Jr. (1982). Conjugal succession: Reentering marriage after divorce. In P. B. Baltes & O. G. Brim, Jr. (Eds.), *Life-span development and behavior* (Vol. 5, pp. 108–146). New York: Academic Press.

Furstenberg, F. F., Jr., & Nord, C. W. (1985). Parenting apart: Patterns of childbearing after marital disruption. *Journal of Marriage and the Family, 47,* 893–912.

Futterman, A., Gallagher, D., Thompson, L. W., Lovett, S., & Gilewski, M. (1990). Retrospective assessment of marital adjustment and depression during the first two years of spousal bereavement. *Psychology and Aging, 5,* 277–283.

Gailey, C. W. (1987). Evolutionary perspectives on gender hierarchy. In B. B. Hess & M. M. Feree (Eds.), *Analyzing gender* (pp. 32–67). Newbury Park, CA: Sage Publications.

Gajdusek, D. C. (1977). Unconventional viruses and the origin and disappearance of kuru. *Science, 197,* 943–960.

Gallagher, D., & Thompson, L. W. (1983). Depression. In P. M. Lewinsohn & L. Teri (Eds.), *Clinical geropsychology* (pp. 7–37). New York: Pergamon Press.

Garber, J., & Seligman, M. E. P. (Eds.). (1980). *Human helplessness: Theory and applications.* New York: Academic Press.

Garland, C., Barrett-Connor, E., Suarez, L., Criqui, M. H., & Wingard, D. L. (1985). Effects of passive smoking on ischemic heart disease mortality of nonsmokers: A prospective study. *American Journal of Epidemiology, 121,* 645–650.

Garn, S. M. (1975). Bone loss and aging. In R. Goldman & M. Rockstein (Eds.), *The physiology and pathology of aging* (pp. 39–57). New York: Academic Press.

Gatz, M., & Siegler, I. C. (1981, August). *Locus of control: A retrospective.* Paper presented at the meeting of the American Psychological Association, Los Angeles.

Gaylord, S. A., & Zung, W. W. K. (1987). Affective disorders among the aging. In L. L. Carstensen & B. A. Edelstein

(Eds.), *Handbook of clinical gerontology* (pp. 76–95). New York: Pergamon Press.

Gentry, M., & Schulman, A. D. (1988). Remarriage as a coping response for widowhood. *Psychology and Aging, 3*, 191–196.

George, L. K. (1980). *Role transitions in later life.* Pacific Grove, CA: Brooks/Cole.

George, L. K., Fillenbaum, G., & Palmore, E. (1984). Sex differences in the antecedents and consequences of retirement. *Journal of Gerontology, 39*, 364–371.

George, L. K., & Gwyther, L. P. (1986). Caregiver well-being: A multi-dimensional examination of family caregivers of demented adults. *The Gerontologist, 26*, 253–259.

Gerard, L., Zacks, R. T., Hasher, L., & Radvansky, G. A. (1991). Age deficits in retrieval: The fan effect. *Journal of Gerontology: Psychological Sciences, 46*, P131–P136.

Gerner, R. H., & Jarvik, L. F. (1984). Antidepressant drug treatment in the elderly. In E. Friedman, F. Mann, & S. Gerson (Eds.), *Depression and antidepressants: Implications for considera-tion and treatment.* New York: Raven Press.

Giambra, L. M., & Quilter, R. E. (1988). Sustained attention in adulthood: A unique, large-sample, longitudinal and multicohort analysis using the Mackworth Clock Test. *Psychology and Aging, 3*, 75–83.

Gibbs, J. C., Gajdusek, D. C., Asher, D. M., Alpers, M. P., Beck, E., Daniel, P. M., & Matthews, W. B. (1968). Creutzfeld-Jakob disease (spongiform encephalopathy): Transmission to the chimpanzee. *Science, 161*, 388–389.

Gibson, R. C. (1986). *Blacks in an aging society.* New York: Carnegie Corporation.

Gibson, R. C. (1987). Reconceptualizing retirement for Black Americans. *The Gerontologist, 27*, 691–698.

Gibson, R. C. (1991). The subjective retirement of black Americans. *Journal of Gerontology: Social Sciences, 46*, S204–S209.

Gilewski, M. J., & Zelinski, E. M. (1986). Questionnaire assessments of memory complaints. In L. W. Poon (Ed.), *Handbook for clinical memory assessment of older adults* (pp. 93–107). Washington, DC: American Psychological Association.

Gilewski, M. J., Zelinski, E. M., & Schaie, K. W. (1990). The Memory Functioning Questionnaire for assessment of memory complaints in adulthood and old age. *Psychology and Aging, 5*, 482–490.

Gilford, R. (1984). Contrasts in marital satisfaction throughout old age: An exchange theory analysis. *Journal of Gerontology, 39*, 325–333.

Gilhooly, M. L. M. (1984). The impact of caregiving on caregivers: Factors associated with the psychological well-being of people supporting a demented relative in the community. *British Journal of Medical Psychology, 57*, 35–44.

Gilhooly, M. L. M. (1986). Senile dementia: Factors associated with caregivers' preference for institutional care. *British Journal of Medical Psychology, 59*, 165–171.

Gill, J. S., Zezulka, A. V., Shipley, M. J., Gill, S. K., & Beevers, D. G. (1986). Stroke and alcohol consumption. *New England Journal of Medicine, 315*, 1041–1046.

Gilleard, C. J., & Gurkan, A. A. (1987). Socioeconomic development and the status of elderly men in Turkey: A test of modernization theory. *Journal of Gerontology, 42*, 353–357.

Gilligan, C. (1982). *In a different voice: Psychological theory and women's development.* Cambridge, MA: Harvard University Press.

Glamser, F., & Hayslip, B., Jr. (1985). The impact of retirement on participation in leisure activities. *Therapeutic Recrea-tion Journal, 19*, 28–38.

Glascock, A. P., & Feinman, S. (1981). Social asset of social burden: Treatment of the aged in non-industrial societies. In C. L. Fry (Ed.), *Dimensions: Aging, culture, and health* (pp. 13–32). New York: Praeger.

Glaser, B. G., & Strauss, A. L. (1965). *Awareness of dying.* Chicago: Aldine-Atherton.

Glaser, B. G., & Strauss, A. L. (1968). *Time for dying.* Chicago: Aldine-Atherton.

Glenn, N. D., & McLanahan, S. (1981). The effects of offspring on the psychological well-being of older adults. *Journal of Marriage and the Family, 43*, 409–421.

Glenn, N. D., & McLanahan, S. (1982). Children and marital happiness: A further specification of the relationship. *Journal of Marriage and the Family, 44*, 63–72.

Glenn, N. D., & Supancic, M. (1984). The social and demographic correlates of divorce and separation in the United States: An update and reconsideration. *Journal of Marriage and the Family, 46*, 563–575.

Glenn, N. D., & Weaver, C. N. (1978). The marital happiness of remarried divorced persons. *Journal of Marriage and the Family, 40*, 269–282.

Glick, I. O., Weiss, R. S., & Parkes, C. M. (1974). *The first year of bereavement.* New York: Wiley.

Glick, P. C., & Lin, S.-L. (1986). Recent changes in divorce and remarriage. *Journal of Marriage and the Family, 48*, 737–748.

Glick, P. C., & Norton, A. J. (1979). Marrying, divorcing, and living together in the U. S. today. *Population Bulletin, 32*, 1–41.

Goate, A., Chartier-Harlin, M.-C., Mullan, M., Brown, J., Crawford, F., Fidani, L., Guiffra, L., Haynes, A., Irving, N., James, L., Mant, R., Newton, P., Rooke, K., Roques, P., Talbot, C., Williamson, R., Rossor, M., Owen, M., & Hardy, J. (1991). Segregation of a missense mutation in the amyloid precursor protein gene with familial Alzheimer's disease. *Nature, 349*, 704–706.

Goggin, N. L., & Stelmach, G. E. (1990). Age-related deficits in cognitive-motor skills. In E. A. Lovelace (Ed.), *Aging and cognition: Mental processes, self-awareness, and interventions* (pp. 135–155). Amsterdam: North-Holland.

Golant, S. M. (1984). The effects of residential and activity behaviors on old people's environmental experiences. In I. Altman, J. Wohlwill, & M. P. Lawton (Eds.), *Human behavior and the environment: Elderly people and the environment* (pp. 239–278). New York: Plenum.

Golant, S. M. (1988). Housing in the year 2020: What does the future hold? In S. M. Golant, D. L. Gutmann, B. L. Neugarten, & S. S. Tobin (Eds.), *The aging society: A look toward the year 2020* (pp. 8–28). Chicago: Center for Applied Gerontology.

Gold, D. T. (1990). Late-life sibling relationships: Does race affect typological distribution? *The Gerontologist, 30,* 741–748.

Goldstein, A., & Goldstein, S. (1986). The challenge of an aging population in the People's Republic of China. *Research on Aging, 8,* 179–199.

Goldstein, E. (1979). Effect of same-sex and cross-sex role models on the subsequent academic productivity of scholars. *American Psychologist, 34,* 407–410.

Gonda, J. (1980). Relationship between formal education and cognitive functioning: A historical perspective. *Educational Gerontology, 5,* 283–291.

Goode, W. J. (1956). *After divorce.* Glencoe, IL: Free Press.

Goody, J. (1976). Aging in non-industrial societies. In R. H. Binstock & E. Shanas (Eds.), *Handbook of aging and the social sciences* (2nd ed., pp. 117–129). New York: Van Nostrand Reinhold.

Gordon, C., Gaitz, C. M., & Scott, J. (1976). Leisure and lives: Personal expressivity across the life span. In R. H. Binstock & E. Shanas (Eds.), *Handbook of aging and the social sciences* (2nd ed., pp. 310–341). New York: Van Nostrand Reinhold.

Gordon, T., & Doyle, J. T. (1987). Drinking and mortality : The Albany study. *American Journal of Epidemiology, 125,* 263–270.

Gordon, T., & Kannel, W. B. (1984). Drinking and mortality: The Framingham study. *American Journal of Epidemiology, 120,* 97–107.

Gordon-Salant, S. (1987). Age-related differences in speech recognition performance as a function of test format and paradigm. *Ear and Hearing, 8,* 277–282.

Gottfries, C. G. (1985). Alzheimer's disease and senile dementia: Biochemical characteristics and aspects of treatment. *Psychopharmacology, 86,* 245–252.

Gottfries, C. G., Gottfries, I., & Roos, B. E. (1969). The investigation of homovanillic acid in the human brain and its correlation to senile dementia. *British Journal of Psychiatry, 115,* 563–574.

Gottfries, C. G., Roos, B. E., & Winblad, B. (1976). Monoamine and monoamine metabolites in the human brain post mortem in senile dementia. *Aktuelle Gerontologie, 6,* 429–435.

Gottsdanker, R. (1982). Age and simple reaction time. *Journal of Gerontology, 37,* 342–348.

Granick, S., & Friedman, A. S. (1973). Effect of education on decline of psychometric test performance with age. *Journal of Gerontology, 22,* 191.

Gratzinger, P., Sheikh, J. I., Friedman, L., & Yesavage, J. A. (1990). Cognitive interventions to improve face-name recall: The role of personality trait differences. *Developmental Psychology, 26,* 889–893.

Green, A. L., & Boxer, A. M. (1986). Daughters and sons as young adults. In N. Datan, A. L. Green, & H. W. Reese (Eds.), *Life-span developmental psychology: Intergenerational relations* (pp. 125–150). Hillsdale, NJ: Erlbaum.

Green, R. F. (1969). Age-intelligence relationships between ages sixteen and sixty-four: A rising trend. *Developmental Psychology, 1,* 618–627.

Greenberg, J. B. (1979). Single parenting and intimacy: A comparison of mothers and fathers. *Alternative Lifestyles, 2,* 308–330.

Greene, V. L., & Monahan, D. J. (1982). The impact of visitation on patient well-being in nursing homes. *The Gerontologist, 22,* 418–423.

Greenwood, J., Love, E. R., & Pratt, O. E. (1983). The effects of alcohol or of thiamine deficiency upon reproduction in the female rat and fetal development. *Alcohol and Alcoholism, 18,* 45–51.

Grey, R. (1756). *Memoria technica* (4th ed.). London: Hinton.

Grimby, G., & Saltin, B. (1983). The aging muscle. *Clinical Physiology, 3,* 209–218.

Guelzow, M. G., Bird, G. W., & Koball, E. H. (1991). An exploratory path analysis of the stress process for dual-career men and women. *Journal of Marriage and the Family, 53,* 151–164.

Guigoz, Y., & Munro, H. N. (1985). Nutrition and aging. In C. E. Finch & E. L. Schneider (Eds.), *Handbook of the biology of aging* (2nd ed., pp. 878–893). New York: Van Nostrand Reinhold.

Guilford, J. P. (1959). *Personality.* New York: McGraw-Hill.

Guilford, J. P. (1980). Fluid and crystallized intelligence: Two fanciful concepts. *Psychological Bulletin, 88,* 406–412.

Gurland, B. J. (1973). A broad clinical assessment of psychopathology in the aged. In C. Eisdorfer & M. P. Lawton (Eds.), *The psychology of adult development and aging* (pp. 343–377). Washington, DC: American Psychological Association.

Gutmann, D. (1978). *Personal transformation in the post-parental period: A cross-cultural view.* Washington, DC: American Association for the Advancement of Science.

Gutmann, D. L. (1987). *Reclaimed powers: Toward a new psychology of men and women in later life.* New York: Basic Books.

Haan, N. (1976). Personality organization of well-functioning younger people and older adults. *International Journal of Aging and Human Development, 7,* 117–127.

Haan, N. (1981). Common dimensions of personality: Early adolescence to middle life. In D. H. Eichorn, N. Haan, J. Clausen, M. Honzik, & P. Mussen (Eds.), *Present and past in middle life* (pp. 117–151). New York: Academic Press.

Haan, N. (1985). Common personality dimensions or common organization across the life span? In J. M. Munnichs, P. Mussen, E. Olbrich, & P. G. Coleman (Eds.), *Life-span and change in gerontological perspective* (pp. 17–44). New York: Academic Press.

Haan, N., Millsap, R., & Hartka, E. (1986). As time goes by: Change and stability in personality over fifty years. *Psychology and Aging, 1,* 220–232.

Hachinski, V. C., Lassen, N. A., & Marshall, J. (1974). Multi-infarct dementia — A cause of mental deterioration in the elderly. *Lancet, 2,* 207–210.

Hacker, H. M. (1981). Blabbermouths and clams — Sex differences in self-disclosure in same-sex and cross-sex friendship dyads. *Psychology of Women Quarterly, 5,* 385–401.

Hagestad, G. (1978). *Patterns of communication and influence between grandparents and grandchildren.* Paper presented at the World Conference on Sociology, Helsinki, Finland.

Hagestad, G. O., & Neugarten, B. L. (1985). Age and the life course. In R. H. Binstock & E. Shanas (Eds.), *Handbook of aging and the social sciences* (2nd ed., pp. 35–61). New York: Van Nostrand Reinhold.

Haggstrom, G. W., Kanouse, D. E., & Morrison, P. A. (1986). Accounting for education shortfalls of mothers. *Journal of Marriage and the Family, 48,* 175–186.

Hakim, S., & Adams, R. D. (1965). The special clinical problem of symptomatic hydrocephalus with normal cerebrospinal fluid pressure: Observations on cerebrospinal fluid hydrodynamics. *Journal of the Neurological Sciences, 2,* 307–327.

Haley, J. (1971). Family therapy. *International Journal of Psychiatry, 9,* 233–242.

Haley, W. E., Levine, E. G., Brown, S. L., Berry, J. W., & Hughes, G. H. (1987). Psychological, social, and health consequences of caring for a relative with senile dementia. *Journal of the American Geriatrics Society, 35,* 405–411.

Halperin, R. H. (1987). Age in cross-cultural perspective: An evolutionary approach. In P. Silverman (Ed.), *The elderly as modern pioneers* (pp. 228–252). Bloomington: Indiana University Press.

Halpern, J. (1987). *Helping your aging parents.* New York: McGraw-Hill.

Hamberger, K., & Lohr, J. (1984). *Stress and stress management: Research and applications.* New York: Springer.

Hamilton, J. (1978). Grandparents as grievers. In J. O. Sahler (Ed.), *The child and death.* St. Louis: C. V. Mosby.

Hamilton, M. (1967). Development of a rating scale for primary depressive illness. *British Journal of Social and Clinical Psychology, 6,* 278–296.

Hamon, R. R., & Blieszner, R. (1990). Filial responsibility expectations among adult child-older parent pairs. *Journal of Gerontology: Psychological Sciences, 45,* P110–P112.

Harbin, T. J., & Blumenthal, J. A. (1985). Relationship among age, sex, the Type A behavior pattern, and cardiovascular reactivity. *Journal of Gerontology, 40,* 714–720.

Harel, Z. (1981). Quality of care, congruence, and well-being among institutionalized aged. *The Gerontologist, 21,* 523–531.

Harker, J. O., Hartley, J. T., & Walsh, D. A. (1982). Understanding discourse: A life-span approach. In B. A. Hutson (Ed.), *Advances in reading/language research* (Vol. 1, pp. 155–202). Greenwich, CT: JAI.

Harkins, S. W., & Kwentus, J. (1990). Pain, discomfort, and suffering in the elderly. In J. J. Bonica (Ed.), *Management of pain.* Philadelphia: Lea & Febinger.

Harman, D. (1987). The free radical theory of aging. In H. R. Warner, R. N. Butler, R. L. Sprott, & E. L. Schneider (Eds.), *Modern biological theories of aging* (pp. 81–87). New York: Raven Press.

Harman, S. M., & Talbert, G. B. (1985). Reproductive aging. In C. E. Finch & E. L. Schneider (Eds.), *Handbook of the biology of aging* (2nd ed., pp. 457–510). New York: Van Nostrand Reinhold.

Harrell, S. (1981). Growing old in rural Taiwan. In P. Amoss & S. Harrell (Eds.), *Other ways of growing old.* Palo Alto, CA: Stanford University Press.

Harris, J. E. (1980). Memory aids people use: Two interview studies. *Memory and Cognition, 8,* 31–38.

Harris, J. E. (1984a). Methods of improving memory. In B. Wilson & N. Moffat (Eds.), *Clinical management of memory problems* (pp. 46–62). Rockville, MD: Aspen.

Harris, J. E. (1984b). Remembering to do things: A forgotten topic. In J. E. Harris & P. E. Morris (Eds.), *Everyday memory, actions, and absentmindedness* (pp. 71–92). London: Academic Press.

Harris, J. E., & Sunderland, A. (1981). A brief survey of the management of memory disorders in rehabilitation units in Britain. *International Rehabilitation Medicine, 3,* 206–209.

Harris, L., & Associates (1975). *The myth and reality of aging in America.* Washington, DC: National Council on the Aging.

Harris, L., & Associates (1981). *Aging in the 80s: America in transition.* Washington, DC: National Council on the Aging.

Harris, M. B., & Turner, P. H. (1986). Gay and lesbian parents. *Journal of Homosexuality, 12,* 101–113.

Harris, R. L., Ellicott, A. M., & Holmes, D. S. (1986). The timing of psychosocial transitions and changes in women's lives: An examination of women aged 45 to 60. *Journal of Personality and Social Psychology, 51,* 409–416.

Harrison, D. E. (1985). Cell and tissue transplantation: A means of studying the aging process. In C. E. Finch & E. L. Schneider (Eds.), *Handbook of the biology of aging* (2nd ed., pp. 322–356). New York: Van Nostrand Reinhold.

Hart, J., & Fleming, R. (1985). An experimental evaluation of reality orientation therapy with geriatric patients in a state mental hospital. *Clinical Gerontologist, 1,* 45–52.

Hartford, M. E. (1980). The use of group methods for work with the aged. In J. E. Birren & R. B. Sloane (Eds.), *Handbook of mental health and aging* (pp. 806–826). Englewood Cliffs, NJ: Prentice-Hall.

Hartley, A. A., & McKenzie, C. R. M. (1991). Attentional and perceptual contributions to the identification of extrafoveal stimuli: Adult age comparisons. *Journal of Gerontology: Psychological Sciences, 46,* P202–P206.

Hartley, J. T. (1989). Memory for prose: Perspectives on the reader. In L. W. Poon, D. C. Rubin, & A. Wilson (Eds.), *Everyday cognition in adult and late life* (pp. 135–156). New York: Cambridge University Press.

Hasher, L., & Zacks, R. T. (1988). Working memory, comprehension, and aging: A review and new view. In G. T. Bower (Ed.), *The psychology of learning and motivation* (Vol. 22, pp. 193–225). New York: Academic Press.

Haskell, W. L., Camargo, C., Jr., Williams, P. T., Vranizan, K. M., Krauss, R. M., Lindgren, F. T., & Wood, P. D. (1984). The effect of cessation and resumption of moderate alcohol intake on serum high-density lipoprotein subfractions. *New England Journal of Medicine, 310,* 805–810.

Hatfield, E., & Walster, E. (1978). *A new look at love.* Reading, MA: Addison-Wesley.

Haun, P. (1965). *Recreation: A medical viewpoint.* New York: Teachers College, Columbia University Press.

Hauri, P. (1982). *The sleep disorders.* Kalamazoo, MI: Upjohn.

Havighurst, R. J. (1982). The world of work. In B. B. Wolman (Ed.), *Handbook of developmental psychology* (pp. 771–787). Englewood Cliffs, NJ: Prentice-Hall.

Hayes, W. C., & Mindel, C. (1973). Extended kinship relations in Black and White families. *Journal of Marriage and the Family, 35,* 51–56.

Hayflick, L. (1987). Origins of longevity. In H. R. Warner, R. N. Butler, R. L. Sprott, & E. L. Schneider (Eds.), *Modern biological theories of aging* (pp. 21–34). New York: Raven Press.

Hayslip, B., Jr. (1986, August). *Alternative mechanisms for improvements in fluid ability in the aged.* Paper presented at the meeting of the American Psychological Association, Washington, DC.

Hayslip, B., Jr. (1988). Personality-ability relationships in aged adults. *Journal of Gerontology, 43,* P79–P84.

Healey, E. S., Kales, A., Monroe, L. J., Bixler, E. O., Chamberlin, K., & Soldatos, C. R. (1981). Onset of insomnia: Role of life-stress events. *Psychosomatic Medicine, 43,* 439–451.

Heaney, R. P., Gallagher, J. C., Johnston, C. C., Neer, R., Parfitt, A. M., & Whedon, G. D. (1982). Calcium nutrition and bone health in the elderly. *American Journal of Clinical Nutrition, 36,* 987–1013.

Heintz, K. M. (1976). *Retirement communities.* New Brunswick, NJ: Rutgers University Center for Urban Policy Research.

Helson, R., & Moane, G. (1987). Personality change in women from college to midlife. *Journal of Personality and Social Psychology, 52,* 1176–1186.

Hendel-Sebestyen, G. (1979). Role diversity: Toward the development of community in a total institutional setting. *Anthropological Quarterly, 52,* 19–28.

Henderson, K. A. (1990). The meaning of leisure for women: An integrative review of the research. *Journal of Leisure Reseach, 22,* 228–243.

Hendricks, J. (1982). The elderly in society: Beyond modernization. *Social Science History, 6,* 321–345.

Hennon, C. B. (1983). Divorce and the elderly: A neglected area of research. In T. H. Brubaker (Ed.), *Family relationships in later life* (pp. 149–172). Beverly Hills, CA: Sage Publications.

Hensel, H. (1981). *Thermoreception and temperature regulation.* New York: Academic Press.

Herberman, R. B., & Callewaert, D. M. (Eds.). (1985). *Mechanisms of cytotoxicity by NK cells.* Orlando, FL: Academic Press.

Herbert, V. (1988). Megavitamins, food fads, and quack nutrition in health promotion: Myths and risks. In R. Chernoff & D. A. Lipschitz (Eds.), *Health promotion and disease prevention in the elderly* (pp. 45–66). New York: Raven Press.

Herr, J., & Weakland, J. (1979). *Counseling elders and their families: Practical techniques for applied gerontology.* New York: Springer.

Hertzog, C., Dixon, R. A., Schulenberg, J., & Hultsch, D. F. (1987). On the differentiation of memory beliefs from memory knowledge: The factor structure of the Metamemory in Adulthood scale. *Experimental Aging Research, 13,* 101–107.

Hertzog, C., Hultsch, D. F., & Dixon, R. A. (1989). Evidence for the convergent validity of two self-report metamemory questionnaires. *Developmental Psychology, 25,* 687–700.

Herzog, A. R., Kahn, R. L., Morgan, J. N., Jackson, J. S., & Antonucci, T. C. (1989). Age differences in productive activities. *Journal of Gerontology: Social Sciences, 44,* S129–S138.

Hess, T. M., & Slaughter, S. J. (1990). Schematic knowledge influences on memory for scene information in young and older adults. *Developmental Psychology, 26,* 855–865.

Hesse, M. (1980). *Revolutions and reconstructions in the philosophy of science.* Bloomington: Indiana University Press.

Hetherington, E. M., Cox, M., & Cox, R. (1982). Effects of divorce on parents and children. In M. E. Lamb (Ed.), *Nontraditional families: Parenting and child development.* Hillsdale, NJ: Erlbaum.

Heumann, L., & Boldy, D. (1982). *Housing for the elderly: Policy and planning formulation in Western Europe and North America.* London: Croom Helm.

Hill, C. D., Thompson, L. W., & Gallagher, D. (1988). The role of anticipatory bereavement in older women's adjustment to widowhood. *The Gerontologist, 28,* 792–796.

Hill, R., Foote, N., Aldonus, J., Carlson, R., & MacDonald, R. (1970). *Family development in three generations.* New York: Schenkman.

Himmelfarb, S. (1984). Age and sex differences in the mental health of older persons. *Journal of Consulting and Clinical Psychology, 52,* 844–856.

Hinton, J. M. (1967). *Dying.* Harmondsworth, England: Penguin.

Hirschfield, R. M. A., & Cross, C. K. (1982). Epidemiology of affective disorders: Psychosocial risk factors. *Archives of General Psychiatry, 39,* 35–46.

Hobart, C. (1988). The family system in remarriage: An exploratory study. *Journal of Marriage and the Family, 50,* 649–661.

Hochschild, A. R. (1973). *The unexpected community.* Englewood Cliffs, NJ: Prentice-Hall.

Hoff, S. F., Scheff, S. W., Bernardo, L. S., & Cotman, C. W. (1982). Lesion-induced synaptogenesis in the dentate gyrus of aged rats. 1: Loss and reacquisition of normal synaptic density. *Journal of Comparative Neurology, 205,* 246–252.

Hoff, S. F., Scheff, S. W., & Cotman, C. W. (1982). Lesion-induced synaptogenesis in the dentate gyrus of the aged rat. 2: Demonstration of an impaired degeneration clearing response. *Journal of Comparative Neurology, 205,* 253–259.

Hofland, B. F. (1988). Autonomy in long term care: Background issues and a programmatic response. *The Gerontologist, 28(Suppl.),* 3–9.

Holland, J. L. (1973). *Making vocational choices: A theory of careers.* Englewood Cliffs, NJ: Prentice-Hall.

Holland, J. L. (1985). *Making vocational choices: A theory of vocational personalities and work environments.* Englewood Cliffs, NJ: Prentice-Hall.

Hollander, C. F., & Becker, H. A. (1988). Planning for health services for the elderly. In D. Evered & J. Whelan (Eds.), *Symposium on research and the ageing population* (pp. 221–228). Chichester, England: Wiley.

Holyroyd, K. A., Appel, M. A., & Andrasik, F. (1983). A cognitive-behavioral approach to psychophysiological disorders. In D. Meichenbaum & M. E. Jarenko (Eds.), *Stress reduction and prevention.* New York: Plenum.

Holzberg, C. S. (1982). Ethnicity and aging: Anthropological perspectives on more than just the minority elderly. *The Gerontologist, 22,* 249–257.

Holzberg, C. S. (1983). Anthropology, life histories, and the aged: The Toronto Baycrest Center. *International Journal of Aging and Human Development, 18,* 255–275.

Hooper, C. (1991). To be or not two bees: Verbs, nouns and the brain. *Journal of NIH Research, 3*(6), 49–54.

Hopkins, D. R., Murrah, B., Hoeger, W. W. K., & Rhodes, R. C. (1990). Effect of low-impact aerobic dance on the functional fitness of elderly women. *The Gerontologist, 30,* 189–192.

Horn, J. L. (1978). Human ability systems. In P. B. Baltes & O. G. Brim, Jr. (Eds.), *Life-span development and behavior* (Vol. 1, pp. 211–256). New York: Academic Press.

Horn, J. L. (1982). The aging of human abilities. In B. B. Wolman (Ed.), *Handbook of developmental psychology* (pp. 847–870). Englewood Cliffs, NJ: Prentice-Hall.

Horn, J. L., & Donaldson, G. (1980). Cognitive development in adulthood. In O. G. Brim, Jr., & J. Kagan (Eds.), *Constancy and change in human development* (pp. 445–529). Cambridge, MA: Harvard University Press.

Horn, J. L., Donaldson, G., & Engstrom, R. (1981). Apprehension, memory, and fluid intelligence decline through the "vital years" of adulthood. *Research on Aging, 3,* 33–84.

Hornblum, J. N., & Overton, W. F. (1976). Area and volume conservation among the elderly: Assessment and training. *Developmental Psychology, 12,* 68–74.

Horowitz, M. J., & Schulz, R. (1983). The relocation controversy: Criticism and commentary on five recent studies. *The Gerontologist, 23,* 229–234.

Hounsfield, G. N. (1973). Computerized transverse axial scanning (tomography). *British Journal of Radiology, 46,* 1016–1022.

Howard, A. (1984, August). *Cool at the top: Personality characteristics of successful executives.* Paper presented at the meeting of the American Psychological Association, Toronto.

Howard, A. (in press). Work and family crossroads along the career. In S. Zedeck (Ed.), *Work and family.* San Francisco: Jossey-Bass.

Howard, A., & Bray, D. W. (1980, August). *Career motivation in mid-life managers.* Paper presented at the meeting of the American Psychological Association, Montreal.

Howard, D. V., Heisey, J. G., & Shaw, R. J. (1986). Aging and the priming of newly learned associations. *Developmental Psychology, 22,* 78–85.

Howe, M. L. (1988). Measuring memory development in adulthood: A model-based approach to disentangling storage-retrieval contributions. In M. L. Howe & C. J. Brainerd (Eds.), *Cognitive development in adulthood* (pp. 39–64). New York: Springer-Verlag.

Hoyer, W. J. (1987, November). *Domains of attention.* Paper presented at the National Institute on Aging Conference on Aging and Attention, Washington, DC.

Huff, F. J., Growdon, J. H., Corkin, S., & Rosen, T. J. (1987). Age at onset and rate of progression of Alzheimer's disease. *Journal of the American Geriatrics Association, 35,* 27–30.

Hughston, G. A., & Protinsky, H. W. (1978). Conservation abilities of elderly men and women: A comparative investigation. *Journal of Psychology, 98,* 23–26.

Hulin, C. L., & Smith, P. C. (1965). A linear model of job satisfaction. *Journal of Applied Psychology, 49,* 209–216.

Hultsch, D. F. (1971). Adult age differences in free classification and free recall. *Developmental Psychology, 4,* 338–342.

Hultsch, D. F., & Dixon, R. A. (1983). The role of pre-experimental knowledge in text processing in adulthood. *Experimental Aging Research, 9,* 17–22.

Hultsch, D. F., & Dixon, R. A. (1984). Memory for text materials in adulthood. In P. B. Baltes & O. G. Brim, Jr. (Eds.), *Life-span development and behavior* (Vol. 6, pp. 77–108). New York: Academic Press.

Hultsch, D. F., & Dixon, R. A. (1990). Learning and memory in aging. In J. E. Birren & K. W. Schaie (Eds.), *Handbook of the psychology of aging* (3rd ed., pp. 258–274). San Diego: Academic Press.

Hultsch, D. F., Masson, M. E. J., & Small, B. J. (1991). Adult age differences in direct and indirect tests of memory. *Journal of Gerontology: Psychological Sciences, 46,* P22–P30.

Hultsch, D. F., & Plemons, J. K. (1979). Life events and life-span development. In P. B. Baltes & O. G. Brim, Jr. (Eds.), *Life-span development and behavior* (Vol. 2, pp. 1–36). New York: Academic Press.

Huyck, M. H. (1982). From gregariousness to intimacy: Marriage and friendship over the adult years. In T. M. Field, A. Huston, H. C. Quay, L. Troll., & G. E. Finley (Eds.), *Review of human development* (pp. 471–484). New York: Wiley.

Huyck, M. H. (1990). Gender differences in aging. In J. E. Birren & K. W. Schaie (Eds.), *Handbook of the psychology of aging* (3rd ed., pp. 124–132). San Diego: Academic Press.

Hyde, J. S., Krajnik, M., & Skuldt-Niederberger, K. (1991). Androgyny across the life span: A replication and longitudinal follow-up. *Developmental Psychology, 27,* 516–519.

Iammarino, N. K. (1975). Relationship between death anxiety and demographic variables. *Psychological Reports, 17,* 262.

Ingraham, M. (1974). *My purpose holds: Reactions and experiences in retirement of TIAA-CREF annuitants.* New York: Educational Research Division, Teachers Insurance and Annuity Association College Retirement Equities Fund.

Irelan, L. M., & Bell, D. B. (1972). Understanding subjectively defined retirement: A pilot analysis. *The Gerontologist, 12,* 354–356.

Irion, J. C., & Blanchard-Fields, F. (1987). A cross-sectional comparison of adaptive coping in adulthood. *Journal of Gerontology, 42,* 502–504.

Isaksson, B. (1973). Clinical nutrition: Requirements of energy and nutrients in diseases. *Bibliography of Nutrition and Dietetics, 19,* 1.

Ivancevich, J. M., & Matteson, M. T. (1988). Type A behavior and the healthy individual. *British Journal of Medical Psychology, 61,* 37–56.

Jackson, B., Taylor, J., & Pyngolil, M. (1991). How age conditions the relationship between climacteric status and health symptoms in African American women. *Research in Nursing and Health, 14,* 1–9.

Jackson, J. J. (1985). Race, national origin, ethnicity, and aging. In R. H. Binstock & E. Shanas (Eds.), *Handbook of aging and the social sciences* (2nd ed., pp. 264–303). New York: Van Nostrand Reinhold.

Jackson, J. J., & Walls, B. E. (1978). Myths and realities about aged Blacks. In M. R. Brown (Ed.), *Readings in gerontology* (2nd ed., pp. 95–113). St. Louis: C. V. Mosby.

Jackson, J. S., & Gibson, R. C. (1985). Work and retirement among the black elderly. In Z. Blau (Ed.), *Current perspectives on aging and the life cycle* (pp. 193–222). Greenwich, CT: JAI.

Jackson, M., Kolodny, B., & Wood, J. L. (1982). To be old and Black: The case for double jeopardy on income and health. In R. C. Manuel (Ed.), *Minority aging, sociological and social psychological issues* (pp. 161–170). Westport, CT: Greenwood.

Jackson, M., & Wood, J. L. (1976). *Aging in America: Implications for the Black aged.* Washington, DC: National Council on the Aging.

Jacobs, J. (1974). *Fun city: An ethnographic study of a retirement community.* New York: Holt, Rinehart & Winston.

Jacobs, J. (1975). *Older persons and retirement communities.* Springfield, IL: Charles C Thomas.

Jacobson, E. (1938). *Progressive relaxation.* Chicago: University of Chicago Press.

James, L. R., & Jones, A. P. (1980). Perceived job characteristics and job satisfaction: An examination of reciprocal causation. *Personnel Psychology, 33,* 97–135.

James, W. (1890). *The principles of psychology.* New York: Holt.

Jamison, K. R., Gerner, R. H., & Goodwin, F. K. (1979). Patient and physician attitudes toward lithium: Relationships to compliance. *Archives of General Psychiatry, 36,* 866–869.

Janson, P., & Ryder, L. K. (1983). Crime and the elderly: The relationship between risk and fear. *The Gerontologist, 23,* 207–212.

Jaques, E. (1965). Death and the mid-life crisis. *International Journal of Psychoanalysis, 46,* 502–514.

Jaremko, M. E. (1983). Stress inoculation training for social anxiety with emphasis on dating anxiety. In D. Meichenbaum & M. E. Jaremko (Eds.), *Stress reduction and prevention.* New York: Plenum.

Jeffko, W. G. (1979, July 6). Redefining death. *Commonweal,* pp. 394–397.

Jemmott, J. B., Borysenko, J. Z., Borysenko, M., McClelland, D. C., Chapman, R., Meyer, D., & Benson, H. (1983). Academic stress, power motivation, and decrease in secretion rate of salivary secretory immunoglobulin A. *Lancet, 1,* 1400–1402.

Jencks, C., Bartlett, S., Corcorin, M., Crouse, J., Eaglesfield, D., Jackson, G., McClelland, K., Mueser, P., Olneck, M., Schwartz, J., Ward, S., & Williams, J. (1979). *Who gets ahead? The determinants of economic success in America.* New York: Basic Books.

Jirovec, R. L., Jirovec, M. M., & Bossé, R. (1985). Environmental determinants of neighborhood satisfaction among urban elderly men. *The Gerontologist, 24,* 261–265.

Johnson, C. L. (1983). A cultural analysis of the grandmother. *Research on Aging, 5,* 547–567.

Johnson, C. L. (1987). The institutional segregation of the elderly. In P. Silverman (Ed.), *The elderly as modern pioneers* (pp. 307–319). Bloomington: Indiana University Press.

Johnson, C. L. (1988). Active and latent functions of grandparenting during the divorce process. *The Gerontologist, 28,* 185–191.

Johnson, C. L., & Barer, B. (1987). Marital instability and the changing kinship networks of grandparents. *The Gerontologist, 27,* 330–335.

Johnson, C. L., & Grant, L. (1985). *The nursing home in American society.* Baltimore: Johns Hopkins University Press.

Jones, L. Y. (1980). *Great expectations: America and the baby boom generation.* New York: Coward, McCann, & Geoghegan.

Jones, M. K., & Jones, B. M. (1980). The relationship of age and drinking habits to the effects of alcohol on memory in women. *Journal of Studies on Alcohol, 41,* 179–186.

Kahana, B., & Kahana, E. (1970). Grandparenthood from the perspective of the developing grandchild. *Developmental Psychology, 3,* 98–105.

Kahana, E. (1982). A congruence model of person-environment interaction. In M. P. Lawton, P. G. Windley, & T. O. Byerts (Eds.), *Aging and the environment: Theoretical approaches* (pp. 97–121). New York: Springer.

Kahana, E., & Kahana, B. (1983). Environmental continuity, futurity, and adaptation of the aged. In G. D. Rowles & R. J. Ohta (Eds.), *Aging and milieu: Environmental perspectives on growing old* (pp. 205–230). New York: Academic Press.

Kahn, R. L., Goldfarb, A. I., Pollack, M., & Peck, A. (1960). Brief objective measures for the determination of mental status in the aged. *American Journal of Psychiatry, 117,* 326–328.

Kales, A., Allen, W. C., Scharf, M. B., & Kales, J. D. (1970). Hypnotic drugs and effectiveness: All-night EEG studies of insomniac subjects. *Archives of General Psychiatry, 23,* 226–232.

Kales, A., Scharf, M. B., & Kales, J. D. (1978). Rebound insomnia: A new clinical syndrome. *Science, 201,* 1039–1040.

Kalish, R. A. (1975). *Late adulthood.* Pacific Grove, CA: Brooks/Cole.

Kalish, R. A. (1976). Death in a social context. In R. H. Binstock & E. Shanas (Eds.), *Handbook of aging and the social sciences* (pp. 483–507). New York: Van Nostrand Reinhold.

Kalish, R. A. (1981). *Death, grief, and caring relationships.* Pacific Grove, CA: Brooks/Cole.

Kalish, R. A. (1984). *Death, grief, and caring relationships* (2nd ed.). Pacific Grove, CA: Brooks/Cole.

Kalish, R. A. (1985). The social context of death and dying. In R. H. Binstock & E. Shanas (Eds.), *Handbook of aging and the social sciences* (2nd ed., pp. 149–170). New York: Van Nostrand Reinhold.

Kalish, R. A. (1987). Death and dying. In P. Silverman (Ed.), *The elderly as modern pioneers* (pp. 320–334). Bloomington: Indiana University Press.

Kalish, R. A., & Reynolds, D. (1976). *Death and ethnicity: A psychocultural study*. Los Angeles: University of Southern California Press.

Kalish, R. A., & Reynolds, D. K. (1981). *Death and ethnicity: A psychocultural study*. Farmingdale, NY: Baywood.

Kallman, D. A., Plato, C. C., & Tobin, J. D. (1990). The role of muscle loss in the age-related decline of grip strength: Cross-sectional and longitudinal perspectives. *Journal of Gerontology: Medical Sciences, 45,* M82–M88.

Kallmann, F. J. (1957). Twin data on the genetics of aging. In G. E. Wolstenhoime & C. M. O'Connor (Eds.), *Methodology of the study of ageing* (pp. 131–143). London: Churchill.

Kaminsky, M. (1978). Pictures from the past: The use of reminiscence in casework with the elderly. *Journal of Gerontological Social Work, 1,* 19–31.

Kamouri, A., & Cavanaugh, J. C. (1986). The impact of pre-retirement education programs on workers' pre-retirement socialization. *Journal of Occupational Behavior, 7,* 245–256.

Kane, R. L., Evans, J. G., & Macfadyen, D. (Eds.). (1990). *Improving the health of older people: A world view*. Oxford, England: Oxford University Press.

Kannel, W. B. (1985). Hypertension and aging. In C. E. Finch & E. L. Schneider (Eds.), *Handbook of the biology of aging* (2nd ed., pp. 859–877). New York: Van Nostrand Reinhold.

Kannel, W. B., & Thom, T. J. (1984). Declining cardiovascular mortality. *Circulation, 70,* 331–336.

Kanter, R. M. (1976, May). Why bosses turn bitchy. *Psychology Today*, pp. 56–59.

Kaplan, M. (1983). The issue of sex bias in DSM III: Comments on articles by Spitzer, Williams, and Kass. *American Psychologist, 38,* 802–803.

Karacen, I., & Williams, R. L. (1983). Sleep disorders in the elderly. *American Family Physicians, 27,* 143–152.

Kastenbaum, R. (1975). Is death a life crisis? On the confrontation with death in theory and practice. In N. Datan & L. Ginsberg (Eds.), *Life-span developmental psychology: Normative life crises* (pp. 19–50). New York: Academic Press.

Kastenbaum, R. (1985). Dying and death: A life-span approach. In J. E. Birren & K. W. Schaie (Eds.), *Handbook of the psychology of aging* (2nd ed., pp. 619–643). New York: Van Nostrand Reinhold.

Kastenbaum, R., & Aisenberg, R. B. (1976). *The psychology of death* (rev. ed.). New York: Springer.

Kastenbaum, R., & Briscoe, L. (1975). The street corner: Laboratory for the study of life-threatening behavior. *Omega: Journal of Death and Dying, 6,* 33–44.

Katzman, R. (1987). Alzheimer's disease: Advances and opportunities. *Journal of the American Geriatrics Society, 35,* 69–73.

Kaufman, D. W., Rosenberg, L., Helmrich, S. P., & Shapiro, S. (1985). Alcohol beverages and myocardial infarction in young men. *American Journal of Epidemiology, 121,* 548–554.

Kausler, D. H. (1982). *Experimental psychology and human aging*. New York: Wiley.

Kausler, D. H. (1985). Episodic memory: Memorizing performance. In N. Charness (Ed.), *Aging and human performance* (pp. 101–141). Chichester, England: Wiley.

Kausler, D. H., & Hakami, M. K. (1983). Memory for activities: Adult age differences and intentionality. *Developmental Psychology, 19,* 889–894.

Kegan, R. (1982). *The evolving self*. Cambridge, MA: Harvard University Press.

Keith, J. (1990). Age in social and cultural context: Anthropological perspectives. In R. H. Binstock & L. K. George (Eds.), *Handbook of aging and the social sciences* (3rd ed., pp. 91–111). San Diego: Academic Press.

Keith, J., Fry, C. L., & Ikels, C. (1990). Community as context for successful aging. In J. Sokolovsky (Ed.), *The cultural context of aging* (pp. 245–261). New York: Bergin & Garvey.

Keith, P. M. (1979). Life changes and perceptions of life and death among older men and women. *Journal of Gerontology, 34,* 870–878.

Keller, J. W., Sherry, D., & Piotrowski, C. (1984). Perspectives on death: A developmental study. *Journal of Psychology, 116,* 137–142.

Kelley, C. M. (1986). Depressive mood effects on memory and attention. In L. W. Poon (Ed.), *Handbook for the clinical memory assessment of older adults* (pp. 238–243). Washington, DC: American Psychological Association.

Kelley, H. H. (1967). Attribution theory in social psychology. *Nebraska Symposium on Motivation, 15,* 192–241.

Kelly, J. B. (1982). Divorce: The adult perspective. In B. B. Wolman (Ed.), *Handbook of developmental psychology* (pp. 734–750). Englewood Cliffs, NJ: Prentice-Hall.

Kelly, J. R., Steinkamp, M. W., & Kelly, J. R. (1987). Later-life satisfaction: Does leisure contribute? *Leisure Sciences, 9,* 189–200.

Kemper, S. (1988). Geriatric psycholinguistics: Syntactic limitations of oral and written language. In L. L. Light & D. M. Burke (Eds.), *Language, memory, and aging* (pp. 58–76). New York: Cambridge University Press.

Kendig, N. E., & Adler, W. H. (1990). The implications of acquired immunodeficiency syndrome for gerontology research and geriatric medicine. *Journal of Gerontology: Medical Sciences, 45,* M77–M81.

Kenney, R. A. (1982). *Physiology of aging: A synopsis*. Chicago: Yearbook Medical.

Kenshalo, D. R. (1977). Age changes in touch, vibration, temperature, kinesthesis, and pain sensitivity. In J. E. Birren & K. W. Schaie (Eds.), *Handbook of the psychology of aging* (pp. 562–579). New York: Van Nostrand Reinhold.

Kenshalo, D. R. (1979). Changes in the vestibular and somasthetic systems as a function of age. In J. M. Ordy & K. Brizzee (Eds.), *Aging: Vol. 10. Sensory systems and communication in the elderly* (pp. 269–282). New York: Raven Press.

Kertzer, D. I., & Madison, O. B. B. (1981). Women's age-set systems in Africa: The Latuka of southern Sudan. In C. L. Fry (Ed.), *Dimensions: Aging, culture, and health* (pp. 109–130). New York: Praeger.

Kiecolt-Glaser, J. K., Speicher, C. E., Holliday, J. E., & Glaser, R. (1984). Stress and the transformation of lymphocytes in Epstein-Barr virus. *Journal of Behavioral Medicine, 7,* 1–12.

Kiefer, C. W., Kim, S., Choi, K., Kim, L., Kim, B.-L., Shon, S., & Kim, T. (1985). Adjustment problems of Korean-American elderly. *The Gerontologist, 25*, 477–482.

Kieffer, G. H. (1979). *Bioethics: A textbook of issues.* Reading, MA: Addison-Wesley.

Kieffer, J. A. (1986). The older volunteer resource. In Committee on an Aging Society (Ed.), *Productive roles in an older society* (pp. 51–72). Washington, DC: National Academy Press.

Kii, T. (1981). Status changes of the elderly in Japan's legal, family, and economic institutions. In C. Nusberg & M. M. Osako (Eds.), *The situation of the Asian/Pacific elderly.* Washington, DC: International Federation on Aging.

Kimmel, D. C. (1978). Adult development and aging: A gay perspective. *Journal of Social Issues, 34*, 113–130.

Kimmel, D. C., Price, K. F., & Walker, J. W. (1978). Retirement choice and retirement satisfaction. *Journal of Gerontology, 33*, 575–585.

King, P. M., Kitchener, K. S., Wood, P. K., & Davison, M. L. (1989). Relationships across developmental domains: A longitudinal study of intellectual, moral, and ego development. In M. L. Commons, J. D. Sinnott, F. A. Richards, & C. Armon (Eds.), *Adult development: Vol. 1. Comparisons and applications of adolescent and adult developmental models.* New York: Praeger.

Kingston, P. W., & Nock, S. L. (1987). Time together among dual-earner couples. *American Sociological Review, 52*, 391–400.

Kinney, J. M., & Stephens, M. A. P. (1989). Hassles and uplifts of giving care to a family member with dementia. *Psychology and Aging, 4*, 402–408.

Kirasic, K. C. (1980, November). *Spatial problem solving in elderly adults: A hometown advantage.* Paper presented at the meeting of the Gerontological Society of America, San Diego.

Kirasic, K. C. (1981, April). *Studying the "hometown advantage" in elderly adults' spatial cognition and spatial behavior.* Paper presented at the meeting of the Society for Research in Child Development, Boston.

Kirasic, K. C. (1991). Spatial cognition and behavior in young and elderly adults: Implications for learning new environments. *Psychology and Aging, 6*, 10–18.

Kirasic, K. C., & Allen, G. L. (1985). Aging, spatial performance, and spatial competence. In N. Charness (Ed.), *Aging and human performance* (pp. 191–223). Chichester, England: Wiley.

Kirkwood, T. B. L. (1985). Comparative and evolutionary aspects of longevity. In C. E. Finch & E. L. Schneider (Eds.), *Handbook of the biology of aging* (2nd ed., pp. 27–44). New York: Van Nostrand Reinhold.

Kitchener, K. S., & King, P. M. (1989). The reflective judgment model: Ten years of research. In M. L. Commons, J. D. Sinnott, F. A. Richards, & C. Armon (Eds.), *Adult development: Vol. 1. Comparisons and applications of adolescent and adult developmental models.* New York: Praeger.

Kitson, G. L., & Sussman, M. B. (1982). Marital complaints, demographic characteristics, and symptoms of mental distress in divorce. *Journal of Marriage and the Family, 44*, 87–101.

Kivett, V. R. (1991). Centrality of the grandfather role among older rural black and white men. *Journal of Gerontology: Social Sciences, 46*, S250–S258.

Kivnick, H. Q. (1982). *The meaning of grandparenthood.* Ann Arbor, MI: UMI Research.

Klatsky, A. L., Friedman, G. D., & Siegelaub, A. B. (1981). Alcohol and mortality: A ten-year Kaiser-Permanente experience. *Annals of Internal Medicine, 95*, 139–145.

Klerman, G. L. (1986, March). *Evidence for increases in rates of depression in North America and Western Europe in recent decades.* Paper presented at the Conference on New Research in Depression, Murnau, West Germany.

Kline, D. W., & Schieber, F. (1985). Vision and aging. In J. E. Birren & K. W. Schaie (Eds.), *Handbook of the psychology of aging* (2nd ed., pp. 296–331). New York: Van Nostrand Reinhold.

Kline, T. J. B., Ghali, L. M., Kline, D. W., & Brown, S. (1990). Visibility distance of highway signs among young, middle-aged, and older observers: Icons are better than text. *Human Factors, 32*, 609–619.

Klingman, A. M., Grove, G. L., & Balin, A. K. (1985). Aging of human skin. In C. E. Finch & E. L. Schneider (Eds.), *Handbook of the biology of aging* (2nd ed., pp. 820–841). New York: Van Nostrand Reinhold.

Klingman, L. H., Aiken, F. J., & Klingman, A. M. (1982). Prevention of ultraviolet damage to the dermis of hairless mice by sunscreens. *Journal of Investigative Dermatology, 78*, 181–189.

Koestenbaum, P. (1976). *Is there an answer to death?* Englewood Cliffs, NJ: Prentice-Hall.

Koff, T. H. (1981). *Hospice: A caring community.* Cambridge, MA: Winthrop.

Koh, J. Y., & Bell, W. G. (1987). Korean elderly in the United States: Intergenerational relations and living arrangements. *The Gerontologist, 27*, 66–71.

Kohlberg, L. (1969). Stage and sequence: The cognitive-developmental approach to socialization. In D. Goslin (Ed.), *Handbook of socialization theory and research.* Chicago: Rand McNally.

Kohlberg, L. (1976). Moral stages and moralization: The cognitive developmental approach. In T. Lickona (Ed.), *Moral development and behavior: Theory, research, and social issues.* New York: Holt, Rinehart & Winston.

Kohlberg, L. (1984). *Essays on moral development: Vol. II. The psychology of moral development.* San Francisco: Harper & Row.

Kohlberg, L. (1987). The development of moral judgment and moral action. In L. Kohlberg (Ed.), *Child development and childhood education: A cognitive-developmental view.* New York: Longman Press.

Kohn, R. R. (1985). Aging and age-related diseases: Normal processes. In H. A. Johnson (Ed.), *Relations between normal aging and disease* (pp. 1–43). New York: Raven Press.

Kornhaber, A. (1985). Grandparenthood and the "new social contract." In V. L. Bengtson & J. F. Robertson (Eds.), *Grandparenthood* (pp. 159–172). Beverly Hills, CA: Sage Publications.

Kornhaber, A., & Woodward, K. L. (1981). *Grandparent/grandchildren: The vital connection.* Garden City, NJ: Anchor.

Kosnik, W., Winslow, L., Kline, D. W., Rasinski, K., & Sekular, R. (1988). Visual changes in everyday life throughout adulthood. *Journal of Gerontology, 43,* P63–P70.

Kotre, J. (1984). *Outliving the self: Generativity and the interpretation of lives.* Baltimore: Johns Hopkins University Press.

Kozma, A., & Stones, M. J. (1983). Predictors of happiness. *Journal of Gerontology, 38,* 626–628.

Kram, K. E. (1980). *Mentoring processes at work: Developmental relationships in managerial careers.* Unpublished doctoral dissertation, Yale University, New Haven, CT.

Kram, K. E. (1985). *Mentoring at work: Developmental relationships in organizational life.* Glenview, IL: Scott, Foresman.

Kram, K. E., & Isabella, L. (1985). Mentoring alternatives: The role of peer relationships in career development. *Academy of Management Journal, 21,* 110–132.

Kramer, D. A. (1983). Post-formal operations? A need for further conceptualization. *Human Development, 26,* 91–105.

Kramer, D. A. (1989). A developmental framework for understanding conflict resolution processes. In J. D. Sinnott (Ed.), *Everyday problem solving: Theory and applications* (pp. 138–152). New York: Praeger.

Kramer, D. A., Angiuld, N., Crisafi, L., & Levine, C. (1991, August). *Cognitive processes in real-life conflict resolution.* Paper presented at the annual meeting of the American Psychological Association, San Francisco.

Kramer, D. A. & Woodruff, D. S. (1986). Relativistic and dialectical thought in three adult age-groups. *Human Development, 29,* 280–290.

Krause, N. (1991). Stress and isolation from close ties in later life. *Journal of Gerontology: Social Sciences, 46,* S183–S194.

Kremer, J. M. (1990). Severe rheumatoid arthritis: Current options in drug therapy. *Geriatrics, 45(12),* 43–48.

Krieger, S., Epsting, F., & Leitner, L. M. (1974). Personal constructs, threat, and attitudes toward death. *Omega: Journal of Death and Dying, 5,* 289.

Krout, J. A. (1988a). Community size differences in service awareness among elderly adults. *Journal of Gerontology, 43,* 528–530.

Krout, J. A. (1988b). Rural versus urban differences in elderly parents' contacts with their children. *The Gerontologist, 28,* 198–203.

Kübler-Ross, E. (1969). *On death and dying.* New York: Macmillan.

Kübler-Ross, E. (1974). *Questions and answers on death and dying.* New York: Macmillan.

Kuhn, D., & Angelev, J. (1976). An experimental study of the development of formal operational thought. *Child Development, 47,* 697–706.

Kuhn, D., Ho, V., & Adams, C. (1979). Formal reasoning among pre- and late adolescents. *Child Development, 50,* 1128–1135.

Kuhn, D., Langer, J., Kohlberg, L., & Haan, N. S. (1977). The development of formal operations in logical and moral judgment. *Genetic Psychology Monographs, 95,* 97–188.

Kurdek, L. A. (1991a). Predictors of increases in marital distress in newlywed couples: A 3–year prospective longitudinal study. *Developmental Psychology, 27,* 627–636.

Kurdek, L. A. (1991b). The relations between reported well-being and divorce history, availability of a proximate adult, and gender. *Journal of Marriage and the Family, 53,* 71–78.

Kurdek, L. A., & Schmitt, J. P. (1986). Early development of relationship quality in heterosexual married, heterosexual cohabiting, gay, and lesbian couples. *Developmental Psychology, 22,* 305–309.

Labouvie-Vief, G. (1977). Adult cognitive development: In search of alternative interpretations. *Merrill-Palmer Quarterly, 23,* 227–263.

Labouvie-Vief, G. (1980). Beyond formal operations: Uses and limits of pure logic in life-span development. *Human Development, 23,* 141–161.

Labouvie-Vief, G. (1981). Proactive and reactive aspects of constructivism: Growth and aging in life-span perspective. In R. M. Lerner & N. A. Busch-Rossnagel (Eds.), *Individuals as producers of their development* (pp. 197–230). New York: Academic Press.

Labouvie-Vief, G. (1984). Logic and self-regulation from youth to maturity: A model. In M. L. Commons, F. A.

Richards, & C. Armon (Eds.), *Beyond formal operations: Late adolescent and adult cognitive development* (pp. 158–179). New York: Praeger.

Labouvie-Vief, G. (1985). Intelligence and cognition. In J. E. Birren & K. W. Schaie (Eds.), *Handbook of the psychology of aging* (2nd ed., pp. 500–530). New York: Van Nostrand Reinhold.

Labouvie-Vief, G., Adams, C., Hakim-Larson, J., Hayden, M., & Devoe, M. (1985). *Logical problem solving and metalogical knowledge from preadolescence to adulthood.* Unpublished manuscript, Wayne State University, Detroit.

Labouvie-Vief, G., & Gonda, J. N. (1976). Cognitive strategy training and intellectual performances in the elderly. *Journal of Gerontology, 31,* 327–332.

Labouvie-Vief, G., Hakim-Larson, J., & Hobart, C. J. (1987). Age, ego level, and the life-span development of coping and defense processes. *Psychology and Aging, 2,* 286–293.

Lachman, J. L., & Lachman, R. (1980). Age and the actualization of world knowledge. In L. W. Poon, J. L. Fozard, L. S. Cermak, D. Arenberg, & L. W. Thompson (Eds.), *New directions in memory and aging* (pp. 285–311). Hillsdale, NJ: Erlbaum.

Lachman, M. E. (1983). Perceptions of intellectual aging: Antecedent or consequence of intellectual functioning? *Developmental Psychology, 19,* 482–498.

Lachman, M. E. (1985). Personal efficacy in middle and old age: Differential and normative patterns of change. In G. H. Elder, Jr. (Ed.), *Life-course dynamics: Trajectories and transitions, 1968–1980.* Ithaca, NY: Cornell University Press.

Lachman, M. E. (1986). Locus of control in aging research: A case for multidimensional and domain-specific assessment. *Psychology and Aging, 1,* 34–40.

Lachman, R., Lachman, J. L., & Butterfield, E. C. (1979). *Cognitive psychology and information processing: An introduction.* Hillsdale, NJ: Erlbaum.

Lacks, P., Bertelson, A. D., Gans, L., & Kunkel, J. (1983). The effectiveness of three behavioral treatments for different degrees of sleep onset insomnia. *Behavior Therapy, 14,* 593–605.

LaCroix, A. Z., Lang, J., Scherr, P., Wallace, R. B., Cornoni-Huntley, J., Berkman, L., Curb, J. D., Evans, D., & Hennekens, C. H. (1991). Smoking and mortality among older men and women in three communities. *New England Journal of Medicine, 324,* 1619–1625.

Lajer, M. (1982). Unemployment and hospitalization among bricklayers. *Scandinavian Journal of Social Medicine, 10,* 3–10.

Lakatta, E. G. (1985). Heart and circulation. In C. E. Finch & E. L. Schneider (Eds.), *Handbook of the biology of aging* (2nd ed., pp. 377–413). New York: Van Nostrand Reinhold.

Lando, H. A. (1977). Successful treatment of smokers with a broad-spectrum behavioral approach. *Journal of Consulting and Clinical Psychology, 45,* 361–366.

Langer, E. J. (1985). Playing the middle against both ends: The usefulness of older adult cognitive activity as a model for cognitive activity in childhood and old age. In S. Yussen (Ed.), *The growth of reflection in children* (pp. 267–285). New York: Academic Press.

Langer, E. J., & Rodin, J. (1976). The effects of choice and enhanced personal responsibility for the aged: A field experiment in an institutional setting. *Journal of Personality and Social Psychology, 34,* 191–198.

Larson, R. (1978). Thirty years of research on the subjective well-being of older Americans. *Journal of Gerontology, 33,* 109–125.

Larson, R., Mannell, R., & Zuzanek, J. (1986). Daily well-being of older adults with friends and family. *Psychology and Aging, 1,* 117–126.

LaRue, A., Dessonville, C., & Jarvik, L. F. (1985). Aging and mental disorders. In J. E. Birren & K. W. Schaie (Eds.), *Handbook of the psychology of aging* (2nd ed., pp. 664–702). New York: Van Nostrand Reinhold.

Latack, J. C. (1984). Career transitions within organizations: An exploratory study of work, nonwork, and coping strategies. *Organizational Behavior and Human Performance, 34,* 296–322.

Lavey, R. S., & Taylor, C. B. (1985). The nature of relaxation therapy. In S. R. Burchfield (Ed.), *Stress: Psychological and physiological interactions* (pp. 329–358). Washington, DC: Hemisphere.

Lawton, M. P. (1980). *Environment and aging.* Pacific Grove, CA: Brooks/Cole.

Lawton, M. P. (1982). Competence, environmental press, and the adaptation of old people. In M. P. Lawton, P. G. Windley, & T. O. Byerts (Eds.), *Aging and the environment: Theoretical approaches* (pp. 33–59). New York: Springer.

Lawton, M. P. (1985a). Activities and leisure. In M. P. Lawton & G. L. Maddox (Eds.), *Annual review of gerontology and geriatrics* (Vol. 5, pp. 127–164). New York: Springer.

Lawton, M. P. (1985b). Housing and living environments of older people. In R. H. Binstock & E. Shanas (Eds.), *Handbook of aging and the social sciences* (2nd ed., pp. 450–478). New York: Van Nostrand Reinhold.

Lawton, M. P., & Cohen, J. (1974). The generality of housing impact on the well-being of older people. *Journal of Gerontology, 29,* 194–204.

Lawton, M. P., Moss, M. S., & Fulcomer, M. (1986–1987). Objective and sub-jective uses of time by older people. *International Journal of Aging and Human Development, 24,* 171–188.

Lawton, M. P., Moss, M., & Moles, E. (1984). The supra-personal neigh-borhood context of older people: Age heterogeneity and well-being. *Environment and Behavior, 16,* 89–109.

Lawton, M. P., & Nahemow, L. (1973). Ecology of the aging process. In C. Eisdorfer & M. P. Lawton (Eds.), *The psychology of adult development and aging* (pp. 619–674). Washington, DC: American Psychological Association.

Lawton, M. P., & Nahemow, L. (1979). Social areas and the well-being of tenants in housing for the elderly. *Multivariate Behavior Research, 14,* 463–484.

Lawton, M. P., & Yaffe, S. (1980). Victimization and fear of crime in elderly public housing tenants. *Journal of Gerontology, 35,* 768–779.

Layde, P. M., Ory, H. W., & Schlesselman, J. J. (1982). The risk of myocardial infarction in former users of oral contraceptives. *Family Planning Perspectives, 14,* 78–80.

Lazarus, R. S. (1984). Puzzles in the study of daily hassles. *Journal of Behavioral Medicine, 7,* 375–389.

Lazarus, R. S., DeLongis, A., Folkman, S., & Gruen, R. (1985). Stress and adaptational outcomes. *American Psychologist, 40,* 770–779.

Lazarus, R. S., & Folkman, S. (1984). *Stress, appraisal, and coping.* New York: Springer.

Leacock, E. (1978). Women's status in egalitarian society: Implications for social evolution. *Current Anthropology, 19,* 247–275.

Leaf, P. J., Berkman, C. S., Weissman, M. M., Holzer, C. E., Tischler, G. L., & Myers, J. K. (1988). The epidemiology of late-life depression. In J. A. Brody & G. L. Maddox (Eds.), *Epidemiology and aging: An international perspective* (pp. 117–133). New York: Springer.

Lebowitz, M. D. (1988). Respiratory changes of aging. In B. Kent & R. Butler (Eds.), *Human aging research: Concepts and techniques* (pp. 263–276). New York: Raven Press.

Lee, G. R. (1985). Kinship and social support of the elderly: The case of the United States. *Aging and Society, 5,* 19–38.

Lee, G. R. (1988). Marital satisfaction in later life: The effects of nonmarital roles. *Journal of Marriage and the Family, 50,* 775–783.

Lee, G. R., & Ellithorpe, E. (1982). Inter-generational exchange and subjective well-being among the elderly. *Journal of Marriage and the Family, 44,* 217–224.

Lee, R. B. (1968). What hunters do for a living, or how to make out on scarce resources. In R. B. Lee and I. DeVore (Eds.), *Man the hunter.* Chicago: Aldine-Atherton.

Lee, T. R., Mancini, J. A., & Maxwell, J. W. (1990). Sibling relationships in adult-hood: Contact patterns and motivation. *Journal of Marriage and the Family, 52,* 431–440.

Lehmann, H. E. (1981). Classification of depressive disorders. In T. A. Ban, R. Gonzalez, A. S. Jablensky, N. A. Sartorius, & F. E. Vartanian (Eds.), *Prevention and treatment of depression* (pp. 3–17). Baltimore: University Park Press.

Lehtonen, L., Eskola, J., Vainio, O., & Lehtonen, A. (1990). Changes in lymphocyte subsets and immune competence in very advanced age. *Journal of Gerontology: Medical Sciences, 45*, M108–M112.

Lemon, B. W., Bengtson, V. L., & Peterson, J. A. (1972). An exploration of the activity theory of aging: Activity types and life satisfactions among in-movers to a retirement community. *Journal of Gerontology, 27*, 511–523.

Lent, R. W., & Hackett, G. (1987). Career self-efficacy: Empirical status and future directions. *Journal of Vocational Behavior, 30*, 347–382.

Leon, G. R., Gillum, B., Gillum, R., & Gouze, M. (1979). Personality stability and change over a 30-year period: Middle to old age. *Journal of Consulting and Clinical Psychology, 47*, 517–524.

Leonard, J. A., & Newman, R. C. (1965). On the acquisition and maintenance of high speed and high accuracy on a key-board task. *Ergonomics, 8*, 281–304.

Lepp, I. (1968). *Death and its mysteries.* New York: Macmillan.

Lerner, M. (1970). When, why, and where people die. In O. G. Brim, Jr., H. E. Freeman, S. Levine, & N. A. Scotch (Eds.), *The dying patient* (pp. 5–29). New York: Russell Sage Foundation.

Lerner, R. M. (1986). *Concepts and theories of human development* (2nd ed.). New York: Random House.

Le Shan, L. (1969). Psychotherapy and the dying patient. In L. Pearson (Ed.), *Death and dying.* Cleveland: Case Western Reserve University Press.

Lesser, J., Lazarus, L. W., Frankel, R., & Havasy, S. (1981). Reminiscence group therapy with psychotic geriatric inpatients. *The Gerontologist, 21*, 291–296.

LeVine, R. (1978). Adulthood and aging in cross-cultural perspective. *Items, 31/32*, 1–5.

Levinson, D. J., Darrow, C., Kline, E., Levinson, M., & McKee, B. (1978). *The seasons of a man's life.* New York: Knopf.

Lewin, K. (1936). *Principles of topological psychology.* New York: McGraw-Hill.

Lewinsohn, P. M. (1975). The behavioral study and treatment of depression. In M. Hersen, R. M. Eisler, & P. M. Miller (Eds.), Progress in behavior modification (Vol. 1, pp. 19–64). New York: Academic Press.

Lewinsohn, P. M., Steinmetz, J. L., Antonuccio, D. O., & Teri, L. (1984).

The coping with depression course. Eugene, OR: Castalia.

Lewis, R. A. (1979). Macular degeneration in the aged. In S. S. Han & D. H. Coons (Eds.), *Special senses and aging.* Ann Arbor: Institute of Gerontology, University of Michigan.

Liang, J., & Warfel, B. L. (1983). Urbanism and life satisfaction among the aged. *Journal of Gerontology, 38*, 97–106.

Lieberman, A. (1974). Parkinson's disease: A clinical review. *American Journal of Medical Science, 267*, 66–80.

Lieberman, A., Dzietolowski, M., Kupersmith, M., Serby, M., Goodgold, A., Korein, J., & Goldstein, M. (1979). Dementia in Parkinson's disease. *Annals of Neurology, 6*, 255–259.

Light, K. E., & Spirduso, W. W. (1990). Effects of aging on the movement complexity factor of response programming. *Journal of Gerontology: Psychological Sciences, 45*, P107–P109.

Light, L. L. (1990). Interactions between memory and language in old age. In J. E. Birren & K. W. Schaie (Eds.), *Handbook of the psychology of aging* (3rd ed., pp. 275–290). San Diego, CA: Academic Press.

Light, L. L., & Anderson, P. A. (1975). Working-memory capacity, age, and memory for discourse. *Journal of Gerontology, 45*, 737–747.

Light, L. L., & Zelinski, E. M. (1983). Memory for spatial information in young and old adults. *Developmental Psychology, 19*, 901–906.

Lincoln, Y. S., & Guba, E. G. (1985). *Naturalistic inquiry.* Beverly Hills, CA: Sage Publications.

Lipman, P. D. (1991). Age and exposure differences in acquisition of route information. *Psychology and Aging, 6*, 128–133.

Lipowski, Z. J. (1975). Physical illness, the patient and his environment: Psychosocial foundations of medicine. In M. Rieser (Ed.), *American handbook of psychiatry* (Vol. 4, pp. 1–42). New York: Basic Books.

Lipowski, Z. J. (1980). *Delirium.* Springfield, IL: Charles C Thomas.

Lishman, W. A. (1978). *Organic psychiatry: The psychological consequences of cerebral disorder.* Oxford, England: Blackwell Scientific.

List, N. (1987). Perspectives in career screening in the elderly. *Geriatric Clinic, 3*, 433–445.

List, N. D. (1988). Cancer screening in the elderly. In R. Chernoff & D. A. Lipschitz (Eds.), *Health promotion and disease prevention in the elderly* (pp. 113–129). New York: Raven Press.

Livson, F. B. (1981). Paths to psychological health in the middle years: Sex differences. In D. Eichorn, N. Haan, J. Clausen, M. Honzik, & P. Mussen (Eds.), *Past and present in middle life* (pp. 183–194). New York: Academic Press.

Locke, E. A. (1976). The natures and causes of job satisfaction. In M. Dunnette (Ed.), *Handbook of industrial/organizational psychology.* Chicago: Rand McNally.

Lockshin, R. A., & Zakeri, Z. F. (1990). MINIREVIEW: Programmed cell death: New thoughts and relevance to aging. *Journal of Gerontology: Biological Sciences, 45*, B135–B140.

Loevinger, J. (1976). *Ego development.* San Francisco: Jossey-Bass.

Logan, R. D. (1986). A reconceptualization of Erikson's theory: The repetition of existential and instrumental themes. *Human Development, 29*, 125–136.

Lombardo, N. E. (1988). ADRDA: Birth and evolution of a major voluntary health association. In M. K. Aronson (Ed.), *Understanding Alzheimer's disease* (pp. 323–326). New York: Scribner's.

Lomranz, J., Bergman, S., Eyal, N., & Shmotkin, D. (1988). Indoor and outdoor activities of aged women and men as related to depression and well-being. *International Journal of Aging and Human Development, 26*, 303–314.

Longino, C. F. (1982). American retirement communities and residential relocation. In M. A. Warnes (Ed.), *Geographical perspectives on the elderly* (pp. 239–262). London: Wiley.

Longino, C. F., Jr., Jackson, D. J., Zimmerman, R. S., & Bradsher, J. E. (1991). The second move: Health and geographical mobility. *Journal of Gerontology: Social Sciences, 46*, S218–S224.

Lopata, H. Z. (1973). *Widowhood in an American city.* Cambridge, MA: Schenkman.

Lopata, H. Z. (1975). Widowhood: Societal factors in life-span disruptions and alternatives. In N. Datan & L. H. Ginsberg (Eds.), *Life-span developmental psychology: Normative life crises* (pp. 217–234). New York: Academic Press.

Lorayne, H., & Lucas, J. (1974). *The memory book.* New York: Ballantine.

Lovelace, E. A., Marsh, G. R., & Oster, O. J. (1982). *Prediction and evaluation of memory performance by young and old adults.* Paper presented at the meeting of the Gerontological Society of America, Boston.

Lowenthal, M. F. (1972). Some potentialities of a life-cycle approach to the study of retirement. In F. M. Carp (Ed.), *Retirement* (pp. 307–338). New York: Behavioral Publications.

Lowenthal, M., Thurnher, M., & Chiriboga, D. (1975). *Four stages of life.* San Francisco: Jossey-Bass.

Löwik, M. R. H., Wedel, M., Kok, F. J., Odink, J., Westenbrink, S., & Meulmeester, J. F. (1991). Nutrition and serum cholesterol levels among elderly men and women (Dutch nutrition surveillance system). *Journal of Gerontology: Medical Sciences, 46,* M23–M28.

Luborsky, M., & Rubinstein, R. L. (1987). Ethnicity and lifetimes: Self-concepts and situational contexts of ethnic identity in late life. In D. E. Gelfand & C. M. Barresi (Eds.), *Ethnic dimensions of aging.* New York: Springer.

Luborsky, M. R., & Rubinstein, R. L. (1990). Ethnic identity and bereavement in later life: The case of older widowers. In J. Sokolovsky (Ed.), *The cultural context of aging* (pp. 229–240). New York: Bergin & Garvey.

Lund, D. A., Dimond, M. S., Caserta, M. F., Johnson, R. J., Poulton, J. L., & Connelly, J. R. (1985–1986). Identifying elderly with coping difficulties after two years of bereavement. *Omega: Journal of Death and Dying, 16,* 213–224.

Lundgren, B. K., Steen, G. B., & Isaksson, B. (1987). Dietary habits in 70- and 75-year-old males and females: Longitudinal and cohort data from a population study. *Näringsforskning.*

Lundin, T. (1984). Morbidity following sudden and unexpected bereavement. *British Journal of Psychiatry, 144,* 84–88.

Lyons, N. (1983). Two perspectives: On self, relationships, and morality. *Harvard Educational Review, 53,* 125–145.

Maas, H. S. (1985). The development of adult development: Recollections and reflections. In J. M. A. Munnichs, P. Mussen, E. Olbrich, & P. G. Coleman (Eds.), *Life-span and change in a gerontological perspective* (pp. 161–175). New York: Academic Press.

Maas, H. S., & Kuypers, J. A. (1974). *From thirty to seventy.* San Francisco: Jossey-Bass.

Maas, J. W. (1978). Clinical and biochemical heterogeneity of depressive disorders. *Annals of Internal Medicine, 88,* 556–563.

Mace, N. L., & Rabins, P. V. (1981). *The 36-hour day.* Baltimore: Johns Hopkins University Press.

Macklin, E. D. (1978). Review of research on nonmarital cohabitation in the United States. In B. I. Murstein (Ed.), *Exploring intimate life styles* (pp. 197–243). New York: Springer.

Macklin, E. D. (1988). Heterosexual couples who cohabit nonmaritally: Some common problems and issues. In C. S. Chilman, E. W. Nunnally, and F. M. Cox (Eds.), *Variant family forms* (pp. 56–72). Newbury Park, CA: Sage Publications.

Madden, D. J. (1990). Adult age differences in the time course of visual attention. *Journal of Gerontology: Psychological Sciences, 45,* P9–P16.

Madden, D. J., & Nebes, R. D. (1980). Aging and the development of automaticity in visual search. *Developmental Psychology, 16,* 377–384.

Maddox, G. L., & Campbell, R. T. (1985). Scope, concepts, and methods in the study of aging. In R. H. Binstock & E. Shanas (Eds.), *Handbook of aging and the social sciences* (2nd ed., pp. 3–31). New York: Van Nostrand Reinhold.

Mahoney, M. J. (1980). *Abnormal psychology.* New York: Harper & Row.

Maletta, G. J. (1984). Use of antipsychotic medication in the elderly. In C. Eisdorfer (Ed.), *Annual review of gerontology and geriatrics* (Vol. 4, pp. 174–220). New York: Springer.

Malinak, D. P., Hoyt, M. F., & Patterson, V. (1979). Adults' reactions to the death of a parent: A preliminary study. *American Journal of Psychiatry, 136,* 1152–1156.

Mandel, R. G., & Johnson, N. S. (1984). A developmental analysis of story recall and comprehension in adulthood. *Journal of Verbal Learning and Verbal Behavior, 23,* 643–659.

Manton, K. G., Wrigley, J. M., Cohen, H. J., & Woodbury, M. A. (1991). Cancer mortality, aging, and patterns of comorbidity in the United States: 1968 to 1986. *Journal of Gerontology: Social Sciences, 46,* S225–S234.

Margolin, L., & White, J. (1987). The continuing role of physical attractiveness in marriage. *Journal of Marriage and the Family, 49,* 21–27.

Markides, K., Boldt, J. S., & Ray, L. A. (1986). Sources of helping and intergenerational solidarity: A three generation study of Mexican Americans. *Journal of Gerontology, 41,* 506–511.

Markides, K., Liang, J., & Jackson, J. S. (1990). Race, ethnicity, and aging: Conceptual and methodological issues. In R. H. Binstock & L. K. George (Eds.), *Handbook of aging and the social sciences* (3rd ed., pp. 112–129). San Diego: Academic Press.

Markides, K., & Martin, H. W. (1983). *Older Mexican Americans: A study in an urban barrio.* Austin: University of Texas Press.

Markus, H., & Nurius, P. (1986). Possible selves. *American Psychologist, 41,* 954–969.

Marlatt, G. A., & Gordon, J. R. (1980). Determinants of relapse: Implication for the maintenance of behavior change. In P. O. Davidson & S. M. Davidson (Eds.), *Behavioral medicine: Changing health lifestyles* (pp. 410–452). New York: Brunner/Mazel.

Marshall, V. (1980). *Last chapters: A sociology of aging and dying.* Pacific Grove, CA: Brooks/Cole.

Martin, L. G. (1988). The aging of Asia. *Journal of Gerontology, 43,* S99–S113.

Martin, M. A. (1990). The homeless elderly: No room at the end. In Z. Harel, P. Ehrlich, & R. Hubbard (Eds.), *The vulnerable aged* (pp. 149–166). New York: Springer.

Martin, T. R., & Bracken, M. B. (1986). Association of low birth weight with passive smoke exposure in pregnancy. *American Journal of Epidemiology, 124,* 633–642.

Masako, O., & Liu, W. T. (1986). Intergenerational relations and the aged

Japanese Americans. *Research on Aging,* 8, 125–155.

Masheter, C. (1991). Postdivorce relationships between ex-spouses: The roles of attachment and interpersonal conflict. *Journal of Marriage and the Family, 53,* 103–110.

Maslow, A. H. (1968). *Toward a psychology of being* (2nd ed.). New York: Van Nostrand Reinhold.

Mason, S. E. (1981, November). *Age group comparisons of memory ratings, predictions, and performance.* Paper presented at the meeting of the Gerontological Society of America, Toronto.

Mason, S. E. (1986). Age and gender as factors in facial recognition. *Experimental Aging Research, 12,* 151–154.

Masoro, E. J. (1988). Food restriction in rodents: An evaluation of its role in the study of aging. *Journal of Gerontology: Biological Sciences, 43,* B59–B64.

Materi, M. (1977). Assertiveness training: A catalyst for behavior change. *Alcohol Health and Research World, 1,* 23–26.

Matthews, R., & Matthews, A. M. (1986). Infertility and involuntary childlessness: The transition to nonparenthood. *Journal of Marriage and the Family, 48,* 641–649.

Mattis, S. (1976). Mental status examination for organic mental syndrome in the elderly patient. In L. Bellak & T. B. Karasu (Eds.), *Geriatric psychiatry: A handbook for psychiatrists and primary health care physicians* (pp. 79–121). New York: Grune & Stratton.

Maxwell, R. J., Silverman, P., & Maxwell, E. K. (1982). The motive for gerontocide. In J. Sokolovsky (Ed.), *Aging and the aged* (Part 1, pp. 67–84). Williamsburg, VA: Studies in Third World Societies (Public No. 22).

Maybury-Lewis, D. (1984). Age and kinship: A structural view. In D. I. Kertzer & J. Keith (Eds.), *Age and anthropological theory* (pp. 123–140). Ithaca, NY: Cornell University Press.

Mayer, K. U., & Muller, W. (1986). The state and the structure of the life course. In A. B. Sorenson, F. W. Weinert, & L. R. Sherrod (Eds.), *Human development and the life course: Multidisciplinary perspectives.* Hillsdale, NJ: Erlbaum.

McAllister, T. W. (1981). Cognitive functioning in the affective disorders. *Comprehensive Psychiatry, 22,* 572–586.

McClelland, J. L., Rumelhart, D. E., & the PDP Research Group (1986). *Parallel distributed processing: Explorations in the microstructure of cognition.* Cambridge, MA: MIT Press.

McCrae, R. R., & Costa, P. T., Jr. (1983). Psychological maturity and subjective well-being: Toward new synthesis. *Developmental Psychology, 19,* 243–248.

McCrae, R. R., & Costa, P. T., Jr. (1984). *Emerging lives, enduring dispositions.* Boston: Little, Brown.

McCrae, R. R., & Costa, P. T., Jr. (1987). Validation of the five-factor model of personality across instruments and observers. *Journal of Personality and Social Psychology, 52,* 81–90.

McCrae, R. R., Costa, P. T., Jr., & Busch, C. M. (1986). Evaluating comprehensiveness in personality systems. *Journal of Personality, 54,* 430–446.

McDonald, R. S. (1986). Assessing treatment effects: Behavior rating scales. In L. W. Poon (Ed.), *Handbook for the clinical memory assessment of older adults* (pp. 129–138). Washington, DC: American Psychological Association.

McDowd, J. M., & Birren, J. E. (1990). Aging and attentional processes. In J. E. Birren & K. W. Schaie (Eds.), *Handbook of the psychology of aging* (3rd ed., pp. 222–233). San Diego: Academic Press.

McDowd, J. M., & Craik, F. I. M. (1988). Effects of aging and task difficulty on divided attention performance. *Journal of Experimental Psychology: Human Perception and Performance, 14,* 267–280.

McDowd, J. M, Filion, D. L., & Oseas-Kreger, D. M. (1991, June) *Inhibitory deficits in selective attention and aging.* Paper presented at the meeting of the American Psychological Society, Washington, DC.

McEvoy, C. L., & Moon, J. R. (1988). Assessment and treatment of everyday memory problems in the elderly. In M. M. Gruneberg, P. E. Morris, & R. N. Sykes (Eds.), *Practical aspects of memory: Current research and issues* (Vol. 2, pp. 155–160). Chichester, England: Wiley.

McGeer, E., & McGeer, P. L. (1980). Aging and neurotransmitter systems. In M. Goldstein, D. B. Caine, A. Liegerman, & M. O. Thorner (Eds.), *Advances in biochemical psychopharmacology: Vol. 23. Ergot compounds and brain function:*

Neuroendocrine and neuropsychiatric aspects (pp. 305–314). New York: Raven Press.

McGuire, F. A., Dottavio, D., & O'Leary, J. T. (1986). Constraints to participation in outdoor recreation across the life span: A nationwide study of limitors and prohibitors. *The Gerontologist, 26,* 538–544.

McKellin, W. H. (1985). Passing away and loss of life: Aging and death among the Managalese of Papua New Guinea. In D. A. Counts & D. R. Counts (Eds.), *Aging and its transformations* (pp. 181–202). Lanham, MD: University Press of America.

McKhann, G., Drachman, D., Folstein, M., Katzman, R., Prince, D., & Stadlam, E. M. (1984). Clinical diagnosis of Alzheimer's disease: Report of the NINCDS-ADRDA Work Group under the auspices of the Department of Health and Human Services Task Force on Alzheimer's disease. *Neurology, 34,* 939–944.

McKnight, A. J. (1988). Driver and pedestrian training. In *Transportation in an aging society: Improving mobility and safety for older persons* (Special Report 218, pp. 101–133). Washington, DC: National Research Council, Transportation Research Board.

Meacham, J. A. (1982). A note on remembering to execute planned actions. *Journal of Applied Developmental Psychology, 3,* 121–133.

Meichenbaum, D. (1985). *Stress inoculation training.* New York: Pergamon Press.

Meichenbaum, D., & Cameron, R. (1983). Stress inoculation training: Toward a general paradigm for training coping skills. In D. Meichenbaum & M. E. Jaremko (Eds.), *Stress reduction and prevention* (pp. 115–154). New York: Plenum.

Meier, D. E. (1988). Skeletal aging. In B. Kent & R. Butler (Eds.), *Human aging research: Concepts and techniques* (pp. 221–244). New York: Raven Press.

Mellinger, G. D., Balter, M. B., & Uhlenhuth, E. H. (1985). Insomnia and its treatment. *Archives of General Psychiatry, 42,* 225–232.

Menaghan, E. G., & Lieberman, M. A. (1986). Changes in depression following divorce: A panel study. *Journal of Marriage and the Family, 48,* 319–328.

Mendelson, M. (1982). Psychodynamics of depression. In E. S. Paykel (Ed.), *Handbook of affective disorders* (pp. 162–174). New York: Guilford.

Merriam, S. (1980). The concept and function of reminiscence: A review of research. *The Gerontologist, 20,* 604–609.

Messer, M. (1967). The possibility of an age-concentrated environment becoming a normative system. *The Gerontologist, 7,* 247–251.

Messer, M. (1968). Age grouping and social status of the elderly. *Sociologist and Social Research, 52,* 271–279.

Meyer, B. J. F. (1983). Text structure and its use in studying comprehension across the adult life span. In B. A. Huston (Ed.), *Advances in reading/ language research* (Vol. 2, pp. 9–54). Greenwich, CT: JAI.

Meyer, B. J. F. (1987). Reading comprehension and aging. In K. W. Schaie (Ed.), *Annual review of gerontology and geriatrics* (Vol. 7, pp. 93–115). New York: Springer.

Meyer, B. J. F., & Rice, G. E. (1981). Information recalled from prose by young, middle, and old adults. *Experimental Aging Research, 7,* 253–268.

Meyer, B. J. F., & Rice, G. E. (1983). Learning and memory from text across the adult life span. In J. Fine & R. O. Freedle (Eds.), *Developmental studies in discourse* (pp. 291–306). Norwood, NJ: Ablex.

Meyer, B. J. F., & Rice, G. E. (1989). Prose processing in adulthood: The text, the reader, and the task. In L. W. Poon, D. C. Rubin, & B. Wilson (Eds.), *Everyday cognition in adulthood and late life* (pp. 157–194). Cambridge: Cambridge University Press.

Meyer, B. J. F., Rice, G. E., Knight, C. C., & Jessen, J. L. (1979). *Effects of comparative and descriptive discourse types on the reading performance of young, middle, and old adults* (Prose Learning Series No. 7). Tempe: Department of Educational Psychology, Arizona State University Press.

Meyer, B. J. F., Young, C. J., & Bartlett, B. J. (1986, August). *A prose learning strategy: Effects on young and old adults.* Paper presented at the meeting of the American Psychological Association, Washington, DC.

Meyer, J. W. (1986). The self and the life course: Institutionalization and its effects. In A. B. Sorenson, F. W. Weinert, & L. R. Sherrod (Eds.), *Human development and the life course: Multidisciplinary perspectives.* Hillsdale, NJ: Erlbaum.

Meyer, J. W. (1987). A regional scale temporal analysis of the net migration patterns of elderly persons over time. *Journal of Gerontology, 42,* 366–375.

Meyerhoff, B. (1978). *Number our days.* New York: Simon & Schuster.

Meyers, G. C. (1985). Aging and worldwide population change. In R. H. Binstock & E. Shanas (Eds.), *Handbook of aging and the social sciences* (2nd ed., pp. 173–198). New York: Van Nostrand Reinhold.

Miles, C. C., & Miles, W. R. (1932). The correlation of intelligence scores and chronological age from early to late maturity. *American Journal of Psychology, 44,* 44–78.

Miller, S. S., & Cavanaugh, J. C. (1990, August). The meaning of grandparenthood and its relationship to demographic, relationship, and social participation variables. Paper presented at the meeting of the American Psychological Association, New York.

Miller, W. R., & Hester, R. K. (1980). Treating the problem drinker: Modern approaches. In W. R. Miller (Ed.), *The addictive behaviors* (pp. 11–142). Oxford: Pergamon Press.

Minkler, M., & Pasick, R. J. (1986). Health promotion and the elderly: A critical perspective on the past and future. In K. Dychtwald (Ed.), *Wellness and health promotion for the elderly* (pp. 39–54). Rockville, MD: Aspen.

Mobily, K. E., Lemke, J. H., & Gisin, G. J. (1991). The idea of leisure repertoire. *Journal of Applied Gerontology, 10,* 208–223.

Mohs, R. C., Kim, Y., Johns, C. A., Dunn, D. D., & Davis, K. I. (1986). Assessing changes in Alzheimer's disease: Memory and language. In L. W. Poon (Ed.), *Handbook for the clinical memory assessment of older adults* (pp. 149–155). Washington, DC: American Psychological Association.

Monczunski, J. (1991). That incurable disease. *Notre Dame Magazine, 20 (1),* 37.

Moody, R. A., Jr. (1975). *Life after life.* Atlanta: Mockingbird.

Moody, R. A., Jr. (1977). *Reflections on life after life.* New York: Bantam.

Moody, R. A., Jr. (1988). *The light beyond.* New York: Bantam.

Moon, J.-H., & Pearl, J. H. (1991). Alienation of elderly Korean American immigrants as related to place of residence, gender, age, years of education, time in the U. S., living with or without children, and living with or without a spouse. *International Journal of Aging and Human Development, 32,* 115–124.

Moore, S. F. (1978). Old age in a lifeterm social arena: Some Chagga in Kilimanjaro in 1974. In B. G. Meyerhoff & A. Simic (Eds.), *Life's career: Aging* (pp. 23–76). Beverly Hills, CA: Sage Publications.

Moos, R. H., & Lemke, S. (1984). *Multiphasic environmental assessment procedure: Manual.* Palo Alto, CA: Social Ecology Laboratory, Stanford University Press.

Moos, R. H., & Lemke, S. (1985). Specialized living environments for older people. In J. E. Birren & K. W. Schaie (Eds.), *Handbook of the psychology of aging* (2nd ed., pp. 864–889). New York: Van Nostrand Reinhold.

Moran, J. A., & Gatz, M. (1987). Group therapies for nursing home adults: An evaluation of two treatment approaches. *The Gerontologist, 27,* 588–591.

Morewitz, J. (1988). Evaluation of excessive daytime sleepiness in the elderly. *Journal of the American Geriatrics Society, 36,* 324–330.

Moritani, T., & deVries, H. A. (1980). Potential for gross muscle hypertrophy in older men. *Journal of Gerontology, 35,* 672–682.

Morris, J. N. (1975). Changes in morale experienced by elderly institutional applicants along the institutional path. *The Gerontologist, 15,* 345–349.

Morris, J. N., & Sherwood, S. (1984). Informal support resources for vulnerable elderly persons: Can they be counted on, why do they work? *International Journal of Aging and Human Development, 18,* 1–17.

Morrow, P. C., & McElroy, J. C. (1987). Work commitment and job satisfaction over three career stages. *Journal of Vocational Behavior, 30*, 330–346.

Mortimer, J. T., Finch, M. D., & Kumka, D. (1982). Persistence and change in development: The multidimensional self-concept. In P. B. Baltes & O. G. Brim, Jr. (Eds.), *Life-span development and behavior* (Vol. 4, pp. 263–313). New York: Academic Press.

Mortimer, R. G. (1989). Older drivers' visibility and comfort in night driving: Vehicle safety factors. In *Proceedings of the Human Factors Society 33rd Annual Meeting* (pp. 154–158). Santa Monica, CA: Human Factors Society.

Moscovitch, M. C. (1982). A neuropsychological approach to perception and memory in normal and pathological aging. In F. I. M. Craik & S. Trehub (Eds.), *Aging and cognitive processes* (pp. 55–78). New York: Plenum.

Moss, M. S., & Lawton, M. P. (1982). Time budgets of older people: A window on four life-styles. *Journal of Gerontology, 37*, 115–123.

Mourant, R. R., & Langolf, G. D. (1976). Luminance specifications for automobile instrument panels. *Human Factors, 18*, 71–84.

Mulrow, C. D., Feussner, J. R., Williams, B. C., & Vokaty, K. A. (1987). The value of clinical findings in the detection of normal pressure hydrocephalus. *Journal of Gerontology, 42*, 277–279.

Munro, H. N., & Young, V. R. (1978). New approaches to the assessment of protein status in man. In A. N. Howard & I. M. Baird (Eds.), *Recent advances in clinical nutrition* (pp. 33–41). London: Libby.

Murphy, C. (1985). Cognitive and chemosensory influences in age-related changes in the ability to identify blended foods. *Journal of Gerontology, 40*, 47–52.

Murphy, C. (1986). Taste and smell in the elderly. In H. L. Meiselman & R. S. Rivlin (Eds.), *Clinical measurement of taste and smell* (pp. 343–371). New York: Macmillan.

Murphy, M. D., Sanders, R. E., Gabriesheski, A. S., & Schmitt, F. A. (1981). Metamemory in the aged. *Journal of Gerontology, 36*, 185–193.

Murphy, Y., & Murphy, R. F. (1974). *Women of the forest.* New York: Columbia University Press.

Murray, H. A. (1938). *Explorations in personality.* New York: Oxford University Press.

Murray, J. (1979). Subjective retirement. *Social Security Bulletin, 42*, 20–25, 43.

Murstein, B. I. (1982). Marital choice. In B. B. Wolman (Ed.), *Handbook of developmental psychology* (pp. 652–666). Englewood Cliffs, NJ: Prentice-Hall.

Muschkin, C., & Myers, G. C. (1989). Migration and household family structure: Puerto Ricans in the United States. *International Migration Review, 23*, 495–501.

Mussen, P. (1985). Early adult antecedents of life satisfaction at age 70. In J. M. A. Munnichs, P. Mussen, E. Olbrich, & P. G. Coleman (Eds.), *Lifespan and change in a gerontological perspective* (pp. 45–61). New York: Academic Press.

Myers, J. E., Wass, H., & Murphey, M. (1980). Ethnic differences in death anxiety among the elderly. *Death Education, 4*, 237–244.

Myers, T. (1983). Corroboration of self-reported alcohol consumption — A comparison of the accounts of a group of male prisoners and those of their wives/cohabitees. *Alcohol and Alcoholism, 18*, 67–74.

Myerson, J., Hale, S., Wagstaff, D., Poon, L. W., & Smith, G. A. (1990). The information-loss model: A mathematical theory of age-related cognitive slowing. *Psychological Review, 97*, 475–487.

Nachtigall, L. E., & Nachtigall, L. B. (1990). Protecting older women from their growing risk of cardiac disease. *Geriatrics, 45*(5), 24–34.

Nagel, J. E., & Adler, W. H. (1988). Immunology. In B. Kent & R. Butler (Eds.), *Human aging research: Concepts and techniques* (pp. 299–310). New York: Raven Press.

National Center for Health Statistics. (1988). *Annual survey of births, marriages, divorces, and deaths: United States, 1987.* Hyattsville, MD: U.S. Public Health Service.

National Center for Health Statistics. (1991). *Annual survey of births, marriages, divorces, and deaths: United States, 1990.* Hyattsville, MD: U.S. Public Health Service.

National Highway Traffic Safety Administration. (1988). *Traffic safety plan for older drivers.* Washington, DC: U.S. Department of Transportation.

National Institute of Aging. (1980). Senility reconsidered. *Journal of the American Medical Association, 244*, 259–263.

National Institute of Alcoholism and Alcohol Abuse (NIAAA). (1983). *Fifth special report to the U.S. Congress on alcohol and health.* (DHHS Publication No. ADM 84–1291). Washington, DC: U.S. Government Printing Office.

National Research Council. (1988). *The emerging population in the twenty-first century: Statistics for health policy.* Washington, DC: National Academy Press.

National Urban League. (1964). *Double-jeopardy — The older Negro in America today.* New York: Author.

Nebes, R. D., Boller, F., & Holland, A. (1986). Use of semantic context by patients with Alzheimer's disease. *Psychology and Aging, 1*, 261–269.

Nehrke, M. F., Bellucci, G., & Gabriel, S. J. (1977). Death anxiety, locus of control, and life satisfaction in the elderly. *Omega: Journal of Death and Dying, 8*, 359–368.

Neimark, E. D. (1975). Longitudinal development of formal operational thought. *Genetic Psychology Monographs, 91*, 171–225.

Neisser, U. (1976). *Cognition and reality.* San Francisco: W. H. Freeman.

Neisser, U., & Winograd, E. (Eds.). (1988). *Remembering reconsidered.* New York: Cambridge University Press.

Nesselroade, J. R., & Labouvie, E. W. (1985). Experimental design in research on aging. In J. E. Birren & K. W. Schaie (Eds.), *Handbook of the psychology of aging* (2nd ed., pp. 35–60). New York: Van Nostrand Reinhold.

Neugarten, B. L. (1969). Continuities and discontinuities of psychological issues into adult life. *Human Development, 12*, 121–130.

Neugarten, B. L. (1973). Personality change in later life: A developmental perspective. In C. Eisdorfer & M. P. Lawton (Eds.), *The psychology of adult development and aging.* Washington, DC: American Psychological Association.

Neugarten, B. L. (1977). Personality and aging. In J. E. Birren & K. W. Schaie (Eds.), *Handbook of the psychology of aging* (pp. 626–649). New York: Van Nostrand Reinhold.

Neugarten, B. L., & Associates (Eds.). (1964). *Personality in middle and late life.* New York: Atherton.

Neugarten, B. L., & Datan, N. (1973). Sociological perspectives on the life cycle. In P. B. Baltes & K. W. Schaie (Eds.), *Life-span developmental psychology: Personality and socialization* (pp. 53–69). New York: Academic Press.

Neugarten, B. L., & Hagestad, G. O. (1976). Age and the life course. In R. H. Binstock & E. Shanas (Eds.), *Handbook of aging and the social sciences* (pp. 35–55). New York: Van Nostrand Reinhold.

Neugarten, B. L., & Weinstein, K. K. (1964). The changing American grandparent. *Journal of Marriage and the Family, 26,* 299–304.

Newman, B. M. (1982). Mid-life development. In B. B. Wolman (Ed.), *Handbook of developmental psychology* (pp. 617–635). Englewood Cliffs, NJ: Prentice-Hall.

Newmann, J. P., Engel, R. J., & Jensen, J. E. (1990). Depressive symptom patterns among older women. *Psychology and Aging, 5,* 101–118.

Newmann, J. P., Engel, R. J., & Jensen, J. E. (1991). Changes in depressive-symptom experiences among older women. *Psychology and Aging, 6,* 212–222.

Nisan, M., & Kohlberg, L. (1982). Universality and cross-cultural variation in moral development: A longitudinal and cross-sectional study in Turkey. *Child Development, 53,* 856–876.

Nock, S. L. (1981). Family life transitions: Longitudinal effects on family members. *Journal of Marriage and the Family, 43,* 703–714.

Nock, S. L. (1982). The life-cycle approach to family analysis. In B. B. Wolman (Ed.), *Handbook of developmental psychology* (pp. 636–651). Englewood Cliffs, NJ: Prentice-Hall.

Noe, R. A. (1987). *An exploratory investigation of the antecedents and consequences of mentoring.* Unpublished manuscript, University of Minnesota, Minneapolis.

Nolen-Hoeksema, S. (1988). Life-span views on depression. In P. B. Baltes & R. M. Lerner (Eds.), *Life-span development and behavior* (Vol. 9, pp. 203–241). Hillsdale, NJ: Erlbaum.

Norris, F. N., & Murrell, S. A. (1987). Older adult family stress and adaptation before and after bereavement. *Journal of Gerontology, 42,* 606–612.

Norris, M. L., & Cunningham, D. R. (1981). Social impact of hearing loss in the aged. *Journal of Gerontology, 36,* 727–729.

Norton, A. J., & Moorman, J. E. (1987). Current trends in marriage and divorce among American women. *Journal of Marriage and the Family, 49,* 3–14.

Nydegger, C. N. (1986). Asymmetrical kin and the problematic son-in-law. In N. Datan, A. L. Greene, & H. W. Reese (Eds.), *Life-span developmental psychology: Intergenerational relations* (pp. 99–124). Hillsdale, NJ: Erlbaum.

O'Brien, S. J., & Vertinsky, P. A. (1991). Unfit survivors: Exercise as a resource for aging women. *The Gerontologist, 31,* 347–357.

O'Donohue, W. T. (1987). The sexual behavior and problems of the elderly. In L. L. Carstensen & B. A. Edelstein (Eds.), *Handbook of clinical gerontology* (pp. 66–75). New York: Pergamon Press.

Ochs, A. L., Newberry, J., Lenhardt, M. L., & Harkins, S. W. (1985). Neural and vestibular aging associated with falls. In J. E. Birren & K. W. Schaie (Eds.), *Handbook of the psychology of aging* (2nd ed., pp. 378–399). New York: Van Nostrand Reinhold.

Ohta, R. J. (1981). Spatial problem-solving: The response selection tendencies of young and elderly adults. *Experimental Aging Research, 7,* 81–84.

Ohta, R. J., & Kirasic, K. C. (1983). The investigation of environmental learning in the elderly. In G. Rowles & R. J. Ohta (Eds.), *Aging and milieu* (pp. 83–95). New York: Academic Press.

Ohta, R. J., Walsh, D. A., & Krauss, I. K. (1981). Spatial perspective-taking ability in young and elderly adults. *Experimental Aging Research, 7,* 45–63.

Olian, J. D., Carroll, S. J., Giannantonia, C. M., & Feren, D. B. (1988). What do protégés look for in a mentor? Results from three experimental studies. *Journal of Vocational Behavior, 33,* 15–37.

Olsho, L. W., Harkins, S. W., & Lenhardt, M. L. (1985). Aging and the auditory system. In J. E. Birren & K. W. Schaie (Eds.), *Handbook of the psychology of aging* (2nd ed., pp. 332–377). New York: Van Nostrand Reinhold.

Olson, D. H., & McCubbin, H. (1983). *Families: What makes them work.* Beverly Hills, CA: Sage Publications.

Ortner, S. (1974). Is female to male as nature is to culture? In M. Z. Rosaldo & L. Lamphere (Eds.), *Women, culture, and society* (pp. 67–88). Palo Alto, CA: Stanford University Press.

Ortner, S. B. (1978). *Sherpas through their rituals.* New York: Cambridge University Press.

Osgood, N. J. (1985). *Suicide in the elderly.* Rockville, MD: Aspen.

Ostrow, A. C. (1980). Physical activity as it relates to the health of the aged. In N. Datan & N. Lohman (Eds.), *Transitions of aging* (pp. 41–56). New York: Academic Press.

Overstall, P. W., Johnson, A. L., & Exton-Smith, A. N. (1978). Instability and falls in the elderly. *Age and Ageing, 7* (Supplement 6), 92–96.

Paffenbarger, R. S., Hyde, R. T., Wing, A. L., & Hsieh, C. (1986). Physical activity, all cause mortality and longevity of college alumni. *New England Journal of Medicine, 314,* 605–613.

Palmore, E. (1975). *The honorable elders: A cross-cultural analysis of aging in Japan.* Durham, NC: Duke University Press.

Palmore, E., & Maeda, D. (1985). *The honorable elders revisited.* Durham, NC: Duke University Press.

Panek, P. E., Barrett, G. V., Sterns, H. L., & Alexander, R. A. (1977). A review of age changes in perceptual information processing ability with regard to driving. *Experimental Aging Research, 3,* 387–449.

Panek, P. E., & Reardon, J. R. (1986). *Age and gender effects on accident types for rural drivers.* Paper presented at the meeting of the Gerontological Society of America, Chicago.

Panek, P. E., & Sterns, H. L. (1985). Self-evaluation, actual performance, and preference across the life-span. *Experimental Aging Research, 11,* 221–223.

Papalia, D. E. (1972). The status of several conservation abilities across the life-span. *Human Development, 15,* 229–243.

Papalia, D. E., & Bielby, D. (1974). Cognitive functioning in middle and old age adults: A review of research based on Piaget's theory. *Human Development, 17,* 424–443.

Papalia, D. E., Salverson, S. M., & True, M. (1973). An evaluation of quantity conservation performance during old age. *International Journal of Aging and Human Development, 4,* 103–109.

Papalia-Finlay, D. E., Blackburn, J., Davis, E., Dellmann, M., & Roberts, P. (1980). Training cognitive functioning in the elderly — Inability to replicate previous findings. *International Journal of Aging and Human Development, 12,* 111–117.

Parasuraman, R. (1987, November). *Aging and sustained attention.* Paper presented at the National Institute on Aging Conference on Aging and Attention, Washington, DC.

Parasuraman, R., Nestor, P., & Greenwood, P. (1989). Sustained-attention capacity in young and older adults. *Psychology and Aging, 4,* 339–345.

Pargament, K. I. (1990). God help me: Toward a theoretical framework of coping for the psychology of religion. *Research in the Social Scientific Study of Religion, 2,* 195–224.

Pargament, K. I., Ensing, D. S., Falgout, K., Olsen, H., Reilly, B., Van Haitsma, K., & Warren, R. (1990). God help me (I): Religious coping efforts as predictors of the outcomes to significant negative life events. *American Journal of Community Psychology, 18,* 793–824.

Pargament, K. I., Olsen, H., Reilly, B., Falgout, K., Ensing, D., & Van Haitsma, K. (1991). *God help me (II): Studies of the ecology of religious coping.* Unpublished manuscript, Bowling Green State University, Bowling Green, OH.

Park, D. C., Cherry, K. E., Smith, A. D., & Lafronza, V. N. (1990). Effects of distinctive context on memory for objects and their locations in young and elderly adults. *Psychology and Aging, 5,* 250–255.

Park, D. C., Puglisi, J. T., & Smith, A. D. (1986). Memory for pictures: Does an age-related decline exist? *Psychology and Aging, 1,* 11–17.

Park, D. C., Puglisi, J. T., & Sovacool, M. (1983). Memory for pictures, words, and spatial location in older adults: Evidence for pictorial superiority. *Journal of Gerontology, 38,* 582–588.

Park, D. C., Puglisi, J. T., & Sovacool, M. (1984). Picture memory in older adults: Effects of contextual detail at encoding and retrieval. *Journal of Gerontology, 39,* 213–215.

Park, D. C., Royal, D., Dudley, W., & Morrell, R. (1988). Forgetting of pictures over a long retention interval in young and older adults. *Psychology and Aging, 3,* 94–95.

Parkes, C. M. (1972). *Bereavement.* New York: International Universities Press.

Parkes, C. M. (1975). Determinants of outcome following bereavement. *Omega: Journal of Death and Dying, 6,* 303–323.

Parmelee, P. A., & Lawton, M. P. (1990). The design of special environments for the aged. In J. E. Birren & K. W. Schaie (Eds.), *Handbook of the psychology of aging* (3rd ed., pp. 464–488). San Diego: Academic Press.

Passuth, P. M. (1984). *Children's socialization to age hierarchies within the peer group and family.* Unpublished doctoral dissertation, Northwestern University, Evanston, IL.

Passuth, P. M., & Bengtson, V. L. (1988). Sociological theories of aging: Current perspectives and future directions. In J. E. Birren & V. L. Bengtson (Eds.), *Emergent theories of aging* (pp. 333–355). New York: Springer.

Pastalan, L. A. (1982). Research in environment and aging: An alternative to theory. In M. P. Lawton, P. G. Windley, & T. O. Byerts (Eds.), *Aging and the environment: Theoretical approaches* (pp. 122–131). New York: Springer.

Patel, V. L., & Groen, G. J. (1986). Knowledge based solution strategies in medical reasoning. *Cognitive Science, 10,* 91–116.

Pattison, E. M. (1977a). The dying experience — Retrospective analysis. In E. M. Pattison (Ed.), *The experience of dying.* Englewood Cliffs, NJ: Prentice-Hall.

Pattison, E. M. (Ed.). (1977b). *The experience of dying.* Englewood Cliffs, NJ: Prentice-Hall.

Pauls, J. (1985). Review of stair safety research with an emphasis on Canadian studies. *Ergonomics, 28,* 999–1010.

Pearlin, L. I., & Johnson, J. (1977). Marital status, life strains, and depression. *American Sociological Review, 42,* 704–715.

Pearlman, J., Stotsky, B. A., & Dominick, J. R. (1969). Attitudes toward death among nursing home personnel. *Journal of Genetic Psychology, 114,* 63–75.

Peele, S. (1984). The cultural context of psychological approaches to alcoholism: Can we control the effects of alcohol? *American Psychologist, 39,* 1337–1351.

Peplau, L., & Gordon, S. L. (1985). Women and men in love: Sex differences in close heterosexual relationships. In V. O'Leary, R. K. Unger, & B. S. Wallston (Eds.), *Women, gender, and social psychology* (pp. 257–292). Hillsdale, NJ: Erlbaum.

Pepper, S. C. (1942). *World hypotheses.* Berkeley: University of California Press.

Perkins, H. W., & Harris, L. B. (1990). Familial bereavement and health in adult life course perspective. *Journal of Marriage and the Family, 52,* 233–241.

Perlmuter, L. C., & Monty, R. A. (1989). Motivation and aging. In L. W. Poon, D. C. Rubin, & B. Wilson (Eds.), *Everyday cognition in adulthood and late life* (pp. 373–393). Cambridge: Cambridge University Press.

Perlmutter, M. (1978). What is memory aging the aging of? *Developmental Psychology, 14,* 330–345.

Perlmutter, M., Adams, C., Berry, J., Kaplan, M., Person, D., & Verdonik, F. (1987). Aging and memory. In K. W. Schaie (Ed.), *Annual review of gerontology and geriatrics* (Vol. 7, pp. 57–92). New York: Springer.

Perlmutter, M., Metzger, R., Miller, R., & Nezworski, T. (1980). Memory for historical events. *Experimental Aging Research, 6,* 47–60.

Perry, W. I. (1970). *Forms of intellectual and ethical development in the college years.* New York: Holt, Rinehart & Winston.

Pershagen, G., Hrubec, Z., & Svensson, C. (1987). Passive smoking and lung cancer in Swedish women. *American Journal of Epidemiology, 125,* 17–24.

Person, D. C., & Wellman, H. M. (1989). *Older adults' theories of memory difficulties*. Unpublished manuscript, Department of Psychology, University of Michigan, Ann Arbor.

Peterson, J. T. (1990). Sibling exchanges and complementarity in the Philippine highlands. *Journal of Marriage and the Family, 52*, 441–451.

Peterson, J. W. (1990). Age of wisdom: Elderly Black women in family and church. In J. Sokolovsky (Ed.), *The cultural context of aging* (pp. 213–227). New York: Bergin & Garvey.

Pezdek, K. (1983). Memory for items and their spatial locations by young and elderly adults. *Developmental Psychology, 19*, 895–900.

Phillis, D. E., & Stein, P. J. (1983). Sink or swing? The lifestyles of single adults. In E. R. Allgeier & N. B. McCormick (Eds.), *Changing boundaries: Gender roles and sexual behavior* (pp. 202–225). Palo Alto, CA: Mayfield.

Piaget, J. (1970). Piaget's theory. In P. H. Mussen (Ed.), *Carmichael's manual of child psychology: Vol. 1* (3rd ed., pp. 703–732). New York: Wiley.

Piaget, J. (1972). Intellectual evolution from adolescence to adulthood. *Human Development, 15*, 1–12.

Pincus, L. (1976). *Death and the family: The importance of mourning*. New York: Pantheon.

Pino, C. J., Rosica, C. M., & Carter, T. J. (1978). The differential effects of relocation on nursing home patients. *The Gerontologist, 18*, 167–172.

Plath, D. W. (1980). *Long engagements: Maturity in modern Japan*. Palo Alto, CA: Stanford University Press.

Pleck, J. H. (1983). Husbands' paid work and family roles: Current research issues. In H. Z. Lopata & J. H. Pleck (Eds.), *Research on the interweave of social roles: Vol. 3. Families and jobs* (pp. 251–333). Greenwich, CT: JAI.

Plude, D. J. (1986, August). *Age and visual search for features vs. conjunctions*. Paper presented at the meeting of the American Psychological Association, Washington, DC.

Plude, D. J., & Doussard-Roosevelt, J. A. (1989). Aging, selective attention, and feature integration. *Psychology and Aging, 4*, 98–105.

Plude, D. J., & Doussard-Roosevelt, J. A. (1990). Aging and attention: Selectivity, capacity, and arousal. In E. A. Lovelace (Ed.), *Aging and cognition: Mental processes, self-awareness, and interventions* (pp. 97–133). Amsterdam: North-Holland.

Plude, D. J., & Hoyer, W. J. (1981). Adult age differences in visual search as a function of stimulus mapping and processing level. *Journal of Gerontology, 36*, 598–604.

Plude, D. J., & Hoyer, W. J. (1985). Attention and performance: Identifying and localizing age deficits. In N. Charness (Ed.), *Aging and human performance* (pp. 47–99). Chichester, England: Wiley.

Plude, D. J., Murphy, L. J., & Gabriel-Byrne, J. (1989, August). *Aging, divided attention, and visual search*. Paper presented at the meeting of the American Psychological Association, New Orleans.

Ponzio, F., Calderini, G., Lomuscio, G., Vantini, G., Toffano, G., & Algeri, S. (1982). Changes in monoamines and their metabolite levels in some brain regions of aged rats. *Neurobiology of Aging, 3*, 23–29.

Poon, L. W. (1985). Differences in human memory with aging: Nature, causes, and clinical implications. In J. E. Birren & K. W. Schaie (Eds.), *Handbook of the psychology of aging* (2nd ed., pp. 427–462). New York: Academic Press.

Poon, L. W. (Ed.). (1986). *Handbook for the clinical memory assessment of older adults*. Washington, DC: American Psychological Association.

Poon, L. W., & Fozard, J. L. (1980). Age and word frequency effects in continuous recognition memory. *Journal of Gerontology, 35*, 77–86.

Poon, L. W., Gurland, B. J., Eisdorfer, C., Crook, T., Thompson, L. W., Kaszniak, A. W., & Davis, K. L. (1986). Integration of experimental and clinical precepts in memory assessments: A tribute to George Talland. In L. W. Poon (Ed.), *Handbook for clinical memory assessment of older adults* (pp. 3–10). Washington, DC: American Psychological Association.

Poon, L. W., & Schaffer, G. (1982). *Prospective memory in young and elderly adults*. Paper presented at the meeting

of the American Psychological Association, Washington, DC.

Popkin, S. J., Gallagher, D., Thompson, L. W., & Moore, M. (1982). Memory complaint and performance in normal and depressed older adults. *Experimental Aging Research, 8*, 141–145.

Posner, J. D., Gorman, K. M., Gitlin, L. N., et al. (1990). Effects of exercise training in the elderly on the occurrence and time to onset of cardiovascular diagnoses. *Journal of the American Geriatrics Association, 38*, 205–210.

Posner, M. I., & Boies, S. J. (1971). Components of attention. *Psychological Review, 78*, 391–408.

Post, F. (1987). Paranoid and schizophrenic disorders among the aging. In L. L. Carstensen & B. A. Edelstein (Eds.), *Handbook of clinical gerontology* (pp. 43–56). New York: Pergamon Press.

Powell, L. A., & Williamson, J. B. (1985). The mass media and the aged. *Social Policy, 16*, 38–49.

Powers, T. G., & Parke, R. D. (1982). Play as a context for early learning: Lab and home analyses. In E. Siegel & L. M. Laosa (Eds.), *The family as a learning environment*. New York: Plenum.

Pratt, M. W., Golding, G., & Kerig, P. (1987). Life-span differences in adult thinking about hypothetical and personal moral issues: Reflection or regression? *International Journal of Behavioral Development, 10*, 359–376.

Pratt, O. E. (1980). The fetal alcohol syndrome: Transport of nutrients and transfer of alcohol and acetaldehyde from mother to fetus. In M. Sandler (Ed.), *Psychopharmacology of alcohol* (pp. 229–258). New York: Raven Press.

Pratt, O. E. (1982). Alcohol and the developing fetus. *British Medical Bulletin, 38*, 48–52.

Price, D. L., Whitehouse, P. J., Struble, R. G., Clark, A. W., Coyle, J. T., DeLong, M. R., & Hedreen, J. C. (1982). Basal forebrain cholinergic systems in Alzheimer's disease and related dementias. *Neuroscience Commentaries, 1*, 84–92.

Price, J. G. (1991). Great expectations: Hallmark of the midlife woman learner. *Educational Gerontology, 17*, 167–174.

Prinz, P. N., & Raskind, M. (1978). Aging and sleep disorders. In R. Williams & I. Karacan (Eds.), *Sleep disorders:*

Diagnosis and treatment (pp. 303–322). New York: Wiley.

Protinsky, H., & Hughston, G. (1978). Conservation in elderly males: An empirical investigation. *Developmental Psychology, 14*, 114.

Pruchno, R. A., & Resch, N. L. (1988). Intrainstitutional relocation: Mortality effects. *The Gerontologist, 28*, 311–317.

Puder, R., Lacks, P., Bertelson, A. D., & Storandt, M. (1983). Short-term stimulus control treatment of insomnia in older adults. *Behavior Therapy, 14*, 424–429.

Quadagno, J. (1982). *Aging in early industrial society: Work, family and social policy in nineteenth century England.* New York: Academic Press.

Quayhagen, M. P., & Quayhagen, M. (1988). Alzheimer's stress: Coping with the caregiving role. *The Gerontologist, 28*, 391–396.

Quigley, M. W. (1979, June 19). Executive corps: Free advice pays off for both sides. *Newsday*, p. 9.

Quinn, R. P., & Staines, G. L. (1979). *The 1977 quality of employment survey.* Ann Arbor: Institute for Social Research, University of Michigan.

Rabbitt, P. (1977). Changes in problem solving ability in old age. In J. E. Birren & K. W. Schaie (Eds.), *Handbook of the psychology of aging* (pp. 606–625). New York: Van Nostrand Reinhold.

Rabinowitz, J. C., Ackerman, B. P., Craik, F. I. M., & Hinchley, J. L. (1982). Aging and metamemory: The roles of relatedness and imagery. *Journal of Gerontology, 37*, 688–695.

Rabinowitz, J. C., Craik, F. I. M., & Ackerman, B. P. (1982). A processing resource account of age differences in recall. *Canadian Journal of Psychology, 36*, 325–344.

Rackoff, N. S., & Mourant, R. R. (1979). Driving performance of the elderly. *Accident Analysis and Prevention, 11*, 247–253.

Radloff, L. S. (1977). The CES-D Scale: A self-report depression scale for research in the general population. *Applied Psychological Measurement, 1*, 385.

Ragland, O. R., & Brand, R. J. (1988). Type A behavior and mortality from coronary heart disease. *New England Journal of Medicine, 318*, 65–69.

Ramig, L. A., & Ringel, R. L. (1983). Effects of physiological aging on selected acoustic characteristics of voice. *Journal of Speech and Hearing Research, 26*, 22–30.

Raphael, B. (1983). *The anatomy of bereavement.* New York: Basic Books.

Rapoport, R., & Rapoport, R. N. (1975) *Leisure and the family life cycle.* London: Routledge & Kegan Paul.

Rapoport, R., & Rapoport, R. N. (1980). Three generations of dual-career family research. In F. Pepitone-Rockwell (Ed.), *Dual career couples.* Beverly Hills, CA: Sage Publications.

Redmore, C. D., & Loevinger, J. (1979). Ego development in adolescence: Longitudinal studies. *Journal of Youth and Adolescence, 8*, 129–134.

Reedy, M. N., Birren, J. E., & Schaie, K. W. (1981). Age and sex differences in satisfying love relationships across the adult life span. *Human Development, 24*, 52–66.

Reese, H. W., & Rodeheaver, D. (1985). Problem solving and complex decision making. In J. E. Birren & K. W. Schaie (Eds.), *Handbook of the psychology of aging* (2nd ed., pp. 474–499). New York: Van Nostrand Reinhold.

Register, J. C. (1981). Aging and race: A Black-White comparative analysis. *The Gerontologist, 21*, 438–443.

Regnier, V. (1983). Urban neighborhood cognition: Relationships between functional and symbolic community elements. In G. D. Rowles & R. J. Ohta (Eds.), *Aging and milieu: Environmental perspectives on growing old* (pp. 63–82). New York: Academic Press.

Reinke, B. J., Holmes, D. S., & Harris, R. L. (1985). The timing of psycho-social change in women's lives: The years 25 to 45. *Journal of Personality and Social Psychology, 48*, 1353–1364.

Reisberg, B., Ferris, S. H., Anand, R., de Leon, M. J., Schneck, M. K., & Crook, T. (1985). Clinical assessment of cognitive decline in normal aging and primary degenerative dementia: Concordant ordinal measures. In P. Pinchot, P. Berner, R. Wolf, & K. Thau (Eds.), *Psychiatry* (Vol. 5, pp. 333–338). New York: Plenum.

Reisberg, B., Ferris, S. H., Borenstein, J., Sinaiko, E., de Leon, M. J., & Buttinger, C. (1986). Assessment of presenting symptoms. In L. W. Poon (Ed.), *Hand-*

book for clinical memory assessment of older adults (pp. 108–128). Washington, DC: American Psychological Association.

Reisberg, B., Ferris, S. H., de Leon, M. J., & Crook, T. (1982). The global deterioration scale for assessment of primary degenerative dementia. *American Journal of Psychiatry, 139*, 1136–1139.

Reynolds, C. F., Kupfer, D. J., Taska, L. S., Hoch, C. C., Sewitch, D. E., & Spiker, D. G. (1985). Sleep of healthy seniors: A revisit. *Sleep, 8*, 20–29.

Reynolds, D. K., & Kalish, R. A. (1974). Anticipation of futurity as a function of ethnicity and age. *Journal of Gerontology, 29*, 224–231.

Rhyne, D. (1981). Basis of marital satisfaction among men and women. *Journal of Marriage and the Family, 43*, 941–955.

Rice, D. M., Buchsbaum, M. S., Hardy, D., & Burgwald, L. (1991). Focal left temporal slow EEG activity is related to verbal recent memory deficit in a non-demented elderly population. *Journal of Gerontology: Psychological Sciences, 46*, P144–P151.

Rice, G. E., & Meyer, B. J. F. (1985). Reading behavior and prose recall performance of young and older adults with high and average verbal ability. *Educational Gerontology, 11*, 57–72.

Richards, O. W. (1977). Effects of luminance and contrast on visual acuity, ages 16 to 90 years. *American Journal of Optometry and Physiological Optics, 54*, 178–184.

Richardson, V., & Kilty, K. M. (1989). Retirement financial planning among black professionals. *The Gerontologist, 29*, 32–37.

Ricklefs, R. (1988, May 19). Adult children of elderly parents hire "surrogates" to oversee care. *Wall Street Journal*, p. 29.

Riegel, K. F. (1973). Dialectic operations: The final period of cognitive development. *Human Development, 16*, 371–381.

Riegel, K. F. (1976). The dialectics of human development. *American Psychologist, 31*, 689–700.

Rikli, R., & Busch, S. (1986). Motor performance of women as a function of age and physical activity level. *Journal of Gerontology, 41*, 645–649.

Riley, M. W. (1971). Social gerontology and the age stratification of society. *The Gerontologist, 11,* 79–87.

Riley, M. W. (1979). Introduction. In M. W. Riley (Ed.), *Aging from birth to death: Interdisciplinary perspectives* (pp. 3–14). Boulder, CO: Westview.

Riley, M. W. (1985). Age strata in social systems. In R. H. Binstock & E. Shanas (Eds.), *Handbook of aging and the social sciences* (2nd ed., pp. 369–411). New York: Van Nostrand Reinhold.

Riley, M. W. (1987). On the significance of age in sociology. *American Sociological Review, 52,* 1–14.

Riley, M. W., & Foner, A. (1968). *Aging and society: An inventory of research findings.* New York: Russell Sage Foundation.

Riley, M. W., Johnson, M., & Foner, A. (1972). *Aging and society: Vol. 3. A sociology of age stratification.* New York: Russell Sage Foundation.

Riley, V. (1981). Psychoneuroendocrine influences on immunocompetence and neoplasia. *Science, 212,* 1100–1109.

Rindfuss, R. R., & Stephen, E. H. (1990). Marital noncohabitation: Separation does not make the heart grow fonder. *Journal of Marriage and the Family, 52,* 259–270.

Ritzer, G. (1977). *Working: Conflict and change* (2nd ed.). Englewood Cliffs, NJ: Prentice-Hall.

Roach, M. (1985). *Another name for madness.* New York: Houghton Mifflin.

Roberto, K. A., & Scott, J. P. (1986). Equity considerations in the friendships of older adults. *Journal of Gerontology, 41,* 241–247.

Roberts, P., & Newton, P. M. (1987). Levinsonian studies of women's adult development. *Psychology and Aging, 2,* 154–163.

Roberts, R. E. (1987). An epidemiological perspective on the mental health of people of Mexican origin. In R. Rodriguez & M. T. Coleman (Eds.), *Mental health issues of the Mexican origin population in Texas* (pp. 55–70). Austin, TX: Hogg Foundation for Mental Health.

Robertson, J. F. (1976). Significance of grandparents: Perceptions of young adult grandchildren. *The Gerontologist, 16,* 137–140.

Robertson, J. F. (1977). Grandmotherhood: A study of role concepts. *Journal of Marriage and the Family, 39,* 165–174.

Robinson, B., & Thurnher, M. (1979). Taking care of aged parents: A family cycle transition. *The Gerontologist, 19,* 586–593.

Robinson, J. K. (1983). Skin problems of aging. *Geriatrics, 38,* 57–65.

Rockstein, M., & Sussman, M. (1979). *Biology of aging.* Belmont, CA: Wadsworth.

Rodeheaver, D., & Datan, N. (1988). The challenge of double jeopardy: Toward a mental health agenda for aging women. *American Psychologist, 43,* 648–654.

Rodeheaver, D., & Thomas, J. L. (1986). Family and community networks in Appalachia. In N. Datan, A. L. Greene, & H. W. Reese (Eds.), *Life-span developmental psychology: Intergenerational relations* (pp. 77–98). Hillsdale, NJ: Erlbaum.

Rodin, J., & Langer, E. J. (1977). Long-term effects of a control-relevant intervention with the institutionalized aged. *Journal of Personality and Social Psychology, 35,* 897–902.

Rodin, J., McAvay, G., & Timko, C. (1988). A longitudinal study of depressed mood and sleep disturbances in elderly adults. *Journal of Gerontology, 43,* P45–P53.

Rogers, A., Watkins, J. F., & Woodward, J. A. (1990). Interregional elderly migration and population redistribution in four industrialized countries: A comparative analysis. *Research on Aging, 12,* 251–293.

Rogers, C. S., & Levitin, P. M. (1987). Osteoarthritis. In C. S. Rogers, J. D. McCue, & P. Gal (Eds.), *Managing chronic disease* (pp. 299–305). Oradell, NJ: Medical Economics Press.

Rogers, J., & Bloom, F. E. (1985). Neurotransmitter metabolism and function in the aging central nervous system. In C. E. Finch & E. L. Schneider (Eds.), *Handbook of the biology of aging* (2nd ed., pp. 645–691). New York: Van Nostrand Reinhold.

Roodin, P. A., Rybash, J. M., & Hoyer, W. J. (1984). Affect in adult cognition: A constructivist view of moral thought and action. In C. Malatesta & C. Izard (Eds.), *The role of affect in adult development and aging.* Beverly Hills: Sage Publications.

Roper Organization. (1980). *The 1980 Virginia Slims American women's opinion poll.* Storrs: Roper Center, University of Connecticut.

Rosenthal, C., & Marshall, V. (1988). Generational transmission of family ritual. *American Behavioral Scientist, 31,* 669–684.

Rosenthal, M. J., & Goodwin, J. S. (1985). Cognitive effects of nutritional deficiency. In H. H. Draper (Ed.), *Advances in nutritional research* (Vol. 7, pp. 71–100). New York: Plenum.

Rosow, I. (1967). *Social integration of the aged.* New York: Free Press.

Rosow, I. (1985). Status and role change through the life cycle. In R. H. Binstock & E. Shanas (Eds.), *Handbook of aging and the social sciences* (2nd ed., pp. 62–93). New York: Van Nostrand Reinhold.

Ross, J. K. (1977). *Old people, new lives.* Chicago: University of Chicago Press.

Rossi, A. S. (1980). Aging and parenthood in the middle years. In P. B. Baltes & O. G. Brim, Jr. (Eds.), *Life-span development and behavior* (Vol. 3, pp. 137–205). New York: Academic Press.

Rowe, J. W., & Kahn, R. L. (1987). Human aging: Usual and successful. *Science, 237,* 143–149.

Rowles, G. D. (1980). Growing old "inside": Aging and attachment to place in an Appalachian community. In N. Datan & N. Lohman (Eds.), *Transitions of aging* (pp. 153–170). New York: Academic Press.

Rowles, G. D. (1983). Geographical dimensions of social support in rural Appalachia. In G. D. Rowles & R. J. Ohta (Eds.), *Aging and milieu: Environmental perspectives on growing old* (pp. 111–130). New York: Academic Press.

Rowles, G. D., & Ohta, R. J. (1983). Emergent themes and new directions: Reflections on aging and milieu research. In G. D. Rowles & R. J. Ohta (Eds.), *Aging and milieu: Environmental perspectives on growing old* (pp. 231–240). New York: Academic Press.

Royce, A. P. (1982). *Ethnic identity: Strategies of diversity.* Bloomington: Indiana University Press.

Rubinstein, R. L. (1987). Never-married elderly as a social type: Reevaluating some images. *The Gerontologist, 27,* 108–113.

Rudzitis, G. (1984). Geographical research and gerontology: An overview. *The Gerontologist, 24,* 536–542.

Ryan, C. (1982). Alcoholism and premature aging: A neuropsychological perspective. *Alcoholism: Clinical and Experimental Research, 6,* 22–30.

Ryan, C., & Butters, N. (1980). Learning and memory complaints in young and old alcoholics: Evidence for the premature aging hypothesis. *Alcoholism: Clinical and Experimental Research, 4,* 288–293.

Rybash, J. M., Hoyer, W. J., & Roodin, P. A. (1986). *Adult cognition and aging.* New York: Pergamon.

Rybash, J. M., Roodin, P. A., & Hoyer, W. J. (1983). Expression of moral thought in later adulthood. *The Gerontologist, 23,* 254–260.

Ryckman, R. M., & Malikioski, M. (1975). Relationship between locus of control and chronological age. *Psychological Reports, 36,* 655–658.

Ryff, C. D. (1991). Possible selves in adulthood and old age: A tale of shifting horizons. *Psychology and Aging, 6,* 286–295.

Rykken, D. E. (1987). Sex in the later years. In P. Silverman (Ed.), *The elderly as modern pioneers* (pp. 125–144). Bloomington: Indiana University Press.

Safilios-Rothschild, C. (1977). *Love, sex, and sex roles.* Englewood Cliffs, NJ: Prentice-Hall.

Sainsbury, P. (1986). The epidemiology of suicide. In A. Roy (Ed.), *Suicide* (pp. 17–40). Baltimore: Williams & Wilkins.

Salamon, S. (1982). Sibling solidarity as an operating strategy in Illinois agriculture. *Rural Sociology, 47,* 349–368.

Salthouse, T. A. (1984). Effects of age and skill in typing. *Journal of Experimental Psychology: General, 113,* 345–371.

Salthouse, T. A. (1985). Speed of behavior and its implications for cognition. In J. E. Birren & K. W. Schaie (Eds.), *Handbook of the psychology of aging* (2nd ed., pp. 400–426). New York: Van Nostrand Reinhold.

Salthouse, T. A. (1988). The role of processing resources in cognitive aging. In

M. L. Howe & C. J. Brainerd (Eds.), *Cognitive development in adulthood* (pp. 185–239). New York: Springer-Verlag.

Salthouse, T. A. (1991, August). *Status of working memory as a mediator of adult age differences in cognition.* Invited address presented at the American Psychological Association, San Francisco.

Salthouse, T. A., Kausler, D. H., & Saults, J. S. (1988). Utilization of path analytic procedures to investigate the role of processing resources in cognitive aging. *Psychology and Aging, 3,* 158–166.

Salthouse, T. A., Rogan, J. D., & Prill, K. (1984). Division of attention: Age differences on a visually presented memory task. *Memory and Cognition, 12,* 613–620.

Salthouse, T. A., & Somberg, B. L. (1982). Isolating the age deficit in speeded performance. *Journal of Gerontology, 37,* 59–63.

Salzman, C. (1975). Electroconvulsive therapy. In R. Shader (Ed.), *Manual of psychiatric therapeutics* (pp. 115–124). Boston: Little, Brown.

Salzman, C. (1984). *Clinical geriatric psychopharmacology.* New York: McGraw-Hill.

Salzman, C., & Shader, R. I. (1979). Clinical evaluation of depression in the elderly. In A. Raskin & L. F. Jarvik (Eds.), *Psychiatric symptoms and cognitive loss in the elderly* (pp. 39–72). Washington, DC: Hemisphere.

Samet, J., Hunt, W., & Key, C. (1986). Choice of cancer therapy varies with age of patient. *Journal of the American Medical Association, 255,* 3385–3390.

Sanders, C. M. (1980–1981). Comparison of younger and older spouses in bereavement outcome. *Omega: Journal of Death and Dying, 11,* 217–232.

Sandler, D. P., Everson, R. B., & Wilcox, A. J. (1985). Passive smoking in adulthood and cancer risk. *American Journal of Epidemiology, 121,* 37–48.

Sangree, W. (1989). Age and power: Life course trajectories and age structuring of power relations in East and West Africa. In D. Kertzer & K. W. Schaie (Eds.), *Age structuring in comparative perspective* (pp. 23–46). New York: Springer.

Sanjek, R. (1984). *Crowded out: Homelessness and the elderly poor in New York*

City. New York: Coalition for the Homeless.

Saunders, C. (1977). Dying they live: St. Christopher's Hospice. In H. Feifel (Ed.), *New meanings of death.* New York: McGraw-Hill.

Schachter, S. (1982). Recidivism and self-cure of smoking and obesity. *American Psychologist, 37,* 436–444.

Schaie, K. W. (1965). A general model for the study of developmental change. *Psychological Bulletin, 64,* 92–107.

Schaie, K. W. (1977). Quasi-experimental designs in the psychology of aging. In J. E. Birren & K. W. Schaie (Eds.), *Handbook of the psychology of aging* (pp. 38–58). New York: Van Nostrand Reinhold.

Schaie, K. W. (1977–1978). Toward a stage theory of adult cognitive development. *International Journal of Aging and Human Development, 8,* 129–138.

Schaie, K. W. (1979). The primary mental abilities in adulthood: An exploration in the development of psychometric intelligence. In P. B. Baltes & O. G. Brim, Jr. (Eds.), *Life-span development and behavior* (Vol. 2, pp. 67–115). New York: Academic Press.

Schaie, K. W. (1983). The Seattle longitudinal study: A twenty-one year exploration of psychometric intelligence in adulthood. In K. W. Schaie (Ed.), *Longitudinal studies of adult psychological development* (pp. 64–155). New York: Guilford.

Schaie, K. W. (1984). Historical time and cohort effects. In K. A. McCluskey & H. W. Reese (Eds.), *Life-span developmental psychology: Historical and generational effects* (pp. 1–45). New York: Academic Press.

Schaie, K. W. (1990). Intellectual development in adulthood. In J. E. Birren & K. W. Schaie (Eds.), *Handbook of the psychology of aging* (3rd ed., pp. 291–309). San Diego: Academic Press.

Schaie, K. W., & Hertzog, C. (1983). Fourteen-year cohort-sequential studies of adult intelligence. *Developmental Psychology, 19,* 531–543.

Schaie, K. W., & Hertzog, C. (1985). Measurement in the psychology of adulthood and aging. In J. E. Birren & K. W. Schaie (Eds.), *Handbook of the psychology of aging* (2nd ed., pp. 61–92). New York: Van Nostrand Reinhold.

Schaie, K. W., & Labouvie-Vief, G. (1974). Generational versus ontogenetic components of change in adult cognitive behavior: A fourteen-year cross-sequential study. *Developmental Psychology, 10*, 305–320.

Schaie, K. W., Orchowsky, S., & Parham, I. A. (1982). Measuring age and socio-cultural change: The case of race and life satisfaction. In R. C. Manuel (Ed.), *Minority aging, sociological and social psychological issues* (pp. 223–230). Westport, CT: Greenwood.

Schaie, K. W., & Parham, I. A. (1977). Cohort-sequential analysis of adult intellectual development. *Developmental Psychology, 13*, 649–653.

Schaie, K. W., & Strother, C. R. (1968). A cross-sequential study of age changes in cognitive behavior. *Psychological Bulletin, 70*, 671–680.

Schaie, K. W., & Willis, S. L. (1986). Can decline in adult intellectual functioning be reversed? *Developmental Psychology, 22*, 223–232.

Scheibel, A. B. (1982). Age-related changes in the human forebrain. *Neurosciences Research Progress Bulletin, 20*, 577–583.

Scheidt, R. J., & Schaie, K. W. (1978). A situational taxonomy for the elderly: Generating situational criteria. *Journal of Gerontology, 33*, 848–857.

Scheidt, R. J., & Windley, P. G. (1985). The ecology of aging. In J. E. Birren & K. W. Schaie (Eds.), *Handbook of the psychology of aging* (2nd ed., pp. 245–258). New York: Van Nostrand Reinhold.

Schermerhorn, R. A. (1970). *Comparative ethnic relations: A framework for theory and research.* Chicago: University of Chicago Press.

Schiffman, S., & Covey, E. (1984). Changes in taste and smell with age: Nutritional aspects. In J. M. Ordy, D. Harman, & R. B. Alfin-Slater (Eds.), *Aging: Vol. 26. Nutrition in gerontology* (pp. 43–64). New York: Raven Press.

Schiffman, S., & Pasternak, M. (1979). Decreased discrimination of food odors in the elderly. *Journal of Gerontology, 34*, 73–79.

Schmitt, F. A., Murphy, M. D., & Sanders, R. E. (1981). Training older adults free recall rehearsal strategies. *Journal of Gerontology, 36*, 329–337.

Schneider, E. L., & Reed, J. D. (1985). Modulations of aging processes. In C. E. Finch & E. L. Schneider (Eds.), *Handbook of the biology of aging* (2nd ed., pp. 45–76). New York: Van Nostrand Reinhold.

Schneider, M. S. (1986). The relationship of cohabiting lesbian and heterosexual couples: A comparison. *Psychology of Women Quarterly, 10*, 234–239.

Schooler, K. K. (1982). Response of the elderly to environment: A stress-theoretical perspective. In M. P. Lawton, P. G. Windley, & T. O. Byerts (Eds.), *Aging and the environment: Theoretical approaches* (pp. 80–96). New York: Springer.

Schuknecht, H. (1974). *Pathology of the ear.* Cambridge, MA: Harvard University Press.

Schultz, N. W. (1980). A cognitive-developmental study of the grandchild-grandparent bond. *Child Study Journal, 10*, 7–26.

Schulz, R. (1978). *The psychology of death, dying and bereavement.* Reading, MA: Addison-Wesley.

Schulz, R. (1985). Emotion and affect. In J. E. Birren & K. W. Schaie (Eds.), *Handbook of the psychology of aging* (2nd ed., pp. 531–543). New York: Van Nostrand Reinhold.

Schulz, R., & Hanusa, B. H. (1978). Long-term effects of control and pre-dictability enhancing interventions: Findings and ethical issues. *Journal of Personality and Social Psychology, 35*, 1194–1201.

Schulz, R., & Hanusa, B. H. (1979). Environmental influences on the effectiveness of control- and competence-enhancing interventions. In L. C. Perlmuter & R. A. Monty (Eds.), *Choice and perceived control* (pp. 315–337). Hillsdale, NJ: Erlbaum.

Schulz, R., Tompkins, C. A., & Rau, M. T. (1988). A longitudinal study of the psychosocial impact of stroke on primary support persons. *Psychology and Aging, 3*, 131–141.

Schwab, D. P., & Heneman, H. G., III. (1977). Age and satisfaction with dimensions of work. *Journal of Vocational Behavior, 10*, 212–222.

Scialfa, C. T., Guzy, L. T., Leibowitz, H. W., Garvey, P. M., & Tyrrell, R. A. (1991). Age differences in estimating vehicle velocity. *Psychology and Aging, 6*, 60–66.

Scott, R. B., & Mitchell, M. C. (1988). Aging, alcohol, and the liver. *Journal of the American Geriatrics Society, 36*, 255–265.

Sears, P. S., & Barbee, A. H. (1978). Career and life satisfaction among Terman's gifted women. In J. C. Stanley, W. C. George, & C. H. Solano (Eds.), *The gifted and the creative: Fifty year perspective* (pp. 28–66). Baltimore: Johns Hopkins University Press.

Selye, H. (1956). *The stress of life.* New York: Macmillan.

Selye, H. (1979). *The stress of my life: A scientist's memoirs.* New York: Van Nostrand Reinhold.

Selye, H. (1982). History and present status of the stress concept. In L. Goldberger & S. Breznitz (Eds.), *Handbook of stress: Theoretical and clinical aspects* (pp. 7–17). New York: Free Press.

Sendbeuhler, J. M., & Goldstein, S. (1977). Attempted suicide among the aged. *Journal of the American Geriatrics Society, 25*, 245–248.

Shainess, N. (1984). *Sweet suffering: Woman as victim.* Indianapolis: Bobbs-Merrill.

Shanas, E. (1972). Adjustment to retirement. In F. M. Carp (Ed.), *Retirement* (pp. 219–244). Berkeley, CA: Behavioral Publications.

Shanas, E. (1980). Older people and their families: The new pioneers. *Journal of Marriage and the Family, 42*, 9–15.

Shand, A. E. (1920). *The foundations of character.* London: Macmillan.

Shapiro, D. H. (1985). Meditation and behavioral medicine: Application of a self-regulation strategy to the clinical management of stress. In S. R. Burchfield (Ed.), *Stress: Psychological and physiological interactions* (pp. 307–328). Washington, DC: Hemisphere.

Sheehy, G. (1976). *Passages.* New York: Dutton.

Sheehy, G. (1981). *Pathfinders.* New York: Morrow.

Shekelle, R. B., Gale, M., & Norusis, M. (1985). Type A score (Jenkins Activity Survey) and risk of recurrent heart disease in the aspirin myocardial infarction study. *American Journal of Cardiology, 56*, 221–225.

Shephard, R. J. (1978). *Physical activity and aging.* Chicago: Yearbook Medical.

Shephard, R. J. (1981). Cardiovascular limitations in the aged. In E. L. Smith & R. C. Serfass (Eds.), *Exercise and aging: The scientific basis* (pp. 19–30). Hillsdale, NJ: Erlbaum.

Shephard, R. J. (1982). *Physiology and biochemistry of exercise.* New York: Praeger.

Sheppard, H. L. (1976). Work and retirement. In R. H. Binstock & E. Shanas (Eds.), *Handbook of aging and the social sciences* (2nd ed., pp. 286–309). New York: Van Nostrand Reinhold.

Sherwood, S., Ruchlin, H. S., & Sherwood, C. C. (1989). CCRCs: An option for aging in place. In D. Tillson & C. J. Fahey (Eds.), *Support of the frail elderly in residential environments.* Glenview, IL: Scott Foresman.

Shinar, D., McDowell, E. D., Rackoff, N. J., & Rockwell, T. H. (1978). Field dependence and driver visual search behavior. *Human Factors, 20,* 553–559.

Shirom, A., & Mazeh, T. (1988). Periodicity in seniority-job satisfaction relationship. *Journal of Vocational Behavior, 33,* 38–49.

Shneidman, E. S. (1973). *Deaths of man.* New York: Quadrangle/New York Times.

Shock, N. W. (1977). Biological theories of aging. In J. E. Birren & K. W. Schaie (Eds.), *Handbook of the psychology of aging* (pp. 103–115). New York: Van Nostrand Reinhold.

Siedler, H., & Malamud, N. (1963). Creutzfeld-Jakob disease: Clinicopathologic report of 15 cases and review of the literature. *Journal of Neuropathology and Experimental Neurology, 22,* 381–402.

Siegel, J. M. (1990). Stressful life events and use of physician services among the elderly: The moderating effect of pet ownership. *Journal of Personality and Social Psychology, 58,* 1081–1086.

Siegel, R. K. (1980). The psychology of life after death. *American Psychologist, 35,* 911–931.

Siegler, I. C., & Gatz, M. (1985). Age patterns in locus of control. In E. Palmore, E. Bossé, G. Maddox, J. Nowlin, & I. C. Siegler (Eds.), *Normal aging 3.* Durham, NC: Duke University Press.

Siegler, I. C., George, L. K., & Okun, M. A. (1979). A cross-sequential analysis of adult personality. *Developmental Psychology, 15,* 350–351.

Silverman, P. (1987). Community settings. In P. Silverman (Ed.), *The elderly as modern pioneers* (pp. 185–210). Bloomington: Indiana University Press.

Simmons, L. W. (1945). *Role of the aged in primitive society.* New Haven, CT: Yale University Press.

Simons, A. D., McGowan, C. R., Epstein, L. H., Kupfer, D. J., & Robertson, R. J. (1985). Exercise as a treatment for depression: An update. *Clinical Psychology Review, 5,* 553–568.

Simonton, D. K. (1990). Creativity and wisdom in aging. In J. E. Birren & K. W. Schaie (Eds.), *Handbook of the psychology of aging* (3rd ed., pp. 320–329). San Diego: Academic Press.

Singleton, W. T. (1979). Safety and risk. In W. T. Singleton (Ed.), *The study of real skills: Vol. 2. Compliance and excellence* (pp. 137–156). Baltimore: University Park Press.

Sinnott, J. D. (1984a). *Everyday memory and solution of everyday problems.* Paper presented at the meeting of the American Psychological Association, Toronto.

Sinnott, J. D. (1984b). Postformal reasoning: The relativistic stage. In M. L. Commons, F. A. Richards, & C. Armon (Eds.), *Beyond formal operations: Late adolescent and adult cognitive development* (pp. 298–325). New York: Praeger.

Sinnott, J. D. (1986). Sex roles and aging: Theory and research from a systems perspective. *Contributions to human development* (Vol. 15). New York: Karger.

Sivak, M., & Olson, P. L. (1982). Nighttime legibility of traffic signs: Conditions eliminating the effects of driver age and disability glare. *Accident Analysis and Prevention, 14,* 87–93.

Sivak, M., Olson, P. L., & Pastalan, L. A. (1981). Effect of driver's age on nighttime legibility of highway signs. *Human Factors, 23,* 59–64.

Sjogren, T., Sjogren, H., & Lindgren, A. G. H. (1952). Morbus Alzheimer and morbus Pick. *Acta Psychiatrica Scandinavica, 82(Suppl.),* 68–108.

Slivinske, L. R., & Fitch, V. L. (1987). The effect of control enhancing intervention on the well-being of elderly individuals living in retirement communities. *The Gerontologist, 27,* 176–181.

Smallegan, M. (1989). Level of depressive symptoms and life stresses for culturally diverse older adults. *The Gerontologist, 29,* 45–50.

Smith, A. D. (1975). Aging and interference with memory. *Journal of Gerontology, 30,* 319–325.

Smith, A. D. (1977). Adult age differences in cued recall. *Developmental Psychology, 13,* 326–331.

Smith, A. D., & Park, D. C. (1990). Adult age differences in memory for pictures and images. In E. A. Lovelace (Ed.), *Aging and cognition: Mental processes, self-awareness, and interventions* (pp. 69–96). Amsterdam: North-Holland.

Smith, D. B. D. (1990). Human factors and aging: An overview of research needs and application opportunities. *Human Factors, 32,* 509–526.

Smith, E. L., & Serfass, R. C. (Eds.). (1981). *Exercise and aging: The scientific basis.* Hillsdale, NJ: Erlbaum.

Smith, J., & Baltes, P. B. (1990). Wisdom-related knowledge: Age/cohort differences in responses to life-planning problems. *Developmental Psychology, 26,* 494–505.

Smith, M., Colligan, M., Horning, R. W., & Hurrell, J. (1978). *Occupational comparison of stress-related disease incidence.* Cincinnati: National Institute for Occupational Safety and Health.

Smith, S. W., Rebok, G. W., Smith, W. R., Hall, S. E., & Alvin, M. (1983). Adult age differences in the use of story structure in delayed free recall. *Experimental Aging Research, 9,* 191–195.

Snyder, C. J., & Barrett, G. V. (1988). The Age Discrimination in Employment Act: A review of court decisions. *Experimental Aging Research, 14,* 3–47.

Sokolovsky, J. (1990). Bringing culture back home: Aging, ethnicity, and family support. In J. Sokolovsky (Ed.), *The cultural context of aging* (pp. 201–211). New York: Bergin & Garvey.

Sokolovsky, J., & Cohen, C. (1983). The cultural meaning of being a "loner" among the inner-city elderly. In J. Sokolovsky (Ed.), *Growing old in different societies* (pp. 189–201). Belmont, CA: Wadsworth.

Soldatos, C. R., Kales, J. D., Scharf, M. B., Bixler, E. O., & Kales, A. (1980). Cigarette smoking associated with sleep difficulty. *Science, 207,* 551–553.

Solnick, R. L., & Corby, N. (1983). Human sexuality and aging. In D. S. Woodruff & J. E. Birren (Eds.), *Aging: Scientific perspectives and social issues* (2nd ed., pp. 202–224). Pacific Grove, CA: Brooks/Cole.

Somberg, B. L., & Salthouse, T. A. (1982). Divided attention abilities in young and old adults. *Journal of Experimental Psychology: Human Perception and Performance, 8,* 651–663.

Somers, A. R. (1987). Insurance for long-term care: Some definitions, problems, and guidelines for action. *New England Journal of Medicine, 317,* 23–29.

Sontag, S. (1972, September 23). The double standard of aging. *Saturday Review,* pp. 29–38.

Spasoff, R. A., Kraus, A. S., Beattie, E. J., Holden, D. E. W., Lawson, J. S., Rodenburg, M., & Woodcock, G. M. (1978). Longitudinal study of elderly residents of long-stay institutions 1: Early response to institutional care. *The Gerontologist, 18,* 281–292.

Spayd, C. S., & Smyer, M. A. (1988). Interventions with agitated, disoriented, or depressed residents. In M. A. Smyer, M. D. Cohn, & D. Brannon (Eds.), *Mental health consultation in nursing homes* (pp. 123–141). New York: New York University Press.

Speare, A., Jr., Avery, R., & Lawton, L. (1991). Disability, residential mobility, and changes in living arrangements. *Journal of Gerontology: Social Sciences, 46,* S133–S142.

Speare, A., Jr., & Meyer, J. W. (1988). Types of elderly residential mobility and their determinants. *Journal of Gerontology, 43,* S74–S81.

Spilich, G. J. (1985). Discourse comprehension across the life span. In N. Charness (Ed.), *Aging and human performance* (pp. 143–190). Chichester, England: Wiley.

Spirduso, W. W. (1980). Physical fitness, aging, and psychomotor speed: A review. *Journal of Gerontology, 35,* 850–865.

Spirduso, W. W., & MacRae, P. G. (1990). Motor performance and aging. In J. E. Birren & K. W. Schaie (Eds.), *Handbook of the psychology of aging* (3rd ed., pp. 183–200). San Diego: Academic Press.

Spitzer, M. E. (1988). Taste acuity in institutionalized and noninstitu-

tionalized elderly men. *Journal of Gerontology, 43,* P71–P74.

Spitzer, R. L., Endicott, J., & Robins, E. (1978). Research Diagnostic Criteria: Rationale and reliability. *Archives of General Psychiatry, 35,* 773–782.

Spokane, A. R. (1985). A review of research on person-environment congruence in Holland's theory of careers. *Journal of Vocational Behavior, 26,* 306–343.

Sporakowski, M. J., & Axelson, L. J. (1984). Long-term marriages: A critical review. *Lifestyles: A Journal of Changing Patterns, 7*(2), 76–93.

Stack, C. (1972). *All our kin: Strategies for survival in a Black community.* New York: Harper & Row.

Stall, R. D., Coates, T. J., & Hoff, C. (1988). Behavioral risk reduction for HIV infection among gay and bisexual men: A review of results in the United States. *American Psychologist, 43,* 878–885.

Stanford, E. P., Happersett, C. J., Morton, D. J., Molgaard, C. A., & Peddecord, K. M. (1991). Early retirement and functional impairment from a multi-ethnic perspective. *Research on Aging, 13,* 5–38.

Stanford, E. P., & Lockery, S. A. (1984). Aging and social relations in the black community. In W. H. Quinn & G. A. Hughston (Eds.), *Independent aging: Family and social systems perspectives* (pp. 164–181). Rockville, MD: Aspen.

Stearns, P. N. (1977). *Old age in European society.* London: Croon Helm.

Steen, B. (1987). Nutrition and the elderly. In M. Bergener (Ed.), *Psychogeriatrics* (pp. 349–361). New York: Springer.

Stein, P. (1978). The lifestyles and life changes and the never married. *Marriage and Family Review, 1,* 1–11.

Stelmach, G. E., Amrhein, P. C., & Goggin, N. L. (1988). Age differences in bimanual coordination. *Journal of Gerontology: Psychological Sciences, 43,* P18–P23.

Stelmach, G. E., Goggin, N. L., & Amrhein, P. C. (1988). Aging and reprogramming: The restructuring of planned movements. *Psychology and Aging, 3,* 151–157.

Stelmach, G. E., Goggin, N. L., & Garcia-Colera, A. (1987). Movement specifi-

cation time with age. *Experimental Aging Research, 13,* 39–46.

Stenback, A. (1980). Depression and suicidal behavior in old age. In J. E. Birren & R. B. Sloane (Eds.), *Handbook of mental health and aging* (pp. 616–652). Englewood Cliffs, NJ: Prentice-Hall.

Stephens, J. (1976). *Loners, losers, and lovers.* Seattle: University of Washington Press.

Stephens, L. R. (Ed.). (1975). *Reality orientation* (rev. ed.). Washington, DC: American Psychiatric Association.

Stern, C., Prather, P., Swinney, D., & Zurif, E. (1991). The time course of automatic lexical access and aging. *Brain and Language, 40,* 359–372.

Sternberg, R. J. (1980). Sketch of a componential sub-theory of human intelligence. *Behavioral and Brain Sciences, 3,* 573–584.

Sternberg, R. J. (1985). *Beyond IQ: A triarchic theory of human intelligence.* Cambridge: Cambridge University Press.

Sternberg, R. J. (1986). A triangular theory of love. *Psychological Review, 93,* 119–135.

Sternberg, R. J., Conway, B. E., Ketron, J. L., & Bernstein, M. (1981). People's conceptions of intelligence. *Journal of Personality and Social Psychology, 41,* 37–55.

Sterns, H. L., Barrett, G. V., & Alexander, R. A. (1985). Accidents and the aging individual. In J. E. Birren & K. W. Schaie (Eds.), *Handbook of the psychology of aging* (2nd ed., pp. 703–724). New York: Van Nostrand Reinhold.

Sterns, H. L., Barrett, G. V., Alexander, R. A., Valasek, D., Forbringer, L. R., & Avolio, B. J. (1978). *Training and evaluation of older adult skills critical for effective driving performance.* Final report prepared for the Andrus Foundation of the NRTA/AARP. Cited in Sterns et al. (1985).

Sterns, H. L., Barrett, G. V., Alexander, R. A., Valasek, D., & McIlvried, J. (1985). *Research to improve diagnostic testing and training of older drivers.* Interim report prepared for the Andrus Foundation of the NRTA/AARP. Cited in Sterns et al. (1985).

Sterns, H. L., & Sanders, R. E. (1980). Training and education of the elderly. In R. R. Turner & H. W. Reese (Eds.),

Life-span developmental psychology: Intervention (pp. 307–330). New York: Academic Press.

Stevens, J. C., Bartoshuk, L. M., & Cain, W. S. (1984). Chemical senses and aging: Taste versus smell. *Chemical Senses, 9,* 167–179.

Stevens, J. C., & Cain, W. S. (1985). Age-related deficiency in the perceived strength of six odorants. *Chemical Senses, 10,* 517–529.

Stevens, J. C., & Cain, W. S. (1986). Smelling via the mouth: Effect of aging. *Perception and Psychophysics, 40,* 142–146.

Stevens, J. C., & Cain, W. S. (1987). Old-age deficits in the sense of smell as gauged by thresholds, magnitude matching, and odor identification. *Psychology of Aging, 2,* 36–42.

Stevens, J. C., Plantinga, A., & Cain, W. S. (1982). Reduction of odor and nasal pungency associated with aging. *Neurobiology of Aging, 3,* 125–132.

Stevens-Long, J. (1988). *Adult life* (3rd ed.). Mountain View, CA: Mayfield.

Stine, E. L. (1990). The way reading and listening work: A tutorial review of discourse processing and aging. In E. A. Lovelace (Ed.), *Aging and cognition: Mental processes, self-awareness, and interventions* (pp. 301–327). Amsterdam: North-Holland.

Stine, E. L., & Wingfield, A. (1987). Process and strategy in memory for speech among younger and older adults. *Psychology and Aging, 2,* 272–279.

Stine, E. L., Wingfield, A., & Poon, L. W. (1986). How much and how fast: Rapid processing of spoken language in later adulthood. *Psychology and Aging, 1,* 303–311.

Stoller, E. (1983). Parental caregiving by adult children. *Journal of Marriage and the Family, 45,* 851–858.

Stoller, E., & Earl, E. L. (1983). Help with activities of everyday life: Sources of support for the noninstitutionalized elderly. *The Gerontologist, 23,* 64–70.

Storandt, M., & Wittels, I. (1975). Maintenance of functioning in relocation of community-dwelling older adults. *Journal of Gerontology, 30,* 608–612.

Storandt, M., Wittels, I., & Botwinick, J. (1975). Predictors of a dimension of well-being in relocated healthy aged. *Journal of Gerontology, 30,* 97–102.

Storck, P. A., Looft, R., & Hooper, F. H. (1972). Interrelationships among Piagetian tasks and traditional measures of cognitive abilities in mature and aged adults. *Journal of Gerontology, 27,* 461–465.

Strauss, A. L., & Glaser, B. G. (1970). *Anguish.* Mill Valley, CA: Sociology Press.

Strayer, D. L., Wickens, C. D., & Braune, R. (1987). Adult age differences in the speed and capacity of information processing: 2. An electrophysiological approach. *Psychology and Aging, 2,* 99–110.

Streib, G. F. (1985). Social stratification and aging. In R. H. Binstock & E. Shanas (Eds.), *Handbook of aging and the social sciences* (2nd ed., pp. 339–368). New York: Van Nostrand Reinhold.

Streib, G. F., & Schneider, C. J. (1971). *Retirement in American society.* Ithaca, NY: Cornell University Press.

Super, D. E. (1957). *The psychology of careers.* New York: Harper & Row.

Super, D. E. (1980). A life span, life space approach to career development. *Journal of Vocational Behavior, 16,* 282–298.

Surwillo, W. W., & Quilter, R. E. (1964). Vigilance, age, and response time. *American Journal of Psychology, 77,* 614–620.

Sweer, L., Martin, D. C., Ladd, R. A., Miller, J. K., & Karpf, M. (1988). The medical evaluation of elderly patients with major depression. *Journal of Gerontology, 43,* M53–M58.

Swenson, C. H., Eskew, R. W., & Kohlhepp, K. A. (1981). Stages of the family life cycle, ego development, and the marriage relationship. *Journal of Marriage and the Family, 43,* 841–853.

Swenson, C. H., & Trahaug, G. (1985). Commitment and the long-term marriage relationship. *Journal of Marriage and the Family, 47,* 939–945.

Taietz, P. (1975). Community complexity and knowledge of facilities. *Journal of Gerontology, 30,* 357–362.

Taietz, P., & Milton, S. (1979). Rural-urban differences in the structure of

services for the elderly in upstate New York counties. *Journal of Gerontology, 34,* 429–437.

Talley, T., & Kaplan, J. (1956). The Negro aged. *Newsletter of the Gerontological Society, 6(December).*

Tanfer, K. (1987). Patterns of premarital cohabitation among never-married women in the United States. *Journal of Marriage and the Family, 49,* 483–497.

Tate, N. (1983). The black aging experience. In R. McNeely & J. Colen (Eds.), *Aging in minority groups.* Beverly Hills, CA: Sage Publications.

Taylor, R., & Chatters, L. (1986). Church-based informal supports. *The Gerontologist, 26,* 637–642.

Teachman, J. (1986). First and second marital dissolution: A decomposition exercise for whites and blacks. *Sociological Quarterly, 27,* 571–590.

Teaff, J. D., Lawton, M. P., Nahemow, L., & Carlson, D. (1978). Impact of age integration on well-being of elderly tenants in public housing. *Journal of Gerontology, 33,* 126–133.

Templer, D., Ruff, C., & Franks, C. (1971). Death anxiety: Age, sex, and parental resemblance in diverse populations. *Developmental Psychology, 4,* 108–114.

Templer, D. I. (1972). Death anxiety in religiously very involved persons. *Psychological Reports, 31,* 361–362.

Teri, L., Truax, P., Logsdon, R. G., Uomoto, J., & Zarit, S. (1990). *Assessment of behavioral problems in dementia: The Revised Memory and Behavior Problems Checklist.* Unpublished manuscript, University of Washington, Seattle.

Terkel, S. (1974). *Working.* New York: Pantheon.

Terpenning, M. S., & Bradley, S. F. (1991). Why aging leads to increased susceptibility to infection. *Geriatrics, 46(2),* 77–80.

Teski, M. (1981). *Living together: An ethnography of a retirement hotel.* Washington, DC: University Press of America.

Thal, L. J. (1988). Treatment strategies. In M. K. Aronson (Ed.), *Understanding Alzheimer's disease.* New York: Scribner's.

Thomae, H. (1970). Cognitive theory of personality and theory of aging. *Human Development, 13,* 1–10.

Thomae, H. (Ed.). (1976). *Patterns of aging*. Basel: Karger.

Thomae, H. (1980). Personality and adjustment to aging. In J. E. Birren & R. B. Sloane (Eds.), *Handbook of mental health and aging* (pp. 285–301). Englewood Cliffs, NJ: Prentice-Hall.

Thomas, G. S., & Rutledge, J. H. (1986). Fitness and exercise for the elderly. In K. Dychtwald (Ed.), *Wellness and health promotion for the elderly* (pp. 165–178). Rockville, MD: Aspen.

Thomas, J. L. (1985). Visual memory: Adult age differences in map recall and learning strategies. *Experimental Aging Research, 11*, 93–95.

Thomas, J. L. (1986a). Age and sex differences in perceptions of grandparenthood. *Journal of Gerontology, 41*, 417–423.

Thomas, J. L. (1986b). Gender differences in satisfaction with grandparenting. *Psychology and Aging, 1*, 215–219.

Thomas, J. L. (1988). Predictors of satisfaction with children's help for younger and older elderly parents. *Journal of Gerontology: Social Sciences, 43*, S9–S14.

Thomas, J. L., Bence, S. L., & Meyer, S. M. (1988, August). *Grandparenting satisfaction: The roles of relationship meaning and perceived responsibility*. Paper presented at the meeting of the American Psychological Association, Atlanta.

Thomas, P. D., Hunt, W. C., Garry, P. J., Hood, R. B., Goodwin, J. M., & Goodwin, J. S. (1983). Hearing acuity in a healthy elderly population: Effects on emotional, cognitive, and social status. *Journal of Gerontology, 38*, 321–325.

Thompson, A. D. (1978). Alcohol and nutrition. *Clinics in Endocrinology and Metabolism, 7*, 405–428.

Thompson, L. W., & Gallagher, D. (1986). Treatment of depression in elderly outpatients. In G. Maletta & F. J. Pirozzolo (Eds.), *Advances in neurogerontology: Vol. 4. Assessment and treatment of the elderly patient*. New York: Praeger.

Thompson, L. W., Gallagher-Thompson, D., Futterman, A., Gilewski, M. J., & Peterson, J. (1991). The effects of late-life spousal bereavement over a 30–month interval. *Psychology and Aging, 6*, 434–441.

Thurstone, L. L. (1938). *Primary mental abilities*. Chicago: University of Chicago Press.

Tice, R. R. (1987). Summary and discussion of Part V. In H. R. Warner, R. N. Butler, R. L. Sprott, & E. L. Schneider (Eds.), *Modern biological theories of aging* (pp. 211–215). New York: Raven Press.

Tietjen, A. M., & Walker, L. J. (1985). Moral reasoning and leadership among men in a Papua, New Guinea society. *Developmental Psychology, 21*, 982–992.

Tobin, J. J. (1987). The American idealization of old age in Japan. *The Gerontologist, 27*, 53–58.

Tobin, S. S., & Lieberman, M. A. (1976). *Last home for the aged*. San Francisco: Jossey-Bass.

Toffler, A. (1970). *Future shock*. New York: Random House.

Tomlinson, B. E., Blessed, G., & Roth, M. (1970). Observations on the brains of demented old people. *Journal of the Neurological Sciences, 11*, 205–242.

Tomlinson-Keasey, C. (1972). Formal operations in females from eleven to fifty-four years of age. *Developmental Psychology, 6*, 364.

Tomporowski, P. D., & Ellis, N. R. (1986). Effects of exercise on cognitive processes: A review. *Psychological Bulletin, 99*, 338–346.

Torrey, B. B. (1985). Sharing increasing costs on declining income: The visible dilemma of the invisible aged. *Milbank Memorial Fund Quarterly Health and Society, 63*, 377–394.

Treat, N. J., Poon, L. W., Fozard, J. L., & Popkin, S. J. (1978). Toward applying cognitive skill training to memory problems. *Experimental Aging Research, 4*, 305–319.

Treisman, A., & Gelade, G. (1980). A feature-integration theory of attention. *Cognitive Psychology, 12*, 97–136.

Troll, L. E. (1971). The family of later life: A decade review. *Journal of Marriage and the Family, 33*, 263–290.

Troll, L. E. (1975). *Early and middle adulthood: The best is yet to be — Maybe*. Pacific Grove, CA: Brooks/Cole.

Troll, L. E., & Bengtson, V. (1982). Intergenerational relations throughout the life span. In B. B. Wolman (Ed.), *Handbook of developmental psychology* (pp. 890–911). Englewood Cliffs, NJ: Prentice-Hall.

Troll, L. E., Miller, S. J., & Atchley, R. C. (1979). *Families in later life*. Belmont, CA: Wadsworth.

Trujillo, K. M., Walsh, D. M., & Brougham, R. R. (1991). *Age differences in exercise motivations*. Paper presented at the annual meeting of the American Psychological Society, Washington, DC.

Tuokko, H., Gallie, K. A., & Crocker, D. J. (1990). Patterns of deterioration in normal and memory impaired elderly. *Developmental Neuropsychology, 6*, 291–300.

Turner, B. F. (1982). Sex-related differences in aging. In B. B. Wolman (Ed.), *Handbook of developmental psychology* (pp. 912–936). Englewood Cliffs, NJ: Prentice-Hall.

Turner, B. F. (1987). Mental health and the older woman. In G. Lesnoff-Caravaglia (Ed.), *Handbook of applied gerontology* (pp. 201–230). New York: Human Sciences Press.

Turner, R. M., & Ascher, L. M. (1982). Therapist factor in the treatment of insomnia. *Behavior Research and Therapy, 17*, 107–112.

Udry, J. R. (1971). Marital alternatives and marital disruption. *Journal of Marriage and the Family, 43*, 889–897.

Uhlenberg, P. (1987). A demographic perspective on aging. In P. Silverman (Ed.), *The elderly as modern pioneers* (pp. 145–160). Bloomington: Indiana University Press.

Uhlenberg, P. (1988). Aging and the social significance of cohorts. In J. E. Birren & V. L. Bengtson (Eds.), *Emergent theories of aging* (pp. 405–425). New York: Springer.

Uhlenberg, P., & Chew, K. S. Y. (1986). Changing place of remarriage in the life course. In D. Kertzer (Ed.), *Family relations in life course perspective*. Greenwich, CT: JAI.

Unger, R. K. (1979). *Female and male*. New York: Harper & Row.

United States Bureau of the Census. (1991). *Statistical abstract of the United States*. Washington, DC: U.S. Government Printing Office.

United States Department of Health and Human Services. (1984). *The health consequences of smoking: Chronic obstructive lung disease* (DHHS Publication No. PHS-50205). Washington, DC: U.S. Government Printing Office.

United States Department of Health and Human Services. (1988). *Vital statistics of the United States, 1985: Vol. 2. Mortality* (Part A). Hyattsville, MD: U.S. Public Health Service.

United States Department of Health and Human Services. (1991). *Vital statistics of the United States, 1988: Vol 2. Mortality* (Part A). Hyattsville, MD: U.S. Public Health Service.

United States Department of Labor. (1988). *Bureau of Labor Statistics.* Washington, DC: U.S. Government Printing Office.

United States Department of Transportation. (1986). *1983–1984 Nationwide personal transportation study* (Vol. 11). Washington, DC: Author.

United States Office of Technology Assessment. (1984). *Technology and aging in America.* Washington, DC: U.S. Government Printing Office.

VandenBos, G. R., DeLeon, P. H., & Pallack, M. S. (1982). An alternative to traditional medical care for the terminally ill. *American Psychologist, 37,* 1245–1248.

van Geert, P. (1987). The structure of Erikson's model of eight stages: A generative approach. *Human Development, 30,* 236–254.

Van Hoose, W. H., & Worth, M. R. (1982). *Adulthood in the life cycle.* Dubuque, IA: William C. Brown.

Van Maanen, J., & Schein, E. H. (1977). Career development. In R. J. Hackman & J. L. Suttle (Eds.), *Improving life at work* (pp. 30–95). New York: Goodyear.

Vernon, S. W., & Roberts, R. E. (1982). Use of the SADS-RDS in a tri-ethnic community survey. *Archives of General Psychiatry, 39,* 47–52.

Verrillo, R. T., & Verrillo, V. (1985). Sensory and perceptual performance. In N. Charness (Ed.), *Aging and human performance* (pp. 1–46). Chichester, England: Wiley.

Verwoerdt, A. (1980). Anxiety, dissociative and personality disorders in the elderly. In E. W. Busse & D. G. Blazer (Eds.), *Handbook of geriatric psychiatry* (pp. 368–380). New York: Van Nostrand Reinhold.

Verwoerdt, A. (1981). *Clinical gero-psychiatry* (2nd ed.). Baltimore: Williams & Wilkins.

Vickio, C. J., & Cavanaugh, J. C. (1985). Relationships among death anxiety, attitudes toward aging, and experience with death in nursing home employees. *Journal of Gerontology, 40,* 347–349.

Vickio, C. J., Cavanaugh, J. C., & Attig, T. (1990). Perceptions of grief among university students. *Death Studies, 14,* 231–240.

Vijg, J., & Papaconstantinou, J. (1990). EURAGE workshop report: Aging and longevity genes: Strategies for identifying DNS sequences controlling life span. *Journal of Gerontology, 45,* B179–B182.

Viney, L. L. (1987). A sociophenomenological approach to life-span development complementing Erikson's sociodynamic approach. *Human Development, 30,* 125–136.

Waddell, K. J., & Rogoff, B. (1981). Effect of contextual organization on spatial memory of middle-aged and older women. *Developmental Psychology, 17,* 878–885.

Wagenaar, W. A., & Groeneweg, J. (1990). The memory of concentration camp survivors. *Applied Cognitive Psychology, 4,* 77–87.

Walford, R. L. (1983). Supergenes histocompatibility: Immunologic and other parameters in aging. In W. Regelson (Ed.), *Intervention in the aging process: Basic research, pre-clinical screening and clinical programs* (pp. 53–68). New York: Liss.

Walker, J. I., & Brodie, H. K. H. (1980). Neuropharmacology of aging. In E. W. Busse & D. G. Blazer (Eds.), *Handbook of geriatric psychiatry* (pp. 102–124). New York: Van Nostrand Reinhold.

Walker, L. J., deVries, B., & Trevethan, S. D. (1987). Moral stages and moral orientations in real-life and hypothetical dilemmas. *Child Development, 58,* 842–858.

Wall, P. D. (1975). Signs of plasticity and reconnection in spinal cord damage. In R. Porter & D. W. Fitzsimons (Eds.), *Outcome of severe damage to the central nervous system* (pp. 35–54). Amsterdam: Elsevier.

Wall, S. D., Brant-Zawadski, M., Jeffrey, R. B., & Barnes, B. (1981). High frequency CT findings within 24 hours after cerebral infarction. *American Journal of Neuroradiology, 2,* 553–557.

Wallace, A. F. C. (1971). Handsome Lake and the decline of the Iroquois matriarchate. In F. L. K. Hsu (Ed.), *Kinship and culture* (pp. 367–376). Chicago: Aldine-Atherton.

Wallace, J. (1985). Behavior modification methods as adjuncts to psychotherapy. In S. Zimberg, J. Wallace, & S. B. Blume (Eds.), *Practical approaches to alcoholism psychotherapy* (2nd ed., pp. 109–130). New York: Plenum.

Wallack, S. S., & Cohen, M. A. (1988). Costs of long-term care: Distribution and responsibility. In D. Evered & J. Whelan (Eds.), *Symposium on research and the aging population* (pp. 235–245). Chichester, England: Wiley.

Wallerstein, J. S., & Kelly, J. B. (1980). *Surviving the breakup: How children and parents cope with divorce.* New York: Basic Books.

Walsh, D. A., Krauss, I. K., & Regnier, V. A. (1981). Spatial ability, environmental knowledge, and environmental use: The elderly. In L. S. Liben, A. H. Patterson, & N. Newcombe (Eds.), *Spatial representation and behavior across the lifespan* (pp. 321–357). New York: Academic Press.

Walsh, E. K., & Cavanaugh, J. C. (1984, November). *Does hospice meet the needs of dying clients?* Paper presented at the meeting of the Gerontological Society of America, San Antonio.

Wantz, M. S., & Gay, J. E. (1981). *The aging process: A health perspective.* Cambridge, MA: Winthrop.

Ward, R. A. (1984a). *The aging experience: An introduction to social gerontology* (2nd ed.). New York: Harper & Row.

Ward, R. A. (1984b). The marginality and salience of being old: When is age relevant? *The Gerontologist, 24,* 227–232.

Ward, R. A., & Kilburn, H. (1983). Community access and life satisfaction: Racial differences in later life. *International Journal of Aging and Human Development, 16,* 209–219.

Wattis, J. P. (1983). Alcohol and old people. *British Journal of Psychiatry, 143,* 306–307.

Webb, W. B. (1975). *Sleep: The gentle tyrant.* New York: Spectrum.

Webb, W. B. (1982). Sleep in older persons: Sleep structures of 50- to 60-year-old men and women. *Journal of Gerontology, 37,* 581–586.

Webb, W. B., & Campbell, S. S. (1980). Awakenings and the return to sleep in an older population. *Sleep, 3,* 41–46.

Webb, W. B., & Levy, C. M. (1982). Age, sleep deprivation and performance. *Psychophysiology, 19,* 272–276.

Webb, W. B., & Swinburne, H. (1971). An observational study of sleep in the aged. *Perceptual and Motor Skills, 32,* 895–898.

Wechsler, D. (1958). *The measurement and appraisal of adult intelligence* (4th ed.). Baltimore: Williams & Wilkins.

Weg, R. B. (1983). The physiological perspective. In R. B. Weg (Ed.), *Sexuality in the later years* (pp. 39–80). New York: Academic Press.

Weibel-Orlando, J. (1990). Grandparenting styles: Native American perspectives. In J. Sokolovsky (Ed.), *The cultural context of aging* (pp. 109–125). New York: Bergin & Garvey.

Weiner, M. B., Brok, A. J., & Snadowski, A. M. (1987). *Working with the aged* (2nd ed.). Norwalk, CT: Appleton-Century-Crofts.

Weiner, R. D. (1979). The psychiatric use of electrically induced seizures. *American Journal of Psychiatry, 136,* 1507–1517.

Weingartner, H., Cohen, R. M., & Bunney, W. E. (1982). Memory-learning impairments in progressive dementia and depression. *American Journal of Psychiatry, 139,* 135–136.

Weingartner, H., & Silberman, E. (1982). Models of cognitive impairment: Cognitive changes in depression. *Psychopharmacology Bulletin, 18,* 27–42.

Weishaus, S., & Field, D. (1988). A half century of marriage: Continuity or change? *Journal of Marriage and the Family, 50,* 763–774.

Weisman, A. D. (1972). *On dying and denying.* New York: Behavioral Publications.

Weiss, R. S. (1975). *Marital separation.* New York: Basic Books.

Weitzman, L. J. (1985). *The divorce revolution: The unexpected social and economic consequences for women and children in America.* New York: Free Press.

Weksler, M. E. (1990). Protecting the aging immune system to prolong quality of life. *Geriatrics, 45*(7), 72–76.

Welford, A. T. (1977). Motor performance. In J. E. Birren & K. W. Schaie (Eds.), *Handbook of the psychology of aging* (pp. 450–496). New York: Van Nostrand Reinhold.

Welford, A. T. (1988). Reaction time, speed of performance, and age. In J. A. Joseph, (Ed.), *Central determinants of age-related declines in motor functioning* (pp. 1–17). New York: New York Academy of Sciences.

Wells, C. E. (1979). Pseudodementia. *American Journal of Psychiatry, 136,* 895–900.

Wells, L., & Macdonald, G. (1981). Interpersonal networks and post-relocation adjustment of the institutionalized elderly. *The Gerontologist, 21,* 177–183.

Wentkowski, G. (1985). Older women's perceptions of great-grandparenthood: A research note. *The Gerontologist, 25,* 593–596.

Wessler, R., Rubin, M., & Sollberger, A. (1976). Circadian rhythm of activity and sleep-wakefulness in elderly institutionalized patients. *Journal of Interdisciplinary Cycle Research, 7,* 333.

West, R. L. (1984, August). *An analysis of prospective everyday memory.* Paper presented at the meeting of the American Psychological Association, Toronto.

West, R. L. (1986a). Everyday memory and aging. *Developmental Neuropsychology, 2,* 323–344.

West, R. L. (1986b). *Memory fitness over 40.* Gainesville, FL: Triad.

West, R. L., & Walton, M. (1985, March). *Practical memory functioning in the elderly.* Paper presented at the National Forum on Research in Aging, Lincoln, NE.

Wetzler, M. A., & Feil, N. (1979). *Validation therapy with disoriented elders who use fantasy.* Cleveland: Edward Feil Productions.

Whitbourne, S. K. (1985). *The aging body.* New York: Springer.

Whitbourne, S. K. (1986). *The me I know: A study of adult identity.* New York: Springer-Verlag.

Whitbourne, S. K. (1987). Personality development in adulthood and old age: Relationships among identity style, health, and well-being. In K. W. Schaie (Ed.), *Annual review of gerontology and geriatrics* (Vol. 7, pp. 189–216). New York: Springer.

White, A. T., & Spector, P. E. (1987). An investigation of age-related factors in the age-job satisfaction relationship. *Psychology and Aging, 2,* 261–265.

White, L. K., & Booth, A. (1985). The quality and stability of remarriages: The role of stepchildren. *American Sociological Review, 50,* 689–698.

Whitlock, F. A. (1986). Suicide and physical illness. In A. Roy (Ed.), *Suicide* (pp. 151–170). Baltimore: Williams & Wilkins.

Wickens, C. D., Braune, R., & Stokes, A. (1987). Age differences in the speed and capacity of information processing. 1: A dual task approach. *Psychology and Aging, 2,* 70–78.

Wiener, J. M. (1988, Winter). Financing options for long-term care. *Living-at-Home,* pp. 1–3.

Wiener, Y., & Vaitenas, R. (1977). Personality and developmental correlates of voluntary and mid-career change in enterprising occupations. *The Gerontologist, 17,* 132.

Wiens, A. N., & Menustik, C. E. (1983). Treatment outcome and patient characteristics in an aversion therapy program for alcoholism. *American Psychologist, 38,* 1089–1096.

Wilkie, F., & Eisdorfer, C. (1971). Intelligence and blood-pressure in the aged. *Science, 172,* 959.

Williams, A. F., & Carsten, O. (1989). Driver age and crash involvement. *American Journal of Public Health, 79,* 326–327.

Williams, J. E., & Best, D. L. (1990). *Measuring sex stereotypes: A thirty-nation study* (rev. ed.). Newbury Park, CA: Sage Publications.

Williams, J. H. (1977). *Psychology of women.* New York: Norton.

Williams, S. A., Denney, N. W., & Schadler, M. (1983). Elderly adults' perception of their own cognitive development during the adult years. *International Journal of Aging and Human Development, 16,* 147–158.

Willis, S. L. (1987). Cognitive training and everyday competence. In K. W. Schaie (Ed.), *Annual review of gerontology and geriatrics* (Vol. 7, pp. 159–188). New York: Springer.

Willis, S. L. (1990). Current issues in cognitive training research. In E. A. Lovelace (Ed.), *Aging and cognition: Mental processes, self-awareness, and interventions* (pp. 263–280). Amsterdam: North-Holland.

Willis, S. L., & Nesselroade, C. S. (1990). Long-term effects of fluid ability training in old-old age. *Developmental Psychology, 26,* 905–910.

Willis, S. L., Schaie, K. W., & Lueers, N. (1983, April). *Fluid-crystallized ability correlates of real life tasks.* Paper presented at the meeting of the Society for Research in Child Development, Detroit.

Wilson, B., & Moffat, N. (Eds.). (1984). *Clinical management of memory problems.* Rockville, MD: Aspen.

Wingfield, A., & Stine, E. L. (1986). Organizational strategies in immediate recall of rapid speeds by young and elderly adults. *Experimental Aging Research, 12,* 79–83.

Wiseman, R. F. (1981). Community environments for the elderly. In F. J. Berghorn, D. E. Schafer, and Associates (Eds.), *The dynamics of aging.* Boulder, CO: Westview.

Wiswell, R. A. (1980). Relaxation, exercise, and aging. In J. E. Birren & R. B. Sloane (Eds.), *Handbook of mental health and aging* (pp. 943–958). Englewood Cliffs, NJ: Prentice-Hall.

Wittels, I., & Botwinick, J. (1974). Survival in relocation. *Journal of Gerontology, 29,* 440–443.

Wittkowski, J. (1981). *Attitudes toward death and dying in older persons and their dependence on life satisfaction and death-related experiences.* Paper presented at the International Congress of Gerontology, Hamburg.

Wolf, E. (1960). Glare and age. *Archives of Ophthalmology, 60,* 502–514.

Wood, V., & Robertson, J. F. (1978). Friendship and kinship interaction: Differential effect on morale of the elderly. *Journal of Marriage and the Family, 40,* 367–375.

Woodruff-Pak, D. S. (1988). *Psychology and aging.* Englewood Cliffs, NJ: Prentice-Hall.

Yanik, A. J. (1988). *Vehicle design considerations for older drivers* (SAE 885090). Warrendale, PA: Society of Automotive Engineers.

Yankelovich, D. (1981). *New rules: Searching for self-fulfillment in a world turned upside down.* New York: Random House.

Yates, F. A. (1966). *The art of memory.* Middlesex, England: Penguin.

Yee, D. (1985). A survey of the traffic safety needs and problems of drivers 55 and over. In J. L. Malfetti (Ed.), *Drivers 55 + : Needs and problems of the older drivers: Survey results and recommendations* (pp. 96–128). Falls Church, VA: AAA Foundation for Traffic Safety.

Yesavage, J. A. (1983). Imagery pretraining and memory training in the elderly. *Gerontology, 29,* 271–275.

Yesavage, J. A., Brink, T. L., Rose, T. L., Lum, O., Huang, V., Adey, M., & Leirer, V. O. (1983). Development and validation of a geriatric depression scale: A preliminary report. *Journal of Psychiatric Research, 17,* 37–49.

Yesavage, J. A., Sheikh, J., Tanke, E. D., & Hill, R. (1988). Response to memory training and individual differences in verbal intelligence and state anxiety. *American Journal of Psychiatry, 145,* 636–639.

Yllo, A. (1978). Nonmarital cohabitation. *Alternative Lifestyles, 1,* 37–54.

Young, L. J., Percy, C. L., & Asire, A. J. (Eds.). (1981). *Incidence and mortality data: 1973–1977.* (National Cancer Institute Monograph 57, DHHS No. NIH 81–2330). Washington, DC: U. S. Government Printing Office.

Zarit, S. H. (1982). Affective correlates of self-reports about memory of older people. *International Journal of Behavioral Geriatrics, 1,* 25–34.

Zarit, S. H., & Anthony, C. (1986). Interventions with dementia patients and their families. In M. Gilhooly, S. Zarit, & J. E. Birren (Eds.), *The dementias: Policy and management* (pp. 104–121). Englewood Cliffs, NJ: Prentice-Hall.

Zarit, S. H., Cole, K. D., & Guider, R. L. (1981). Memory training strategies and subjective complaints of memory in the aged. *The Gerontologist, 21,* 158–164.

Zarit, S. H., Eiler, J., & Hassinger, M. (1985). Clinical assessment. In J. E. Birren & K. W. Schaie (Eds.), *Handbook of the psychology of aging* (2nd ed., pp. 725–754). New York: Van Nostrand Reinhold.

Zarit, S. H., Todd, P. A., & Zarit, J. M. (1986). Subjective burden of husbands and wives as caregivers: A longitudinal study. *The Gerontologist, 26,* 260–266.

Zarit, S. H., & Zarit, J. M. (1983). Cognitive impairment. In P. M. Lewinsohn & L. Teri (Eds.), *Clinical geropsychology* (pp. 38–80). New York: Pergamon Press.

Zegans, L. S. (1982). Stress and the development of somatic disorders. In L. Goldberger & S. Breznitz (Eds.), *Handbook of stress: Theoretical and clinical aspects* (pp. 134–152). New York: Free Press.

Zelinski, E. M., Gilewski, M. J., & Anthony-Bergstone, C. R. (1990). Memory Functioning Questionnaire: Concurrent validity with memory performance and self-reported memory failures. *Psychology and Aging, 5,* 388–399.

Zelinski, E. M., Gilewski, M. J., & Thompson, L. W. (1980). Do laboratory tests relate to self assessment of memory ability in the young and old? In L. W. Poon, J. L. Fozard, L. S. Cermak, D. Arenberg, & L. W. Thompson (Eds.), *New directions in memory and aging* (pp. 519–544). Hillsdale, NJ: Erlbaum.

Zepelin, H. (1973). A survey of age differences in sleep patterns and dream recall among well-educated men and women. *Sleep Research, 2,* 81.

Zgola, J. M. (1987). *Doing things: A guide to programming activities for persons with Alzheimer's disease and related disorders.* Baltimore: Johns Hopkins University Press.

Zimberg, S. (1985). Principles of alcoholism psychotherapy. In S. Zimberg, J. Wallace, & S. B. Blume (Eds.), *Practical approaches to alcoholism psychotherapy* (pp. 3–22). New York: Plenum.

Zsembik, B. A., & Singer, A. (1990). The problem of defining retirement among minorities: The Mexican Americans. *The Gerontologist, 30,* 749–757.

Zung, W. A. (1965). A self-rating depression scale. *Archives of General Psychiatry, 12,* 63–70.

ACKNOWLEDGMENTS

p. 14: © Barbara Rios/Photo Researchers; p. 18: © Kathy Sloane/Jeroboam; p. 20: Dorothea Lange/Library of Congress; p. 38: © Bob Daemmrich; p. 52: © Joel Gordon; p. 62: P. & D. Maybury-Lewis/Anthro-Photos; p. 67: Ilka Hartmann/Jeroboam; p. 95: Michael Hayman/Stock, Boston; p. 102: © Gordon K. Morioka; p. 119: Michael Hayman/Stock, Boston; p. 121: © Martha Tabor; p. 133: Ulrike Welsch/Photo Researchers; p. 135: © Rod Schmall; p. 156: © Lara Hartley; p. 169: © Lara Hartley; p. 183: Ilka Hartmann/Jeroboam; p. 192: © Lara Hartley; p. 208: © Nita Winter; p. 209: © Lara Hartley; p. 237: J. L. Atlan/Sygma; p. 246: Robert Ginn/EKM-Nepenthe; p. 247: Robert Capa/Magnum; p. 261: © Lara Hartley; p. 266: Larry Merkle/Courtesy American Conservatory Theatre, San Francisco; p. 270: Rick Reinhard/Black Star; p. 275: Charles Gatewood/The Image Works; p. 298: © Drayden Hebb; p. 312: Reprinted by permission of the Alzheimer's Association; p. 320: © Martha Tabor; p. 329: © Nita Winter; p. 339: © Marianne Gontarz; p. 358: © Lionel J-M Delevingne/Stock, Boston; p. 360: © Zephyr Pictures/Melanie Carr; p. 368: © Joel Gordon; p. 386: Laimute E. Druskis/Jeroboam; p. 399: Royal Photo Company Collection/University of Louisville Photographic Archives; p. 400: Craig Litherland/Jeroboam; p. 405: Gale Zucker/Stock, Boston; p. 418: © Ethan Hoffman; p. 422: © Zephyr Pictures/Melanie Carr; p. 425: Steve Kagan/NYT Pictures; p. 431: © Steve Skjold; p. 450: © Owen Seumptewa; p. 461: Janice Fullman/The Picture Cube; p. 466: AP/Wide World Photos; p. 468: © Marcel Miranda/The Names Project; p. 475: © Lara Hartley; p. 485: © Lara Hartley; p. 487: © Elizabeth Crews

NAME INDEX

GLOSSARY/SUBJECT INDEX